Work Your Stars!

 USING ASTROLOGY TO

NAVIGATE YOUR CAREER PATH, SHINE ON THE JOB,

AND GUIDE YOUR BUSINESS DECISIONS

Matthew "Dr. Matt" Abergel

A FIRESIDE BOOK

Published by Simon & Schuster

 FIRESIDE
Rockefeller Center
1230 Avenue of the Americas
New York, NY 10020

FIRESIDE and colophon are registered trademarks
of Simon & Schuster Inc.

Designed by Gretchen Achilles

Manufactured in the United States of America

10   9   8   7   6   5   4   3   2   1

Library of Congress Cataloging-in-Publication Data
Abergel, Matthew.
    Work your stars! : using astrology to navigate your career path,
shine on the job, and guide your business decisions / Matthew
Abergel.
        p.   cm.
    1. Astrology and business.   2. Success in business—Miscellanea.
I. Title.
BF1729.B8A24   1999
133.5—dc21   99-22000
                                                                CIP

ISBN 0-684-84995-X

Grateful acknowledgment is given to Astro Communications Services, San
Diego, CA, for all astrological charts, tables, and map, reprinted by permission.
Pages 163–66, "Stellar Negotiations: [Some Final Lessons on] How to Schmooz
Any Schmo in the Universe" originally appeared on *Idea Cafe: The Small Business
Channel*, www.ideacafe.com. Copyright 1997 by Matthew Abergel.

Acknowledgments

Many people contributed to this book's content and production, and it's my pleasure to thank them. I especially want to thank

★ the experts who advised me on business relationships and psychology, including social workers Kama Brockmann and Christine Duffy; law professor Eric San Juan; syndicated columnist Rhonda Abrams; and the clients who shared their stars and experiences

★ the creative pros who put this book in your hands, including my insanely bright editorial assistant Daniel Sullivan; computer whiz David Cunningham; and the awesome Simon & Schuster editors Becky Cabaza and Carrie D. Thornton

★ the loving and lovely folks who kept me sane (barely!) during this process, including my supportive family in California; the very cool staff of Caribou Coffee on Broadway in Chicago; my office companion, Ginger the Dog; and my partner, Bob Cooner, who deserves more gratitude than I could express in a hundred books.

Work Your Stars!
is dedicated to my dad, Ike Abergel,
at whose side I learned to run a business,
tell a story, and play a killer game of blackjack.

Contents

Introduction

They say opportunity knocks once—and then walks away. Not destiny. Your destiny calls many times. But do you answer it? Or do you put it on hold? This book is about answering your destiny when it calls; finding a career or starting a business that's right for you; and paying the rent while you're at it. So stick with me—together we'll stop staring at the want ads and start listening to those calls from destiny.

Not too long ago my friend and former client Laura was totally preoccupied with her future. She didn't know what she wanted to do. She hoped a New York editor would call with a book contract. She dreamed Prince Charming's Lost and Found Department would call about a lost glass slipper—8½, just her size. Someday, she was sure, her destiny would call. Meanwhile she just sat around, waiting for the phone to ring.

Then one day (we later found out this was around the time Saturn entered the career sector of her horoscope), she got sick of waiting. She asked me to cast her business and career horoscope. We talked about the symbols in her chart—how they resonated with what she wanted to do, what talents she yearned to express in the marketplace, what the stars whispered about her destiny. Laura listened. She searched her soul. She developed a plan.

As the plan was emerging, the beautiful and rich symbols of Laura's horoscope helped point the way. She landed a job that keeps her energized and well paid, and she's currently at work on her first novel after publishing several very clever freelance articles. As for Prince Charming—no, he hasn't shown up yet, but you never know about some of those frogs!

That's what astrology can do for you: open a few doors you hadn't bothered to knock on, remind you to answer some phone calls you've neglected—until now. This book will show you that astrology doesn't dictate your destiny. Destiny might call, but you still have to get up and answer it! *Work Your Stars!* is based on my many years of writing for and consulting with curious professionals, mostly small-business owners and entrepreneurs, who wanted more than a job, more than a comfortable lifestyle. They wanted to fulfill their personal missions—and have a good time and a few laughs along the way. I wish you the same.

Business Astrology Is Booming!

But don't take my word for it. My readers and clients aren't the only ones capitalizing on the wealth of astrological insight available to executives and entrepreneurs these days. Many high-profile companies are taking advantage of this 5,000-year-old study of the stars. For example:

★ Traders at major Wall Street brokerage firms are using astrology to track the cycles of financial markets, especially the futures markets. In fact, many investment funds and investment newsletters use planetary indicators in their predictions. (See *Financial World,* May 11, 1993.)

★ A major Brazilian bank relied on business astrologers to help navigate a risky foray into the European capital markets. The bank's venture was successful, and the astrology consulting business is growing leaps and bounds in both Brazil and Argentina. (See *The Economist,* Feb. 11, 1995.)

★ One of the oldest and most renowned vineyards in France carries out all vineyard operations according to astrological rhythms. (See *Wine Spectator,* Feb. 15, 1989.)

★ A number of Western European marketing firms are using astrological demographics to match consumers with the products that target their needs and interests. And in Taiwan, demographers are doing astrological research on families and business startups. (See *Demograph,* May 1993.)

★ Executives and human resources departments are using astrology to assess their employees' strengths, to maximize their talents, and to help them become more productive. (See *Personnel Journal,* Sept. 1995.)

★ In Hong Kong, even food is served with stars: Want to pick a fine wine? Choose a dessert? Check your horoscope! (See *Gourmet,* April 1989.)

Bringing It Down to Earth—and Today's Job Market

You might wonder how these big shots are reaping so much valuable information from their two-sentence horoscopes in the newspapers. Well, they're not! They're using professional business astrology consultants—to the tune of $300 to $5,000 per consultation. Why so much? The costs are high because these consultations involve much more than the typical Sun signs you read while waiting to get your haircut.

Exercising the meticulous methods of traditional and experimental astrology, these consultants must cast an entire chart—sometimes several—of the Sun, all the planets, and the intricate relationships between them. In fact, it's a whole astrological profile, unique to the person or business in question.

So let's say you're thinking about starting your own business. Or you've just finished school and you're eager to enter a career that's more than a job. Or the career's going great but you'd like to impress a crucial client. Can you benefit from the same astrological techniques as the French vineyard and the Wall Street traders? Yes! In this book, you can look at the many factors of your horoscope to start assembling the information you need to get on the business or career fast track—or whatever track answers your calling.

Let's Get Started: How to Use This Book

No reputable horoscope intends to tell you exactly who you are and what you ought do with your life. It does propose, however, to bring to your awareness parts of yourself you might not see. Throughout this book you'll read many descriptions of your planets, the archetypal symbols of the various elements that comprise this portrait of you. Before you say, "No way, that's not me," consider how the description might be you. Or how you'd like it to be. Or how you'd like to avoid it like the plague! This process will help you to know yourself, what you want, and how to succeed in a career or business.

Of course all of these symbols fold in on one another, and you can't really take any one of them as an isolated part of your professional self. For example, Mars represents your leadership energy, but in any leadership position you'll also draw on your interpersonal talents (Venus energy) and ability to meet challenges (Saturn energy).

So it's important to assemble your Professional Planetary Profile (your PPP), explained in part three of this book. It's exactly what a professional business and career astrologer would do. They would look at your entire chart, certainly not just your Sun sign, and figure out your strengths, your inclinations, and your drives—a composite of the individual, unique professional you.

Here's a quick look at the four components of the PPP, an all-important astrological tool. Do not fear! All you need to know is your birth time and place.

1. Your Sun sign

2. Your rising sign

3. Your Moon sign

4. Your planetary signs (Mercury, Venus, Mars, Jupiter, and Saturn)

You'll find charts for your rising sign, Moon sign, and planetary signs at the end of each corresponding chapter in part two (your Sun sign, and its dates, are given in part one). As you work through part two, fill in that

section of your PPP. For instance, the PPP will ask you for the position of Mars on your birthday. You'll find the information to answer that question after you read the Mars chapter, in the charts that follow it.

Part three contains a blank PPP work sheet for you to photocopy. There is room for you to write in your answers, as well as a completed sample PPP, but here's a preview of all the questions in the PPP:

Professional Planetary Profile Work Sheet

Profile for _____

Birth date _____ Birth time _____ Birthplace _____

Profile creation date _____

MISSION

Sun in _____

The greatest inspiration for my career is _____.

My hero(es) is/are _____
_____.

My guiding motivation is a desire to _____.

The personal strengths and assets I most want to capitalize on are _____
_____.

The personal weaknesses and liabilities I want to overcome are _____
_____.

PUBLIC AND PROFESSIONAL IMAGE

Rising sign: _____

The image I most want to present in the workplace is of someone who is _____
_____.

I want to enhance my public and professional image by _____
_____.

ENVIRONMENT

Moon in _____

I thrive in an environment where _____.
I can handle stress by _____.
Eventually I want to work in a setting where I can _____.

ORGANIZATION AND COMMUNICATION

Mercury in _____

I communicate effectively by _____.
I excel at organizing by _____.
I can achieve my peak performance by _____.

PROMOTION AND MARKETING

Venus in _____

I am a great networker when I _____.
My sales savvy shines when I _____.
I want to improve my networking and sales by _____.

LEADERSHIP

Mars in _____

I want to develop my leadership qualities by _____.
When conflicts arise, I can resolve them by _____.
I want to express my entrepreneurial spirit by/with _____.
I can become more self-empowered by _____.

OPPORTUNITY

Jupiter in _____

My key to opening up greater opportunities is _____.
I want to develop this quality by _____.

REACHING OPTIMUM POTENTIAL

Saturn in _____

I sometimes hold myself back by _____.
Recognizing this, I can break free by _____.

If you follow my instructions and work through the Professional Planetary Profile as you read through *Work Your Stars!*, by the end of the book, your profile will be completely filled in.

Where's Mine?

The planetary charts in *Work Your Stars!* cover the years 1940 to 1980. The rising sign charts (pages 183–89) cover time zones throughout North America, Alaska, and Hawaii. But what if you were born, say, in 1937 in West Africa, like my dad? Sorry, you're out of luck. We had to draw the line somewhere, you know. But wait! Everyone, including my dad, should be able to use every part of *Work Your Stars!* So for any birthday before 1940 or after 1980, and for any birthplace outside North America, I'll gladly provide you with a customized computer-calculated horoscope chart, totally for free. Just send me your birth day, birthplace, and time via e-mail to stars@drmatt.net (on "subject" line, write "my chart"). Or send a self-addressed, stamped envelope with the above information to Dr. Matt, ICM Enterprises, 430 East Alisal Street, Salinas, CA 93905.

If you just can't wait to get a fancy computerized chart for yourself or a colleague, call the pros who designed the astrological tables for this book—right now. For approximately the price of a cappuccino, they'll send or fax one on the double. Contact Astro Communications Services at their toll-free number: (800) 888-9983, Monday through Friday, 8:00 A.M. to 5:00 P.M., Pacific Time.

Work Your Stars!

Part One

☛ SOLAR POWER—GET PLUGGED
INTO YOUR POTENTIAL

"Know yourself."
FROM APOLLO'S TEMPLE AT DELPHI, GREECE

Ah, the Sun! I used to take it for granted. Then I moved from California to Chicago, where the Sun shines less than my grandmother's tarnished silverware. Now I pop vitamin D tablets and worship the Sun, thankful for every beam that pierces the gloom.

To classical stargazers the Sun was Apollo, a good-looking guy with the gifts of eternal youth and many lovers. Apollo presided over the arts, culture, and the law—the stone and mortar of civilization. On his chariot he carried light and warmth to the world every day.

In your business and career horoscope, the Sun represents the part of you that feels alive. It stands for the center of your internal universe. Around it everything else revolves—including all the pieces of your personal and professional self. From its location in your birth chart you can behold your sense of purpose. Here you'll glimpse your greatest assets and liabilities, the ball of fire that sizzles with the potential to reach everyone and everything in its orbit.

When your inner Sun is shining, your energy is contagious and customers or colleagues actually crack smiles. But without a developed sense of your solar energy, you walk around with little purpose and direction, your assets, talents, and potentials largely untapped.

> **"Not till the sun excludes you do I exclude you."**
> AMERICAN POET
> WALT WHITMAN

In your Professional Planetary Profile (PPP), the Sun occupies the most important place. If you're familiar with business plans, think of the Sun as your mission statement and executive summary. It's the chairman of the board. The other forces—Mercury, Venus, Mars, and all—better work together with the Sun, or you've got problems.

The Sun is your sense of self, the impulse to be you, just you, in abundant and rich complexity.

What to Look For

Because of the Sun's immense importance in your horoscope and your Professional Planetary Profile, each Sun sign is broken up into several sections:

THE MYTH

The story behind the sign. Who is Taurus anyway? What did Cancer the cranky crab do to get prime real estate in the night sky? Each sign is backed by a rich mythology. Let the symbols sink in. They may inspire you to create a few myths of your own!

MOTIVATION

What drives you to succeed? What gets you out of bed in the morning? Here's the irresistible impulse behind all that you do, the energy you need to survive, your ultimate goal. Knowledge of what drives you will help you realize your goals by clarifying the most important elements of your life. Get ideas here for your personal mission statement.

ASSETS

These are the good aspects of your sign, your character. What folks like about you, how you affect other people positively. Where you succeed interpersonally and professionally. These are the traits you ought to capitalize on and invest in.

LIABILITIES

These are the traits you ought to be careful of. They'll drag you down. Often you'll find that your greatest assets can also be your greatest liabilities. You may be really good at saving money (an asset) but forget that money's useless unless you invest (liability). Understanding your faults multiplies your successes. You can't avoid falling into a chasm unless you know it's there.

DR. MATT'S TIPS FOR SUCCESS

At the end of your Sun sign, I've highlighted a few strategic pointers for making the most of your solar potential.

ALLIANCES

Here's where you find out how your sign interacts with others. This section is just about as big as all the above sections combined. That's because business and professional alliances matter—a lot. The roots of the words *economics* and *commerce* don't have anything to do with money. They're about relationships. And in the marketplace relationships make all the difference, whether you're partners, teammates, or employer and employee.

Remember, the Sun symbolizes the *vision* you have for your business or career and, in fact, for your life. Grab your suntan lotion—now it's time to look up your Sun sign and its corresponding chapter in part one.

GET SOME SUNSHINE:
THE BENEFITS OF UNDERSTANDING
YOUR SOLAR POWERS @ WORK

★ Turn on and turn up your motivation.

★ Connect with the deepest promise of what you can become.

★ Discover the ancient myths behind your solar powers.

★ Let go of the stereotypes of tabloid horoscopes.

★ Take stock of your assets and liabilities.

Aries @ Work

MARCH 21 TO APRIL 19

ARIES

The Myth

There are many Aries myths, and all of them are about one thing: going for what you want. Consider the circumstances of the celebrated ram's birth: Neptune (god of the sea and surfing) loved a woman who rejected him. So the mighty god turned both himself and his beloved into sheep. As you might imagine, one thing led to another and they soon gave birth to a little baby sheep: Aries, the first constellation of the zodiac.

But Aries wasn't your garden variety of ram. He was a magical, flying ram, and the Golden Fleece—more valuable than a Burberry's cashmere sweater—came off his back. Everybody wanted it, but it was protected by a ferocious dragon. Finally Jason and the Argonauts snagged the Golden Fleece and won fame and fortune. The hero was Jason, but the moral of the story is all Aries: What's a little stiff competition when it comes to getting what you want?

Motivation

Aries is driven to boldly do what no one's done before. A maker of break-throughs, you're like Captain Kirk with a briefcase and a cellular phone. The way things are usually done is one thing, and the way you do them is quite another.

"Because it's there."
MOUNTAIN CLIMBER GEORGE MALLORY (EXPLAINING WHY HE CLIMBED MT. EVEREST)

Needless to say you're not one to be lost in the crowd with poor puny Waldo. No one has to wonder where you are; your very presence screams, "Here I am!" No one forgets you when you make your exit because the impression you leave behind is like a solitary trail of great bear prints among the millions of tiny gull prints in the sand. When papers are scattered and deadlines rear their ugly heads, you, like an Atlas of the workplace, rise up against the mighty force of chaos with order on your shoulders—and refuse to shrug.

And you were born this way, you lucky innovator. Born to buck. Most Aries have little trouble getting motivated. It's innate. You wake up with your eyes wide open ready to do, do, do. Problems arise when you can't figure out what to *do* with all that motivation.

Assets

I never met an Aries who didn't go gaga for bright colors. Taurus may be the sign of the bull, but it's Aries that charges at the sight of red, the smell of blood, the taste of success. Aries likes to take the lead. And Aries does. And Aries is good at it.

Your leadership abilities spark others into action. You're an adrenaline junkie with enough to spare. You ooze energy and your companions soak it up like espresso. If people are languid and lazy at the meeting, you'll perk them up with the electric shock of your personality. Things get done when you're around. Papers are filed, copy is written, forms are processed. You can goad an elephantine bureacracy into outrunning a leopard.

Aries won't tolerate lumbering. If rules must be broken in order to get things done, so be it. Long lines? Cut in front. Inventory problems? De-mand what you need. Unfair policies? Charge up the steps of City Hall. Your mother may have told you time and again, "Haste makes waste," but for you nothing's so wasteful as wasted time.

And when something stands in your way? Well, darn it, you ram right through it like a Mack truck through crepe paper. In fact, you're eager to confront challenges—you even kind of like them. What's life without a struggle, anyway? You'll not only climb the highest mountain, you'll seek it out. When someone says, "Impossible," you say, "Try me!"

Feisty, that's what you are, sort of like the Tasmanian devil in a suit.

Liabilities

When the road is clear and straight, Aries runs the fastest. But a few pebbles can trip up even a herd of stampeding elephants. Passion, courage, a boom box blaring Baroque or heavy metal—you need these things, and you need a sensible secretary, too.

Sometimes, though, you run up against a stone wall. Aries has a hard time facing the fact that impossibilities do exist. You risk becoming like poor old Captain Ahab in *Moby Dick*, trying to harpoon a white whale that just can't be killed. It's an honorable enterprise—the stuff of great books—but you're setting yourself up for a loss. If you invest everything in a whale of an impossible venture, it might sink you and your crew in a dark sea of bankruptcy.

Likewise, in your single-minded pursuit of a certain goal, you're sometimes insensitive to the feelings of others. Everything's about impulse and reflex with you, and sometimes you kick back a little too hard. Compromise does not come easily. You'd rather knock antlers with the opposition than admit that you, too, might be wrong on certain points. Because you love the rush of battle, you sometimes forget to cushion your blows among more tender souls.

Remember, you need help as much as everyone else, and you don't want to alienate your helpers: the guy who brings you coffee, the postal clerk, and so on. Sometimes folks just don't have the time to do everything as efficiently as you'd like. You're not always realistic about limits and even overestimate yourself. Asking for help is difficult. You want to be the Lone Ranger, but you forget that even he needed Tonto at his side.

Discipline bores you. You want to jump to the finish line without training for the marathon, and this drive for instant gratification is both your asset and your curse. You will probably make it to the finish line (after all, you want it so bad), but only if you successfully harness your inner warrior and train it to get the job done.

Aries might climb the highest mountain successfully from time to time, but if you aren't careful, if you don't take breaks on the way up, you

might run out of steam. Even with all that adrenaline pumping through your veins, every engine burns its gas and has to stop for refueling. You might think you can handle several projects at once, but take care you don't have to stay up 24/7 to do it. Do the things you can. Don't do the things you can't. And know the difference.

Dr. Matt's Tips for Aries Success

★ Don't choose a career that will take 20 years to hit the big time. Instant gratification tickles your fancy. Get some.

★ You don't always get what you want. Shoot for half and you're doing well. Meanwhile, make that half worth getting.

★ Cultivate the endurance to sustain your enthusiastic commitment. Discipline bores you, but some savvy Aries successfully harness their inner warrior and train it to get the job done.

★ Ask for help. People won't think less of you. They might even identify with you.

DON'T MESS WITH THIS BROAD!

Aries is typically caricatured as a warrior. But not all of you dress in camouflage fatigues and drink testosterone for breakfast. Aries is also the sign of the strong woman. Consider Bette Davis, Joan Crawford, Gloria Swanson, and Diana Ross—four Aries in high heels. All of them forged careers on their strong personalities, gaining renown for their indomitable will and drive to succeed in a tough-guys' world. In fact, Crawford and Davis pioneered Hollywood's damsels-*not*-in-distress character type.

Aries in Alliance

ARIES @ WORK WITH ARIES

☛ **Kowabunga!**

You two are a couple of dynamos, and together you have more explosive power than a bundle of dynamite. It's a fight to get a word in edgewise.

You challenge each other. You bicker instead of banter. You keep a little rivalry going just to keep the adrenaline pumping. But like any explosive material, your alliance lacks staying power. Together you take risks heedlessly and burn out quickly. With two sets of eyes always fixed on the ultimate target, you neglect the bills, deadlines, and other sideline distractions. Figure out both your Saturn signs and get a grip on making this alliance last past the initial infatuation stage.

> **"I love war and responsibility and excitement. Peace is going to be hell on me."**
> U.S. ARMY GENERAL
> GEORGE S. PATTON

IF THE OTHER ARIES IS BOSS: Learn to take direction. Fantasize you're the Big Cheese. How would you want to be treated? Give it to them. Don't try to overpower them. Someday you'll be promoted. Meanwhile, don't become anyone's whipping boy. You won't last long in *that* role.

IF YOU'RE IN CHARGE: You know what *not* to do. Don't rub their noses in their inferiority. Don't make your Aries employees wait around feeling useless. *Do* offer them plenty of opportunities to prove themselves.

ARIES @ WORK WITH TAURUS

☞ **Great expectations!**

In this alliance Taurus seems to compensate for all your flaws, and vice versa, and together you look like an unbeatable team. Taurus keeps you steady. They fix a budget and, quite miraculously, ensure you both stick to it. You start it, they finish it, and with combined forces you can accomplish big tasks. Before you get too comfortable, however, anticipate the pitfalls of working with someone who'll want to restrain you from running too fast.

IF TAURUS IS BOSS: Impress them with your hard work and determination. Do what you say you're going to do. And have some patience. While Taureans can be great strategizers, they lack your quick reflexes. Respect their "Do Not Enter" signs.

IF YOU'RE IN CHARGE: Forget about tactics like screaming, threatening, or demanding it yesterday. Taurus will tune you out. Instead, make them feel secure, with enough chances to go to the bathroom and stare out the window. Raises work well, too. Delegate your long-term projects to Taureans.

ARIES @ WORK WITH GEMINI

☛ New improved formula!

An idea whose time has come (that's you, baby!) doesn't go far without a good marketing plan. That's where Gemini comes in. You're the flame; they're the breeze. Together you can reach people. You find new approaches. You inspire each other. You may come to feel, though, that your Gemini partner is all talk and no action. This is one alliance where you'll definitely want to make a plan—and stick to it. No wishy-washiness allowed!

IF GEMINI IS BOSS: They'll appreciate your speed, but maybe not your independence. Be there for them. Don't expect consistency. Geminis seldom say the same thing twice.

IF YOU'RE IN CHARGE: Realize Gemini will take on more than they can handle (sound familiar?). Help them focus. Set deadlines. Ask them to keep you informed of any and all changes. They will. They're good at it.

ARIES @ WORK WITH CANCER

☛ All's fair in love and war!

A couple of ardent survivors—that's you two. Though your alliance is rockier than the coast of Brittany, you both have a flair for extreme measures and single-mindedness of purpose. Respect your deep-set differences. Cancer, for example, isn't reckless; they'll want to account for every penny. You're a forward-thinker, while Cancer rummages through the past.

IF CANCER IS BOSS: You'll probably get tired of them checking up on you. Convince them you're on task. Allay their worries, or learn to ignore them while feigning heartfelt sympathy.

IF YOU'RE IN CHARGE: Be sensitive to Cancer's feelings. Don't take their pouting as a sign of attack. Give them lots of chances. You'll chomp at the bit to coax them out of their shell—probably a good thing. They really can share your enthusiasm, but don't expect a fireworks display.

ARIES @ WORK WITH LEO

☞ Look out, Las Vegas!

Here come two of the world's biggest gamblers, a couple of high rollers out to paint the town red—or any other flashy color you two can agree to disagree about. This alliance is loud. Sometimes it's obnoxious. It's never on autopilot, since you both love the cockpit so much. Despite your fun, take precautions to define who owns what—and who (if anyone) has the right to write checks or buy and sell assets. This is a double-occupancy partnership—it needs room for two leaders, two egos, two winners.

IF LEO IS BOSS: Show them the admiration you actually feel. Let them bask in the spotlight, but define a sphere where you can shine, too—otherwise you'll resent them. Meanwhile, offer a few distractions. Leo can't resist a distraction—it brings out their creativity.

IF YOU'RE IN CHARGE: Fight the temptation to knock Leo down a couple of notches. Give them strokes and opportunities to impress the public and junior staff. Show them who's boss, but never deny their dignity or talent. In fact, if you become their biggest fan, they'll become your hardest worker.

ARIES @ WORK WITH VIRGO

☞ Roll up your sleeves and get crackin'!

So you don't have much in common besides work. Who cares? You don't have to marry them; you have to work with them. Virgos find you haphazard; they neglect to capitalize on your energy. Meanwhile you tend to pass up Virgo's hidden talents. You think their priorities are mixed up. So by all means, appreciate one another; exploit one another's strengths if you have to! You have lots to learn from each other. Get Virgo to help perfect what you start.

IF VIRGO IS BOSS: You can bet they'll be a demanding taskmaster. They'll pick at you. They'll expect lots of help and good service. Don't let yourself feel as if you don't do anything right. You do. Just don't be late.

IF YOU'RE IN CHARGE: You'll be tempted to crack the whip and kick your spurs. "Why are they so damned slow and methodical about everything?" you wonder. But these by-the-book employees will ensure you never pay late fees or look like a lost lamb again. Greet Virgo's fussiness with good humor. Hand over your paperwork hassles to these conscientious workers.

ARIES @ WORK WITH LIBRA

☛ Beauty and the Beast

You figure out which is which! This alliance can work, but not without a constant tug-of-war or seesaw—and of course *you'll* decide what and when to play. In this parnership it's important to establish a rhythm that works for both of you. Will you take breaks while Libra minds the shop, or will you both punch the clock together? Libra will cling to you. You will secretly depend on their people skills and light touch. Hey, sometimes codependency ain't so bad!

IF LIBRA IS BOSS: Stop rushing! A Libra is a classy kind of boss, and they appreciate the *process*, not just the product. They'll call on you in a crisis, but they won't appreciate your love of constructive chaos. Almost certainly they'll try to reform you, raise your standards, correct your grammar. If this is all you have to put up with, just deal! Chances are they won't invade your turf.

IF YOU'RE IN CHARGE: You may have found your ideal right-hand person or aide-de-camp. Libra is loyal, charming, and can still keep up with you. But be forewarned! They ask lots of questions and won't want to make a move without you. Clarify just how much autonomy you expect them to exercise.

ARIES @ WORK WITH SCORPIO

☛ "Go ahead, make my day."

You've got horns, they've got stingers. Imagine the gratuitous violence in this Hollywood blockbuster! Whether this alliance can work all depends on where you two focus your overflowing energies—preferably the focus is on the job, not on each other. Otherwise, you two have the potential to be as antagonistic as a couple of gunslingers in a standoff at the OK Corral. You take the direct approach. Scorpio does anything but. You risk a lot. They never gamble without hedging their bets. (You think

> **"To grow and know what one is growing towards— that is the source of all strength and confidence in life."**
>
> AUTHOR JAMES BAILLIE

I jest? Just wait till it's time to buy insurance!) But when the two of you are on the same wavelength, this team is a massive powerhouse.

IF SCORPIO IS BOSS: Stop trying to figure them out. You won't. You will no doubt run headlong into that Scorpionic deep and serious side. Don't

dismiss what they value. And remember, they may forgive, but they never forget, whereas you're not one to hold a grudge.

IF YOU'RE IN CHARGE: Stop worrying what they're doing behind your back. Or if you can't, then bring it into the open. When subtlety and special tactics are called for, call in the Scorpio.

ARIES @ WORK WITH SAGITTARIUS

☛ **Anchors away!**

The world is your oyster. Aries is the quintessential pioneer, Sagittarius the consummate adventurer. Together you're addicted to conquering the marketplace like a feverish game of Risk or Monopoly. In this partnership, make sure there's plenty of seed money—you'll need it. And don't forget the bandages—you'll need those, too, when Saj gets their tie caught in the paper shredder, which you've cranked up to its highest setting. Neither of you is big in the tact department, so be careful negotiating a loan for your Ram-Centaur new business. Other than that, have a good time!

IF SAGITTARIUS IS BOSS: You're sure to win all sorts of special favors and exceptions to the rules. But practice restraint in those animated "discussions" that consistently turn nasty. Both of you tend to escalate!

IF YOU'RE IN CHARGE: With Saj around, you'll always have someone close by who speaks your language. But they'll also ask you to consider other options, listen to different points of view. Occasionally indulge your Saj's need to deliberate and ponder—it'll yield bountiful ideas.

ARIES @ WORK WITH CAPRICORN

☛ **Welcome to the Big League!**

A good pairing for business in the penthouse suite, this alliance thrives on loads of mutual ambition. You contribute the enthusiasm and innovation, Capricorn the pragmatism and respectability. But be forewarned! You're likely to bristle under Capricorn's authority, which threatens to squash Aries's energies. And then, too, you'll be tempted to seize the upper hand at your earliest convenience. For this partnership to work, the secret ingredient is respecting each other.

IF CAPRICORN IS BOSS: Face it: It won't be easy. But even in your haste you must realize the Capricorn boss can open a lot of doors for you. Sure,

they'll expect you to pay your dues. So what? Deliver only as much lip service as you're comfortable with and let your work speak for itself.

IF YOU'RE IN CHARGE: Don't be a bossy boss and never run out of projects for this diligent worker. Besides a paycheck, you'll have to remunerate them with plenty of recognition and rewards—and no, a pat on the back isn't good enough. Try taking out a full-page ad in *USA Today*.

ARIES @ WORK WITH AQUARIUS

☛ **Let's start a revolution!**

You've got the zeal, Aquarius the doctrine, and together you're bound to rock your world. With a combined effort you can be major trendsetters, the founders of the latest fad or fashion. Expect the unexpected. But bear in mind that long-range plans will take a backseat to instant gratification, so spend a little time on strategy—or hire a Scorpio.

IF AQUARIUS IS BOSS: You may have found the perfect job—except, of course, working for yourself. Though the Aquarian head honcho can be cool and passionless, they tend to admire individuality and quick thinking, which is good news for you. But don't expect special treatment just because you're buddy-buddy. Aquarius plays fair.

IF YOU'RE IN CHARGE: You've got an ally in your pursuit of new experiences, your quest to break new ground. Set a good example—these folks need to believe they're fighting the good fight. And watch out for jealousy. Since you're the boss, it's the Aquarius who's likely to be popular with the crowds.

ARIES @ WORK WITH PISCES

☛ **Fire and water make smoke.**

You decide if it's the smoke of a productive factory or an opium den of shattered ambitions. You're both a couple of unshakable dream chasers. The similarities pretty much end there. But in a team, you can work like peanut butter and jelly—one sticky, one squishy, the perfect combination. But don't forget the bread—this alliance needs plenty of working capital, a practical plan, and a reality check at regular intervals.

IF PISCES IS BOSS: Impress them with your strong personality—they'll eat it up so long as they don't find it threatening. With the Pisces boss, you're almost sure, though, to suffer from too much management, none at all, or

a constant flip-flop between the two. Ask your Pisces boss to lay out your responsibilities. Then do your own thing. Help them realize they can't get by without you.

IF YOU'RE IN CHARGE: You'll be pleased with your loyal, biddable Pisces who's so eager to serve. But watch out! They're sensitive. Don't lash out too sharply—or if you do, don't expect them to have recovered when you're suddenly back to being Mr. or Ms. Nice. Allow them plenty of room to be creative. Call them in to solve problems no one else can even begin to understand.

Taurus @ Work

"Success to me is having ten honeydew melons and eating
only the top half of each one."
TAURUS ENTERTAINER BARBRA STREISAND

TAURUS

The Myth

In classical mythology, Taurus the bull sidled up to a beautiful country girl who petted him and eventually hopped on his back for a ride. Faster than the Concorde, Taurus whisked her off to a Greek island, where it turned out he was not a beast at all, but Zeus, king of the gods and CEO of Mount Olympus. The moral of the fable: Taurus may seem simple—practical, reliable, and stubborn—but underneath that bovine-of-burden exterior is an Armani toga and unshakable quest for all things beautiful.

Motivation

Taurus craves security. Not too much razzle-dazzle, thank you, just the good old-fashioned Good Life. It's not that you give two hoots about out-doing the Joneses, but you were born a class act, and it's de rigueur that all you do and have be classy. (For more on Taurus's well-concealed

down-and-dirty side, check out page 307.) You're also pretty fond of results. The vision of an Aquarius, the intricate ideas of a Gemini—those are nice to talk about over coffee and all, but things you can touch and fondle and toss around are more your cup of tea—a very good cup of tea served in bone china, if you please.

Assets

You were born with a green thumb—if not for petunias, certainly for growing a business. Like a gardener, you sink your hands right into the mud and start making stuff. Once you get off your comfy spot on the couch, you throw yourself into your work as if your life depends on it. It does. Taurus thrives on paychecks and profits. When it comes to the Good Life, more is better.

Taurus doesn't leave things to chance. You want to know where your next meal is coming from. That's why you're so darned dependable. Your fridge is always full. Coworkers come to you for help and cookies. Customers come to you because they know what they're dealing with—and exactly how much it's going to cost 'em. No sudden whammies from your bull pen!

Sure, there's that lazy side of yours. It takes a hallelujah chorus to jolt you out of bed in the morning. But once up and properly nourished, you finish what you start. You stay on top of things. In a team, Taurus makes sure everything goes according to plan. Leave the scheduling to Virgo—Taurus is here for quality control. A lot of opera singers are Taureans. They'd rather sing with the lights out than sing off-key.

Work is a big part of every Taurus's life. When you get your own office, you move in photos of Mom and enough hot cocoa to get you and your pals through the winter. You make friends on the job. And since you shine in a suit, you might even meet your sweetheart over a power lunch.

Impracticality bothers Taurus. It's not that Taurus isn't a dreamer. It's just that Taurus's dreams are predicated on dollars and cents and a strong sense of what you'll wear to the White House to accept the Businessperson of the Year award.

Whether a partner, collaborator, or a close working associate, Taurus the Bull can always be depended on, in any kind of situation, ranging from putting together a surprise birthday party to instantly coming to the rescue in a crisis. Steadiness, predictability, ongoing support—all of these qualities are in the Taurean portfolio of assets.

Liabilities

Taurus can get stuffy and complacent. Once you're settled, you're as hard to budge as an 800-pound gorilla on a banana plantation. If your goal is simply to have your own cubicle and enough petty cash to buy a new angora sweater every month, then fine. But if you dream of loftier things, you must nudge yourself. Besides, somebody else wants to sit in the La-Z-Boy awhile.

> **"It's just a job. Grass grows, birds fly, waves pound the sand. I beat people up."**
> BOXING CHAMPION
> MUHAMMAD ALI

Unfortunately, many a Taurus settles for a job beneath them just to get security. The modern Taurean entrepreneur also runs the risk of getting lost in cyberspace and losing touch with the physical world and life's simple pleasures. If you're stumped for business ideas, think basics: food, shelter, chocolate.

Dr. Matt's Tips for Taurus Success

★ Promote your talent for follow-through. While everyone *appreciates* results, you take the cake for delivering the goods.

★ Rehearse saying the word *no!* Sure, the boss and lots of clients adore your dependability. But you need to have a life, too, not just a to-do list. Besides, if you're always available, it means you're never scarce, which means your value drops.

★ Ease your grip on the purse strings before your knuckles turn any whiter! If you're looking for a happy compromise to stop the battle between your inner cheapskate and your latent spendthrift, try this: Spend sensibly on personal indulgences that will pay off in the long run, like a dapper professional wardrobe, fine art for the office, or an educational retreat. Bonus: *Some* of these treats are even tax-deductible as allowable by law!

★ Do more dreaming. Remember, it doesn't cost extra to dream big. And although many dreams don't come true, dreaming can lead to pretty viable *plans* that do.

★ Take a ride on the wild side. Not often, but once in a while. You might like it there after all.

ANY WAY YOU LOOK AT IT, A "BULL MARKET" MEANS GROWTH

With their affinity for the finer things in life, many Taureans gravitate toward the glamour of the performing arts. Shakespeare, for example, was born under Taurus, as were singers Ella Fitzgerald, Barbra Streisand, and Cher. But even away from the bright lights of the stage, Taurus is determined to "grow" a prosperous career—or even an entire country. Case in point: Golda Meir, who transplanted herself from Milwaukee to a kibbutz in Palestine, helped establish the Jewish homeland of Israel, and eventually became that nation's fourth prime minister. With the determination typical of a Taurus, Golda Meir revered hard work and gracefully shouldered one job after another wherever she was most needed. As prime minister, she made good use of her Taurean diplomacy in her relentless efforts toward peace, a necessity of that Taurean Good Life.

Taurus in Alliance

TAURUS @ WORK WITH ARIES

☞ **Don't rush me!**

This alliance goes at its own pace. After all, Ariens are all about speed (Aries is ruled by Mars, planet of raw, driving energy), while Taureans absolutely can only move forward in their own measured gait. Can you two work together? Yes, if Taurus understands Aries is truly an innovator, and if Aries accepts the fact that though you move slowly, you provide a wealth of sound backup and no-nonsense loyalty.

> "Work is the rent you pay for the room you occupy on earth."
> TAURUS BRITISH MONARCH ELIZABETH II

IF ARIES IS BOSS: Keep on your toes and don't let their slapdash way of doing things throw you off balance. Also, tell them that though you may lumber, you can carry a heavy load; you're methodical but darn productive in the end.

IF YOU'RE IN CHARGE: Use Aries to bolster your ability to improvise; or have them field problems that were unforeseen in the overall plan. Aries is good on the front lines, while you're better off with the generals.

TAURUS @ WORK WITH TAURUS

☞ **"The perfect blend of art and machine."**

You two understand each other perfectly. In fact, there's often a loyalty to one another that may last long after the original alliance has come to a close. But, if Taurus and Taurus should seriously disagree about anything, the two bulls will each take a fixed stance and not budge. What a waste, because together you two can do just about anything you set out to do. To keep it going, the light touch is required. One caution: It's easy to get jealous of each other.

IF THE OTHER TAURUS IS BOSS: You'll be admired and treated well, until you get on their nerves. If your Taurus boss gets snippy, avoid confronting them about it until you think matters over. Their snippiness and your frustration are probably a result of mutual boredom. Try livening things up.

IF YOU'RE IN CHARGE: You may start to find familiar little failings in your Taurus employee, like a marked lack of sponteneity. But you can change that. Try leading your employee, and yourself, into some risky waters. Meanwhile, though, carry lifeboats stocked with plenty of resources in reserve.

TAURUS @ WORK WITH GEMINI

☞ **Quiet, please!**

This can be a bright and sunny alliance for Taurus. Gemini's ruling planet, Mercury (mascot of communications), brings new ideas, new people, and new projects to the forefront. But all the talk and commotion of this genial air sign may be too overwhelming for the earthy Taurus, who often needs peace and quiet to function best. You two will have your most serious discussions at the point when the noise gets to be too much. Speak up!

IF GEMINI IS BOSS: Remember: Opposites can attract. The combination of your stolidity and Gemini's flightiness can inject fun, laughter, and joie de vivre into grunt work. But if you shun pleasure and dwell on productivity and promotions, you'll probably wind up resenting Gemini's easy-come, easy-go authority and move on to pursue a career where your roots can be better grounded.

IF YOU'RE IN CHARGE: Be wary of confining Geminis; they aren't good prisoners of scheduling. You'll profit most if you let them indulge in a variety

jobs. Keep them focused, but not *too* narrowly—Gemini needs a wide angle to see clearly.

TAURUS @ WORK WITH CANCER

☞ **Good vibrations.**

Both Taurus and Cancer really care about accomplishing something of value. Cancer's planetary mascot, the Moon, represents the subconscious mind, while Taurus is ruled by Venus, the planet of creativity. But if Cancer's uneven moods ever encounter Taurus's stubborn disposition, then everything comes to a screeching halt. Fortunately, you two know you've got a good thing going and are careful not to mess it up. You take turns changing moods, from uneven to steady, from stubborn to flexible.

IF CANCER IS BOSS: A shared interest in comfort and security ought to make you cozy allies. You'll rarely feel Cancer is taking you for a ride. But if they seem a little too emotionally needy for the demands of their position, offer comfort before you walk out on what can be a beautiful alliance.

IF YOU'RE IN CHARGE: It'll help if you take an interest in Cancer's well-being, checking in regularly to see if everything's OK. Cancer's emotions are like water building behind a dike: Spot the leaks and plug them up before the whole thing bursts. The best way to do this is through open and honest communication.

TAURUS @ WORK WITH LEO

☞ **And ne'er the twain shall meet.**

While both Taurus and Leo absolutely thrive in any atmosphere where ease and luxury are highlighted, these two are still fixed signs—set in your ways and a bit compromise-resistant. Each wants to control the situation, the project, and, above all, the money involved. Flexibility is in short supply and tension seems almost inevitable. The one way it can work is for you each to have an assigned role. Don't trespass on the other's turf. Watch out for mutual bossiness!

IF LEO IS BOSS: Get ready for everything to turn into a big deal! While this boss might appreciate your bottom-line mentality, Leo's likely to expect a whole lot more, too, like your taking the initiative to network and innovate. Play an advisory role, but don't give orders.

IF YOU'RE IN CHARGE: Try to avoid falling into a hot-and-cold holding pattern with this enthusiastic employee. Sure, you two will get along better some days than others, but it's exhausting to ride a roller coaster of conflict, crisis, and resolution (though it may appeal to Leo's dramatic inclinations). Occasionally let them feel big, even though they're smaller than you.

TAURUS @ WORK WITH VIRGO

☛ **Working like clockwork.**

This is a very good combination for you. With Virgo, another earth sign, a Taurus is neither rushed nor pushed. Both of you feel secure in each other's predictability and reliability. As a result, you can focus totally on the objective. Success is a given. However, Virgo has a sharp tongue, and criticism of any kind causes Taurus to falter. This is one alliance where you'll have to ask Virgo to reexamine their delivery, time and again, because, as you know, Taurus is just too valuable to lose! Whatever you do, don't get mixed in *process*. It's essential you both get a life away from the partnership.

IF VIRGO IS BOSS: Be confident and prepared for derisive remarks. Virgo will pick up on, and make note of, the smallest wrinkle in an otherwise solid report. Smooth it out, and take Virgo's occasional nit-picking in stride. If your work is good, they really do appreciate it.

IF YOU'RE IN CHARGE: Try and bring out the earthiness in Virgo. Though a solid worker, Virgo lacks your rugged realism, and this may lead to difficulty when Virgo has to deal with the unpredictable outside world. Make them color outside the lines once in a while.

TAURUS @ WORK WITH LIBRA

☛ **Nice but not easy.**

Whenever beauty and luxury are involved, you two are in total agreement. Nothing is too good nor too expensive for you and the development of your mutual projects. Only when Taurus's approach to deal-making directly conflicts with Libra's flitting, flirting, and networking does real trouble arise. But your shared mascot planet, Venus, comes to the rescue by opening the problem-solving discussions between you two. Hint: Allow plenty of time for working out the kinks, or even just agreeing on a restaurant.

IF LIBRA IS BOSS: This is no time to just sit back and crank out more widgets. Offer your consulting services when an important decision must be made. Libra needs advice. They think in terms of "maybes," so you can help them find direction. But be subtle, and remember your position.

IF YOU'RE IN CHARGE: The distant and aloof boss behind closed doors doesn't elicit Libra's best. Cut through Libra's apprehensiveness by working with them directly, convincing them you won't hide behind your mahogany desk when problems arise. If you need Libra, let them know it; it's in their nature to flirt with possibilities—and they may even go so far as to send their résumés to your competitors.

TAURUS @ WORK WITH SCORPIO

☞ **Who's the boss?**

When a substantial alliance between Taurus and Scorpio actually exists, it is extremely successful. It's purely a matter of "opposites attract." However, you two are often the rare alliance, for each is a fixed sign, and each must control unconditionally. There is very little flexibility here, because everything—even the smallest transaction—is so important. But when it works, this is truly a gorgeous joint venture.

IF SCORPIO IS BOSS: You may find Scorpio callous and cold. In truth, your boss is deeply committed to the working relationship. They don't know how to show it because they fear you're not as committed as they are. If you're loyal, let them know it.

IF YOU'RE IN CHARGE: Treat Scorpio with tender loving care. Patience and tact are necessities. Joke with Scorpio very carefully, and never at their expense. If Scorpio feels slighted, you'll either be abandoned or worse: Scorpio may strike back.

TAURUS @ WORK WITH SAGITTARIUS

☞ **Marching to the beat of different drummers.**

Sagittarius causes Taurus to do things in a totally new way. It's usually a good thing, but it's always expansive; Sagittarius has "think big" built into their nervous system. Meanwhile, Sagittarius values Taurus's sound backup and attention to detail. Sagittarius is here, there, and everywhere, while Taurus tends to be, well, here. For this alliance to be the success story it can be, you two will have to respect one another's pacing.

IF SAGITTARIUS IS BOSS: Don't try and keep up with Saj's lickety-split pace. Haste can get the job done, but it can also make waste. Your Taurean instincts let you know the difference. Share your knowledge with Saj—tactfully, of course.

IF YOU'RE IN CHARGE: It is important to adapt to their style. If you try and force Saj to do things your way, you'll stifle their productivity. Demanding too much control will alienate and anger them. There is some method to their madness.

TAURUS @ WORK WITH CAPRICORN

☛ **Attached at the hip.**

For Taurus, this is nearly the perfect alliance, the one in which everything comes together, on all levels, at all times. With scant effort, Taurus and Capricorn create, organize, and develop their goals—and see them realized—nearly as easily as breathing. This is actually that good. But the warning bells should ring when you fall into a workaday rut. Hopefully Capricorn will remember what's at stake and create a new goal right on the spot.

IF CAPRICORN IS BOSS: Understand that Capricorn takes work very seriously. It's part of their sense of self. Treating business too lightly may make Capricorn see you as a jokester. Or it may simply hurt their feelings.

IF YOU'RE IN CHARGE: Encourage Capricorn to open their mind. Both of you dislike change. But change is a prerequisite for the successful business. As the more expressive sign, and the boss, you'll have to start the wheels of innovation turning.

TAURUS @ WORK WITH AQUARIUS

☛ **A glass menagerie.**

Not usually one another's first choice. But if the climate is right—and the project, collaboration, or assignment benefits from well-defined guidelines—then Taurus and Aquarius can form a limited but extremely favorable alliance. Taurus can help realize Aquarius's vision.

It's always a matter of Taurus's predictability and methods versus Aquarian surprise tactics and left-field brilliant ideas. These two simply see the world differently. And should any pressure, real or imagined, be brought to bear on this fragile alliance, it shall suddenly terminate.

> **"He is well paid that is well satisfied."**
> TAURUS POET
> AND PLAYWRIGHT
> WILLIAM SHAKESPEARE

IF AQUARIUS IS BOSS: At first you'll be aggravated by Aquarius's dreamy demeanor, but if you're willing try new things, Aquarius can lead you on ventures you'd never conceive. Open your mind.

IF YOU'RE IN CHARGE: Use Aquarius for inspiration and energy, while toning down their ideas to keep them manageable. Bring them down to earth, but don't pin them down or they'll slip through your fingers.

TAURUS @ WORK WITH PISCES

☛ **Use protection!**

This is a very, very casual alliance. In fact, you two just sort of fall into it. No hard lines, no rough edges. Certainly no problems with pacing. Taurus will be able to create. Pisces will be given encouragement. Quiet is the order of the day—and plenty of room to think things through. Still, should Taurus ever need rock-solid backup, well, then, Taurus will learn what others have learned: If bored, unhappy, or merely curious, Pisces the Fish may decide to explore new waters.

IF PISCES IS BOSS: You're a bull and Pisces is a drifter. Learn to be flexible, but don't get carried away on Pisces's roller-coaster dreams. Your Pisces boss will learn to appreciate your experience learned in the school of hard knocks.

IF YOU'RE IN CHARGE: Gosh, Pisces seems moody. One day cheerful, the next gloomy. But they have good ideas—though some are pies in the sky. Bring things down to earth: Be an anchor as well as a boss.

Gemini @ Work

"We all have our *things*. I'm an infomaniac."
GEMINI MEDICAL JOURNALIST ENID VASQUEZ

MAY 21 TO JUNE 20

GEMINI

The Myth

In Greek and Roman mythology, the Geminis were a couple of brothers—twins, actually, but not identical—who liked to make mischief. The problem was that one of them, Pollux, was immortal, while Castor was just a regular guy. So one day as a prank, they crashed a double wedding and kidnapped the two brides. As you might expect, the grooms got mad and Castor was killed.

Pollux was grief-stricken. He begged Zeus, king of the gods, to let Castor live. So Zeus placed the brothers together in the sky. But on one condition: They could live there only half the year. Their time would be split. So they lived six months on Mount Olympus and the rest of the year in Hades, the underworld. Moral of the story: Gemini wants it all: to be both mortal and immortal, to change directions regularly, and to have that cozy little brownstone in Manhattan as well as the condo in Miami Beach.

Motivation

When it comes to Gemini's motivation, one will never do. Why narrow it down when you can have 16? Variety is more than the spice of your life—it *is* your life. It might look like greed or gluttony, but it's not. Pigging out doesn't tempt your taste buds. But tasting everything life has to offer—now there's an idea you'll invest in.

Geminis are idea people. A whopping retirement fund appeals to you as much as the next guy, but only for the free time it will afford you to pursue sketching and ice-skating in your 80s. But for now, today's ideas suffice. Money just pays the electric bill so you can devour the newspaper before nodding off in bed, dreaming of new and exciting vacation destinations.

In the morning you chew on raw data. By the afternoon you're spitting out brainstorms like watermelon seeds. Hey, the boss needs a proposal drafted? No problem. You produce. Meanwhile, the great American novel might be sprouting in your head.

But contrary to popular superstition, not all Geminis are writers and teachers. Though you tend to excel at such challenges, you grow bored doing just one thing. You're the type who sells hearing aids by day and moonlights as the 1-900-DOMINATRIX by night. And then, of course, you'll write the definitive book on the subject!

Assets

You may not be able to leap tall buildings in a single bound, but you're a lot like Superman. On the one hand you're Clark Kent, the roving reporter, sopping up information like a thirsty sponge. Boy, how you ought to excel in this information age, lapping up ideas on the Internet and redistributing factoids! Then, emerging from the phone booth, you're the superhero himself, making sense of a problem and fixing it in no time flat. Those dastardly quarterly reports and Post-it Notes deter most professionals. But you knock them down to earth so the rest of humanity can manage them. And you fly from task to task, *almost* as fast as a speeding bullet.

> **"An executive is someone who makes a decision quickly and gets somebody else to do the work."**
> TV NEWS COMMENTATOR
> JOE MOORE

You've seen those want ads: ". . . able to juggle multiple tasks." Gem-

ini's the quintessential multitasker. You can brew coffee, balance your checkbook, and close that deal in San Francisco all at the same time. If the average professional changes careers six times in a lifetime, you change at least a dozen, probably a baker's dozen.

You know a lot. Your insatiable curiosity drives you to collect facts and figures as obsessively as Martha Stewart collects recipes—thanks to that trusty Gemini hard drive of yours. You're resourceful. You know where to look for things and process information quickly. Where other folks see scraps of paper and torn-up photos, you see a collage. And your attention to detail is impeccable. You read the print, the fine print, and the space in between.

Gemini's the journalist of the zodiac. Even if you're a tax attorney and not a reporter, you're always after a good scoop. You tackle your briefs and analyze stats with a keen eye. Like a foreign correspondent, the Gemini mind roves far and wide even if its body's stuck in a swivel chair. Lots of Geminis take desk jobs, but it's agony for them to sit still. Gemini needs to get around. I knew one who worked in three countries in a year, and she wasn't even a flight attendant.

> **"To me creativity is one body; it just has different limbs—poetry, acting, music, whatever. I'm sure I'm not alone when I say that I need many different things to express myself fully."**
> GEMINI SINGER, SONGWRITER, AND POET
> JEWEL

You're a talker. Aries may tell people where to go, and Capricorn is likely to tell them what to do, but Gemini can tell them what they want to hear. You make friends and contacts easily, though you may not cultivate them into deep working relationships because, well, who has time? Networking's a cinch. (If not, check out your Venus sign to pump up your networking muscles.)

Want to know what Gemini's biggest material asset is? No, it's not your computer, your Fabergé egg, or even your astrological mutual fund account. It's your Rolodex—or address book, database, or wherever you store all those names and numbers. If you haven't captialized on this yet, start now.

You thrive in a team. As one of the gang you quickly make friends and allies. Small teams and defined projects work best—large, unwieldy groups or assignments might force you to spread yourself too thin, a danger every Gemini should avoid.

Great networking and big sales go together. If you've got the soul of a salesperson, flaunt it, preferably by outselling your less quick-witted competition. A career in public relations might be for you. Or advertising. Anything that exercises your communication skills. And if you don't like

your career, do what you do best: Change it and move on to bigger and better things.

Liabilities

Sure, you're a Jack or Jill of all trades, but master of how many? Potentially scatterbrained, you flit from task to task and wonder how to prioritize. As soon as one task starts, another intrigues you. If the mind wanders, so can profits.

You're a born people person, but sometimes your smooth-talkin' ways are mistaken for con artistry. Friendliness works, but keep it genuine. And don't let your inner roving reporter become a tabloid journalist with a gossip column. Fight the paparazzi within.

Dr. Matt's Tips for Gemini Success

★ Find something to be passionate about, work that'll get you out of bed not only tomorrow but for years to come.

★ Identify what you value, what's meaningful. Learn to distinguish great opportunities from enticing distractions.

★ Be flexible, even if it's within a framework of consistency and long-range plans. And be careful not to get bogged down in the busy work.

★ Practice the art of conversation, receiving as well as giving, in order to communicate more effectively. Controversy might sell a scandalous hard-rock album, but agreements make for a friendlier work environment.

★ This above all: Take a chill pill. Take a walk. Stress kills more business-people than wayward buses. The great ideas will still be there when you get back from the spa.

TWIN FORTUNES

Geminis can talk and Geminis can sell—the essential skills of the multi-billion dollar advertising industry. Nobody knows this better than Charles and Maurice Saatchi—not twins, but brothers, both of whom are Geminis. Together they founded Saatchi & Saatchi, the London-based multinational advertising agency with some of the world's biggest, best-recognized accounts. From market research to production to media scheduling, advertising agencies juggle many responsibilities—another Gemini talent that makes the Saatchi brothers perfectly suited to spreading the word about every conceivable product.

Gemini in Alliance

GEMINI @ WORK WITH ARIES

☛ Faster! Faster!

This speedy alliance starts fast. Let's hope it doesn't end fast, too. You and Aries share a natural attraction. Aries pushes you, directs your dynamism, sets ablaze your own latent hopes and ambitions. They can help you rise to the top of your field or to gain influence in professional organizations, labor groups, or the public at large. You, meanwhile, help articulate their plans, giving words and form to their passion. But since you both get bored quickly, find a way, right now, to stay on track and turn ideas into profits.

IF ARIES IS BOSS: They'll push you hard. They'll like your speed but won't quite grasp your curiosity or eye for detail. When you burst in with three new ways to double profit margins, they'll have trouble pulling themselves away from objective number one. The trick? Distill your three ideas into one palpable plan of attack and show Aries how it'll beat the competition. That'll get their attention!

IF YOU'RE IN CHARGE: Help Aries understand that living in the moment is a great Zen philosophy but that they still need to plan for tomorrow. Put them on a schedule. Make them pace themselves. Give them definite goals with achievable rewards.

GEMINI @ WORK WITH TAURUS

☞ A marriage of convenience.

Taurus looks at you, sees the lightbulbs going off over your head, and is dazzled. You look into their eyes and see dollar signs, which reminds you the bills need to be paid. Obviously you need each other. Taurus brings value and quality, you sell it to the highest bidder. What's more, Taurus backs you up and supports you behind the scenes. They tap resources. You call attention to the stones they've left unturned and nudge Taurus out of the office and into the marketplace. But while your strategies may complement each other's, this partnership won't prosper until you've decided on mutually agreeable goals and priorities.

IF TAURUS IS BOSS: You're bound to make them nervous. Though you're a great asset to any Taurus, they're likely to think of you as a complicated piece of technology—awfully promising but hard to figure out and operate. So now you know what to do: Be self-reliant. Don't tax their limited ability to cope with stress. In fact, you'll score big points for managing the complexities of office life while they amass their fortunes.

IF YOU'RE IN CHARGE: Rely on them. They want to help. So delegate, share responsibility, and ask their opinion. It might not please you, but it's still a good way to sort through your own thoughts. And don't forget to ask the Bull for help with quality control—it's their specialty.

GEMINI @ WORK WITH ANOTHER GEMINI

☞ Thirty-one flavors!

Two Geminis in one office? Wow! This is a lively alliance, full of intellectual stimulation and fascinating debates. The schedules are full; activity never runs out; ideas abound like tulips in springtime. But together you're awfully restless, and completing your chores looms largest among your mutual challenges. In your effort to stay on top of the newest innovations, hold back from criticizing each other. A strong team spirit and an eye on the bottom line will work wonders.

IF THE OTHER GEMINI IS BOSS: Be ready for the winds to change at any minute. Gemini goes with the flow and follows sudden inspirations. They'll expect you to be right there at the turning point with them. But if you can help them stay focused, you've done everybody a big favor.

IF YOU'RE IN CHARGE: Be in charge! Every employee needs rules and limits. Communicate these up front. But there's no need to be insanely rigid. One great Gemini feature is how you respond effectively to individual problems, the ones not covered in the procedure manual. Empower your Gemini employee to do the same, but in a way that's consistent with *your* style.

GEMINI @ WORK WITH CANCER

☛ **A profitable enterprise.**

Together you have a good sense of how to please the market. With your perspicacity and Cancer's instincts, you can combine forces to identify bargains and anticipate rapidly appreciating market sectors. And when you burn out, Cancer can help revive you. Meanwhile, you drag them out of their shell. Despite these mutual advantages, however, you must vigilantly address your partnership's division of labor. Does one of you do all the fun stuff while the other's stuck with drudgery? By the same token, make sure each of you is profiting fairly.

IF CANCER IS BOSS: Don't let them down. Make sure they know you're on their side. Ask, for example, before you make your niece's wedding shower invitations on the office copy machine. Cancers in charge are generous but hate to be cheated.

IF YOU'RE IN CHARGE: It won't be easy to shape Cancer in your image. They'll try to make you happy, but it's no use trying to cook lasagna in a pie tin. Instead, tap Cancer's inherent resources. Assign them projects that need careful and ongoing attention. Let them interact with clients who need the personal touch.

GEMINI @ WORK WITH LEO

☛ **Forget guerrilla marketing—here comes King Kong!**

Publicity is this alliance's forte. Leo packages, you promote—together you could successfuly evangelize for everything from deodorant to world peace. In this partnership there's no shortage of contacts or creativity. But are you both a couple of "front men" or cover girls? Does anybody file the quarterly payroll taxes? Rather than bicker over whose voice is on the answering machine, perform a duet and consider hiring or contracting a bookkeeper and other support staff.

IF LEO IS BOSS: They're the boss! You won't find lots of room to experiment. But don't get discouraged. First, prove yourself. The Leo boss admires talent. Next, present your ideas in a nice tidy package, never scattered or half-baked. Finally, have fun. Leo loosens up when he knows it's safe to come off the pedestal to play.

IF YOU'RE IN CHARGE: Test your Leo's ability to manage responsibility. Leos tend to promise more than they can deliver, but not often, especially if their pride's at stake. Then get them to help you solidify your ideas and ship them to market. Leo wants to stand up for an award-winning product or service.

GEMINI @ WORK WITH VIRGO

☛ **Twins—but definitely not identical!**

Both your signs share the same mascot planet, Mercury, which means neither of you is a slouch in the intellectual department. But like a couple of rivalrous siblings, you may have so much in common that you're nothing alike. You find Virgo boring. They consider you superficial. Virgo's critical, you're tactless, and together you argue over just about everything. Even a simple discussion of office decor may send the poor interior designer running for prescription drugs. (Look up both of your Jupiter signs to see how you can complement one another's talents and opportunities.)

IF VIRGO IS BOSS: Don't expect them to let you run wild. Virgos are as protective of their workers as they are of their work, which they tend to treat like a holy pilgrimage. They can squeeze productivity out of you like the last drop of toothpaste in the tube. Definitely honor their priorities, but don't stress out with performance anxiety.

IF YOU'RE IN CHARGE: If Virgo understands your objective, and if you don't bother them with too many tangents, Virgo will serve you devotedly. But like a seasoned English butler, your Virgo employee needs their own territory to administer and polish. Give them something that needs improving and reworking, then you'll be free to move on, without Virgo nagging you about the office climate control.

GEMINI @ WORK WITH LIBRA

☛ **Fun and games.**

This is a playful alliance, potentially full of wit and good humor, and a constant competition to seem more ingenious than the other. Between

the two of you, compromise flows effortlessly. The conversations never run dry. Broadening your professional horizons is equally valued. It's not, however, the ideal alliance for laying solid foundations or holding out against the competition. Build on your easy friendship with Libra by limiting conversation (an egg timer works well!) and highlighting tangible accomplishments.

IF LIBRA IS BOSS: You'll think you can get away with murder—or anything else! But it ain't necessarily so. Libras are patient. They put up with a lot. And then, bam! Libra zeroes in on anything sneaky, suspicious, or unfair. Win their trust and you've won an undeterrable advocate.

IF YOU'RE IN CHARGE: You'll find Libra an agreeable employee, full of the words *yes, you've got it* and *have a nice day!* They may lack your initiative to sell, sell, sell, but they sure know how to follow up with customers and keep the public happy. But before the other employees start complaining, beware of playing favorites.

GEMINI @ WORK WITH SCORPIO

☛ **Sharp as diamonds.**

The brain power in this alliance is so monumental it seems ready to topple over like the Leaning Tower of Pisa. Let's hope no one gets hurt! Scorpio's a planner. You're an improviser. Together you can put on a good show, as long as there's room for your flexibility and their rigidity. They'll want to control the money—fine, but request receipts and spreadsheets or you'll quickly drift from the solid facts of the business. While Scorpio enjoys your cleverness most days, on others your charm will get you nowhere.

IF SCORPIO IS BOSS: You can probably bear it when they try to control your every move. But it's another matter when they demand that you concentrate. Train yourself to communicate in a simple, direct fashion. While Geminis love to flirt with corporate headhunters or sudden job openings elsewhere, the Scorpio boss is ruthlessly possessive—training you is an investment they won't obligingly part with.

IF YOU'RE IN CHARGE: Scorpio will hold you to your word—a promise made is a promise kept with these guys. Honor Scorpio's affinity for privacy. It might seem they're holed up scheming a world takeover, but they're really getting your work done. When you need to focus with the exactitude of a laser beam, call in Scorpio.

GEMINI @ WORK WITH SAGITTARIUS

☛ **Big picture, little picture.**

Sagittarius looks up, out, and beyond. You focus on the nitty-gritty. Together, nothing escapes your mutual examination—four eyes fixed on a cosmos full of things to know. Who knows more, you or Saj? Hard to say, but you can bet the issue will underly most of your disputes. In this team you'll spend lots of time at the drawing board, united in the pursuits of bluffing, brainstorming, and concocting. The missing links are practicality and staying power. Get some or you'll study lots of fish and catch nothing but seaweed.

IF SAGITTARIUS IS BOSS: Count on stretching your mind. Once they discover you're a quick thinker, Saj'll expect you to keep up. *If* you have time, question them about the meaning of life or the Sydney Stock Exchange— they'll love you for it. They'll also appreciate your attention to detail, but don't rub their noses in it.

IF YOU'RE IN CHARGE: You may never see your Saj. Even more than you, they relish their freedom. Out in the world, moving from task to task is their favorite modus operandi. This can work for you, but only if Saj is a phone call away. Give them a pager, cell phone, and e-mail—plus a request to check in *regularly.*

GEMINI @ WORK WITH CAPRICORN

☛ **This is serious business.**

Like diplomats from two contrary cultures, you start out on your best behavior. Together you can unlock big money and achieve high-stakes objectives worthy of the world's kudos. But differences of opinion abound. Capricorn naturally assumes they can steer you like a Tonka Toy. They want a routine. Routine stifles you. They want a sure thing. You prefer open options. Communication is key, even if you have to pry it out of them.

IF CAPRICORN IS BOSS: They'll expect consistency. Anything newfangled will conflict with their tried-and-true sensibilities—unless, of course, you can make a case for necessary advancement and keeping up with industry standards.

IF YOU'RE IN CHARGE: You might quickly forget who's the boss! They're natural leaders and you're, well, not. Don't worry. They'll respect your intel-

ligence—so, then, intelligently tell them what to do. Establish guidelines and standards. Give Capricorn a sense of authority by making them responsible for a few routine tasks. Evaluate them with concrete examples, not casual remarks.

GEMINI @ WORK WITH AQUARIUS

☛ **Time for the question-answer period.**

A couple of skeptics, you two challenge the existing order and wonder how to fix it. Spotting flaws in the room, you, Gemini, tend to rearrange the furniture, whereas Aquarius throws it out and starts from scratch. But at heart you both advocate the new and original, even if it's really the outrageous and recycled. This alliance brings out the teacher in each of you, and the two of you are forever debating issues of law, commerce, and marketing gimmicks.

> **"Every successful enterprise requires three [people]—a dreamer, a businessman, and a son-of-a-bitch."**
> AUTHOR PETER MCARTHUR

Someday, however, somebody's got to make a decision. Dr. Matt doesn't recommend tossing a coin, so force yourself to draw conclusions before quitting time.

IF AQUARIUS IS BOSS: You'll inevitably run into their strong beliefs and elaborate theories. This can inspire you to new heights, a beacon to guide your work with a sense of purpose. Then again, Aquarius can frustrate the hair off your head, especially when they greet your ideas with their trademark indifference. So stay objective. Don't take it personally. Aquarius doesn't.

IF YOU'RE IN CHARGE: You've got yourself a comrade. With this instant rapport, you don't have to explain everything 27 times. But look out! Your protégé is in demand. You may suddenly discover you don't have the biggest Rolodex or the busiest schedule in the office anymore.

GEMINI @ WORK WITH PISCES

☛ **Everything to lose, everything to gain.**

This alliance can make you or break you. First the bad news. A Pisces teammate will drive you berserk. Accept it. See, you tell it how it is, whereas Pisces holds back, often skirting the real issue. Able to fill many niches, Gemini will try anything once. Forever carving out their own niche, Pisces is fussy, with hard-to-predict reactions to your multitudinous suggestions. But when it's good between you, it's *real* good. Like magic. Like reaching the Promised Land. You communicate so well it's like

telepathy. Pisces lifts your work out of its mundane existence and into the sky, contributing value you never thought possible.

IF PISCES IS BOSS: Crank up your creativity and imagination and watch your brownie points rack up fast. But to really succeed with the Pisces boss, look beyond the surface. In leadership roles they often *play* a role. So borrow some good instincts for human nature and figure out what your Pisces boss really wants.

IF YOU'RE IN CHARGE: Depend on Pisces to soothe your worries; don't let them strain your already tender nerves. Sensitive and hard to assess, Pisces may require more management effort than you're willing to exert. Careful training is key. Once you're on the same wavelength, you'll prefer the Pisces employee to an electric blanket on a cold night.

Cancer @ Work

**"Be like a duck, my mother used to tell me. Remain calm on
the surface and paddle like hell underneath."**
CANCER ACTOR MICHAEL CAINE

CANCER

The Myth

Cancer has always understood the value of "location, location, location."
To Mesopotamian stargazers, the stars of Cancer were the portal that souls
crossed on their way from heaven to earth. Just imagine the foot traffic!

How Cancer the Crab acquired this prestigious address is told by Greek
mythology. Full of jealousy, the goddess Hera hated Hercules. When Hercules
was a baby, Hera tried killing him with two snakes in his bed. That
didn't work, so Hera sent the Hydra monster after Hercules. In the midst
of the swampy battle, a crab emerged from the muck and bit Hercules on
the foot. Hercules was a feisty fellow and he crushed the crab, but Hera
was so grateful to the shelled nipper that she placed Cancer among the
stars in the sky. Moral of the story: Cancer is loyal, helpful, fiercely protective,
and always finds its way to prime real estate.

Motivation

Crabs swim around in the deep. And your motivation, Cancer, springs from the depth of your heart. Better than most, you understand that the great goal in life isn't success but fulfillment. Not just your own. You're motivated to nurture loved ones, the little people, the bankrupt business in distress that you picked up for a song at auction.

The phrase "Make something of yourself" speaks the essence of Cancer. It's not the pride and glory of Leo that coaxes you out of bed, nor is it Capricorn's drive to forge a legacy. It is simply the fulfillment of a rich life, warm and comfortable, safe and nourishing.

But fulfillment and nurturing takes more than a pat on the back and enough pocket money for popcorn at the movies. It takes a strong foundation. It takes a healthy environment. Without the right supportive habitat—whether it's Rodeo Drive or cyberspace—no business can survive. You're a survivor. You promote the climate and conditions to grow a strong organization or career—one that'll stick around long enough to ensure the survival of you and what you value.

You value sustained growth and the promise of better tomorrows. Aries, that determined rascal, may plant the seeds, and Leo may sell the crop before it's ripe, but you water the seeds and scatter your own personal brand of Miracle-Gro till the garden is bright in bloom.

Assets

Your feelings run deep. As an employee, you're devoted; as an entrepreneur, passionate. People trust you, like a favorite old movie they watch again and again. As a manager, you get a lot of requests for free advice and good counsel. Everybody senses you've seen it all before, even if you're just as green as the rest of the junior staff.

Cancers make great consultants, managers, and teachers. No, not because you're incurable masochists. It's because you help people, projects, and companies reach self-sufficiency, inviting them to define their own lives and purposes. "Go, fly away, and soar!" you tell them. And you're the wind beneath their wings. Cancer also makes things safe. You step in and ask, "What do we need and how are we going to fulfill those needs?" Then you fill 'er up.

You're a born salesperson because you know *what* to sell to your

customers. Sure, Gemini and Sagittarius are more outgoing and blabber-mouthy, but you know how to meet people's needs. Which is what sales is all about anyway. Or should be. After all, the laws of supply and de-mand are all about *responding* to the marketplace.

Another asset in the Cancer portfolio is a knack for merchandising. Satisfied customers mean a lot to you. In your work there's humanity and personality. Cancer cares. You almost always find something to care about, or it finds you.

But don't let all this touchy-feely talk make you think you're just plain squishy. Can-cer's a force to reckon with. You defend what's yours. The Crab knows how to protect itself. The ocean crashes, the sands blow, the sharks bite—meanwhile, the Crab is cozy and care-free in a home of its own making. So go ahead, swim with the sharks.

Like Taurus, you value security. But while the Bull luxuriates in security like a cat on a catnip farm, you stock it up like canned foods on an aircraft carrier—always ready in an emergency. That's Cancer, the pack rat of the zodiac, the creator of nest eggs bigger than a pterodactyl's.

> "Perhaps it is time the 'work ethic' was redefined. . . . In a world of cybernetics, of an almost runaway technology, things are increasingly making things. It is for our species, it would seem, to go on to other matters. Human matters."
> AUTHOR STUDS TERKEL

The longest day of the year is when the Sun enters Cancer, the start of summer: the season of family barbecues, grape harvests, and hot-blooded revolutions (the French and American revolutions were both Cancer af-fairs). This sign is about creating life. Now, before you run off snickering like a kid in Sex Ed, think about where you want to grow more life, more bounty, more summertime. That is where you'll find your next big break.

Liabilities

You're no soft-shelled crab, but sometimes you act like one. Constructive criticism can send you into fits of despair. You brood. Oh, how you brood.

Fearing rejection, you isolate. Fearing insecurity, you hesitate. But be-ware that you don't hide away from the world because it's so damn scary. Sure it is, but you've got the inner strength to weather it. If things start getting you down, change them. Cancer has the power.

Sometimes Cancer cares too much. "Let me help you with that" be-comes an excuse to take over and manage everybody's life. Don't grow dependent on others' dependency on you. The stress can be too great.

Carry the burden you can, but don't beg for the straw that'll break your back. The world needs you. *Really.* It's just a matter of finding your niche.

> **"Inside myself is a place where I live all alone and that's where you renew your springs that never dry up.**
> HUMANITARIAN AND NOBEL LAUREATE IN LITERATURE PEARL S. BUCK

Once settled in the niche, learn the difference between business and pleasure. You take business personally and schedule your trip to London with "appointments" at Westminster Abbey and Parliament. Clearly you're invested in whatever you do. But boundaries matter. Don't turn all your colleagues into bosom buddies, and don't pencil in all of your friends as contacts.

Finally, in your quest to amass resources, you can lose sight of what you want. Trinkets and toys become your reason for living. Try not to overspend on things you'll never use—you're better off letting someone else order the office supplies.

Dr. Matt's Tips for Cancer Success

★ Establish some base level of security—a nest egg, a down payment on a house, someone to help with the kids while you brave the marketplace—and then stop fretting. Complete security is a myth.

★ Don't run from stormy weather. Stay and face the thunder.

★ Chase some dreams.

★ Cultivate your sense of humor and lightheartedness.

★ Above all, don't let the world knock you down. Though you're not the toughest sign out there, you're the best at bouncing back.

LIFE, LIBERTY, AND THE PURSUIT OF HAPPINESS

In modern history, Cancer's the sign of revolution. The American, then the French, then the Russian revolutions all started under the Sun in Cancer. That may seem odd since Cancer's not intrinsically rebellious like Aquarius, nor naturally idealistic like Sagittarius. But Cancer wants to *rebuild*. "Let's start a better world," said those revolutionists, like the American Founding Fathers who wrote about life, liberty, and the pursuit of happiness. Cancer is urgent. They respond to *need*. Cancer feels the need, the urgency, the mood of the people, and they act accordingly. "Liberty, equality, fraternity," cried the French revolutionists. No, not idealistic, not rebellious. Just a good idea whose time had come.

Cancer in Alliance

CANCER @ WORK WITH ARIES

☛ **Good cop, bad cop.**

Equally determined, you're both initiators. But sustaining this relationship is tough. You're sensitive. They're less than sensitive. You scrimp and save. Aries spends whatever it takes. The power struggle is constant. Will Aries dominate, or will you smother them with parental guidance? Still, if you want to play in the big leagues, you can't beat Aries as a teammate. Forthrightness is essential. Discuss feelings and fears. Don't gloss over the rough edges before you smooth them out. Just spit it out.

IF ARIES IS BOSS: You'll need an extralarge dose of assertiveness not to get squashed. Don't be a pushover and don't hold a grudge. Aries won't let you hide in your shell, but it's OK—even necessary, perhaps—to make them aware of your comfort zone.

IF YOU'RE IN CHARGE: Don't let Aries walk all over you. Do make use of their abundant energy, compensating what you may lack in willpower. This employee will be your champion, but only if you're their hero.

CANCER @ WORK WITH TAURUS

☛ **Working hard *and* smart.**

You make a good team, sharing a passion, even a downright lust, for security. Your combined retirement plans probably exceed the GNP of a small country. Cancer contributes creativity. Taurus supplies steadiness. You're both careful investors and dependable businesspersons. Together you forge an alliance that people trust, banks invest in, and customers count on. This combination lacks some excitement, but if the profits meet your expectations, you're both likely to stick around.

IF TAURUS IS BOSS: You'll work hard, aim to please, and deserve a slap on the back. But Taurus doesn't always want to invest so much time in development and planning as you do. Prove your approach pays off in the long run.

IF YOU'RE IN CHARGE: Motivate your Taurus employee and help them understand what they're working toward. Reward them with tangible bonuses and perks, not just praise and plaques.

CANCER @ WORK WITH GEMINI

☛ **Mind over matter.**

The twins move just a little too fast for you. They like change. You like stability and a natural evolution of things. It's hard to extract from scatterbrained Gemini the level of commitment you'd appreciate. But you make a superduper sales team. Gemini's flair for reporting facts and figures and your warm, personal touch make it a cinch to clinch the deal. To keep this relationship running smoothly, listen to Gemini's ideas. Tell them your qualms. You both lack the head-on approach, so stop skirting issues. When this alliance is ready to make a deal, skip irrelevant steps and try just going for it.

IF GEMINI IS BOSS: Keep this in mind: What they say is not etched in gold, as it might be for you. Gemini tends to think out loud. What you interpret as *The Plan* may well be a "kinda-sorta-maybe" proposition. Be Gemini's sounding board and you'll be doing them a huge favor.

IF YOU'RE IN CHARGE: You'll want to groom and coach this young whippersnapper. Give them an anchor, but don't keep them desk-bound. Take advantage of Gemini's talent: multitasking. Gemini requires variety. Still, though, limit distractions.

CANCER @ WORK WITH CANCER

☞ There's a fighter in there!

A couple of Cancers, eh? Well, you're both territorial. Despite lots of generosity, heaven help the unsuspecting employee who steals your sta-pler. Neither of you likes people to mess with your stuff or trespass on your territory! So in this partnership, make the boundaries as visi-ble as the old Berlin Wall. Though this alliance is great at bringing people together, you each need your space. Confrontation doesn't come easy. Find a trick or tactic for resolving conflicts, making decisions—anything to fall back on besides your feeling of the moment. And most of all, get in sync with each other's moods or get out of the office!

> **"Wherever your treasure is, there will your heart be also."**
> THE GOSPEL OF MATTHEW

IF THE OTHER CANCER IS BOSS: Remember every Cancer's got a center as soft as a cherry cordial. Someday you might get to see it. But for now, realize they're no softie to deal with. The Cancer boss can't stand uncertainty, so deliver a sure thing and you've got a friend in high places.

IF YOU'RE IN CHARGE: Don't let your Cancer employee feel expendable or ob-solete. To be replaced by a machine or made "redundant" by a kid half their age—this is what they fear, so a safe, solvent environment will yield the best performance from this dedicated worker.

CANCER @ WORK WITH LEO

☞ A good name.

Comfortable and robust, this alliance likes the bottom line, especially when it's big. Leo's strength increases your security. They're more willing to take risks—and if anyone can convince you to put your money or good name on the line, it's Leo. Sure, Leo's arrogance is a bit of a turn-off, but their optimism brightens your outlook. You give Leo what they need: ad-miration. They look at your work and say, "Yeah, this'll sell!" When all's OK, you're both loyal to the max. If you start taking advantage of one an-other, maximum loyalty may transform into maximum enmity.

IF LEO IS BOSS: Admire their leadership, even if it does strike you as unre-strained and extravagant. By playing on Leo's team, you may find you've suddenly got the confidence and determination you need to go forward. Only you can decide when it's time to cut the cord and move on.

IF YOU'RE IN CHARGE: Test your Leo. They need challenges and rise to the occasion. Ask for Leo's input when a situation looks hopeless—they can always squeeze lemonade out of lemons. If tensions arise, remember a Leo approaches conflict differently than a Cancer. Whereas you may keep silent and strike without warning, the Lion tends to roar loudly but seldom bites.

CANCER @ WORK WITH VIRGO

☞ **Worrywarts.**

Together you're never without a contingency plan. The two of you like to consider *every* conceivable option and outcome. Nothing misses your attention, including all of the things that *can* go wrong but probably never will. Dr. Matt recommends optimism and accentuating what's probable, not just possible in a million years. Focus more effort on executing Plan A and less on dreaming up Plans B and C. It'd also be nice if you'd tolerate each other's idiosyncrasies.

IF VIRGO IS BOSS: Be really concrete with Virgo. Touchy-feely they're not! Put suggestions in writing. Account for how you're spending your time. And if an assignment makes you unhappy, don't pout. Explain it to your Virgo boss in terms of diminished productivity.

IF YOU'RE IN CHARGE: Don't let Virgo fill up their agenda with busywork. You see, Virgo may look self-sufficient, but if you don't explain the to-do list point by point, Virgo will take the initiative and start sharpening pencils with the gusto of an infomercial knife salesman.

CANCER @ WORK WITH LIBRA

☞ **From the heart or the head?**

This partnership can work if, and only if, it's a true partnership. That's not easy, considering you two are so incongruous, especially in conflict resolution. You, for example, react fervently to threats or problems that Libra might dismiss as inconsequential. Help them see that in a team, your problem is their problem. Definitely don't withdraw from a Libra teammate! It freaks them out.

IF LIBRA IS BOSS: You may be expected to put on a happy face, all the time, in sunshine or killer tornadoes. Help them understand there are days when you perform smashingly, and days when you'd rather stay home

and make passionate love to your pillow. Besides, it's how well you do your work that counts, not how well you can smile on command.

IF YOU'RE IN CHARGE: This employee will gobble up your attention—and pay you back with excellent listening skills. But if Libra feels stifled, possessed, or subjected to too many brouhahas, look out! They can lose their warmth and zest faster than leftovers can in the fridge.

CANCER @ WORK WITH SCORPIO

☛ **A tinderbox.**

Don't be the one to drop the match on this potential inferno. Business is highly personal for the both of you. So it's crucial to put agreements in writing and talk frankly. Otherwise, every incidental clash will take place under the surface until one of you, seemingly out of nowhere, exclaims, "To heck with it! I'm going to Fairbanks to start a dog-sledding business." But you can sidestep explosions by transforming bitterness or hard feelings into a friendly rivalry. Engines run by spark and boom. Likewise, you can stoke each other's creativity and productivity to optimum capacity— as long as this alliance stays professional with no hidden agendas.

IF SCORPIO IS BOSS: Now is the time to communicate honestly or risk total failure. When it comes to being indirect and tough to pin down, Scorpio's got you beat, so don't get caught in a game of second-guessing. More than anyone, you have the gift of sincerity. Use it with Scorpio and they'll be pleasantly surprised.

IF YOU'RE IN CHARGE: You'll earn Scorpio's respect by proving insight is more effective than brute force. Since you already know the value of intuition, capitalize on Scorpio's gut feelings and ability to size up a situation. Let Scorpio in on important decisions. It might spark disagreement, but that'll ultimately strengthen the discussion.

CANCER @ WORK WITH SAGITTARIUS

☛ **Let's get this show on the road!**

You two look like a pair of mismatched socks. You want a roof over your head. Sagittarius wanders off seeking a safari. Still, though, this alliance can do great things—especially if you, Cancer, are looking to expand your horizons. Saj offers a passport out of the same old thing, helping place your achievements in a larger context, pointing out how

your contributions really *matter*. And together you can create a breeding ground for the imagination and good deeds aplenty. But watch the bottom line! No matter how interesting your work with Saj, it's got to be solvent to keep going. Work for work's sake is called a hobby.

IF SAGITTARIUS IS BOSS: They'll expect you to *absorb* a lot, from critical information to "in" jokes to where they left their power of attorney. If you can soak it up, they'll fork it over, making you indispensable. But remember! Saj—especially in a high position—says what they think when they think it, regardless of innocent bystanders' feelings. Let them know you are neither innocent nor a bystander!

IF YOU'RE IN CHARGE: Use Sagittarius to bring coherence and purpose to your plans. Assign them intellectually engaging tasks. Allow them to roam to whichever hinterlands you'd prefer to avoid. But foremost, Saj needs to understand the motive—particularly when it's a profit motive.

CANCER @ WORK WITH CAPRICORN

☛ **Built to last.**

Once you get beyond your differences, this alliance promises longevity. Fleeting ventures and fly-by-night schemes don't interest you. Tradition both stimulates and stymies this partnership. Together you lack a taste for adventure. Develop a willingness to participate in the early stages of growing a business. Remember, if you're in a dark, unfamiliar room—like today's marketplace—you have to fumble for the light switch before you can get comfy in a plush chair.

IF CAPRICORN IS BOSS: Don't expect a lot of personal attention, but do good work and it won't go unnoticed. If you have practical input, speak up. Capricorn doesn't want employees to hold their tongues for fear of hurting people's feelings. To them, feelings aren't the issue—what matters is what works, what doesn't, and how to fix it.

IF YOU'RE IN CHARGE: Provide a stable, *and* supportive, environment. Capricorn exudes self-reliance. Don't let that fool you. They need strokes as much as the next person, but they also need challenges to maximize their potential.

CANCER @ WORK WITH AQUARIUS

☞ **Oh, the tension!**

This alliance takes you places you never dreamed possible. But are you sure you want to go there? The unconventionality of Aquarius opens the door to trouble as well as opportunity. You may find them too data-hungry—too dependent on stats, studies, and think-tank proclamations. Except for a strong sense of duty and the desire to do the right thing, you have little in common. Don't overestimate business problems and devalue personal problems, especially when they come between you.

IF AQUARIUS IS BOSS: Try to go with the flow. They'll push you to innovate, which has its rewards. Yet your respect for convention can help Aquarius to recognize that the wacky ain't always where the money is.

IF YOU'RE IN CHARGE: Get Aquarius to keep you on the cutting edge, handling new technology, Internet solutions, and a generation of uncanny consumers. While they'll want to be paid what they're worth, Aquarius needs more than big bucks for inspiration. Try an inflatable robotic coworker.

CANCER @ WORK WITH PISCES

☞ **Dreaming the *possible* dream.**

This alliance lacks many, if not most, of the virtues taught in MBA programs. Get over it. Concentrate on your supreme strength: a talent for empathizing with your consumers. You feed their stomachs. Pisces feeds their souls. Reaching them in the first place, however, is essential. Increase your business's visibility in the marketplace—if you aren't seen, you aren't believed. With Pisces, always make room for a few eccentricities. Sometimes they're geniuses, sometimes loonies. It's your job (lucky you!) to bring out their best, and keep their worst out of bankruptcy.

IF PISCES IS BOSS: Let them know your boundaries. Your moods don't have to depend on their moods. Your work's not their work. But go along with their dream. Even if you don't believe in it, Pisces needs to think you do. Help them create a safe environment (your specialty!) where dreams can be realized responsibly.

IF YOU'RE IN CHARGE: You've got in the Pisces employee a true *assistant*. They want to *help*. Let them. But make it clear what kind of help you need, and what's just a nuisance. You don't need worshipers, you need workers.

Leo @ Work

JULY 23 TO AUGUST 22

LEO

The Myth

In one ancient Greek myth, the constellation Leo isn't a lion but a beautiful fur coat. It came off the back of a terrbily mean lion that tormented the locals. So when Hercules graduated from hero school, his first job was to stop that lion. Hercules and the lion wrestled. In the fray, Hercules lost a finger and the lion lost its coat. Victorious, and praised by the townspeople, Hercules used Leo's coat as a magical coat of armor and its mane as a helmet to protect him from enemies—and bad hair. Moral of the story: What's a hard day at work as long as you're well dressed and the toast of the town?

Motivation

Leo goes for glory. Not wealth, not power—these are just the *accoutrements* of glory. Deep down, you want to *feel* glorious! The red carpet is the road you aim to walk in this life. And as you walk it, the bright lights bathe your face, the roar of the crowd deafens your doubts, and the heady perfume of roses thrown at your feet reinforces the fact you've done your job not just well but superbly. You are, in fact, liked and valued. If money comes with the red carpet (and it usually does), so be it. But what's money without style?

Style, another Leo motivator, can turn everything into art. The artist Marcel Duchamp was a Leo. He'd sign his name to household objects (like a cup or a napkin) and call it art. Leo likes to put on a good show. In the musical version of *Working* by Studs Terkel there's a song called "It's an Art" sung by two waitresses serving burgers at a greasy spoon. They must have been Leos. Everything's an event with Leo. You never merely have a *job*. It's always a career. Even Leo dishwashers pride themselves on removing all the spots on the glasses while the breakfast dishes stack up. Why find a silver lining when you can find gold?

You want to whistle while you work, maybe even cha-cha and fox-trot. Job satisfaction ranks high among your priorities. It's hard to find; it might take a lifetime. To you, couch potato–hood is more terrifying than going down with the *Titanic*. At least then you'd get your picture in the paper.

Assets

You Leos take pride in your work. "I made this!" is your mantra. To the right employer you're more loyal than a golden retriever. You stand behind a brand, a name, or an ideal unfailingly—as long as you believe in it. But as soon that belief is betrayed or compromised, look out! Given how much you emotionally invest in whatever you do, if you feel slighted, you'll invest even more emotion into reaping revenge. When lions roar, they *roar!*

Your joie de vivre is contagious. When you're in high spirits, the workplace whirs like a carnival and the workday is both fun and productive. Leo can make any routine job satisfying, rewarding, and worthy of admiration. You'd find the quickest, most efficient way to stuff envelopes,

and darn it, you'd be proud. Routine jobs, however, are not really what you're cut out for!

Leo makes an entrance. In an economy like ours where the competition is stiff and there's nothing new under the Sun, Leo announces, "I'm here. Let the party begin!" Like a good actor, you're always prepared. You won't get caught with your zipper down on the sales floor. You check it on your way out of the dressing room. You comb your hair. You squirt cologne. You look organized, whether you are or not. Your car, for example, may be a pigsty—but if it is, you'll master the art of the one-minute makeover, dumping the junk in the trunk before tooling your clients around town.

> **"Art is not a mirror to reflect the world, but a hammer with which to shape it."**
> POLITICO AND POET
> VLADIMIR MAYAKOVSKY

You're always *on*. When you go for a job interview, you don't just sit in the waiting room twiddling your thumbs and reading your horoscope. You work the room, schmoozing the secretaries, fully aware that any so-called idle banter will prove you can fit into the company culture—before you've even met the big shots.

Contrary to popular opinion, not all Leos are attention hogs and narcissistic self-promoters. It's just that even the most modest felines realize they have to sell personality in order to sell a business or idea. Stand before a crowd and it hardly matters what you're saying: The crowd listens with perked ears and glued eyeballs. You've got them in the palm of your hand. You have a knack (when you want to use it) for making people feel important and good about themselves. You'll often find yourself running seminars and solving interoffice squabbles—because you're pretty darn good at it.

God may be in the details, but they still drive you crazy. Organizing a budget? Managing a database? No thanks. Your organizational talents lie elsewhere. "Come on, everybody," you say, "let's put on a show!"

Creative outlets are a must for Leo. You need to give of yourself—leadership, the arts, teaching children. It doesn't matter. So long as you express your personality and make a contribution.

Liabilities

You've got a big ego. That's not necessarily a bad thing. It often takes a big ego to make it big. But you have the potential to get too big for your britches and alienate all those folks who'd love you otherwise. You end up looking like a control freak, a high-maintenance individual who needs too

much attention. Or if you're the shy type, your ego might not ask for too much but it bruises as easily as a ripe tomato. Without affirmation your performance lags, which makes you less likely to receive affirmation—it's a vicious cycle that does you no good.

Leo hates to be a bit player. You dislike sharing power or control and sometimes reject the need to plan ahead. While you like to travel with an entourage and kindly accept assistance, you resent any interference with your plans. Justifying your actions to anyone seems such a bother, even a downright insult to your intelligence. You defy the advice of friends and every worthwhile book you've ever read and count on overnight success. "Leo knows best!" is a mighty costly golden rule to live by.

A little flexibility could do wonders for your creativity. It's a funny thing about creativity—it takes, ironically, both a strong ego and a healthy dose of vulnerability to put yourself and your opuses on display for public consumption. But the promise of success and reverence can lure you away from your Muse, the mythological mistress who whispers inspiration in your ear. Only you can decide whether you'd rather listen to applause or your heart.

Dr. Matt's Tips for Leo Success

★ Forge a job where your personality isn't just tolerated but lionized. Cookie-cutter careers are not for you.

★ Plan ahead. You like glitz, glory, and improvisation, but keep yourself grounded by coworkers who know the value of budgeting time. Quick, knee-jerk work can often be shoddy.

★ Beware of playing the prima donna. Make sure when you get the leading role you can actually execute it.

★ Surround yourself with a few skeptics and other independent thinkers, not just a team of colleagues who say, "Yes! You're so right!"

★ *Beware of flattery!* You, proud Leo, are particularly susceptible to praise even when it's false.

★ Share power and control, and be a team player even if you are the leader of the pack. Ask for help and use it.

★ Try to understand your coworkers and bosses, remembering their motives are probably different from yours. Not everyone wants to be king of the jungle. Some folks are content where they are.

★ Listen when people resist and question your ideas. Learn from them. Have justification for your actions. Avoid tyranny. It's the tyrants, after all, who most frequently wind up at the guillotine.

THE LION'S GOT STYLE—AND POPULARITY, TOO!

Leos have always had their paws in the arts and entertainment fields, earning fame for their creations. But from a business viewpoint, Leo's true talent is not creating culture but *popularizing* culture, making it marketable not to the few but to the many. In fashion, for example, Leo designers Coco Chanel and Yves Saint Laurent liberated middle-class women from expensive tailor-made dresses with affordable ready-to-wear designs. Leo chef Julia Child spearheaded the TV cooking shows that brought haute cuisine to home kitchens across a nation. With his assembly line, Leo carmaker Henry Ford was the first to supply automobiles to a mass market interested in transportation, not joy rides. Actress and producer Lucille Ball, another Leo, helped make the half-hour TV sitcom the world's most popular form of entertainment. And Leo pop artist Andy Warhol created art from everyday objects for everyday people. The list goes on. If a Leo roars in the forest, somebody'd better hear it!

Leo in Alliance

LEO @ WORK WITH ARIES

☛ The battle for center stage.

Leo thinks grandiosely. Aries acts impulsively. Together you think you can conquer the world. Or you just think the world of yourselves. Since you won't like it if Aries competes against *you*, direct the competitive spirit outward. Brace yourself for ego conflicts, with Aries defying your natural dominance. But bring Leo endurance to Aries's courage and you've got a winner!

IF ARIES IS BOSS: You've found a leader. Are you ready to follow? Chances are you'll serve the Aries boss dutifully, so long as they're generous and don't homogenize your work to look just like theirs. If, however, they push you too far too hard, you'll say, *"In your ear, Aries,"* digging in your

claws like a cat in a tall tree. Watch out! Arguments can take nasty turns since both of you know how to dish it out.

IF YOU'RE IN CHARGE: Put a leash (a long leash!) on Aries and send them out to guard the business. Make them do your dirty work. Deputize them to fight the battles that would make you sweat unattractively. Most importantly, take the heat *off* your relationship and put it *on* the task at hand. Together you can achieve aggressive business growth.

LEO @ WORK WITH TAURUS

☛ **A brick wall.**

This alliance is as staunch and stubborn as they come. When hassled, neither of you budges. You withhold commitment. Taurus is stingy with admiration. You surge confidently ahead, aggrandizing your mission, while Taurus plods onward with caution and determination. Taurus will tolerate your need for fame and fortune, but not if it comes at their expense. So to make this team work, don't stand in each other's way. Don't threaten Taurus's humbler but possibly more sensible goals. And indulge once in a while in your mutual weakness: luxury goods!

IF TAURUS IS BOSS: You'll crave elbow room. Whereas you like to cut through the red tape, Taurus wants to play by the rules and avoid trouble. Taurus's tedium might irritate you, so try to earn enough independence to manage your own output. Eventually Taurus won't care *how* you did it, as long as you did it.

IF YOU'RE IN CHARGE: Tell Taurus what you need and how you need it. Give them plenty of time and they'll come through—and you won't even have to spend a lot of management effort, which you always resent. If you appreciate Taurus's quality workmanship, they'll keep it coming.

LEO @ WORK WITH GEMINI

☛ **Positive attitude.**

One thing's for sure: You keep each other interested. Sharing a positive outlook and love of life, Leo and Gemini work well together in groups, especially if you both feel like part of a winning team, not a couple of individuals with something to prove. As the more potent, more tenacious partner, provide Gemini with structure. Gemini will return the favor by supporting your big plans and calculated gambles. But if it's a true partnership, share the glory *and* the headaches.

IF GEMINI IS BOSS: You might like this arrangement. What the typical Gemini boss lacks in leadership they make up for in stimulation and encouragement. And of course they've got contacts galore, so get to know a Gemini and you will have gotten to know an entire industry, not to mention some really cool trade secrets!

IF YOU'RE IN CHARGE: Give Gemini a sense of purpose. Offer them true leadership, not just management, and constructively reinforce your mission and purpose. A few incentives along the way wouldn't hurt either, so occasionally single out Gemini's accomplishments as examples of good work. Since you like trophies, add them to the personnel budget.

LEO @ WORK WITH CANCER

☛ **Maybe, maybe not.**

You say, "Yes!" Cancer says, "Maybe. I'll consider it." You draw up the marketing plan. Cancer devises the contingency plan—because, hey, something might go wrong. You're willing to risk it all (except maybe your pride!), but Cancer risks *nada*. Yet in your separate ways, you both aim to please. You impress people. Cancer satisfies them. Together you produce happy customers who come back for more. Only in times of setback will this alliance suffer. Look after each other's well-being. Never view Cancer as a means to an end. They hate anything disposable—napkins, diapers, partnerships.

IF CANCER IS BOSS: They'll butt into your business. They'll ask lots of questions, many of which you find silly. Get used to it. Try to see it more as mothering, less as a play for control. If you stick with Cancer and prove your professional "ripeness," they'll hand over the keys to the car and lean on you.

IF YOU'RE IN CHARGE: You've got a fan. Cancer will admire you, perhaps from afar. You won't, however, live up to their expectations of heroism (no one could!). So be real with them from day one. For a few minutes each month, say, shoot the breeze with them at the watercooler. You need an effective employee, not a worshipful groupie!

LEO @ WORK WITH LEO

☛ **Song and dance routine.**

Leo is the zodiac's master of ceremonies and maven of schtick. Performance anxiety stalls other professionals. But with you it just fuels your

fire. So charisma is the hallmark of this alliance. Never ever will this duo be lost in the crowd. Everything you produce together will bear your paw prints and distinct character. But at the bottom of most famous paintings is one signature, not two. Though in the worst of times two Leos may bolster one another, in the best of times it's hard to share the glory as well as the throne.

IF THE OTHER LEO IS BOSS: You've enlisted for some ambitious objectives! They'll describe the outline of what they want and expect you to supply the substance. So occasionally you may have to report what they want isn't possible—a task no Leo relishes! Ask for more instruction, less hot air, and take yourselves less seriously. Everyone has their price. You'll put up with your Leo boss if the rewards are big and shiny enough!

> **"Ours is the country where, in order to sell your product, you don't so much point out its merits as you first work like hell to sell yourself."**
> BUSINESS COMMENTATOR
> LOUIS KRONENBERGER

IF YOU'RE IN CHARGE: Give your Leo employee plenty to work with, so they don't have to scurry around trying to anticipate what'll gratify you. Provide concrete examples. Start out teaching, not disciplining. Don't delay gratification too long. This worker needs to see their name in lights *today*.

LEO @ WORK WITH VIRGO

☛ Put out the fire!

You start fires. Virgo rings the alarm. You're eager. Virgo is sober. You demand progress, tying Virgo to schedules and standards. Virgo deflates your ego, silencing your roar. You like hype. Virgo goes for substance. Obviously your common ground is no bigger than a broom closet in Tokyo. Still, though, it can work, especially in the profit department. Value Virgo's efficiency. Help them see how their contribution makes all the rest possible. And whatever you do, spend more time making money than fighting over it!

IF VIRGO IS BOSS: Make sure the criteria are clear. Find out in advance what the rules are—and live up to them. That way you've covered the seat of your pants and won't take flack—a combustible substance in this relationship—for failing. Moderate your enthusiasm so you can sustain it. No wham, bam, thank-you ma'ams with this boss!

IF YOU'RE IN CHARGE: Tell Virgo, "Time's up!" They can't take all week to perfect one project while the rest sit there. Explain you want the report *written*, not worthy of a Pulitzer Prize. Integrate Virgo into a team and they'll consume less of your management time. As long as neither of you is yelling, "Don't bother me!" you know you're getting along.

LEO @ WORK WITH LIBRA

☛ Jumbo price tag.

Neither of you comes cheap. So for this alliance you need one of two things, preferably both: (1) profitability and enough perks to keep you comfortable and (2) outlets for expression and panache. This alliance leaves the nuts and bolts to the grease monkeys and fixates on the showroom decor. The challenge to reach ever greater levels of sophistication and specialization keeps you on your toes like a couple of ballerinas. But who will win the popularity contest? Hard to say, but make sure there's room for both of you in the spotlight.

> **"I won't congratulate you or wish you good luck. It's obvious you're destined to do great things."**
> LITERATURE PROFESSOR
> KATHY SMITH

IF LIBRA IS BOSS: If they waffle or waver even a little, you won't be able to resist jumping in and seizing control. But despite your inclinations, playing nice always works best with this boss, whose inner dictator you don't want to meet. Instead of staging a coup, crank up your Leo magnetism and get into Libra's good graces.

IF YOU'RE IN CHARGE: You'll treasure Libra's social skills, as long as they don't overshadow yours. Check in with Libra frequently—they thrive on contact, and besides, they can offer you a variety of different points of view you hadn't considered before.

LEO @ WORK WITH SCORPIO

☛ Dynamic duo or mortal enemies.

Consider the Scorpios you know. Natural allies you are *not*. Resentment's a constant danger. Leo spends money to make money. Scorpio deliberates over every penny. Leo implements programs immediately. Scorpio first hires a focus group and conducts a survey. You do, however, share passion. In fact, watch out for sexual tension! Scorpio is steamy under the surface while Leo steams all over. In a healthy business venture, Scorpio lays the groundwork, Leo acts on it. Keep in mind Scorpio wants

to reduce decisions and tactics to a formula. So to convince your Scorpio teammate, talk formula, talk tactics, don't gush.

IF SCORPIO IS BOSS: You may chafe under their command. You want to make 20 sales and they want to ask 20 questions about your sales report. Don't take it personally when they scrutinize your work. Of course that's not easy for a Leo, so just to be on the safe side, keep your résumé ready and up to date. It's hard for this work relationship to last.

IF YOU'RE IN CHARGE: Watch this person! Don't let Scorpio undermine your authority. Be confident. Create an environment where Scorpio feels secure. Assure them, quite genuinely, that your success is their success, that you won't forget their name and contributions when you're promoted to the 34th floor. Remember, Scorpio's a born power broker—get them on your side so they can broker *you* some!

LEO @ WORK WITH SAGITTARIUS

☛ **Party animals.**

Both of you like a good time. Not just on the weekend, but in the office, too. In fact, if you're both ambitious, you may forget the weekends and "play" at your jobs Monday to Monday. Chores are your mutual downfall. You're more determined than Saj to just do it, so take turns taking out the garbage after your all-night brainstorming sessions. Together, your creativity skyrockets. You fabricate wild stories and schemes that belong in a dime store novel yet somehow make it to the bestseller list. To solve internal problems, talk specifics and work toward a resolution—don't turn it into a bitch fest.

IF SAGITTARIUS IS BOSS: You'll undoubtedly elicit this boss's two extremes: one day deep and philosophical; the next, flamboyant and irreverent. Don't you climb on the seesaw, too! Instead, figure out what they're really aspiring to. Then participate in getting there. Saj will give you room to be yourself, but only if you humor them, exercise your creativity to the limit, and drop everything and grab a pencil when they're feeling inspired.

IF YOU'RE IN CHARGE: Saj might—at least in the beginning—require daily monitoring. Don't hover, but let them know a competent adult is in the room. Later you can ease up, doling out privileges for good performance. Whatever you do, eventually give Saj opportunities to volunteer their wisdom and experience. Drudgery is not for this person!

LEO @ WORK WITH CAPRICORN

☛ Climb every mountain.

The idea of "making it" is the glue that binds this alliance. You've got talents. Capricorn's got skills. They're obsessed with production. You cherish packaging and presentation. Recognition for success drives you equally onward and upward. The only thing missing is fun. Neither of you likes getting down in the trenches. You wonder, "Couldn't they lighten up?" They wonder why you want to hang fine art on the bathroom walls. To really make this work, don't order each other around. In fact, treat each other like visiting dignitaries, each with your own chunk of sovereignty.

IF CAPRICORN IS BOSS: Expect calluses on your fingertips—this jefe will make you *work!* They love your personality; they adore the sense of style and savoir faire you bestow on the company. But once you show a little potential, they'll want to "tap" all your talent like an oil well in the desert.

IF YOU'RE IN CHARGE: You've lucked out. It won't be easy. You'll both struggle. Capricorn might rain on your parade. But if they don't, Capricorn will sure as heck make the parade happen, no matter what the odds. This employee treats you right—with dignity, chivalry, and a slap on the wrist when the coffers run empty.

LEO @ WORK WITH AQUARIUS

☛ Prerogative versus principles.

This alliance rides on a commitment to negotiating what's important. Aquarius has high ideals. You don't always have time for ideals. Aquarius considers the theories and accounts for the unexpected. You act first, ask questions later. So you make a good team, as long as you don't get too settled in your ways. You, for example, need to listen when Aquarius talks about shelf life. And Aquarius needs to pay attention when you talk about what the product *looks* like on the shelf. Remember, everything's negotiable. These days, nothing's written in stone—just in cyberspace.

IF AQUARIUS IS BOSS: Don't come on too strong. Don't approach this boss with a do-it-now! attitude, but with a what-do-you-think? perspective. They'll appreciate intelligence and patience, or anything approximating a method. Most importantly, don't cheat! Integrity will put you on their A-list faster than a tidy desk.

IF YOU'RE IN CHARGE: Recognize Aquarius's loyalty and commitment. Acknowledge their contribution, openly and repeatedly. Aquarius won't be a squeaky wheel, but give them the grease anyway.

LEO @ WORK WITH PISCES

☛ **Smoke gets in your eyes.**

You're fire, Pisces is water, and together you produce either boiling water or a smoky mess. In business dealings, you're up front while Pisces lurks and watches. You clown around and Pisces ponders the consequences. It must seem as though you're from different worlds. But it can work. You're both dreamers. Pisces listens. You talk. And since both of you know how to work a crowd and please the people—each in your own way, of course—together you enjoy an adoring public. In this alliance, shoot for sterling customer service and don't step on each other's tail. After all, lions bite and fish stink!

> **"Anyone who says businessmen deal in facts, not fiction, has never read old five-year projections"**
> LEO PUBLISHER MALCOM FORBES

IF PISCES IS BOSS: You probably won't get the special attention you crave. But don't count on aggression or temper tantrums to prompt a response from Pisces. Instead, let them get to know you. In a crisis you might even bond. They want to ferret out your hidden talents, to "discover" you. Eventually the well-positioned Pisces may turn out to be the patron or sponsor you've been waiting for.

IF YOU'RE IN CHARGE: You're likely to find Pisces overly sensitive. You'll want to rush in and rescue them. You might crowd them, coaxing them forward, since you tend to associate activity with productivity. Not so with this employee, who needs time and space to do your bidding.

Virgo @ Work

VIRGO

The Myth

In the *Metamorphoses*, Ovid's masterpiece of Roman mythology, humankind fell from the prosperous golden age into a life of chaos, competition, and crime (sound familiar?). The gods, wanting to get away from it all, bought up real estate on Mount Olympus and other heavenly retirement communities, and flew the coop. All of them, that is, except one young goddess who came to be known in the zodiac as Virgo. This virgin goddess hung out long enough to help the measly mortals. She endowed them with civilization and fertility. She gave them advice and a little taste of heaven. Moral of the story: When the going gets tough, Virgo sticks around to save the day and make valuable home improvements.

Motivation

Money matters. So does approval, so a letter of appreciation or a bonus in your paycheck can really keep you going. But none of it motivates you like a job well done. Whether it's a seven-course meal with all the right wines or a financial plan itemized down to the last lightbulb, you aim for precision. Flaws violate your vision of how the world ought to look.

> **"Never do today what you can do tomorrow. Something may occur to make you regret your premature action."**
> REVOLUTIONARY WAR HERO
> AARON BURR

Feeling down? Looking for a change? Let the quest for perfection guide you. Will you attain it? Hard to say. Columbus set sail for the East Indies and never found them. He did, however, stumble across the Americas, so the trip didn't turn out a total failure. Neither will yours. Find what you love to *do*. Use your hands, your brain, whatever fidgets the most. You're destined to make things better. Self-improvement and world-improvement go hand in hand.

Virgo also needs to be needed. It must have been a Virgo who first said, "When you help others, you help yourself." Once you find the right cause, you serve it religiously. It takes a peculiar mixture of guts and blind faith to fix a problem that your capricious Aries and tentative Libra colleagues fled long ago. But you stay. It needs you as much as the stray kittens you rescued in grade school did. It brings out the best in you. And, after all, the best is what you're after.

Assets

There's a stereotype out there of Virgo as a workaholic and hypochondriac, a schoolmarm type who carries a can of Lysol in her purse. Now really, does that sound like *you?* Sometimes I think Leo, the sign right before yours, was so greedy for attention that Virgo got stuck with all the boring leftover characteristics. Sure, Virgos can be persnickety, but they're more than tax clerks and scullery maids, you know.

Virgo strives to make things right—to bring order to chaos, beauty to an ugly landscape; to extract substance from behind the hoopla. In other words, you've got the right stuff to operate a business and organize an occupation.

"Modest and shy." "Meticulous and reliable." "Practical and diligent." Maybe you've heard these accusations from colleagues or your local

horoscope column. A lot of astrologers advise Virgo to lighten up and not be so "anal retentive." Not me. In many jobs, that's exactly what's called for. Imagine an administrative assistant who wasn't fastidious! Papers would be lost, messages scattered, meeting dates forgotten. For many years a Virgo CEO headed Boeing, the world's largest passenger aircraft manufacturer. I always flew confidently knowing the 747 was engineered under a Virgo head honcho.

Without organization, creativity flops. You can't start a business selling widgets without a budget and careful analysis of the widget market. Virgo analyzes. You detect the leak in the roof before the building collapses—always an important skill in big business where a tiny oversight can result in economic agonies. "That decimal point is over one place too far!" As you know and never fail to point out, decimal points make all the difference.

In entrepreneurial ventures, your plan of attack is solid. The business you build can be a *Titanic* that doesn't sink, because *your* map includes the icebergs. Then you avoid them. In the arts, Virgos excel wherever thoroughness is called for. Think of a ballet dancer spinning flawless pirouettes. Think of a jeweler cutting priceless diamonds. And if I ever have surgery, sign me up with a Virgo doctor.

In the workforce, Virgo's industrious. Hard work doesn't scare you. You strive to do it right the first time. Otherwise you start over. In order to restore your nerves, you like breaks, but while you're sipping a decaf cappuccino in the staff lounge, the project du jour still cries out to you. It needs you. Your customers, many of whom you may never meet, need you. At the end of the day, you want to feel you've been useful.

Your orderly methods, attention to detail, productive velocity, and drive for perfection make you a highly functioning work machine. You may often hear people whispering of Virgo behind their backs, "How do they *do* all that?!" You just smile. When you like your work, it's your refuge. Not a chore. Not a challenge. Just something you're darned good at.

Liabilities

The goal of perfection can inspire all of us to do better, but it's not a religion. Forever on a mission to improve, you fuss. You pick. You meddle. Cool it! Cut the world some slack. While you're at it, take it easier on yourself, too.

Before you know it, you can slip into drudgery, going about your tasks like a phone on automatic redial. You occasionally forget you have Mom and Dad to thank for your life, not an IBM engineer! Keep the work alive and meaningful, one eye on the project and another on the goal.

I firmly believe every Virgo longs to get in touch with her inner slob. Though repression never did a body good, with Virgo it's downright dangerous. Normally a paragon of moderation, you turbulently let loose, bingeing on excess. Rather than slack at work, you'll play hooky. Or quit altogether. If you're sick of selling widgets, you might burn them all with a bottle of Scotch rather than take a few deep breaths and resolve to sell fewer to keep sane. Work on accepting your limitations without succumbing to them.

> "When I call on a client. I come by cab, and I am sleek and clean and foursquare. I carry myself as though I've made a quiet killing on the stock market, and have come to call more as a public service than anything else."
>
> NOVELIST KURT VONNEGUT

Utilitarianism and attention to detail are valuable assets to any company or home business—unless it becomes pedantic, nitpicking, and dogmatic. Don't turn into the stuffy school librarian with a ruler, smacking palms indiscriminately. Virgo is prime breeding ground for obsessive-compulsive disorder, which could result in your downfall.

At times, your relentless purging of imperfections (especially when it comes to imperfect people) may come across as downright inhuman. Working on your own can be just as bad, if you turn that critical eye too hard on yourself. OK, so you didn't bargain well with the widget supplier. Forgive yourself. Do better next time. Don't collapse under the pressure of your own demands.

Dr. Matt's Tips for Virgo Success

★ Find work you *like*. If you must, sacrifice a few perks. Your dream job won't arrive tomorrow, but meanwhile find some joy in what you do.

★ Cultivate as much appreciation for the extraordinary as you have for the ordinary. Things that might look frivolous to you can in fact serve a valuable purpose.

★ Schedule (you must schedule!), but make room for accidents and ripe new opportunities.

★ Scrutinize your boss, coworkers, and workplace, but don't give them a lot of bad press. Gossip hurts.

★ If you're considering starting your own business, remember: You'll gain freedom but lose control. Entrepreneurial income's unpredictable. But if you love what you do, you can always look forward to getting up in the morning.

WHEN THIS VIRGIN SPEAKS, PEOPLE LISTEN!

He's been called the Billion Dollar Brain, the Oracle of Omaha, and the Greatest Investor of All Time. Simply by setting a good example, Warren Buffet has spawned international investment trends like "Buffetology" and "Buffetmania." He is probably the second richest American, and a quintessential Virgo, though he's not your typical Wall Street stock trader. Still residing in his native Nebraska, he steers clear of high-stake gambles and prefers to seek out individual companies that meet his long list of Virgin criteria. Exacting, methodical, and skeptical, Buffet is renowned for identifying undervalued companies with good managment and avoiding industries, like high tech, that he doesn't understand completely. Yes, he's as picky as any Virgo, but it's that Virgin pickiness that has sent him straight to the top.

Virgo in Alliance

VIRGO @ WORK WITH ARIES

☛ **Fast and hard, slow and easy.**

You both respond well to challenge. Other than that, however, you have less in common than a firefighter and an arsonist. Aries has speed, you've got endurance. Together you can go far fast. But the issue is whether you can *stay* together long enough to reach the finish line.

IF ARIES IS BOSS: Let them challenge and dare you. You can afford a little excitement—relish it! Aries encourages you to mix meticulous work with a vigor you're unaccustomed to. This work relationship may help you get in touch with your inner slob, but at least it's a productive slob.

IF YOU'RE IN CHARGE: Aries may injure your sense of propriety by refusing to take orders or act cautiously. Mentor your Aries employee, but don't expect to recreate them in your own image. They'll take your guidance, albeit grudgingly, as long as it's constructive, not personal.

VIRGO @ WORK WITH TAURUS

☛ **Growth potential.**

Taurus may help you grow into that businessperson you've always dreamed of being. Potentially, this is a very fruitful alliance. You're both practical and like methods and routines you can trust. Use your skills right, and this close-knit crew can accumulate heaps of money. Virgo has the technique and Taurus implements it. But set realistic goals—both of you tend to tackle more duties than anyone can handle. In this alliance, learn to solicit the talents of the right pros and specialists.

IF TAURUS IS BOSS: You'll appreciate that they never ask you to cut corners. But if they do, convince them the corners matter! Though you share comparable work ethics, Taurus takes genuine pleasure in their work. Maybe some of it will rub off on you.

IF YOU'RE IN CHARGE: You'll find Taurus employees cheerfully follow orders, and as long as you don't exploit them, these workers will bring an energy to your business that you'll soon count on.

VIRGO @ WORK WITH GEMINI

☛ **The one versus the many.**

As a Virgo, you have discriminating taste; you separate the wheat from the chaff. Gemini, on the other hand, takes it all in. Virgo resents Gemini's insistence on freedom and will seek to limit it. From you Gemini can learn practicality. You two share a flair for the intellectual. With luck and effort, this alliance can realize the truth of "many in one and one in many." Look for the qualities you share and the qualities you don't. You'll find your differences are complementary.

IF GEMINI IS BOSS: They'll make sure your quality workmanship doesn't get stuck in the back room. If you've got the product, they've got the market. But since Gemini tends to label everything "miscellaneous," you can help them find, refine, and target the *right* market.

IF YOU'RE IN CHARGE: Train Gemini to ask the right questions. They're information junkies—a good thing. But not all information is created equal. Get them to categorize by relevance—a better thing.

VIRGO @ WORK WITH CANCER

☞ **The philosopher and the poet.**

Cancer's perceptive. You're analytic. Together you can diagnose whatever ails your company. You're mutually interested in serving and comforting those who need it. This alliance works particularly well in any business dedicated to some humanitarian purpose. But watch out! You're both potentially critical, and your relationship will last only if criticism is kind and serves a purpose. Virgo steadies Cancer, assessing and actualizing their intuitions. In the strongest alliance, Virgo gives form to Cancer's content.

IF CANCER IS BOSS: Try to curb your tendency to organize the workplace *your* way. Cancer may not be authoritarian, but if they're the boss, they're the boss. Be helpful. Do your best. That's all Cancer asks, and they'll appreciate it.

IF YOU'RE IN CHARGE: Bounce your ideas off Cancer. They'll come back to you with a new spin. Don't criticize and nag Cancer too much. Really: They can be oh, so soft and tender, despite the crusty exterior.

VIRGO @ WORK WITH LEO

☞ **The reserved and the flamboyant.**

You two make a very divergent pair, yet success is possible. Virgo is short on praise and long on criticism. Leo thrives on numerous "pats on the back," which you resist giving. And you refuse to be dominated. Leo can inspire you, pointing out how your work will influence millions or transcend the ordinary. The alliance works when Leo's grandeur elevates your pettiness, and your attention to detail reminds Leo that even they cannot turn copper into gold.

IF LEO IS BOSS: You're drawn to their dazzling qualities and colorful baubles. You know it. Leo knows it. Try a few kind words without resorting to kissing up. You'll be rewarded!

IF YOU'RE IN CHARGE: Send the lion out into the world as your ambassador. They're suave and know how to win the respect of buyers or the competition. You're best at managing the home front.

VIRGO @ WORK WITH VIRGO

☛ **A model of efficiency.**

This alliance advances under mutual resourcefulness. Each of you masters many skills. But if they're all the same skills, other areas of your partnership will suffer. Success involves the cultivation of a little difference, a little complementarity. This is a responsible, intelligent, and serious alliance characterized by constant adaptation. Neither dominates the other completely. But you need to keep busy to avoid overanalyzing one another. Each of you is wary of praising the other, and an inability to express gratitude is one thing that could spell the end of a beautiful friendship.

IF THE OTHER VIRGO IS BOSS: Remember, Virgo's infatuated with having a place for everything and everything in its place. These places may, however, differ radically from where you'd put them.

IF YOU'RE IN CHARGE: Curb the criticism. You can identify with how it can melt a Virgo! Critique the product or the performance, not the person.

VIRGO @ WORK WITH LIBRA

☛ **Common sense versus common ground.**

Common sense is your textbook. Libra, on the other hand, acts out of whimsy, inspiration, or just because they like it. You're known for being uptight; Libra's got a reputation for being easygoing. Virgo wants to make Libra focused and decisive. Libra interprets Virgo reserve as rejection. What you do share is an aversion to messing up. Libra pushes you to profit from your labor. Their imagination can breathe life into your common sense. If you can imagine big bucks, there's a greater motivation to earn them. The alliance may be push and pull, but the overall motion is forward.

> *"Pas de souci. Soyez content."*
> FRENCH FOR "DON'T WORRY. BE HAPPY."

IF LIBRA IS BOSS: They'll value your good work, but that's not enough. They expect a good attitude, a presentable appearance, and a *few* dirty details about your love life.

IF YOU'RE IN CHARGE: Libra won't get it when you don't buy into their "irresistible" ideas. Hear them out but explain the limits on your budget.

VIRGO @ WORK WITH SCORPIO

☛ **Crisis Control Center.**

You need control. Scorpio demands power. Together you're bound to butt heads. But you both respond swimmingly in a crisis, plugging the dike before it bursts. You share mutual respect of your intelligence. But a lack of communication can plague this alliance because Scorpio is as secretive as you are reserved. Honest give-and-take is a must—and the only way to tell when there are leaks in the dike. Benefits of this alliance are a mutual willingness to compromise and the development of a sense of purpose (as long as it's shared). Marshalling your investigative skills may lead to important and profitable discoveries. This alliance drives at securing answers, but don't be too quick to pass judgment.

IF SCORPIO IS BOSS: Since they're naturally suspicious, give them nothing to worry about regarding how you do your job.

IF YOU'RE IN CHARGE: Use Scorpio to push you into thinking about financial consequences and profiting from your labor.

VIRGO @ WORK WITH SAGITTARIUS

☛ **Don't sweat the small stuff.**

Sagittarius always knows how to gouge you where it counts—even if they aren't aware they're doing it. In this partnership cling to your identity at all costs. Definitely don't tell each other how to live. Virgo plans ahead. Sagittarius follows the moment. Sagittarius can broaden your mind. You think progressively in an orderly fashion. If Saj's accidental jabs don't get you, and your plans don't stifle Saj's creativity, this can be a highly successful relationship. There's a real potential for innovation—the kind that works.

IF SAGITTARIUS IS BOSS: Embrace the challenge this relationship presents. It may look as though this boss doesn't work hard, but they do. Meanwhile, make yourself indisposable and Saj may try to adopt you.

IF YOU'RE IN CHARGE: Tutor your Saj in the importance of procedure, policies, and having a consistent method for achieving results. But by the same token, appreciate Saj's ability to find the best shortcut to any destination.

VIRGO @ WORK WITH CAPRICORN

☛ There's a job to do.

This alliance concentrates on workmanship and know-how, and tends to neglect the individuals involved. Spend more time with your customers; develop worthwhile relationships with suppliers. Because Capricorn stabilizes volatile situations, this relationship makes you willing to take risks you wouldn't on your own. Together you're ambitious, hardworking, and goal oriented. But don't forget the human element. Be respectful of each other.

IF CAPRICORN IS BOSS: The stability of the Capricorn-headed place will be welcome to your Virgin sensibility. You work hard and Capricorn loves you for it. If they don't show it, respond by showing how much you appreciate working for them. Chances are, they'll let you know that the feeling's mutual.

IF YOU'RE IN CHARGE: Don't let Capricorn's diligence make you forget they need a pat on the back. Show your appreciation every once in a while. It'll also be to your benefit to talk over risky decisions with Capricorn whenever possible, because the Goat always provides a soaring reality check.

VIRGO @ WORK WITH AQUARIUS

☛ Out of the frying pan and into the fire.

Aquarius's vision for a better tomorrow really brings out the workaholic in you. You'll bust your keester for them, perhaps quite literally if you don't beware of stressing out. Don't be frustrated by Aquarius's slowness to action; they care deeply. Treat them well and they'll give you their loyalty. They seem aloof and self-sufficient, but that doesn't mean they are. You are both rational intellectuals, inquisitive and problem-solving, but you have different goals: You're concerned with personal advancement, while Aquarius wants to advance the world at large. Incorporate your sense of purpose with a modified version of Aquarian reform, and the alliance may result in sound business sense.

IF AQUARIUS IS BOSS: Though their approach is different from yours, trust that Aquarius knows what they're doing. They probably do. Remember: in matters of pacing, to each their own.

IF YOU'RE IN CHARGE: Don't spend too much time smashing Aquarius's dreamy visions of change. A little imagination never hurt business. Sometimes

it can actually help. Just don't start believing there's always a pot of gold at the end of the rainbow. You have to work for it.

VIRGO @ WORK WITH PISCES

☛ **Strength in numbers.**

You and Pisces share a bond, but whether it's one of love or obligation is hard to say. You're always trying to get Pisces to see things your way, but when you look carefully, you may see more of yourself in them than you care to admit. You look for tangible evidence and data, whereas Pisces accepts anecdotes and personal testimonies. The important thing here is to jointly reveal weaknesses and expose vulnerabilities rather than cover them up. Then you can really capitalize on one another's strengths.

IF PISCES IS BOSS: Pisces will most likely value your ordered approach. If not, business may not run so smoothly. Without being overbearing, demonstrate that your methods are an asset your Pisces boss shouldn't do without.

IF YOU'RE IN CHARGE: Be aware of Pisces's sensitivity, and try not to injure it. You might not like their seeming impracticality right off, but you can learn from it. What expands your view of things ultimately helps you.

Libra @ Work

SEPTEMBER 23 TO OCTOBER 22

LIBRA

The Myth

In Greek mythology, Libra symbolized a golden chariot. One day Pluto, branch manager of the Underworld, drove Libra up to the doorstep of the beautiful heiress Persephone and kidnapped her. When Persephone's high-profile mother, Demeter, the goddess of agriculture, discovered her daughter had been abducted, she got so furious she stopped allowing crops to grow on earth. To keep everyone from starving, Zeus, the big boss, drew up an agreement: Once every year, Libra the golden chariot would transport Persephone to Pluto's Underworld where she'd stay a few months. During this time the fields would remain barren. Then Libra the golden chariot would shuttle Persephone back to earth and flowers and grain would flourish. The plan worked. Earthlings could eat. All the big shots got what they wanted. And Libra made a killing on ticket sales. Moral of the story: Libra facilitates compromise, offers top-notch service, and never forgets along the way to accrue an attractive commission.

Motivation

More than 2,000 years ago Plato asked, "What is the good life?" Libra is still asking this question. In fact you're living it, by forever searching for the right way, the best way, the most beautiful way to lead a life. Along the way you consider many opinions and theories. Each receives your full attention. You make no quick decisions. To you La Dolce Vita isn't an Italian restaurant—it's a way of life, the sweet life.

Libra pines for luxury. Forget Leo's flash, it's too garish. And don't bother with Sagittarius's bigger-is-better philosophy. In the taste department, you appreciate one rum truffle over a whole box of cheap hard candy. After all, it is good taste that Libra longs for. More to the point, Libra reaches for harmony—everything (or everyone) working together. To turn noise into music—that is the Libra endeavor.

So it's no surprise that Libra's the classic sign of the diplomat. Whether it's feng shui for the office or a carefully chosen empowered team that exceeds profit projections, Libra strives to find the right formula to create balance.

Assets

Eek! A fire breaks out in your office's waiting room. Everyone panics. They flee their desks and fight over the watercooler jugs—all except Libra. You stay calm. Chaos won't get the best of you. There's a right way to handle this, and you'll find it. In the meantime, why mess up your hair or risk losing the document you've been correcting?

> **"Question: If you could change one thing about yourself, what would it be? Answer: I'd lose the ability to see things from both sides."**
> FILMMAKER JAMES L. BROOKS, IN *VANITY FAIR*

Libra's got the gentle touch. You're a born consultant, who can easily turn a profit by telling companies things they should already know in an unassuming way that makes them feel comfortable with their oversights. Working on your own, you may not excel at self-promotion, but people are drawn to you naturally. They'll buy your product or service because behind it they see a kind, fair, and trustworthy person.

Flattery will get you everywhere. Every Libra has the potential to be as charming as a graduate of Miss Muff's Academy for Promising Pubescents. You possess that rare ability to look more innocent than you really

are, seeming both approachable and formidable. More than just a "team player," you're an active participant. It doesn't take much arm-twisting before you say, "OK, I'll do it. When should I start?"

> **"Life is what happens while you are making other plans."**
> LIBRA MUSICIAN JOHN LENNON

Libra excels at synthesizing many parts into a functional whole. You're often the one who gets stuck finding a consensus, whipping into shape a team of freethinkers and rugged individualists. How do you take your colleagues' 12 company mission statements and squeeze them into one viable plan? You'll figure it out and have them all wearing matching bowling shirts by the end of the day.

Persuasion is one of your assets. So is cooperation. It fits, then, that in bygone days Libra was the sign of the matchmaker. Suave and sociable, you make a great representative, able to convey a message or a brand identity that builds relationships. You also have a knack for improving on the ideas of your competitors because you understand them. For example, if Gobo and Gortz starts to sell goggles in the swimwear department, you'll say, "Hey, I like that concept, but why not get closer to the action and sell at pools?"

Libra creates culture. Whether it's corporate culture or high culture, you use it to get people on your side. The Libran artist says, "Look at my painting—that's how I see the world." The Libran manager says, "Read our employee handbook—it represents our company culture and keeps all of us on the same page."

Normally content to get your kicks listening to old, sad songs and rearranging the furniture, you occasionally enjoy the cheap thrills of teaming up with a semishady coworker or a partner in the fast lane. You might even in-line skate to work and drink regular instead of decaf. But as a rule you stay calm and predictable. Thank heaven someone does!

Liabilities

Libra doesn't like to rock the boat. You prefer peace at any price. You start out cooperating and wind up complying. "This is how it is," says Libra. "But why?" asks the skeptic. "Hmm, well, because *they* say so." You are often too easily influenced by others. Trying to understand everyone's side can result in gullibility if you don't approach things critically.

Indecision plagues the Libra professional who sees all sides of every issue. Should you or should you not sell your invention's patent to

Microsoft? You hesitate and vacillate. But unless you want some whiz kid in his dad's garage to beat your invention to market, you've got to sell (or

"Trust is the highest form of human motivation."
AUTHOR STEVEN COVEY

not) and put what's behind you behind you. Likewise, when the boss asks you the best way to market widgets, eventually you have to decide what *is* the best way—even if other ways have their high points. Otherwise you risk paralysis in the face of dizzying alternatives.

Nothing if not idealistic, you keep waiting—and waiting—for your dreams to be realized. But the world often fails to live up to Libra's lofty expectations: customers who say please and thank-you, and employees who show up on time simply because they love their jobs so much. Till then, you have an incredible talent for improvising harmony in a world that sounds more like a rush-hour traffic jam in Tokyo.

Dr. Matt's Tips for Libra Success:

★ Whatever your profession, get in touch with your public relations talents. Don't underestimate the value of your flair for networking.

★ Take advantage of opportunities to expand your areas of expertise. While specialization sometimes pays off, don't rely exclusively on one or two talents to get you through your career.

★ Overcome "decidaphobia." Repeatedly listing the pros and cons of a tough choice seldom works better than flipping a coin. And asking for so-called "expert" advice eventually fails, too. After careful but not excessive consideration, just make up your mind!

★ Before you start your own business, work for someone else to see how it's done, so you can do it better.

★ Spend some time analyzing the tension between what you want to do and what you ought to do. Find a way to integrate them.

★ Don't make unnecessary compromises just to please other people. If the boat needs rocking, rock it, or risk going down with the ship.

A BUBBLE BATH EMPIRE

Aahhh! Imagine soaking in a hot bath surrounded by the soothing scents of peppermint and dewberry. It sounds more like a vacation than a business—but not for Anita Roddick, the Libra entrepreneur who founded The Body Shop, a leading retailer of bath, skin, and aromatherapy products. Like most Libras who want their personal and professional goals to cooperate, Roddick set out to create what she calls "profits with principles." With more than 1,500 branches worldwide, Roddick and her retail chain led the movement toward cosmetics *not* tested on animals. And by campaigning for social and environmental causes, The Body Shop has earned lots of free publicity and saved a ton of money on advertising. True to the spirit of Libra, this resourceful Englishwoman didn't compromise her principles—or her profits!

Libra in Alliance

LIBRA @ WORK WITH ARIES

☞ **No more Mr. Nice Guy!**

Aries rocks the boat. You prefer smooth sailing. Unfortunately for you, this alliance is no Caribbean cruise! It's an attraction that instantly appeals but quickly wears off, a constant competition to determine who's way is better. Aries *insists* where you persuade. You try to pacify crisis situations while Aries continues the frenzy, yelling "Fix it, *now!*" While you see both sides of the issue, Aries sees one side: theirs. For this duet to succeed—and it can—stand up to Aries, but don't play their game. You can temper Aries's approach and Aries can empower yours.

IF ARIES IS BOSS: They'll expect you to accommodate them. Go for it, but don't become a whipping boy. If Aries acts like a totalitarian dictator, let them know that if you understand the reasons behind your work, it'll improve the efficiency and quality of what you do.

IF YOU'RE IN CHARGE: In Aries lies the heart of a warrior. Let them use it. Put Aries in an active position, possibly one involving self-assertion and bargaining. Just don't let them turn the office into a bloodbath.

LIBRA @ WORK WITH TAURUS

☞ The long arm of justice.

Though neither of you is a big risk-taker, this alliance can empower you both to be bigger fish in a bigger pond. Taurus is reverent, eager to work, and willing to extend the effort required. You carry the wisdom of the scales, approach business with an eye on morality, and see the ins and outs of every decision. So Taurus helps you make the decision, and is a master of implementation. But let the relationship grow, slowly, to its highest productivity. Beware of commingling bank accounts too abruptly, before trust has evolved. First see if you can agree on a simple purchase order!

IF TAURUS IS BOSS: You'll find them fair and equitable, but a little too stodgy. To get in good, build in a lot of safeguards. For example, keep liability insurance policies up to date and put a "Do Not Enter" sign on the plugged-up facilities. Any cost-saving suggestions will also be music to their ears.

IF YOU'RE IN CHARGE: Assign Taurus some of the responsibilities you tend to overlook. Ask them, say, to lock up at closing time or investigate complaints. They're careful, they pay attention, and they won't get in your way, as long as you don't get in theirs.

LIBRA @ WORK WITH GEMINI

☞ Something to think about.

This partnership makes you think. Together you spout theories, discuss the meaning of life, debate the merits and defects of supply-side economics. But is either of you prepared to break a nail putting theory into practice? Cultivate the stamina to stick it out in tough times. In Gemini's congenial company, there's an urge to grow too far too fast. Optimism is good, but do your homework. Pass a few driving tests before you start that trucking company.

IF GEMINI IS BOSS: They'll overwhelm you with information. When you only have time to fill 20 orders, they give you 40. The key is not to freak out. Despite outward appearances, Gemini isn't trying to work you into an early grave. They just don't know the difference between 20 and 40! Gently enlighten them.

IF YOU'RE IN CHARGE: You've got a dynamo on your hands. Your Gemini employee can—and will—fill many gaps. Whether it's the receptionist or the

marketing VP who calls in sick, Gemini can step in and improvise with less advance notice than it takes to order a pizza. But train them. Someday they'll need to use software they never met before.

LIBRA @ WORK WITH CANCER

☛ **First things first.**

Every budget is limited. No business has enough time. It's how you allocate these resources that counts. And unfortunately, your two agendas fundamentally collide. Cancer, for instance, may want to pay off all your debt at once, whereas you'd rather take advantage of low interest rates to keep expanding. But you're both willing to commit, and with a good rapport, you've got a shot at working out your differences. First, though, you have to acknowledge that your differences *exist.* Don't sabotage your Cancer teammate (especially not in public), but be sure to tell them how you feel (*definitely* not in public!). Don't worry, they won't break.

IF CANCER IS BOSS: They'll want to put you in the public eye, to show you off, to have you be the neon sign on their used car lot. If you like the role of meeter and greeter, fine. If not, prove you've got other talents. But whatever you wind up doing, get ready for plenty of responsibility.

IF YOU'RE IN CHARGE: Cancer may remain aloof, and will certainly try to look terribly professional and composed. Take it easy on them. Compliment their new haircut as well as their new sales record. Don't force them out of their shell, but give them an open invitation to crawl out whenever they like. Most of all, give them something *important* to sink their claws into.

LIBRA @ WORK WITH LEO

☛ **Not *what* you know, but *whom* you know.**

This is an alliance of two people persons. Together you benefit from good contacts, knowing the right people. As a team, you'll be magnetically drawn to the cutting edge. Any drab enterprise with room for colorful improvement can succeed under this partnership.

IF LEO IS BOSS: They'll expect a high degree of self-reliance and resourcefulness, counting on you to create a masterpiece without handing you a paint-by-number set. This boss wants you to articulate your goals and go above and beyond the precepts of your job description. But don't worry— they'll give you plenty of chances.

IF YOU'RE IN CHARGE: Leo will enjoy rocking your world. They'll goad you, talk three decibels too loudly, and propose radical changes. No harm's intended—Leo just doesn't want you to forget they're in the room. If you ask for their advice or expertise, they'll quickly become your biggest devotee.

LIBRA @ WORK WITH VIRGO

☛ **Professional polish.**

This alliance produces a nice and neat finished product. But getting there might test your renowned Libran people power. Get Virgo to take you seriously. Break it to them gently—they don't know everything already. Virgo focuses on the task, getting it done. When it comes to pleasing the client, Virgo fulfills the contract to the letter. You, on the other hand, tend to put the client *before* the contract. Convince Virgo that without your schmoozing skills, there *is* no contract.

IF VIRGO IS BOSS: They'll find all your flaws, all of the unexplained holes in your résumé. Either sew up the holes or grin and bear the criticism. On the bright side, however, Virgo also challenges you to be *more* than you thought you could be, without even having to join the army.

IF YOU'RE IN CHARGE: Get the most out of your Virgo employee by acknowledging their expertise, and making sure it's never idle. Overlook petty comments but don't wait around to resolve ongoing personality conflicts. Appeal to Virgo's collaborative professionalism, not their insecurities.

LIBRA @ WORK WITH LIBRA

☛ **Killer brand names.**

The stunning asset of this alliance is how well the Libra team reaches its market and brands its product. Branding is about building an ongoing relationship between you and your customers, something Libra excels at. But if you make a promise to your market—or to your Libra colleague—don't break it. That's the fastest way to devastate a brand and this partnership. Now, get busy designing your Libra label!

IF THE OTHER LIBRA IS BOSS: This isn't the place to explore your latent competitive spirit. The Libra boss wants a team player, not a beauty pageant contestant or rugged individualist with something to prove. Look sharp, conduct yourself appropriately, and don't dicker over puny clauses in your contract. This exec will adore you.

IF YOU'RE IN CHARGE: Find out which kind of Libra employee you've hired: A total Yes! person or Mary, Mary, Quite Contrary. Either way, this well-meaning worker tends to take sides—maybe yours, maybe the opposite. Help them find a happy middle ground.

LIBRA @ WORK WITH SCORPIO

☛ **Check your balances.**

No matter what your idea or suggestion, Scorpio's first question or response will be, "Is it profitable?" or, "How much does it cost?" This is bound to rankle you. But before you stew and steam, see if Scorpio's budgetary fascism inspires you to reach more creative solutions. No, you won't see eye to eye. Libra looks at the bright side. Scorpio looks at *every* side. Try, though, not to see Scorpio as a naysayer but as someone with a valuable perspective—one that you tend to ignore. If that doesn't work, show Scorpio there's life beyond the bottom line.

IF SCORPIO IS BOSS: Keep in mind they've got a personal stake in your performance. If you don't look good, they don't look good. And Scorpio *hates* to look bad. The high standards they enforce on you are the same standards to which they hold themselves. Develop a working relationship with this boss that's based on more than how you figure into their career objectives.

IF YOU'RE IN CHARGE: Realize Scorpio is always calculating the value of things—the value of getting on your good side, the equity accruing in their retirement plans, the merits of building up their résumé at your organization. Fine, but show them other values count, too—like the quality of the work they do for you.

LIBRA @ WORK WITH SAGITTARIUS

☛ **Fast friends, slow movers.**

In this alliance, there's a lot of busyness, but how's business? Collaboration comes easy. You both have a good time, valuing the partnership over the product. Sagittarius bolsters your self-confidence. You provide Saj with a ready and willing playmate. But tough decisions are, well, tough. Nobody wants to spoil the fun. Work toward building a true joint venture, not just a quickie. Set a routine. Stick to it.

IF SAGITTARIUS IS BOSS: You may have found the support and positive feedback on which you thrive. Don't expect Saj, however, to pick up on the

nuances of your daily grind. Workplace politics aren't their specialty. Don't hesitate to specify your individual needs. Charm works well, too.

IF YOU'RE IN CHARGE: Saj will appeal to your strong sense of ethics and camaraderie. You may, in fact, have a soft spot for this employee. But guide them. And don't expect the same level of commitment you'd expect from yourself. Saj is hard to pin down.

LIBRA @ WORK WITH CAPRICORN

☛ **Someone to watch over you.**

This alliance may demand more compromise than even *you* can gracefully dispense. Capricorn misses nothing. If you want their approval, you'll have to fight for it, which most Libras hate to do. Capricorn is always going to set limits on your plans and your duties—not stopping you, but reminding you of reality. But you can succeed together. Draw from Capricorn support and sustenance, but stop chasing their approval. Relate to each other like equals, no matter who's bossing you.

IF CAPRICORN IS BOSS: Hang on tightly to your sense of who you are. When a Libra sings backup for Capricorn, they tend to get lost behind Capricorn's booming voice. So preserve your voice, even if it means breaking it to this boss there's more than one way to get to Memphis. Just don't steal the show.

IF YOU'RE IN CHARGE: Portray yourself as an important person to know, a real top dog so you can feel confident that Capricorn won't question your authority. This employee can be trusted to supervise many of the tasks you dread, but don't expect them to stay long in a subservient role.

LIBRA @ WORK WITH AQUARIUS

☛ **And a good time was had by all.**

Uninhibited and easygoing, you can loosen your tie and let down your hair with Aquarius. This alliance values originality over conformity. From popular culture and the mass market you two glean a good idea of what's next to hit the charts. But in your willingness—even eagerness—to try new things, have you tested their profitability? Remember that most inventors never make a penny off their inventions—the big winners are the entrepreneurs who develop them. Be original, but think dollars and cents.

IF AQUARIUS IS BOSS: It may seem that anything goes. They're lenient, it's cool, and your contribution is valued. But as soon as you cross some unknown line, they'll suddenly throw a fit. Keep a sense of humor with this one—ultraprofessionalism can kill a good thing.

IF YOU'RE IN CHARGE: You'll find this employee eminently agreeable, but determined not to compromise who they are or how they work. No problem—let them take the work home if that's their style—just as long as it's done by tomorrow morning. If you want to make sure, put them on commision.

LIBRA @ WORK WITH PISCES

☛ **Deal with it!**

This alliance seldom takes the direct approach. When the going gets tough, Libra and Pisces get going, with a two-for-one ticket to Fantasy Island. Decision-making is your common enemy. But it's too costly if you both fritter away an entire afternoon choosing a new letterhead. Still, though, you do look out for one another's welfare, and give and take comes easy, so don't jump ship at the first sign of trouble. Lean on each other. The power in numbers is the secret to your mutual success.

IF PISCES IS BOSS: Pisces may expect you to invent your own tasks to identify what needs to be done without telling you. Great efforts on your part may go unrecognized or unrewarded, whereas someone else's casual help may get them an Employee of the Month award. They may take it personally when you aren't exemplary. Figure out what their priorities are and make them yours as well.

IF YOU'RE IN CHARGE: To get the most out of your Pisces employee, create a casual work setting that's still very productive. Don't encourage laziness, but then again don't encourage martyrdom or total indentured servitude, either. Pisces may be uncomfortable with a democracy, but by the same token they won't reach their full creativity under a dictatorship.

Scorpio @ Work

"Sooner or later I'm going to die, but I'm not going to retire."
SCORPIO AND SOCIOLOGIST MARGARET MEAD

SCORPIO

The Myth

Throughout the world, myths about Scorpio are good and juicy. To ancient Chinese astrologers, Scorpio was a dragon; to the Polynesians, a giant fishhook for lifting islands and volcanoes from the ocean floor; and to the Egyptians, Scorpio was a phoenix, the magical desert bird that lives 500 years and then sets itself on fire, rising renewed from the ashes to start another long life.

In Greek mythology, Scorpio represented the bug that Artemis, the young goddess of wild animals, picked up and threw at Orion the hunter when he got fresh with her. Orion had boasted that no animal could harm him, but he was sorely wrong. Scorpio stung him with poison, sending frisky Orion scampering away to lick his wounds and zip up his toga. Moral of the story: Scorpio may look small and squashable, but he always sticks up for allies, never fears a bully, and abounds with surprises.

Motivation

Scorpio is full of riddles, so here's one for you: What motivation may be simple to name but hard to catch? Power. You like it. You want it. You won't stop till you get some.

So Scorpio hungers for power. It sounds like a bad word, but it's not. The word *power* comes from the Latin verb *potere,* which means "to be able to." That's you: With a can-do attitude, you have an unquenchable thirst for *ability.* You don't so much want the Ferrari as you *need the speed.* The rush of vigor, force, and strength drives Scorpio to push limits and break records.

With power comes influence. Motivated to reach the crowds and a broad range of people, you want to be in a position to sway public opinion. As far as you're concerned, Capricorn can keep their prestige and Aries is welcome to hog all the authority, while Cancer and Taurus hoard the stocks and bonds. None of it, you realize, matters more than the power to change people's minds and experience life on the edge.

Scorpio also gets a kick out of the power of transformation. Unlike Pisces, you don't chase after rainbows. You work with what you've got. "This is how it is and I'm going to do something about it," is Scorpio's motto. If something is old and withering, you breathe new life into it. In people, ideas, or a spooky supply closet, you probe the dark depths. You examine motives, determined to know what makes people tick. In your dexterous hands, a dull, lifeless job turns into a career where you're indispensable. In short, one person's garbage is Scorpio's buried treasure.

Assets

Scorpio is a crisis-buster. When the you-know-what hits the fan, who you gonna call? Try 1-800-SCORPIO. You work so well under pressure that you might even want to consider a career defusing bombs. When corporate profits lag, when a takeover is imminent, when bankruptcy looms too close for comfort, Scorpio resurrects the prospect of success.

If Aries plants the seeds of business and Taurus grows them, you're the one who comes in later with the Weed Eater. You're what business professors call a "turnaround artist," someone who can rescue a company from the claws of calamity. Just in the nick of time, you turn liabilities into assets. You're often—probably too often—called in to clean up other people's messes.

But Scorpio just can't seem to shirk a reputation for shrewdness. You sit back and watch, figuring out what motivates clients and coworkers before taking action. Lots of Scorpios wouldn't take an elected official position for all the free lunches in Washington, but the truth is, you've got a political sixth sense. You size up workplace situations with the observational skills of a surveillance camera.

> **"Every act of creation is first of all an act of destruction."**
> ARTIST PABLO PICASSO

Inquiring minds want to know! And so does Scorpio. In fact, Scorpio is practically the private dick of the zodiac. You snoop around for information, separating genuine leads from red herrings. You ferret out advantageous interest rates. You dig up bargains and dust off hidden treasures. When most managers see a problem, they tinker till they fix it. Not you. Probing and passionate, Scorpio's not interested in symptoms. You diagnose the problem's *source*. Who's got time for shots in the dark? If you're gonna tinker, you're going to solve the heart of the matter.

Intensity is another Scorpio asset. Often driven by sheer willpower, you lock onto objectives like a pit bull with a leg of lamb, and concentrate on one task to the exclusion of all distractions. I've never known commitment like Scorpio commitment. You don't commit quickly—first you demand loyalty, sacrifice, or sheer bribery—but once you do, that project, task, or career is your mistress forever. Or at least until it betrays you. But even then Scorpio is resilient and almost always bounces back.

Years ago, Scorpio and Aries used to share Mars as a planetary mascot. Now Pluto has come into the picture and current astrologers know better. Under Mars, Aries charges straight ahead. That's not you. Pluto suits Scorpio's sideways, diagonal, and zigzag movements. Though you never follow the straight and narrow, you sometimes lead. But more often you hang back among the ranks where you know you can find the pulse of the regiment, the key to the power behind the megaphone. If I want the answers that *aren't* in the back of the book, I ask a Scorpio.

Liabilities

Scorpio gets paranoid. You harbor conspiracy theories. You anticipate the worst and lose sight of the rest. Case in point: A Scorpio school chum of mine, now a yuppie credit analyst, bemoaned his fate one day over coffee: "I attract *%$@! My whole life is a failure." The very next week he landed a fancy job with an international commercial bank. He's typical of Scorpio types—you like to think you have a monopoly on misfortune. Your life

has been *so* hard. First you were born (a traumatic birth) and, well, it was downhill from there. Oh yes, I feel your pain.

Your shrewdness sometimes makes you seem sneaky and insincere. Clients and coworkers don't want to work with someone whose hidden agenda slips through their grin like a rush of bad breath. You are tempted to flirt with big money; you're drawn to shady dealings and suitcases of unmarked bills—who cares where it comes from? Like a youthful daredevil, you think you're indestructible when the money's rolling in, but beware of treading on ambiguous ethical territory.

You're into outsmarting people, which can serve your purposes, but can also alienate your comrades. Eventually even you, clandestine Scorpio, will be found out. Though at times you can become an island of efficiency, you can also get lost in the fantasy of your own potency. For your power to remain productive, you must cooperate with others, and if your presence is too alienating, others will kick you out the door.

Scorpio has a deep capacity to become jaded. An optimistic Scorpio is rare, but if you can find one—or better yet, if you can become one—you'd see a magnificent sight, a human who could reach the heights of whatever mountain captured his or her gaze.

Dr. Matt's Tips for Scorpio Success

★ Use power. Don't abuse it.

★ Develop your ability to read people objectively.

★ In meetings and discussions, be ready to argue your point with facts, figures, and clear logic. Yes, your urge to appeal to the emotions can work too, but why not hedge your bets?

★ Make sure you can deliver on your promises.

★ Find specific projects on which to focus your gung-ho attitude. Otherwise you'll end up scaring the uptight big shots with your seemingly unwarranted enthusiasm.

★ Relax into the fact you may occasionally lose your magic tiara and no longer have to be wonder worker. Maybe then you'll start seeing those things that make you truly excellent. Embrace your human foibles, dandruff, obsessive neuroses—if not, they may embrace you.

★ Keep perspective. Though you seesaw between excess and asceticism, a little moderation wouldn't hurt.

SCORPIO TO THE MAX!

Whether you love him or hate him, you've got to admire Scorpio computer tycoon Bill Gates, founder and CEO of Microsoft, the world's first micro-computer software company. As one of the youngest, biggest, wealthiest industrialists in the world, Gates exemplifies the telltale Scorpio characteristic of extremism. When he does it, he does it to the max, just like all successful Scorpios. Often showing more interest in power than in profits, Gates is a master of making his Microsoft products indispensable to nearly every computer owner. Clearly he wants worldwide technology to bear his stamp. True to the Scorpio spirit, he's known for competing shrewdly and rescuing faltering computer businesses.

Scorpio in Alliance

SCORPIO @ WORK WITH ARIES

☞ **Cutthroat.**

The two of you make an aggressive team, a couple of control freaks who will conquer an industry, or exhaust each other trying. Aries grabs for power, you consolidate it. Aries cares about the business's public image, you're more concerned with its credit and credibility. You share a short fuse and a winner's instinct. This alliance is urgent and crisis-oriented. Friendly competiton spurs you on, but avoid a belligerent clash of wills. Together you can build a superpower, but only with a division of labor that allows each of you to do what you do best.

IF ARIES IS BOSS: Treat them like a four-star general. They'll appreciate your discipline, but probably not your lack of sponteneity. Aries will come to rely on your crisis-management skills. Keep a first-aid kit close at hand.

IF YOU'RE IN CHARGE: Teach Aries the art of strategy. Aries is a fighter and trailblazer, deploying a full frontal assault where you prefer a little subtle espionage. Help Aries learn from previous mistakes.

SCORPIO @ WORK WITH TAURUS

☛ **Value judgments.**

You're both hard workers committed to achieving goals and high standards, but you don't always share compatible visions and values. Make sure the partnership is equal—that rewards are commensurate with contributions, but not "tit for tat" where everyone's always keeping score; a relationship isn't a balance sheet. Support Taurus. Impress them with a stellar track record before you go near their purse strings or

> **"Power corrupts, but lack of power corrupts absolutely."**
> POLITICIAN ADLAI STEVENSON

a contract to incorporate. Even if this partnership is one for all and all for one, let Taurus maintain a few goodies of their own.

IF TAURUS IS BOSS: Don't throw out the coffee grounds. They might want them for their rose garden. In fact, don't do anything that jostles their universe or wastes precious, or not-so-precious, resources. Treat them like a high-quality martini: Don't shake them too much—it taints their delicate consistency. A gentle stirring will do the trick.

IF YOU'RE IN CHARGE: Make Taurus feel that you won't drop them through the booby-hatch if their third-quarter sales don't live up to expectations. Remember, Taurus needs a nice, even, steady pace. Unlike you, they won't obligingly pull all-nighters for tommorow morning's video conference call.

SCORPIO @ WORK WITH GEMINI

☛ **Too much information!**

Gemini's an information junkie, whereas too much information annoys you. You prefer what's relevant. You may, however, come to admire Gemini when you see how much entrée and carte blanche they have up their sleeve. Just wait till you see the size of their Rolodex! You expect a lot of each other, and a lot you may get. Gemini lacks focus, but not new ideas. This alliance works best when you decide on a division of labor and avoid trespassing on one another's territory.

IF GEMINI IS BOSS: You may find their budgeting frivolous and their questioning nature nerve-wracking. But this boss can turn your tap-dancing routine into a Broadway hit, so don't write them off till you've learned all Gemini's tricks of the trade.

IF YOU'RE IN CHARGE: Get ready for this employee to tax your flexibility more than a yoga guru would. They'll have special requests, wacky ideas, and a distressing habit of yelling, "Stop the presses!" But Gemini may come to idolize you. And you know, of course, imitation is the most sincere form of flattery.

SCORPIO @ WORK WITH CANCER

☛ **The competitive edge.**

You want profit margins. Cancer wants a satisfied customer. When Cancer finds a good thing, they stick with it. You, on the other hand, want to make it better. Shall the twain ever meet? Yes, if you realize customer satisfaction guarantees future earnings and Cancer learns to operate within their means. In this alliance, avoid feast or famine. Bear in mind Cancer wants security. You make a lot of guarantees, Cancer expects you to fulfill them. This alliance does well if you draw out one another from your respective cocoons by creating a safe environment with plenty of warm running water.

IF CANCER IS BOSS: They may want to integrate you into the organization faster and more thoroughly than you're comfortable with. Cancer wants to know you're going to gel with the rest of the crowd and stick around.

IF YOU'RE IN CHARGE: Make Cancer look around. They've got a knack for spotting underserved markets, locations waiting to be discovered, or opportunities for collective buying power. Though Cancer likes to nest, send them out to talk to the folks on the street. Without knowing your market, Cancer can't determine which will sell better, Tutti-Frutti or Ballistic Banana.

SCORPIO @ WORK WITH LEO

☛ **Just grow up!**

You don't like Leo, certainly not at first. Frivolous and pompous, they offend you. Their personality intimidates you. "Can't they control themselves?" you wonder. Power trips plague this alliance. Both of you identify each other's weaknesses and immediately start to amputate. But you need Leo. Maybe not today, or even tomorrow. But someday. Leo knows where the action is and, more than any other sign, how to put *you* at Ground Zero. Don't burn yourselves out with petty squabbles over who does the hiring and firing. Give up some inconsequential control if it ultimately

gets you where you want to be—and with Leo, that's always on the front page.

IF LEO IS BOSS: They want to be in the driver's seat. Get used to it. But you'll discover they're more than happy to let you do everything else, from pumping the gas to rebuilding the engine.

IF YOU'RE IN CHARGE: Temper your desire to humble Leo—that might risk irreparable damage. Leo will work their bushy little tail off if you dangle promises of promotion before them—and then deliver. Make room for individual accomplishment as well as team success.

SCORPIO @ WORK WITH VIRGO

☛ **No funny business.**

You two are very serious together. Lighten up. In a moment of crisis, you, Scorpio, respond with whatever's needed, the end usually justifying the means. But Virgo wants to do it by the book, no exceptions. In disagreements, resist the urge (you both have it) to isolate. Share viewpoints. Realize one story can—and should!—produce multiple interpretations. And whatever you do, don't reinforce one another's inferiority complexes. Treat each other like champions. Even if it feels fake today, by day after tomorrow it might be for real.

IF VIRGO IS BOSS: Always keep the customer in mind. Ask yourself, "How is what I'm doing right now going to benefit the end user?" If the answer is a big zilch, Virgo won't be happy, no matter how much your efforts help outsmart competitors. Virgo wants productivity with purpose.

IF YOU'RE IN CHARGE: Tell Virgo to get to the heart of the problem. Virgo works hard, but may not always know where to direct their efforts. Help them learn to identify the *source* of the mess, not just how to clean it up.

SCORPIO @ WORK WITH LIBRA

☛ **Persuasion power.**

Together you and Libra can coerce, cajole, or compel just about anyone to do anything at any price. But unless you two retain your individuality, say *adios* to any dreams of harmony in this partnership. While you, Scorpio, tend to determine exactly what's needed for success, Libra is less sure, always weighing the options. For getting along with Libra and

all-around better negotiations, Dr. Matt recommends asking lots of open-ended questions—not the yes-or-no variety, but invitations for people to impart valuable information.

IF LIBRA IS BOSS: Listen to them. Try not to let personality conflicts disturb your plans to do a good job. Libra plays evenhandedly, so even if you aren't Libra's pet employee, don't worry. You'll get your fair share of goodies.

IF YOU'RE IN CHARGE: Consider the human factor. Before barraging Libra with systems, procedures, and policies, try working on their attitude. With a mind-set attuned to your wavelength, the Libra will learn faster and uphold your vision. And remember, Libra's a social animal—solitary confinement yields poor work, so team them up with a more junior or senior buddy.

SCORPIO @ WORK WITH SAGITTARIUS

☛ **Fierce negotiators.**

No street vendor or real estate broker wants to encounter this team! You and Saj drive a hard bargain. The typical Scorpio hates to be cheated, whereas Saj loves to haggle for the heck of it. In your dickering and deal-making, just make sure you don't alienate the person on the other end—or each other! And bear in mind that if your joint venture falls on hard times, Saj may hit the road even though you'd prefer to stay and resurrect the rubble. Iron out ownership issues today.

IF SAGITTARIUS IS BOSS: Don't fudge the truth. Saj appreciates honesty, even when it hurts. They may miss the little stuff (so catch it for them), but Saj is surprisingly alert to new ideas for professional growth, and happy to have you tag along. Saj isn't your ideal boss, but if served conscientiously, Saj can, and will, catapult you to bigger and better places.

IF YOU'RE IN CHARGE: Delegate authority as well as responsibility. Saj needs to branch out, learning to be accountable. But they can't do it if you're holding a safety net below them or an iron fist above. Test Saj with a few start-to-finish projects of their own. Don't, however, set them up to fail. Nothing's sadder or more wasteful than a forlorn centaur.

SCORPIO @ WORK WITH CAPRICORN

☛ Survival of the fittest.

You and Capricorn make an effective management team. Capricorn brings know-how and a talent for sniffing out opportunities like a blood-hound. You supply the discipline to employ it without wasting a drop. Together and independently, ask yourselves what you truly value. Capricorn's rigid. You adapt to the environment. Strike a balance between these extremes, constantly reevaluting and stating in

> **"People should know what you stand for. They should also know what you won't stand for."**
> ANONYMOUS

no uncertain terms what needs to be done and who's supposed to do it. As a bloc, you command awesome respect and deference, and many underlings as well as clients may never make a move without consulting you first.

IF CAPRICORN IS BOSS: Work smarter, not harder. From you, Scorpio, this boss expects insights into human nature and consumer behavior. Even if it's not in your job description, you'll earn extra points for making contacts and bringing in clients. The Capricorn boss has few confidants, but you may find yourself among this elite.

IF YOU'RE IN CHARGE: Capricorn will finish the job and aim to please, but don't send any quirky or unfamiliar tasks across their desk without due warning. Despite that confident exterior, Capricorn looks silly when asked to juggle apples and oranges.

SCORPIO @ WORK WITH AQUARIUS

☛ Bound to stick around.

This alliance delivers—again and again. Together with Aquarius, you see a job through to the finish line, working purposefully on one job at a time, one step at a time. But since you're both headstrong, brace yourself for dissension. Aquarius, in your view, wastes too much time and money on networking, charities, or dream-chasing when you'd like them to focus on continued fiscal viability. Help them see that one can't exist without the other. "Visionary but managerially challenged" sums up the typical Aquarius professional. Success lies in combining your mangerial skills with Aquarius's visions.

IF AQUARIUS IS BOSS: Let them know what you're good at. Ultimately Aquarius appreciates innovation over blind obedience. No one—especially not

you!—*is* their job description. So expose your talents. Without making it a big deal, identify a problem that's fallen through the cracks, catch it, and make it *your* baby.

IF YOU'RE IN CHARGE: Don't pass judgment on Aquarius too quickly. They hate to be pigeonholed, and once they feel "sized up," Aquarius immediately wants to shatter any preconception you may have of them. Encourage them to hone multiple talents.

SCORPIO @ WORK WITH PISCES

☞ **Rescue and retreat.**

Given our economy's growing stress-relief sectors, from tourism to aromatherapy, this alliance can strike it rich saving the day. Full of an inner vitality, a uniquely human quality that makes everyone in your environment feel taken care of or rejuvenated, you and Pisces *relieve* problems. Your motto says, "Hey, look, there's more to life than paying taxes!" Customers and coworkers want to believe you and refuel at your gurgling fountains. But beware! This alliance musn't ever let itself run ragged. Practice what you preach. Take a spa day.

IF PISCES IS BOSS: They may look oblivious, but these folks are very aware. Your chances of success are greater if you don't double-cross the Fish. Wager that Pisces is watching, even if they seem sound asleep.

IF YOU'RE IN CHARGE: Be a boss worth admiring. Pisces needs a hero, a role model to emulate. And give Pisces a sense of belonging. More than most, Pisces knows there are lots of fish in the sea—and if they feel undirected or left out, Pisces may just swim away. If Pisces is valuable, let them know it.

Sagittarius @ Work

NOVEMBER 22 TO DECEMBER 21

SAGITTARIUS

The Myth

Like the happy-go-lucky souls it represents, the Sagittarius myth gets around. In China, this constellation represents a tiger; in India, a horse. In Arab mythology, Sagittarius is a flock of ostriches: some are coming, some are going, and one's in the middle acting like a traffic cop.

In ancient Greece, Sagittarius was quite a party animal. Half horse and half human, this centaur was born out of the illicit affair between a frisky father and a provocative cloud masquerading as a beautiful goddess. Eventually Sagittarius matured, published several bestselling scrolls, and taught courses at an elite university for young heroes. Moral of these fables: Saj is cosmopolitan, fun-loving, and unrealistic—but after playtime's over, Saj reveals a wealth of wisdom and a Madison Avenue flair for selling ideas.

Motivation

More than fortune, more than fame, Sagittarius shoots for freedom. Freedom of thought, liberty to pursue happiness, but mostly *free time*. That's not to say your life is a cabaret, old chum; a career of sunbathing on Miami Beach would wear you out faster than hard labor in Alcatraz. But basically, you thrive on having enough time, freedom, and resources to do what you want. That's all. Of course, that's a lot.

"The Prime Minister would stay in bed till 9 A.M. Then he'd sit up, looking like a pink cherub, and read the latest war reports. If the news was good, he bounced up and down with joy looking like a small boy. If it was bad, he'd pull up the sheet till his face was barely visible, looking like my grandmother, as if to keep out the bad news. But then he'd start the day's business."

WRITTEN ON A LONDON MUSEUM WALL ABOUT SAGITTARIAN WINSTON CHURCHILL AFTER WORLD WAR II

Not lazy but gluttonous, Sagittarius always wants more. It's not greed but some kind of bizarre quest for understanding that your friends gave up trying to understand years ago. Not content to be one or the other, the Centaur is half human, half beast, galloping through the forest with a bow and arrow. Nowadays maybe it's a camcorder. Whichever, Sagittarius shoots at everything, insatiable for new experiences and challenges. Hey, if you use enough arrows or film, you're bound to catch something interesting.

"Interesting and fun" are prerequisites for maintaining your motivation. Sagittarius seeks a life of adventure. The daily routine seems like a treadmill. You'd rather run on the beach, dashing waves, skipping stones, befriending the sea otters. You learn. You travel. You talk to people—all *sorts* of people. Wisdom is the destination. Pleasure is the journey. So above all, what you desire is a passport. It might cost big bucks. It may take years to acquire. But you cheerfully bear the struggle if it produces the carte blanche to be who you are, do what you fancy, and go where your curiosity calls.

Assets

"What's out there?" you wonder. So with passport in hand, you cross borders and explore frontiers, the consummate prospector. "Can't you see?" says Sagittarius. "Out there are worlds waiting to be discovered, untapped

markets dying for what we've got." At any corner of the global village you can make your home and set up shop. Whatever your field, you've got the heart of an import-export mogul. Foreign cultures and faraway places—from Timbuktu to cyberspace—animate your wanderlust.

But not all adventures require long-distance travel. Sagittarius studies. You possess a masterful brain demanding constant employment. Ensconced in your armchair, absorbed in books or software, you take many turbocharged journeys in your mind. Saj is a lifetime learner, and any job that won't let you expand your horizons needs to be shot. But don't worry, your expertise is in demand; it's bound to dazzle the boss and tantalize clients.

Optimism is the Sagittarian birthright. Incurably romantic, you take obstacles in stride and make contacts easily. There's an innocent, genuine quality that makes you popular. You don't, however, like to kiss up. Honesty's your best policy. You wouldn't think of complimenting the emperor's new clothes when he's really wearing nothing more than his birthday suit.

Sajs without a long list of goals ought to forfeit their zodiac membership cards. The future beckons. You've always got your eye on the big picture. Far-reaching ramifications and down-the-road possibilities number among the greatest insights you bring to any strategy meeting. Philosophy courses through your veins. A fierce defender of your principles, you ponder the impact of your decisions on your company, its people, and society at large. Injustice infuriates you. On the other hand, expansion delights you. Expanding a business, opening up markets, arguing a precedent-setting case before a high court—these are all Sagittarian endeavors.

In the Sagittarian worldview, "Life is a daring adventure or nothing at all" (to quote Helen Keller). So when it comes to growing a career, you can choose to approach the situation in one of two ways: Your career is either a laborious distraction that merely pays the bills while you pursue your real passions after-hours, *or* your career is a fundamental part of the adventure, a tangible expression of your character and calling.

Liabilities

Many a Sagittarius suffers from growing pains, particularly in the early stages of career development. Blind optimism gets you in trouble. You overestimate earnings and underestimate how long it'll take to earn them. Caution escapes you. No matter how hard you work to locate the solution

to a problem, when you find it you skip steps, carelessly risking a nasty spill.

What business leaders call "project procurement" is your specialty. Project *completion,* however, is your potential downfall. You lose interest and change directions. You neglect to read the

> **"Beavis, like, free your mind, or something."**
> CARTOON CHARACTER
> BUTTHEAD

fine print. You're as restless as a hyena in a pet shop. Where do you start? How do you organize your plan of attack? Who might catch you in flagrante delicto? "Oh, who cares!" says the peripatetic Sagittarius.

In fact one Sagittarian playwright I worked with used to say that all of the world's Sajs should move to a tropical island where, unencumbered by the daily nuisances of paying bills and punching a clock, they could reflect on life and produce great works of art and scholarship. To maintain the infrastructure, like sewage and housing, they could hire a crew of efficient Virgos. Perhaps that's a little extreme. Irresponsibility needn't plague you all the days of your life. But then again, that tropical island idea doesn't sound half bad, does it?

Whether among mango trees or city skyscrapers, the robust Sagittarian career needs to encompass *wholeness*. It needs room for the mundane and the philosophical. A little drudgery doesn't have to eclipse your potential. Take breaks. Use routine chores like vacuuming the staples off the floor to relax your mind and rejuvenate your soul.

Dr. Matt's Tips for Sagittarius Success

★ Develop self-discipline. Make it second nature to use proven time-management skills. Leave room for tangents, but don't let them overtake your entire workday.

★ Buy pencils. Get a chalkboard. You need to doodle and brainstorm in anything but ink—it'll scare away your creativity.

★ Be realistic about how much money you need. Many Sagittarians settle for lower pay to get work they love. That's great, but take precautions like staying up to date in other fields and ensuring you're covered for health care.

★ Even if your résumé doesn't fit perfectly with the job you want, give it a shot. Given your adaptability, use a cover letter or interview to convince a potential employer your background has indeed prepared you for this challenge. Turn your enthusiasm into hire-ability.

★ You're in the habit of turning pipe dreams into skyscrapers. But with all this eagerness to push upward, it's easy to neglect the plans and very imagination that nourished the roots. Pause and remember why you bothered in the first place. Glance back at your mission statement. You won't lose momentum, you'll gain support.

THAT'S A "FUNNY" WAY TO MAKE A LIVING

The sign of explorers and "navel-gazers," Sagittarius arrives at a unique, sometimes twisted, but always philosophical outlook on life—and then feels compelled to pronounce an opinion. But whether Saj bitches about their worldview or laughs about it, they sure like to profit from it. *Peanuts* creator Charles Schultz, a Saj, humorously transformed his childhood foibles into the world's favorite comic strip. Another Saj comic, James Thurber, wrote funny and satirical books on topics ranging from the mundane to the inhumane. *New York Times* columnist, pundit, and Sagittarian William Safire freely and mercilessly comments on everything from grammar to politics. In his spare time, Sagittarian Prime Minister Winston Churchill published books of history, warfare, and scathing remarks. Two examples par excelence of the Sagittarian mentality are Mark Twain and Woody Allen. Both have created funny but pointed stories about the serious issues of their times, and both are (and were, in the case of Twain), well, characters in their own right. It's true that staring into your navel usually isn't a profitable activity, but if you're like these guys you can turn vision into power, prestige, and *mucho dinero.*

Sagittarius in Alliance

SAGITTARIUS @ WORK WITH ARIES

☛ Independence Day celebration!

A couple of freedom addicts, you both have a thing for doing your own thing. Working with Aries is always an impulsive, energized experience, full of sudden decisions and quick changes. Together, your mutual love of riskiness isn't just doubled; it's cubed. But in the long run, Saj, you're willing to wager less than Aries. At first sight of a beautiful island, you jump ship looking for buried treasure while Aries sticks to the mission, regardless of icebergs. Spend resources prudently. Fight laziness. Cut down on caffeine.

IF ARIES IS BOSS: Try to keep up. Timeliness counts. Aries believes "time is money." Help Aries understand your motives and methods, the rationale behind your strong convictions. Otherwise he'll think you're just wasting time.

IF YOU'RE IN CHARGE: Constantly revive Aries. Keep the job fresh, the challenges unpredictable. For even better results, appeal to Aries's inner entrepreneur—they've all got one. Aries is right at home in an empowered team or semiautonomous department. If these tactics fail, try shock therapy.

SAGITTARIUS @ WORK WITH TAURUS

☛ **The opportunist meets the loan officer!**

Here's an alliance between an extravagant idealist (you) and a sober pragmatist (Taurus). You broaden Taurus's worldview. They get you to stop staring at the view and start looking at the bottom line. Clearly, compromise is the best policy. Side by side, you're as hard-working as a team of oxen, but *first* you'll have to negotiate which field to plow. In the best of times, you complement each other's assets and liabilities, yielding an optimistic team with a sense of "anything's possible." In the worst of times, you go your separate ways. Try sticking it out a little longer.

IF TAURUS IS BOSS: Earn their trust. Taurus worries. Don't give them anything to worry about. Anticipate problems. Report mistakes. And don't confuse Taurus with too much information. *Do* convince them with plenty of facts and figures.

IF YOU'RE IN CHARGE: You'll appreciate Taurus's dependability. But don't take it for granted! Taurus expects more than a pat on the back—like a sensible dental plan, or workplace safety and easy parking. Forget about promoting Taurus to a new job title unless it comes with a salary boost.

SAGITTARIUS @ WORK WITH GEMINI

☛ **Big picture, little picture.**

You've got pie in the sky. Gemini's got 18 pie recipes but no vision for starting a nationwide brand. It's a natural attraction. You feed on one another's cleverness. Is there ever a dull moment? Just don't go into the library together—you'll get kicked out for excessive banter. When problems crop up, it's no battle of wills but an all-out war of wits. Mutually,

you lack discretion. Can either of you keep a secret? Better leave the safe deposit keys with a reliable Scorpio. And establish a clear direction.

IF GEMINI IS BOSS: Pay attention to the details. Don't absentmindedly talk about this boss behind closed doors—it always, without fail, gets back to them. To get Gemini's attention, always get a second opinion and quote the experts. Footnotes help too.

IF YOU'RE IN CHARGE: Put everything in writing. Don't expect Gemini to assume what you mean. And acknowledge their ideas, no matter how much or how little you've been able to use them. Gemini's ingenuity flourishes in an environment where it's OK to ask dumb questions.

SAGITTARIUS @ WORK WITH CANCER

☛ **Very important problems.**

In this alliance everything's a big deal. You assert your priorities. Cancer insists their pet projects matter more. Hassles turn into ordeals. Frequently you'd both like to shout, "You just don't *understand!*" But this duet isn't doomed. Helping to define your purpose, Cancer makes you a rebel *with* a cause. Furthermore, since you tend to overlook the obvious, Cancer shifts your gaze to opportunities, motives, and pitfalls—often right under your nose. And probably more than any other colleague, Cancer appeals to your latent sense of financial security, urging you, for instance, to set up a retirement fund or start a life insurance policy (preferably with themselves as beneficiary). So with Cancer, bounce back from adversity. Don't panic over a box of lost paper clips.

> **"The purpose of life? To cultivate enthusiasm."**
>
> *THE 1001 NIGHTS*

IF CANCER IS BOSS: Stay calm. Your typically frantic condition won't go over well here. Cancer craves stability. And remember, with an eager beast like you, this boss tends to be overprotective, even a bit parental. Let Cancer know when you're ready to grow up and borrow the car keys.

YOU'RE IN CHARGE: Cancer can help you create an environment where people come first. Cancer never forgets a client's face. This employee can absorb complaints and please difficult personalities. But don't betray their confidence! That brings out drastic measures.

SAGITTARIUS @ WORK WITH LEO

☛ **Good buddies, lazy partners.**

They're fire, you're fire, and together you blaze. The jokes are flying, the aspirations are bubbling over, and working together is more fun than a bonfire at the beach in summertime. And potentially every bit as unproductive. Teamed up, you derail one another, pursuing various tangents. Still, the chance to learn from and promote one another is boundless. Don't let it get to the point where you're saying, "Anything you can do I can do better." Bear in mind the goal of a win-win situation. Neither of you likes to lose.

IF LEO IS BOSS: Be clear on the concepts. Try to understand where Leo's coming from, allowing for the fact their idea may be in the germination stage—not fully grown—and you're supposed to help it evolve. Look, every Leo-headed business or department has a *style* all its own. Figure it out, dress and act accordingly, and you're halfway home.

IF YOU'RE IN CHARGE: Create opportunities for Leo to shine, to prove they're as smart as you, to organize your clutter, even while you remain the boss. Tap Leo's expertise. Give prizes, not only for performance but also for service and commitment. Leo seldom walks away from the trust someone places in them.

SAGITTARIUS @ WORK WITH VIRGO

☛ **The odd couple.**

I don't have to spell out who's the neat freak and who's the slob, do I? This alliance absolutely, positively has to allow elbow room for each of you. Don't crowd, don't meddle, don't look over each other's shoulder. You can help Virgo overcome their fear of screwing up in front of a judgmental world. Meanwhile, Virgo's user-friendly packaging can move your big ideas out of the test lab and into the laps of your consumers. Since you and Virgo are always building a better mousetrap, watch out for changing your image too radically. Familiarity doesn't breed contempt; it breeds brand loyalty.

IF VIRGO IS BOSS: Be clear about what you need to do your job *right*. Supplies? New software? A can of air freshener? Virgo doesn't expect you to improvise, but necessities like these can escape their attention. Typically, as long as you work within a reasonable budget, Virgo's happy to help you work more efficiently. (Sorry, a stretch limo probably isn't reasonable!)

IF YOU'RE IN CHARGE: Take this insight from Dr. Matt: Virgins are not easy! As long as it's business as usual, Virgo produces. But watch out for straining them with overtime, unfamiliar technology, or goofy projects. Tending toward an erratic management style, you Sagittarians can maximize Virgo's potential by providing schedules, directions, and clean floors without cookie crumbs.

SAGITTARIUS @ WORK WITH LIBRA

☛ **Mutual beneficiaries.**

This alliance takes teamwork seriously. Together you and Libra encourage active participation—and usually get it from anyone who hears your cheerleading cheers. Insecurities disappear. When one of you carps, "I can't do it!" the other insists, "Yes, you can! We'll do it together." When it comes to public relations and diplomacy, however, you see the world quite differently. Libra likes to keep the peace; you can't help but make waves. Live with it. Make this a relationship where you're both free—and urged!—to be who you are, not the other's fantasy of the ideal partner.

IF LIBRA IS BOSS: Don't disappoint them! Keep promises, don't throw a tantrum when you feel like a failure and, while keeping one eye on the competition, don't insist that another company manufacturers plastic grass that's greener than yours. Commitment—not a typical Sagittarian virtue—scores big with this boss.

IF YOU'RE IN CHARGE: Focus on quality, not quantity. Arbitrary and dogmatic quotas ignore Libra's talent for creating the most *appropriate* results, whether big or little. Furthermore, let Libra be a soothing influence on you and your workplace. Libra stays reasonable even in the most unreasonable situations.

SAGITTARIUS @ WORK WITH SCORPIO

☛ **Very intriguing!**

This alliance is prone to exaggeration. Problems seem enormous. Achievements feel like tickets to Easy Street. Late at night you're ready to compete against IBM; the next morning, bleary-eyed and hungry, you fear changing a printer ribbon. Still, though, you can learn a lot from Scorpio's ability to watch and scrutinize before throwing away punches or money. Likewise, Scorpio can learn from your breezy talent for bluffing and sidestepping obstacles. But nobody learns if you don't communicate!

Assume nothing. Don't try to read minds! Even if you could, Scorpio's language would sound like Greek to you.

IF SCORPIO IS BOSS: Don't be careless. Keep "trade secrets" secret. Call attention to potential problems before they fester. And don't abuse power with which you're entrusted. The Scorpio boss will peg you for promotion if you project a sense of knowing what you want and how to get it.

IF YOU'RE IN CHARGE: Get ready for tough questions. Scorpio knows how to ask them. This employee pushes you to solve puzzles you've pondered for years but never concluded. In turn, rev up Scorpio's potential by supportively asking how they see this job fitting into their life plans. If necessary, dig deeper: Every Scorpio has a plan!

SAGITTARIUS @ WORK WITH SAGITTARIUS

☛ **Never heard the word *impossible*.**

With mutual self-confidence or contagious self-delusion, a Saj alliance is bound to defy limits. You produce unwritten plays. You start software companies without knowing how to turn on a computer. Somewhere along the way you'll learn—from a book, on the Internet, eavesdropping at a party—*somehow*. Cross that bridge when you come to it, or take a hang glider. If you want to expand your mind, if you want to have a good time, this alliance works. If you want to compete with less idealistic folks, get some outside input, *fast*. And unless you write for daytime TV, avoid unnecessary melodrama.

IF THE OTHER SAGITTARIUS IS BOSS: Don't be average. And don't think you're going to befriend this boss by *not* having an opinion. When you hide your personality and panache from Saj, they simply assume you don't have any. Stand up for your principles and act like you've got a lot of action going on upstairs.

IF YOU'RE IN CHARGE: Make this employee stay in touch. As you know, Sagittarians tend to stray! These diversions often yield good results and bright ideas but leave coworkers and customers hanging. Establish a "call-back policy," whereby Saj has to return messages and e-mail within 24 to 48 hours. Even a few sentences can let the world know Saj is still alive and open for business!

SAGITTARIUS @ WORK WITH CAPRICORN

Delayed gratification.

This alliance rains on your parade. Capricorn slows down your lofty ambitions, forcing you to heed the yellow warning lights. But as for profits, this team goes full speed ahead. Always with one eye on the bottom line, Capricorn nags you about the price point—always wanting you to get top dollar—but they'll also urge you to spend money to make money. Just remember: It's the *making it* part that counts. You're willing to go farther out on a limb than the goat, but whether it's out of confidence or recklessness is hard to say. Ask for support, not just skepticism.

IF CAPRICORN IS BOSS: Think *long term*. In the event of a flood, plan to commute to work on your inflatable raft. Discuss where you'd like your career to be in 5, 10, 15 years. Put forth ideas that show this organization will outlive the latest fad.

IF YOU'RE IN CHARGE: Give Capricorn plenty of direction. They'll need definite goals and other indications, like a promotion and pointers, to feel they're moving up in the world.

SAGITTARIUS @ WORK WITH AQUARIUS

☛ **Watch out for the long-distance bills!**

In this alliance, you love to talk shop and exchange ideas, all of which are out of proportion with reality—but hey, that's OK! Imagination flows freely. You do, though, run the risk of locking horns ideologically. Aquarius has their conviction, you have your beliefs, and a happy agreement to disagree might be more profitable than trying to convince each other who's right. Aquarius seems too analytic, a little dry for your taste, but if you can add the caviar to their melba toast, it's a winning combination. As partners, you're both wary of commitment, but since you're equally goal-oriented you make great teammates.

IF AQUARIUS IS BOSS: Don't sell out. Don't treat coworkers like competitors for this boss's favor. Aquarius wants a real team, not a band of mercenaries. A pro with integrity wins this boss's Most Valuable Player award.

IF YOU'RE IN CHARGE: Get Aquarius to help you refine your ideas and ship them to market. Think of Aquarius as a theatrical agent working on your behalf, a matchmaker who connects you with the right person, the right tool, the right caterer for your next shindig.

SAGITTARIUS @ WORK WITH PISCES

☛ Dreamers of the world unite!

When you two get together something magical happens. It's like arriving at a place you've always dreamed of. Is it Oz or is it purgatory? This
alliance lacks discipline. When you two work together you get careless,
forgetting that sky-writing isn't the most effective form of advertising. But
then again, you engender one another's talents and creativity. Resist the
urge to grow too fast. Bigger isn't better, only bigger and harder to manage.

IF PISCES IS BOSS: Stop trying to understand them. You won't. Just do what
they say, respect their position, and don't overreact. If something bothers
you, renegotiate—preferably without losing the least bit of professional
composure. Pisces is almost always open to working things out but resents
having to get mean and feisty.

IF YOU'RE IN CHARGE: Look beyond this employee's job satisfaction to a bigger
sense of their personal fulfillment. No, you're not Pisces's fairy godmother,
but contributing to their overall success and well-being ensures that Pisces
remains one of your most committed workers. Always treat Pisces like a
whole person, not "just" an assistant. Pisces is never *just* anything!

Capricorn @ Work

> "You are not here merely to make a living. You are here to enable the world to live more amply, with greater vision, with a finer spirit of hope and achievement. You are here to enrich the world, and you impoverish yourself if you forget the errand."
>
> CAPRICORN U.S. PRESIDENT WOODROW WILSON

DECEMBER 22 TO JANUARY 19

CAPRICORN

The Myth

In worldwide mythology of the stars, Capricorn ranks among the oldest, most enduring constellations. To the Greeks, Capricorn depicted the mountain god Pan who worked as a shepherd by day and a musician by night. A bit of a workaholic, he mostly kept to himself—except for those numerous occasions when, legend has it, he seduced nymphs in the forest. Life was good, but Pan's feelings still got hurt when the nearby citizens of Athens didn't invite him to their parties and festivals. But instead of getting mad, Pan voluntarily showed up on the eve of a terrible battle and helped the Athenians to victory. After that, they never failed to honor and celebrate their new ally. Moral of the story: Capricorn works hard, loves emphatically, and often saves the day—but for all that effort there better be a trophy and a free lunch!

Motivation

Capricorn is built to last. Here today, gone tomorrow is not your style. Capricorn wants mastery. Mastery takes time. That's OK. Capricorn builds—brick by brick—till the building is complete. Forget disposable accomplishments. You want to create an opus

> **"I like work; it fascinates me. I can sit and look at it for hours."**
> ENGLISH PLAYWRIGHT
> JEROME K. JEROME

that lasts—a monument, a new artistic technique, a legacy. Your Capricorn essence drives you to get so good at whatever you choose to do that your peers and your inner critic regard you as a master. It might take a lifetime, but you'll do it.

After your death—or even before—you'd really appreciate a statue of your dignified self. On a superficial level, Capricorn craves society's acceptance and praise. On a deeper level, what you really want is to do the deeds that merit a statue. Capricorn is motivated to become a *mensch*, the Yiddish word for an honorable person of integrity, a noble character with a sense of what's right and responsible. Unlike Aquarius, you don't need to change the world. You're a knight who sticks to your own code of chivalry. Tradition matters. You won't break old rules without good reason. But neither will you let tradition interfere with doing the right thing.

"Adversity won't get me down!" is Capricorn's motto. And by golly, a little adversity can get you up! You excel in a struggle. When the opposition closes in, you're at your best, composed, poised, and prepared to defend your interests like a karate black belt.

Assets

Your parents called you precocious. Your teachers called you a smart aleck. And Hindu astrologers call you an old soul. The fact is, Capricorns mature fast, especially in the professional world. You're tough cookies who don't crumble in spilled milk.

You people ooze class. You're born with more breeding than a thoroughbred pony. Even the Capricorns raised in a trailer park know how to act like Old Money. You've got connections to all the best people in town. Your evident sense of propriety guarantees you won't sell their secrets to the *National Enquirer*. To get what you want, you have more effective means at your disposal!

Ambitious and determined, Capricorn likes to call shotgun on the driver's seat. But you're patient—to a point. When objectives falter, you can wait it out. Capricorn proceeds prudently, more like the stately *Queen Elizabeth II* luxury liner than the brisk new 777s. Exception! When going in for the kill or clinching the deal, the Goat strikes faster than a cobra in a mouse hotel!

You work by the book. Often, you *write* the book! When duty calls, you salute. In the usual course of things, you display a rare talent for separating business and pleasure, preventing irrational factors like, say, emotions, from tampering with the cash register. Faced with scarcity or deficits, you respond like a hero. Oddly enough, however, prosperity can freak you out. "Let the good times roll!" isn't a typical Capricorn philosophy. There's too much work to be done.

You don't like your fortunes left to chance. Whether you shelter cash in unnumbered Swiss bank accounts or sew silver dollars into the hem of your curtains, you're already ready for a rainy day. If infants could talk, you would've asked for certain guarantees (in writing!) at your birth.

Despite your patience, slow service and mediocrity exasperate your efficient sensibilities. Anywhere, anytime, you identify room for improvement. Capricorn could, I've no doubt, find the profit potential in raw sewage. Sell it to former Soviet republics? Turn it into nonfossil fuel? Convince tourists to ride submarines through the Indianapolis sewer treatment plant? You'll think of something.

Every Capricorn must choose one of two possibilities: (1) Shrink from the heavy responsibilities the universe yokes to your back, kvetching all the way about skyrocketing costs and conspiracies in banana republics to undermine your market share, or (2) accept your role as a guide and exemplar to colleagues and employees, arriving at the unexpected conclusion that yes, you have what it takes to be a mensch.

Liabilities

You're probably too busy to realize it, but the rest of us are fed up with your discipline. It makes us look bad, feel nincompoopish. "But what discipline?" you ask. That's even more infuriating. You make the hard stuff look easy without breaking a sweat. You see, that's why it's so hard for you to find sympathy when you just want to knock back a few beers with the gang. That's why we all want your secret when you don't even know you have one. If you did, you'd mass-market it.

When rules and schedules replace ingenuity, Capricorn stagnates. Instead of buying into an imposed regime, you adopt an arbitrary code of conduct that runs your life and career. Look, an enterprising spirit depends on invention, and invention requires a break with tradition. A

"No one can make you feel inferior without your consent."
SOCIAL REFORMER
ELEANOR ROOSEVELT

little competition reminds you of this, but without a mountain to climb or a challenge to tackle, you Caps seem to let your potential go to waste like leftovers forgotten at the back of the fridge.

Unfortunately, Capricorn has a tendency to fall into "social-climber mode"—when self-esteem doesn't satisfy your greed for prestige. You grovel for stature and status. You sell out for a medal or an invitation to join the country club. You apply to the Stanford Business School for a piece of parchment, not for an education, not even for fun in the Sun.

So much more than the rest of us indecisive mortals, you Capricorns always seem to know what you desire and how to bag it. But underneath your Rock of Gibraltar complexion, do you fret about serving red wine with fish? Do you notice that you're formidable and hard to approach? Or recognize that financial and emotional security may look alike but aren't? I sure hope you do! With flaws and all, humanity's a terrible thing to waste.

Dr. Matt's Tips for Capricorn Success

★ Unleash your habitually locked-up wild side. In our Info Age economy, creativity isn't frivolous.

★ Forget about keeping up with the Joneses. Who the heck *are* the Joneses, anyway? And more importantly, why do you want to be like them? Define success in your own terms.

★ Get comfortable with risks, both personal and financial, if you want to get ahead. Be ready to make a fool of yourself. If everyone laughs, at least it's certain you had their attention.

★ Consider your feelings, family, and other nonquantifiable factors in major economic and career decisions. There's a cool job in Tierra del Fuego? Great, but what will your significant other do while you feed penguins?

★ Accessorize your wardrobe with colors other than black, brown, and gray. *No!* Navy blue does *not* count as a color!

"YES, DARLING, I SEE THE POTENTIAL!"

Drawn to power and prestige, Capricorns have always played in the big leagues—like Capricorn entrepreneurs Conrad Hilton (founder of Hilton Hotels) and Howard Hughes (eccentric airplane and nightclub tycoon). But my personal favorite was a little Capricorn lady, a former client of Dr. Matt. This so-called "housewife" made a fortune in real estate. The funny thing is, she'd never intended to get rich; she simply wanted quality time with the kids while saving for a rainy day. So, seeing potential where others saw a dumpy Victorian mansion, she planted flowers and rented out rooms, turning it into a showplace. Her kitchen counter was her office. She'd negotiate over a cup of tea while the dogs and kids rushed in and out. Over the years she accumulated one apartment house after another, gifted at finding gold in the unlikeliest places. Last I heard, she still works at her kitchen counter, stirring soup while wheeling and dealing over the phone with New York real estate agents. That's Capricorn. They do things slowly, but ever so surely, one apartment house after another.

Capricorn in Alliance

CAPRICORN @ WORK WITH ARIES

☞ **Above and beyond the call of duty.**

This alliance has too many cooks in the kitchen. Willing to assume tremendous personal responsibility, you both excel as leaders—but what about as workers? To get the job done, immediately settle on individual job descriptions. And forget the trophies—help people achieve what's really important. Since you, Capricorn, demand solid foundations while Aries hates to wait around, you'll have to painstakingly explain, for example, why you need a database system *before* Aries sends off 500 ad hoc sales letters to an incomplete mailing list. If it's truly a partnership, work together. If not, it's not a partnership.

IF ARIES IS BOSS: Don't play the blame game. Pointing fingers, Aries wants to know who made the mess. But by passing the buck, you lose allies among coworkers. So as for the mess, show initiative and just clean it up. Let Aries know you're a force to be reckoned with, but not that you're trying to steal their territory.

IF YOU'RE IN CHARGE: Let Aries know it. Try to avoid, however, a traditional "I'm the boss" relationship. Instead of ordering Aries around, try rallying their urge to feel productive. If Aries loses self-esteem, *you've* lost one of this employee's greatest motivators.

CAPRICORN @ WORK WITH TAURUS

☛ Eye on the prize.

This alliance thrives on mutual admiration. Good craftsmanship turns you on. Together, you select talented personnel. You choose outstanding raw materials. You wait for the best vintage. There's no compromise. That's fine for production standards, but with each other and your market, Dr. Matt recommends adaptability. If all you're hearing is no, find new ways to reach a yes!

IF TAURUS IS BOSS: Give them a KISS: keep it short and simple. Don't overload their circuits. Taurus wants problems and information presented in a way that makes decision-making possible and profits probable.

IF YOU'RE IN CHARGE: Keep Taurus energized. Don't depend on their dependability *too* much or they'll grow bored, too uninspired to accomplish more than the bare minimum required to do the job. Force Taurus to see a few fields over the horizon.

CAPRICORN @ WORK WITH GEMINI

☛ A tight ship.

Hesitant to delegate and desperate for approval, this alliance can easily fall into a rut. Together you label and alphabetize every customer and each postage stamp that leaves the office. Gemini is speedy, you're thorough, and consequently your styles clash and you may find yourselves arguing over things like white versus manila envelopes or sugar versus saccharine. But if you can get beyond the petty details, you and Gemini are eminently resourceful, able to handle massive projects that crush other teams. Mutually decide the reasons behind your efforts.

IF GEMINI IS BOSS: Take notes! Remember, Gemini's a fast talker with too much technical knowledge for their own good. This boss needs an employee with an excellent memory and time-management skills. Frequently exasperating but eternally grateful, Gemini really wants to lean on you.

IF YOU'RE IN CHARGE: Set boundaries for the scope of the work. If work's not getting done the way you want, try this policy: "We're not leaving this room till we've settled on a plan." Gemini will write fast enough to spark a paper fire.

CAPRICORN @ WORK WITH CANCER

☛ Security blanket.

This alliance clings to survival. Together you tend to fear the worst, anticipating every shift in the wind, dwelling on past mistakes. As a result, you build a viable business, but not necessarily a prosperous one. Furthermore, Cancer's personal life and responsibilities may unwelcomely intrude on your reputation as a serious professional. To make it work, set goals that speak to your sense of fulfillment, not just success. When a fantastic but grueling opportunity arrives, ask yourselves, "Is this worth it?"

IF CANCER IS BOSS: Act as though you need them. Not for just a paycheck, but also for mentoring, guidance, and the occasional fashion pointer. Do a tidy job, consistently performing in a way they can count on. Cancer will reciprocate by looking out for your best interests, too.

IF YOU'RE IN CHARGE: Take Cancer under your wing. Regularly check to see how things are going. No, you don't have to look over their shoulder while they stamp an envelope, but bear in mind Cancer thrives on supportive guidance and the chance to show off their progress to head honchos.

CAPRICORN @ WORK WITH LEO

☛ No more mediocrity!

In terms of a finished product, this alliance tolerates nothing but the finest. Second best embarrasses you into working harder, the two of you competing for stardom and VIP status. In terms of just getting along, however, this alliance can succumb to immaturity. Without enough to do, you're bound to squabble, with at least of one of you declaring, "There's

only room for one leading star in this production!" If you fight, make sure it's worth fighting for. Too often the smallest stakes ignite the biggest fires.

IF LEO IS BOSS: Learn to improvise. With Leo you never know what's next. If you want to keep them happy, go along with their every whim. If you want to do them a favor, point out reality. If you want to do both, you're on your own.

IF YOU'RE IN CHARGE: Reduce stress in the environment, but don't eliminate it completely. According to actors and professional public speakers, some stage fright keeps them motivated and sharp. Learning this employee's limits, put a stop to Leo's stress before it turns into a soap opera.

CAPRICORN @ WORK WITH VIRGO

☛ Step by step.

This alliance has a strong sense of order. Seldom skipping steps, you and Virgo follow the 1-2-3 process that leads to the goal. Virgo knows things—or how to find out, supplying answers, or at least the right questions to ask. But in your dependence on data and studies, you two can lose sight of the human element. Tools are useful, but they're not gods. Don't kowtow to a machine. Remember, you bought the computer, not vice versa. Learn to respond to emergencies or other out-of-the-ordinary priorities that suddenly crop up. Master chefs don't follow recipes on the back of a box!

IF VIRGO IS BOSS: Learn to put up with idiosyncrasies. Virgo likes things just *so*—"A place for everything, everything in its place." "A lid for every pot." That sort of thing. But Virgo hates to have their methods challenged. Instead, gradually demonstrate time-saving measures that leave time for activities other than, say, signing payroll checks. A rubber stamp's a wonderful gift!

IF YOU'RE IN CHARGE: Virgo likes to show off their handiwork and may look to you to provide the showcase. Things that appear trivial to you may matter greatly to Virgo.

CAPRICORN @ WORK WITH LIBRA

☛ A class act.

This alliance brings out your best—and your worst. On the bright side you and Libra dazzle the world with fine manners and superior service.

You don't need ads on billboards. You've got clout and cachet. On the dark side, though, you're stuffy and snooty. Libra expects overnight success with all the trimmings. You overlook opportunities that smell of the common folk. The key here is to connect with your market, whether that's your customers or supervisors, and be *classy*, not class-conscious.

IF LIBRA IS BOSS: Don't get stuck in your same old tried-and-true routine. The Libra boss wants *participation*, and that means staying on top of industry news and building relationships with key players. Libra will glance at your résumé but stare at your list of references and contacts.

IF YOU'RE IN CHARGE: Capitalize on Libra's soft touch. Want customer service with more finesse than you care to exert? Put Libra at the counter. Planning a merger or acquisition? Send Libra to woo the right partner. Like a savvy Hollywood director, Libra's bound to show you off in the best light.

CAPRICORN @ WORK WITH SCORPIO

☛ **Serious contenders.**

This alliance aims high. In the thick of things, among the big shots is where you want to be. The small time holds little appeal for this dynamic duo. More than most, Scorpio can convince you to change with the times. Don't, however, let this semireclusive cohort lock you up in a back office plotting a world takeover. If you want to make it in the market, you've got to *go* to the market and mingle with the masses.

IF SCORPIO IS BOSS: Respond *now*. Give them an answer *today*. And don't even *think* about making up excuses. You Capricorns take your time, reveling in a job done thoroughly. The Scorpio boss, however, sometimes loses sight of the goal and simply *must* see nose-to-the-grindstone labor and toil. Either learn to look busy or help this boss feel confident without commotion.

IF YOU'RE IN CHARGE: Ask Scorpio to navigate. If you're driving to Saint Louis, for example, have Scorpio read the map. If you're building a business, appoint Scorpio to vigilantly watch where you've been and where you're headed. With a good rapport, this relationship can excel like no other at surveying the economic landscape and crossing it without casualties.

CAPRICORN @ WORK WITH SAGITTARIUS

☛ Two heads are better than one.

In this alliance two philosophies butt heads. You say, "If you're going to do it, do it right." Sagittarius says, *"C'est la vie."* You think in terms of fundamentals. Saj gazes out the window. If you two run a bakery, you'll study wheat futures in the world commodities markets while Saj hunts for the perfect croissant recipe. It must often feel you're cleaning up Saj's kitchen. But when the recipe works, this expert team produces gourmet results. Find common ground and start promoting your complementary qualifications.

IF SAGITTARIUS IS BOSS: Think out loud. Join their brainstorming. You'll like it. For an hour. Then you'll tire of it and want to move on to making something happen. Saj won't shut up. Their brains are like industrial-size washers at the Laundromat—they just keep spinning and agitating. The only way to stop them is to take their quarters away and tell them how much it costs to keep going.

IF YOU'RE IN CHARGE: Minimize paperwork, bureaucratic red tape, and reporting requirements. While this employee wants to do a job with integrity, Sagittarius chafes at silly rules and inane procedures. Help them see the big picture and their enthusiasm will go up faster than a Bull Market.

CAPRICORN @ WORK WITH CAPRICORN

☛ Image conscious.

This alliance always wants to put the best foot forward. If you don't have heart attacks from working too hard, your Capricorn team can distinguish itself as the best in the field. Overnight success is not your style. A certificate of quality and authenticity comes with everything you do. But don't get hung up on public approval ratings. Consider Rolls Royce. For decades it epitomized luxury but consistently failed to make a profit. Decide if you want to be impoverished aristocrats or successful professionals.

IF THE OTHER CAPRICORN IS BOSS: Be careful what you ask for. You might get it. This high-profile boss can put you in the position you've aspired to. But once there, are you sure you want it? With your Capricorn boss demanding top-notch performance, it's hard to live up to your own expectations let alone theirs. Don't compromise your standards for bootlicking.

IF YOU'RE IN CHARGE: Don't burn out this overachiever. Ask for a commitment to one set of tasks or projects. Then don't distract them. Since your Capricorn employee is already so goal-oriented, emphasize ongoing concerns like learning along the way, maintaining healthy relationships, and having a few kicks.

CAPRICORN @ WORK WITH AQUARIUS

☛ **Do the right thing.**

This alliance wants to do business while keeping ethics and values intact. You're interested in principles with quantifiable results, like "How many customers' lives have we saved?" Aquarius shoots for a less definable target, such as, "How have we improved their quality of life?" But trying to do good, this team confronts real-world obstacles, like profit margins, and here you and Aquarius are bound to disagree. Persuade Aquarius that to run an ethical business you have to *stay* in business.

> **"If you build a business up big enough, it's respectable."**
> HUMORIST WILL ROGERS

IF AQUARIUS IS BOSS: Stay on the inside track. Aquarius respects cutting-edge expertise. Be able to talk shop like a pro, not a dabbler. Score with Aquarius by reading trade publications, taking postgrad courses, and updating your wardrobe. Knowing the newest in-spots for lunch wouldn't hurt either.

IF YOU'RE IN CHARGE: Allow Aquarius to fail as well as succeed. Like the mad scientists that they are at heart, Aquarius needs room to experiment. Your Aquarius graphic designer, for instance, might test 400 colors before choosing the best for your logo. But rest assured your customers won't quickly forget that quirky shade of purple.

CAPRICORN @ WORK WITH PISCES

☛ **Head in the clouds, feet on the ground.**

This alliance pulls in different directions. Pisces admires your results but doesn't necessarily like your methods, finding them too arbitrary. You dig Pisces's ideals but see a lack of savvy for making them flourish. You're a political animal, able to play all the angles. Pisces can't be bothered. But with combined forces, you two create a safe harbor. This team attracts coworkers looking for answers and customers seeking TLC—tender loving care. Package it, but save some for each other, too.

IF PISCES IS BOSS: Take them seriously! Feeling tempted to run roughshod over this boss? Tsk, tsk! Pisces looks like a pushover. Get over that idea right now! You may crave a more stable work environment because Pisces always keeps you guessing. But one thing's for sure: Prioritize people over problems and agendas.

IF YOU'RE IN CHARGE: Treat Pisces like a machine and they'll break down faster than a British sports car. Treat them like a human being and they'll give all they've got—and then some. Listen to Pisces. You don't have to agree with them, but do nod and grunt occasionally.

Aquarius @ Work

> "I refuse to be muzzled. . . . Free speech not only lives, it rocks. . . . I will continue to use my voice."
> AQUARIAN TV HOST AND PRODUCER OPRAH WINFREY

JANUARY 20 TO FEBRUARY 18

AQUARIUS

The Myth

In the eastern Mediterranean, the "cradle of civilization," the Aquarius legend was very popular. To the Babylonians and the Hebrews, the jug-carrying Aquarius represented the hand of God feeding the rivers and flooding the seas, sometimes benevolently, sometimes vengefully, as in the tale of Noah and the flood. Noah's story expresses a characteristically Aquarian theme: Save all the animals! Create a new world! Start fresh!

To the Greeks, Aquarius symbolized the handsome prince called Ganymede. One day, tired of his workaday routine, Ganymede spotted an eagle and flew away with the great bird. Not knowing what to expect, Ganymede wound up atop Mount Olympus, where the eagle turned out to be Zeus, king of the gods, who offered Ganymede a new career as his personal cup-bearer and confidant. Moral of the story: No matter how rich or beautiful, Aquarius gets bored fast and longs for meaningful work among the world's movers and shakers.

Motivation

Aquarius doesn't want much. You simply want to change the world. Idealistic and original, you're always dressed and ready for *The Revolution*. Perhaps you'll revolutionize health care or the independent cinema scene. Maybe you'll modernize your workplace window-washing system. Whatever the case, you like to shake up this tired world like a bottle of salad dressing.

> **"Continual innovation is essential to meeting the demands of the consumer, stockholders, and the media."**
>
> ALUMNI 1998 PUBLICATION OF STANFORD UNIVERSITY'S GRADUATE SCHOOL OF BUSINESS

You're an inventor and innovator. Either ahead of your time or off your rocker—sometimes it's hard to tell the difference—you tinker. You experiment like a kid with a chemistry set. You challenge the status quo. Ultimately, Aquarius aims to translate theories and concepts into real-life actions. Profits and prestige matter less than the vision, but they come in handy when you want a new laboratory to test your latest formulas.

Of course, not all Aquarians are flaming rebels or card-carrying Party Members. Most of you are upstanding citizens with a flair for the unusual, a penchant for sharing your vision. You'd really like to get all of us to work together to find our common humanity, but failing that you'd settle for changing your job title.

Assets

Aquarius is the zodiac's prophet of progress. Even if you're a technophobe who regards the electric can opener as state-of-the-art technology, you possess a special talent for introducing new ideas and helping other people get comfortable with different modes of operating. Thanks to you, change seems possible. Worn-out bad habits wither away.

As a paradigm-buster, you aren't afraid to implement radical changes, to reorganize an already existing but ailing organization, or to simply start a new one. A former client of mine, an Aquarian psychology instructor, was famous for saying, "There is a better way." If there is, you'll find it. Rules were meant to be broken, and Aquarius was meant to break them. Nothing's a sacred cow with you around. You design the sacred cows of the future.

Big and logical, the Aquarian mind can handle abstract thinking. Be-

cause you can detach yourself from a subject long enough to analyze it objectively, you're a valuable asset to any meeting or discussion—and a natural at playing devil's advocate or applying the scientific method. You've got built-in bionic binoculars, able to spot choices and options the rest of the world is too shortsighted to see.

One benefit you often see is that there's power in numbers. Despite your love of independence, you inevitably find your way to the hub of any industry. Where it's happening is where you like to be, building community, seeking strategic alliances, and joining the clubs and associations where the leaders of your field converge. Meanwhile, back on your company's homefront, you fill people with esprit de corps and trailblazing techniques.

Unlike some professionals who always have one eye on reaching the top of the ladder, Aquarians seem to succeed in spite of themselves, often more motivated by missions than by money. For example, the Aquarian anthropologist Mary Leakey dedicated a long lifetime to digging up fossils. She discovered 3.5-million-year-old human footprints in Tanzania and radically shifted the scientific community's theories of our species' origins.

Undeniably hip, you're a trendy trendsetter. Charismatic and popular with the public, you've got an eye for fads. What's the next craze, rage, or vogue? The best new restaurant to wine and dine a prospective client? When I want to know, I ask an Aquarius. Almost instinctively, you understand consumer preferences and demographics. That's kind of ironic for a professional eccentric who'd rather invent a product than mingle with the masses who buy it!

Liabilities

Danger! Aquarius risks trendiness to the point of following a movement blindly. Wall Street's suddenly big on rutabaga futures? Gee, you better hop on the bandwagon—don't want to get left behind! The attraction of the seemingly progressive and the flash of new ideas, whether brilliant or not, can suck you into a tragic chain of events. Be careful you don't leap to the support of a "groundbreaking expert" who claims the world's actually octagonal. Before subscribing to an innovation, check the facts. New isn't better; it's just new. Bear in mind the disastrous results of Coca-Cola changing its classic formula!

Strange but true: You can be insensitive. Though you relate well to the "market," you don't always relate well to real people. You love innovation, but do you empower employees and coworkers to innovate? Do you

allow them the freedom you crave? Are you a team player? Occasionally your devotion to your own concepts and visions blinds you to other points of view. Aquarius is a great reformer, but, like all reformers, can lapse into totalitarian measures, using the ends to justify the means. Make sure the means don't alienate the people around you *too* much, or you'll be neck deep in invoices with no one to help you pay them.

Freedom. Space. Independence. Free-thinking. These stereotypical Aquarian words sound like the lyrics to a 1960s ballad sung by a long-haired guitarist who knows only two chords. It's no coincidence, you know, that the civil rights movement coincided with the dawning of the Age of Aquarius. Now it's here and everybody's wondering what all the fuss is about. Cell phones? Liposuction? *This* is the progress we fought for? But you know better. You know you don't have to wear tie-dye to make a difference. When the revolution finally does come, the Libras will be better dressed, but at least you'll know what we're fighting for. You will, won't you?

Dr. Matt's Tips for Aquarius Success

Don't think it's easy to be a professional Aquarius! More of you than any other sign wind up in the Hall of Fame. That, plus all your lofty ideals, is a lot to live up to. Fortunately, the current economy needs you Aquarius types.

★ Find a niche for your originality.

★ Stay on top of the latest technology and industry developments.

★ Patent your inventions.

★ Seek a work environment that values saving the whales, or whatever you're into this month.

★ Know when to tinker and when to leave well enough alone. If it ain't broke, why fix it?

★ Value "praxis" as much as theory—that is, implement what you design; the blueprint isn't the building.

★ Value people. Get to know them. Accept their human flaws and inconsistencies while urging them to do better.

★ Examine your overall goals continuously. It's important that they be in line with who you are now, today, and with the current state of your

business or career—not where it was when you first started out pushing a wheelbarrow with some turnips for sale.

NERDS HAVE MORE FUN!

Typical of an Aquarius, one of the owners of a large electronics corporation was considered too daft and nerdy to manage production, so he spent all day wandering around the plant. One day he saw engineers working on a pocket-sized tape recorder for the business market. They were struggling because the tiny gadget's motor had space for a playback mechanism, but not a recorder. The owner recommended attaching headphones and calling it a Walkman, because teenagers would use it to listen to music while they walked. Market researchers gasped: Who would buy a tape recorder that couldn't record? Against conventional wisdom, this Aquarian-spirited owner insisted on its production, and I guess you know where the story goes from there. A lot of happy teenagers and massive profit!

Aquarius in Alliance

AQUARIUS @ WORK WITH ARIES

☛ **Movers and shakers.**

Often quite high-profile, this alliance knows people who know people. Together you can benefit from a wealth of contacts and plenty of free press, whether good, bad, or simply sensational. Goals, however, are hard to agree on. You think Aries doesn't think first—or ever. Aries thinks you think too much. Strike a balance between theory and practice, discussion and implementation. Listen carefully when Aries wants to promote the packaging more than the product. Will that compromise your values, or competently reach the people you want to reach? With Aries, tough decisions are par for the course!

IF ARIES IS BOSS: Go the extra distance. This boss might look too busy to notice, but Aries really admires personal initiative. Don't wait around for Aries to tell you to fix a problem. If you see the screws coming loose on the skylight, grab the toolbox!

IF YOU'RE IN CHARGE: Respond to Aries as an individual, not just "one of the staff" you manage. Be accessible. Make room for this overachiever. If they see your Aquarian pie in the sky but no chance of getting a piece for themselves, Aries will find a new trip.

AQUARIUS @ WORK WITH TAURUS

☛ **Back and forth.**

Though on the outside you appear strong and durable, from an insider's viewpoint you and Taurus seem to be hitting each over the head with pots and pans. Taurus disapproves of your forward thinking. You feel suffocated by Taurus's "same old thing." Yes, indeed, you bring out each other's stubborn streak. But if this alliance can be as strong as it looks, steady progress is guaranteed. To keep Taurus happy, change only what needs to be changed. To keep everyone else happy, announce new developments as soon as they're ready—or risk sounding like old news in a world that craves the latest and freshest in everything.

> **"It is often easier to fight for principles than to live up to them."**
> STATESMAN ADLAI STEVENSON

IF TAURUS IS BOSS: Practice common sense. Don't fuss too much with making the report *look* pretty. Taurus wants genuine information, not hoopla or conjecture. Illustrate your point with real-life examples instead of kooky hypothetical situations.

IF YOU'RE IN CHARGE: Provide the resources Taurus needs to get the job done. Give them, for example, clear-cut decisions, not wishy-washy suggestions. Promote an open-door policy among supervisors so Taurus can be your eyes and ears in the trenches. And for Taurus, a spacious, modestly plush work space does wonders.

AQUARIUS @ WORK WITH GEMINI

☛ **Fast on your feet.**

This alliance lays waste to preconceived notions and outdated modes of operation. A couple of quick thinkers, you and Gemini respond to problems faster than firefighters. Armed and ready, you've got your bags packed, operators standing by, and your shelves fully stocked and prepped for immediate shipment to your consumers. But beware of hyperactivity that's counterproductive. To steer clear of misunderstandings, practice active listening and don't jump to conclusions.

IF GEMINI IS BOSS: Increasing public visibility can only help your credibility. Attract favorable media attention. Do something newsworthy, not scandalous. Network at the ballpark. And as for business cards at social functions—don't leave home without them!

IF YOU'RE IN CHARGE: Give Gemini opportunities to be clever. This cunning employee can figure out how to shave precious minutes off a time-consuming procedure or compose an advertising jingle that radio listeners just can't stop humming. Without such outlets, bored but sly Gemini might start counterfeiting gift certificates on the new laser printer!

AQUARIUS @ WORK WITH CANCER

☛ The good old days.

This alliance is bound to disagree over the definition of success. You seek progress. Cancer wants maintenance. You depend on what you *see* to achieve your goals. Cancer depends on what they *feel*. You tend to downplay conflicts and tension whereas Cancer blows them out of proportion. But maybe because you're so idealistic, or maybe because you've got something to prove, you work harder when Cancer's around.

IF CANCER IS BOSS: Put them at ease by creating a sense of community. This boss has trouble with your characteristic Aquarian aloofness. When appropriate, instead of saying *you* and *me,* try using *we* and *us.* Help define *our* market and build community bonds with it. Without trying to be their best friend, shower Cancer with a few pleasantries and pieces of personal chitchat.

IF YOU'RE IN CHARGE: Expect devotion but not heroism. Cancer's a creature of habit. Don't sporadically assign them tasks unfamiliar to their job description or typical schedule. If you ask for *help,* Cancer will try their best, but be reasonable. And when the computer cheats Cancer's paycheck of $300, apologize profusely and make it up to them before the end of the day— before they have time to mope over it.

AQUARIUS @ WORK WITH LEO

☛ You say tomato, I say to-mah-to.

Seldom harmonious, the soul of this alliance says, "Let's take the world by storm!" Leo turns you on. Despite their characteristic superficiality and self-absorption, you realize the value of having Leo on your team. You may, in fact, rely on their publicity skills and built-in fortitude. Leo's rigid

rules, however, will send you hunting for a crowbar to pry them open. For good or ill, Leo pushes your buttons like a kid hogging the TV remote. Totally frustrating, utterly electrifying, this partnership is bound to elicit your best qualities and worst anxieties. Listen to each other. Keep in touch with reality. And remember, loyalty's a two-way street.

IF LEO IS BOSS: Contradicting them doesn't work. On rare occasions you can reason with a Leo boss. But most often you'll have to do it Leo's way—or *show* them a better way, being careful not to offend them. Stay cool. Stick to the business at hand. Dress for the part—or whatever part you want.

IF YOU'RE IN CHARGE: Throw a party. Leo needs periodic reminders they're on the right track. Celebrate victories and cook up excuses for special occasions. Though Aquarian managers usually strive for solidarity, that doesn't mean you can't honor individual talents and achievements. Just don't play favorites!

AQUARIUS @ WORK WITH VIRGO

☛ **Make it better.**

This inquisitive alliance fixes things, and is able to reduce big problems to little pieces on a Monopoly board. Since you both adore toys, gadgets, and gizmos, this team milks technology for all it's worth. Problems arise, though, when one of you, often Virgo, becomes resentful of getting stuck with the grunt work. Also, for all your fascination with whatzits and widgets, you have a tendency to overlook the *whozits,* and end up treating colleagues carelessly. Don't take the familiar for granted—in your work *or* in your coworkers.

IF VIRGO IS BOSS: Remember that criticism is a form of feedback. It might not always *sound* like it, but Virgo probably *does* like you. They just have a funny way of showing it—especially with you Aquarians—and that's by constantly examining your work and suggesting changes. This boss will really test your virtue of open-mindedness!

IF YOU'RE IN CHARGE: Encourage Virgo to get to know customers. Although Virgo functions perfectly well in a back room crunching numbers, Virgo reaches their highest potential when they can see that they're improving the quality of a real person's life. Given the chance, your Virgo employee will memorize how all your top clients take their tea or martinis!

AQUARIUS @ WORK WITH LIBRA

☛ Membership has its privileges.

Smart and innovative, this alliance inspires a sense of belonging. You and Libra get people involved, even reaching beyond workplace walls to the wider community. You've figured out that a feeling of membership keeps customers loyal, employees dedicated, and suppliers supportive. It's great to embrace diversity and encourage multiple viewpoints; when it come to decision-making, though, you two can't please all of the people all of the time. If you try, you'll eventu-

Hmaro mata emsis maa el hmir. **"His donkey doesn't go with the other donkeys."**
A MOROCCAN SAYING

ally please all of the people *none* of the time. Now try to convince decida-phobic, doesn't-like-to-make-waves Libra of that!

IF LIBRA IS BOSS: It might be love at first sight. Well, maybe not love, but you certainly start out adulating Libra. Appreciating your uniqueness, clearing space for your experiments, Libra wins your vote. But Libra has goals, too, many of which eventually will take precedence. Avoid future disillusion-ment by being who you are, no beguiling facades allowed.

IF YOU'RE IN CHARGE: Make Libra feel like a partner, someone with a place in your organization. Alienation and anonymity quickly debilitate this re-fined employee. Give Libra a title and letterhead stationery. Ask them to represent you at trade shows and conferences. Invite them to sit in on im-portant meetings. And don't forget their birthday.

AQUARIUS @ WORK WITH SCORPIO

Destiny calls.

Though it can often be frustrating, this alliance feels *important,* as if your greatest work can be accomplished at Scorpio's side—and indeed it can. You, Aquarius, love a good discussion, and with Scorpio's frequent contradictions, topics for debate aren't scarce. While it irks you that Scor-pio doesn't lay all their cards on the table, it irks you even more when Scorpio delays action, sniffing out a more advantageous time to strike. And it *really* drives you nuts when Scorpio tells you how to act in public. Nonetheless, you and Scorpio share a strong sense of purpose. *Do* some-thing with it! Remain professional. Set time limits on meetings. And when referring to this esteemed colleague, avoid four-letter words.

IF SCORPIO IS BOSS: Justify your actions. This boss needs ongoing reassurance that they made the right choice when they hired you. So without bragging, report your accomplishments on a regular basis, even if they seem trivial. To Scorpio, nothing they do or oversee is unimportant.

IF YOU'RE IN CHARGE: Tell Scorpio up front what to expect. Salary, working hours, performance goals—save yourself some grief and make these circumstances explicit. Scorpio works better and harder for an attainable goal rather than just doing a good job to get on the boss's good side—not that they'll reject a surprise bonus for an exceptional month!

AQUARIUS @ WORK WITH SAGITTARIUS

☛ **Problem-solvers.**

Consumed by curiosity, this alliance likes to ask questions and find answers. Unsolved mysteries and bewildering dilemmas drive you and Saj to bond. In areas like hi-tech adventures and cinematic experiments, you two open up opportunities in a jiffy. But if you're founding a company, *first* find out Saj's long-term plans—for life as well as work. Most Sagittarians harbor romantic fantasies that involve dropping everything. Do you drop well? In a business built on ideas, who owns the intellectual property? These questions need answers before you start tracking UFOs in the hopes of exporting imitation Rolexes to Uranus.

IF SAGITTARIUS IS BOSS: Stay open to new ideas. Forget what you learned in college or your last job—this boss will appreciate that experience but probably not want to perpetuate it. Show a willingness, even an eagerness, to constantly remold yourself. And remember, with Saj it's not *what* you know that counts, it's what you can *do* with what you know.

IF YOU'RE IN CHARGE: Encourage ongoing intellectual growth. Instead of a simple bonus, reward Saj with a "growth grant" for pursuing higher education or travel budgets for attending conferences. Make books and Internet access available. The fastest way to stifle a Saj is to take away their reading material!

AQUARIUS @ WORK WITH CAPRICORN

☛ **Rules were meant to be broken!**

Don't expect a walk in the park with this alliance. Capricorn upholds the status quo. Defying Capricorn's conventional business models, you lead the avant-garde. On good days, this duet deals effectively with large

institutions and surpasses expectations. Capricorn earns the market's respect while you capture their awe—the perfect combination for, say, introducing new technology. On bad days, you two bicker, citing chapter and verse of the latest economics textbooks. To succeed, don't treat Capricorn like a stick in the mud! Elicit their fun factor. Appeal to their love of calculated risks. And most importantly, never embarrass a Capricorn in public!

IF CAPRICORN IS BOSS: Definitely leave at home any chip you may carry around on your shoulder. No matter if they're chairman of the board or middle management, Capricorn highly regards authority. So if you want to make the world, or just your job, a better place, change the system from within—don't topple the whole institution!

IF YOU'RE IN CHARGE: Don't let this employee stagnate at a low-level position forever. Capricorn wonders, "Where's my promotion?" while you say, "But look what we've accomplished as a team." Capricorn needs tangible rewards, not just a warm and fuzzy feeling.

AQUARIUS @ WORK WITH AQUARIUS

☛ **Champions of progress.**

With both of you desperately seeking stimulation, it makes sense you'd gravitate toward one another. Craving independence and bucking interference, your minds snap together like a plug in a socket and you'll have a blast discussing shared interests and brainstorming the future of your joint venture. But to really purr, this alliance needs to develop a true friendship, or at least a mutual tolerance, that goes beyond abstract concepts like opening a franchise on the first public space stations. Definitely treat this comrade as more than just a meal ticket

IF THE OTHER AQUARIUS IS BOSS: Be a great sounding board. Frequently the Aquarius boss needs to try out a new idea—when they do, be there to talk it up. Though you undoubtedly cling to strong convictions of your own, an open mind and flair for turning the world topsy-turvy pushes this head honcho's joy buzzer.

IF YOU'RE IN CHARGE: Find ways to make their job easier. Better yet, let this employee find ways. You can probably identify: Aquarian morale is damaged by wasted efforts and outmoded methods. But remember, they're not your clone. It'll take this more junior Aquarius time to reach your level of experience and expertise. Help their growth, don't force it.

AQUARIUS @ WORK WITH PISCES

☛ **At any cost.**

Individually, these two are hardly the biggest gamblers of the zodiac. Nonetheless Aquarius and Pisces are willing to risk it all together. Sacrifices go with the territory. Hardships don't deter you. It's not a job; it's a *mission*. Or possibly, if you two clash, a calamity waiting to happen. You want Pisces to think more with their head, less with their gut. As a team, you're hard to pin down, changing directions and canceling meetings at the last minute. For smooth sailing, don't force your thinking on Pisces but try to make them see the light. And be reasonable about how much you're prepared to give up to get what you supposedly want.

> **"I want people to rush right out and change the world."**
> AQUARIAN PSYCHOTHERAPIST
> AND AUTHOR NADYA GIUSI

IF PISCES IS BOSS: Show your humanity. No kidding: The fastest way to win favor with Pisces is to express a little vulnerability, share a few outrageous ambitions, and ask for guidance. Pisces wants to see you're not cold and calculating. And it'll really turn them on if you include their organization in your life plans, right up there with the birth of your first child.

IF YOU'RE IN CHARGE: Eureka! Pisces can see your vision, the beauty of what you hope to accomplish. Now, instead of letting it be a mirage on the horizon, help Pisces see what it takes to go there. Foster pragmatism and an ability to detach emotionally from a vexing situation. Provide incentives for Pisces to distill the best from technology and personnel. And reassure Pisces that success is OK.

Pisces @ Work

> "'Just pay me your money and hop right aboard!'
> So they clambered inside. Then the big machine roared.
> And it klonked. And it bonked. And it jerked. And it berked.
> And it bopped them about. But the thing really worked!"

PISCES AUTHOR AND CARTOONIST DR. SEUSS

FEBRUARY 19 TO MARCH 20

PISCES

The Myth

In ancient mythology, Pisces were a couple of fish in the river near Mount Olympus, headquarters of the gods. When the gruesome monster Typhon attacked the palace, these savvy fish escaped unnoticed, avoiding the beast's lava-spewing bad breath. Tying their tails together so as not to get separated, the fish swam all the way to the Nile River where they turned out not to be fish at all, but the beautiful goddess Venus and her hunky son Cupid, ready to start a new life on the beaches of Egypt. Moral of the story: Pisces may be kind, creative, and even a bit slippery, but underneath that sensitive fish stick facade is a resourceful soul who turns setbacks into opportunities.

Motivation

Frequently stereotyped as the wishy-washiest of zodiac signs, Pisces actually aspires to the biggest of ambitions: to make dreams come true. No frivolous dreams of flying magic carpets—we're talking the American Dream, Martin Luther King's dream for equality, the artist's dream of a masterpiece. You're a sucker for a rags-to-riches story and any real-life Cinderella fairy tale that proves the impossible wasn't so impossible after all.

> **"And after they had explored all the suns in the universe and all the planets in each sun they realized they were alone, and they were glad, because they now knew they would have to become all of the things they had hoped to find."**
> PLAYWRIGHT LANFORD WILSON

Doing your job isn't enough. You want to *contribute*. You long to make a contribution to the world that extends beyond your individual self, like a teacher who inspires hundreds of students over the course of her career, thereby changing thousands of lives. Whether the teacher's name is remembered for generations or forgotten on graduation day, the dream endures. On this planet, that's as close as you can get to immortality.

Pisces doesn't bound out of bed with Taurus's determination or Saj's enthusiasm. You emerge from the boudoir just to prove, to yourself and the world, that there's still something worth believing in. To marvel at sunlight slicing through the curtains. To curiously explore a marketplace so full of faithless, jaded consumers that you have no trouble convincing them to buy what you're selling.

Assets

A couple of fusty British astrology books describe Pisces as "selfless and other-worldly" and "weak-willed and sympathetic." Maybe that's you on a Zen retreat, but in business and career spheres you're more like a killer whale than a jellyfish. Sure, you keep your teeth concealed, but when pushed to the limit, you can be every bit as ferocious as a loudmouth Aries. Possibly even more so, since you know better how to tread in the shadows. But before I paint too much of an Edgar Allen Poe kind of scene here, just keep in mind the power of your personality, your uncanny ability to sway the stubbornest old fogeys.

Life is hard. Work is extrahard. That's old news to Pisces, the tradi-

tional sign of saints and sufferers. But you can make it all tolerable, even joyful, by placing each little chore and every grueling day within the context of a higher purpose. In your hands, a worthwhile project or organization adds up to more than the sum of its individual parts. "Someday, somehow," preaches Pisces, "this thing will be bigger than all of us."

You've got that Pisces mystique. Rich in fantasies, you like to live in a world of your own fabrication. When reality stinks, you burn incense and imagine you're in a French perfume factory. Pretty soon every nose within 300 feet is smelling roses. You make expert ad men and amazing campaigners because you've got a knack for triggering subconscious drives, endowing people and products with romantic, mystical, or healing properties. Whereas Cancer appeals to consumers' needs and Leo and Scorpio tug on their desires, you speak to their dreams. Fortunately for you, dreams always command higher prices than food, shelter, or cheap thrills.

Pisces is often accused of being a space case. It's true. Imagination occupies a big chunk of your psyche. But sometimes retreating into outer space can be a good thing. During the 1960s, for example, astronauts took the first photographs of earth seen from space, a god's-eye view of one totally undivided planet. These popular new pictures, according to many media experts, greatly propelled the public's interest in environmentalism and worldwide human rights. That's Pisces—the humble hero who transcends the ordinary and returns to help others make it extraordinary. And in this age of the global economy, a global perspective means extraordinary profits.

Let's face it. You're not the no-nonsense business type. You rely on intuition. You hesitate to make decisions that might harm less fortunate folks. You take leaps of faith as wide as the Grand Canyon. To the boss who's your hero you swear undying allegiance, but with the villainous boss, you tune out completely. As an entrepreneur, you resist growth that threatens your lifestyle. To Pisces, work and life are inseparable. Work expresses who you are and therefore it shouldn't be boring unless you're boring.

Liabilities

Pisces would rather not deal with reality. When your head's in the clouds, you overlook anything ugly or unappetizing. But when you return to earth, you wonder why the bank declined your application for a small business loan. "Not enough qualifications?" you ask, mystified and indignant. Artistic Pisces—like actors, writers, and basket-weavers—tend to excel at their craft but fall flat when it comes to marketing their skill in an

arena where talent matters less than connections. The same goes for you corporate Pisces seeking a promotion. Get to know the real world inti-

> **"You can dream, create, design, and build the most wonderful place in the world, but it requires people to make the dream a reality."**
> FILM INNOVATOR WALT DISNEY

mately. Take off the rose-tinted Ray•Bans and buy yourself some street smarts.

A dreamer and wish-maker, Pisces also runs the risk of disillusionment. You knock on the marble pillars of a castle at Disneyland and discover they're hollow. Or you learn your company's CEO, an executive you've idolized for years, was embezzling from the pension fund. Suddenly your whole world comes crashing down and the dream turns into a nightmare.

Then it feels like Karma has singled you out for an extraagonizing lifetime. You become a martyr without a mission. Cynicism sets in like gangrene and self-pity takes root like nettles. Escape seems like the only option. You'll never make another sacrifice. You'll never believe again.

In our world of virtual reality and cybershopping, the distinctions between fact and fantasy blur. If you can navigate the fine line, opportunities abound for you in the 21st-century economy. If you can't, invest in a life jacket.

Dr. Matt's Tips for Pisces Success

★ Don't let a minor setback send you packing for the Himalayas (unless llama futures are up). You're made of tougher stuff than that.

★ Learn to act—don't just be acted upon. When the director shouts, "Lights, camera, action!" be ready to shake your booty or lose the part to a newcomer with more get-up-and-go.

★ Let neither circumstance nor coworkers have the power to determine how you feel or whether you reach your goals.

★ Master your own destiny. While there is such a thing as fate, don't give away your power to determine how you feel or whether you reach your goals.

★ Practice creative visualization. If that's too corny, cut out magazine photos of your dream house and ideal job and paste them to your bathroom mirror—anything to align your vibrant imagination with your workaday world. You can't create what you can't imagine.

> ### SOMEWHERE OVER THE RAINBOW
>
> A quintessential Pisces, Nobel Prize–winning author John Steinbeck passionately loved the American dream but was often discouraged by how hard it was to reach. In many of Steinbeck's best novels and screenplays, like *The Grapes of Wrath* and *Of Mice and Men,* downtrodden characters are seeking some version of the Promised Land, a little piece of Utopia where they can live in peace, free of discrimination, working the earth and reaping its bounty. They can never make it on their own. It always takes a collective effort and a common faith—two of Steinbeck's favorite themes and two of Pisces's best strategies for success.

Pisces in Alliance

PISCES @ WORK WITH ARIES

☛ **A pressure cooker.**

When this alliance runs well, Aries instills you with bravery and enables you to act on your convictions and realize your strength of character. When it runs poorly, Aries haunts you. When unhappy, Aries strays from unpleasant situations, sticking you with loneliness and responsibility. Aries is so many things you're not, and vice versa. You two simply must share—not just profits, but spirit. Here's a recipe: Mix equal parts Pisces awareness and Aries do-it-now vitality.

IF ARIES IS BOSS: Don't jump on their stress-makes-me-feel-alive bandwagon. To meet this boss's demands, work fast and furiously, but never forget both you and Aries need to do quality work with sufficient time for creative incubation to be happy (even if they don't know it). If Aries barks at you, don't take it personally. They may be rams but they've got some Irish wolfhound in them, too!

IF YOU'RE IN CHARGE: Spare Aries from long meetings and dictionary-sized reports. Aries wants to achieve objectives. Distractions vex their overachiever sensibilities. Don't, however, exempt them from ongoing education and technical training. There's nothing worse than an Aries who thinks they can operate Windows, and then complains there's no glass cleaner!

PISCES @ WORK WITH TAURUS

☞ **Let's wait and see.**

Together, you and Taurus command awesome powers of observation. Taurus sees what they're supposed to see, while you look behind the veil. In a partnership, Taurus gets you to look down the road a piece, to firmly locate your goals in a very real geography. You, meanwhile, turn Taurus's gaze up to the stars, energizing this teammate with validation and team spirit. But watch out! With such wide-open eyes this alliance may be too busy ogling to get the job done. Be less impressionable. Initiate more often.

IF TAURUS IS BOSS: Don't drift. Stay focused on the task, whatever it takes. Taurus isn't interested in how it *coulda* been or *shoulda* been—simply how it is, right here, right now. With this boss, don't embellish the truth or run from problems. From you, Pisces, Taurus wants participation in a concrete game plan, and I'm not talking about tiddledywinks.

IF YOU'RE IN CHARGE: Bring out the best in Taurus by reinforcing job security and providing simple but cozy surroundings. A comfortable desk chair, for instance, inexpensively inspires this employee to sit and toil for hours without glancing at the clock. Give your Taurus employee firm deadlines and instructions; they need a structured environment in order to work well.

PISCES @ WORK WITH GEMINI

☞ **Every which way.**

This alliance tries to do and have it all. But as an old business saying says, "If you chase two rabbits, both will escape." The Pisces-Gemini team needs to define its identity—before wasting resources. Who are you? What do you want? And most importantly, how do you position your-selves in the organization or market? Without answers to questions like these, you surrender to fate. Once you both start *acting* rather than being acted *upon*, Gemini's the best person to make you into an irreplaceable, celebrated leader in your field.

IF GEMINI IS BOSS: There's no escape. They check *everything*, keeping you on your toes more than a prima ballerina. Then, suddenly, they stop check-ing—but who knows for how long? So practice consistency. Stop trying to prove your intrinsic self-worth by writing eloquent memos that are occa-sionally appreciated, more frequently trashed. Under this boss it'll take

you longer to make it big—but when you do, it'll be bigger than ever before.

IF YOU'RE IN CHARGE: Delegate the nitty-gritty to Gemini. Though you like to do a job thoroughly, the details of modern life—like returning messages and filing correspondence—freak you out. Gemini, on the other hand, can turn your office into a model of efficiency, where the phone is always answered by the second ring.

PISCES @ WORK WITH CANCER

☞ The artists' colony.

What this alliance lacks in realism it makes up for in creativity. Side by side with Cancer you can foster a safe and stimulating milieu where personnel look forward to each day and the chance to express their inner artist or latent tycoonery. Elegant and even poetic, you and Cancer apply your talents to causes and projects that guarantee success not only on the job but also after hours. First, though, convince Cancer of your "Go ahead and try it" attitude. To get started, try this formula: If reality stinks, don't leave. Make it smell better.

IF CANCER IS BOSS: Secretly (or maybe overtly!) insecure, this boss is bound to keep you under their thumb. For best results, pacify their doubts and worries. If they're middle management, help Cancer look good in the eyes of *their* boss. Meanwhile, brace yourself for boundary issues, like when they summon you back to work at 3 A.M. to investigate a missing payroll stub. Volatility's the name of this game—but Dr. Matt's sure you're ready for the ride.

IF YOU'RE IN CHARGE: Invite Cancer to your inner circle. Cancer doesn't want to feel left out. Consider offering stock options, profit sharing, or simply more public recognition. Cancer will faithfully protect your interests, but only when they've got a stake in the struggle. Remember: You don't like the role of disciplinarian—but in a pinch you'll go there! To prevent a harsh encounter with Cancer, set parameters in advance, especially regarding Cancer's tendency to crowd the workplace with personal issues. It's easier to be a jerk up front and gradually get nicer than to start out sweet and become a monster.

> **"What a bother this world can be."**
> *VANITY FAIR* ASTROLOGER
> MICHAEL LUTIN

PISCES @ WORK WITH LEO

☞ Games of chance.

Enormously entertaining, this alliance likes to overdo it. The stupidest things you'll ever do, you'll do with Leo, who scorns you for reflecting and deliberating and urges you into reckless situations. But don't overlook this relationship's serious virtues. Together you know what you're doing and you're good at it. As a team, you're popular, in demand, and able to reach nonmainstream markets like kids, seniors, and pets. To ensure success, buy an alarm clock. Don't take too many sick days. Find secure tax shelters. And make definite plans to be *out* of the workplace and *away* from Leo to rejuvenate.

IF LEO IS BOSS: Act like you want to be there. By merely going through the motions you'll quickly alienate this boss. Leo won't tolerate apathy. In this job, love it, leave it—or do something about it! The Leo boss almost always prefers disagreeable but constructive confrontation to passive-aggression of any kind—even yours.

IF YOU'RE IN CHARGE: Tell Leo why their job *matters*. Leo fears becoming a wage slave, a drudge whose work anyone could do. But like an indestructible pickup truck, they've got perseverance. Undesirable chores don't deter them. Even when you feel like escaping a nasty chore, Leo will stick with it.

PISCES @ WORK WITH VIRGO

☞ Customer Service Award.

You and Virgo both want to serve the customer well. But you go about it differently. Virgo tends to institute policies and codes of behavior. You prefer to empower employees to relate personally with whoever walks through the door. In this alliance, each of you mystifies the other. Virgo's rigidity is foreign but attractive. In Virgo, however, you probably recognize your own nagging conscience and fear of making mistakes. So create a team culture where, instead of waiting and worrying, you just do it. When you encounter setbacks, let them be a reason to grow, not to kick yourselves. And once in a while, you perfectionists should settle for *finishing*—no more finishing touches allowed!

IF VIRGO IS BOSS: Stand up for yourself. Virgo usually means well, but sometimes their constant pushing feels like nagging. Don't be too compliant and don't flee. Learn Virgo's language. Though it sounds a lot like the in-

structions for assembling a microcomputer, after you translate it into standard English, you'll see all Virgo wants is productivity and efficiency.

IF YOU'RE IN CHARGE: Treat Virgo the way you want them to treat your customers. Virgo can imitate your model to a T, and keep your clientele coming back for more. Virgo wants—quite desperately, actually—to do a good job. Help them by being a role model and providing straightforward, attainable goals. Virgo's not dense, they just like tangible, doable tasks.

PISCES @ WORK WITH LIBRA

☛ Go with the flow.

Charming on the surface, this alliance is easygoing and laid back—but knock on it and this duet sounds hollow. Libra tries to be everyone's buddy, which works in the beginning. But eventually every organization meets opposition. You're not afraid of plunging into the dark, unseemly side of business and you'd like to see Libra get their hands dirty more often. Still, you enter into this alliance wary of disturbing Libra's harmony. There's a tendency for you and Libra to be fair-weather friends—storm clouds may send one or both of you packing. Early on, investigate the partnership's tax consequences. And establish ownership issues *before* trying to slice the Picasso in two equal halves.

IF LIBRA IS BOSS: Disagree once in a while! Although saying Yes! may seem like the fastest way to your leader's heart, an ambitious Libra boss actually wants to examine issues from several points of view. By challenging Libra—always in a professional way, of course—you'll enhance their problem-solving skills, meanwhile scoring points for yourself.

IF YOU'RE IN CHARGE: Let Libra make a few important decisions. It'll build their confidence and build your trust in their abilities. If you don't want to be kissed up to, explain right away you'll be evaluating Libra on less fluffy criteria! Maximize Libra's diplomatic skills by having them represent you at press conferences, networking events, or any other venue where you'd prefer to wield power from a distance.

PISCES @ WORK WITH SCORPIO

☛ Defying the odds.

You two are natural allies, ready to jump to one another's defense. As a team you have the capacity to defy critics and break through to the most resistant clients or supervisors. Though rejection terrifies most Pisces, at

Scorpio's side you can persist, undaunted by mean people and competitive circumstances. This alliance is in jeopardy, however, of becoming totally *reactive* rather than proactive. Emotions unduly influence your decisions. You tend to view everyone—maybe even each other—as a potential threat. So cool it! Figure out if your feelings are appropriate to the situation. And remember: Breathe deeply and avoid scissors, letter openers, and other sharp office equipment!

IF SCORPIO IS BOSS: Never give up. Scorpio forbids surrender. So when you're really desperate for answers, don't beat your head against the desk—halt! Compose yourself. Look around. Is there another route, a shortcut, an indirect approach to this problem? Think creatively, but always legalistically, and you'll earn the key to Scorpio's good graces.

IF YOU'RE IN CHARGE: Put Scorpio to work on planning and problem-solving. Sharp and savvy, Scorpio knows what to look for. Like a rare Arctic flower, Scorpio blooms in a severe climate. Catastrophe calls on all of their diagnostic and fix-it acumen. But don't manufacture crises—or let Scorpio do it—just to give them something to do. A lot of emergencies are false alarms.

PISCES @ WORK WITH SAGITTARIUS

☛ **Diversity is Job 1.**

This alliance can tap the treasures of a diverse workforce and a multi-faceted marketplace. In collaboration you and Saj are eclectic—you take the best, ignore the rest, and turn a hodgepodge into a gourmet delight. Together you tolerate and even capitalize on people from all walks of life, but your open-mindedness often stops short of accepting other opinions or philosophies. With a couple of jabberers like you, this duet can float away on a puff of hot air. Keep ad hoc meetings and discussions to a minimum. And don't let Saj's enthusiasm fool you—they won't put their money where your mouth is till you've both done your homework.

> **"This world is but canvas to our imaginations."**
> NATURALIST AUTHOR HENRY DAVID THOREAU

IF SAGITTARIUS IS BOSS: Go with the flow. Have a sense of humor. Be willing to change gears often. In the midst of conflict, don't withdraw. Saj gets mad—and then gets over it. If you hold a grudge, it'll only confuse Sagittarius.

IF YOU'RE IN CHARGE: Uphold morale. In doom and gloom Saj will slump. But as long as there's a common goal and a chance to make a difference for some potential client, even a goldfish with cleaner water, Saj carries the torch. Having a good time motivates Saj more than the threat of dire consequences.

PISCES @ WORK WITH CAPRICORN

☛ **A star is born.**

This alliance attracts attention. Capricorn puts you in the public eye. A softer soul, you help Capricorn connect with individuals on deeper levels—tugging on their heartstrings, their pocketbooks, or both. Capricorn contributes follow-through and long-term direction. You, in turn, are one of the best at eliciting stuffy Capricorn's fun, spontaneous, and creative side. Together you work well in exclusive businesses with discriminating clients. Beware, however, of becoming cliquish. Embrace all sorts of people. Heck, the more embracing the better!

IF CAPRICORN IS BOSS: Always act like a pro. Capricorn respects, and rewards, knowledgeable, skilled professionals who can build valuable connections with the community. The key to upward mobility in this job is to obey Capricorn's tried-and-trusted methods—and occasionally introduce some new ideas of your own.

IF YOU'RE IN CHARGE: Always treat Capricorn like a *somebody*, never a nobody. Capricorn will respect your authority, but only if you acknowledge their talents and advance their career. Avoid questioning or second-guessing their every move. Persuade Capricorn to stop worrying about what other people think—lots of the best actors have never won Academy Awards.

PISCES @ WORK WITH AQUARIUS

☛ **A kinder, gentler business.**

This alliance benefits from high ideals and sound values. With mutual effort, you can retain talented employees, transform a motley crew into a cohesive team, and succeed in the marketplace without cheating or sacrificing. Aquarius acts like your conscience, questioning the ultimate ramifications of the work you do together. You tend to admire their patience, but hate their stubbornness, and distrust their theories. Don't leave all the strategizing and number-crunching to Aquarius, or you'll risk failing to reach your potential. Keep one another down to earth. Business ain't done in the clouds.

IF AQUARIUS IS BOSS: Position yourself as a team player. Even if you know you perform best when left to your own devices, this boss wants a staff who can unite behind a common cause. Formulate your ideas in a way that makes them accessible to everyone—no secret decoder ring required!

IF YOU'RE IN CHARGE: Don't hover. Doling out freedom for good work, let Aquarius find more productive methods and make friends with their own personal computer. If you offer management advice as a chance to learn new tricks, rather than commands to obey, Aquarius will respond as fast and cleverly as a trained seal.

PISCES @ WORK WITH PISCES

☛ **To dream the impossible dream.**

Can two Pisces professionals be anything more than drinking buddies? Together you wallow. The world looks bleak. So much potential, so little progress. You reinforce each other's feeling of being trapped by circumstances, restricted by forces beyond your control. Unless, of course, you choose to confront the issues. Push the envelope. Ask for help. Fight the flake factor. Then dreams come true. You give of yourselves. And the world stands in awe that such wondrous deeds were possible.

IF THE OTHER PISCES IS BOSS: Direct communication is essential, but not easy to achieve. Even if your Pisces boss is unclear, don't you be too! Pin them down. Ask for specific dates, amounts, and objectives. In this boss you may have found the warm and caring authority figure you've been looking for—but watch out for mixed messages like "Take care of yourself" followed by "Work overtime every night this week!"

IF YOU'RE IN CHARGE: Teach moderation. Help this employee work within real-world limits without succumbing to them. Goals, personal development, profits and wages, workplace relationships, hanging out at the watercooler—all of these matter, and your Pisces employee needs to know "bingeing" in one place means fasting in another. And remember, your Pisces employee needs your ample consideration. They'll follow you to the end of Wall Street, but don't snap or growl.

Stellar Negotiations

Some Final Lessons on How to Schmooz Any Schmo in the Universe

According to one shrewd Capricorn entrepreneur (is there any other kind?) the single most important business negotiation strategy is this: To get what you want, first figure out what the other guy wants. So true. Sure, it helps to know your own goals and objectives and have a plan for reaching them. But nobody works in a vacuum. We all need something from the other guy.

Stellar negotiations aren't manipulation. In the long run, you'll never get what you want by manipulating people. But if we learn how to negotiate each person's needs and idiosyncrasies, and to unite them with our own, then we can arrive at the most productive happy middle ground.

To get you off on the right foot, here's Dr. Matt's guide to schmoozing any schmo in the universe. If you cater to a person's sign, you'll easily charm the pants, or anything else, off 'em.

ARIES

Want to make friends with an Aries? Let them initiate—at least in the beginning. Ask them to choose the restaurant (loud music helps). Aries needs to take charge and stay one step ahead of the game. Don't ever let them think you'll take advantage of them or get the upper hand. You needn't bother offering Aries all the answers in a tidy prospectus. They live the questions, thrive on challenge. Turn on an Aries by turning a job into an adventure. Don't bog them down with details. They'll leave you in the dust.

TAURUS

Relax. No need to get huffy or overeager with Taurus. They appreciate patience, a job done right, a crème brûlée baked to perfection. Surround them with good food and music. "Food is love," declared one Taurus professional. She wasn't kidding. Fast food is not an option! Neither is elevator music. In negotiations, make them feel certain they aren't risking too much. These guys like a sure thing.

GEMINI

Keep talking. Silence is death with Gemini. Give them lots of options. Ask them questions. They love telling you the answers. If they don't know something (rarely the case), they'll find out and send it pronto by fax, phone, and e-mail. Don't play games. Gemini knows all the rules. They probably wrote them. These guys spout ideas a mile a minute. Encourage brainstorming. You can get away with insulting their mother. Don't insult their ideas.

CANCER

Don't insult their mother! In fact, it's best to take a sincere interest in Cancer's family. And take the time to get to know them and their secret soft spots. Like a dog, they have to sniff you before you can pet them. Make Cancer feel at home. Sit them down and ask their advice. Appreciate their little gestures (not so little to them). Help them feel they're building something that's gonna last. Don't hurt their feelings.

LEO

Take them to in-spots popular with movie stars and politicos. Make them feel important. Leos were all born with VIP badges. Compliment their hair, their teeth, the jewelry (all of it's fake, but who cares?). Flatter them. Tell them how much you appreciate them. They're loyal. You should be, too.

VIRGO

Get your facts straight. Don't try to pull anything over on these people. Forget about faking it—Virgos are the Virgins, after all, and they can fake it better than the rest of us. But they don't. They do it right the first time, every time. You better too, if you want to deal with them. One more thing—they're good at fixing things. Praise their problem-solving handiwork and you've got Virgo on your side.

LIBRA

Flirt with them. Shake their hand a little too long. Make them feel you'll stick around forever. For an icebreaker, ask about their sweetie pies. Talk slowly and deliberately. Eloquence and style probably count for more than substance. These gentle souls can get insecure about money, espe-

cially when there's not enough of it. Threaten their sense of cash flow or aesthetics and count yourself thrown out of their ball club.

SCORPIO

Cut to the chase. Scorpio can spot BS from the 32nd floor with the naked eye. Whatever you do, don't double-cross them. If you even *seem* calculated, Scorpio gets suspicious and does one of those famous disappearing acts. Wining and dining and otherwise buttering them up just makes them slipperier. Lay yourself on the line with Scorpio. Forget about second-guessing what they want. They're too good at it. Win Scorpio's confidence by divulging a secret.

SAGITTARIUS

To get in good with Saj, take 'em to ethnic restaurants where everybody sits on the floor and eats with their hands. Get them talking about their experiences and travels—Sajs have all been somewhere the rest of us haven't even heard about. Sagittarius generally comes across as confident and breezy. But watch out: They all have little pet insecurities. Don't go there. Instead, laugh at their jokes; it loosens them up better than a martini. Don't make a big fuss if they're late. They've always got the best excuses.

CAPRICORN

Dealing with a stiff-necked Capricorn, eh? Don't worry. It's not impossible to deal with the Goat—it just takes effort. Inspire confidence. Wear sensible clothes that cost a lot and last forever. Be authentic and classy. They sidestep anything chintzy or rinky-dink. One caution: It takes a lot to impress these guys. You've got a Ph.D. from Southern State College? That's nice—they're best friends with an Ivy League provost. Appeal to their sense of quality. These guys set the standards. Don't be late.

AQUARIUS

Get to know their friends. If you're in good with their friends, chances are good you're in good with them. What's more, find out what they believe in. Talk about it. Tell them what you care about. If they don't like your politics, they don't like you—unless you convince them you believe what you believe for good reason. One more thing: Aquarius gets their

jollies on gadgets and toys. Talk to them in techno lingo, if that's their thing.

PISCES

Wow Pisces with *who* you are, not *what* you are. Impress them with integrity. Make time for them. They hate to be rushed or neglected. Thank them profusely for their generosity, which they always deny. Almost every Pisces has a weird sense of luck, destiny, gut feelings—whatever you want to call it. Make them think you're lucky. They'll want to rub your belly. Tell them your rough-draft fantasies. They'll fill in the fuzzy spots.

Part Two

YOUR BOARD OF DIRECTORS:

YOUR RISING SIGN AND THE PLANETS, TOO

You've met your Sun sign, your horoscope's chairman of the board. It's the Sun that represents your sense of purpose, the motivation and vision for your career or business. But that's only the beginning. Now it's time to meet your rising sign, plus your planets, so that you can get to know your entire birth chart and complete your Professional Planetary Profile.

For effective professionals, all the planets' energies work in harmony. Think of it as a successful corporation with the Sun at the helm *plus* a board of directors and administrative staff that carries out the chairman's vision. You may be a by-the-book Capricorn Sun who dreams of building a lasting legacy. But if you have Venus in Sagittarius, you'll approach the marketing of your vision with less seriousness, more humor, and a sense that anything's possible. People are complex—so astrology is, too!

The planets you'll meet include the Moon, Mercury, Venus, Mars, Jupiter, and Saturn, plus your rising sign, which isn't a planet but an astrological point. A special chapter will deal with the "macro" planets: Uranus, Neptune, and Pluto.

Remember, we all have all of the planets and their symbolic energies in our charts. So pay attention to what unique insights each planet has to say about your professional work style.

How to Get Your Foot in the Door—Your Rising Sign

"I'm a salesman. I play a role all day long."
A SCORPIO-RISING REGIONAL SALES MANAGER

How many times have you walked out of an interview kicking yourself? "If only I'd made a better first impression. If only they'd seen the real me. If only I'd worn stripes instead of polka dots, they'd have hired me on the spot." Probably true. But of course they didn't see the real you. They saw the polka dots.

More to the point, they saw your first impression, your outward professional persona. While most people don't spend a lot of time thinking about this aspect of themselves, it is important to know what kind of image you're projecting and to consciously develop this crucial part of your professional identity. Why bother? Because in our economy of sound bites and infomercials, they won't see the real you till *after* you've got the gig—if you get the gig.

Your rising sign (also called an "Ascendant") represents this part of yourself, the one that's constantly auditioning—or refusing to. It's how you come across at a party, during an interview, on the ski slopes making a deal. It's your calling card, the face you show to the world.

In my astrological interviews, professionals from all different fields gave similar advice for success: You've got to develop a positive public persona. It's not a mask. It doesn't hide the real you. It does, however, let you

navigate the world gracefully and efficiently, remaining true to yourself and your goals. With the wrong approach, you lose the interview or the audition in the first two minutes. Use your rising sign strategically, and you'll make a great first impression—and maybe get the chance to make a second.

Dr. Matt's Advice: By all means, express your rising sign. It's part of you. But it's not the whole you. Don't bother inventing an elaborate theatrical role that demands 24-hour maintenance. To determine your personal rising sign, see "Rising Sign Tables," page 181.

THE BENEFITS OF WORKING YOUR RISING SIGN

★ You'll revamp your professional image

★ You'll consciously project your positive public persona

★ You'll get your foot out of your mouth and in the door

If Your Rising Sign Is . . .

ARIES

☛ **Big ego, big personality, big deal.**

You come across as bubbly, full of life, as restless as a toddler who can't choose between Legos and Lincoln Logs. Are you ever *not* in a rush? Your public persona screams, "Try me, I'll take anything on!" But you have to decide beforehand how much you can (or simply want!) to handle.

> **"My job is not just my job. I'm also an actor."**
> A COMMERCIAL INSURANCE BROKER WITH $1 BILLION IN ANNUAL SALES

Even if you coasted to success on a trust fund, you look like a self-made person, independent and ambitious, like someone who won't take to bed at the first sign of sniffles. Though you may not believe yourself to be competitive, you appear to be, and you may have to convince new coworkers you're not running a race against them. Watch out! It's easy to be branded the company troublemaker. Try speaking softer, carrying a bigger stick. If you're stuck for a new image, try the benevolent dictator routine.

INTERVIEW INSIGHT: Be nice! Practice being tactful. Ponder questions before blurting out the answer. Be careful what you ask for—with your quest for challenges, you might get more work than you wanted. Display your ambition like a medal, but demonstrate the discipline to make good on your goals. Play up your experiences as a team player to counter the impression that you're out only for yourself. Do your homework to prove you can fit into the company culture. Keep a rein—but not too tight—on runaway optimism and speed-demon recklessness.

TAURUS

☞ **As solid as a house.**

That's you from the outside—feet on the ground and a roof that doesn't leak. What we see in you right away is good taste and common sense. Even if money burns a hole in your pocket when nobody's looking, you project financial savvy and stability. You seem like someone with realistic expectations, and you often connect with people on the most practical of levels. Maybe you don't look like the fastest kid to ever climb a corporate ladder, but at least we think you'll still be here when the others have lost their balance and tumbled down.

One word of caution in the image department: You seem to constantly appraise things and evaluate people. You may not notice, but others probably do. Beware of this tendency to stick a label—whether it be a price tag or a personality judgment—on *everything* in your environment.

INTERVIEW INSIGHT: Don't talk dollar figures too fast. Sell yourself, not just your previous performance figures. No need to stand on formality: Talk to strangers, they've got leads. Point out that you can adapt to change, adopt new methods. Move fast: Return calls quickly, provide references immediately, show up early. Though you seem pretty dependable, it doesn't always look as though you're very action-oriented. Prospective employers or clients will want to know if you will get the job done with any degree of creativity or originality. Shine. Make a fuss over your latest personal achievement.

GEMINI

☞ **Busy, busy, busy.**

Right off the bat you impress everyone with your long list of accomplishments and witty way with words. You seem so agile, both at expressing yourself and just moving around the room as if you'd designed it yourself. People quickly note your curiosity and the fact you catch on

quickly. What's harder to see is the substance behind your quick wit and self-assurance. Do you have real opinions and deep convictions? Stop hiding them behind all that chatter. Your image of the devastatingly bright wonder child can easily give way to your scatterbrained tendencies—that notorious ditzy-geeky facade that is the mark of none other than a strong Gemini influence. This kind of Woody Allen image works for some of you with this rising sign, but not for others.

INTERVIEW INSIGHT: Relax. Breathe. Hiring agents can see you've got the requirements for the position, but show them you do indeed have time to squeeze an actual *job* into your hectic life. And let them know you'll stick around awhile—that you won't be running off with the next circus that comes to town. Emphasize your versatility but show some depth. Quote a few footnotes to back up all those amazing factoids. Don't turn up the wit to full volume till *after* you get the gig.

CANCER

☛ **Firm but tender.**

Like the crab that symbolizes the sign, this is the calling card of Cancer rising. Behind a tough, shy, and hard-to-crack exterior, it looks as though there's a sensitive creature who could even win the heart of a tax collector. In fact, it's downright dangerous how much people trust you. You could be embezzling their mother's pension, but they'd still think of you as a fairy godmother, sincere, affectionate, and familiar, though simultaneously very elusive. You're as warm and cozy as a mug of hot chocolate but you guard your privacy like the last marshmallows left on earth. Even if you just go home and watch TV and eat mac and cheese from a box, folks at the office suspect you enjoy a rich and varied outside life and strong sense of self. Superhelpful, you appear to be someone who'd rescue a spider instead of squashing it, so it's easy to get stuck in the role of the savior, even when you'd rather be saved yourself.

You're more impressionable than the rest of us, and respond to different people like Zelig, the human chameleon. You can be hypersensitive to your environment. If it helps, take a familiar blanket to your next interview—just don't wear it! "I don't come cheap!" seems to be tattooed across your forehead. If you don't work for bargain basement prices, fine. But if the big bucks matter less than getting the gig, let employers know you won't require the upkeep expenses of a thoroughbred racehorse.

INTERVIEW INSIGHT: Put your fear of rejection on hold. Let go of a little caution. Milk your talent to come across as sincere, affectionate, devoted.

Prove you've got the organizational skills and fortitude to make a go of it. Convince potential employers or clients they need you.

LEO

☛ **Image matters.**

Leo rising can wear many hats, all of them pretty flashy. Eager to make a stupendous first impression, you seem to be "on" all the time. Have you ever been seen with your hair a mess or your desk disorganized? Abundant self-assurance seems like your birthright, and we often get the idea you've known what you wanted since kindergarten. At the end of the workweek coworkers automatically assume you've got a date for Friday night. Who wouldn't want to pal around with such a charismatic companion? Thanks to your flair for extroversion and sensationalism, your outward personality is not easily forgotten, but a few acquaintances may wonder why you're so prone to blowing everything out of proportion. Your first impression promises a lot, but people seldom doubt you'll deliver.

They do wonder, however, if *they* can live up to your demanding expectations. Pushing the Leo rising image too far, you can appear high-maintenance, someone who needs round-the clock attention and praise.

INTERVIEW INSIGHT: Go easy on the eau de cologne. Don't gloat. Sometimes your high level of confidence can be off-putting, so try to stay humble when you're trying to make a good impression. Identify and promote some special, hard-to-find quality or talent, but avoid flaunting just the great features of you and your résumé; stress instead the benefits you bring to a company or investor. Use your self-assurance to encourage the people around you to shine—it makes them feel wonderful about themselves *and* you. Laugh, cry, express your undying gratitude. We shouldn't buy it, but we do.

VIRGO

☛ **You've got it together.**

Or you seem to, anyhow. Even if you're deep down a rebel waiting to break free, you project the persona of someone who'll read the directions and follow the rules, an organized professional who knows how to put paper in the fax machine and balance the company checkbook. The words "May I help you?" seem to flash over your head like a neon sign. You're always ready to lend a hand, but maybe we shouldn't ask since you're

already so frightfully busy. Are you preoccupied with something? It usually looks like it.

On first meeting, you often seem as prim and proper as an English butler or governess—polite and well-composed. But unlike Mary Poppins, not all nannies help the medicine go down with a spoonful of sugar. You risk coming across as a fussbudget; so try to loosen up a little.

INTERVIEW INSIGHTS: Take pride in previous achievements. Good grooming comes naturally, but add a dab of pizzazz to your appearance. Be upbeat. Cut the self-criticism—the world is hard enough. Resist sounding critical, picky, or overly skeptical about a person's or project's chances of success, including your own. Gush with health and vitality, but curb your nervous energy and the urge to tinker and fiddle. Don't let distractions get to you. Express genuine interest in the work you want to do. Laugh at dumb jokes.

LIBRA

☞ Mr. NiceGuy.

Libra rising is the mark of a real charmer. Refined, suave, and hopelessly social, you seem like someone who keeps commitments, who's always cooperative, and is maybe a bit of a pushover. In fact, you're capable of being pretty sly and persuasive, but never without offering a smile, a pat on the back, a free cup of coffee. Since you're always respectful of those around you, it's not hard for you to command a lot of respect in return.

In contrast to people with Leo rising, who tend to blow everything out of proportion, people with Libra rising smooth out the surface. You pacify strangers. You make friends with the enemy. Coworkers may often implore you to take their side, or at least to mediate tough situations and take on the role of judge of character.

INTERVIEW INSIGHT: Take a stand. Sound sure of your goals and ultimate destination. Exhibit your ability to be your own person, not an empty vessel into which other people pour their leftovers. Don't kiss up, and when problems arise, don't pass the buck. Negotiate nicely but fiercely (even if they resent paying you more, they'll know you've got the right stuff). Don't be easily deterred. No need to contradict or second-guess yourself.

SCORPIO

☛ **The person with a past.**

Though you may in fact have never done anything more scandalous than pilfer an abandoned quarter from a pay phone, you seem full of secrets, mystery, and intrigue. You don't seem to miss a move. Being observant and aware is a big part of your persona, and you seem sensitive to office politics, corruption, and the games people play. And though you're no blabbermouth, nobody doubts you'll keep those around you honest. You always seem to be where the excitement is—and if there's none going on, you start some. Others may mistake your strong-mindedness and willfulness as an attempt to exert control. So share power. Help coworkers feel you're not keeping a CIA file on their last-known name and whereabouts.

INTERVIEW INSIGHT: Concentrate on this job, this client. Make them see they've got your full attention. Convey honesty and candor, but stay tactful—no need to tell the boss about the run in her stockings! Express tolerance and a willingness to participate. Don't come on too strong. Help interviewers understand your motives.

SAGITTARIUS

☛ **Cutie pie.**

Your breezy smile and wide-open eyes make you look like Mr. Easygoing, Ms. Happy-Go-Lucky. You seem to take everything in stride while never coming off as flighty or fickle. But despite your firm grounding, there are times you struggle to buck the system, eager to run free.

One of your greatest gifts is a big, hearty laugh, but your image comes with a serious side, too. You seem to know more than you could—more than anyone could, given your age and résumé. So don't be surprised when you're called on and expected to know the answer to the $64,000 question. You're tremendously absorbed in your work—be sure to make time for yourself somewhere in that busy schedule. Your amiability makes you a lot of friends in the office, but you run the risk of not being taken seriously by your coworkers or clients. Make sure you emphasize your work over your socializing. Finally, though, since you look like someone with grand ideas and amazing plans, you'll have to make The People in

> "Acting is a nice childish profession—pretending you're someone else and, at the same time, selling yourself."
> ACTRESS KATHARINE HEPBURN

Charge believe you won't gamble away the farm or procrastinate on the little stuff.

INTERVIEW INSIGHT: Sit still for five minutes. By all means express your profound *interest* in the job, the project, the gig. But convince them you're doing it for more than curiosity's sake, more than just another neat learning experience among your countless others. Resist the temptation to embellish the truth—we all know you love a good story, but stick to the facts. Say something open-minded. Call attention to what motivates you, and how that translates into results. In your enthusiasm to accept the job once it's offered, make sure you know the specifics—are you really ready to transfer to Abu Dhabi?

CAPRICORN

☛ **One tough cookie.**

That's your image, at least till you pop a few buttons. It looks like you've got all your ducks in a row—and when you say "Jump!" we say "Quack!" It's amazing how, even with a hangover or a nasty head cold, you can pull off gray-flannel seriousness better than the stuffy actors on *Masterpiece Playhouse.*

It doesn't matter if you're a bulldozer driver or a corporate VP—you present a formal and austere first impression, always the on-the-ball professional. Yes, you mean business! Possibly a late bloomer in the personality department, you try to bloom extrabright and fancy to make up for lost time. You project competence. You project so much competence it can intimidate people or make them jealous. Employees and underlings appreciate your experience but fear your scowl.

Your strong ambition comes through right away, and so does the strong work ethic that backs it up. What's that, you don't feel like you have a work ethic? All your packaging suggests the contrary, so make the most of it. But don't be surprised when your broad shoulders attract the weight of the world. Fight the snob factor. With Capricorn rising you may tend to work extrahard to have the right look, the right résumé, the right attitude. Right on! But many sloppier folks can mistake this professionalism for pretentiousness, so be careful not to come on too strong. Make friends with the common folk.

INTERVIEW INSIGHT: Show us you're a self-starter. And by all means be confident, but keep your plans to take over the company to yourself—at least till the second interview. Crack a casual smile while maintaining your professional poise. Let loose a little. Talk *more* than shop talk. Avoid name-

dropping. Keep your promises: It's one of your greatest untapped assets. Slouch once in a while, it makes you seem more human.

AQUARIUS

☛ **"I did it my way."**

Some people introduce themselves with a handshake, others with a business card. But not *you*. You do it with a theme song. All the Brooks Brothers suits in the world couldn't make you look totally conventional. There's an air of difference about you. You electrify a room with your magnetic personality—a little remote, quite zany, definitely intriguing.

Since you come across as such a rare edition, it's not always easy to live up to people's first impressions of you. Always being different can be pretty tiring. The world gives you lots of space because you seem to need it. But in spite of your large investment in individuality, you're hardly cut out for a career in left field. Your devil-may-care attitude doesn't stop you from being a people person, a team player who wears the suit but keeps the sneakers.

INTERVIEW INSIGHT: Capitalize on your aura of brilliance—the million-ideas-a-minute person—but stay focused and on topic. Steer clear of political hot potatoes, at least for now. Help interviewers understand those off-the-beaten-track experiences on your résumé. Resist the urge to form a hasty alliance or partnership. Talk specifics, not just theories and abstractions. Support ideas with concrete examples and game plans. Convince them you *know how* to play by the rules. Appeal to their sense of vision and imagination.

PISCES

☛ **Space Cadet.**

Your rising sign seems outfitted with its own space suit—or maybe a mermaid costume, halo, or black beret. Whichever, an initial meeting with you often leaves people wondering if they've just had an encounter with a being from another world or a different dimension. Once that first radioactive fog clears, however, you emerge as highly imaginative, compassionate, as devoted to worthwhile work as a Zen monk to his vows. And you're quite capable of leaving a deep, heartfelt impression on the most heartless customer.

A little on the shy side, you project a go-with-the-flow attitude. Your public persona seems to say, "I'm easy, I'm flexible, and I'm willing." Maybe too willing. You'll have to make it clear you're not always eager to

pick up breakfast for the staff meeting just because the donut shop's on your way to work. And when a project you *do* want comes along, put aside any sign of your inhibitions. Banish a ditzy image by knowing how to tap resources, turn dreams into goals, and carve a niche in your environment.

Generally a soothing influence wherever you go, you seem sensitive, maybe even too sensitive. As a result, you may have to persuade colleagues that you do have both feet planted on the ground and that your head's in the clouds for good reason, not just for the pretty view. Though you may know what you mean in word and deed, the rest of us might not get it. Don't run the risk of sounding vague. In most cases, guide us to just one possible interpretation: yours!

INTERVIEW INSIGHT: Be here now! Shake hands firmly and make eye contact. Exude a strong work ethic. Imply how much you're willing to sacrifice for this job, but don't nail yourself to a cross or you might get stuck there. Be proactive, not passive. Check the facts and ignore the fiction. Stimulate our ability to care.

RISING SIGN TABLES
How to Find Your Rising Sign

It's easy to find your rising sign using these tables for all three "zones" in the continental United States, plus Alaska and Hawaii. If you were born outside the United States, please refer to page 17.

1. Determine your time of birth—*the more accurate the better!* Check your birth certificate, ask a relative, or write to the county where you were born. *And if you were born during Daylight Savings Time, subtract one hour from your given birth time.*

2. Now look at the diagram on page 182 to determine in which zone you were born.

3. Turn to the rising sign tables for that zone and find the listing for your birth date. If your date is not listed, choose the date just before your birth date.

4. In the tables, find the time you were born (already determined in the above step 1) by looking at the time entries to the right of the date. Again, if your birth time is not listed, select the time just before your birth time.

5. Subtract four minutes from the time shown for each (if any) day you were born after the listed date to get the sign change time for your birth date. If the adjusted time is after your birth time, see one column to the left.

6. Hooray! The sign noted at the top of the column should be your rising sign.*

Example

1. The birth data I have for Oprah Winfrey says she was born January 29, 1954, at 12:00 P.M. (noon) in Noxapater, Mississippi.

*Please note: These rising signs are approximations. If you were born close to the time change or near the edges of the "zone," the only way to verify your rising sign is to have a computerized chart calculated. For more information about that, see page 17.

2. If we look at the map diagram, we see all of Mississippi falls in Zone 2. So for Oprah's rising sign, we'll look in the tables under Zone 2.

3. Under Zone 2 in the rising sign tables, we skim down to Oprah's birth date, January 29. It *is* listed. (If it weren't, we'd have chosen the nearest date *before* her birth date.)

4. In the row to the right of "January 29," Oprah's precise birth time is not listed, so we choose the nearest time *before* her birth time, which happens to be 10:45 A.M.

5. We don't have to subtract any minutes because Oprah's birth date is listed.

6. At the top of the column with 10:45 A.M. in it, we see the sign Taurus. If Oprah's birth data is correct, she has Taurus rising—Taurus is her rising sign.

WHERE WERE YOU BORN?*

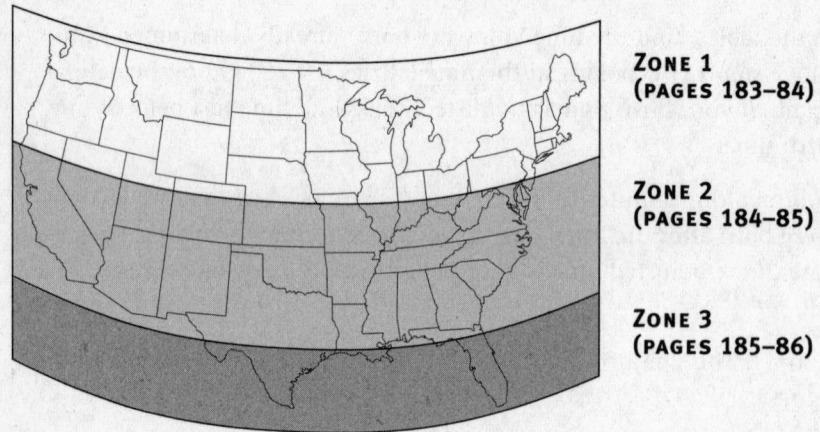

ZONE 1
(PAGES 183–84)

ZONE 2
(PAGES 184–85)

ZONE 3
(PAGES 185–86)

RISING SIGN TABLES

Zone 1	Aries	Taurus	Gemini	Cancer	Leo	Virgo	Libra	Scorpio	Sagittarius	Capricorn	Aquarius	Pisces
Jan. 1	11:17 A.M.	12:47 P.M.	2:28 P.M.	4:29 P.M.	6:45 P.M.	9:06 P.M.	11:19 P.M.	1:32 A.M.	3:49 A.M.	6:04 A.M.	8:06 A.M.	9:47 A.M.
Jan. 8	10:49 A.M.	12:19 P.M.	2:01 P.M.	4:02 P.M.	6:17 P.M.	8:38 P.M.	10:51 P.M.	1:04 A.M.	3:21 A.M.	5:37 A.M.	7:38 A.M.	9:20 A.M.
Jan. 15	10:22 A.M.	11:51 A.M.	1:33 P.M.	3:34 P.M.	5:50 P.M.	8:11 P.M.	10:22 P.M.	12:37 A.M.	2:54 A.M.	5:09 A.M.	7:10 A.M.	8:52 A.M.
Jan. 22	9:54 A.M.	11:24 A.M.	1:06 P.M.	3:07 P.M.	5:22 P.M.	7:43 P.M.	9:56 P.M.	12:09 A.M.	2:26 A.M.	4:42 A.M.	6:43 A.M.	8:25 A.M.
Jan. 29	9:27 A.M.	10:56 A.M.	12:38 P.M.	2:39 P.M.	4:55 P.M.	7:16 P.M.	9:29 P.M.	11:42 P.M.	1:59 A.M.	4:14 A.M.	6:15 A.M.	7:57 A.M.
Feb. 5	8:59 A.M.	10:29 A.M.	12:11 P.M.	2:12 P.M.	4:27 P.M.	6:44 P.M.	9:01 P.M.	11:14 P.M.	1:31 A.M.	3:47 A.M.	5:48 A.M.	7:30 A.M.
Feb. 12	8:32 A.M.	10:01 A.M.	11:43 A.M.	1:44 P.M.	4:00 P.M.	6:17 P.M.	8:34 P.M.	10:47 P.M.	1:04 A.M.	3:19 A.M.	5:20 A.M.	7:02 A.M.
Feb. 19	8:04 A.M.	9:34 A.M.	11:16 A.M.	1:17 P.M.	3:32 P.M.	5:49 P.M.	8:06 P.M.	10:19 P.M.	12:36 A.M.	2:52 A.M.	4:53 A.M.	6:35 A.M.
Feb. 26	7:37 A.M.	9:06 A.M.	10:48 A.M.	12:49 P.M.	3:05 P.M.	5:22 P.M.	7:39 P.M.	9:52 P.M.	12:09 A.M.	2:24 A.M.	4:25 A.M.	6:07 A.M.
March 5	7:09 A.M.	8:39 A.M.	10:20 A.M.	12:22 P.M.	2:37 P.M.	4:54 P.M.	7:11 P.M.	9:24 P.M.	11:41 P.M.	1:57 A.M.	3:58 A.M.	5:39 A.M.
March 12	6:42 A.M.	8:11 A.M.	9:53 A.M.	11:54 A.M.	2:10 P.M.	4:27 P.M.	6:40 P.M.	8:57 P.M.	11:14 P.M.	1:29 A.M.	3:30 A.M.	5:12 A.M.
March 19	6:14 A.M.	7:44 A.M.	9:25 A.M.	11:27 A.M.	1:42 P.M.	3:59 P.M.	6:12 P.M.	8:29 P.M.	10:46 P.M.	1:02 A.M.	3:03 A.M.	4:44 A.M.
March 26	5:47 A.M.	7:16 A.M.	8:58 A.M.	10:59 A.M.	1:15 P.M.	3:32 P.M.	5:45 P.M.	8:02 P.M.	10:18 P.M.	12:34 A.M.	2:35 A.M.	4:17 A.M.
April 2	5:19 A.M.	6:49 A.M.	8:30 A.M.	10:32 A.M.	12:47 P.M.	3:04 P.M.	5:17 P.M.	7:34 P.M.	9:51 P.M.	12:07 A.M.	2:08 A.M.	3:49 A.M.
April 9	4:52 A.M.	6:21 A.M.	8:03 A.M.	10:04 A.M.	12:20 P.M.	2:37 P.M.	4:50 P.M.	7:06 P.M.	9:23 P.M.	11:39 P.M.	1:40 A.M.	3:22 A.M.
April 16	4:24 A.M.	5:54 A.M.	7:35 A.M.	9:36 A.M.	11:52 A.M.	2:09 P.M.	4:22 P.M.	6:35 P.M.	8:56 P.M.	11:12 P.M.	1:13 A.M.	2:54 A.M.
April 23	3:56 A.M.	5:26 A.M.	7:08 A.M.	9:09 A.M.	11:25 A.M.	1:42 P.M.	3:55 P.M.	6:08 P.M.	8:28 P.M.	10:44 P.M.	12:45 A.M.	2:27 A.M.
April 30	3:29 A.M.	4:59 A.M.	6:40 A.M.	8:41 A.M.	10:57 A.M.	1:14 P.M.	3:27 P.M.	5:40 P.M.	8:01 P.M.	10:16 P.M.	12:18 A.M.	1:59 A.M.
May 7	3:01 A.M.	4:31 A.M.	6:13 A.M.	8:14 A.M.	10:30 A.M.	12:46 P.M.	2:59 P.M.	5:12 P.M.	7:33 P.M.	9:49 P.M.	11:50 P.M.	1:32 A.M.
May 14	2:34 A.M.	4:04 A.M.	5:45 A.M.	7:46 A.M.	10:02 A.M.	12:19 P.M.	2:32 P.M.	4:45 P.M.	7:06 P.M.	9:21 P.M.	11:23 P.M.	1:04 A.M.
May 21	2:06 A.M.	3:36 A.M.	5:18 A.M.	7:19 A.M.	9:34 A.M.	11:51 A.M.	2:04 P.M.	4:17 P.M.	6:34 P.M.	8:54 P.M.	10:55 P.M.	12:37 A.M.
May 28	1:39 A.M.	3:09 A.M.	4:50 A.M.	6:51 A.M.	9:07 A.M.	11:24 A.M.	1:37 P.M.	3:50 P.M.	6:07 P.M.	8:26 P.M.	10:28 P.M.	12:09 A.M.
June 4	1:11 A.M.	2:41 A.M.	4:23 A.M.	6:24 A.M.	8:39 A.M.	10:56 A.M.	1:09 P.M.	3:22 P.M.	5:39 P.M.	7:59 P.M.	10:00 P.M.	11:42 P.M.
June 11	12:44 A.M.	2:13 A.M.	3:55 A.M.	5:56 A.M.	8:12 A.M.	10:29 A.M.	12:42 P.M.	2:55 P.M.	5:12 P.M.	7:31 P.M.	9:32 P.M.	11:14 P.M.
June 18	12:16 A.M.	1:46 A.M.	3:28 A.M.	5:29 A.M.	7:44 A.M.	10:01 A.M.	12:14 P.M.	2:27 P.M.	4:44 P.M.	7:04 P.M.	9:05 P.M.	10:47 P.M.
June 25	11:49 P.M.	1:18 A.M.	3:00 A.M.	5:01 A.M.	7:17 A.M.	9:34 A.M.	11:47 A.M.	2:00 P.M.	4:17 P.M.	6:32 P.M.	8:37 P.M.	10:19 P.M.
July 2	11:21 P.M.	12:51 A.M.	2:33 A.M.	4:34 A.M.	6:49 A.M.	9:06 A.M.	11:19 A.M.	1:32 P.M.	3:49 P.M.	6:05 P.M.	8:10 P.M.	9:52 P.M.
July 9	10:54 P.M.	12:23 A.M.	2:05 A.M.	4:06 A.M.	6:22 A.M.	8:39 A.M.	10:52 A.M.	1:05 P.M.	3:22 P.M.	5:37 P.M.	7:42 P.M.	9:24 P.M.
July 16	10:26 P.M.	11:56 P.M.	1:38 A.M.	3:39 A.M.	5:54 A.M.	8:11 A.M.	10:24 A.M.	12:37 P.M.	2:54 P.M.	5:10 P.M.	7:15 P.M.	8:57 P.M.
July 23	9:59 P.M.	11:28 P.M.	1:10 A.M.	3:11 A.M.	5:27 A.M.	7:44 A.M.	9:57 A.M.	12:10 P.M.	2:27 P.M.	4:42 P.M.	6:43 P.M.	8:29 P.M.
July 30	9:31 P.M.	11:01 P.M.	12:42 A.M.	2:44 A.M.	4:59 A.M.	7:16 A.M.	9:29 A.M.	11:42 A.M.	1:59 P.M.	4:15 P.M.	6:16 P.M.	8:01 P.M.
Aug. 6	9:04 P.M.	10:33 P.M.	12:15 A.M.	2:16 A.M.	4:32 A.M.	6:49 A.M.	9:02 A.M.	11:15 A.M.	1:32 P.M.	3:47 P.M.	5:48 P.M.	7:34 P.M.
Aug. 13	8:36 P.M.	10:06 P.M.	11:47 P.M.	1:49 A.M.	4:04 A.M.	6:21 A.M.	8:34 A.M.	10:47 A.M.	1:04 P.M.	3:20 P.M.	5:21 P.M.	7:06 P.M.
Aug. 20	8:09 P.M.	9:38 P.M.	11:20 P.M.	1:21 A.M.	3:37 A.M.	5:54 A.M.	8:07 A.M.	10:20 A.M.	12:37 P.M.	2:52 P.M.	4:53 P.M.	6:35 P.M.
Aug. 27	7:41 P.M.	9:11 P.M.	10:52 P.M.	12:54 A.M.	3:09 A.M.	5:26 A.M.	7:39 A.M.	9:52 A.M.	12:09 P.M.	2:25 P.M.	4:26 P.M.	6:07 P.M.
Sept. 3	7:14 P.M.	8:43 P.M.	10:25 P.M.	12:26 A.M.	2:42 A.M.	4:59 A.M.	7:12 A.M.	9:25 A.M.	11:42 A.M.	1:57 P.M.	3:58 P.M.	5:40 P.M.
Sept. 10	6:42 P.M.	8:16 P.M.	9:57 P.M.	11:59 P.M.	2:14 A.M.	4:31 A.M.	6:44 A.M.	8:57 A.M.	11:14 A.M.	1:30 P.M.	3:31 P.M.	5:12 P.M.
Sept. 17	6:15 P.M.	7:48 P.M.	9:30 P.M.	11:31 P.M.	1:47 A.M.	4:04 A.M.	6:17 A.M.	8:30 A.M.	10:46 A.M.	1:02 P.M.	3:03 P.M.	4:45 P.M.
Sept. 24	5:47 P.M.	7:21 P.M.	9:02 P.M.	11:03 P.M.	1:19 A.M.	3:36 A.M.	5:49 A.M.	8:02 A.M.	10:19 A.M.	12:35 P.M.	2:36 P.M.	4:17 P.M.
Oct. 1	5:20 P.M.	6:49 P.M.	8:35 P.M.	10:36 P.M.	12:52 A.M.	3:08 A.M.	5:21 A.M.	7:34 A.M.	9:51 A.M.	12:07 P.M.	2:08 P.M.	3:50 P.M.
Oct. 8	4:52 P.M.	6:22 P.M.	8:07 P.M.	10:08 P.M.	12:24 A.M.	2:41 A.M.	4:54 A.M.	7:07 A.M.	9:24 A.M.	11:40 A.M.	1:41 P.M.	3:22 P.M.
Oct. 15	4:24 P.M.	5:54 P.M.	7:40 P.M.	9:41 P.M.	11:56 P.M.	2:13 A.M.	4:26 A.M.	6:39 A.M.	8:56 A.M.	11:12 A.M.	1:13 P.M.	2:55 P.M.

(continued on next page)

RISING SIGN TABLES (continued)

Zone 1	Aries	Taurus	Gemini	Cancer	Leo	Virgo	Libra	Scorpio	Sagittarius	Capricorn	Aquarius	Pisces
Oct. 22	3:57 P.M.	5:27 P.M.	7:12 P.M.	9:13 P.M.	11:29 P.M.	1:46 A.M.	3:59 A.M.	6:12 A.M.	8:29 A.M.	10:44 A.M.	12:46 P.M.	2:27 P.M.
Oct. 29	3:29 P.M.	4:59 P.M.	6:41 P.M.	8:46 P.M.	11:01 P.M.	1:18 A.M.	3:31 A.M.	5:44 A.M.	8:01 A.M.	10:17 A.M.	12:18 P.M.	2:00 P.M.
Nov. 5	3:02 P.M.	4:32 P.M.	6:13 P.M.	8:18 P.M.	10:34 P.M.	12:51 A.M.	3:04 A.M.	5:17 A.M.	7:34 A.M.	9:49 A.M.	11:51 A.M.	1:32 P.M.
Nov. 12	2:34 P.M.	4:04 P.M.	5:46 P.M.	7:51 P.M.	10:06 P.M.	12:23 A.M.	2:36 A.M.	4:49 A.M.	7:06 A.M.	9:22 A.M.	11:23 A.M.	1:05 P.M.
Nov. 19	2:07 P.M.	3:37 P.M.	5:18 P.M.	7:23 P.M.	9:39 P.M.	11:56 P.M.	2:09 A.M.	4:22 A.M.	6:39 A.M.	8:54 A.M.	10:56 A.M.	12:37 P.M.
Nov. 26	1:39 P.M.	3:09 P.M.	4:51 P.M.	6:52 P.M.	9:11 P.M.	11:28 P.M.	1:41 A.M.	3:54 A.M.	6:11 A.M.	8:27 A.M.	10:28 A.M.	12:10 P.M.
Dec. 3	1:12 P.M.	2:41 P.M.	4:23 P.M.	6:24 P.M.	8:44 P.M.	11:01 P.M.	1:14 A.M.	3:27 A.M.	5:44 A.M.	7:59 A.M.	10:00 A.M.	11:42 A.M.
Dec. 10	12:44 P.M.	2:14 P.M.	3:56 P.M.	5:57 P.M.	8:16 P.M.	10:33 P.M.	12:46 A.M.	2:59 A.M.	5:16 A.M.	7:32 A.M.	9:33 A.M.	11:15 A.M.
Dec. 17	12:17 P.M.	1:46 P.M.	3:28 P.M.	5:29 P.M.	7:49 P.M.	10:06 P.M.	12:19 A.M.	2:32 A.M.	4:49 A.M.	7:04 A.M.	9:05 A.M.	10:47 A.M.
Dec. 24	11:49 A.M.	1:19 P.M.	3:01 P.M.	5:02 P.M.	7:21 P.M.	9:38 P.M.	11:51 P.M.	2:04 A.M.	4:21 A.M.	6:37 A.M.	8:38 A.M.	10:20 A.M.
Dec. 31	11:22 A.M.	12:51 P.M.	2:33 P.M.	4:34 P.M.	6:50 P.M.	9:11 P.M.	11:24 P.M.	1:37 A.M.	3:54 A.M.	6:09 A.M.	8:10 A.M.	9:52 A.M.

Zone 2	Aries	Taurus	Gemini	Cancer	Leo	Virgo	Libra	Scorpio	Sagittarius	Capricorn	Aquarius	Pisces
Jan. 1	11:17 A.M.	12:36 P.M.	2:08 P.M.	4:05 P.M.	6:25 P.M.	8:55 P.M.	11:19 P.M.	1:43 A.M.	4:09 A.M.	6:28 A.M.	8:26 A.M.	9:58 A.M.
Jan. 8	10:49 A.M.	12:08 P.M.	1:41 P.M.	3:38 P.M.	5:57 P.M.	8:27 P.M.	10:51 P.M.	1:15 A.M.	3:41 A.M.	6:01 A.M.	7:58 A.M.	9:31 A.M.
Jan. 15	10:22 A.M.	11:41 A.M.	1:13 P.M.	3:10 P.M.	5:30 P.M.	8:00 P.M.	10:24 P.M.	12:48 A.M.	3:14 A.M.	5:33 A.M.	7:31 A.M.	9:03 A.M.
Jan. 22	9:54 A.M.	11:13 A.M.	12:46 P.M.	2:43 P.M.	5:02 P.M.	7:32 P.M.	9:56 P.M.	12:20 A.M.	2:46 A.M.	5:06 A.M.	7:03 A.M.	8:36 A.M.
Jan. 29	9:27 A.M.	10:45 A.M.	12:18 P.M.	2:15 P.M.	4:35 P.M.	7:05 P.M.	9:29 P.M.	11:53 P.M.	2:19 A.M.	4:38 A.M.	6:36 A.M.	8:08 A.M.
Feb. 5	8:59 A.M.	10:18 A.M.	11:50 A.M.	1:48 P.M.	4:07 P.M.	6:33 P.M.	9:01 P.M.	11:25 P.M.	1:51 A.M.	4:11 A.M.	6:08 A.M.	7:40 A.M.
Feb. 12	8:32 A.M.	9:50 A.M.	11:23 A.M.	1:20 P.M.	3:40 P.M.	6:06 P.M.	8:34 P.M.	10:58 P.M.	1:24 A.M.	3:43 A.M.	5:40 A.M.	7:13 A.M.
Feb. 19	8:04 A.M.	9:23 A.M.	10:55 A.M.	12:53 P.M.	3:12 P.M.	5:38 P.M.	8:06 P.M.	10:30 P.M.	12:56 A.M.	3:16 A.M.	5:13 A.M.	6:45 A.M.
Feb. 26	7:37 A.M.	8:55 A.M.	10:28 A.M.	12:25 P.M.	2:45 P.M.	5:11 P.M.	7:39 P.M.	10:03 P.M.	12:29 A.M.	2:48 A.M.	4:45 A.M.	6:18 A.M.
March 5	7:09 A.M.	8:28 A.M.	10:00 A.M.	11:58 A.M.	2:17 P.M.	4:43 P.M.	7:11 P.M.	9:35 P.M.	12:01 A.M.	2:21 A.M.	4:18 A.M.	5:50 A.M.
March 12	6:42 A.M.	8:00 A.M.	9:33 A.M.	11:30 A.M.	1:50 P.M.	4:16 P.M.	6:40 P.M.	9:08 P.M.	11:34 P.M.	1:53 A.M.	3:50 A.M.	5:23 A.M.
March 19	6:14 A.M.	7:33 A.M.	9:05 A.M.	11:03 A.M.	1:22 P.M.	3:48 P.M.	6:12 P.M.	8:40 P.M.	11:06 P.M.	1:26 A.M.	3:23 A.M.	4:55 A.M.
March 26	5:47 A.M.	7:05 A.M.	8:38 A.M.	10:35 A.M.	12:55 P.M.	3:21 P.M.	5:45 P.M.	8:12 P.M.	10:39 P.M.	12:58 A.M.	2:55 A.M.	4:28 A.M.
April 2	5:19 A.M.	6:38 A.M.	8:10 A.M.	10:08 A.M.	12:27 P.M.	2:53 P.M.	5:17 P.M.	7:45 P.M.	10:11 P.M.	12:31 A.M.	2:28 A.M.	4:00 A.M.
April 9	4:52 A.M.	6:10 A.M.	7:43 A.M.	9:40 A.M.	12:00 P.M.	2:26 P.M.	4:50 P.M.	7:17 P.M.	9:44 P.M.	12:03 A.M.	2:00 A.M.	3:33 A.M.
April 16	4:24 A.M.	5:43 A.M.	7:15 A.M.	9:13 A.M.	11:32 A.M.	1:58 P.M.	4:22 P.M.	6:46 P.M.	9:16 P.M.	11:36 P.M.	1:33 A.M.	3:05 A.M.
April 23	3:56 A.M.	5:15 A.M.	6:48 A.M.	8:45 A.M.	11:04 A.M.	1:31 P.M.	3:55 P.M.	6:18 P.M.	8:48 P.M.	11:08 P.M.	1:05 A.M.	2:38 A.M.
April 30	3:29 A.M.	4:48 A.M.	6:20 A.M.	8:17 A.M.	10:37 A.M.	1:03 P.M.	3:27 P.M.	5:51 P.M.	8:21 P.M.	10:40 P.M.	12:38 A.M.	2:10 A.M.
May 7	3:01 A.M.	4:20 A.M.	5:53 A.M.	7:50 A.M.	10:09 A.M.	12:36 P.M.	2:59 P.M.	5:23 P.M.	7:53 P.M.	10:13 P.M.	12:10 A.M.	1:43 A.M.
May 14	2:34 A.M.	3:53 A.M.	5:25 A.M.	7:22 A.M.	9:42 A.M.	12:08 P.M.	2:32 P.M.	4:56 P.M.	7:26 P.M.	9:45 P.M.	11:43 P.M.	1:15 A.M.
May 21	2:06 A.M.	3:25 A.M.	4:58 A.M.	6:55 A.M.	9:14 A.M.	11:40 A.M.	2:04 P.M.	4:28 P.M.	6:54 P.M.	9:18 P.M.	11:15 P.M.	12:48 A.M.
May 28	1:39 A.M.	2:58 A.M.	4:30 A.M.	6:27 A.M.	8:47 A.M.	11:13 A.M.	1:37 P.M.	4:01 P.M.	6:27 P.M.	8:50 P.M.	10:48 P.M.	12:20 A.M.
June 4	1:11 A.M.	2:30 A.M.	4:03 A.M.	6:00 A.M.	8:19 A.M.	10:45 A.M.	1:09 P.M.	3:33 P.M.	5:59 P.M.	8:23 P.M.	10:20 P.M.	11:53 P.M.
June 11	12:44 A.M.	2:03 A.M.	3:35 A.M.	5:32 A.M.	7:52 A.M.	10:18 A.M.	12:42 P.M.	3:06 P.M.	5:32 P.M.	7:55 P.M.	9:53 P.M.	11:25 P.M.
June 18	12:16 A.M.	1:35 A.M.	3:08 A.M.	5:05 A.M.	7:24 A.M.	9:50 A.M.	12:14 P.M.	2:38 P.M.	5:04 P.M.	7:28 P.M.	9:25 P.M.	10:58 P.M.
June 25	11:49 P.M.	1:08 A.M.	2:40 A.M.	4:37 A.M.	6:57 A.M.	9:23 A.M.	11:47 A.M.	2:11 P.M.	4:37 P.M.	7:00 P.M.	8:58 P.M.	10:30 P.M.
July 2	11:21 P.M.	12:40 A.M.	2:12 A.M.	4:10 A.M.	6:29 A.M.	8:55 A.M.	11:19 A.M.	1:43 P.M.	4:09 P.M.	6:29 P.M.	8:30 P.M.	10:03 P.M.
July 9	10:54 P.M.	12:12 A.M.	1:45 A.M.	3:42 A.M.	6:02 A.M.	8:28 A.M.	10:52 A.M.	1:16 P.M.	3:42 P.M.	6:01 P.M.	8:03 P.M.	9:35 P.M.

Zone 2		Aries	Taurus	Gemini	Cancer	Leo	Virgo	Libra	Scorpio	Sagittarius	Capricorn	Aquarius	Pisces
July	16	10:26 P.M.	11:45 P.M.	1:17 P.M.	3:15 A.M.	5:34 A.M.	8:00 A.M.	10:24 A.M.	12:48 P.M.	3:14 P.M.	5:34 P.M.	7:35 P.M.	9:07 P.M.
July	23	9:59 P.M.	11:17 P.M.	12:50 A.M.	2:47 A.M.	5:07 A.M.	7:33 A.M.	9:57 A.M.	12:21 P.M.	2:47 P.M.	5:06 P.M.	7:07 P.M.	8:40 P.M.
July	30	9:31 P.M.	10:50 P.M.	12:22 A.M.	2:20 A.M.	4:39 A.M.	7:05 A.M.	9:29 A.M.	11:53 A.M.	2:19 P.M.	4:39 P.M.	6:36 P.M.	8:12 P.M.
Aug.	6	9:04 P.M.	10:22 P.M.	11:55 P.M.	1:52 A.M.	4:12 A.M.	6:38 A.M.	9:02 A.M.	11:26 A.M.	1:52 P.M.	4:11 P.M.	6:08 P.M.	7:45 P.M.
Aug.	13	8:36 P.M.	9:55 P.M.	11:27 P.M.	1:25 A.M.	3:44 A.M.	6:10 A.M.	8:34 A.M.	10:58 A.M.	1:24 P.M.	3:44 P.M.	5:41 P.M.	7:17 P.M.
Aug.	20	8:09 P.M.	9:27 P.M.	11:00 P.M.	12:57 A.M.	3:17 A.M.	5:43 A.M.	8:07 A.M.	10:31 A.M.	12:57 P.M.	3:16 P.M.	5:13 P.M.	6:46 P.M.
Aug.	27	7:41 P.M.	9:00 P.M.	10:32 P.M.	12:30 A.M.	2:49 A.M.	5:15 A.M.	7:39 A.M.	10:03 A.M.	12:29 P.M.	2:49 P.M.	4:46 P.M.	6:18 P.M.
Sept.	3	7:14 P.M.	8:32 P.M.	10:05 P.M.	12:02 A.M.	2:22 A.M.	4:48 A.M.	7:12 A.M.	9:36 A.M.	12:02 P.M.	2:21 P.M.	4:18 P.M.	5:51 P.M.
Sept.	10	6:42 P.M.	8:05 P.M.	9:37 P.M.	11:35 P.M.	1:54 A.M.	4:20 A.M.	6:44 A.M.	9:08 A.M.	11:34 A.M.	1:54 P.M.	3:51 P.M.	5:23 P.M.
Sept.	17	6:15 P.M.	7:37 P.M.	9:10 P.M.	11:07 P.M.	1:26 A.M.	3:53 A.M.	6:17 A.M.	8:40 A.M.	11:07 A.M.	1:26 P.M.	3:23 P.M.	4:56 P.M.
Sept.	24	5:47 P.M.	7:10 P.M.	8:42 P.M.	10:39 P.M.	12:59 A.M.	3:25 A.M.	5:49 A.M.	8:13 A.M.	10:39 A.M.	12:59 P.M.	2:56 P.M.	4:28 P.M.
Oct.	1	5:20 P.M.	6:38 P.M.	8:15 P.M.	10:12 P.M.	12:31 A.M.	2:58 A.M.	5:21 A.M.	7:45 A.M.	10:12 A.M.	12:31 P.M.	2:28 P.M.	4:01 P.M.
Oct.	8	4:52 P.M.	6:11 P.M.	7:47 P.M.	9:44 P.M.	12:04 A.M.	2:30 A.M.	4:54 A.M.	7:18 A.M.	9:44 A.M.	12:04 P.M.	2:01 P.M.	3:33 P.M.
Oct.	15	4:24 P.M.	5:43 P.M.	7:20 P.M.	9:17 P.M.	11:36 P.M.	2:03 A.M.	4:26 A.M.	6:50 A.M.	9:16 A.M.	11:36 A.M.	1:33 P.M.	3:06 P.M.
Oct.	22	3:57 P.M.	5:16 P.M.	6:48 P.M.	8:49 P.M.	11:09 P.M.	1:35 A.M.	3:59 A.M.	6:23 A.M.	8:49 A.M.	11:08 A.M.	1:06 P.M.	2:38 P.M.
Oct.	29	3:29 P.M.	4:48 P.M.	6:21 P.M.	8:22 P.M.	10:41 P.M.	1:07 A.M.	3:31 A.M.	5:55 A.M.	8:21 A.M.	10:41 A.M.	12:38 P.M.	2:11 P.M.
Nov.	5	3:02 P.M.	4:21 P.M.	5:53 P.M.	7:54 P.M.	10:14 P.M.	12:40 A.M.	3:04 A.M.	5:28 A.M.	7:54 A.M.	10:13 A.M.	12:11 P.M.	1:43 P.M.
Nov.	12	2:34 P.M.	3:53 P.M.	5:26 P.M.	7:27 P.M.	9:46 P.M.	12:12 A.M.	2:36 A.M.	5:00 A.M.	7:26 A.M.	9:46 A.M.	11:43 A.M.	1:16 P.M.
Nov.	19	2:07 P.M.	3:26 P.M.	4:58 P.M.	6:55 P.M.	9:19 P.M.	11:45 P.M.	2:09 A.M.	4:33 A.M.	6:59 A.M.	9:18 A.M.	11:16 A.M.	12:48 P.M.
Nov.	26	1:39 P.M.	2:58 P.M.	4:31 P.M.	6:28 P.M.	8:51 P.M.	11:17 P.M.	1:41 A.M.	4:05 A.M.	6:31 A.M.	8:51 A.M.	10:48 A.M.	12:21 P.M.
Dec.	3	1:12 P.M.	2:31 P.M.	4:03 P.M.	6:00 P.M.	8:24 P.M.	10:50 P.M.	1:14 A.M.	3:38 A.M.	6:04 A.M.	8:23 A.M.	10:21 A.M.	11:53 A.M.
Dec.	10	12:44 P.M.	2:03 P.M.	3:36 P.M.	5:33 P.M.	7:56 P.M.	10:22 P.M.	12:46 A.M.	3:10 A.M.	5:36 A.M.	7:56 A.M.	9:53 A.M.	11:26 A.M.
Dec.	17	12:17 P.M.	1:36 P.M.	3:08 P.M.	5:05 P.M.	7:29 P.M.	9:55 P.M.	12:19 A.M.	2:43 A.M.	5:09 A.M.	7:28 A.M.	9:26 A.M.	10:58 A.M.
Dec.	24	11:49 A.M.	1:08 P.M.	2:40 P.M.	4:38 P.M.	7:01 P.M.	9:27 P.M.	11:51 P.M.	2:15 A.M.	4:41 A.M.	7:01 A.M.	8:58 A.M.	10:31 A.M.
Dec.	31	11:22 A.M.	12:40 P.M.	2:13 P.M.	4:10 P.M.	6:30 P.M.	9:00 P.M.	11:24 P.M.	1:48 A.M.	4:14 A.M.	6:33 A.M.	8:30 A.M.	10:03 A.M.

Zone 3		Aries	Taurus	Gemini	Cancer	Leo	Virgo	Libra	Scorpio	Sagittarius	Capricorn	Aquarius	Pisces
Jan.	1	11:17 A.M.	12:21 P.M.	1:42 P.M.	3:33 P.M.	5:58 P.M.	8:41 P.M.	11:19 P.M.	1:57 A.M.	4:35 A.M.	7:00 A.M.	8:52 A.M.	10:12 A.M.
Jan.	8	10:49 A.M.	11:54 A.M.	1:14 P.M.	3:06 P.M.	5:31 P.M.	8:13 P.M.	10:51 P.M.	1:29 A.M.	4:08 A.M.	6:33 A.M.	8:25 A.M.	9:45 A.M.
Jan.	15	10:22 A.M.	11:26 A.M.	12:47 P.M.	2:38 P.M.	5:03 P.M.	7:46 P.M.	10:24 P.M.	1:02 A.M.	3:40 A.M.	6:05 A.M.	7:57 A.M.	9:17 A.M.
Jan.	22	9:54 A.M.	10:59 A.M.	12:19 P.M.	2:11 P.M.	4:36 P.M.	7:18 P.M.	9:56 P.M.	12:34 A.M.	3:13 A.M.	5:38 A.M.	7:30 A.M.	8:50 A.M.
Jan.	29	9:27 A.M.	10:31 A.M.	11:51 A.M.	1:43 P.M.	4:08 P.M.	6:47 P.M.	9:29 P.M.	12:07 A.M.	2:45 A.M.	5:10 A.M.	7:02 A.M.	8:22 A.M.
Feb.	5	8:59 A.M.	10:04 A.M.	11:24 A.M.	1:16 P.M.	3:41 P.M.	6:19 P.M.	9:01 P.M.	11:39 P.M.	2:18 A.M.	4:43 A.M.	6:34 A.M.	7:55 A.M.
Feb.	12	8:32 A.M.	9:36 A.M.	10:56 A.M.	12:48 P.M.	3:13 P.M.	5:52 P.M.	8:34 P.M.	11:12 P.M.	1:50 A.M.	4:15 A.M.	6:07 A.M.	7:27 A.M.
Feb.	19	8:04 A.M.	9:09 A.M.	10:29 A.M.	12:21 P.M.	2:46 P.M.	5:24 P.M.	8:06 P.M.	10:44 P.M.	1:23 A.M.	3:48 A.M.	5:39 A.M.	7:00 A.M.
Feb.	26	7:37 A.M.	8:41 A.M.	10:01 A.M.	11:53 A.M.	2:18 P.M.	4:57 P.M.	7:39 P.M.	10:17 P.M.	12:55 A.M.	3:20 A.M.	5:12 A.M.	6:32 A.M.
March	5	7:09 A.M.	8:14 A.M.	9:34 A.M.	11:26 A.M.	1:51 P.M.	4:29 P.M.	7:11 P.M.	9:49 P.M.	12:28 A.M.	2:53 A.M.	4:44 A.M.	6:05 A.M.
March	12	6:42 A.M.	7:46 A.M.	9:06 A.M.	10:58 A.M.	1:23 P.M.	4:02 P.M.	6:40 P.M.	9:22 P.M.	12:00 A.M.	2:25 A.M.	4:17 A.M.	5:37 A.M.
March	19	6:14 A.M.	7:19 A.M.	8:39 A.M.	10:31 A.M.	12:56 P.M.	3:34 P.M.	6:12 P.M.	8:54 P.M.	11:33 P.M.	1:58 A.M.	3:49 A.M.	5:09 A.M.
March	26	5:47 A.M.	6:51 A.M.	8:11 A.M.	10:03 A.M.	12:28 P.M.	3:07 P.M.	5:45 P.M.	8:27 P.M.	11:05 P.M.	1:30 A.M.	3:22 A.M.	4:42 A.M.
April	2	5:19 A.M.	6:24 A.M.	7:44 A.M.	9:36 A.M.	12:01 P.M.	2:39 P.M.	5:17 P.M.	7:59 P.M.	10:38 P.M.	1:03 A.M.	2:54 A.M.	4:14 A.M.

(continued on next page)

RISING SIGN TABLES (continued)

Zone 3	Aries	Taurus	Gemini	Cancer	Leo	Virgo	Libra	Scorpio	Sagittarius	Capricorn	Aquarius	Pisces
April 9	4:52 A.M.	5:56 A.M.	7:16 A.M.	9:08 A.M.	11:33 A.M.	2:12 P.M.	4:50 P.M.	7:32 P.M.	10:10 P.M.	12:35 A.M.	2:27 A.M.	3:47 A.M.
April 16	4:24 A.M.	5:29 A.M.	6:49 A.M.	8:41 A.M.	11:06 A.M.	1:44 P.M.	4:22 P.M.	7:04 P.M.	9:43 P.M.	12:08 A.M.	1:59 A.M.	3:19 A.M.
April 23	3:56 A.M.	5:01 A.M.	6:21 A.M.	8:13 A.M.	10:38 A.M.	1:16 P.M.	3:55 P.M.	6:33 P.M.	9:15 P.M.	11:40 P.M.	1:32 A.M.	2:52 A.M.
April 30	3:29 A.M.	4:34 A.M.	5:54 A.M.	7:45 A.M.	10:10 A.M.	12:49 P.M.	3:27 P.M.	6:05 P.M.	8:47 P.M.	11:12 P.M.	1:04 A.M.	2:24 A.M.
May 7	3:01 A.M.	4:06 A.M.	5:26 A.M.	7:18 A.M.	9:43 A.M.	12:21 P.M.	2:59 P.M.	5:38 P.M.	8:20 P.M.	10:45 P.M.	12:37 A.M.	1:57 A.M.
May 14	2:34 A.M.	3:39 A.M.	4:59 A.M.	6:50 A.M.	9:15 A.M.	11:54 A.M.	2:32 P.M.	5:10 P.M.	7:52 P.M.	10:17 P.M.	12:09 A.M.	1:29 A.M.
May 21	2:06 A.M.	3:11 A.M.	4:31 A.M.	6:23 A.M.	8:48 A.M.	11:26 A.M.	2:04 P.M.	4:42 P.M.	7:25 P.M.	9:50 P.M.	11:42 P.M.	1:02 A.M.
May 28	1:39 A.M.	2:43 A.M.	4:04 A.M.	5:55 A.M.	8:20 A.M.	10:59 A.M.	1:37 P.M.	4:15 P.M.	6:53 P.M.	9:22 P.M.	11:14 P.M.	12:34 A.M.
June 4	1:11 A.M.	2:16 A.M.	3:36 A.M.	5:28 A.M.	7:53 A.M.	10:31 A.M.	1:09 P.M.	3:47 P.M.	6:26 P.M.	8:55 P.M.	10:47 P.M.	12:07 A.M.
June 11	12:44 A.M.	1:48 A.M.	3:09 A.M.	5:00 A.M.	7:25 A.M.	10:04 A.M.	12:42 P.M.	3:20 P.M.	5:58 P.M.	8:27 P.M.	10:19 P.M.	11:39 P.M.
June 18	12:16 A.M.	1:21 A.M.	2:41 A.M.	4:33 A.M.	6:58 A.M.	9:36 A.M.	12:14 P.M.	2:52 P.M.	5:31 P.M.	8:00 P.M.	9:52 P.M.	11:12 P.M.
June 25	11:49 P.M.	12:53 A.M.	2:14 A.M.	4:05 A.M.	6:30 A.M.	9:09 A.M.	11:47 A.M.	2:25 P.M.	5:03 P.M.	7:32 P.M.	9:24 P.M.	10:44 P.M.
July 2	11:21 P.M.	12:26 A.M.	1:46 A.M.	3:38 A.M.	6:03 A.M.	8:41 A.M.	11:19 A.M.	1:57 P.M.	4:36 P.M.	7:05 P.M.	8:57 P.M.	10:17 P.M.
July 9	10:54 P.M.	11:58 P.M.	1:18 A.M.	3:10 A.M.	5:35 A.M.	8:14 A.M.	10:52 A.M.	1:30 P.M.	4:08 P.M.	6:33 P.M.	8:29 P.M.	9:49 P.M.
July 16	10:26 P.M.	11:31 P.M.	12:51 A.M.	2:43 A.M.	5:08 A.M.	7:46 A.M.	10:24 A.M.	1:02 P.M.	3:41 P.M.	6:06 P.M.	8:01 P.M.	9:22 P.M.
July 23	9:59 P.M.	11:03 P.M.	12:23 A.M.	2:15 A.M.	4:40 A.M.	7:19 A.M.	9:57 A.M.	12:35 P.M.	3:13 P.M.	5:38 P.M.	7:34 P.M.	8:54 P.M.
July 30	9:31 P.M.	10:36 P.M.	11:56 P.M.	1:48 A.M.	4:13 A.M.	6:51 A.M.	9:29 A.M.	12:07 P.M.	2:46 P.M.	5:11 P.M.	7:06 P.M.	8:27 P.M.
Aug. 6	9:04 P.M.	10:08 P.M.	11:28 P.M.	1:20 A.M.	3:45 A.M.	6:24 A.M.	9:02 A.M.	11:40 A.M.	2:18 P.M.	4:43 P.M.	6:35 P.M.	7:59 P.M.
Aug. 13	8:36 P.M.	9:41 P.M.	11:01 P.M.	12:53 A.M.	3:18 A.M.	5:56 A.M.	8:34 A.M.	11:12 A.M.	1:51 P.M.	4:16 P.M.	6:07 P.M.	7:32 P.M.
Aug. 20	8:09 P.M.	9:13 P.M.	10:33 P.M.	12:25 A.M.	2:50 A.M.	5:29 A.M.	8:07 A.M.	10:45 A.M.	1:23 P.M.	3:48 P.M.	5:40 P.M.	7:04 P.M.
Aug. 27	7:41 P.M.	8:46 P.M.	10:06 P.M.	11:58 P.M.	2:23 A.M.	5:01 A.M.	7:39 A.M.	10:17 A.M.	12:56 P.M.	3:21 P.M.	5:12 P.M.	6:33 P.M.
Sept. 3	7:14 P.M.	8:18 P.M.	9:38 P.M.	11:30 P.M.	1:55 A.M.	4:34 A.M.	7:12 A.M.	9:50 A.M.	12:28 P.M.	2:53 P.M.	4:45 P.M.	6:05 P.M.
Sept. 10	6:42 P.M.	7:51 P.M.	9:11 P.M.	11:03 P.M.	1:28 A.M.	4:06 A.M.	6:44 A.M.	9:22 A.M.	12:01 P.M.	2:26 P.M.	4:17 P.M.	5:37 P.M.
Sept. 17	6:15 P.M.	7:23 P.M.	8:43 P.M.	10:35 P.M.	1:00 A.M.	3:38 A.M.	6:17 A.M.	8:55 A.M.	11:33 A.M.	1:58 P.M.	3:50 P.M.	5:10 P.M.
Sept. 24	5:47 P.M.	6:52 P.M.	8:16 P.M.	10:07 P.M.	12:32 A.M.	3:11 A.M.	5:49 A.M.	8:27 A.M.	11:06 A.M.	1:31 P.M.	3:22 P.M.	4:42 P.M.
Oct. 1	5:20 P.M.	6:24 P.M.	7:48 P.M.	9:40 P.M.	12:05 A.M.	2:43 A.M.	5:21 A.M.	8:00 A.M.	10:38 A.M.	1:03 P.M.	2:55 P.M.	4:15 P.M.
Oct. 8	4:52 P.M.	5:57 P.M.	7:21 P.M.	9:12 P.M.	11:37 P.M.	2:16 A.M.	4:54 A.M.	7:32 A.M.	10:11 A.M.	12:36 P.M.	2:27 P.M.	3:47 P.M.
Oct. 15	4:24 P.M.	5:29 P.M.	6:49 P.M.	8:45 P.M.	11:10 P.M.	1:48 A.M.	4:26 A.M.	7:05 A.M.	9:43 A.M.	12:08 P.M.	2:00 P.M.	3:20 P.M.
Oct. 22	3:57 P.M.	5:02 P.M.	6:22 P.M.	8:17 P.M.	10:42 P.M.	1:21 A.M.	3:59 A.M.	6:37 A.M.	9:15 A.M.	11:40 A.M.	1:32 P.M.	2:52 P.M.
Oct. 29	3:29 P.M.	4:34 P.M.	5:54 P.M.	7:50 P.M.	10:15 P.M.	12:53 A.M.	3:31 A.M.	6:09 A.M.	8:48 A.M.	11:13 A.M.	1:05 P.M.	2:25 P.M.
Nov. 5	3:02 P.M.	4:07 P.M.	5:27 P.M.	7:22 P.M.	9:47 P.M.	12:26 A.M.	3:04 A.M.	5:42 A.M.	8:20 A.M.	10:45 A.M.	12:37 P.M.	1:57 P.M.
Nov. 12	2:34 P.M.	3:39 P.M.	4:59 P.M.	6:51 P.M.	9:20 P.M.	11:58 P.M.	2:36 A.M.	5:14 A.M.	7:53 A.M.	10:18 A.M.	12:10 P.M.	1:30 P.M.
Nov. 19	2:07 P.M.	3:11 P.M.	4:32 P.M.	6:23 P.M.	8:52 P.M.	11:31 P.M.	2:09 A.M.	4:47 A.M.	7:25 A.M.	9:50 A.M.	11:42 A.M.	1:02 P.M.
Nov. 26	1:39 P.M.	2:44 P.M.	4:04 P.M.	5:56 P.M.	8:25 P.M.	11:03 P.M.	1:41 A.M.	4:19 A.M.	6:58 A.M.	9:23 A.M.	11:15 A.M.	12:35 P.M.
Dec. 3	1:12 P.M.	2:16 P.M.	3:37 P.M.	5:28 P.M.	7:57 P.M.	10:36 P.M.	1:14 A.M.	3:52 A.M.	6:30 A.M.	8:55 A.M.	10:47 A.M.	12:07 P.M.
Dec. 10	12:44 P.M.	1:49 P.M.	3:09 P.M.	5:01 P.M.	7:30 P.M.	10:08 P.M.	12:46 A.M.	3:24 A.M.	6:03 A.M.	8:28 A.M.	10:20 A.M.	11:40 A.M.
Dec. 17	12:17 P.M.	1:21 P.M.	2:42 P.M.	4:33 P.M.	7:02 P.M.	9:41 P.M.	12:19 A.M.	2:57 A.M.	5:35 A.M.	8:00 A.M.	9:52 A.M.	11:12 A.M.
Dec. 24	11:49 A.M.	12:54 P.M.	2:14 P.M.	4:06 P.M.	6:31 P.M.	9:13 P.M.	11:51 P.M.	2:29 A.M.	5:08 A.M.	7:33 A.M.	9:25 A.M.	10:45 A.M.
Dec. 31	11:22 A.M.	12:26 P.M.	1:46 P.M.	3:38 P.M.	6:03 P.M.	8:46 P.M.	11:24 P.M.	2:02 A.M.	4:40 A.M.	7:05 A.M.	8:57 A.M.	10:17 A.M.

Alaska		Aries	Taurus	Gemini	Cancer	Leo	Virgo	Libra	Scorpio	Sagittarius	Capricorn	Aquarius	Pisces
Jan.	1	11:16 A.M.	11:45 A.M.	12:29 P.M.	2:05 P.M.	4:50 P.M.	8:05 P.M.	11:18 P.M.	2:31 A.M.	5:46 A.M.	8:31 A.M.	10:03 A.M.	10:47 A.M.
Jan.	8	10:49 A.M.	11:18 A.M.	12:02 P.M.	1:33 P.M.	4:22 P.M.	7:37 P.M.	10:50 P.M.	2:04 A.M.	5:19 A.M.	8:04 A.M.	9:35 A.M.	10:19 A.M.
Jan.	15	10:21 A.M.	10:50 A.M.	11:34 A.M.	1:06 P.M.	3:55 P.M.	7:10 P.M.	10:23 P.M.	1:36 A.M.	4:51 A.M.	7:36 A.M.	9:08 A.M.	9:52 A.M.
Jan.	22	9:53 A.M.	10:23 A.M.	11:07 A.M.	12:38 P.M.	3:27 P.M.	6:42 P.M.	9:55 P.M.	1:09 A.M.	4:24 A.M.	7:09 A.M.	8:40 A.M.	9:24 A.M.
Jan.	29	9:26 A.M.	9:55 A.M.	10:39 A.M.	12:11 P.M.	3:00 P.M.	6:14 P.M.	9:28 P.M.	12:41 A.M.	3:56 A.M.	6:41 A.M.	8:13 A.M.	8:57 A.M.
Feb.	5	8:58 A.M.	9:28 A.M.	10:12 A.M.	11:43 A.M.	2:32 P.M.	5:47 P.M.	9:00 P.M.	12:14 A.M.	3:28 A.M.	6:14 A.M.	7:45 A.M.	8:29 A.M.
Feb.	12	8:31 A.M.	9:00 A.M.	9:44 A.M.	11:16 A.M.	2:05 P.M.	5:19 P.M.	8:33 P.M.	11:46 P.M.	3:01 A.M.	5:46 A.M.	7:18 A.M.	8:02 A.M.
Feb.	19	8:03 A.M.	8:33 A.M.	9:17 A.M.	10:48 A.M.	1:33 P.M.	4:52 P.M.	8:05 P.M.	11:19 P.M.	2:33 A.M.	5:19 A.M.	6:50 A.M.	7:34 A.M.
Feb.	26	7:36 A.M.	8:05 A.M.	8:49 A.M.	10:21 A.M.	1:06 P.M.	4:24 P.M.	7:38 P.M.	10:51 P.M.	2:06 A.M.	4:51 A.M.	6:23 A.M.	7:07 A.M.
March	5	7:08 A.M.	7:38 A.M.	8:21 A.M.	9:53 A.M.	12:38 P.M.	3:57 P.M.	7:10 P.M.	10:24 P.M.	1:38 A.M.	4:24 A.M.	5:55 A.M.	6:39 A.M.
March	12	6:41 A.M.	7:10 A.M.	7:54 A.M.	9:26 A.M.	12:11 P.M.	3:29 P.M.	6:43 P.M.	9:56 P.M.	1:11 A.M.	3:56 A.M.	5:28 A.M.	6:12 A.M.
March	19	6:13 A.M.	6:42 A.M.	7:26 A.M.	8:58 A.M.	11:43 A.M.	3:02 P.M.	6:15 P.M.	9:29 P.M.	12:43 A.M.	3:28 A.M.	5:00 A.M.	5:44 A.M.
March	26	5:46 A.M.	6:15 A.M.	6:59 A.M.	8:31 A.M.	11:16 A.M.	2:34 P.M.	5:48 P.M.	9:01 P.M.	12:16 A.M.	3:01 A.M.	4:33 A.M.	5:17 A.M.
April	2	5:18 A.M.	5:47 A.M.	6:31 A.M.	8:03 A.M.	10:48 A.M.	2:07 P.M.	5:20 P.M.	8:34 P.M.	11:48 P.M.	2:33 A.M.	4:05 A.M.	4:49 A.M.
April	9	4:51 A.M.	5:20 A.M.	6:04 A.M.	7:36 A.M.	10:21 A.M.	1:35 P.M.	4:53 P.M.	8:06 P.M.	11:21 P.M.	2:06 A.M.	3:38 A.M.	4:21 A.M.
April	16	4:23 A.M.	4:52 A.M.	5:36 A.M.	7:08 A.M.	9:53 A.M.	1:08 P.M.	4:25 P.M.	7:39 P.M.	10:53 P.M.	1:38 A.M.	3:10 A.M.	3:54 A.M.
April	23	3:56 A.M.	4:25 A.M.	5:09 A.M.	6:40 A.M.	9:26 A.M.	12:40 P.M.	3:58 P.M.	7:11 P.M.	10:26 P.M.	1:11 A.M.	2:42 A.M.	3:26 A.M.
April	30	3:28 A.M.	3:57 A.M.	4:41 A.M.	6:13 A.M.	8:58 A.M.	12:13 P.M.	3:30 P.M.	6:44 P.M.	9:58 P.M.	12:43 A.M.	2:15 A.M.	2:59 A.M.
May	7	3:01 A.M.	3:30 A.M.	4:14 A.M.	5:45 A.M.	8:31 A.M.	11:45 A.M.	3:03 P.M.	6:16 P.M.	9:31 P.M.	12:16 A.M.	1:47 A.M.	2:31 A.M.
May	14	2:33 A.M.	3:02 A.M.	3:46 A.M.	5:18 A.M.	8:03 A.M.	11:18 A.M.	2:35 P.M.	5:49 P.M.	9:03 P.M.	11:48 P.M.	1:20 A.M.	2:04 A.M.
May	21	2:06 A.M.	2:35 A.M.	3:19 A.M.	4:50 A.M.	7:36 A.M.	10:50 A.M.	2:08 P.M.	5:21 P.M.	8:36 P.M.	11:21 P.M.	12:52 A.M.	1:36 A.M.
May	28	1:38 A.M.	2:07 A.M.	2:51 A.M.	4:23 A.M.	7:08 A.M.	10:23 A.M.	1:36 P.M.	4:53 P.M.	8:08 P.M.	10:53 P.M.	12:25 A.M.	1:09 A.M.
June	4	1:11 A.M.	1:40 A.M.	2:24 A.M.	3:55 A.M.	6:40 A.M.	9:55 A.M.	1:09 P.M.	4:26 P.M.	7:41 P.M.	10:26 P.M.	11:57 P.M.	12:41 A.M.
June	11	12:43 A.M.	1:12 A.M.	1:56 A.M.	3:28 A.M.	6:13 A.M.	9:28 A.M.	12:41 P.M.	3:58 P.M.	7:13 P.M.	9:58 P.M.	11:30 P.M.	12:14 A.M.
June	18	12:15 A.M.	12:45 A.M.	1:29 A.M.	3:00 A.M.	5:45 A.M.	9:00 A.M.	12:14 P.M.	3:31 P.M.	6:46 P.M.	9:31 P.M.	11:02 P.M.	11:46 P.M.
June	25	11:48 P.M.	12:17 A.M.	1:01 A.M.	2:33 A.M.	5:18 A.M.	8:33 A.M.	11:46 A.M.	3:03 P.M.	6:18 P.M.	9:03 P.M.	10:35 P.M.	11:19 P.M.
July	2	11:20 P.M.	11:50 P.M.	12:34 A.M.	2:05 A.M.	4:50 A.M.	8:05 A.M.	11:18 A.M.	2:36 P.M.	5:51 P.M.	8:36 P.M.	10:07 P.M.	10:51 P.M.
July	9	10:53 P.M.	11:22 P.M.	12:06 A.M.	1:38 A.M.	4:23 A.M.	7:38 A.M.	10:51 A.M.	2:08 P.M.	5:23 P.M.	8:08 P.M.	9:40 P.M.	10:24 P.M.
July	16	10:25 P.M.	10:55 P.M.	11:39 P.M.	1:10 A.M.	3:55 A.M.	7:10 A.M.	10:23 A.M.	1:37 P.M.	4:55 P.M.	7:41 P.M.	9:12 P.M.	9:56 P.M.
July	23	9:58 P.M.	10:27 P.M.	11:11 P.M.	12:43 A.M.	3:28 A.M.	6:42 A.M.	9:56 A.M.	1:09 P.M.	4:28 P.M.	7:13 P.M.	8:45 P.M.	9:29 P.M.
July	30	9:30 P.M.	10:00 P.M.	10:44 P.M.	12:15 A.M.	3:00 A.M.	6:15 A.M.	9:28 A.M.	12:42 P.M.	4:00 P.M.	6:46 P.M.	8:17 P.M.	9:01 P.M.
Aug.	6	9:03 P.M.	9:32 P.M.	10:16 P.M.	11:48 P.M.	2:33 A.M.	5:47 A.M.	9:01 A.M.	12:14 P.M.	3:33 P.M.	6:18 P.M.	7:50 P.M.	8:34 P.M.
Aug.	13	8:35 P.M.	9:05 P.M.	9:48 P.M.	11:20 P.M.	2:05 A.M.	5:20 A.M.	8:33 A.M.	11:47 A.M.	3:05 P.M.	5:51 P.M.	7:22 P.M.	8:06 P.M.
Aug.	20	8:08 P.M.	8:37 P.M.	9:21 P.M.	10:53 P.M.	1:38 A.M.	4:52 A.M.	8:06 A.M.	11:19 A.M.	2:38 P.M.	5:23 P.M.	6:55 P.M.	7:39 P.M.
Aug.	27	7:40 P.M.	8:09 P.M.	8:53 P.M.	10:25 P.M.	1:10 A.M.	4:25 A.M.	7:38 A.M.	10:52 A.M.	2:10 P.M.	4:55 P.M.	6:27 P.M.	7:11 P.M.
Sept.	3	7:13 P.M.	7:42 P.M.	8:26 P.M.	9:58 P.M.	12:43 A.M.	3:57 A.M.	7:11 A.M.	10:24 A.M.	1:39 P.M.	4:28 P.M.	6:00 P.M.	6:44 P.M.
Sept.	10	6:45 P.M.	7:14 P.M.	7:58 P.M.	9:30 P.M.	12:15 A.M.	3:30 A.M.	6:43 A.M.	9:57 A.M.	1:11 P.M.	4:00 P.M.	5:32 P.M.	6:16 P.M.
Sept.	17	6:18 P.M.	6:47 P.M.	7:31 P.M.	9:02 P.M.	11:48 P.M.	3:02 A.M.	6:16 A.M.	9:29 A.M.	12:44 P.M.	3:33 P.M.	5:05 P.M.	5:48 P.M.
Sept.	24	5:50 P.M.	6:19 P.M.	7:03 P.M.	8:35 P.M.	11:20 P.M.	2:35 A.M.	5:48 A.M.	9:02 A.M.	12:16 P.M.	3:05 P.M.	4:37 P.M.	5:21 P.M.
Oct.	1	5:23 P.M.	5:52 P.M.	6:36 P.M.	8:07 P.M.	10:53 P.M.	2:07 A.M.	5:21 A.M.	8:34 A.M.	11:49 A.M.	2:38 P.M.	4:09 P.M.	4:53 P.M.
Oct.	8	4:55 P.M.	5:24 P.M.	6:08 P.M.	7:40 P.M.	10:25 P.M.	1:40 A.M.	4:53 A.M.	8:07 A.M.	11:21 A.M.	2:10 P.M.	3:42 P.M.	4:26 P.M.
Oct.	15	4:28 P.M.	4:57 P.M.	5:41 P.M.	7:12 P.M.	9:58 P.M.	1:12 A.M.	4:26 A.M.	7:39 A.M.	10:54 A.M.	1:39 P.M.	3:14 P.M.	3:58 P.M.

(continued on next page)

RISING SIGN TABLES (continued)

Alaska

	Aries	Taurus	Gemini	Cancer	Leo	Virgo	Libra	Scorpio	Sagittarius	Capricorn	Aquarius	Pisces
Oct. 22	4:00 P.M.	4:29 P.M.	5:13 P.M.	6:45 P.M.	9:30 P.M.	12:45 A.M.	3:58 A.M.	7:12 A.M.	10:26 A.M.	1:11 P.M.	2:47 P.M.	3:31 P.M.
Oct. 29	3:33 P.M.	4:02 P.M.	4:46 P.M.	6:17 P.M.	9:02 P.M.	12:17 A.M.	3:31 A.M.	6:44 A.M.	9:59 A.M.	12:44 P.M.	2:19 P.M.	3:03 P.M.
Nov. 5	3:05 P.M.	3:34 P.M.	4:18 P.M.	5:50 P.M.	8:35 P.M.	11:50 P.M.	3:03 A.M.	6:17 A.M.	9:31 A.M.	12:16 P.M.	1:48 P.M.	2:36 P.M.
Nov. 12	2:38 P.M.	3:07 P.M.	3:51 P.M.	5:22 P.M.	8:07 P.M.	11:22 P.M.	2:36 A.M.	5:49 A.M.	9:04 A.M.	11:49 A.M.	1:20 P.M.	2:08 P.M.
Nov. 19	2:10 P.M.	2:39 P.M.	3:23 P.M.	4:55 P.M.	7:40 P.M.	10:55 P.M.	2:08 A.M.	5:21 A.M.	8:36 A.M.	11:21 A.M.	12:53 P.M.	1:37 P.M.
Nov. 26	1:39 P.M.	2:12 P.M.	2:56 P.M.	4:27 P.M.	7:12 P.M.	10:27 P.M.	1:40 A.M.	4:54 A.M.	8:09 A.M.	10:54 A.M.	12:25 P.M.	1:09 P.M.
Dec. 3	1:11 P.M.	1:40 P.M.	2:28 P.M.	4:00 P.M.	6:45 P.M.	10:00 P.M.	1:13 A.M.	4:26 A.M.	7:41 A.M.	10:26 A.M.	11:58 A.M.	12:42 P.M.
Dec. 10	12:43 P.M.	1:13 P.M.	2:01 P.M.	3:32 P.M.	6:17 P.M.	9:32 P.M.	12:45 A.M.	3:59 A.M.	7:14 A.M.	9:59 A.M.	11:30 A.M.	12:14 P.M.
Dec. 17	12:16 P.M.	12:45 P.M.	1:29 P.M.	3:05 P.M.	5:50 P.M.	9:04 P.M.	12:18 A.M.	3:31 A.M.	6:46 A.M.	9:31 A.M.	11:03 A.M.	11:47 A.M.
Dec. 24	11:48 A.M.	12:18 P.M.	1:02 P.M.	2:37 P.M.	5:22 P.M.	8:37 P.M.	11:50 P.M.	3:04 A.M.	6:19 A.M.	9:04 A.M.	10:35 A.M.	11:19 A.M.
Dec. 31	11:21 A.M.	11:50 A.M.	12:34 P.M.	2:10 P.M.	4:55 P.M.	8:09 P.M.	11:23 P.M.	2:36 A.M.	5:51 A.M.	8:36 A.M.	10:08 A.M.	10:52 A.M.

Hawaii

	Aries	Taurus	Gemini	Cancer	Leo	Virgo	Libra	Scorpio	Sagittarius	Capricorn	Aquarius	Pisces
Jan. 1	11:16 A.M.	12:50 P.M.	2:38 P.M.	4:41 P.M.	6:55 P.M.	9:09 P.M.	11:18 P.M.	1:27 A.M.	3:41 A.M.	5:55 A.M.	7:58 A.M.	9:43 A.M.
Jan. 8	10:49 A.M.	12:22 P.M.	2:11 P.M.	4:13 P.M.	6:28 P.M.	8:41 P.M.	10:50 P.M.	1:00 A.M.	3:13 A.M.	5:28 A.M.	7:30 A.M.	9:15 A.M.
Jan. 15	10:21 A.M.	11:54 A.M.	1:39 P.M.	3:46 P.M.	6:00 P.M.	8:14 P.M.	10:23 P.M.	12:32 A.M.	2:46 A.M.	5:00 A.M.	7:03 A.M.	8:47 A.M.
Jan. 22	9:53 A.M.	11:27 A.M.	1:12 P.M.	3:18 P.M.	5:32 P.M.	7:46 P.M.	9:55 P.M.	12:05 A.M.	2:18 A.M.	4:33 A.M.	6:35 A.M.	8:20 A.M.
Jan. 29	9:26 A.M.	10:59 A.M.	12:44 P.M.	2:51 P.M.	5:05 P.M.	7:19 P.M.	9:28 P.M.	11:37 P.M.	1:51 A.M.	4:05 A.M.	6:08 A.M.	7:52 A.M.
Feb. 5	8:58 A.M.	10:32 A.M.	12:17 P.M.	2:23 P.M.	4:37 P.M.	6:51 P.M.	9:00 P.M.	11:10 P.M.	1:23 A.M.	3:38 A.M.	5:40 A.M.	7:25 A.M.
Feb. 12	8:31 A.M.	10:04 A.M.	11:49 A.M.	1:52 P.M.	4:10 P.M.	6:24 P.M.	8:33 P.M.	10:42 P.M.	12:56 A.M.	3:10 A.M.	5:13 A.M.	6:57 A.M.
Feb. 19	8:03 A.M.	9:37 A.M.	11:22 A.M.	1:24 P.M.	3:42 P.M.	5:56 P.M.	8:05 P.M.	10:14 P.M.	12:28 A.M.	2:43 A.M.	4:45 A.M.	6:30 A.M.
Feb. 26	7:36 A.M.	9:09 A.M.	10:54 A.M.	12:57 P.M.	3:15 P.M.	5:29 P.M.	7:38 P.M.	9:47 P.M.	12:01 A.M.	2:15 A.M.	4:18 A.M.	6:02 A.M.
March 5	7:08 A.M.	8:42 A.M.	10:27 A.M.	12:29 P.M.	2:47 P.M.	5:01 P.M.	7:10 P.M.	9:19 P.M.	11:33 P.M.	1:48 A.M.	3:50 A.M.	5:35 A.M.
March 12	6:41 A.M.	8:14 A.M.	9:59 A.M.	12:02 P.M.	2:20 P.M.	4:34 P.M.	6:43 P.M.	8:52 P.M.	11:06 P.M.	1:20 A.M.	3:22 A.M.	5:07 A.M.
March 19	6:13 A.M.	7:47 A.M.	9:32 A.M.	11:34 A.M.	1:48 P.M.	4:06 P.M.	6:15 P.M.	8:24 P.M.	10:38 P.M.	12:52 A.M.	2:55 A.M.	4:40 A.M.
March 26	5:46 A.M.	7:19 A.M.	9:04 A.M.	11:07 A.M.	1:21 P.M.	3:39 P.M.	5:48 P.M.	7:57 P.M.	10:11 P.M.	12:25 A.M.	2:27 A.M.	4:12 A.M.
April 2	5:18 A.M.	6:52 A.M.	8:37 A.M.	10:39 A.M.	12:53 P.M.	3:11 P.M.	5:20 P.M.	7:29 P.M.	9:43 P.M.	11:57 P.M.	2:00 A.M.	3:45 A.M.
April 9	4:51 A.M.	6:24 A.M.	8:09 A.M.	10:12 A.M.	12:26 P.M.	2:44 P.M.	4:53 P.M.	7:02 P.M.	9:16 P.M.	11:30 P.M.	1:32 A.M.	3:17 A.M.
April 16	4:23 A.M.	5:57 A.M.	7:42 A.M.	9:44 A.M.	11:58 A.M.	2:16 P.M.	4:25 P.M.	6:34 P.M.	8:48 P.M.	11:02 P.M.	1:05 A.M.	2:50 A.M.
April 23	3:56 A.M.	5:29 A.M.	7:14 A.M.	9:16 A.M.	11:31 A.M.	1:45 P.M.	3:58 P.M.	6:07 P.M.	8:21 P.M.	10:35 P.M.	12:37 A.M.	2:22 A.M.
April 30	3:28 A.M.	5:02 A.M.	6:46 A.M.	8:49 A.M.	11:03 A.M.	1:17 P.M.	3:30 P.M.	5:39 P.M.	7:53 P.M.	10:07 P.M.	12:10 A.M.	1:55 A.M.
May 7	3:01 A.M.	4:34 A.M.	6:19 A.M.	8:21 A.M.	10:36 A.M.	12:49 P.M.	3:03 P.M.	5:12 P.M.	7:26 P.M.	9:40 P.M.	11:42 P.M.	1:27 A.M.
May 14	2:33 A.M.	4:07 A.M.	5:51 A.M.	7:54 A.M.	10:08 A.M.	12:22 P.M.	2:35 P.M.	4:44 P.M.	6:58 P.M.	9:12 P.M.	11:15 P.M.	1:00 A.M.
May 21	2:06 A.M.	3:39 A.M.	5:24 A.M.	7:26 A.M.	9:41 A.M.	11:54 A.M.	2:08 P.M.	4:17 P.M.	6:30 P.M.	8:45 P.M.	10:47 P.M.	12:32 A.M.
May 28	1:38 A.M.	3:12 A.M.	4:56 A.M.	6:59 A.M.	9:13 A.M.	11:27 A.M.	1:36 P.M.	3:49 P.M.	6:03 P.M.	8:17 P.M.	10:20 P.M.	12:05 A.M.
June 4	1:11 A.M.	2:44 A.M.	4:29 A.M.	6:31 A.M.	8:46 A.M.	10:59 A.M.	1:09 P.M.	3:22 P.M.	5:35 P.M.	7:50 P.M.	9:52 P.M.	11:37 P.M.
June 11	12:43 A.M.	2:17 A.M.	4:01 A.M.	6:04 A.M.	8:18 A.M.	10:32 A.M.	12:41 P.M.	2:54 P.M.	5:08 P.M.	7:22 P.M.	9:25 P.M.	11:10 P.M.
June 18	12:15 A.M.	1:49 A.M.	3:34 A.M.	5:36 A.M.	7:51 A.M.	10:04 A.M.	12:14 P.M.	2:27 P.M.	4:40 P.M.	6:55 P.M.	8:57 P.M.	10:42 P.M.
June 25	11:48 P.M.	1:21 A.M.	3:06 A.M.	5:09 A.M.	7:23 A.M.	9:37 A.M.	11:46 A.M.	1:55 P.M.	4:13 P.M.	6:27 P.M.	8:30 P.M.	10:14 P.M.
July 2	11:20 P.M.	12:54 A.M.	2:39 A.M.	4:41 A.M.	6:56 A.M.	9:09 A.M.	11:18 A.M.	1:28 P.M.	3:45 P.M.	6:00 P.M.	8:02 P.M.	9:47 P.M.
July 9	10:53 P.M.	12:26 A.M.	2:11 A.M.	4:14 A.M.	6:28 A.M.	8:42 A.M.	10:51 A.M.	1:00 P.M.	3:18 P.M.	5:32 P.M.	7:35 P.M.	9:19 P.M.

Hawaii	Aries	Taurus	Gemini	Cancer	Leo	Virgo	Libra	Scorpio	Sagittarius	Capricorn	Aquarius	Pisces
July 16	10:25 P.M.	11:59 P.M.	1:44 A.M.	3:46 A.M.	6:00 A.M.	8:14 A.M.	10:23 A.M.	12:33 P.M.	2:50 P.M.	5:05 P.M.	7:07 P.M.	8:52 P.M.
July 23	9:58 P.M.	11:31 P.M.	1:16 A.M.	3:19 A.M.	5:33 A.M.	7:47 A.M.	9:56 A.M.	12:05 P.M.	2:23 P.M.	4:37 P.M.	6:40 P.M.	8:24 P.M.
July 30	9:30 P.M.	11:04 P.M.	12:49 A.M.	2:51 A.M.	5:05 A.M.	7:19 A.M.	9:28 A.M.	11:38 A.M.	1:51 P.M.	4:10 P.M.	6:12 P.M.	7:57 P.M.
Aug. 6	9:03 P.M.	10:36 P.M.	12:21 A.M.	2:24 A.M.	4:38 A.M.	6:52 A.M.	9:01 A.M.	11:10 A.M.	1:24 P.M.	3:42 P.M.	5:44 P.M.	7:29 P.M.
Aug. 13	8:35 P.M.	10:09 P.M.	11:54 P.M.	1:56 A.M.	4:10 A.M.	6:24 A.M.	8:33 A.M.	10:42 A.M.	12:56 P.M.	3:15 P.M.	5:17 P.M.	7:02 P.M.
Aug. 20	8:08 P.M.	9:41 P.M.	11:26 P.M.	1:29 A.M.	3:43 A.M.	5:57 A.M.	8:06 A.M.	10:15 A.M.	12:29 P.M.	2:47 P.M.	4:49 P.M.	6:34 P.M.
Aug. 27	7:40 P.M.	9:14 P.M.	10:59 P.M.	1:01 A.M.	3:15 A.M.	5:29 A.M.	7:38 A.M.	9:47 A.M.	12:01 P.M.	2:19 P.M.	4:22 P.M.	6:07 P.M.
Sept. 3	7:13 P.M.	8:46 P.M.	10:31 P.M.	12:34 A.M.	2:48 A.M.	5:02 A.M.	7:11 A.M.	9:20 A.M.	11:34 A.M.	1:48 P.M.	3:54 P.M.	5:39 P.M.
Sept. 10	6:45 P.M.	8:19 P.M.	10:04 P.M.	12:06 A.M.	2:20 A.M.	4:34 A.M.	6:43 A.M.	8:52 A.M.	11:06 A.M.	1:20 P.M.	3:27 P.M.	5:12 P.M.
Sept. 17	6:18 P.M.	7:51 P.M.	9:36 P.M.	11:38 P.M.	1:53 A.M.	4:07 A.M.	6:16 A.M.	8:25 A.M.	10:39 A.M.	12:53 P.M.	2:59 P.M.	4:44 P.M.
Sept. 24	5:50 P.M.	7:24 P.M.	9:08 P.M.	11:11 P.M.	1:25 A.M.	3:39 A.M.	5:48 A.M.	7:57 A.M.	10:11 A.M.	12:25 P.M.	2:32 P.M.	4:17 P.M.
Oct. 1	5:23 P.M.	6:56 P.M.	8:41 P.M.	10:43 P.M.	12:58 A.M.	3:12 A.M.	5:21 A.M.	7:30 A.M.	9:44 A.M.	11:58 A.M.	2:04 P.M.	3:49 P.M.
Oct. 8	4:55 P.M.	6:29 P.M.	8:13 P.M.	10:16 P.M.	12:30 A.M.	2:44 A.M.	4:53 A.M.	7:02 A.M.	9:16 A.M.	11:30 A.M.	1:33 P.M.	3:22 P.M.
Oct. 15	4:28 P.M.	6:01 P.M.	7:46 P.M.	9:48 P.M.	12:03 A.M.	2:16 A.M.	4:26 A.M.	6:35 A.M.	8:49 A.M.	11:03 A.M.	1:05 P.M.	2:54 P.M.
Oct. 22	4:00 P.M.	5:34 P.M.	7:18 P.M.	9:21 P.M.	11:35 P.M.	1:49 A.M.	3:58 A.M.	6:07 A.M.	8:21 A.M.	10:35 A.M.	12:38 P.M.	2:27 P.M.
Oct. 29	3:33 P.M.	5:06 P.M.	6:51 P.M.	8:53 P.M.	11:08 P.M.	1:21 A.M.	3:31 A.M.	5:40 A.M.	7:54 A.M.	10:08 A.M.	12:10 P.M.	1:55 P.M.
Nov. 5	3:05 P.M.	4:39 P.M.	6:23 P.M.	8:26 P.M.	10:40 P.M.	12:54 A.M.	3:03 A.M.	5:12 A.M.	7:26 A.M.	9:40 A.M.	11:43 A.M.	1:28 P.M.
Nov. 12	2:38 P.M.	4:11 P.M.	5:56 P.M.	7:58 P.M.	10:13 P.M.	12:26 A.M.	2:36 A.M.	4:45 A.M.	6:58 A.M.	9:13 A.M.	11:15 A.M.	1:00 P.M.
Nov. 19	2:10 P.M.	3:43 P.M.	5:28 P.M.	7:31 P.M.	9:45 P.M.	11:59 P.M.	2:08 A.M.	4:17 A.M.	6:31 A.M.	8:45 A.M.	10:48 A.M.	12:33 P.M.
Nov. 26	1:39 P.M.	3:16 P.M.	5:01 P.M.	7:03 P.M.	9:18 P.M.	11:31 P.M.	1:40 A.M.	3:50 A.M.	6:03 A.M.	8:18 A.M.	10:20 A.M.	12:05 P.M.
Dec. 3	1:11 P.M.	2:48 P.M.	4:33 P.M.	6:36 P.M.	8:50 P.M.	11:04 P.M.	1:13 A.M.	3:22 A.M.	5:36 A.M.	7:50 A.M.	9:53 A.M.	11:37 A.M.
Dec. 10	12:43 P.M.	2:21 P.M.	4:06 P.M.	6:08 P.M.	8:22 P.M.	10:36 P.M.	12:45 A.M.	2:55 A.M.	5:08 A.M.	7:23 A.M.	9:25 A.M.	11:10 A.M.
Dec. 17	12:16 P.M.	1:49 P.M.	3:38 P.M.	5:41 P.M.	7:55 P.M.	10:09 P.M.	12:18 A.M.	2:27 A.M.	4:41 A.M.	6:55 A.M.	8:58 A.M.	10:42 A.M.
Dec. 24	11:48 A.M.	1:22 P.M.	3:11 P.M.	5:13 P.M.	7:27 P.M.	9:41 P.M.	11:50 P.M.	2:00 A.M.	4:13 A.M.	6:28 A.M.	8:30 A.M.	10:15 A.M.
Dec. 31	11:21 A.M.	12:54 P.M.	2:43 P.M.	4:46 P.M.	7:00 P.M.	9:14 P.M.	11:23 P.M.	1:32 A.M.	3:46 A.M.	6:00 A.M.	8:03 A.M.	9:47 A.M.

There's a Place for You—Visit the Moon

"A sane environment is one in which there is room to be crazy. A crazy environment is one in which there is no room to be sane."
AUTHOR SOLOMON SHORT

Where do you thrive? Under what conditions do you accomplish your best work? What kind of environment nurtures your talents and keeps you purring? If you need answers to these questions, take a look at the Moon. No need to hop on the next space shuttle out of Cape Canaveral—just ascertain your Moon sign in the tables starting on page 202.

The Moon represents your emotions and instincts, the part of you that meets basic needs—your own and other people's. Emotions fluctuate largely because of environmental and stress factors. If the atmosphere and stress of your job make you unhappy in body or mind, you won't perform well for long; if your basic needs aren't met, you can hardly meet career demands.

But you can do something about these things by finding or creating the conditions where you *will* feel healthy and energetic. Your Moon sign may not be able to determine whether you should take a job on an Alaskan oil tanker or at an elementary school, but it can help you answer the fundamental question, "What do I need from my work environment and activities to feel well enough to perform my duties at my best?"

DO YOU SWIM WITH THE SHARKS, DOLPHINS, OR JELLYFISH? YOUR HABITAT FOR PROSPERITY

The word *zodiac* translates to "the parade of animals" and comes from the same Greek root as the word *zoo*. At the best zoos, each species gets its own habitat and special diet. Tigers pace the desert land while penguins swim in the pool. It makes ecological sense, every animal benefiting from the conditions to which nature suited it. So what's your habitat for prosperity? Your Moon sign can help you find it!

TAKE A CHILL PILL! STRESS-BUSTERS!

All work situations cause stress. Some stress is good because it drives you to work harder and smarter. Some stress is bad because it robs you of your peace of mind and can, according to study upon study, cause very real medical problems. You're not a machine! Don't expect yourself to operate like one. Beat toxic stress before it beats you. To your personal list of already tried-and-trusted solutions, add some of Dr. Matt's stress-busters, specially formulated to meet the needs of your individual Moon sign.

Moon in Aries

HABITAT FOR PROSPERITY: Excitement is a must. Exhilaration is even better. While a racetrack may drive away less hearty folks, it's got the kind of loud and competitive atmosphere that would keep you happy as a polar bear on the North Pole. Keep your work environment *fresh*. Dull or worn-out surroundings are bound to plunge you into a rut. Your ideal habitat also needs room for solitude. Though constant commotion is acceptable and even desirable, there's only room for one driver in your zooming race car of a career. Do you have a low-key Sun sign? Doesn't matter—somewhere in you lurks the *need* for *speed*.

STRESS-BUSTERS! Sleep. Get more of it. Even if you *can* go strong on four hours a night, don't. Plan vacations that aren't business trips. And don't bother flying 14 hours to scuba dive off the Great Barrier Reef—a nice, relaxing long weekend in the country (with some spontaneous excitement) will do just fine. If dozing off or getting away isn't an option, start a pet project whose rewards you really *like*, maybe a career-enhancing undertaking that makes you more self-reliant, such as learning to use new software or brewing your own coffee for a change!

Moon in Taurus

HABITAT FOR PROSPERITY: Even more than most, you rely on your environment for sustenance. You need plenty of personal space. If you work from home, make sure you have a proper home office. If you travel from client to client, establish a home base. Look for a milieu where you can get *comfortable*. Your workplace can be small, but it's got to provide a haven from the obnoxious outside world. And let's not forget *functional*. If the work space and its equipment aren't easy to use and downright handy, you'll never get anything done.

STRESS-BUSTERS! Listen to music. Go for retail therapy (i.e., shop till you drop!). Food works too, but overindulgence doesn't, so find one treat that'll keep you going between meetings. While escaping the day-to-day relieves stress for some Moon signs, it'll probably just exacerbate your tension level. So stay put, but take lots of little breaks. With the Moon in Taurus, your five senses are hypersensitive. Lucky you! Stimulate all five, preferably one or two at a time, and the stress will melt away like ice cubes on a hot day.

Moon in Gemini

HABITAT FOR PROSPERITY: Make a wish! Like a dandelion seed in the wind, you seem able to go anywhere and put down roots. Invest in a good backpack or briefcase so wherever you end up, you can get right to work. Ideally, you'll land in an active environment with a constant hubbub—and not stuck under a supervisor's thumb. Visualize an old-fashioned newspaper office with the constant clickety-clack of typewriter keys and ringing of telephones. It ain't glamorous, but it's seldom dull, and it typifies the kind of environment that succors a Gemini Moon. Then again, you might prefer to work out of your car, coming and going as you like, talking on the cell phone, changing gears, slurping coffee, and surfing radio stations. But keep your eyes on the road! With all those distractions it can be easy to get off course.

STRESS-BUSTERS! Stop the chatter. At some point talk becomes counterproductive. Just a few moments of silence—that's what you need. Close the door. Turn off the phone. Assess how you're feeling: hot? cold? angry? accomplished? Maybe all those things at once. You don't have to diagnose

yourself, but *observe* yourself before acting on a jumble of conflicting emotions. If silence fails, stimulate a noncerebral part of your body. My Moon-in-Gemini attorney swims a mile every day; he calls it his moving meditation. Still stressed? Eliminate options. By consciously narrowing down the number of choices you're willing to consider, you'll banish much of the anxiety of decision-making.

Moon in Cancer

HABITAT FOR PROSPERITY: Since climbing back into the womb is not an option, you'll need to look for another kind of nurturing, caring, comforting environment. Steer clear of settings where you'll have to put up with bullies and excessive criticism. Dr. Matt also recommends quality furnishings that won't disintegrate, so no folding chairs or pictures hung with tacks. Even if you spend little time in your work space or anticipate relocating in six months, you'll work *better* while you're there if the place feels more like a castle than a campsite. You may not appreciate absolute solitude, but you don't want just anyone trespassing on your territory or possessions. Don't be afraid to draw boundaries—for example, allow coworkers to borrow your Mont Blanc fountain pen, but only when it's bolted to your desk!

> **"Everyone is under stress. . . . The only human body without stress is a corpse."**
> CERTIFIED MANAGEMENT CONSULTANT AND AUTHOR ROGER HERMAN

STRESS-BUSTERS! Care for something—the supply closet, a desktop gardenia, a goldfish. Don't let emotions overwhelm you—don't hide them, but when they start to get the best of you, focus on something else, preferably a purely cognitive exercise like alphabetizing the bookshelves. Don't just pout, ask for what you really want. Inner calm is essential for you. Prioritize your responsibilities and back out of those that seem unnecessary. For best results, you need to focus on your stress-buster as much as your job. Immerse yourself in relaxation. The object is to return *renewed*, not just rested.

Moon in Leo

HABITAT FOR PROSPERITY: You've heard of "dress for success." Well, with Moon in Leo you need to *decorate* for success. The rustic work environment isn't for you. Your ideal work space should display bright colors, with interesting shapes and designs. You'll have a hard time in a work setting that demands you leave your personality at home; in fact, your area really needs to exude the right image—preferably *your* image. If this sounds out of line with reality, don't lose heart. Until you have your own private office suite, embellish your desk or even your uniform with artifacts of your individuality.

STRESS-BUSTERS! Take up a creative hobby—preferably, since you hate to wait around, something that yields near-immediate gratification. Or designate yourself the company photographer; in moments of stress, tell everyone to stop, take a deep breath, and say *cheese*. Find a work rhythm that is guided by your needs rather than by external forces—canceling one appointment to make another. Make time for each thing and give it the time it deserves. Pamper yourself. Get a massage, a haircut—anything that caters to you. If that fails, try "tricking" yourself into vacation mode. Grab a pal, head for the nearest bar and order a tall drink with extra cherries and paper umbrellas—even if it's just a Diet Coke you can pretend you're vacationing somewhere far, far away.

Moon in Virgo

HABITAT FOR PROSPERITY: You do best in a workplace where everyone is self-sufficient and behaves like an adult. If they need help, they ask for it; they don't wait for someone to rescue them. You need to know what to expect and can get painfully uneasy when too many curve balls are thrown in your direction. You need to be able to stay on top of all you have to do. Enough to do is just right for you—not too little, not too much, just enough. You can't stand nebulous assignments or evasive coworkers. In your ideal situation, everybody's on the same page and equally committed to getting the job done without too much overtime. Keep it neat! You'll have a hard time reaching your full potential in a setting where you have to look hard to find the Yellow Pages.

STRESS-BUSTERS! Complain. Piss and moan. Get it off your chest, for a little while, but then let it rest. Upchucking your grievances eventually *induces* stress rather than relieves it. Instead, find one *little* activity over which you can exert total control. Clean off your desk. Organize your computer. Write a to-do list. If you just can't leave the stressful problem alone, go back to square one. Pare it down to its most fundamental, most manageable core. Proceed from there. Before you reach for the aspirin or a fourth cup of coffee, ask yourself, "Do I want the stress to disappear, or do I need the stress to make me feel alive and important?" Look for serenity, not just the absence of stress, they're not the same.

Moon in Libra

HABITAT FOR PROSPERITY: A pretty place brings out your best. Try earthy, soothing colors. Fresh flowers. Maybe even a view. If you've got to have clutter, arrange it esthetically. A congenial atmosphere fulfills your need to have not only coworkers but friends in the workplace, too. Although it's impossible, not to mention potentially unwise, to become bosom buddies with everyone on the job, you won't fare well in an environment where the intimacy never goes beyond first names. On the other hand, constant companionship will drive you batty. Remember! Make your work space pleasant and refined, even a little artsy, without too many obnoxious noises, odors, or rude people.

STRESS-BUSTERS! Talk to a friend—a good friend. If there's not one around, make friends with a book, or anything else that reminds you you're not alone in your stress. Stop stewing. Don't dwell on gruff or discourteous remarks made by jerks. Do something *civilized*. Get dressed up—if you look like a million bucks you're more likely to *feel* like a million bucks. Go on a harmless "date"—like take your assistant out for a banana split. Invite a client to tea at the Ritz or coffee at Starbucks. Be nice to the person who's bothering you. It might not make him less difficult, but you'll feel better having done the noble deed.

Moon in Scorpio

HABITAT FOR PROSPERITY: Do not disturb, *s'il vous plaît*. While you do fine with lots of commotion *around* you, full-fledged interruptions disrupt your work

style. Lack of privacy or other interference makes you queasy. You won't take kindly to a long line of auditors and supervisors checking up on your work. So in your optimal occupational habitat, trust is a necessity. Even if you're good at putting up a front, don't spend too much time wearing a facade. Constant performance will burn you out. Getting work done, however, will make you glow like an Olympic medal. You need a nonthreatening work environment with plenty of room for self-improvement—so say "Thanks, but no thanks" to the job where your work is limited to one area and you never learn another skill. It's all about taking chances. For a clean bill of mental health, you need to take chances, ones that make you grow as a professional and a human being. Choose a career landscape that breeds risk-taking and change.

STRESS-BUSTERS! Accomplish something—any little thing at all. Wash out your coffee mug. Polish your shoes. You won't eliminate the stress, but you can contain it by feeling you're making progress. Enforce periodic breaks. Though you may be able to immerse yourself in work for hours on end, it will leave you depleted and vulnerable to mind-altering, physically painful tension. Remember to pace yourself and conserve energy for the final approaching deadline. Meanwhile, warn coworkers about your darker side. That way, when your hidden idiosyncrasies erupt during a stressful situation, coworkers will be prepared—and won't compound your problems by wondering how Dr. Jekyll just turned into Mr. Hyde.

Moon in Sagittarius

HABITAT FOR PROSPERITY: You've got major claustrophobia, so pay special attention to picking a work environment where you don't feel trapped. Try a job that involves travel, calling on clients in different locales, or maybe even driving around in a semi. It helps if you walk or bicycle to work, or hop on your in-line skates and whiz by the cars stuck in traffic. If you've got far too long a commute for that, try listening to books on tape on your way. No matter what, remember to *never stop learning*. For you, an office without sufficient reading material and a little view of the changing leaves may as well be a Medieval torture chamber. At the very least, adorn your cubicle with a three-dollar poster of Niagara Falls and a thought-provoking quotation from Aristotle or your favorite rock 'n' roll guru.

STRESS-BUSTERS! Get out. Get physical. Stop beating your head against a stressful situation. How? Simplify. Reduce the problem to its lowest com-

mon denominator. Try to objectively ascertain whether it's as big a deal as it feels right now. In rectifying the situation, think about the long term—don't just patch it with a piece of tape! If you realize it's not as big a deal as you thought, let it go. Fortunately, you have one of the least stress-sensitive Moon signs, and are able to laugh off situations that would crush the rest of us. Developing your game plan in advance can save you from having to make last-minute decisions.

Moon in Capricorn

HABITAT FOR PROSPERITY: You can master many environments, from desk job to football field. The respectability matters more than the actual location of your occupational environment. You won't last long anywhere you don't feel proud to walk through the doors every morning. Your ideal professional habitat would also provide the right tools for the job—equipment that functions, support staff with proper training, and the conveniences that go along with being a professional in your industry. Don't forget about room to rest, too, especially since you tend to burn the midnight oil.

> **"If your desk isn't cluttered, you probably aren't doing your job."**
> ITT CORPORATION CHAIRMAN
> HAROLD GENEEN

STRESS-BUSTERS! Haste makes you crazy. Be persistent, though; running from the eye of the storm won't be a relief, it will only make you feel out of the loop. Don't deprive yourself too much—not of food, sleep, or companionship. Throw out useless clutter; it's bound to raise your blood pressure. Have a conversation with an older person, an expert, someone you admire—just call them up, offer to buy lunch, and indulge in picking their brain and hearing their stories. You'll find yourself energized by their wisdom. Whatever you do, take stress-busting seriously. Don't let anxiety fry your circuits. An overloaded Capricorn Moon can sabotage the rest of your Professional Planetary Profile.

Moon in Aquarius

HABITAT FOR PROSPERITY: It doesn't matter what your Sun sign is; with an Aquarius Moon, you need to work someplace where you can let loose a little, maybe a lot—so *no blank white walls!* Unconventional settings make

you feel right at home. Surround yourself with unusual colors and quirky designs. It's a boon if you can work for or among your "identity community." Consider, for example, an African American business district, a gay and lesbian chamber of commerce, an Episcopalian agency. In any case, solidarity in the workplace counts for more than oak paneling. You'd like every day to be Casual Friday, and probably won't maximize your abilities in an environment that emphasizes bureaucracies or traditional hierarchical role models. Most importantly, find friends. "Strictly professional" workplace relations will leave you feeling adrift at sea.

STRESS-BUSTERS! Cut through red tape before it chokes you. If the stress of nine to five gets you down, look into becoming a consultant or finding a job with "flex time." Let your mind wander to big open spaces. Dust off your list of goals or (if you've already completed one) reread your Professional Planetary Profile. Is it time for new goals? Where do you want to be in five years? A born thinker, you'll benefit from stress-busters that are more than mind-numbing distractions. Volunteer for instance, to start a company-wide canned food drive. Redesign your work environment. Break a few outmoded rules. And remain optimistic. If you can choose to see the glass as half empty or half full, the Aquarian Moon part of you will appreciate the half full perspective. Stay grounded. Your mind, emotions, and imagination like to soar. That's grand! But prevent the stress of flying too high by holding on to something familiar, like a tried-and-trusted routine.

Moon in Pisces

HABITAT FOR PROSPERITY: Whereas a Moon-in-Aquarius professional instinctively seeks an unconventional workplace, you go for a downright off-the-beaten-track career environment. Perhaps you'd excel in a huge public institution where you could get lost among the hordes—at least during the lunch hour. Or maybe you'd find it reassuring to work somewhere secluded, or piloting an airplane 30,000 feet above civilization. You can handle many settings that others can't, like hospitals, prisons, or outer space research labs. Cramped quarters won't likely get the best of you, mostly because your surroundings matter less than your *inner* landscape. It's the space between your ears where you need to be comfortable in order to do your best work. So decorate your desk with one or two objects that hold special meaning—they'll comfort you in tense times. But remember: Wherever you go, there you are. Don't forget to do spring cleaning up there in the attic of your mind once in a while!

STRESS-BUSTERS! Listen to your instincts. Start anticipating critical situations before they reach their peak. If a lucrative project sets off your internal fire alarm, think twice about accepting it. Be your own best friend. This is the secret to self-sufficiency in any environment. So don't berate yourself for "failure" or demand that impossible goals be met by tomorrow morning 9 A.M. Have you tried yoga? Or meditation? You can do many exercises without leaving your desk, all of which serve to *separate you from stress* long enough to get your bearings back. Another technique is to write a letter, spilling your guts on the page, and seal it in envelope addressed to no one; give the stress *away,* and get on with your day. Finally, since the Moon rules feelings and Pisces the feet, don't overlook the stress-busting benefits of a good foot rub!

How to Find Your Moon Sign—Easy as 1-2-3

1. In the following Moon tables, look up the year of your birth, and, within that year, find the month of your birth.

2. In that month, run your finger down the far-left column until you find your birth *day.*

3. Eureka! Directly to the right of your birthday is your Moon sign. When you find your Moon sign, write it down in your Planetary Positions Chart on page 377.

But wait! The Moon moves very fast, changing signs every two and a half days, so there's an almost 50-50 chance it changed signs right *on* your birthday. Uh oh! If your birthday lists *two* signs (starting with one sign and, farther to the right, changing to another later that same day), you'll want to determine if you were born *before* or *after* the change.

DETERMINING YOUR SIGN DOWN TO THE MINUTE

There are just two simple steps in converting your birth time to see if the Moon (or any planet) changed signs before or after you were born.

Step 1: Convert to Eastern Time. As you know, when it's high noon in New York, it's 9:00 A.M. in Los Angeles. Those cities are three time zones apart. So a kid born at noon in Los Angeles is actually born at 3:00 P.M. in New York time. Well, the Moon and other planetary tables in this book are calculated for Eastern Standard Time (like New York), so you'll want to

make sure you're comparing apples and apples (not apples and oranges) by converting *your* birth time zone to the Eastern Time Zone.

If you were born in the Eastern Time Zone (like New York, Boston, Tallahassee), you're all set. Go to Step 2.

If you were born in the Central Time Zone (like Chicago, St. Louis, Houston), *add one hour* to convert your birth time to Eastern time.

If you were born in the Mountain Time Zone (like Sante Fe, Denver), *add two hours* to get Eastern Time.

If you were born in the Pacific Time Zone (like Los Angeles, San Francisco, Las Vegas, Seattle), *add three hours* to get Eastern Time.

If you were born outside the continental United States, try to figure out how many time zones away from Eastern Time (or, simply, New York) you were born. Remember! If you were born in the opposite direction, you'll *subtract* hours instead of add. (For example, if you were born in London, subtract five hours from your birth time to get Eastern Time.)

Step 2: Convert to Standard Time. Were you born during Daylight Savings Time? That's when most (but not all!) places in American "spring" the clocks forward in April and "fall" back in October. If you were born between April and October, chances are that Daylight Savings Time was in effect. To be sure, ask Mom or call the library. If the clocks were indeed on Daylight Savings Time, *subtract one hour* from the Eastern Time you found in Step 1. Now you have the Eastern *Standard* Time of your birth.

If you were born between November and March (fall and winter babies!) you were definitely *not* born during Daylight Savings Time, so in Step 1 you already determined the Eastern Standard Time of your birth.

Hurray! Now, in these Moon tables, you can check to see if you were born before or after the Moon changed signs.

EXAMPLE

For a trial run, let's figure out Oprah Winfrey's Moon sign using the above guidelines.

According to one source, Oprah was born on January 29, 1954, at 12:00 P.M. (noon) in Noxapater, Mississippi.

1. In the Moon tables we turn to 1954, then to January.

2. We look in the far-left column to find the day, 29.

3. To the right of 29 is written Sagittarius. That's it! Oprah has the Moon in Sagittarius, so she'd write that down in her Planetary Positions Chart on page 377, and in this chapter she'd check out the entry for Moon in Sagittarius.

The Moon didn't change signs on Oprah's birthday (Sagittarius is the only sign listed), so she doesn't need to convert her birth time. But just for the sake of practice, let's pretend she was born instead on the *first* of January, 1954, at noon in Mississippi.

You'll notice in the Moon tables that on January 1, 1954, the Moon moved from Scorpio to Sagittarius at 11:39 A.M. Eastern Standard Time. Was that before or after Oprah was born?

Step 1: Convert to Eastern Time. Mississippi is in the Central Time Zone. That means we *add one hour* to Oprah's birth time. Twelve P.M. (noon) plus one hour comes to 1:00 P.M. That's Oprah's Eastern Time of birth.

Step 2: Convert to Standard Time. Oprah was born in January. That's not the season for Daylight Savings Time. So her birth time is already Standard. (We do *not* subtract an hour for Daylight Savings Time.)

Aha! Oprah, we've discovered, was born at 1:00 P.M. Eastern Standard Time. Now we look again at the Moon table for January 1, 1954. At that time, was the Moon in Scorpio or Sagittarius? Well, it may have started off the day in Scorpio, but at 11:39 A.M. Eastern Standard Time it *moved* to Sagittarius. Oprah was born almost an hour and twenty-one minutes *after* the Moon shifted to Sagittarius, so even in this example Oprah still has the Moon in Sagittarius.

If you need to, you can determine any planet's change down to the minute!

MOON SIGN TABLES
1940

JANUARY

1	Virgo	5:43 A.M.	Libra
2	Libra		
3	Libra	9:36 A.M.	Scorpio
4	Scorpio		
5	Scorpio	3:12 P.M.	Sagittarius
6	Sagittarius		
7	Sagittarius	10:30 P.M.	Capricorn
8	Capricorn		
9	Capricorn		
10	Capricorn	7:42 A.M.	Aquarius
11	Aquarius		
12	Aquarius	7:03 P.M.	Pisces
13	Pisces		
14	Pisces		
15	Pisces	7:56 A.M.	Aries
16	Aries		
17	Aries	8:15 P.M.	Taurus
18	Taurus		
19	Taurus		
20	Taurus	5:32 A.M.	Gemini
21	Gemini		
22	Gemini	10:35 A.M.	Cancer
23	Cancer		
24	Cancer	12:10 P.M.	Leo
25	Leo		
26	Leo	12:12 P.M.	Virgo
27	Virgo		
28	Virgo	12:43 P.M.	Libra
29	Libra		
30	Libra	3:17 P.M.	Scorpio
31	Scorpio		

FEBRUARY

1	Scorpio	8:36 P.M.	Sagittarius
2	Sagittarius		
3	Sagittarius		
4	Sagittarius	4:27 A.M.	Capricorn
5	Capricorn		
6	Capricorn	2:21 P.M.	Aquarius
7	Aquarius		
8	Aquarius		
9	Aquarius	1:58 A.M.	Pisces
10	Pisces		
11	Pisces	2:49 P.M.	Aries
12	Aries		
13	Aries		
14	Aries	3:36 A.M.	Taurus
15	Taurus		
16	Taurus	2:10 P.M.	Gemini
17	Gemini		
18	Gemini	8:46 P.M.	Cancer
19	Cancer		
20	Cancer	11:19 P.M.	Leo
21	Leo		
22	Leo	11:11 P.M.	Virgo
23	Virgo		
24	Virgo	10:29 P.M.	Libra
25	Libra		
26	Libra	11:13 P.M.	Scorpio
27	Scorpio		
28	Scorpio		
29	Scorpio	2:54 A.M.	Sagittarius

MARCH

1	Sagittarius		
2	Sagittarius	10:02 A.M.	Capricorn

(March continued)

3	Capricorn		
4	Capricorn	8:07 P.M.	Aquarius
5	Aquarius		
6	Aquarius		
7	Aquarius	8:07 P.M.	Pisces
8	Pisces		
9	Pisces	9:01 P.M.	Aries
10	Aries		
11	Aries		
12	Aries	9:44 A.M.	Taurus
13	Taurus		
14	Taurus	8:53 P.M.	Gemini
15	Gemini		
16	Gemini		
17	Gemini	4:57 A.M.	Cancer
18	Cancer		
19	Cancer	9:15 A.M.	Leo
20	Leo		
21	Leo	10:20 A.M.	Virgo
22	Virgo		
23	Virgo	9:47 A.M.	Libra
24	Libra		
25	Libra	9:33 A.M.	Scorpio
26	Scorpio		
27	Scorpio	11:31 A.M.	Sagittarius
28	Sagittarius		
29	Sagittarius	5:00 P.M.	Capricorn
30	Capricorn		
31	Capricorn		

APRIL

1	Capricorn	2:13 A.M.	Aquarius
2	Aquarius		
3	Aquarius	2:11 P.M.	Pisces
4	Pisces		
5	Pisces		
6	Pisces	3:10 A.M.	Aries
7	Aries		
8	Aries	3:39 P.M.	Taurus
9	Taurus		
10	Taurus		
11	Taurus	2:32 A.M.	Gemini
12	Gemini		
13	Gemini	11:04 A.M.	Cancer
14	Cancer		
15	Cancer	4:44 P.M.	Leo
16	Leo		
17	Leo	7:34 P.M.	Virgo
18	Virgo		
19	Virgo	8:23 P.M.	Libra
20	Libra		
21	Libra	8:33 P.M.	Scorpio
22	Scorpio		
23	Scorpio	9:48 P.M.	Sagittarius
24	Sagittarius		
25	Sagittarius		
26	Sagittarius	1:50 A.M.	Capricorn
27	Capricorn		
28	Capricorn	9:39 A.M.	Aquarius
29	Aquarius		
30	Aquarius	8:56 P.M.	Pisces

MAY

1	Pisces		
2	Pisces		
3	Pisces	9:52 A.M.	Aries
4	Aries		

(May continued)

5	Aries	10:12 P.M.	Taurus
6	Taurus		
7	Taurus		
8	Taurus	8:34 A.M.	Gemini
9	Gemini		
10	Gemini	4:33 P.M.	Cancer
11	Cancer		
12	Cancer	10:22 P.M.	Leo
13	Leo		
14	Leo		
15	Leo	2:18 A.M.	Virgo
16	Virgo		
17	Virgo	4:40 A.M.	Libra
18	Libra		
19	Libra	6:12 A.M.	Scorpio
20	Scorpio		
21	Scorpio	8:00 A.M.	Sagittarius
22	Sagittarius		
23	Sagittarius	11:35 A.M.	Capricorn
24	Capricorn		
25	Capricorn	6:19 P.M.	Aquarius
26	Aquarius		
27	Aquarius		
28	Aquarius	4:39 A.M.	Pisces
29	Pisces		
30	Pisces	5:18 P.M.	Aries
31	Aries		

JUNE

1	Aries		
2	Aries	5:44 A.M.	Taurus
3	Taurus		
4	Taurus	3:49 P.M.	Gemini
5	Gemini		
6	Gemini	11:02 P.M.	Cancer
7	Cancer		
8	Cancer		
9	Cancer	4:00 A.M.	Leo
10	Leo		
11	Leo	7:41 A.M.	Virgo
12	Virgo		
13	Virgo	10:43 A.M.	Libra
14	Libra		
15	Libra	1:31 P.M.	Scorpio
16	Scorpio		
17	Scorpio	4:34 P.M.	Sagittarius
18	Sagittarius		
19	Sagittarius	8:44 P.M.	Capricorn
20	Capricorn		
21	Capricorn		
22	Capricorn	3:15 A.M.	Aquarius
23	Aquarius		
24	Aquarius	12:55 P.M.	Pisces
25	Pisces		
26	Pisces		
27	Pisces	1:13 A.M.	Aries
28	Aries		
29	Aries	1:52 P.M.	Taurus
30	Taurus		

JULY

1	Taurus		
2	Taurus	12:15 A.M.	Gemini
3	Gemini		
4	Gemini	7:10 A.M.	Cancer
5	Cancer		
6	Cancer	11:12 A.M.	Leo

7	Leo		
8	Leo	1:44 P.M.	Virgo
9	Virgo		
10	Virgo	4:07 P.M.	Libra
11	Libra		
12	Libra	7:07 P.M.	Scorpio
13	Scorpio		
14	Scorpio	11:05 P.M.	Sagittarius
15	Sagittarius		
16	Sagittarius		
17	Sagittarius	4:17 A.M.	Capricorn
18	Capricorn		
19	Capricorn	11:22 A.M.	Aquarius
20	Aquarius		
21	Aquarius	8:58 P.M.	Pisces
22	Pisces		
23	Pisces		
24	Pisces	9:01 A.M.	Aries
25	Aries		
26	Aries	9:56 P.M.	Taurus
27	Taurus		
28	Taurus		
29	Taurus	9:04 A.M.	Gemini
30	Gemini		
31	Gemini	4:32 P.M.	Cancer

AUGUST

1	Cancer		
2	Cancer	8:20 P.M.	Leo
3	Leo		
4	Leo	9:50 P.M.	Virgo
5	Virgo		
6	Virgo	10:50 P.M.	Libra
7	Libra		
8	Libra		
9	Libra	12:46 A.M.	Scorpio
10	Scorpio		
11	Scorpio	4:29 A.M.	Sagittarius
12	Sagittarius		
13	Sagittarius	10:15 A.M.	Capricorn
14	Capricorn		
15	Capricorn	6:07 P.M.	Aquarius
16	Aquarius		
17	Aquarius		
18	Aquarius	4:10 A.M.	Pisces
19	Pisces		
20	Pisces	4:14 P.M.	Aries
21	Aries		
22	Aries		
23	Aries	5:17 A.M.	Taurus
24	Taurus		
25	Taurus	5:13 P.M.	Gemini
26	Gemini		
27	Gemini		
28	Gemini	1:53 A.M.	Cancer
29	Cancer		
30	Cancer	6:31 A.M.	Leo
31	Leo		

SEPTEMBER

1	Leo	7:57 A.M.	Virgo
2	Virgo		
3	Virgo	7:54 A.M.	Libra
4	Libra		
5	Libra	8:16 A.M.	Scorpio
6	Scorpio		
7	Scorpio	10:36 A.M.	Sagittarius
8	Sagittarius		
9	Sagittarius	3:45 P.M.	Capricorn
10	Capricorn		
11	Capricorn	11:51 P.M.	Aquarius
12	Aquarius		
13	Aquarius		
14	Aquarius	10:25 A.M.	Pisces
15	Pisces		
16	Pisces	10:43 P.M.	Aries
17	Aries		
18	Aries		
19	Aries	11:45 A.M.	Taurus
20	Taurus		
21	Taurus		
22	Taurus	12:05 A.M.	Gemini
23	Gemini		
24	Gemini	9:57 A.M.	Cancer
25	Cancer		
26	Cancer	4:09 P.M.	Leo
27	Leo		
28	Leo	6:41 P.M.	Virgo
29	Virgo		
30	Virgo	6:46 P.M.	Libra

OCTOBER

1	Libra		
2	Libra	6:12 P.M.	Scorpio
3	Scorpio		
4	Scorpio	6:54 P.M.	Sagittarius
5	Sagittarius		
6	Sagittarius	10:28 P.M.	Capricorn
7	Capricorn		
8	Capricorn		
9	Capricorn	5:44 A.M.	Aquarius
10	Aquarius		
11	Aquarius	4:18 P.M.	Pisces
12	Pisces		
13	Pisces		
14	Pisces	4:50 A.M.	Aries
15	Aries		
16	Aries	5:49 P.M.	Taurus
17	Taurus		
18	Taurus		
19	Taurus	5:59 A.M.	Gemini
20	Gemini		
21	Gemini	4:18 P.M.	Cancer
22	Cancer		
23	Cancer	11:51 P.M.	Leo
24	Leo		
25	Leo		
26	Leo	4:10 A.M.	Virgo
27	Virgo		
28	Virgo	5:37 A.M.	Libra
29	Libra		
30	Libra	5:25 A.M.	Scorpio
31	Scorpio		

NOVEMBER

1	Scorpio	5:21 A.M.	Sagittarius
2	Sagittarius		
3	Sagittarius	7:22 A.M.	Capricorn
4	Capricorn		
5	Capricorn	1:03 P.M.	Aquarius
6	Aquarius		
7	Aquarius	10:46 P.M.	Pisces
8	Pisces		
9	Pisces		
10	Pisces	11:13 A.M.	Aries
11	Aries		
12	Aries		
13	Aries	12:13 A.M.	Taurus
14	Taurus		
15	Taurus	12:00 P.M.	Gemini
16	Gemini		
17	Gemini	9:52 P.M.	Cancer
18	Cancer		
19	Cancer		
20	Cancer	5:38 A.M.	Leo
21	Leo		
22	Leo	11:11 A.M.	Virgo
23	Virgo		
24	Virgo	2:25 P.M.	Libra
25	Libra		
26	Libra	3:44 P.M.	Scorpio
27	Scorpio		
28	Scorpio	4:18 P.M.	Sagittarius
29	Sagittarius		
30	Sagittarius	5:50 P.M.	Capricorn

DECEMBER

1	Capricorn		
2	Capricorn	10:12 P.M.	Aquarius
3	Aquarius		
4	Aquarius		
5	Aquarius	6:35 A.M.	Pisces
6	Pisces		
7	Pisces	6:26 P.M.	Aries
8	Aries		
9	Aries		
10	Aries	7:27 A.M.	Taurus
11	Taurus		
12	Taurus	7:08 P.M.	Gemini
13	Gemini		
14	Gemini		
15	Gemini	4:20 A.M.	Cancer
16	Cancer		
17	Cancer	11:16 A.M.	Leo
18	Leo		
19	Leo	4:35 P.M.	Virgo
20	Virgo		
21	Virgo	8:37 P.M.	Libra
22	Libra		
23	Libra	11:30 P.M.	Scorpio
24	Scorpio		
25	Scorpio		
26	Scorpio	1:36 A.M.	Sagittarius
27	Sagittarius		
28	Sagittarius	3:58 A.M.	Capricorn
29	Capricorn		
30	Capricorn	8:09 A.M.	Aquarius
31	Aquarius		

MOON SIGN TABLES
1941

JANUARY

1	Aquarius	3:35 P.M.	Pisces
2	Pisces		
3	Pisces		
4	Pisces	2:34 A.M.	Aries
5	Aries		
6	Aries	3:28 P.M.	Taurus
7	Taurus		
8	Taurus		
9	Taurus	3:27 A.M.	Gemini
10	Gemini		
11	Gemini	12:33 P.M.	Cancer
12	Cancer		
13	Cancer	6:39 P.M.	Leo
14	Leo		
15	Leo	10:45 P.M.	Virgo
16	Virgo		
17	Virgo		
18	Virgo	2:00 A.M.	Libra
19	Libra		
20	Libra	5:04 A.M.	Scorpio
21	Scorpio		
22	Scorpio	8:16 A.M.	Sagittarius
23	Sagittarius		
24	Sagittarius	12:01 P.M.	Capricorn
25	Capricorn		
26	Capricorn	5:06 P.M.	Aquarius
27	Aquarius		
28	Aquarius		
29	Aquarius	12:34 A.M.	Pisces
30	Pisces		
31	Pisces	11:02 A.M.	Aries

FEBRUARY

1	Aries		
2	Aries	11:41 P.M.	Taurus
3	Taurus		
4	Taurus		
5	Taurus	12:09 P.M.	Gemini
6	Gemini		
7	Gemini	9:57 P.M.	Cancer
8	Cancer		
9	Cancer		
10	Cancer	4:07 A.M.	Leo
11	Leo		
12	Leo	7:21 A.M.	Virgo
13	Virgo		
14	Virgo	9:07 A.M.	Libra
15	Libra		
16	Libra	10:52 A.M.	Scorpio
17	Scorpio		
18	Scorpio	1:37 P.M.	Sagittarius
19	Sagittarius		
20	Sagittarius	5:54 P.M.	Capricorn
21	Capricorn		
22	Capricorn		
23	Capricorn	12:02 A.M.	Aquarius
24	Aquarius		
25	Aquarius	8:18 A.M.	Pisces
26	Pisces		
27	Pisces	6:54 P.M.	Aries
28	Aries		

MARCH

1	Aries		
2	Aries	7:23 A.M.	Taurus
3	Taurus		

4	Taurus	8:12 P.M.	Gemini
5	Gemini		
6	Gemini		
7	Gemini	7:04 A.M.	Cancer
8	Cancer		
9	Cancer	2:19 P.M.	Leo
10	Leo		
11	Leo	5:51 P.M.	Virgo
12	Virgo		
13	Virgo	6:51 P.M.	Libra
14	Libra		
15	Libra	7:03 P.M.	Scorpio
16	Scorpio		
17	Scorpio	8:08 P.M.	Sagittarius
18	Sagittarius		
19	Sagittarius	11:25 P.M.	Capricorn
20	Capricorn		
21	Capricorn		
22	Capricorn	5:34 A.M.	Aquarius
23	Aquarius		
24	Aquarius	2:30 P.M.	Pisces
25	Pisces		
26	Pisces		
27	Pisces	1:39 A.M.	Aries
28	Aries		
29	Aries	2:14 P.M.	Taurus
30	Taurus		
31	Taurus		

APRIL

1	Taurus	3:06 A.M.	Gemini
2	Gemini		
3	Gemini	2:44 P.M.	Cancer
4	Cancer		
5	Cancer	11:26 P.M.	Leo
6	Leo		
7	Leo		
8	Leo	4:21 A.M.	Virgo
9	Virgo		
10	Virgo	5:54 A.M.	Libra
11	Libra		
12	Libra	5:31 A.M.	Scorpio
13	Scorpio		
14	Scorpio	5:07 A.M.	Sagittarius
15	Sagittarius		
16	Sagittarius	6:38 A.M.	Capricorn
17	Capricorn		
18	Capricorn	11:31 A.M.	Aquarius
19	Aquarius		
20	Aquarius	8:07 P.M.	Pisces
21	Pisces		
22	Pisces		
23	Pisces	7:34 A.M.	Aries
24	Aries		
25	Aries	8:23 P.M.	Taurus
26	Taurus		
27	Taurus		
28	Taurus	9:11 A.M.	Gemini
29	Gemini		
30	Gemini	8:56 P.M.	Cancer

MAY

1	Cancer		
2	Cancer		
3	Cancer	6:34 A.M.	Leo
4	Leo		
5	Leo	1:06 P.M.	Virgo

6	Virgo		
7	Virgo	4:11 P.M.	Libra
8	Libra		
9	Libra	4:34 P.M.	Scorpio
10	Scorpio		
11	Scorpio	3:49 P.M.	Sagittarius
12	Sagittarius		
13	Sagittarius	4:04 P.M.	Capricorn
14	Capricorn		
15	Capricorn	7:15 P.M.	Aquarius
16	Aquarius		
17	Aquarius		
18	Aquarius	2:33 A.M.	Pisces
19	Pisces		
20	Pisces	1:34 P.M.	Aries
21	Aries		
22	Aries		
23	Aries	2:26 A.M.	Taurus
24	Taurus		
25	Taurus	3:10 P.M.	Gemini
26	Gemini		
27	Gemini		
28	Gemini	2:36 A.M.	Cancer
29	Cancer		
30	Cancer	12:15 P.M.	Leo
31	Leo		

JUNE

1	Leo	7:38 P.M.	Virgo
2	Virgo		
3	Virgo		
4	Virgo	12:17 A.M.	Libra
5	Libra		
6	Libra	2:13 A.M.	Scorpio
7	Scorpio		
8	Scorpio	2:24 A.M.	Sagittarius
9	Sagittarius		
10	Sagittarius	2:31 A.M.	Capricorn
11	Capricorn		
12	Capricorn	4:41 A.M.	Aquarius
13	Aquarius		
14	Aquarius	10:33 A.M.	Pisces
15	Pisces		
16	Pisces	8:30 P.M.	Aries
17	Aries		
18	Aries		
19	Aries	9:03 A.M.	Taurus
20	Taurus		
21	Taurus	9:44 P.M.	Gemini
22	Gemini		
23	Gemini		
24	Gemini	8:51 A.M.	Cancer
25	Cancer		
26	Cancer	5:55 P.M.	Leo
27	Leo		
28	Leo		
29	Leo	1:03 A.M.	Virgo
30	Virgo		

JULY

1	Virgo	6:17 A.M.	Libra
2	Libra		
3	Libra	9:33 A.M.	Scorpio
4	Scorpio		
5	Scorpio	11:13 A.M.	Sagittarius
6	Sagittarius		
7	Sagittarius	12:21 P.M.	Capricorn

8	Capricorn		
9	Capricorn	2:36 P.M.	Aquarius
10	Aquarius		
11	Aquarius	7:42 P.M.	Pisces
12	Pisces		
13	Pisces		
14	Pisces	4:35 A.M.	Aries
15	Aries		
16	Aries	4:30 P.M.	Taurus
17	Taurus		
18	Taurus		
19	Taurus	5:10 A.M.	Gemini
20	Gemini		
21	Gemini	4:15 P.M.	Cancer
22	Cancer		
23	Cancer		
24	Cancer	12:48 A.M.	Leo
25	Leo		
26	Leo	7:03 A.M.	Virgo
27	Virgo		
28	Virgo	11:41 A.M.	Libra
29	Libra		
30	Libra	3:09 P.M.	Scorpio
31	Scorpio		

AUGUST

1	Scorpio	5:49 P.M.	Sagittarius
2	Sagittarius		
3	Sagittarius	8:17 P.M.	Capricorn
4	Capricorn		
5	Capricorn	11:32 P.M.	Aquarius
6	Aquarius		
7	Aquarius		
8	Aquarius	4:51 A.M.	Pisces
9	Pisces		
10	Pisces	1:13 P.M.	Aries
11	Aries		
12	Aries		
13	Aries	12:32 A.M.	Taurus
14	Taurus		
15	Taurus	1:09 P.M.	Gemini
16	Gemini		
17	Gemini		
18	Gemini	12:37 A.M.	Cancer
19	Cancer		
20	Cancer	9:15 A.M.	Leo
21	Leo		
22	Leo	2:53 P.M.	Virgo
23	Virgo		
24	Virgo	6:21 P.M.	Libra
25	Libra		
26	Libra	8:49 P.M.	Scorpio
27	Scorpio		
28	Scorpio	11:13 P.M.	Sagittarius
29	Sagittarius		
30	Sagittarius		
31	Sagittarius	2:18 A.M.	Capricorn

SEPTEMBER

1	Capricorn		
2	Capricorn	6:39 A.M.	Aquarius
3	Aquarius		
4	Aquarius	12:52 P.M.	Pisces
5	Pisces		
6	Pisces	9:28 P.M.	Aries
7	Aries		
8	Aries		
9	Aries	8:32 A.M.	Taurus
10	Taurus		
11	Taurus	9:06 P.M.	Gemini
12	Gemini		
13	Gemini		
14	Gemini	9:09 A.M.	Cancer
15	Cancer		
16	Cancer	6:36 P.M.	Leo
17	Leo		
18	Leo		
19	Leo	12:29 A.M.	Virgo
20	Virgo		
21	Virgo	3:17 A.M.	Libra
22	Libra		
23	Libra	4:24 A.M.	Scorpio
24	Scorpio		
25	Scorpio	5:24 A.M.	Sagittarius
26	Sagittarius		
27	Sagittarius	7:44 A.M.	Capricorn
28	Capricorn		
29	Capricorn	12:17 P.M.	Aquarius
30	Aquarius		

OCTOBER

1	Aquarius	7:18 P.M.	Pisces
2	Pisces		
3	Pisces		
4	Pisces	4:37 A.M.	Aries
5	Aries		
6	Aries	3:52 P.M.	Taurus
7	Taurus		
8	Taurus		
9	Taurus	4:23 A.M.	Gemini
10	Gemini		
11	Gemini	4:53 P.M.	Cancer
12	Cancer		
13	Cancer		
14	Cancer	3:29 A.M.	Leo
15	Leo		
16	Leo	10:36 A.M.	Virgo
17	Virgo		
18	Virgo	1:54 P.M.	Libra
19	Libra		
20	Libra	2:25 P.M.	Scorpio
21	Scorpio		
22	Scorpio	2:00 P.M.	Sagittarius
23	Sagittarius		
24	Sagittarius	2:40 P.M.	Capricorn
25	Capricorn		
26	Capricorn	6:02 P.M.	Aquarius
27	Aquarius		
28	Aquarius		
29	Aquarius	12:51 A.M.	Pisces
30	Pisces		
31	Pisces	10:38 A.M.	Aries

NOVEMBER

1	Aries		
2	Aries	10:19 P.M.	Taurus
3	Taurus		
4	Taurus		
5	Taurus	10:52 A.M.	Gemini
6	Gemini		
7	Gemini	11:26 P.M.	Cancer
8	Cancer		
9	Cancer		
10	Cancer	10:49 A.M.	Leo

11	Leo		
12	Leo	7:29 P.M.	Virgo
13	Virgo		
14	Virgo		
15	Virgo	12:22 A.M.	Libra
16	Libra		
17	Libra	1:40 A.M.	Scorpio
18	Scorpio		
19	Scorpio	12:53 A.M.	Sagittarius
20	Sagittarius		
21	Sagittarius	12:11 A.M.	Capricorn
22	Capricorn		
23	Capricorn	1:46 A.M.	Aquarius
24	Aquarius		
25	Aquarius	7:09 A.M.	Pisces
26	Pisces		
27	Pisces	4:26 P.M.	Aries
28	Aries		
29	Aries		
30	Aries	4:18 A.M.	Taurus

DECEMBER

1	Taurus		
2	Taurus	5:00 P.M.	Gemini
3	Gemini		
4	Gemini		
5	Gemini	5:22 A.M.	Cancer
6	Cancer		
7	Cancer	4:43 P.M.	Leo
8	Leo		
9	Leo		
10	Leo	2:12 A.M.	Virgo
11	Virgo		
12	Virgo	8:46 A.M.	Libra
13	Libra		
14	Libra	11:51 A.M.	Scorpio
15	Scorpio		
16	Scorpio	12:10 P.M.	Sagittarius
17	Sagittarius		
18	Sagittarius	11:26 A.M.	Capricorn
19	Capricorn		
20	Capricorn	11:53 A.M.	Aquarius
21	Aquarius		
22	Aquarius	3:33 P.M.	Pisces
23	Pisces		
24	Pisces	11:24 P.M.	Aries
25	Aries		
26	Aries		
27	Aries	10:43 A.M.	Taurus
28	Taurus		
29	Taurus	11:27 P.M.	Gemini
30	Gemini		
31	Gemini		

MOON SIGN TABLES
1942

JANUARY

1 Gemini	11:42 A.M.	Cancer
2 Cancer		
3 Cancer	10:32 P.M.	Leo
4 Leo		
5 Leo		
6 Leo	7:42 A.M.	Virgo
7 Virgo		
8 Virgo	2:48 P.M.	Libra
9 Libra		
10 Libra	7:24 P.M.	Scorpio
11 Scorpio		
12 Scorpio	9:31 P.M.	Sagittarius
13 Sagittarius		
14 Sagittarius	10:07 P.M.	Capricorn
15 Capricorn		
16 Capricorn	10:52 P.M.	Aquarius
17 Aquarius		
18 Aquarius		
19 Aquarius	1:43 A.M.	Pisces
20 Pisces		
21 Pisces	8:08 A.M.	Aries
22 Aries		
23 Aries	6:18 P.M.	Taurus
24 Taurus		
25 Taurus		
26 Taurus	6:44 A.M.	Gemini
27 Gemini		
28 Gemini	7:03 P.M.	Cancer
29 Cancer		
30 Cancer		
31 Cancer	5:37 A.M.	Leo

FEBRUARY

1 Leo		
2 Leo	1:57 P.M.	Virgo
3 Virgo		
4 Virgo	8:18 P.M.	Libra
5 Libra		
6 Libra		
7 Libra	12:56 A.M.	Scorpio
8 Scorpio		
9 Scorpio	4:06 A.M.	Sagittarius
10 Sagittarius		
11 Sagittarius	6:19 A.M.	Capricorn
12 Capricorn		
13 Capricorn	8:27 A.M.	Aquarius
14 Aquarius		
15 Aquarius	11:51 A.M.	Pisces
16 Pisces		
17 Pisces	5:46 P.M.	Aries
18 Aries		
19 Aries		
20 Aries	2:57 A.M.	Taurus
21 Taurus		
22 Taurus	2:47 P.M.	Gemini
23 Gemini		
24 Gemini		
25 Gemini	3:15 A.M.	Cancer
26 Cancer		
27 Cancer	2:06 P.M.	Leo
28 Leo		

MARCH

1 Leo	10:06 P.M.	Virgo
2 Virgo		
3 Virgo		
4 Virgo	3:23 A.M.	Libra
5 Libra		
6 Libra	6:50 A.M.	Scorpio
7 Scorpio		
8 Scorpio	9:28 A.M.	Sagittarius
9 Sagittarius		
10 Sagittarius	12:08 P.M.	Capricorn
11 Capricorn		
12 Capricorn	3:30 P.M.	Aquarius
13 Aquarius		
14 Aquarius	8:09 P.M.	Pisces
15 Pisces		
16 Pisces		
17 Pisces	2:41 A.M.	Aries
18 Aries		
19 Aries	11:39 A.M.	Taurus
20 Taurus		
21 Taurus	11:00 P.M.	Gemini
22 Gemini		
23 Gemini		
24 Gemini	11:33 A.M.	Cancer
25 Cancer		
26 Cancer	11:04 P.M.	Leo
27 Leo		
28 Leo		
29 Leo	7:36 A.M.	Virgo
30 Virgo		
31 Virgo	12:36 P.M.	Libra

APRIL

1 Libra		
2 Libra	2:54 P.M.	Scorpio
3 Scorpio		
4 Scorpio	4:04 P.M.	Sagittarius
5 Sagittarius		
6 Sagittarius	5:42 P.M.	Capricorn
7 Capricorn		
8 Capricorn	8:56 P.M.	Aquarius
9 Aquarius		
10 Aquarius		
11 Aquarius	2:19 A.M.	Pisces
12 Pisces		
13 Pisces	9:49 A.M.	Aries
14 Aries		
15 Aries	7:18 P.M.	Taurus
16 Taurus		
17 Taurus		
18 Taurus	6:37 A.M.	Gemini
19 Gemini		
20 Gemini	7:10 P.M.	Cancer
21 Cancer		
22 Cancer		
23 Cancer	7:21 A.M.	Leo
24 Leo		
25 Leo	5:02 P.M.	Virgo
26 Virgo		
27 Virgo	10:50 P.M.	Libra
28 Libra		
29 Libra		
30 Libra	12:59 A.M.	Scorpio

MAY

1 Scorpio		
2 Scorpio	1:03 A.M.	Sagittarius
3 Sagittarius		
4 Sagittarius	1:04 A.M.	Capricorn
5 Capricorn		
6 Capricorn	2:56 A.M.	Aquarius
7 Aquarius		
8 Aquarius	7:44 A.M.	Pisces
9 Pisces		
10 Pisces	3:31 P.M.	Aries
11 Aries		
12 Aries		
13 Aries	1:37 A.M.	Taurus
14 Taurus		
15 Taurus	1:15 P.M.	Gemini
16 Gemini		
17 Gemini		
18 Gemini	1:49 A.M.	Cancer
19 Cancer		
20 Cancer	2:21 P.M.	Leo
21 Leo		
22 Leo		
23 Leo	1:07 A.M.	Virgo
24 Virgo		
25 Virgo	8:22 A.M.	Libra
26 Libra		
27 Libra	11:32 A.M.	Scorpio
28 Scorpio		
29 Scorpio	11:39 A.M.	Sagittarius
30 Sagittarius		
31 Sagittarius	10:43 A.M.	Capricorn

JUNE

1 Capricorn		
2 Capricorn	10:59 A.M.	Aquarius
3 Aquarius		
4 Aquarius	2:14 P.M.	Pisces
5 Pisces		
6 Pisces	9:11 P.M.	Aries
7 Aries		
8 Aries		
9 Aries	7:16 A.M.	Taurus
10 Taurus		
11 Taurus	7:11 P.M.	Gemini
12 Gemini		
13 Gemini		
14 Gemini	7:50 A.M.	Cancer
15 Cancer		
16 Cancer	8:19 P.M.	Leo
17 Leo		
18 Leo		
19 Leo	7:33 A.M.	Virgo
20 Virgo		
21 Virgo	4:04 P.M.	Libra
22 Libra		
23 Libra	8:50 P.M.	Scorpio
24 Scorpio		
25 Scorpio	10:09 P.M.	Sagittarius
26 Sagittarius		
27 Sagittarius	9:30 P.M.	Capricorn
28 Capricorn		
29 Capricorn	9:00 P.M.	Aquarius
30 Aquarius		

JULY

1 Aquarius	10:46 P.M.	Pisces
2 Pisces		
3 Pisces		
4 Pisces	4:10 A.M.	Aries
5 Aries		
6 Aries	1:22 A.M.	Taurus
7 Taurus		

8	Taurus		
9	Taurus	1:10 A.M.	Gemini
10	Gemini		
11	Gemini	1:51 P.M.	Cancer
12	Cancer		
13	Cancer		
14	Cancer	2:08 A.M.	Leo
15	Leo		
16	Leo	1:08 P.M.	Virgo
17	Virgo		
18	Virgo	10:02 P.M.	Libra
19	Libra		
20	Libra		
21	Libra	4:02 A.M.	Scorpio
22	Scorpio		
23	Scorpio	6:58 A.M.	Sagittarius
24	Sagittarius		
25	Sagittarius	7:38 A.M.	Capricorn
26	Capricorn		
27	Capricorn	7:37 A.M.	Aquarius
28	Aquarius		
29	Aquarius	8:49 A.M.	Pisces
30	Pisces		
31	Pisces	12:55 P.M.	Aries

AUGUST

1	Aries		
2	Aries	8:47 P.M.	Taurus
3	Taurus		
4	Taurus		
5	Taurus	7:54 A.M.	Gemini
6	Gemini		
7	Gemini	8:30 P.M.	Cancer
8	Cancer		
9	Cancer		
10	Cancer	8:39 A.M.	Leo
11	Leo		
12	Leo	7:09 P.M.	Virgo
13	Virgo		
14	Virgo		
15	Virgo	3:31 A.M.	Libra
16	Libra		
17	Libra	9:38 A.M.	Scorpio
18	Scorpio		
19	Scorpio	1:35 P.M.	Sagittarius
20	Sagittarius		
21	Sagittarius	3:46 P.M.	Capricorn
22	Capricorn		
23	Capricorn	5:07 P.M.	Aquarius
24	Aquarius		
25	Aquarius	6:55 P.M.	Pisces
26	Pisces		
27	Pisces	10:39 P.M.	Aries
28	Aries		
29	Aries		
30	Aries	5:29 A.M.	Taurus
31	Taurus		

SEPTEMBER

1	Taurus	3:40 P.M.	Gemini
2	Gemini		
3	Gemini		
4	Gemini	4:00 A.M.	Cancer
5	Cancer		
6	Cancer	4:15 P.M.	Leo
7	Leo		
8	Leo		
9	Leo	2:31 A.M.	Virgo
10	Virgo		
11	Virgo	10:05 A.M.	Libra
12	Libra		
13	Libra	3:19 P.M.	Scorpio
14	Scorpio		
15	Scorpio	6:58 P.M.	Sagittarius
16	Sagittarius		
17	Sagittarius	9:48 P.M.	Capricorn
18	Capricorn		
19	Capricorn		
20	Capricorn	12:27 A.M.	Aquarius
21	Aquarius		
22	Aquarius	3:34 A.M.	Pisces
23	Pisces		
24	Pisces	7:57 A.M.	Aries
25	Aries		
26	Aries	2:35 P.M.	Taurus
27	Taurus		
28	Taurus		
29	Taurus	12:05 A.M.	Gemini
30	Gemini		

OCTOBER

1	Gemini	12:03 P.M.	Cancer
2	Cancer		
3	Cancer		
4	Cancer	12:35 A.M.	Leo
5	Leo		
6	Leo	11:13 A.M.	Virgo
7	Virgo		
8	Virgo	6:33 P.M.	Libra
9	Libra		
10	Libra	10:46 P.M.	Scorpio
11	Scorpio		
12	Scorpio		
13	Scorpio	1:10 A.M.	Sagittarius
14	Sagittarius		
15	Sagittarius	3:13 A.M.	Capricorn
16	Capricorn		
17	Capricorn	6:01 A.M.	Aquarius
18	Aquarius		
19	Aquarius	10:05 A.M.	Pisces
20	Pisces		
21	Pisces	3:37 P.M.	Aries
22	Aries		
23	Aries	10:52 P.M.	Taurus
24	Taurus		
25	Taurus		
26	Taurus	8:18 A.M.	Gemini
27	Gemini		
28	Gemini	8:00 P.M.	Cancer
29	Cancer		
30	Cancer		
31	Cancer	8:48 A.M.	Leo

NOVEMBER

1	Leo		
2	Leo	8:19 P.M.	Virgo
3	Virgo		
4	Virgo		
5	Virgo	4:21 A.M.	Libra
6	Libra		
7	Libra	8:27 A.M.	Scorpio
8	Scorpio		
9	Scorpio	9:47 A.M.	Sagittarius
10	Sagittarius		
11	Sagittarius	10:18 A.M.	Capricorn
12	Capricorn		
13	Capricorn	11:48 A.M.	Aquarius
14	Aquarius		
15	Aquarius	3:28 P.M.	Pisces
16	Pisces		
17	Pisces	9:30 P.M.	Aries
18	Aries		
19	Aries		
20	Aries	5:38 A.M.	Taurus
21	Taurus		
22	Taurus	3:35 P.M.	Gemini
23	Gemini		
24	Gemini		
25	Gemini	3:17 A.M.	Cancer
26	Cancer		
27	Cancer	4:09 P.M.	Leo
28	Leo		
29	Leo		
30	Leo	4:29 A.M.	Virgo

DECEMBER

1	Virgo		
2	Virgo	1:55 P.M.	Libra
3	Libra		
4	Libra	7:06 P.M.	Scorpio
5	Scorpio		
6	Scorpio	8:34 P.M.	Sagittarius
7	Sagittarius		
8	Sagittarius	8:07 P.M.	Capricorn
9	Capricorn		
10	Capricorn	7:57 P.M.	Aquarius
11	Aquarius		
12	Aquarius	9:56 P.M.	Pisces
13	Pisces		
14	Pisces		
15	Pisces	3:04 A.M.	Aries
16	Aries		
17	Aries	11:16 A.M.	Taurus
18	Taurus		
19	Taurus	9:46 P.M.	Gemini
20	Gemini		
21	Gemini		
22	Gemini	9:46 A.M.	Cancer
23	Cancer		
24	Cancer	10:35 P.M.	Leo
25	Leo		
26	Leo		
27	Leo	11:10 A.M.	Virgo
28	Virgo		
29	Virgo	9:44 P.M.	Libra
30	Libra		
31	Libra		

MOON SIGN TABLES
1943

JANUARY
1	Libra	4:40 A.M.	Scorpio
2	Scorpio		
3	Scorpio	7:34 A.M.	Sagittarius
4	Sagittarius		
5	Sagittarius	7:35 A.M.	Capricorn
6	Capricorn		
7	Capricorn	6:42 A.M.	Aquarius
8	Aquarius		
9	Aquarius	7:03 A.M.	Pisces
10	Pisces		
11	Pisces	10:21 A.M.	Aries
12	Aries		
13	Aries	5:22 P.M.	Taurus
14	Taurus		
15	Taurus		
16	Taurus	3:39 A.M.	Gemini
17	Gemini		
18	Gemini	3:53 P.M.	Cancer
19	Cancer		
20	Cancer		
21	Cancer	4:44 A.M.	Leo
22	Leo		
23	Leo	5:03 P.M.	Virgo
24	Virgo		
25	Virgo		
26	Virgo	3:47 A.M.	Libra
27	Libra		
28	Libra	11:51 A.M.	Scorpio
29	Scorpio		
30	Scorpio	4:34 P.M.	Sagittarius
31	Sagittarius		

FEBRUARY
1	Sagittarius	6:15 P.M.	Capricorn
2	Capricorn		
3	Capricorn	6:10 P.M.	Aquarius
4	Aquarius		
5	Aquarius	6:08 P.M.	Pisces
6	Pisces		
7	Pisces	8:00 P.M.	Aries
8	Aries		
9	Aries		
10	Aries	1:17 A.M.	Taurus
11	Taurus		
12	Taurus	10:25 A.M.	Gemini
13	Gemini		
14	Gemini	10:24 P.M.	Cancer
15	Cancer		
16	Cancer		
17	Cancer	11:18 A.M.	Leo
18	Leo		
19	Leo	11:20 P.M.	Virgo
20	Virgo		
21	Virgo		
22	Virgo	9:30 A.M.	Libra
23	Libra		
24	Libra	5:25 P.M.	Scorpio
25	Scorpio		
26	Scorpio	10:59 P.M.	Sagittarius
27	Sagittarius		
28	Sagittarius		

MARCH
1	Sagittarius	2:19 A.M.	Capricorn
2	Capricorn		
3	Capricorn	3:56 A.M.	Aquarius

APRIL
4	Aquarius		
5	Aquarius	4:54 A.M.	Pisces
6	Pisces		
7	Pisces	6:41 A.M.	Aries
8	Aries		
9	Aries	10:53 A.M.	Taurus
10	Taurus		
11	Taurus	6:39 P.M.	Gemini
12	Gemini		
13	Gemini		
14	Gemini	5:51 A.M.	Cancer
15	Cancer		
16	Cancer	6:41 P.M.	Leo
17	Leo		
18	Leo		
19	Leo	6:43 A.M.	Virgo
20	Virgo		
21	Virgo	4:21 P.M.	Libra
22	Libra		
23	Libra	11:23 P.M.	Scorpio
24	Scorpio		
25	Scorpio		
26	Scorpio	4:23 A.M.	Sagittarius
27	Sagittarius		
28	Sagittarius	8:05 A.M.	Capricorn
29	Capricorn		
30	Capricorn	10:57 A.M.	Aquarius
31	Aquarius		

APRIL
1	Aquarius	1:27 P.M.	Pisces
2	Pisces		
3	Pisces	4:17 P.M.	Aries
4	Aries		
5	Aries	8:37 P.M.	Taurus
6	Taurus		
7	Taurus		
8	Taurus	3:41 A.M.	Gemini
9	Gemini		
10	Gemini	2:03 P.M.	Cancer
11	Cancer		
12	Cancer		
13	Cancer	2:39 A.M.	Leo
14	Leo		
15	Leo	2:59 P.M.	Virgo
16	Virgo		
17	Virgo		
18	Virgo	12:41 A.M.	Libra
19	Libra		
20	Libra	7:04 A.M.	Scorpio
21	Scorpio		
22	Scorpio	10:56 A.M.	Sagittarius
23	Sagittarius		
24	Sagittarius	1:40 P.M.	Capricorn
25	Capricorn		
26	Capricorn	4:21 P.M.	Aquarius
27	Aquarius		
28	Aquarius	7:36 P.M.	Pisces
29	Pisces		
30	Pisces	11:39 P.M.	Aries

MAY
1	Aries		
2	Aries		
3	Aries	4:57 A.M.	Taurus
4	Taurus		
5	Taurus	12:16 P.M.	Gemini

(continued)
6	Gemini		
7	Gemini	10:17 P.M.	Cancer
8	Cancer		
9	Cancer		
10	Cancer	10:39 A.M.	Leo
11	Leo		
12	Leo	11:21 P.M.	Virgo
13	Virgo		
14	Virgo		
15	Virgo	9:44 A.M.	Libra
16	Libra		
17	Libra	4:19 P.M.	Scorpio
18	Scorpio		
19	Scorpio	7:33 P.M.	Sagittarius
20	Sagittarius		
21	Sagittarius	9:00 P.M.	Capricorn
22	Capricorn		
23	Capricorn	10:23 P.M.	Aquarius
24	Aquarius		
25	Aquarius		
26	Aquarius	12:58 A.M.	Pisces
27	Pisces		
28	Pisces	5:16 A.M.	Aries
29	Aries		
30	Aries	11:25 A.M.	Taurus
31	Taurus		

JUNE
1	Taurus	7:29 P.M.	Gemini
2	Gemini		
3	Gemini		
4	Gemini	5:45 A.M.	Cancer
5	Cancer		
6	Cancer	6:03 P.M.	Leo
7	Leo		
8	Leo		
9	Leo	7:03 A.M.	Virgo
10	Virgo		
11	Virgo	6:22 P.M.	Libra
12	Libra		
13	Libra		
14	Libra	1:59 A.M.	Scorpio
15	Scorpio		
16	Scorpio	5:36 A.M.	Sagittarius
17	Sagittarius		
18	Sagittarius	6:30 A.M.	Capricorn
19	Capricorn		
20	Capricorn	6:33 A.M.	Aquarius
21	Aquarius		
22	Aquarius	7:36 A.M.	Pisces
23	Pisces		
24	Pisces	10:52 A.M.	Aries
25	Aries		
26	Aries	4:52 P.M.	Taurus
27	Taurus		
28	Taurus		
29	Taurus	1:27 A.M.	Gemini
30	Gemini		

JULY
1	Gemini	12:13 P.M.	Cancer
2	Cancer		
3	Cancer		
4	Cancer	12:39 A.M.	Leo
5	Leo		
6	Leo	1:45 P.M.	Virgo
7	Virgo		

8	Virgo		
9	Virgo	1:44 A.M.	Libra
10	Libra		
11	Libra	10:40 A.M.	Scorpio
12	Scorpio		
13	Scorpio	3:37 P.M.	Sagittarius
14	Sagittarius		
15	Sagittarius	5:06 P.M.	Capricorn
16	Capricorn		
17	Capricorn	4:46 P.M.	Aquarius
18	Aquarius		
19	Aquarius	4:30 P.M.	Pisces
20	Pisces		
21	Pisces	6:08 P.M.	Aries
22	Aries		
23	Aries	10:53 P.M.	Taurus
24	Taurus		
25	Taurus		
26	Taurus	7:04 A.M.	Gemini
27	Gemini		
28	Gemini	6:04 P.M.	Cancer
29	Cancer		
30	Cancer		
31	Cancer	6:43 A.M.	Leo

AUGUST

1	Leo		
2	Leo	7:45 P.M.	Virgo
3	Virgo		
4	Virgo		
5	Virgo	7:51 A.M.	Libra
6	Libra		
7	Libra	5:40 P.M.	Scorpio
8	Scorpio		
9	Scorpio		
10	Scorpio	12:08 A.M.	Sagittarius
11	Sagittarius		
12	Sagittarius	3:09 A.M.	Capricorn
13	Capricorn		
14	Capricorn	3:36 A.M.	Aquarius
15	Aquarius		
16	Aquarius	3:06 A.M.	Pisces
17	Pisces		
18	Pisces	3:32 A.M.	Aries
19	Aries		
20	Aries	6:39 A.M.	Taurus
21	Taurus		
22	Taurus	1:34 P.M.	Gemini
23	Gemini		
24	Gemini		
25	Gemini	12:07 A.M.	Cancer
26	Cancer		
27	Cancer	12:49 P.M.	Leo
28	Leo		
29	Leo		
30	Leo	1:47 A.M.	Virgo
31	Virgo		

SEPTEMBER

1	Virgo	1:33 P.M.	Libra
2	Libra		
3	Libra	11:20 P.M.	Scorpio
4	Scorpio		
5	Scorpio		
6	Scorpio	6:38 A.M.	Sagittarius
7	Sagittarius		
8	Sagittarius	11:13 A.M.	Capricorn
9	Capricorn		
10	Capricorn	1:18 P.M.	Aquarius
11	Aquarius		
12	Aquarius	1:46 P.M.	Pisces
13	Pisces		
14	Pisces	2:09 P.M.	Aries
15	Aries		
16	Aries	4:14 P.M.	Taurus
17	Taurus		
18	Taurus	9:42 P.M.	Gemini
19	Gemini		
20	Gemini		
21	Gemini	7:10 A.M.	Cancer
22	Cancer		
23	Cancer	7:34 P.M.	Leo
24	Leo		
25	Leo		
26	Leo	8:30 A.M.	Virgo
27	Virgo		
28	Virgo	7:56 P.M.	Libra
29	Libra		
30	Libra		

OCTOBER

1	Libra	5:04 A.M.	Scorpio
2	Scorpio		
3	Scorpio	12:03 P.M.	Sagittarius
4	Sagittarius		
5	Sagittarius	5:11 P.M.	Capricorn
6	Capricorn		
7	Capricorn	8:39 P.M.	Aquarius
8	Aquarius		
9	Aquarius	10:44 P.M.	Pisces
10	Pisces		
11	Pisces		
12	Pisces	12:12 A.M.	Aries
13	Aries		
14	Aries	2:26 A.M.	Taurus
15	Taurus		
16	Taurus	7:07 A.M.	Gemini
17	Gemini		
18	Gemini	3:28 P.M.	Cancer
19	Cancer		
20	Cancer		
21	Cancer	3:12 A.M.	Leo
22	Leo		
23	Leo	4:10 P.M.	Virgo
24	Virgo		
25	Virgo		
26	Virgo	3:38 A.M.	Libra
27	Libra		
28	Libra	12:14 P.M.	Scorpio
29	Scorpio		
30	Scorpio	6:14 P.M.	Sagittarius
31	Sagittarius		

NOVEMBER

1	Sagittarius	10:37 P.M.	Capricorn
2	Capricorn		
3	Capricorn		
4	Capricorn	2:10 A.M.	Aquarius
5	Aquarius		
6	Aquarius	5:16 P.M.	Pisces
7	Pisces		
8	Pisces	8:10 A.M.	Aries
9	Aries		
10	Aries	11:32 A.M.	Taurus

11	Taurus		
12	Taurus	4:31 P.M.	Gemini
13	Gemini		
14	Gemini		
15	Gemini	12:22 A.M.	Cancer
16	Cancer		
17	Cancer	11:27 A.M.	Leo
18	Leo		
19	Leo		
20	Leo	12:21 A.M.	Virgo
21	Virgo		
22	Virgo	12:19 P.M.	Libra
23	Libra		
24	Libra	9:09 P.M.	Scorpio
25	Scorpio		
26	Scorpio		
27	Scorpio	2:35 P.M.	Sagittarius
28	Sagittarius		
29	Sagittarius	5:43 A.M.	Capricorn
30	Capricorn		

DECEMBER

1	Capricorn	8:01 A.M.	Aquarius
2	Aquarius		
3	Aquarius	10:36 A.M.	Pisces
4	Pisces		
5	Pisces	2:00 P.M.	Aries
6	Aries		
7	Aries	6:30 P.M.	Taurus
8	Taurus		
9	Taurus		
10	Taurus	12:32 A.M.	Gemini
11	Gemini		
12	Gemini	8:46 A.M.	Cancer
13	Cancer		
14	Cancer	7:37 P.M.	Leo
15	Leo		
16	Leo		
17	Leo	8:22 A.M.	Virgo
18	Virgo		
19	Virgo	8:55 P.M.	Libra
20	Libra		
21	Libra		
22	Libra	6:46 A.M.	Scorpio
23	Scorpio		
24	Scorpio	12:44 P.M.	Sagittarius
25	Sagittarius		
26	Sagittarius	3:24 P.M.	Capricorn
27	Capricorn		
28	Capricorn	4:21 P.M.	Aquarius
29	Aquarius		
30	Aquarius	5:17 P.M.	Pisces
31	Pisces		

MOON SIGN TABLES
1944

JANUARY

1	Pisces	7:34 P.M.	Aries
2	Aries		
3	Aries	11:58 P.M.	Taurus
4	Taurus		
5	Taurus		
6	Taurus	6:44 A.M.	Gemini
7	Gemini		
8	Gemini	3:48 P.M.	Cancer
9	Cancer		
10	Cancer		
11	Cancer	2:58 A.M.	Leo
12	Leo		
13	Leo	3:38 P.M.	Virgo
14	Virgo		
15	Virgo		
16	Virgo	4:29 A.M.	Libra
17	Libra		
18	Libra	3:27 P.M.	Scorpio
19	Scorpio		
20	Scorpio	10:53 P.M.	Sagittarius
21	Sagittarius		
22	Sagittarius		
23	Sagittarius	2:26 A.M.	Capricorn
24	Capricorn		
25	Capricorn	3:09 A.M.	Aquarius
26	Aquarius		
27	Aquarius	2:48 A.M.	Pisces
28	Pisces		
29	Pisces	3:15 A.M.	Aries
30	Aries		
31	Aries	6:07 A.M.	Taurus

FEBRUARY

1	Taurus		
2	Taurus	12:17 P.M.	Gemini
3	Gemini		
4	Gemini	9:40 P.M.	Cancer
5	Cancer		
6	Cancer		
7	Cancer	9:20 A.M.	Leo
8	Leo		
9	Leo	10:08 P.M.	Virgo
10	Virgo		
11	Virgo		
12	Virgo	10:54 A.M.	Libra
13	Libra		
14	Libra	10:24 P.M.	Scorpio
15	Scorpio		
16	Scorpio		
17	Scorpio	7:15 A.M.	Sagittarius
18	Sagittarius		
19	Sagittarius	12:33 P.M.	Capricorn
20	Capricorn		
21	Capricorn	2:27 P.M.	Aquarius
22	Aquarius		
23	Aquarius	2:09 P.M.	Pisces
24	Pisces		
25	Pisces	1:31 P.M.	Aries
26	Aries		
27	Aries	2:36 P.M.	Taurus
28	Taurus		
29	Taurus	7:06 P.M.	Gemini

MARCH

1	Gemini		
2	Gemini		
3	Gemini	3:38 A.M.	Cancer
4	Cancer		
5	Cancer	3:19 P.M.	Leo
6	Leo		
7	Leo		
8	Leo	4:18 A.M.	Virgo
9	Virgo		
10	Virgo	4:55 P.M.	Libra
11	Libra		
12	Libra		
13	Libra	4:12 A.M.	Scorpio
14	Scorpio		
15	Scorpio	1:31 P.M.	Sagittarius
16	Sagittarius		
17	Sagittarius	8:13 P.M.	Capricorn
18	Capricorn		
19	Capricorn	11:55 P.M.	Aquarius
20	Aquarius		
21	Aquarius		
22	Aquarius	12:59 A.M.	Pisces
23	Pisces		
24	Pisces	12:42 A.M.	Aries
25	Aries		
26	Aries	1:01 A.M.	Taurus
27	Taurus		
28	Taurus	3:58 A.M.	Gemini
29	Gemini		
30	Gemini	10:59 A.M.	Cancer
31	Cancer		

APRIL

1	Cancer	9:54 P.M.	Leo
2	Leo		
3	Leo		
4	Leo	10:49 A.M.	Virgo
5	Virgo		
6	Virgo	11:22 P.M.	Libra
7	Libra		
8	Libra		
9	Libra	10:12 A.M.	Scorpio
10	Scorpio		
11	Scorpio	7:02 P.M.	Sagittarius
12	Sagittarius		
13	Sagittarius		
14	Sagittarius	1:56 A.M.	Capricorn
15	Capricorn		
16	Capricorn	6:46 A.M.	Aquarius
17	Aquarius		
18	Aquarius	9:28 A.M.	Pisces
19	Pisces		
20	Pisces	10:35 A.M.	Aries
21	Aries		
22	Aries	11:29 A.M.	Taurus
23	Taurus		
24	Taurus	1:59 P.M.	Gemini
25	Gemini		
26	Gemini	7:49 P.M.	Cancer
27	Cancer		
28	Cancer		
29	Cancer	5:36 A.M.	Leo
30	Leo		

MAY

1	Leo	6:04 P.M.	Virgo
2	Virgo		
3	Virgo		
4	Virgo	6:40 A.M.	Libra

JUNE

5	Libra		
6	Libra	5:18 P.M.	Scorpio
7	Scorpio		
8	Scorpio		
9	Scorpio	1:27 A.M.	Sagittarius
10	Sagittarius		
11	Sagittarius	7:33 A.M.	Capricorn
12	Capricorn		
13	Capricorn	12:10 P.M.	Aquarius
14	Aquarius		
15	Aquarius	3:35 P.M.	Pisces
16	Pisces		
17	Pisces	6:03 P.M.	Aries
18	Aries		
19	Aries	8:15 P.M.	Taurus
20	Taurus		
21	Taurus	11:26 P.M.	Gemini
22	Gemini		
23	Gemini		
24	Gemini	5:04 A.M.	Cancer
25	Cancer		
26	Cancer	2:04 P.M.	Leo
27	Leo		
28	Leo		
29	Leo	1:58 A.M.	Virgo
30	Virgo		
31	Virgo	2:37 P.M.	Libra

JUNE

1	Libra		
2	Libra		
3	Libra	1:32 A.M.	Scorpio
4	Scorpio		
5	Scorpio	9:27 A.M.	Sagittarius
6	Sagittarius		
7	Sagittarius	2:41 P.M.	Capricorn
8	Capricorn		
9	Capricorn	6:12 P.M.	Aquarius
10	Aquarius		
11	Aquarius	8:58 P.M.	Pisces
12	Pisces		
13	Pisces	11:41 P.M.	Aries
14	Aries		
15	Aries		
16	Aries	2:52 A.M.	Taurus
17	Taurus		
18	Taurus	7:11 A.M.	Gemini
19	Gemini		
20	Gemini	1:28 P.M.	Cancer
21	Cancer		
22	Cancer	10:25 P.M.	Leo
23	Leo		
24	Leo		
25	Leo	9:58 A.M.	Virgo
26	Virgo		
27	Virgo	10:40 P.M.	Libra
28	Libra		
29	Libra		
30	Libra	10:10 A.M.	Scorpio

JULY

1	Scorpio		
2	Scorpio	6:38 P.M.	Sagittarius
3	Sagittarius		
4	Sagittarius	11:42 P.M.	Capricorn
5	Capricorn		
6	Capricorn		

7	Capricorn	2:14 A.M.	Aquarius
8	Aquarius		
9	Aquarius	3:39 A.M.	Pisces
10	Pisces		
11	Pisces	5:18 A.M.	Aries
12	Aries		
13	Aries	8:16 A.M.	Taurus
14	Taurus		
15	Taurus	1:11 P.M.	Gemini
16	Gemini		
17	Gemini	8:21 P.M.	Cancer
18	Cancer		
19	Cancer		
20	Cancer	5:51 A.M.	Leo
21	Leo		
22	Leo	5:24 P.M.	Virgo
23	Virgo		
24	Virgo		
25	Virgo	6:08 A.M.	Libra
26	Libra		
27	Libra	6:16 P.M.	Scorpio
28	Scorpio		
29	Scorpio		
30	Scorpio	3:50 A.M.	Sagittarius
31	Sagittarius		

AUGUST

1	Sagittarius	9:42 A.M.	Capricorn
2	Capricorn		
3	Capricorn	12:10 P.M.	Aquarius
4	Aquarius		
5	Aquarius	12:35 P.M.	Pisces
6	Pisces		
7	Pisces	12:43 P.M.	Aries
8	Aries		
9	Aries	2:20 P.M.	Taurus
10	Taurus		
11	Taurus	6:38 P.M.	Gemini
12	Gemini		
13	Gemini		
14	Gemini	2:03 A.M.	Cancer
15	Cancer		
16	Cancer	12:08 P.M.	Leo
17	Leo		
18	Leo		
19	Leo	12:01 A.M.	Virgo
20	Virgo		
21	Virgo	12:45 P.M.	Libra
22	Libra		
23	Libra		
24	Libra	1:13 A.M.	Scorpio
25	Scorpio		
26	Scorpio	11:52 A.M.	Sagittarius
27	Sagittarius		
28	Sagittarius	7:12 P.M.	Capricorn
29	Capricorn		
30	Capricorn	10:44 P.M.	Aquarius
31	Aquarius		

SEPTEMBER

1	Aquarius	11:14 P.M.	Pisces
2	Pisces		
3	Pisces	10:27 P.M.	Aries
4	Aries		
5	Aries	10:28 P.M.	Taurus
6	Taurus		
7	Taurus		
8	Taurus	1:14 A.M.	Gemini
9	Gemini		
10	Gemini	7:47 A.M.	Cancer
11	Cancer		
12	Cancer	5:50 P.M.	Leo
13	Leo		
14	Leo		
15	Leo	6:00 A.M.	Virgo
16	Virgo		
17	Virgo	6:48 P.M.	Libra
18	Libra		
19	Libra		
20	Libra	7:11 A.M.	Scorpio
21	Scorpio		
22	Scorpio	6:16 P.M.	Sagittarius
23	Sagittarius		
24	Sagittarius		
25	Sagittarius	2:55 A.M.	Capricorn
26	Capricorn		
27	Capricorn	8:10 A.M.	Aquarius
28	Aquarius		
29	Aquarius	9:58 A.M.	Pisces
30	Pisces		

OCTOBER

1	Pisces	9:30 A.M.	Aries
2	Aries		
3	Aries	8:46 A.M.	Taurus
4	Taurus		
5	Taurus	9:59 A.M.	Gemini
6	Gemini		
7	Gemini	2:56 P.M.	Cancer
8	Cancer		
9	Cancer		
10	Cancer	12:03 A.M.	Leo
11	Leo		
12	Leo	12:04 P.M.	Virgo
13	Virgo		
14	Virgo		
15	Virgo	12:55 A.M.	Libra
16	Libra		
17	Libra	1:03 P.M.	Scorpio
18	Scorpio		
19	Scorpio	11:50 P.M.	Sagittarius
20	Sagittarius		
21	Sagittarius		
22	Sagittarius	8:48 A.M.	Capricorn
23	Capricorn		
24	Capricorn	3:19 P.M.	Aquarius
25	Aquarius		
26	Aquarius	6:53 P.M.	Pisces
27	Pisces		
28	Pisces	7:54 P.M.	Aries
29	Aries		
30	Aries	7:45 P.M.	Taurus
31	Taurus		

NOVEMBER

1	Taurus	8:28 P.M.	Gemini
2	Gemini		
3	Gemini		
4	Gemini	12:04 A.M.	Cancer
5	Cancer		
6	Cancer	7:44 A.M.	Leo
7	Leo		
8	Leo	6:59 P.M.	Virgo
9	Virgo		
10	Virgo		
11	Virgo	7:45 A.M.	Libra
12	Libra		
13	Libra	7:48 P.M.	Scorpio
14	Scorpio		
15	Scorpio		
16	Scorpio	6:02 A.M.	Sagittarius
17	Sagittarius		
18	Sagittarius	2:20 P.M.	Capricorn
19	Capricorn		
20	Capricorn	8:47 P.M.	Aquarius
21	Aquarius		
22	Aquarius		
23	Aquarius	1:18 A.M.	Pisces
24	Pisces		
25	Pisces	3:57 A.M.	Aries
26	Aries		
27	Aries	5:22 A.M.	Taurus
28	Taurus		
29	Taurus	6:55 A.M.	Gemini
30	Gemini		

DECEMBER

1	Gemini	10:17 A.M.	Cancer
2	Cancer		
3	Cancer	4:53 P.M.	Leo
4	Leo		
5	Leo		
6	Leo	3:04 A.M.	Virgo
7	Virgo		
8	Virgo	3:28 P.M.	Libra
9	Libra		
10	Libra		
11	Libra	3:42 A.M.	Scorpio
12	Scorpio		
13	Scorpio	1:50 P.M.	Sagittarius
14	Sagittarius		
15	Sagittarius	9:22 P.M.	Capricorn
16	Capricorn		
17	Capricorn		
18	Capricorn	2:44 A.M.	Aquarius
19	Aquarius		
20	Aquarius	6:39 A.M.	Pisces
21	Pisces		
22	Pisces	9:42 A.M.	Aries
23	Aries		
24	Aries	12:24 P.M.	Taurus
25	Taurus		
26	Taurus	3:26 P.M.	Gemini
27	Gemini		
28	Gemini	7:44 P.M.	Cancer
29	Cancer		
30	Cancer		
31	Cancer	2:19 A.M.	Leo

MOON SIGN TABLES
1945

JANUARY

1	Leo		
2	Leo	11:49 A.M.	Virgo
3	Virgo		
4	Virgo	11:44 P.M.	Libra
5	Libra		
6	Libra		
7	Libra	12:13 P.M.	Scorpio
8	Scorpio		
9	Scorpio	10:55 P.M.	Sagittarius
10	Sagittarius		
11	Sagittarius		
12	Sagittarius	6:28 A.M.	Capricorn
13	Capricorn		
14	Capricorn	10:57 A.M.	Aquarius
15	Aquarius		
16	Aquarius	1:27 P.M.	Pisces
17	Pisces		
18	Pisces	3:21 P.M.	Aries
19	Aries		
20	Aries	5:48 P.M.	Taurus
21	Taurus		
22	Taurus	9:35 P.M.	Gemini
23	Gemini		
24	Gemini		
25	Gemini	3:05 A.M.	Cancer
26	Cancer		
27	Cancer	10:33 A.M.	Leo
28	Leo		
29	Leo	8:09 P.M.	Virgo
30	Virgo		
31	Virgo		

FEBRUARY

1	Virgo	7:46 A.M.	Libra
2	Libra		
3	Libra	8:22 P.M.	Scorpio
4	Scorpio		
5	Scorpio		
6	Scorpio	7:57 A.M.	Sagittarius
7	Sagittarius		
8	Sagittarius	4:29 P.M.	Capricorn
9	Capricorn		
10	Capricorn	9:12 P.M.	Aquarius
11	Aquarius		
12	Aquarius	10:52 P.M.	Pisces
13	Pisces		
14	Pisces	11:12 P.M.	Aries
15	Aries		
16	Aries		
17	Aries	12:05 A.M.	Taurus
18	Taurus		
19	Taurus	3:01 A.M.	Gemini
20	Gemini		
21	Gemini	8:42 A.M.	Cancer
22	Cancer		
23	Cancer	4:58 P.M.	Leo
24	Leo		
25	Leo		
26	Leo	3:13 A.M.	Virgo
27	Virgo		
28	Virgo	2:57 P.M.	Libra

MARCH

1	Libra		
2	Libra		
3	Libra	3:32 A.M.	Scorpio

4	Scorpio		
5	Scorpio	3:45 P.M.	Sagittarius
6	Sagittarius		
7	Sagittarius		
8	Sagittarius	1:37 A.M.	Capricorn
9	Capricorn		
10	Capricorn	7:40 A.M.	Aquarius
11	Aquarius		
12	Aquarius	9:50 A.M.	Pisces
13	Pisces		
14	Pisces	9:32 A.M.	Aries
15	Aries		
16	Aries	8:54 A.M.	Taurus
17	Taurus		
18	Taurus	10:04 A.M.	Gemini
19	Gemini		
20	Gemini	2:31 P.M.	Cancer
21	Cancer		
22	Cancer	10:32 P.M.	Leo
23	Leo		
24	Leo		
25	Leo	9:11 A.M.	Virgo
26	Virgo		
27	Virgo	9:15 P.M.	Libra
28	Libra		
29	Libra		
30	Libra	9:50 A.M.	Scorpio
31	Scorpio		

APRIL

1	Scorpio	10:08 P.M.	Sagittarius
2	Sagittarius		
3	Sagittarius		
4	Sagittarius	8:51 A.M.	Capricorn
5	Capricorn		
6	Capricorn	4:28 P.M.	Aquarius
7	Aquarius		
8	Aquarius	8:10 P.M.	Pisces
9	Pisces		
10	Pisces	8:38 P.M.	Aries
11	Aries		
12	Aries	7:40 P.M.	Taurus
13	Taurus		
14	Taurus	7:31 P.M.	Gemini
15	Gemini		
16	Gemini	10:14 P.M.	Cancer
17	Cancer		
18	Cancer		
19	Cancer	4:52 A.M.	Leo
20	Leo		
21	Leo	3:03 P.M.	Virgo
22	Virgo		
23	Virgo		
24	Virgo	3:15 A.M.	Libra
25	Libra		
26	Libra	3:52 P.M.	Scorpio
27	Scorpio		
28	Scorpio		
29	Scorpio	3:56 A.M.	Sagittarius
30	Sagittarius		

MAY

1	Sagittarius	2:40 P.M.	Capricorn
2	Capricorn		
3	Capricorn	11:06 P.M.	Aquarius
4	Aquarius		
5	Aquarius		

6	Aquarius	4:21 A.M.	Pisces
7	Pisces		
8	Pisces	6:25 A.M.	Aries
9	Aries		
10	Aries	6:24 A.M.	Taurus
11	Taurus		
12	Taurus	6:12 A.M.	Gemini
13	Gemini		
14	Gemini	7:51 A.M.	Cancer
15	Cancer		
16	Cancer	12:57 P.M.	Leo
17	Leo		
18	Leo	9:56 P.M.	Virgo
19	Virgo		
20	Virgo		
21	Virgo	9:43 A.M.	Libra
22	Libra		
23	Libra	10:21 P.M.	Scorpio
24	Scorpio		
25	Scorpio		
26	Scorpio	10:11 A.M.	Sagittarius
27	Sagittarius		
28	Sagittarius	8:24 P.M.	Capricorn
29	Capricorn		
30	Capricorn		
31	Capricorn	4:35 A.M.	Aquarius

JUNE

1	Aquarius		
2	Aquarius	10:25 A.M.	Pisces
3	Pisces		
4	Pisces	1:51 P.M.	Aries
5	Aries		
6	Aries	3:23 P.M.	Taurus
7	Taurus		
8	Taurus	4:15 P.M.	Gemini
9	Gemini		
10	Gemini	6:02 P.M.	Cancer
11	Cancer		
12	Cancer	10:20 P.M.	Leo
13	Leo		
14	Leo		
15	Leo	6:07 A.M.	Virgo
16	Virgo		
17	Virgo	5:06 P.M.	Libra
18	Libra		
19	Libra		
20	Libra	5:36 A.M.	Scorpio
21	Scorpio		
22	Scorpio	5:27 P.M.	Sagittarius
23	Sagittarius		
24	Sagittarius		
25	Sagittarius	3:14 A.M.	Capricorn
26	Capricorn		
27	Capricorn	10:36 A.M.	Aquarius
28	Aquarius		
29	Aquarius	3:51 P.M.	Pisces
30	Pisces		

JULY

1	Pisces	7:29 P.M.	Aries
2	Aries		
3	Aries	10:04 P.M.	Taurus
4	Taurus		
5	Taurus		
6	Taurus	12:20 A.M.	Gemini
7	Gemini		

8	Gemini	3:10 A.M.	Cancer
9	Cancer		
10	Cancer	7:43 A.M.	Leo
11	Leo		
12	Leo	2:58 P.M.	Virgo
13	Virgo		
14	Virgo		
15	Virgo	1:13 A.M.	Libra
16	Libra		
17	Libra	1:29 P.M.	Scorpio
18	Scorpio		
19	Scorpio		
20	Scorpio	1:36 A.M.	Sagittarius
21	Sagittarius		
22	Sagittarius	11:29 A.M.	Capricorn
23	Capricorn		
24	Capricorn	6:16 P.M.	Aquarius
25	Aquarius		
26	Aquarius	10:26 P.M.	Pisces
27	Pisces		
28	Pisces		
29	Pisces	1:07 A.M.	Aries
30	Aries		
31	Aries	3:29 A.M.	Taurus

AUGUST

1	Taurus		
2	Taurus	6:23 A.M.	Gemini
3	Gemini		
4	Gemini	10:23 A.M.	Cancer
5	Cancer		
6	Cancer	3:53 P.M.	Leo
7	Leo		
8	Leo	11:24 P.M.	Virgo
9	Virgo		
10	Virgo		
11	Virgo	9:21 A.M.	Libra
12	Libra		
13	Libra	9:24 P.M.	Scorpio
14	Scorpio		
15	Scorpio		
16	Scorpio	9:56 A.M.	Sagittarius
17	Sagittarius		
18	Sagittarius	8:31 P.M.	Capricorn
19	Capricorn		
20	Capricorn		
21	Capricorn	3:32 A.M.	Aquarius
22	Aquarius		
23	Aquarius	7:05 A.M.	Pisces
24	Pisces		
25	Pisces	8:30 A.M.	Aries
26	Aries		
27	Aries	9:34 A.M.	Taurus
28	Taurus		
29	Taurus	11:47 A.M.	Gemini
30	Gemini		
31	Gemini	4:00 P.M.	Cancer

SEPTEMBER

1	Cancer		
2	Cancer	10:20 P.M.	Leo
3	Leo		
4	Leo		
5	Leo	6:36 A.M.	Virgo
6	Virgo		
7	Virgo	4:48 P.M.	Libra
8	Libra		
9	Libra		
10	Libra	4:48 A.M.	Scorpio
11	Scorpio		
12	Scorpio	5:37 P.M.	Sagittarius
13	Sagittarius		
14	Sagittarius		
15	Sagittarius	5:11 A.M.	Capricorn
16	Capricorn		
17	Capricorn	1:19 P.M.	Aquarius
18	Aquarius		
19	Aquarius	5:19 P.M.	Pisces
20	Pisces		
21	Pisces	6:10 P.M.	Aries
22	Aries		
23	Aries	5:53 P.M.	Taurus
24	Taurus		
25	Taurus	6:32 P.M.	Gemini
26	Gemini		
27	Gemini	9:38 P.M.	Cancer
28	Cancer		
29	Cancer		
30	Cancer	3:47 A.M.	Leo

OCTOBER

1	Leo		
2	Leo	12:34 P.M.	Virgo
3	Virgo		
4	Virgo	11:17 P.M.	Libra
5	Libra		
6	Libra		
7	Libra	11:24 A.M.	Scorpio
8	Scorpio		
9	Scorpio		
10	Scorpio	12:17 A.M.	Sagittarius
11	Sagittarius		
12	Sagittarius	12:33 P.M.	Capricorn
13	Capricorn		
14	Capricorn	10:07 P.M.	Aquarius
15	Aquarius		
16	Aquarius		
17	Aquarius	3:34 A.M.	Pisces
18	Pisces		
19	Pisces	5:09 A.M.	Aries
20	Aries		
21	Aries	4:30 A.M.	Taurus
22	Taurus		
23	Taurus	3:49 A.M.	Gemini
24	Gemini		
25	Gemini	5:11 A.M.	Cancer
26	Cancer		
27	Cancer	9:55 A.M.	Leo
28	Leo		
29	Leo	6:12 P.M.	Virgo
30	Virgo		
31	Virgo		

NOVEMBER

1	Virgo	5:08 A.M.	Libra
2	Libra		
3	Libra	5:29 P.M.	Scorpio
4	Scorpio		
5	Scorpio		
6	Scorpio	6:18 A.M.	Sagittarius
7	Sagittarius		
8	Sagittarius	6:35 P.M.	Capricorn
9	Capricorn		
10	Capricorn		
11	Capricorn	4:59 A.M.	Aquarius
12	Aquarius		
13	Aquarius	12:05 P.M.	Pisces
14	Pisces		
15	Pisces	3:24 P.M.	Aries
16	Aries		
17	Aries	3:48 P.M.	Taurus
18	Taurus		
19	Taurus	3:02 P.M.	Gemini
20	Gemini		
21	Gemini	3:14 P.M.	Cancer
22	Cancer		
23	Cancer	6:12 P.M.	Leo
24	Leo		
25	Leo		
26	Leo	12:59 A.M.	Virgo
27	Virgo		
28	Virgo	11:18 A.M.	Libra
29	Libra		
30	Libra	11:43 P.M.	Scorpio

DECEMBER

1	Scorpio		
2	Scorpio		
3	Scorpio	12:30 P.M.	Sagittarius
4	Sagittarius		
5	Sagittarius		
6	Sagittarius	12:23 A.M.	Capricorn
7	Capricorn		
8	Capricorn	10:34 A.M.	Aquarius
9	Aquarius		
10	Aquarius	6:20 P.M.	Pisces
11	Pisces		
12	Pisces	11:15 P.M.	Aries
13	Aries		
14	Aries		
15	Aries	1:30 A.M.	Taurus
16	Taurus		
17	Taurus	2:03 A.M.	Gemini
18	Gemini		
19	Gemini	2:27 A.M.	Cancer
20	Cancer		
21	Cancer	4:30 A.M.	Leo
22	Leo		
23	Leo	9:44 A.M.	Virgo
24	Virgo		
25	Virgo	6:45 P.M.	Libra
26	Libra		
27	Libra		
28	Libra	6:43 A.M.	Scorpio
29	Scorpio		
30	Scorpio	7:32 P.M.	Sagittarius
31	Sagittarius		

MOON SIGN TABLES
1946

JANUARY

1	Sagittarius		
2	Sagittarius	7:11 A.M.	Capricorn
3	Capricorn		
4	Capricorn	4:38 P.M.	Aquarius
5	Aquarius		
6	Aquarius	11:47 P.M.	Pisces
7	Pisces		
8	Pisces		
9	Pisces	4:56 A.M.	Aries
10	Aries		
11	Aries	8:25 A.M.	Taurus
12	Taurus		
13	Taurus	10:42 A.M.	Gemini
14	Gemini		
15	Gemini	12:32 P.M.	Cancer
16	Cancer		
17	Cancer	3:04 P.M.	Leo
18	Leo		
19	Leo	7:40 P.M.	Virgo
20	Virgo		
21	Virgo		
22	Virgo	3:31 A.M.	Libra
23	Libra		
24	Libra	2:40 P.M.	Scorpio
25	Scorpio		
26	Scorpio		
27	Scorpio	3:27 A.M.	Sagittarius
28	Sagittarius		
29	Sagittarius	3:18 P.M.	Capricorn
30	Capricorn		
31	Capricorn		

FEBRUARY

1	Capricorn	12:23 A.M.	Aquarius
2	Aquarius		
3	Aquarius	6:32 A.M.	Pisces
4	Pisces		
5	Pisces	10:38 A.M.	Aries
6	Aries		
7	Aries	1:47 P.M.	Taurus
8	Taurus		
9	Taurus	4:45 P.M.	Gemini
10	Gemini		
11	Gemini	7:59 P.M.	Cancer
12	Cancer		
13	Cancer	11:50 P.M.	Leo
14	Leo		
15	Leo		
16	Leo	5:03 A.M.	Virgo
17	Virgo		
18	Virgo	12:36 P.M.	Libra
19	Libra		
20	Libra	11:05 P.M.	Scorpio
21	Scorpio		
22	Scorpio		
23	Scorpio	11:41 A.M.	Sagittarius
24	Sagittarius		
25	Sagittarius		
26	Sagittarius	12:01 A.M.	Capricorn
27	Capricorn		
28	Capricorn	9:34 A.M.	Aquarius

MARCH

1	Aquarius		
2	Aquarius	3:25 P.M.	Pisces
3	Pisces		

4	Pisces	6:23 P.M.	Aries
5	Aries		
6	Aries	8:08 P.M.	Taurus
7	Taurus		
8	Taurus	10:12 P.M.	Gemini
9	Gemini		
10	Gemini		
11	Gemini	1:29 A.M.	Cancer
12	Cancer		
13	Cancer	6:14 A.M.	Leo
14	Leo		
15	Leo	12:32 P.M.	Virgo
16	Virgo		
17	Virgo	8:40 P.M.	Libra
18	Libra		
19	Libra		
20	Libra	7:04 P.M.	Scorpio
21	Scorpio		
22	Scorpio	7:30 P.M.	Sagittarius
23	Sagittarius		
24	Sagittarius		
25	Sagittarius	8:18 A.M.	Capricorn
26	Capricorn		
27	Capricorn	6:51 P.M.	Aquarius
28	Aquarius		
29	Aquarius		
30	Aquarius	1:26 A.M.	Pisces
31	Pisces		

APRIL

1	Pisces	4:16 A.M.	Aries
2	Aries		
3	Aries	4:56 A.M.	Taurus
4	Taurus		
5	Taurus	5:25 A.M.	Gemini
6	Gemini		
7	Gemini	7:21 A.M.	Cancer
8	Cancer		
9	Cancer	11:37 A.M.	Leo
10	Leo		
11	Leo	6:20 P.M.	Virgo
12	Virgo		
13	Virgo		
14	Virgo	3:13 A.M.	Libra
15	Libra		
16	Libra	2:03 P.M.	Scorpio
17	Scorpio		
18	Scorpio		
19	Scorpio	2:30 A.M.	Sagittarius
20	Sagittarius		
21	Sagittarius	3:28 P.M.	Capricorn
22	Capricorn		
23	Capricorn		
24	Capricorn	2:56 A.M.	Aquarius
25	Aquarius		
26	Aquarius	10:54 A.M.	Pisces
27	Pisces		
28	Pisces	2:45 P.M.	Aries
29	Aries		
30	Aries	3:31 P.M.	Taurus

MAY

1	Taurus		
2	Taurus	3:03 P.M.	Gemini
3	Gemini		
4	Gemini	3:23 P.M.	Cancer
5	Cancer		

6	Cancer	6:04 P.M.	Leo
7	Leo		
8	Leo	11:57 P.M.	Virgo
9	Virgo		
10	Virgo		
11	Virgo	8:53 A.M.	Libra
12	Libra		
13	Libra	8:08 P.M.	Scorpio
14	Scorpio		
15	Scorpio		
16	Scorpio	8:46 A.M.	Sagittarius
17	Sagittarius		
18	Sagittarius	9:42 P.M.	Capricorn
19	Capricorn		
20	Capricorn		
21	Capricorn	9:31 A.M.	Aquarius
22	Aquarius		
23	Aquarius	6:39 P.M.	Pisces
24	Pisces		
25	Pisces		
26	Pisces	12:05 A.M.	Aries
27	Aries		
28	Aries	2:04 A.M.	Taurus
29	Taurus		
30	Taurus	1:54 A.M.	Gemini
31	Gemini		

JUNE

1	Gemini	1:28 A.M.	Cancer
2	Cancer		
3	Cancer	2:39 A.M.	Leo
4	Leo		
5	Leo	6:57 A.M.	Virgo
6	Virgo		
7	Virgo	2:57 P.M.	Libra
8	Libra		
9	Libra		
10	Libra	2:04 A.M.	Scorpio
11	Scorpio		
12	Scorpio	2:50 P.M.	Sagittarius
13	Sagittarius		
14	Sagittarius		
15	Sagittarius	3:39 A.M.	Capricorn
16	Capricorn		
17	Capricorn	3:16 P.M.	Aquarius
18	Aquarius		
19	Aquarius		
20	Aquarius	12:43 A.M.	Pisces
21	Pisces		
22	Pisces	7:19 A.M.	Aries
23	Aries		
24	Aries	10:56 A.M.	Taurus
25	Taurus		
26	Taurus	12:07 P.M.	Gemini
27	Gemini		
28	Gemini	12:10 P.M.	Cancer
29	Cancer		
30	Cancer	12:47 P.M.	Leo

JULY

1	Leo		
2	Leo	3:45 P.M.	Virgo
3	Virgo		
4	Virgo	10:21 P.M.	Libra
5	Libra		
6	Libra		
7	Libra	8:41 A.M.	Scorpio

8	Scorpio		
9	Scorpio	9:20 P.M.	Sagittarius
10	Sagittarius		
11	Sagittarius		
12	Sagittarius	10:05 A.M.	Capricorn
13	Capricorn		
14	Capricorn	9:17 P.M.	Aquarius
15	Aquarius		
16	Aquarius		
17	Aquarius	6:15 A.M.	Pisces
18	Pisces		
19	Pisces	12:59 P.M.	Aries
20	Aries		
21	Aries	5:35 P.M.	Taurus
22	Taurus		
23	Taurus	8:18 P.M.	Gemini
24	Gemini		
25	Gemini	9:44 P.M.	Cancer
26	Cancer		
27	Cancer	10:57 P.M.	Leo
28	Leo		
29	Leo		
30	Leo	1:32 A.M.	Virgo
31	Virgo		

AUGUST

1	Virgo	7:05 A.M.	Libra
2	Libra		
3	Libra	4:23 P.M.	Scorpio
4	Scorpio		
5	Scorpio		
6	Scorpio	4:36 A.M.	Sagittarius
7	Sagittarius		
8	Sagittarius	5:23 P.M.	Capricorn
9	Capricorn		
10	Capricorn		
11	Capricorn	4:23 A.M.	Aquarius
12	Aquarius		
13	Aquarius	12:41 P.M.	Pisces
14	Pisces		
15	Pisces	6:37 P.M.	Aries
16	Aries		
17	Aries	10:59 P.M.	Taurus
18	Taurus		
19	Taurus		
20	Taurus	2:22 A.M.	Gemini
21	Gemini		
22	Gemini	5:06 A.M.	Cancer
23	Cancer		
24	Cancer	7:38 A.M.	Leo
25	Leo		
26	Leo	10:54 A.M.	Virgo
27	Virgo		
28	Virgo	4:15 P.M.	Libra
29	Libra		
30	Libra		
31	Libra	12:49 A.M.	Scorpio

SEPTEMBER

1	Scorpio		
2	Scorpio	12:31 P.M.	Sagittarius
3	Sagittarius		
4	Sagittarius		
5	Sagittarius	1:24 A.M.	Capricorn
6	Capricorn		
7	Capricorn	12:41 P.M.	Aquarius
8	Aquarius		
9	Aquarius	8:46 P.M.	Pisces
10	Pisces		
11	Pisces		
12	Pisces	1:49 A.M.	Aries
13	Aries		
14	Aries	5:03 A.M.	Taurus
15	Taurus		
16	Taurus	7:45 A.M.	Gemini
17	Gemini		
18	Gemini	10:42 A.M.	Cancer
19	Cancer		
20	Cancer	2:13 P.M.	Leo
21	Leo		
22	Leo	6:38 P.M.	Virgo
23	Virgo		
24	Virgo		
25	Virgo	12:40 A.M.	Libra
26	Libra		
27	Libra	9:12 A.M.	Scorpio
28	Scorpio		
29	Scorpio	8:32 P.M.	Sagittarius
30	Sagittarius		

OCTOBER

1	Sagittarius		
2	Sagittarius	9:29 A.M.	Capricorn
3	Capricorn		
4	Capricorn	9:27 P.M.	Aquarius
5	Aquarius		
6	Aquarius		
7	Aquarius	6:09 A.M.	Pisces
8	Pisces		
9	Pisces	11:05 A.M.	Aries
10	Aries		
11	Aries	1:20 P.M.	Taurus
12	Taurus		
13	Taurus	2:37 P.M.	Gemini
14	Gemini		
15	Gemini	4:23 P.M.	Cancer
16	Cancer		
17	Cancer	7:35 P.M.	Leo
18	Leo		
19	Leo		
20	Leo	12:35 A.M.	Virgo
21	Virgo		
22	Virgo	7:33 A.M.	Libra
23	Libra		
24	Libra	4:41 P.M.	Scorpio
25	Scorpio		
26	Scorpio		
27	Scorpio	4:03 A.M.	Sagittarius
28	Sagittarius		
29	Sagittarius	4:59 P.M.	Capricorn
30	Capricorn		
31	Capricorn		

NOVEMBER

1	Capricorn	5:36 A.M.	Aquarius
2	Aquarius		
3	Aquarius	3:32 P.M.	Pisces
4	Pisces		
5	Pisces	9:28 P.M.	Aries
6	Aries		
7	Aries	11:49 P.M.	Taurus
8	Taurus		
9	Taurus		
10	Taurus	12:07 A.M.	Gemini
11	Gemini		
12	Gemini	12:15 A.M.	Cancer
13	Cancer		
14	Cancer	1:53 A.M.	Leo
15	Leo		
16	Leo	6:05 A.M.	Virgo
17	Virgo		
18	Virgo	1:12 P.M.	Libra
19	Libra		
20	Libra	10:58 P.M.	Scorpio
21	Scorpio		
22	Scorpio		
23	Scorpio	10:44 A.M.	Sagittarius
24	Sagittarius		
25	Sagittarius	11:40 P.M.	Capricorn
26	Capricorn		
27	Capricorn		
28	Capricorn	12:30 P.M.	Aquarius
29	Aquarius		
30	Aquarius	11:30 P.M.	Pisces

DECEMBER

1	Pisces		
2	Pisces		
3	Pisces	7:05 A.M.	Aries
4	Aries		
5	Aries	10:48 A.M.	Taurus
6	Taurus		
7	Taurus	11:30 A.M.	Gemini
8	Gemini		
9	Gemini	10:50 A.M.	Cancer
10	Cancer		
11	Cancer	10:46 A.M.	Leo
12	Leo		
13	Leo	1:09 P.M.	Virgo
14	Virgo		
15	Virgo	7:07 P.M.	Libra
16	Libra		
17	Libra		
18	Libra	4:43 A.M.	Scorpio
19	Scorpio		
20	Scorpio	4:48 P.M.	Sagittarius
21	Sagittarius		
22	Sagittarius		
23	Sagittarius	5:50 A.M.	Capricorn
24	Capricorn		
25	Capricorn	6:29 P.M.	Aquarius
26	Aquarius		
27	Aquarius		
28	Aquarius	5:43 A.M.	Pisces
29	Pisces		
30	Pisces	2:31 P.M.	Aries
31	Aries		

MOON SIGN TABLES
1947

JANUARY
1	Aries	8:06 P.M.	Taurus
2	Taurus		
3	Taurus	10:26 P.M.	Gemini
4	Gemini		
5	Gemini	10:28 P.M.	Cancer
6	Cancer		
7	Cancer	9:53 P.M.	Leo
8	Leo		
9	Leo	10:45 P.M.	Virgo
10	Virgo		
11	Virgo		
12	Virgo	2:54 A.M.	Libra
13	Libra		
14	Libra	11:15 A.M.	Scorpio
15	Scorpio		
16	Scorpio	11:03 P.M.	Sagittarius
17	Sagittarius		
18	Sagittarius		
19	Sagittarius	12:10 P.M.	Capricorn
20	Capricorn		
21	Capricorn		
22	Capricorn	12:37 A.M.	Aquarius
23	Aquarius		
24	Aquarius	11:23 A.M.	Pisces
25	Pisces		
26	Pisces	8:10 P.M.	Aries
27	Aries		
28	Aries		
29	Aries	2:45 A.M.	Taurus
30	Taurus		
31	Taurus	6:52 A.M.	Gemini

FEBRUARY
1	Gemini		
2	Gemini	8:38 A.M.	Cancer
3	Cancer		
4	Cancer	9:01 A.M.	Leo
5	Leo		
6	Leo	9:42 A.M.	Virgo
7	Virgo		
8	Virgo	12:39 P.M.	Libra
9	Libra		
10	Libra	7:28 P.M.	Scorpio
11	Scorpio		
12	Scorpio		
13	Scorpio	6:15 A.M.	Sagittarius
14	Sagittarius		
15	Sagittarius	7:12 P.M.	Capricorn
16	Capricorn		
17	Capricorn		
18	Capricorn	7:38 A.M.	Aquarius
19	Aquarius		
20	Aquarius	5:57 P.M.	Pisces
21	Pisces		
22	Pisces		
23	Pisces	1:58 A.M.	Aries
24	Aries		
25	Aries	8:08 A.M.	Taurus
26	Taurus		
27	Taurus	12:47 P.M.	Gemini
28	Gemini		

MARCH
1	Gemini	3:59 P.M.	Cancer
2	Cancer		
3	Cancer	6:00 P.M.	Leo

4	Leo		
5	Leo	7:46 P.M.	Virgo
6	Virgo		
7	Virgo	10:51 P.M.	Libra
8	Libra		
9	Libra		
10	Libra	4:51 A.M.	Scorpio
11	Scorpio		
12	Scorpio	2:34 P.M.	Sagittarius
13	Sagittarius		
14	Sagittarius		
15	Sagittarius	3:00 A.M.	Capricorn
16	Capricorn		
17	Capricorn	3:35 P.M.	Aquarius
18	Aquarius		
19	Aquarius		
20	Aquarius	1:57 A.M.	Pisces
21	Pisces		
22	Pisces	9:23 A.M.	Aries
23	Aries		
24	Aries	2:29 P.M.	Taurus
25	Taurus		
26	Taurus	6:16 P.M.	Gemini
27	Gemini		
28	Gemini	9:26 P.M.	Cancer
29	Cancer		
30	Cancer		
31	Cancer	12:22 A.M.	Leo

APRIL
1	Leo		
2	Leo	3:30 A.M.	Virgo
3	Virgo		
4	Virgo	7:39 A.M.	Libra
5	Libra		
6	Libra	1:57 P.M.	Scorpio
7	Scorpio		
8	Scorpio	11:12 P.M.	Sagittarius
9	Sagittarius		
10	Sagittarius		
11	Sagittarius	11:08 A.M.	Capricorn
12	Capricorn		
13	Capricorn	11:51 P.M.	Aquarius
14	Aquarius		
15	Aquarius		
16	Aquarius	10:47 A.M.	Pisces
17	Pisces		
18	Pisces	6:25 P.M.	Aries
19	Aries		
20	Aries	10:56 P.M.	Taurus
21	Taurus		
22	Taurus		
23	Taurus	1:27 A.M.	Gemini
24	Gemini		
25	Gemini	3:22 A.M.	Cancer
26	Cancer		
27	Cancer	5:44 A.M.	Leo
28	Leo		
29	Leo	9:15 A.M.	Virgo
30	Virgo		

MAY
1	Virgo	2:24 P.M.	Libra
2	Libra		
3	Libra	9:35 P.M.	Scorpio
4	Scorpio		
5	Scorpio		

6	Scorpio	7:09 A.M.	Sagittarius
7	Sagittarius		
8	Sagittarius	6:55 P.M.	Capricorn
9	Capricorn		
10	Capricorn		
11	Capricorn	7:41 A.M.	Aquarius
12	Aquarius		
13	Aquarius	7:20 P.M.	Pisces
14	Pisces		
15	Pisces		
16	Pisces	3:56 A.M.	Aries
17	Aries		
18	Aries	8:51 A.M.	Taurus
19	Taurus		
20	Taurus	10:51 A.M.	Gemini
21	Gemini		
22	Gemini	11:27 A.M.	Cancer
23	Cancer		
24	Cancer	12:18 P.M.	Leo
25	Leo		
26	Leo	2:50 P.M.	Virgo
27	Virgo		
28	Virgo	7:54 P.M.	Libra
29	Libra		
30	Libra		
31	Libra	3:42 A.M.	Scorpio

JUNE
1	Scorpio		
2	Scorpio	1:54 P.M.	Sagittarius
3	Sagittarius		
4	Sagittarius		
5	Sagittarius	1:51 A.M.	Capricorn
6	Capricorn		
7	Capricorn	2:38 P.M.	Aquarius
8	Aquarius		
9	Aquarius		
10	Aquarius	2:47 A.M.	Pisces
11	Pisces		
12	Pisces	12:34 P.M.	Aries
13	Aries		
14	Aries	6:45 P.M.	Taurus
15	Taurus		
16	Taurus	9:21 P.M.	Gemini
17	Gemini		
18	Gemini	9:32 P.M.	Cancer
19	Cancer		
20	Cancer	9:06 P.M.	Leo
21	Leo		
22	Leo	10:01 P.M.	Virgo
23	Virgo		
24	Virgo		
25	Virgo	1:51 A.M.	Libra
26	Libra		
27	Libra	9:17 A.M.	Scorpio
28	Scorpio		
29	Scorpio	7:46 P.M.	Sagittarius
30	Sagittarius		

JULY
1	Sagittarius		
2	Sagittarius	8:03 A.M.	Capricorn
3	Capricorn		
4	Capricorn	8:50 P.M.	Aquarius
5	Aquarius		
6	Aquarius		
7	Aquarius	9:03 A.M.	Pisces

8	Pisces		
9	Pisces	7:34 P.M.	Aries
10	Aries		
11	Aries		
12	Aries	3:12 A.M.	Taurus
13	Taurus		
14	Taurus	7:17 A.M.	Gemini
15	Gemini		
16	Gemini	8:14 A.M.	Cancer
17	Cancer		
18	Cancer	7:34 A.M.	Leo
19	Leo		
20	Leo	7:19 A.M.	Virgo
21	Virgo		
22	Virgo	9:33 A.M.	Libra
23	Libra		
24	Libra	3:41 P.M.	Scorpio
25	Scorpio		
26	Scorpio		
27	Scorpio	1:40 A.M.	Sagittarius
28	Sagittarius		
29	Sagittarius	2:01 P.M.	Capricorn
30	Capricorn		
31	Capricorn		

AUGUST

1	Capricorn	2:50 A.M.	Aquarius
2	Aquarius		
3	Aquarius	2:49 P.M.	Pisces
4	Pisces		
5	Pisces		
6	Pisces	1:20 A.M.	Aries
7	Aries		
8	Aries	9:43 A.M.	Taurus
9	Taurus		
10	Taurus	3:17 P.M.	Gemini
11	Gemini		
12	Gemini	5:49 P.M.	Cancer
13	Cancer		
14	Cancer	6:06 P.M.	Leo
15	Leo		
16	Leo	5:49 P.M.	Virgo
17	Virgo		
18	Virgo	7:04 P.M.	Libra
19	Libra		
20	Libra	11:44 P.M.	Scorpio
21	Scorpio		
22	Scorpio		
23	Scorpio	8:34 A.M.	Sagittarius
24	Sagittarius		
25	Sagittarius	8:31 P.M.	Capricorn
26	Capricorn		
27	Capricorn		
28	Capricorn	9:18 A.M.	Aquarius
29	Aquarius		
30	Aquarius	9:03 P.M.	Pisces
31	Pisces		

SEPTEMBER

1	Pisces		
2	Pisces	7:03 A.M.	Aries
3	Aries		
4	Aries	3:10 P.M.	Taurus
5	Taurus		
6	Taurus	9:18 P.M.	Gemini
7	Gemini		
8	Gemini		

9	Gemini	1:12 A.M.	Cancer
10	Cancer		
11	Cancer	3:03 A.M.	Leo
12	Leo		
13	Leo	3:51 A.M.	Virgo
14	Virgo		
15	Virgo	5:16 A.M.	Libra
16	Libra		
17	Libra	9:11 A.M.	Scorpio
18	Scorpio		
19	Scorpio	4:49 P.M.	Sagittarius
20	Sagittarius		
21	Sagittarius		
22	Sagittarius	3:58 A.M.	Capricorn
23	Capricorn		
24	Capricorn	4:38 P.M.	Aquarius
25	Aquarius		
26	Aquarius		
27	Aquarius	4:24 A.M.	Pisces
28	Pisces		
29	Pisces	1:58 P.M.	Aries
30	Aries		

OCTOBER

1	Aries	9:15 P.M.	Taurus
2	Taurus		
3	Taurus		
4	Taurus	2:44 A.M.	Gemini
5	Gemini		
6	Gemini	6:47 A.M.	Cancer
7	Cancer		
8	Cancer	9:41 A.M.	Leo
9	Leo		
10	Leo	11:57 A.M.	Virgo
11	Virgo		
12	Virgo	2:31 P.M.	Libra
13	Libra		
14	Libra	6:45 P.M.	Scorpio
15	Scorpio		
16	Scorpio		
17	Scorpio	1:53 A.M.	Sagittarius
18	Sagittarius		
19	Sagittarius	12:14 P.M.	Capricorn
20	Capricorn		
21	Capricorn		
22	Capricorn	12:39 A.M.	Aquarius
23	Aquarius		
24	Aquarius	12:45 P.M.	Pisces
25	Pisces		
26	Pisces	10:31 P.M.	Aries
27	Aries		
28	Aries		
29	Aries	5:16 A.M.	Taurus
30	Taurus		
31	Taurus	9:36 A.M.	Gemini

NOVEMBER

1	Gemini		
2	Gemini	12:32 P.M.	Cancer
3	Cancer		
4	Cancer	3:03 P.M.	Leo
5	Leo		
6	Leo	5:55 P.M.	Virgo
7	Virgo		
8	Virgo	9:42 P.M.	Libra
9	Libra		
10	Libra		

11	Libra	3:03 A.M.	Scorpio
12	Scorpio		
13	Scorpio	10:33 A.M.	Sagittarius
14	Sagittarius		
15	Sagittarius	8:37 P.M.	Capricorn
16	Capricorn		
17	Capricorn		
18	Capricorn	8:45 A.M.	Aquarius
19	Aquarius		
20	Aquarius	9:16 P.M.	Pisces
21	Pisces		
22	Pisces		
23	Pisces	7:53 A.M.	Aries
24	Aries		
25	Aries	3:06 P.M.	Taurus
26	Taurus		
27	Taurus	6:55 P.M.	Gemini
28	Gemini		
29	Gemini	8:31 P.M.	Cancer
30	Cancer		

DECEMBER

1	Cancer	9:30 P.M.	Leo
2	Leo		
3	Leo	11:23 P.M.	Virgo
4	Virgo		
5	Virgo		
6	Virgo	3:14 A.M.	Libra
7	Libra		
8	Libra	9:24 A.M.	Scorpio
9	Scorpio		
10	Scorpio	5:49 P.M.	Sagittarius
11	Sagittarius		
12	Sagittarius		
13	Sagittarius	4:14 A.M.	Capricorn
14	Capricorn		
15	Capricorn	4:16 P.M.	Aquarius
16	Aquarius		
17	Aquarius		
18	Aquarius	4:59 A.M.	Pisces
19	Pisces		
20	Pisces	4:37 P.M.	Aries
21	Aries		
22	Aries		
23	Aries	1:11 A.M.	Taurus
24	Taurus		
25	Taurus	5:47 A.M.	Gemini
26	Gemini		
27	Gemini	7:03 A.M.	Cancer
28	Cancer		
29	Cancer	6:41 A.M.	Leo
30	Leo		
31	Leo	6:47 A.M.	Virgo

MOON SIGN TABLES
1948

JANUARY

1	Virgo		
2	Virgo	9:10 A.M.	Libra
3	Libra		
4	Libra	2:51 P.M.	Scorpio
5	Scorpio		
6	Scorpio	11:41 P.M.	Sagittarius
7	Sagittarius		
8	Sagittarius		
9	Sagittarius	10:41 A.M.	Capricorn
10	Capricorn		
11	Capricorn	10:54 P.M.	Aquarius
12	Aquarius		
13	Aquarius		
14	Aquarius	11:35 A.M.	Pisces
15	Pisces		
16	Pisces	11:44 P.M.	Aries
17	Aries		
18	Aries		
19	Aries	9:42 A.M.	Taurus
20	Taurus		
21	Taurus	4:01 P.M.	Gemini
22	Gemini		
23	Gemini	6:23 P.M.	Cancer
24	Cancer		
25	Cancer	6:00 P.M.	Leo
26	Leo		
27	Leo	4:56 P.M.	Virgo
28	Virgo		
29	Virgo	5:29 P.M.	Libra
30	Libra		
31	Libra	9:27 P.M.	Scorpio

FEBRUARY

1	Scorpio		
2	Scorpio		
3	Scorpio	5:26 A.M.	Sagittarius
4	Sagittarius		
5	Sagittarius	4:30 P.M.	Capricorn
6	Capricorn		
7	Capricorn		
8	Capricorn	4:59 A.M.	Aquarius
9	Aquarius		
10	Aquarius	5:37 P.M.	Pisces
11	Pisces		
12	Pisces		
13	Pisces	5:37 A.M.	Aries
14	Aries		
15	Aries	4:08 P.M.	Taurus
16	Taurus		
17	Taurus	11:56 P.M.	Gemini
18	Gemini		
19	Gemini		
20	Gemini	4:09 A.M.	Cancer
21	Cancer		
22	Cancer	5:07 A.M.	Leo
23	Leo		
24	Leo	4:22 A.M.	Virgo
25	Virgo		
26	Virgo	4:05 A.M.	Libra
27	Libra		
28	Libra	6:24 A.M.	Scorpio
29	Scorpio		

MARCH

1	Scorpio	12:41 P.M.	Sagittarius
2	Sagittarius		
3	Sagittarius	10:50 P.M.	Capricorn
4	Capricorn		
5	Capricorn		
6	Capricorn	11:14 A.M.	Aquarius
7	Aquarius		
8	Aquarius	11:53 P.M.	Pisces
9	Pisces		
10	Pisces		
11	Pisces	11:33 A.M.	Aries
12	Aries		
13	Aries	9:40 P.M.	Taurus
14	Taurus		
15	Taurus		
16	Taurus	5:45 A.M.	Gemini
17	Gemini		
18	Gemini	11:14 A.M.	Cancer
19	Cancer		
20	Cancer	1:58 P.M.	Leo
21	Leo		
22	Leo	2:42 P.M.	Virgo
23	Virgo		
24	Virgo	3:01 P.M.	Libra
25	Libra		
26	Libra	4:50 P.M.	Scorpio
27	Scorpio		
28	Scorpio	9:46 P.M.	Sagittarius
29	Sagittarius		
30	Sagittarius		
31	Sagittarius	6:34 A.M.	Capricorn

APRIL

1	Capricorn		
2	Capricorn	6:18 P.M.	Aquarius
3	Aquarius		
4	Aquarius		
5	Aquarius	6:56 A.M.	Pisces
6	Pisces		
7	Pisces	6:28 P.M.	Aries
8	Aries		
9	Aries		
10	Aries	3:58 A.M.	Taurus
11	Taurus		
12	Taurus	11:20 A.M.	Gemini
13	Gemini		
14	Gemini	4:41 P.M.	Cancer
15	Cancer		
16	Cancer	8:16 P.M.	Leo
17	Leo		
18	Leo	10:30 P.M.	Virgo
19	Virgo		
20	Virgo		
21	Virgo	12:16 A.M.	Libra
22	Libra		
23	Libra	2:49 A.M.	Scorpio
24	Scorpio		
25	Scorpio	7:31 A.M.	Sagittarius
26	Sagittarius		
27	Sagittarius	3:22 P.M.	Capricorn
28	Capricorn		
29	Capricorn		
30	Capricorn	2:16 A.M.	Aquarius

MAY

1	Aquarius		
2	Aquarius	2:44 P.M.	Pisces
3	Pisces		
4	Pisces		
5	Pisces	2:28 A.M.	Aries
6	Aries		
7	Aries	11:48 A.M.	Taurus
8	Taurus		
9	Taurus	6:20 P.M.	Gemini
10	Gemini		
11	Gemini	10:38 P.M.	Cancer
12	Cancer		
13	Cancer		
14	Cancer	1:39 A.M.	Leo
15	Leo		
16	Leo	4:14 A.M.	Virgo
17	Virgo		
18	Virgo	7:07 A.M.	Libra
19	Libra		
20	Libra	10:56 A.M.	Scorpio
21	Scorpio		
22	Scorpio	4:22 P.M.	Sagittarius
23	Sagittarius		
24	Sagittarius		
25	Sagittarius	12:08 A.M.	Capricorn
26	Capricorn		
27	Capricorn	10:31 A.M.	Aquarius
28	Aquarius		
29	Aquarius	10:46 P.M.	Pisces
30	Pisces		
31	Pisces		

JUNE

1	Pisces	10:55 A.M.	Aries
2	Aries		
3	Aries	8:43 P.M.	Taurus
4	Taurus		
5	Taurus		
6	Taurus	3:06 A.M.	Gemini
7	Gemini		
8	Gemini	6:28 A.M.	Cancer
9	Cancer		
10	Cancer	8:11 A.M.	Leo
11	Leo		
12	Leo	9:49 A.M.	Virgo
13	Virgo		
14	Virgo	12:33 P.M.	Libra
15	Libra		
16	Libra	5:03 P.M.	Scorpio
17	Scorpio		
18	Scorpio	11:28 P.M.	Sagittarius
19	Sagittarius		
20	Sagittarius		
21	Sagittarius	7:51 A.M.	Capricorn
22	Capricorn		
23	Capricorn	6:15 P.M.	Aquarius
24	Aquarius		
25	Aquarius		
26	Aquarius	6:23 A.M.	Pisces
27	Pisces		
28	Pisces	6:56 P.M.	Aries
29	Aries		
30	Aries		

JULY

1	Aries	5:40 A.M.	Taurus
2	Taurus		
3	Taurus	12:48 P.M.	Gemini
4	Gemini		
5	Gemini	4:07 P.M.	Cancer
6	Cancer		

Day	Sign	Time	Sign
7	Cancer	4:53 P.M.	Leo
8	Leo		
9	Leo	5:04 P.M.	Virgo
10	Virgo		
11	Virgo	6:31 P.M.	Libra
12	Libra		
13	Libra	10:28 P.M.	Scorpio
14	Scorpio		
15	Scorpio		
16	Scorpio	5:11 A.M.	Sagittarius
17	Sagittarius		
18	Sagittarius	2:13 P.M.	Capricorn
19	Capricorn		
20	Capricorn		
21	Capricorn	1:02 A.M.	Aquarius
22	Aquarius		
23	Aquarius	1:13 P.M.	Pisces
24	Pisces		
25	Pisces		
26	Pisces	1:57 A.M.	Aries
27	Aries		
28	Aries	1:34 P.M.	Taurus
29	Taurus		
30	Taurus	10:01 P.M.	Gemini
31	Gemini		

AUGUST

Day	Sign	Time	Sign
1	Gemini		
2	Gemini	2:20 A.M.	Cancer
3	Cancer		
4	Cancer	3:13 A.M.	Leo
5	Leo		
6	Leo	2:32 A.M.	Virgo
7	Virgo		
8	Virgo	2:30 A.M.	Libra
9	Libra		
10	Libra	4:56 A.M.	Scorpio
11	Scorpio		
12	Scorpio	10:49 A.M.	Sagittarius
13	Sagittarius		
14	Sagittarius	7:51 P.M.	Capricorn
15	Capricorn		
16	Capricorn		
17	Capricorn	7:02 A.M.	Aquarius
18	Aquarius		
19	Aquarius	7:23 P.M.	Pisces
20	Pisces		
21	Pisces		
22	Pisces	8:05 A.M.	Aries
23	Aries		
24	Aries	8:03 P.M.	Taurus
25	Taurus		
26	Taurus		
27	Taurus	5:40 A.M.	Gemini
28	Gemini		
29	Gemini	11:34 A.M.	Cancer
30	Cancer		
31	Cancer	1:41 P.M.	Leo

SEPTEMBER

Day	Sign	Time	Sign
1	Leo		
2	Leo	1:20 P.M.	Virgo
3	Virgo		
4	Virgo	12:35 P.M.	Libra
5	Libra		
6	Libra	1:34 P.M.	Scorpio
7	Scorpio		
8	Scorpio	5:52 P.M.	Sagittarius
9	Sagittarius		
10	Sagittarius		
11	Sagittarius	1:56 A.M.	Capricorn
12	Capricorn		
13	Capricorn	12:58 P.M.	Aquarius
14	Aquarius		
15	Aquarius		
16	Aquarius	1:27 A.M.	Pisces
17	Pisces		
18	Pisces	2:02 P.M.	Aries
19	Aries		
20	Aries		
21	Aries	1:45 A.M.	Taurus
22	Taurus		
23	Taurus	11:40 A.M.	Gemini
24	Gemini		
25	Gemini	6:46 P.M.	Cancer
26	Cancer		
27	Cancer	10:35 P.M.	Leo
28	Leo		
29	Leo	11:40 P.M.	Virgo
30	Virgo		

OCTOBER

Day	Sign	Time	Sign
1	Virgo	11:30 P.M.	Libra
2	Libra		
3	Libra	11:58 P.M.	Scorpio
4	Scorpio		
5	Scorpio		
6	Scorpio	2:55 A.M.	Sagittarius
7	Sagittarius		
8	Sagittarius	9:31 A.M.	Capricorn
9	Capricorn		
10	Capricorn	7:42 P.M.	Aquarius
11	Aquarius		
12	Aquarius		
13	Aquarius	8:03 A.M.	Pisces
14	Pisces		
15	Pisces	8:36 P.M.	Aries
16	Aries		
17	Aries		
18	Aries	7:54 A.M.	Taurus
19	Taurus		
20	Taurus	5:15 P.M.	Gemini
21	Gemini		
22	Gemini		
23	Gemini	12:21 A.M.	Cancer
24	Cancer		
25	Cancer	5:10 A.M.	Leo
26	Leo		
27	Leo	7:53 A.M.	Virgo
28	Virgo		
29	Virgo	9:16 A.M.	Libra
30	Libra		
31	Libra	10:31 A.M.	Scorpio

NOVEMBER

Day	Sign	Time	Sign
1	Scorpio		
2	Scorpio	1:10 P.M.	Sagittarius
3	Sagittarius		
4	Sagittarius	6:40 P.M.	Capricorn
5	Capricorn		
6	Capricorn		
7	Capricorn	3:41 A.M.	Aquarius
8	Aquarius		
9	Aquarius	3:34 P.M.	Pisces
10	Pisces		
11	Pisces		
12	Pisces	4:12 A.M.	Aries
13	Aries		
14	Aries	3:24 P.M.	Taurus
15	Taurus		
16	Taurus		
17	Taurus	12:02 A.M.	Gemini
18	Gemini		
19	Gemini	6:11 A.M.	Cancer
20	Cancer		
21	Cancer	10:32 A.M.	Leo
22	Leo		
23	Leo	1:48 P.M.	Virgo
24	Virgo		
25	Virgo	4:33 P.M.	Libra
26	Libra		
27	Libra	7:19 P.M.	Scorpio
28	Scorpio		
29	Scorpio	10:52 P.M.	Sagittarius
30	Sagittarius		

DECEMBER

Day	Sign	Time	Sign
1	Sagittarius		
2	Sagittarius	4:16 A.M.	Capricorn
3	Capricorn		
4	Capricorn	12:32 P.M.	Aquarius
5	Aquarius		
6	Aquarius	11:46 P.M.	Pisces
7	Pisces		
8	Pisces		
9	Pisces	12:30 P.M.	Aries
10	Aries		
11	Aries		
12	Aries	12:09 A.M.	Taurus
13	Taurus		
14	Taurus	8:44 A.M.	Gemini
15	Gemini		
16	Gemini	2:01 P.M.	Cancer
17	Cancer		
18	Cancer	5:03 P.M.	Leo
19	Leo		
20	Leo	7:19 P.M.	Virgo
21	Virgo		
22	Virgo	9:59 P.M.	Libra
23	Libra		
24	Libra		
25	Libra	1:39 A.M.	Scorpio
26	Scorpio		
27	Scorpio	6:29 A.M.	Sagittarius
28	Sagittarius		
29	Sagittarius	12:47 P.M.	Capricorn
30	Capricorn		
31	Capricorn	9:07 P.M.	Aquarius

MOON SIGN TABLES
1949

JANUARY

1	Aquarius		
2	Aquarius		
3	Aquarius	7:58 A.M.	Pisces
4	Pisces		
5	Pisces	8:40 P.M.	Aries
6	Aries		
7	Aries		
8	Aries	9:03 A.M.	Taurus
9	Taurus		
10	Taurus	6:31 P.M.	Gemini
11	Gemini		
12	Gemini	11:57 P.M.	Cancer
13	Cancer		
14	Cancer		
15	Cancer	2:08 A.M.	Leo
16	Leo		
17	Leo	2:52 A.M.	Virgo
18	Virgo		
19	Virgo	4:03 A.M.	Libra
20	Libra		
21	Libra	6:59 A.M.	Scorpio
22	Scorpio		
23	Scorpio	12:09 P.M.	Sagittarius
24	Sagittarius		
25	Sagittarius	7:22 P.M.	Capricorn
26	Capricorn		
27	Capricorn		
28	Capricorn	4:26 A.M.	Aquarius
29	Aquarius		
30	Aquarius	3:26 P.M.	Pisces
31	Pisces		

FEBRUARY

1	Pisces		
2	Pisces	4:04 A.M.	Aries
3	Aries		
4	Aries	4:57 P.M.	Taurus
5	Taurus		
6	Taurus		
7	Taurus	3:40 A.M.	Gemini
8	Gemini		
9	Gemini	10:22 A.M.	Cancer
10	Cancer		
11	Cancer	1:00 P.M.	Leo
12	Leo		
13	Leo	1:05 P.M.	Virgo
14	Virgo		
15	Virgo	12:44 P.M.	Libra
16	Libra		
17	Libra	1:53 P.M.	Scorpio
18	Scorpio		
19	Scorpio	5:49 P.M.	Sagittarius
20	Sagittarius		
21	Sagittarius		
22	Sagittarius	12:50 A.M.	Capricorn
23	Capricorn		
24	Capricorn	10:26 A.M.	Aquarius
25	Aquarius		
26	Aquarius	9:54 P.M.	Pisces
27	Pisces		
28	Pisces		

MARCH

1	Pisces	10:36 A.M.	Aries
2	Aries		
3	Aries	11:33 P.M.	Taurus
4	Taurus		
5	Taurus		
6	Taurus	11:05 A.M.	Gemini
7	Gemini		
8	Gemini	7:21 P.M.	Cancer
9	Cancer		
10	Cancer	11:33 P.M.	Leo
11	Leo		
12	Leo		
13	Leo	12:24 A.M.	Virgo
14	Virgo	11:40 P.M.	Libra
15	Libra		
16	Libra	11:25 P.M.	Scorpio
17	Scorpio		
18	Scorpio		
19	Scorpio	1:30 A.M.	Sagittarius
20	Sagittarius		
21	Sagittarius	7:04 A.M.	Capricorn
22	Capricorn		
23	Capricorn	4:10 P.M.	Aquarius
24	Aquarius		
25	Aquarius		
26	Aquarius	3:50 A.M.	Pisces
27	Pisces		
28	Pisces	4:41 P.M.	Aries
29	Aries		
30	Aries		
31	Aries	5:29 A.M.	Taurus

APRIL

1	Taurus		
2	Taurus	5:03 P.M.	Gemini
3	Gemini		
4	Gemini		
5	Gemini	2:10 A.M.	Cancer
6	Cancer		
7	Cancer	7:59 A.M.	Leo
8	Leo		
9	Leo	10:32 A.M.	Virgo
10	Virgo		
11	Virgo	10:48 A.M.	Libra
12	Libra		
13	Libra	10:27 A.M.	Scorpio
14	Scorpio		
15	Scorpio	11:23 A.M.	Sagittarius
16	Sagittarius		
17	Sagittarius	3:16 P.M.	Capricorn
18	Capricorn		
19	Capricorn	10:59 P.M.	Aquarius
20	Aquarius		
21	Aquarius		
22	Aquarius	10:08 A.M.	Pisces
23	Pisces		
24	Pisces	11:01 P.M.	Aries
25	Aries		
26	Aries		
27	Aries	11:41 A.M.	Taurus
28	Taurus		
29	Taurus	10:48 P.M.	Gemini
30	Gemini		

MAY

1	Gemini		
2	Gemini	7:43 A.M.	Cancer
3	Cancer		
4	Cancer	2:11 P.M.	Leo
5	Leo		
6	Leo	6:11 P.M.	Virgo
7	Virgo		
8	Virgo	8:07 P.M.	Libra
9	Libra		
10	Libra	8:54 P.M.	Scorpio
11	Scorpio		
12	Scorpio	9:57 P.M.	Sagittarius
13	Sagittarius		
14	Sagittarius		
15	Sagittarius	12:57 A.M.	Capricorn
16	Capricorn		
17	Capricorn	7:19 A.M.	Aquarius
18	Aquarius		
19	Aquarius	5:26 P.M.	Pisces
20	Pisces		
21	Pisces		
22	Pisces	6:02 A.M.	Aries
23	Aries		
24	Aries	6:42 P.M.	Taurus
25	Taurus		
26	Taurus		
27	Taurus	5:27 A.M.	Gemini
28	Gemini		
29	Gemini	1:39 P.M.	Cancer
30	Cancer		
31	Cancer	7:36 P.M.	Leo

JUNE

1	Leo		
2	Leo	11:53 P.M.	Virgo
3	Virgo		
4	Virgo		
5	Virgo	2:58 A.M.	Libra
6	Libra		
7	Libra	5:13 A.M.	Scorpio
8	Scorpio		
9	Scorpio	7:24 A.M.	Sagittarius
10	Sagittarius		
11	Sagittarius	10:40 A.M.	Capricorn
12	Capricorn		
13	Capricorn	4:26 P.M.	Aquarius
14	Aquarius		
15	Aquarius		
16	Aquarius	1:38 A.M.	Pisces
17	Pisces		
18	Pisces	1:45 P.M.	Aries
19	Aries		
20	Aries		
21	Aries	2:30 A.M.	Taurus
22	Taurus		
23	Taurus	1:20 P.M.	Gemini
24	Gemini		
25	Gemini	9:01 P.M.	Cancer
26	Cancer		
27	Cancer		
28	Cancer	2:01 A.M.	Leo
29	Leo		
30	Leo	5:27 A.M.	Virgo

JULY

1	Virgo		
2	Virgo	8:22 A.M.	Libra
3	Libra		
4	Libra	11:22 A.M.	Scorpio
5	Scorpio		
6	Scorpio	2:45 P.M.	Sagittarius
7	Sagittarius		

8	Sagittarius	7:02 P.M.	Capricorn
9	Capricorn		
10	Capricorn		
11	Capricorn	1:09 A.M.	Aquarius
12	Aquarius		
13	Aquarius	10:01 A.M.	Pisces
14	Pisces		
15	Pisces	9:43 P.M.	Aries
16	Aries		
17	Aries		
18	Aries	10:36 A.M.	Taurus
19	Taurus		
20	Taurus	9:57 P.M.	Gemini
21	Gemini		
22	Gemini		
23	Gemini	5:52 A.M.	Cancer
24	Cancer		
25	Cancer	10:19 A.M.	Leo
26	Leo		
27	Leo	12:36 P.M.	Virgo
28	Virgo		
29	Virgo	2:20 P.M.	Libra
30	Libra		
31	Libra	4:44 P.M.	Scorpio

AUGUST

1	Scorpio		
2	Scorpio	8:25 P.M.	Sagittarius
3	Sagittarius		
4	Sagittarius		
5	Sagittarius	1:36 A.M.	Capricorn
6	Capricorn		
7	Capricorn	8:34 A.M.	Aquarius
8	Aquarius		
9	Aquarius	5:45 P.M.	Pisces
10	Pisces		
11	Pisces		
12	Pisces	5:20 A.M.	Aries
13	Aries		
14	Aries	6:18 P.M.	Taurus
15	Taurus		
16	Taurus		
17	Taurus	6:23 A.M.	Gemini
18	Gemini		
19	Gemini	3:15 P.M.	Cancer
20	Cancer		
21	Cancer	8:07 P.M.	Leo
22	Leo		
23	Leo	9:56 P.M.	Virgo
24	Virgo		
25	Virgo	10:24 P.M.	Libra
26	Libra		
27	Libra	11:19 P.M.	Scorpio
28	Scorpio		
29	Scorpio		
30	Scorpio	2:00 A.M.	Sagittarius
31	Sagittarius		

SEPTEMBER

1	Sagittarius	7:05 A.M.	Capricorn
2	Capricorn		
3	Capricorn	2:37 P.M.	Aquarius
4	Aquarius		
5	Aquarius		
6	Aquarius	12:26 A.M.	Pisces
7	Pisces		
8	Pisces	12:13 P.M.	Aries
9	Aries		
10	Aries		
11	Aries	1:12 A.M.	Taurus
12	Taurus		
13	Taurus	1:47 P.M.	Gemini
14	Gemini		
15	Gemini	11:52 P.M.	Cancer
16	Cancer		
17	Cancer		
18	Cancer	6:04 P.M.	Leo
19	Leo		
20	Leo	8:34 A.M.	Virgo
21	Virgo		
22	Virgo	8:41 A.M.	Libra
23	Libra		
24	Libra	8:20 A.M.	Scorpio
25	Scorpio		
26	Scorpio	9:21 A.M.	Sagittarius
27	Sagittarius		
28	Sagittarius	1:07 P.M.	Capricorn
29	Capricorn		
30	Capricorn	8:13 P.M.	Aquarius

OCTOBER

1	Aquarius		
2	Aquarius		
3	Aquarius	6:19 A.M.	Pisces
4	Pisces		
5	Pisces	6:27 P.M.	Aries
6	Aries		
7	Aries		
8	Aries	7:26 A.M.	Taurus
9	Taurus		
10	Taurus	8:02 P.M.	Gemini
11	Gemini		
12	Gemini		
13	Gemini	6:51 A.M.	Cancer
14	Cancer		
15	Cancer	2:35 P.M.	Leo
16	Leo		
17	Leo	6:42 P.M.	Virgo
18	Virgo		
19	Virgo	7:48 P.M.	Libra
20	Libra		
21	Libra	7:18 P.M.	Scorpio
22	Scorpio		
23	Scorpio	7:08 P.M.	Sagittarius
24	Sagittarius		
25	Sagittarius	9:10 P.M.	Capricorn
26	Capricorn		
27	Capricorn		
28	Capricorn	2:50 A.M.	Aquarius
29	Aquarius		
30	Aquarius	12:21 P.M.	Pisces
31	Pisces		

NOVEMBER

1	Pisces		
2	Pisces	12:34 A.M.	Aries
3	Aries		
4	Aries	1:37 P.M.	Taurus
5	Taurus		
6	Taurus		
7	Taurus	1:55 A.M.	Gemini
8	Gemini		
9	Gemini	12:35 P.M.	Cancer
10	Cancer		
11	Cancer	9:00 P.M.	Leo
12	Leo		
13	Leo		
14	Leo	2:42 A.M.	Virgo
15	Virgo		
16	Virgo	5:36 A.M.	Libra
17	Libra		
18	Libra	6:18 A.M.	Scorpio
19	Scorpio		
20	Scorpio	6:15 A.M.	Sagittarius
21	Sagittarius		
22	Sagittarius	7:19 A.M.	Capricorn
23	Capricorn		
24	Capricorn	11:24 A.M.	Aquarius
25	Aquarius		
26	Aquarius	7:35 P.M.	Pisces
27	Pisces		
28	Pisces		
29	Pisces	7:18 A.M.	Aries
30	Aries		

DECEMBER

1	Aries	8:22 P.M.	Taurus
2	Taurus		
3	Taurus		
4	Taurus	8:28 A.M.	Gemini
5	Gemini		
6	Gemini	6:31 P.M.	Cancer
7	Cancer		
8	Cancer		
9	Cancer	2:28 A.M.	Leo
10	Leo		
11	Leo	8:31 A.M.	Virgo
12	Virgo		
13	Virgo	12:45 P.M.	Libra
14	Libra		
15	Libra	3:13 P.M.	Scorpio
16	Scorpio		
17	Scorpio	4:32 P.M.	Sagittarius
18	Sagittarius		
19	Sagittarius	6:00 P.M.	Capricorn
20	Capricorn		
21	Capricorn	9:24 P.M.	Aquarius
22	Aquarius		
23	Aquarius		
24	Aquarius	4:20 A.M.	Pisces
25	Pisces		
26	Pisces	3:05 P.M.	Aries
27	Aries		
28	Aries		
29	Aries	3:58 A.M.	Taurus
30	Taurus		
31	Taurus	4:13 P.M.	Gemini

MOON SIGN TABLES
1950

JANUARY

1	Gemini		
2	Gemini		
3	Gemini	1:56 A.M.	Cancer
4	Cancer		
5	Cancer	8:58 A.M.	Leo
6	Leo		
7	Leo	2:06 P.M.	Virgo
8	Virgo		
9	Virgo	6:08 P.M.	Libra
10	Libra		
11	Libra	9:28 P.M.	Scorpio
12	Scorpio		
13	Scorpio		
14	Scorpio	12:16 A.M.	Sagittarius
15	Sagittarius		
16	Sagittarius	3:06 A.M.	Capricorn
17	Capricorn		
18	Capricorn	7:07 A.M.	Aquarius
19	Aquarius		
20	Aquarius	1:41 P.M.	Pisces
21	Pisces		
22	Pisces	11:37 P.M.	Aries
23	Aries		
24	Aries		
25	Aries	12:08 P.M.	Taurus
26	Taurus		
27	Taurus		
28	Taurus	12:43 A.M.	Gemini
29	Gemini		
30	Gemini	10:50 A.M.	Cancer
31	Cancer		

FEBRUARY

1	Cancer	5:34 P.M.	Leo
2	Leo		
3	Leo	9:37 P.M.	Virgo
4	Virgo		
5	Virgo		
6	Virgo	12:19 A.M.	Libra
7	Libra		
8	Libra	2:50 A.M.	Scorpio
9	Scorpio		
10	Scorpio	5:51 A.M.	Sagittarius
11	Sagittarius		
12	Sagittarius	9:45 A.M.	Capricorn
13	Capricorn		
14	Capricorn	2:57 P.M.	Aquarius
15	Aquarius		
16	Aquarius	10:11 P.M.	Pisces
17	Pisces		
18	Pisces		
19	Pisces	8:01 A.M.	Aries
20	Aries		
21	Aries	8:12 P.M.	Taurus
22	Taurus		
23	Taurus		
24	Taurus	9:03 A.M.	Gemini
25	Gemini		
26	Gemini	8:03 P.M.	Cancer
27	Cancer		
28	Cancer		

MARCH

1	Cancer	3:30 A.M.	Leo
2	Leo		
3	Leo	7:24 A.M.	Virgo

4	Virgo		
5	Virgo	9:00 A.M.	Libra
6	Libra		
7	Libra	9:55 A.M.	Scorpio
8	Scorpio		
9	Scorpio	11:37 A.M.	Sagittarius
10	Sagittarius		
11	Sagittarius	3:07 P.M.	Capricorn
12	Capricorn		
13	Capricorn	8:52 P.M.	Aquarius
14	Aquarius		
15	Aquarius		
16	Aquarius	4:59 A.M.	Pisces
17	Pisces		
18	Pisces	3:21 P.M.	Aries
19	Aries		
20	Aries		
21	Aries	3:32 A.M.	Taurus
22	Taurus		
23	Taurus	4:28 P.M.	Gemini
24	Gemini		
25	Gemini		
26	Gemini	4:17 A.M.	Cancer
27	Cancer		
28	Cancer	1:04 P.M.	Leo
29	Leo		
30	Leo	6:01 P.M.	Virgo
31	Virgo		

APRIL

1	Virgo	7:40 P.M.	Libra
2	Libra		
3	Libra	7:35 P.M.	Scorpio
4	Scorpio		
5	Scorpio	7:37 P.M.	Sagittarius
6	Sagittarius		
7	Sagittarius	9:29 P.M.	Capricorn
8	Capricorn		
9	Capricorn		
10	Capricorn	2:24 A.M.	Aquarius
11	Aquarius		
12	Aquarius	10:38 A.M.	Pisces
13	Pisces		
14	Pisces	9:32 P.M.	Aries
15	Aries		
16	Aries		
17	Aries	10:00 A.M.	Taurus
18	Taurus		
19	Taurus	10:54 P.M.	Gemini
20	Gemini		
21	Gemini		
22	Gemini	11:02 A.M.	Cancer
23	Cancer		
24	Cancer	8:57 P.M.	Leo
25	Leo		
26	Leo		
27	Leo	3:30 A.M.	Virgo
28	Virgo		
29	Virgo	6:25 A.M.	Libra
30	Libra		

MAY

1	Libra	6:37 A.M.	Scorpio
2	Scorpio		
3	Scorpio	5:50 A.M.	Sagittarius
4	Sagittarius		
5	Sagittarius	6:08 A.M.	Capricorn

6	Capricorn		
7	Capricorn	9:22 A.M.	Aquarius
8	Aquarius		
9	Aquarius	4:34 P.M.	Pisces
10	Pisces		
11	Pisces		
12	Pisces	3:18 A.M.	Aries
13	Aries		
14	Aries	3:59 P.M.	Taurus
15	Taurus		
16	Taurus		
17	Taurus	4:52 A.M.	Gemini
18	Gemini		
19	Gemini	4:51 P.M.	Cancer
20	Cancer		
21	Cancer		
22	Cancer	3:06 A.M.	Leo
23	Leo		
24	Leo	10:50 A.M.	Virgo
25	Virgo		
26	Virgo	3:26 P.M.	Libra
27	Libra		
28	Libra	5:01 P.M.	Scorpio
29	Scorpio		
30	Scorpio	4:43 P.M.	Sagittarius
31	Sagittarius		

JUNE

1	Sagittarius	4:27 P.M.	Capricorn
2	Capricorn		
3	Capricorn	6:18 P.M.	Aquarius
4	Aquarius		
5	Aquarius	11:57 P.M.	Pisces
6	Pisces		
7	Pisces		
8	Pisces	9:44 A.M.	Aries
9	Aries		
10	Aries	10:12 P.M.	Taurus
11	Taurus		
12	Taurus		
13	Taurus	11:05 A.M.	Gemini
14	Gemini		
15	Gemini	10:45 P.M.	Cancer
16	Cancer		
17	Cancer		
18	Cancer	8:37 A.M.	Leo
19	Leo		
20	Leo	4:31 P.M.	Virgo
21	Virgo		
22	Virgo	10:09 P.M.	Libra
23	Libra		
24	Libra		
25	Libra	1:19 A.M.	Scorpio
26	Scorpio		
27	Scorpio	2:26 A.M.	Sagittarius
28	Sagittarius		
29	Sagittarius	2:48 A.M.	Capricorn
30	Capricorn		

JULY

1	Capricorn	4:19 A.M.	Aquarius
2	Aquarius		
3	Aquarius	8:51 A.M.	Pisces
4	Pisces		
5	Pisces	5:24 P.M.	Aries
6	Aries		
7	Aries		

8	Aries	5:13 A.M.	Taurus
9	Taurus		
10	Taurus	6:02 P.M.	Gemini
11	Gemini		
12	Gemini		
13	Gemini	5:34 A.M.	Cancer
14	Cancer		
15	Cancer	2:52 P.M.	Leo
16	Leo		
17	Leo	10:05 P.M.	Virgo
18	Virgo		
19	Virgo		
20	Virgo	3:34 A.M.	Libra
21	Libra		
22	Libra	7:27 A.M.	Scorpio
23	Scorpio		
24	Scorpio	9:55 A.M.	Sagittarius
25	Sagittarius		
26	Sagittarius	11:39 A.M.	Capricorn
27	Capricorn		
28	Capricorn	1:55 P.M.	Aquarius
29	Aquarius		
30	Aquarius	6:19 P.M.	Pisces
31	Pisces		

AUGUST

1	Pisces		
2	Pisces	2:03 A.M.	Aries
3	Aries		
4	Aries	1:06 P.M.	Taurus
5	Taurus		
6	Taurus		
7	Taurus	1:44 A.M.	Gemini
8	Gemini		
9	Gemini	1:27 P.M.	Cancer
10	Cancer		
11	Cancer	10:36 P.M.	Leo
12	Leo		
13	Leo		
14	Leo	5:03 A.M.	Virgo
15	Virgo		
16	Virgo	9:31 A.M.	Libra
17	Libra		
18	Libra	12:49 P.M.	Scorpio
19	Scorpio		
20	Scorpio	3:36 P.M.	Sagittarius
21	Sagittarius		
22	Sagittarius	6:23 P.M.	Capricorn
23	Capricorn		
24	Capricorn	9:53 P.M.	Aquarius
25	Aquarius		
26	Aquarius		
27	Aquarius	3:02 A.M.	Pisces
28	Pisces		
29	Pisces	10:45 A.M.	Aries
30	Aries		
31	Aries	9:19 P.M.	Taurus

SEPTEMBER

1	Taurus		
2	Taurus		
3	Taurus	9:45 A.M.	Gemini
4	Gemini		
5	Gemini	9:54 P.M.	Cancer
6	Cancer		
7	Cancer		
8	Cancer	7:34 A.M.	Leo
9	Leo		
10	Leo	1:55 P.M.	Virgo
11	Virgo		
12	Virgo	5:28 P.M.	Libra
13	Libra		
14	Libra	7:27 P.M.	Scorpio
15	Scorpio		
16	Scorpio	9:12 P.M.	Sagittarius
17	Sagittarius		
18	Sagittarius	11:49 P.M.	Capricorn
19	Capricorn		
20	Capricorn		
21	Capricorn	3:59 A.M.	Aquarius
22	Aquarius		
23	Aquarius	10:09 A.M.	Pisces
24	Pisces		
25	Pisces	6:32 P.M.	Aries
26	Aries		
27	Aries		
28	Aries	5:08 A.M.	Taurus
29	Taurus		
30	Taurus	5:26 P.M.	Gemini

OCTOBER

1	Gemini		
2	Gemini		
3	Gemini	5:59 A.M.	Cancer
4	Cancer		
5	Cancer	4:40 P.M.	Leo
6	Leo		
7	Leo	11:54 P.M.	Virgo
8	Virgo		
9	Virgo		
10	Virgo	3:29 A.M.	Libra
11	Libra		
12	Libra	4:31 A.M.	Scorpio
13	Scorpio		
14	Scorpio	4:44 A.M.	Sagittarius
15	Sagittarius		
16	Sagittarius	5:55 A.M.	Capricorn
17	Capricorn		
18	Capricorn	9:27 A.M.	Aquarius
19	Aquarius		
20	Aquarius	3:53 P.M.	Pisces
21	Pisces		
22	Pisces		
23	Pisces	12:59 A.M.	Aries
24	Aries		
25	Aries	12:03 P.M.	Taurus
26	Taurus		
27	Taurus		
28	Taurus	12:22 A.M.	Gemini
29	Gemini		
30	Gemini	1:03 P.M.	Cancer
31	Cancer		

NOVEMBER

1	Cancer		
2	Cancer	12:38 A.M.	Leo
3	Leo		
4	Leo	9:21 A.M.	Virgo
5	Virgo		
6	Virgo	2:10 P.M.	Libra
7	Libra		
8	Libra	3:28 P.M.	Scorpio
9	Scorpio		
10	Scorpio	2:51 P.M.	Sagittarius
11	Sagittarius		
12	Sagittarius	2:25 P.M.	Capricorn
13	Capricorn		
14	Capricorn	4:14 P.M.	Aquarius
15	Aquarius		
16	Aquarius	9:38 P.M.	Pisces
17	Pisces		
18	Pisces		
19	Pisces	6:39 A.M.	Aries
20	Aries		
21	Aries	6:08 P.M.	Taurus
22	Taurus		
23	Taurus		
24	Taurus	6:38 A.M.	Gemini
25	Gemini		
26	Gemini	7:13 P.M.	Cancer
27	Cancer		
28	Cancer		
29	Cancer	7:02 A.M.	Leo
30	Leo		

DECEMBER

1	Leo	4:53 P.M.	Virgo
2	Virgo		
3	Virgo	11:29 P.M.	Libra
4	Libra		
5	Libra		
6	Libra	2:19 A.M.	Scorpio
7	Scorpio		
8	Scorpio	2:17 A.M.	Sagittarius
9	Sagittarius		
10	Sagittarius	1:16 A.M.	Capricorn
11	Capricorn		
12	Capricorn	1:34 A.M.	Aquarius
13	Aquarius		
14	Aquarius	5:10 A.M.	Pisces
15	Pisces		
16	Pisces	12:58 P.M.	Aries
17	Aries		
18	Aries		
19	Aries	12:10 A.M.	Taurus
20	Taurus		
21	Taurus	12:49 P.M.	Gemini
22	Gemini		
23	Gemini		
24	Gemini	1:18 A.M.	Cancer
25	Cancer		
26	Cancer	12:45 P.M.	Leo
27	Leo		
28	Leo	10:41 P.M.	Virgo
29	Virgo		
30	Virgo		
31	Virgo	6:20 A.M.	Libra

MOON SIGN TABLES
1951

JANUARY

1	Libra		
2	Libra	10:58 A.M.	Scorpio
3	Scorpio		
4	Scorpio	12:38 P.M.	Sagittarius
5	Sagittarius		
6	Sagittarius	12:32 P.M.	Capricorn
7	Capricorn		
8	Capricorn	12:35 P.M.	Aquarius
9	Aquarius		
10	Aquarius	2:56 P.M.	Pisces
11	Pisces		
12	Pisces	9:05 P.M.	Aries
13	Aries		
14	Aries		
15	Aries	7:10 A.M.	Taurus
16	Taurus		
17	Taurus	7:36 P.M.	Gemini
18	Gemini		
19	Gemini		
20	Gemini	8:06 A.M.	Cancer
21	Cancer		
22	Cancer	7:12 P.M.	Leo
23	Leo		
24	Leo		
25	Leo	4:26 A.M.	Virgo
26	Virgo		
27	Virgo	11:46 A.M.	Libra
28	Libra		
29	Libra	5:04 P.M.	Scorpio
30	Scorpio		
31	Scorpio	8:16 P.M.	Sagittarius

FEBRUARY

1	Sagittarius		
2	Sagittarius	9:52 P.M.	Capricorn
3	Capricorn		
4	Capricorn	11:04 P.M.	Aquarius
5	Aquarius		
6	Aquarius		
7	Aquarius	1:29 A.M.	Pisces
8	Pisces		
9	Pisces	6:43 A.M.	Aries
10	Aries		
11	Aries	3:33 P.M.	Taurus
12	Taurus		
13	Taurus		
14	Taurus	3:18 A.M.	Gemini
15	Gemini		
16	Gemini	3:51 P.M.	Cancer
17	Cancer		
18	Cancer		
19	Cancer	3:01 A.M.	Leo
20	Leo		
21	Leo	11:43 A.M.	Virgo
22	Virgo		
23	Virgo	6:01 P.M.	Libra
24	Libra		
25	Libra	10:31 P.M.	Scorpio
26	Scorpio		
27	Scorpio		
28	Scorpio	1:49 A.M.	Sagittarius

MARCH

1	Sagittarius		
2	Sagittarius	4:29 A.M.	Capricorn
3	Capricorn		

4	Capricorn	7:11 A.M.	Aquarius
5	Aquarius		
6	Aquarius	10:45 A.M.	Pisces
7	Pisces		
8	Pisces	4:16 P.M.	Aries
9	Aries		
10	Aries		
11	Aries	12:33 A.M.	Taurus
12	Taurus		
13	Taurus	11:36 A.M.	Gemini
14	Gemini		
15	Gemini		
16	Gemini	12:06 A.M.	Cancer
17	Cancer		
18	Cancer	11:44 A.M.	Leo
19	Leo		
20	Leo	8:39 P.M.	Virgo
21	Virgo		
22	Virgo		
23	Virgo	2:21 A.M.	Libra
24	Libra		
25	Libra	5:36 A.M.	Scorpio
26	Scorpio		
27	Scorpio	7:40 A.M.	Sagittarius
28	Sagittarius		
29	Sagittarius	9:51 A.M.	Capricorn
30	Capricorn		
31	Capricorn	1:02 P.M.	Aquarius

APRIL

1	Aquarius		
2	Aquarius	5:44 P.M.	Pisces
3	Pisces		
4	Pisces		
5	Pisces	12:16 A.M.	Aries
6	Aries		
7	Aries	8:52 A.M.	Taurus
8	Taurus		
9	Taurus	7:41 P.M.	Gemini
10	Gemini		
11	Gemini		
12	Gemini	8:04 A.M.	Cancer
13	Cancer		
14	Cancer	8:18 P.M.	Leo
15	Leo		
16	Leo		
17	Leo	6:07 A.M.	Virgo
18	Virgo		
19	Virgo	12:13 P.M.	Libra
20	Libra		
21	Libra	2:55 P.M.	Scorpio
22	Scorpio		
23	Scorpio	3:40 P.M.	Sagittarius
24	Sagittarius		
25	Sagittarius	4:20 P.M.	Capricorn
26	Capricorn		
27	Capricorn	6:32 P.M.	Aquarius
28	Aquarius		
29	Aquarius	11:13 P.M.	Pisces
30	Pisces		

MAY

1	Pisces		
2	Pisces	6:26 A.M.	Aries
3	Aries		
4	Aries	3:46 P.M.	Taurus
5	Taurus		

6	Taurus		
7	Taurus	2:51 A.M.	Gemini
8	Gemini		
9	Gemini	3:13 P.M.	Cancer
10	Cancer		
11	Cancer		
12	Cancer	3:49 A.M.	Leo
13	Leo		
14	Leo	2:44 P.M.	Virgo
15	Virgo		
16	Virgo	10:05 P.M.	Libra
17	Libra		
18	Libra		
19	Libra	1:23 A.M.	Scorpio
20	Scorpio		
21	Scorpio	1:44 A.M.	Sagittarius
22	Sagittarius		
23	Sagittarius	1:07 A.M.	Capricorn
24	Capricorn		
25	Capricorn	1:41 A.M.	Aquarius
26	Aquarius		
27	Aquarius	5:05 A.M.	Pisces
28	Pisces		
29	Pisces	11:53 A.M.	Aries
30	Aries		
31	Aries	9:33 P.M.	Taurus

JUNE

1	Taurus		
2	Taurus		
3	Taurus	9:03 A.M.	Gemini
4	Gemini		
5	Gemini	9:31 P.M.	Cancer
6	Cancer		
7	Cancer		
8	Cancer	10:12 A.M.	Leo
9	Leo		
10	Leo	9:47 P.M.	Virgo
11	Virgo		
12	Virgo		
13	Virgo	6:31 A.M.	Libra
14	Libra		
15	Libra	11:17 A.M.	Scorpio
16	Scorpio		
17	Scorpio	12:26 P.M.	Sagittarius
18	Sagittarius		
19	Sagittarius	11:38 A.M.	Capricorn
20	Capricorn		
21	Capricorn	11:04 A.M.	Aquarius
22	Aquarius		
23	Aquarius	12:49 P.M.	Pisces
24	Pisces		
25	Pisces	6:13 P.M.	Aries
26	Aries		
27	Aries		
28	Aries	3:17 A.M.	Taurus
29	Taurus		
30	Taurus	2:51 P.M.	Gemini

JULY

1	Gemini		
2	Gemini		
3	Gemini	3:27 A.M.	Cancer
4	Cancer		
5	Cancer	4:00 P.M.	Leo
6	Leo		
7	Leo		

8	Leo	3:36 A.M.	Virgo
9	Virgo		
10	Virgo	1:04 P.M.	Libra
11	Libra		
12	Libra	7:19 P.M.	Scorpio
13	Scorpio		
14	Scorpio	10:03 P.M.	Sagittarius
15	Sagittarius		
16	Sagittarius	10:14 P.M.	Capricorn
17	Capricorn		
18	Capricorn	9:41 P.M.	Aquarius
19	Aquarius		
20	Aquarius	10:29 P.M.	Pisces
21	Pisces		
22	Pisces		
23	Pisces	2:21 A.M.	Aries
24	Aries		
25	Aries	10:07 A.M.	Taurus
26	Taurus		
27	Taurus	9:08 P.M.	Gemini
28	Gemini		
29	Gemini		
30	Gemini	9:42 A.M.	Cancer
31	Cancer		

AUGUST

1	Cancer	10:08 P.M.	Leo
2	Leo		
3	Leo		
4	Leo	9:18 A.M.	Virgo
5	Virgo		
6	Virgo	6:34 P.M.	Libra
7	Libra		
8	Libra		
9	Libra	1:24 A.M.	Scorpio
10	Scorpio		
11	Scorpio	5:31 A.M.	Sagittarius
12	Sagittarius		
13	Sagittarius	7:18 A.M.	Capricorn
14	Capricorn		
15	Capricorn	7:53 A.M.	Aquarius
16	Aquarius		
17	Aquarius	8:52 A.M.	Pisces
18	Pisces		
19	Pisces	11:58 A.M.	Aries
20	Aries		
21	Aries	6:26 P.M.	Taurus
22	Taurus		
23	Taurus		
24	Taurus	4:27 A.M.	Gemini
25	Gemini		
26	Gemini	4:44 P.M.	Cancer
27	Cancer		
28	Cancer		
29	Cancer	5:10 A.M.	Leo
30	Leo		
31	Leo	4:00 P.M.	Virgo

SEPTEMBER

1	Virgo		
2	Virgo		
3	Virgo	12:32 A.M.	Libra
4	Libra		
5	Libra	6:49 A.M.	Scorpio
6	Scorpio		
7	Scorpio	11:11 A.M.	Sagittarius
8	Sagittarius		
9	Sagittarius	2:06 P.M.	Capricorn
10	Capricorn		
11	Capricorn	4:11 P.M.	Aquarius
12	Aquarius		
13	Aquarius	6:21 P.M.	Pisces
14	Pisces		
15	Pisces	9:47 P.M.	Aries
16	Aries		
17	Aries		
18	Aries	3:41 A.M.	Taurus
19	Taurus		
20	Taurus	12:47 P.M.	Gemini
21	Gemini		
22	Gemini		
23	Gemini	12:34 A.M.	Cancer
24	Cancer		
25	Cancer	1:08 P.M.	Leo
26	Leo		
27	Leo		
28	Leo	12:05 A.M.	Virgo
29	Virgo		
30	Virgo	8:08 A.M.	Libra

OCTOBER

1	Libra		
2	Libra	1:23 P.M.	Scorpio
3	Scorpio		
4	Scorpio	4:48 P.M.	Sagittarius
5	Sagittarius		
6	Sagittarius	7:30 P.M.	Capricorn
7	Capricorn		
8	Capricorn	10:19 P.M.	Aquarius
9	Aquarius		
10	Aquarius		
11	Aquarius	1:46 A.M.	Pisces
12	Pisces		
13	Pisces	6:19 A.M.	Aries
14	Aries		
15	Aries	12:37 P.M.	Taurus
16	Taurus		
17	Taurus	9:22 P.M.	Gemini
18	Gemini		
19	Gemini		
20	Gemini	8:43 A.M.	Cancer
21	Cancer		
22	Cancer	9:25 P.M.	Leo
23	Leo		
24	Leo		
25	Leo	9:01 A.M.	Virgo
26	Virgo		
27	Virgo	5:25 P.M.	Libra
28	Libra		
29	Libra	10:09 P.M.	Scorpio
30	Scorpio		
31	Scorpio		

NOVEMBER

1	Scorpio	12:20 A.M.	Sagittarius
2	Sagittarius		
3	Sagittarius	1:40 A.M.	Capricorn
4	Capricorn		
5	Capricorn	3:43 A.M.	Aquarius
6	Aquarius		
7	Aquarius	7:23 A.M.	Pisces
8	Pisces		
9	Pisces	12:52 P.M.	Aries
10	Aries		
11	Aries	8:07 P.M.	Taurus
12	Taurus		
13	Taurus		
14	Taurus	5:15 A.M.	Gemini
15	Gemini		
16	Gemini	4:28 P.M.	Cancer
17	Cancer		
18	Cancer		
19	Cancer	5:12 A.M.	Leo
20	Leo		
21	Leo	5:35 P.M.	Virgo
22	Virgo		
23	Virgo		
24	Virgo	3:09 A.M.	Libra
25	Libra		
26	Libra	8:32 A.M.	Scorpio
27	Scorpio		
28	Scorpio	10:20 A.M.	Sagittarius
29	Sagittarius		
30	Sagittarius	10:22 A.M.	Capricorn

DECEMBER

1	Capricorn		
2	Capricorn	10:45 A.M.	Aquarius
3	Aquarius		
4	Aquarius	1:08 P.M.	Pisces
5	Pisces		
6	Pisces	6:18 P.M.	Aries
7	Aries		
8	Aries		
9	Aries	2:04 A.M.	Taurus
10	Taurus		
11	Taurus	11:54 A.M.	Gemini
12	Gemini		
13	Gemini	11:22 P.M.	Cancer
14	Cancer		
15	Cancer		
16	Cancer	12:05 P.M.	Leo
17	Leo		
18	Leo		
19	Leo	12:52 A.M.	Virgo
20	Virgo		
21	Virgo	11:41 A.M.	Libra
22	Libra		
23	Libra	6:38 P.M.	Scorpio
24	Scorpio		
25	Scorpio	9:27 P.M.	Sagittarius
26	Sagittarius		
27	Sagittarius	9:24 P.M.	Capricorn
28	Capricorn		
29	Capricorn	8:36 P.M.	Aquarius
30	Aquarius		
31	Aquarius	9:10 P.M.	Pisces

MOON SIGN TABLES
1952

JANUARY

1	Pisces		
2	Pisces		
3	Pisces	12:42 A.M.	Aries
4	Aries		
5	Aries	7:43 A.M.	Taurus
6	Taurus		
7	Taurus	5:42 P.M.	Gemini
8	Gemini		
9	Gemini		
10	Gemini	5:34 A.M.	Cancer
11	Cancer		
12	Cancer	6:19 P.M.	Leo
13	Leo		
14	Leo		
15	Leo	7:00 A.M.	Virgo
16	Virgo		
17	Virgo	6:19 P.M.	Libra
18	Libra		
19	Libra		
20	Libra	2:44 A.M.	Scorpio
21	Scorpio		
22	Scorpio	7:22 A.M.	Sagittarius
23	Sagittarius		
24	Sagittarius	8:39 A.M.	Capricorn
25	Capricorn		
26	Capricorn	8:06 A.M.	Aquarius
27	Aquarius		
28	Aquarius	7:45 A.M.	Pisces
29	Pisces		
30	Pisces	9:33 A.M.	Aries
31	Aries		

FEBRUARY

1	Aries	2:51 P.M.	Taurus
2	Taurus		
3	Taurus	11:55 P.M.	Gemini
4	Gemini		
5	Gemini		
6	Gemini	11:44 A.M.	Cancer
7	Cancer		
8	Cancer		
9	Cancer	12:36 A.M.	Leo
10	Leo		
11	Leo	1:02 P.M.	Virgo
12	Virgo		
13	Virgo		
14	Virgo	12:00 A.M.	Libra
15	Libra		
16	Libra	8:45 A.M.	Scorpio
17	Scorpio		
18	Scorpio	2:42 P.M.	Sagittarius
19	Sagittarius		
20	Sagittarius	5:49 P.M.	Capricorn
21	Capricorn		
22	Capricorn	6:48 P.M.	Aquarius
23	Aquarius		
24	Aquarius	7:01 P.M.	Pisces
25	Pisces		
26	Pisces	8:12 P.M.	Aries
27	Aries		
28	Aries		
29	Aries	12:02 A.M.	Taurus

MARCH

1	Taurus		
2	Taurus	7:36 A.M.	Gemini

3	Gemini		
4	Gemini	6:40 P.M.	Cancer
5	Cancer		
6	Cancer		
7	Cancer	7:30 A.M.	Leo
8	Leo		
9	Leo	7:51 P.M.	Virgo
10	Virgo		
11	Virgo		
12	Virgo	6:16 A.M.	Libra
13	Libra		
14	Libra	2:20 P.M.	Scorpio
15	Scorpio		
16	Scorpio	8:15 P.M.	Sagittarius
17	Sagittarius		
18	Sagittarius		
19	Sagittarius	12:19 A.M.	Capricorn
20	Capricorn		
21	Capricorn	2:55 A.M.	Aquarius
22	Aquarius		
23	Aquarius	4:39 A.M.	Pisces
24	Pisces		
25	Pisces	6:34 A.M.	Aries
26	Aries		
27	Aries	10:05 A.M.	Taurus
28	Taurus		
29	Taurus	4:36 P.M.	Gemini
30	Gemini		
31	Gemini		

APRIL

1	Gemini	2:39 A.M.	Cancer
2	Cancer		
3	Cancer	3:10 P.M.	Leo
4	Leo		
5	Leo		
6	Leo	3:40 A.M.	Virgo
7	Virgo		
8	Virgo	1:56 P.M.	Libra
9	Libra		
10	Libra	9:13 P.M.	Scorpio
11	Scorpio		
12	Scorpio		
13	Scorpio	2:08 A.M.	Sagittarius
14	Sagittarius		
15	Sagittarius	5:41 A.M.	Capricorn
16	Capricorn		
17	Capricorn	8:43 A.M.	Aquarius
18	Aquarius		
19	Aquarius	11:40 A.M.	Pisces
20	Pisces		
21	Pisces	2:56 P.M.	Aries
22	Aries		
23	Aries	7:15 P.M.	Taurus
24	Taurus		
25	Taurus		
26	Taurus	1:40 A.M.	Gemini
27	Gemini		
28	Gemini	11:06 A.M.	Cancer
29	Cancer		
30	Cancer	11:12 P.M.	Leo

MAY

1	Leo		
2	Leo		
3	Leo	11:57 A.M.	Virgo
4	Virgo		

5	Virgo	10:39 P.M.	Libra
6	Libra		
7	Libra		
8	Libra	5:49 A.M.	Scorpio
9	Scorpio		
10	Scorpio	9:50 A.M.	Sagittarius
11	Sagittarius		
12	Sagittarius	12:09 P.M.	Capricorn
13	Capricorn		
14	Capricorn	2:14 P.M.	Aquarius
15	Aquarius		
16	Aquarius	5:05 P.M.	Pisces
17	Pisces		
18	Pisces	9:07 P.M.	Aries
19	Aries		
20	Aries		
21	Aries	2:29 A.M.	Taurus
22	Taurus		
23	Taurus	9:37 A.M.	Gemini
24	Gemini		
25	Gemini	7:06 P.M.	Cancer
26	Cancer		
27	Cancer		
28	Cancer	6:59 A.M.	Leo
29	Leo		
30	Leo	7:57 P.M.	Virgo
31	Virgo		

JUNE

1	Virgo		
2	Virgo	7:26 A.M.	Libra
3	Libra		
4	Libra	3:19 P.M.	Scorpio
5	Scorpio		
6	Scorpio	7:21 P.M.	Sagittarius
7	Sagittarius		
8	Sagittarius	8:46 P.M.	Capricorn
9	Capricorn		
10	Capricorn	9:27 P.M.	Aquarius
11	Aquarius		
12	Aquarius	11:00 P.M.	Pisces
13	Pisces		
14	Pisces		
15	Pisces	2:29 A.M.	Aries
16	Aries		
17	Aries	8:11 A.M.	Taurus
18	Taurus		
19	Taurus	4:03 P.M.	Gemini
20	Gemini		
21	Gemini		
22	Gemini	2:04 A.M.	Cancer
23	Cancer		
24	Cancer	2:02 P.M.	Leo
25	Leo		
26	Leo		
27	Leo	3:06 A.M.	Virgo
28	Virgo		
29	Virgo	3:18 P.M.	Libra
30	Libra		

JULY

1	Libra		
2	Libra	12:25 A.M.	Scorpio
3	Scorpio		
4	Scorpio	5:27 A.M.	Sagittarius
5	Sagittarius		
6	Sagittarius	7:02 A.M.	Capricorn

7	Capricorn		
8	Capricorn	6:54 A.M.	Aquarius
9	Aquarius		
10	Aquarius	6:59 A.M.	Pisces
11	Pisces		
12	Pisces	8:56 A.M.	Aries
13	Aries		
14	Aries	1:45 P.M.	Taurus
15	Taurus		
16	Taurus	9:37 P.M.	Gemini
17	Gemini		
18	Gemini		
19	Gemini	8:05 A.M.	Cancer
20	Cancer		
21	Cancer	8:20 P.M.	Leo
22	Leo		
23	Leo		
24	Leo	9:25 A.M.	Virgo
25	Virgo		
26	Virgo	9:54 P.M.	Libra
27	Libra		
28	Libra		
29	Libra	8:04 A.M.	Scorpio
30	Scorpio		
31	Scorpio	2:37 P.M.	Sagittarius

AUGUST

1	Sagittarius		
2	Sagittarius	5:27 P.M.	Capricorn
3	Capricorn		
4	Capricorn	5:41 P.M.	Aquarius
5	Aquarius		
6	Aquarius	5:05 P.M.	Pisces
7	Pisces		
8	Pisces	5:33 P.M.	Aries
9	Aries		
10	Aries	8:46 P.M.	Taurus
11	Taurus		
12	Taurus		
13	Taurus	3:36 A.M.	Gemini
14	Gemini		
15	Gemini	1:52 P.M.	Cancer
16	Cancer		
17	Cancer		
18	Cancer	2:19 A.M.	Leo
19	Leo		
20	Leo	3:22 P.M.	Virgo
21	Virgo		
22	Virgo		
23	Virgo	3:42 A.M.	Libra
24	Libra		
25	Libra	2:10 P.M.	Scorpio
26	Scorpio		
27	Scorpio	9:53 P.M.	Sagittarius
28	Sagittarius		
29	Sagittarius		
30	Sagittarius	2:24 A.M.	Capricorn
31	Capricorn		

SEPTEMBER

1	Capricorn	4:03 A.M.	Aquarius
2	Aquarius		
3	Aquarius	4:00 A.M.	Pisces
4	Pisces		
5	Pisces	3:57 A.M.	Aries
6	Aries		
7	Aries	5:48 A.M.	Taurus
8	Taurus		
9	Taurus	11:06 A.M.	Gemini
10	Gemini		
11	Gemini	8:24 P.M.	Cancer
12	Cancer		
13	Cancer		
14	Cancer	8:38 A.M.	Leo
15	Leo		
16	Leo	9:42 P.M.	Virgo
17	Virgo		
18	Virgo		
19	Virgo	9:41 A.M.	Libra
20	Libra		
21	Libra	7:43 P.M.	Scorpio
22	Scorpio		
23	Scorpio		
24	Scorpio	3:33 A.M.	Sagittarius
25	Sagittarius		
26	Sagittarius	9:06 A.M.	Capricorn
27	Capricorn		
28	Capricorn	12:24 P.M.	Aquarius
29	Aquarius		
30	Aquarius	1:52 P.M.	Pisces

OCTOBER

1	Pisces		
2	Pisces	2:34 P.M.	Aries
3	Aries		
4	Aries	4:05 P.M.	Taurus
5	Taurus		
6	Taurus	8:15 P.M.	Gemini
7	Gemini		
8	Gemini		
9	Gemini	4:16 A.M.	Cancer
10	Cancer		
11	Cancer	3:50 P.M.	Leo
12	Leo		
13	Leo		
14	Leo	4:51 A.M.	Virgo
15	Virgo		
16	Virgo	4:44 P.M.	Libra
17	Libra		
18	Libra		
19	Libra	2:10 A.M.	Scorpio
20	Scorpio		
21	Scorpio	9:12 A.M.	Sagittarius
22	Sagittarius		
23	Sagittarius	2:28 P.M.	Capricorn
24	Capricorn		
25	Capricorn	6:28 P.M.	Aquarius
26	Aquarius		
27	Aquarius	9:23 P.M.	Pisces
28	Pisces		
29	Pisces	11:34 P.M.	Aries
30	Aries		
31	Aries		

NOVEMBER

1	Aries	1:58 A.M.	Taurus
2	Taurus		
3	Taurus	6:02 A.M.	Gemini
4	Gemini		
5	Gemini	1:12 P.M.	Cancer
6	Cancer		
7	Cancer	11:56 P.M.	Leo
8	Leo		
9	Leo		
10	Leo	12:47 P.M.	Virgo
11	Virgo		
12	Virgo		
13	Virgo	12:57 A.M.	Libra
14	Libra		
15	Libra	10:18 A.M.	Scorpio
16	Scorpio		
17	Scorpio	4:33 P.M.	Sagittarius
18	Sagittarius		
19	Sagittarius	8:40 P.M.	Capricorn
20	Capricorn		
21	Capricorn	11:52 P.M.	Aquarius
22	Aquarius		
23	Aquarius		
24	Aquarius	2:55 A.M.	Pisces
25	Pisces		
26	Pisces	6:09 A.M.	Aries
27	Aries		
28	Aries	9:54 A.M.	Taurus
29	Taurus		
30	Taurus	2:53 P.M.	Gemini

DECEMBER

1	Gemini		
2	Gemini	10:09 P.M.	Cancer
3	Cancer		
4	Cancer		
5	Cancer	8:23 A.M.	Leo
6	Leo		
7	Leo	8:57 P.M.	Virgo
8	Virgo		
9	Virgo		
10	Virgo	9:35 A.M.	Libra
11	Libra		
12	Libra	7:39 P.M.	Scorpio
13	Scorpio		
14	Scorpio		
15	Scorpio	2:00 A.M.	Sagittarius
16	Sagittarius		
17	Sagittarius	5:17 A.M.	Capricorn
18	Capricorn		
19	Capricorn	7:02 A.M.	Aquarius
20	Aquarius		
21	Aquarius	8:45 A.M.	Pisces
22	Pisces		
23	Pisces	11:30 A.M.	Aries
24	Aries		
25	Aries	3:46 P.M.	Taurus
26	Taurus		
27	Taurus	9:48 P.M.	Gemini
28	Gemini		
29	Gemini		
30	Gemini	5:53 A.M.	Cancer
31	Cancer		

MOON SIGN TABLES
1953

JANUARY

1	Cancer	4:17 P.M.	Leo
2	Leo		
3	Leo		
4	Leo	4:41 A.M.	Virgo
5	Virgo		
6	Virgo	5:36 P.M.	Libra
7	Libra		
8	Libra		
9	Libra	4:44 A.M.	Scorpio
10	Scorpio		
11	Scorpio	12:14 P.M.	Sagittarius
12	Sagittarius		
13	Sagittarius	3:55 P.M.	Capricorn
14	Capricorn		
15	Capricorn	4:57 P.M.	Aquarius
16	Aquarius		
17	Aquarius	5:07 P.M.	Pisces
18	Pisces		
19	Pisces	6:08 P.M.	Aries
20	Aries		
21	Aries	9:20 P.M.	Taurus
22	Taurus		
23	Taurus		
24	Taurus	3:21 A.M.	Gemini
25	Gemini		
26	Gemini	12:07 P.M.	Cancer
27	Cancer		
28	Cancer	11:06 P.M.	Leo
29	Leo		
30	Leo		
31	Leo	11:35 A.M.	Virgo

FEBRUARY

1	Virgo		
2	Virgo		
3	Virgo	12:31 A.M.	Libra
4	Libra		
5	Libra	12:21 P.M.	Scorpio
6	Scorpio		
7	Scorpio	9:20 P.M.	Sagittarius
8	Sagittarius		
9	Sagittarius		
10	Sagittarius	2:32 A.M.	Capricorn
11	Capricorn		
12	Capricorn	4:17 A.M.	Aquarius
13	Aquarius		
14	Aquarius	3:58 A.M.	Pisces
15	Pisces		
16	Pisces	3:30 A.M.	Aries
17	Aries		
18	Aries	4:51 A.M.	Taurus
19	Taurus		
20	Taurus	9:27 A.M.	Gemini
21	Gemini		
22	Gemini	5:48 P.M.	Cancer
23	Cancer		
24	Cancer		
25	Cancer	5:05 A.M.	Leo
26	Leo		
27	Leo	5:51 P.M.	Virgo
28	Virgo		

MARCH

1	Virgo		
2	Virgo	6:41 A.M.	Libra
3	Libra		

4	Libra	6:31 P.M.	Scorpio
5	Scorpio		
6	Scorpio		
7	Scorpio	4:20 A.M.	Sagittarius
8	Sagittarius		
9	Sagittarius	11:10 A.M.	Capricorn
10	Capricorn		
11	Capricorn	2:37 P.M.	Aquarius
12	Aquarius		
13	Aquarius	3:17 P.M.	Pisces
14	Pisces		
15	Pisces	2:39 P.M.	Aries
16	Aries		
17	Aries	2:44 P.M.	Taurus
18	Taurus		
19	Taurus	5:35 P.M.	Gemini
20	Gemini		
21	Gemini		
22	Gemini	12:29 A.M.	Cancer
23	Cancer		
24	Cancer	11:14 A.M.	Leo
25	Leo		
26	Leo		
27	Leo	12:04 A.M.	Virgo
28	Virgo		
29	Virgo	12:51 P.M.	Libra
30	Libra		
31	Libra		

APRIL

1	Libra	12:19 A.M.	Scorpio
2	Scorpio		
3	Scorpio	9:58 A.M.	Sagittarius
4	Sagittarius		
5	Sagittarius	5:29 P.M.	Capricorn
6	Capricorn		
7	Capricorn	10:27 P.M.	Aquarius
8	Aquarius		
9	Aquarius		
10	Aquarius	12:49 A.M.	Pisces
11	Pisces		
12	Pisces	1:19 A.M.	Aries
13	Aries		
14	Aries	1:31 A.M.	Taurus
15	Taurus		
16	Taurus	3:27 A.M.	Gemini
17	Gemini		
18	Gemini	8:53 A.M.	Cancer
19	Cancer		
20	Cancer	6:27 P.M.	Leo
21	Leo		
22	Leo		
23	Leo	6:53 A.M.	Virgo
24	Virgo		
25	Virgo	7:40 P.M.	Libra
26	Libra		
27	Libra		
28	Libra	6:52 A.M.	Scorpio
29	Scorpio		
30	Scorpio	3:52 P.M.	Sagittarius

MAY

1	Sagittarius		
2	Sagittarius	10:55 P.M.	Capricorn
3	Capricorn		
4	Capricorn		
5	Capricorn	4:12 A.M.	Aquarius

6	Aquarius		
7	Aquarius	7:46 A.M.	Pisces
8	Pisces		
9	Pisces	9:49 A.M.	Aries
10	Aries		
11	Aries	11:12 A.M.	Taurus
12	Taurus		
13	Taurus	1:27 P.M.	Gemini
14	Gemini		
15	Gemini	6:16 P.M.	Cancer
16	Cancer		
17	Cancer		
18	Cancer	2:47 A.M.	Leo
19	Leo		
20	Leo	2:31 P.M.	Virgo
21	Virgo		
22	Virgo		
23	Virgo	3:16 A.M.	Libra
24	Libra		
25	Libra	2:32 P.M.	Scorpio
26	Scorpio		
27	Scorpio	11:08 P.M.	Sagittarius
28	Sagittarius		
29	Sagittarius		
30	Sagittarius	5:17 A.M.	Capricorn
31	Capricorn		

JUNE

1	Capricorn	9:45 A.M.	Aquarius
2	Aquarius		
3	Aquarius	1:12 P.M.	Pisces
4	Pisces		
5	Pisces	4:01 P.M.	Aries
6	Aries		
7	Aries	6:41 P.M.	Taurus
8	Taurus		
9	Taurus	10:03 P.M.	Gemini
10	Gemini		
11	Gemini		
12	Gemini	3:17 A.M.	Cancer
13	Cancer		
14	Cancer	11:27 A.M.	Leo
15	Leo		
16	Leo	10:37 P.M.	Virgo
17	Virgo		
18	Virgo		
19	Virgo	11:16 A.M.	Libra
20	Libra		
21	Libra	10:57 P.M.	Scorpio
22	Scorpio		
23	Scorpio		
24	Scorpio	7:48 A.M.	Sagittarius
25	Sagittarius		
26	Sagittarius	1:29 P.M.	Capricorn
27	Capricorn		
28	Capricorn	4:51 P.M.	Aquarius
29	Aquarius		
30	Aquarius	7:08 P.M.	Pisces

JULY

1	Pisces		
2	Pisces	9:23 P.M.	Aries
3	Aries		
4	Aries		
5	Aries	12:23 A.M.	Taurus
6	Taurus		
7	Taurus	4:42 A.M.	Gemini

8	Gemini		
9	Gemini	10:54 A.M.	Cancer
10	Cancer		
11	Cancer	7:28 P.M.	Leo
12	Leo		
13	Leo		
14	Leo	6:28 A.M.	Virgo
15	Virgo		
16	Virgo	7:04 P.M.	Libra
17	Libra		
18	Libra		
19	Libra	7:17 A.M.	Scorpio
20	Scorpio		
21	Scorpio	4:59 P.M.	Sagittarius
22	Sagittarius		
23	Sagittarius	11:07 P.M.	Capricorn
24	Capricorn		
25	Capricorn		
26	Capricorn	2:03 A.M.	Aquarius
27	Aquarius		
28	Aquarius	3:07 A.M.	Pisces
29	Pisces		
30	Pisces	3:56 A.M.	Aries
31	Aries		

AUGUST

1	Aries	5:57 A.M.	Taurus
2	Taurus		
3	Taurus	10:10 A.M.	Gemini
4	Gemini		
5	Gemini	4:59 P.M.	Cancer
6	Cancer		
7	Cancer		
8	Cancer	2:16 A.M.	Leo
9	Leo		
10	Leo	1:33 P.M.	Virgo
11	Virgo		
12	Virgo		
13	Virgo	2:08 A.M.	Libra
14	Libra		
15	Libra	2:43 P.M.	Scorpio
16	Scorpio		
17	Scorpio		
18	Scorpio	1:30 A.M.	Sagittarius
19	Sagittarius		
20	Sagittarius	8:53 A.M.	Capricorn
21	Capricorn		
22	Capricorn	12:29 P.M.	Aquarius
23	Aquarius		
24	Aquarius	1:12 P.M.	Pisces
25	Pisces		
26	Pisces	12:46 P.M.	Aries
27	Aries		
28	Aries	1:10 P.M.	Taurus
29	Taurus		
30	Taurus	4:07 P.M.	Gemini
31	Gemini		

SEPTEMBER

1	Gemini	10:30 P.M.	Cancer
2	Cancer		
3	Cancer		
4	Cancer	8:05 A.M.	Leo
5	Leo		
6	Leo	7:47 P.M.	Virgo
7	Virgo		
8	Virgo		
9	Virgo	8:27 A.M.	Libra
10	Libra		
11	Libra	9:05 P.M.	Scorpio
12	Scorpio		
13	Scorpio		
14	Scorpio	8:32 A.M.	Sagittarius
15	Sagittarius		
16	Sagittarius	5:21 P.M.	Capricorn
17	Capricorn		
18	Capricorn	10:30 P.M.	Aquarius
19	Aquarius		
20	Aquarius		
21	Aquarius	12:06 A.M.	Pisces
22	Pisces	11:30 P.M.	Aries
23	Aries		
24	Aries	10:45 P.M.	Taurus
25	Taurus		
26	Taurus		
27	Taurus	12:01 A.M.	Gemini
28	Gemini		
29	Gemini	4:56 A.M.	Cancer
30	Cancer		

OCTOBER

1	Cancer	1:53 P.M.	Leo
2	Leo		
3	Leo		
4	Leo	1:40 A.M.	Virgo
5	Virgo		
6	Virgo	2:28 P.M.	Libra
7	Libra		
8	Libra		
9	Libra	2:56 A.M.	Scorpio
10	Scorpio		
11	Scorpio	2:19 P.M.	Sagittarius
12	Sagittarius		
13	Sagittarius	11:51 P.M.	Capricorn
14	Capricorn		
15	Capricorn		
16	Capricorn	6:34 A.M.	Aquarius
17	Aquarius		
18	Aquarius	9:55 A.M.	Pisces
19	Pisces		
20	Pisces	10:27 A.M.	Aries
21	Aries		
22	Aries	9:47 A.M.	Taurus
23	Taurus		
24	Taurus	10:04 A.M.	Gemini
25	Gemini		
26	Gemini	1:24 P.M.	Cancer
27	Cancer		
28	Cancer	8:55 P.M.	Leo
29	Leo		
30	Leo		
31	Leo	8:04 A.M.	Virgo

NOVEMBER

1	Virgo		
2	Virgo	8:51 P.M.	Libra
3	Libra		
4	Libra		
5	Libra	9:12 A.M.	Scorpio
6	Scorpio		
7	Scorpio	8:06 P.M.	Sagittarius
8	Sagittarius		
9	Sagittarius		
10	Sagittarius	5:18 A.M.	Capricorn
11	Capricorn		
12	Capricorn	12:31 P.M.	Aquarius
13	Aquarius		
14	Aquarius	5:17 P.M.	Pisces
15	Pisces		
16	Pisces	7:35 P.M.	Aries
17	Aries		
18	Aries	8:15 P.M.	Taurus
19	Taurus		
20	Taurus	8:55 P.M.	Gemini
21	Gemini		
22	Gemini	11:31 P.M.	Cancer
23	Cancer		
24	Cancer		
25	Cancer	5:40 A.M.	Leo
26	Leo		
27	Leo	3:41 P.M.	Virgo
28	Virgo		
29	Virgo		
30	Virgo	4:06 A.M.	Libra

DECEMBER

1	Libra		
2	Libra	4:30 P.M.	Scorpio
3	Scorpio		
4	Scorpio		
5	Scorpio	3:09 A.M.	Sagittarius
6	Sagittarius		
7	Sagittarius	11:33 A.M.	Capricorn
8	Capricorn		
9	Capricorn	5:59 P.M.	Aquarius
10	Aquarius		
11	Aquarius	10:46 P.M.	Pisces
12	Pisces		
13	Pisces		
14	Pisces	2:06 A.M.	Aries
15	Aries		
16	Aries	4:22 A.M.	Taurus
17	Taurus		
18	Taurus	6:27 A.M.	Gemini
19	Gemini		
20	Gemini	9:40 A.M.	Cancer
21	Cancer		
22	Cancer	3:23 P.M.	Leo
23	Leo		
24	Leo		
25	Leo	12:24 A.M.	Virgo
26	Virgo		
27	Virgo	12:11 P.M.	Libra
28	Libra		
29	Libra		
30	Libra	12:43 A.M.	Scorpio
31	Scorpio		

MOON SIGN TABLES
1954

JANUARY

1	Scorpio	11:39 A.M.	Sagittarius
2	Sagittarius		
3	Sagittarius	7:45 P.M.	Capricorn
4	Capricorn		
5	Capricorn		
6	Capricorn	1:09 A.M.	Aquarius
7	Aquarius		
8	Aquarius	4:43 A.M.	Pisces
9	Pisces		
10	Pisces	7:27 P.M.	Aries
11	Aries		
12	Aries	10:10 A.M.	Taurus
13	Taurus		
14	Taurus	1:29 P.M.	Gemini
15	Gemini		
16	Gemini	6:01 P.M.	Cancer
17	Cancer		
18	Cancer		
19	Cancer	12:24 A.M.	Leo
20	Leo		
21	Leo	9:14 A.M.	Virgo
22	Virgo		
23	Virgo	8:30 P.M.	Libra
24	Libra		
25	Libra		
26	Libra	9:03 A.M.	Scorpio
27	Scorpio		
28	Scorpio	8:42 P.M.	Sagittarius
29	Sagittarius		
30	Sagittarius		
31	Sagittarius	5:27 A.M.	Capricorn

FEBRUARY

1	Capricorn		
2	Capricorn	10:38 A.M.	Aquarius
3	Aquarius		
4	Aquarius	1:03 P.M.	Pisces
5	Pisces		
6	Pisces	2:14 P.M.	Aries
7	Aries		
8	Aries	3:47 P.M.	Taurus
9	Taurus		
10	Taurus	6:54 P.M.	Gemini
11	Gemini		
12	Gemini		
13	Gemini	12:10 A.M.	Cancer
14	Cancer		
15	Cancer	7:35 A.M.	Leo
16	Leo		
17	Leo	5:00 P.M.	Virgo
18	Virgo		
19	Virgo		
20	Virgo	4:14 A.M.	Libra
21	Libra		
22	Libra	4:43 P.M.	Scorpio
23	Scorpio		
24	Scorpio		
25	Scorpio	5:00 A.M.	Sagittarius
26	Sagittarius		
27	Sagittarius	2:58 P.M.	Capricorn
28	Capricorn		

MARCH

1	Capricorn	9:07 P.M.	Aquarius
2	Aquarius		
3	Aquarius	11:32 P.M.	Pisces

APRIL *(continued from March)*

4	Pisces		
5	Pisces	11:40 P.M.	Aries
6	Aries		
7	Aries	11:32 P.M.	Taurus
8	Taurus		
9	Taurus		
10	Taurus	1:06 A.M.	Gemini
11	Gemini		
12	Gemini	5:37 A.M.	Cancer
13	Cancer		
14	Cancer	1:17 P.M.	Leo
15	Leo		
16	Leo	11:21 P.M.	Virgo
17	Virgo		
18	Virgo		
19	Virgo	10:57 A.M.	Libra
20	Libra		
21	Libra	11:26 P.M.	Scorpio
22	Scorpio		
23	Scorpio		
24	Scorpio	11:56 A.M.	Sagittarius
25	Sagittarius		
26	Sagittarius	10:55 P.M.	Capricorn
27	Capricorn		
28	Capricorn		
29	Capricorn	6:37 A.M.	Aquarius
30	Aquarius		
31	Aquarius	10:16 A.M.	Pisces

APRIL

1	Pisces		
2	Pisces	10:40 A.M.	Aries
3	Aries		
4	Aries	9:43 A.M.	Taurus
5	Taurus		
6	Taurus	9:40 A.M.	Gemini
7	Gemini		
8	Gemini	12:29 P.M.	Cancer
9	Cancer		
10	Cancer	7:05 P.M.	Leo
11	Leo		
12	Leo		
13	Leo	5:03 A.M.	Virgo
14	Virgo		
15	Virgo	4:58 P.M.	Libra
16	Libra		
17	Libra		
18	Libra	5:32 A.M.	Scorpio
19	Scorpio		
20	Scorpio	5:55 P.M.	Sagittarius
21	Sagittarius		
22	Sagittarius		
23	Sagittarius	5:11 A.M.	Capricorn
24	Capricorn		
25	Capricorn	2:02 P.M.	Aquarius
26	Aquarius		
27	Aquarius	7:21 P.M.	Pisces
28	Pisces		
29	Pisces	9:08 P.M.	Aries
30	Aries		

MAY

1	Aries	8:42 P.M.	Taurus
2	Taurus		
3	Taurus	8:06 P.M.	Gemini
4	Gemini		
5	Gemini	9:30 P.M.	Cancer

MAY *(continued)*

6	Cancer		
7	Cancer		
8	Cancer	2:29 A.M.	Leo
9	Leo		
10	Leo	11:23 A.M.	Virgo
11	Virgo		
12	Virgo	11:03 P.M.	Libra
13	Libra		
14	Libra		
15	Libra	11:42 A.M.	Scorpio
16	Scorpio		
17	Scorpio	11:53 P.M.	Sagittarius
18	Sagittarius		
19	Sagittarius		
20	Sagittarius	10:49 A.M.	Capricorn
21	Capricorn		
22	Capricorn	7:48 P.M.	Aquarius
23	Aquarius		
24	Aquarius		
25	Aquarius	2:08 A.M.	Pisces
26	Pisces		
27	Pisces	5:32 P.M.	Aries
28	Aries		
29	Aries	6:33 A.M.	Taurus
30	Taurus		
31	Taurus	6:41 A.M.	Gemini

JUNE

1	Gemini		
2	Gemini	7:46 A.M.	Cancer
3	Cancer		
4	Cancer	11:34 A.M.	Leo
5	Leo		
6	Leo	7:06 P.M.	Virgo
7	Virgo		
8	Virgo		
9	Virgo	5:59 A.M.	Libra
10	Libra		
11	Libra	6:30 P.M.	Scorpio
12	Scorpio		
13	Scorpio		
14	Scorpio	6:37 A.M.	Sagittarius
15	Sagittarius		
16	Sagittarius	5:05 P.M.	Capricorn
17	Capricorn		
18	Capricorn		
19	Capricorn	1:26 A.M.	Aquarius
20	Aquarius		
21	Aquarius	7:37 A.M.	Pisces
22	Pisces		
23	Pisces	11:43 A.M.	Aries
24	Aries		
25	Aries	2:09 P.M.	Taurus
26	Taurus		
27	Taurus	3:41 P.M.	Gemini
28	Gemini		
29	Gemini	5:35 P.M.	Cancer
30	Cancer		

JULY

1	Cancer	9:16 P.M.	Leo
2	Leo		
3	Leo		
4	Leo	3:56 A.M.	Virgo
5	Virgo		
6	Virgo	1:53 P.M.	Libra
7	Libra		

8	Libra		
9	Libra	2:04 A.M.	Scorpio
10	Scorpio		
11	Scorpio	2:19 P.M.	Sagittarius
12	Sagittarius		
13	Sagittarius		
14	Sagittarius	12:40 A.M.	Capricorn
15	Capricorn		
16	Capricorn	8:19 A.M.	Aquarius
17	Aquarius		
18	Aquarius	1:33 P.M.	Pisces
19	Pisces		
20	Pisces	5:07 P.M.	Aries
21	Aries		
22	Aries	7:52 P.M.	Taurus
23	Taurus		
24	Taurus	10:30 P.M.	Gemini
25	Gemini		
26	Gemini		
27	Gemini	1:41 A.M.	Cancer
28	Cancer		
29	Cancer	6:10 A.M.	Leo
30	Leo		
31	Leo	12:50 P.M.	Virgo

AUGUST

1	Virgo		
2	Virgo	10:14 P.M.	Libra
3	Libra		
4	Libra		
5	Libra	10:03 A.M.	Scorpio
6	Scorpio		
7	Scorpio	10:32 P.M.	Sagittarius
8	Sagittarius		
9	Sagittarius		
10	Sagittarius	9:20 A.M.	Capricorn
11	Capricorn		
12	Capricorn	4:54 P.M.	Aquarius
13	Aquarius		
14	Aquarius	9:17 P.M.	Pisces
15	Pisces		
16	Pisces	11:37 P.M.	Aries
17	Aries		
18	Aries		
19	Aries	1:26 A.M.	Taurus
20	Taurus		
21	Taurus	3:56 A.M.	Gemini
22	Gemini		
23	Gemini	7:50 A.M.	Cancer
24	Cancer		
25	Cancer	1:22 P.M.	Leo
26	Leo		
27	Leo	8:44 P.M.	Virgo
28	Virgo		
29	Virgo		
30	Virgo	6:12 A.M.	Libra
31	Libra		

SEPTEMBER

1	Libra	5:49 P.M.	Scorpio
2	Scorpio		
3	Scorpio		
4	Scorpio	6:32 A.M.	Sagittarius
5	Sagittarius		
6	Sagittarius	6:10 P.M.	Capricorn
7	Capricorn		
8	Capricorn		

9	Capricorn	2:31 A.M.	Aquarius
10	Aquarius		
11	Aquarius	6:55 A.M.	Pisces
12	Pisces		
13	Pisces	8:22 A.M.	Aries
14	Aries		
15	Aries	8:44 A.M.	Taurus
16	Taurus		
17	Taurus	9:55 A.M.	Gemini
18	Gemini		
19	Gemini	1:13 P.M.	Cancer
20	Cancer		
21	Cancer	7:04 P.M.	Leo
22	Leo		
23	Leo		
24	Leo	3:11 A.M.	Virgo
25	Virgo		
26	Virgo	1:11 P.M.	Libra
27	Libra		
28	Libra		
29	Libra	12:52 A.M.	Scorpio
30	Scorpio		

OCTOBER

1	Scorpio	1:41 P.M.	Sagittarius
2	Sagittarius		
3	Sagittarius		
4	Sagittarius	2:04 A.M.	Capricorn
5	Capricorn		
6	Capricorn	11:45 A.M.	Aquarius
7	Aquarius		
8	Aquarius	5:17 P.M.	Pisces
9	Pisces		
10	Pisces	6:58 P.M.	Aries
11	Aries		
12	Aries	6:32 P.M.	Taurus
13	Taurus		
14	Taurus	6:10 P.M.	Gemini
15	Gemini		
16	Gemini	7:50 P.M.	Cancer
17	Cancer		
18	Cancer		
19	Cancer	12:41 A.M.	Leo
20	Leo		
21	Leo	8:44 A.M.	Virgo
22	Virgo		
23	Virgo	7:12 P.M.	Libra
24	Libra		
25	Libra		
26	Libra	7:11 A.M.	Scorpio
27	Scorpio		
28	Scorpio	7:59 P.M.	Sagittarius
29	Sagittarius		
30	Sagittarius		
31	Sagittarius	8:36 A.M.	Capricorn

NOVEMBER

1	Capricorn		
2	Capricorn	7:22 P.M.	Aquarius
3	Aquarius		
4	Aquarius		
5	Aquarius	2:34 A.M.	Pisces
6	Pisces		
7	Pisces	5:42 A.M.	Aries
8	Aries		
9	Aries	5:48 A.M.	Taurus
10	Taurus		

11	Taurus	4:50 A.M.	Gemini
12	Gemini		
13	Gemini	4:59 A.M.	Cancer
14	Cancer		
15	Cancer	8:03 A.M.	Leo
16	Leo		
17	Leo	2:52 P.M.	Virgo
18	Virgo		
19	Virgo		
20	Virgo	1:02 A.M.	Libra
21	Libra		
22	Libra	1:13 P.M.	Scorpio
23	Scorpio		
24	Scorpio		
25	Scorpio	2:01 A.M.	Sagittarius
26	Sagittarius		
27	Sagittarius	2:24 P.M.	Capricorn
28	Capricorn		
29	Capricorn		
30	Capricorn	1:19 A.M.	Aquarius

DECEMBER

1	Aquarius		
2	Aquarius	9:38 A.M.	Pisces
3	Pisces		
4	Pisces	2:35 P.M.	Aries
5	Aries		
6	Aries	4:23 P.M.	Taurus
7	Taurus		
8	Taurus	4:16 P.M.	Gemini
9	Gemini		
10	Gemini	4:06 P.M.	Cancer
11	Cancer		
12	Cancer	5:48 P.M.	Leo
13	Leo		
14	Leo	10:54 P.M.	Virgo
15	Virgo		
16	Virgo		
17	Virgo	7:51 A.M.	Libra
18	Libra		
19	Libra	7:43 P.M.	Scorpio
20	Scorpio		
21	Scorpio		
22	Scorpio	8:35 A.M.	Sagittarius
23	Sagittarius		
24	Sagittarius	8:40 A.M.	Capricorn
25	Capricorn		
26	Capricorn		
27	Capricorn	7:00 A.M.	Aquarius
28	Aquarius		
29	Aquarius	3:09 P.M.	Pisces
30	Pisces		
31	Pisces	8:56 P.M.	Aries

MOON SIGN TABLES
1955

JANUARY

Day	Sign	Time	
1	Aries		
2	Aries		
3	Aries	12:24 A.M.	Taurus
4	Taurus		
5	Taurus	2:04 A.M.	Gemini
6	Gemini		
7	Gemini	3:00 A.M.	Cancer
8	Cancer		
9	Cancer	4:41 A.M.	Leo
10	Leo		
11	Leo	8:43 A.M.	Virgo
12	Virgo		
13	Virgo	4:15 P.M.	Libra
14	Libra		
15	Libra		
16	Libra	3:15 A.M.	Scorpio
17	Scorpio		
18	Scorpio	4:01 P.M.	Sagittarius
19	Sagittarius		
20	Sagittarius		
21	Sagittarius	4:09 A.M.	Capricorn
22	Capricorn		
23	Capricorn	1:58 P.M.	Aquarius
24	Aquarius		
25	Aquarius	9:11 P.M.	Pisces
26	Pisces		
27	Pisces		
28	Pisces	2:19 A.M.	Aries
29	Aries		
30	Aries	6:06 A.M.	Taurus
31	Taurus		

FEBRUARY

Day	Sign	Time	
1	Taurus	9:02 A.M.	Gemini
2	Gemini		
3	Gemini	11:36 A.M.	Cancer
4	Cancer		
5	Cancer	2:28 P.M.	Leo
6	Leo		
7	Leo	6:43 P.M.	Virgo
8	Virgo		
9	Virgo		
10	Virgo	1:33 A.M.	Libra
11	Libra		
12	Libra	11:38 A.M.	Scorpio
13	Scorpio		
14	Scorpio		
15	Scorpio	12:07 A.M.	Sagittarius
16	Sagittarius		
17	Sagittarius	12:34 P.M.	Capricorn
18	Capricorn		
19	Capricorn	10:33 P.M.	Aquarius
20	Aquarius		
21	Aquarius		
22	Aquarius	5:09 A.M.	Pisces
23	Pisces		
24	Pisces	9:06 A.M.	Aries
25	Aries		
26	Aries	11:46 A.M.	Taurus
27	Taurus		
28	Taurus	2:24 P.M.	Gemini

MARCH

Day	Sign	Time	
1	Gemini		
2	Gemini	5:40 P.M.	Cancer
3	Cancer		
4	Cancer	9:48 P.M.	Leo
5	Leo		
6	Leo		
7	Leo	3:09 A.M.	Virgo
8	Virgo		
9	Virgo	10:20 A.M.	Libra
10	Libra		
11	Libra	8:04 P.M.	Scorpio
12	Scorpio		
13	Scorpio		
14	Scorpio	8:13 A.M.	Sagittarius
15	Sagittarius		
16	Sagittarius	9:01 P.M.	Capricorn
17	Capricorn		
18	Capricorn		
19	Capricorn	7:47 A.M.	Aquarius
20	Aquarius		
21	Aquarius	2:45 P.M.	Pisces
22	Pisces		
23	Pisces	6:09 P.M.	Aries
24	Aries		
25	Aries	7:31 P.M.	Taurus
26	Taurus		
27	Taurus	8:42 P.M.	Gemini
28	Gemini		
29	Gemini	11:05 P.M.	Cancer
30	Cancer		
31	Cancer		

APRIL

Day	Sign	Time	
1	Cancer	3:20 A.M.	Leo
2	Leo		
3	Leo	9:31 A.M.	Virgo
4	Virgo		
5	Virgo	5:34 P.M.	Libra
6	Libra		
7	Libra		
8	Libra	3:38 A.M.	Scorpio
9	Scorpio		
10	Scorpio	3:41 P.M.	Sagittarius
11	Sagittarius		
12	Sagittarius		
13	Sagittarius	4:40 A.M.	Capricorn
14	Capricorn		
15	Capricorn	4:20 P.M.	Aquarius
16	Aquarius		
17	Aquarius		
18	Aquarius	12:28 A.M.	Pisces
19	Pisces		
20	Pisces	4:29 A.M.	Aries
21	Aries		
22	Aries	5:29 A.M.	Taurus
23	Taurus		
24	Taurus	5:24 A.M.	Gemini
25	Gemini		
26	Gemini	6:09 A.M.	Cancer
27	Cancer		
28	Cancer	9:09 A.M.	Leo
29	Leo		
30	Leo	2:58 P.M.	Virgo

MAY

Day	Sign	Time	
1	Virgo		
2	Virgo	11:26 P.M.	Libra
3	Libra		
4	Libra		
5	Libra	10:04 A.M.	Scorpio
6	Scorpio		
7	Scorpio	10:19 P.M.	Sagittarius
8	Sagittarius		
9	Sagittarius		
10	Sagittarius	11:19 A.M.	Capricorn
11	Capricorn		
12	Capricorn	11:29 P.M.	Aquarius
13	Aquarius		
14	Aquarius		
15	Aquarius	8:53 A.M.	Pisces
16	Pisces		
17	Pisces	2:21 P.M.	Aries
18	Aries		
19	Aries	4:12 P.M.	Taurus
20	Taurus		
21	Taurus	3:56 P.M.	Gemini
22	Gemini		
23	Gemini	3:33 P.M.	Cancer
24	Cancer		
25	Cancer	4:53 P.M.	Leo
26	Leo		
27	Leo	9:16 P.M.	Virgo
28	Virgo		
29	Virgo		
30	Virgo	5:08 A.M.	Libra
31	Libra		

JUNE

Day	Sign	Time	
1	Libra	3:54 P.M.	Scorpio
2	Scorpio		
3	Scorpio		
4	Scorpio	4:24 A.M.	Sagittarius
5	Sagittarius		
6	Sagittarius	5:21 P.M.	Capricorn
7	Capricorn		
8	Capricorn		
9	Capricorn	5:30 A.M.	Aquarius
10	Aquarius		
11	Aquarius	3:32 P.M.	Pisces
12	Pisces		
13	Pisces	10:24 P.M.	Aries
14	Aries		
15	Aries		
16	Aries	1:50 A.M.	Taurus
17	Taurus		
18	Taurus	2:36 A.M.	Gemini
19	Gemini		
20	Gemini	2:15 A.M.	Cancer
21	Cancer		
22	Cancer	2:36 A.M.	Leo
23	Leo		
24	Leo	5:26 A.M.	Virgo
25	Virgo		
26	Virgo	11:55 A.M.	Libra
27	Libra		
28	Libra	10:04 P.M.	Scorpio
29	Scorpio		
30	Scorpio		

JULY

Day	Sign	Time	
1	Scorpio	10:34 A.M.	Sagittarius
2	Sagittarius		
3	Sagittarius	11:29 P.M.	Capricorn
4	Capricorn		
5	Capricorn		
6	Capricorn	11:18 A.M.	Aquarius
7	Aquarius		

8	Aquarius	9:09 P.M.	Pisces
9	Pisces		
10	Pisces		
11	Pisces	4:33 A.M.	Aries
12	Aries		
13	Aries	9:20 A.M.	Taurus
14	Taurus		
15	Taurus	11:43 A.M.	Gemini
16	Gemini		
17	Gemini	12:30 P.M.	Cancer
18	Cancer		
19	Cancer	1:03 P.M.	Leo
20	Leo		
21	Leo	3:06 P.M.	Virgo
22	Virgo		
23	Virgo	8:16 P.M.	Libra
24	Libra		
25	Libra		
26	Libra	5:19 A.M.	Scorpio
27	Scorpio		
28	Scorpio	5:24 P.M.	Sagittarius
29	Sagittarius		
30	Sagittarius		
31	Sagittarius	6:18 A.M.	Capricorn

AUGUST

1	Capricorn		
2	Capricorn	5:52 P.M.	Aquarius
3	Aquarius		
4	Aquarius		
5	Aquarius	3:04 A.M.	Pisces
6	Pisces		
7	Pisces	10:00 A.M.	Aries
8	Aries		
9	Aries	3:03 P.M.	Taurus
10	Taurus		
11	Taurus	6:33 P.M.	Gemini
12	Gemini		
13	Gemini	8:50 P.M.	Cancer
14	Cancer		
15	Cancer	10:34 P.M.	Leo
16	Leo		
17	Leo		
18	Leo	12:57 A.M.	Virgo
19	Virgo		
20	Virgo	5:34 A.M.	Libra
21	Libra		
22	Libra	1:37 P.M.	Scorpio
23	Scorpio		
24	Scorpio		
25	Scorpio	1:03 A.M.	Sagittarius
26	Sagittarius		
27	Sagittarius	1:57 P.M.	Capricorn
28	Capricorn		
29	Capricorn		
30	Capricorn	1:35 A.M.	Aquarius
31	Aquarius		

SEPTEMBER

1	Aquarius	10:23 A.M.	Pisces
2	Pisces		
3	Pisces	4:24 P.M.	Aries
4	Aries		
5	Aries	8:36 P.M.	Taurus
6	Taurus		
7	Taurus	11:58 P.M.	Gemini
8	Gemini		
9	Gemini		
10	Gemini	3:01 A.M.	Cancer
11	Cancer		
12	Cancer	6:02 A.M.	Leo
13	Leo		
14	Leo	9:33 A.M.	Virgo
15	Virgo		
16	Virgo	2:35 P.M.	Libra
17	Libra		
18	Libra	10:18 P.M.	Scorpio
19	Scorpio		
20	Scorpio		
21	Scorpio	9:11 A.M.	Sagittarius
22	Sagittarius		
23	Sagittarius	10:01 P.M.	Capricorn
24	Capricorn		
25	Capricorn		
26	Capricorn	10:07 A.M.	Aquarius
27	Aquarius		
28	Aquarius	7:12 P.M.	Pisces
29	Pisces		
30	Pisces		

OCTOBER

1	Pisces	12:46 A.M.	Aries
2	Aries		
3	Aries	3:52 A.M.	Taurus
4	Taurus		
5	Taurus	5:59 A.M.	Gemini
6	Gemini		
7	Gemini	8:23 A.M.	Cancer
8	Cancer		
9	Cancer	11:41 A.M.	Leo
10	Leo		
11	Leo	4:11 P.M.	Virgo
12	Virgo		
13	Virgo	10:13 P.M.	Libra
14	Libra		
15	Libra		
16	Libra	6:23 A.M.	Scorpio
17	Scorpio		
18	Scorpio	5:07 P.M.	Sagittarius
19	Sagittarius		
20	Sagittarius		
21	Sagittarius	5:52 A.M.	Capricorn
22	Capricorn		
23	Capricorn	6:33 P.M.	Aquarius
24	Aquarius		
25	Aquarius		
26	Aquarius	4:37 A.M.	Pisces
27	Pisces		
28	Pisces	10:46 A.M.	Aries
29	Aries		
30	Aries	1:30 P.M.	Taurus
31	Taurus		

NOVEMBER

1	Taurus	2:23 P.M.	Gemini
2	Gemini		
3	Gemini	3:11 P.M.	Cancer
4	Cancer		
5	Cancer	5:20 P.M.	Leo
6	Leo		
7	Leo	9:36 P.M.	Virgo
8	Virgo		
9	Virgo		
10	Virgo	4:15 A.M.	Libra
11	Libra		
12	Libra	1:12 P.M.	Scorpio
13	Scorpio		
14	Scorpio		
15	Scorpio	12:17 A.M.	Sagittarius
16	Sagittarius		
17	Sagittarius	12:59 P.M.	Capricorn
18	Capricorn		
19	Capricorn		
20	Capricorn	1:58 A.M.	Aquarius
21	Aquarius		
22	Aquarius	1:10 P.M.	Pisces
23	Pisces		
24	Pisces	8:47 P.M.	Aries
25	Aries		
26	Aries		
27	Aries	12:27 A.M.	Taurus
28	Taurus		
29	Taurus	1:11 A.M.	Gemini
30	Gemini		

DECEMBER

1	Gemini	12:46 A.M.	Cancer
2	Cancer		
3	Cancer	1:07 A.M.	Leo
4	Leo		
5	Leo	3:50 A.M.	Virgo
6	Virgo		
7	Virgo	9:48 A.M.	Libra
8	Libra		
9	Libra	6:59 P.M.	Scorpio
10	Scorpio		
11	Scorpio		
12	Scorpio	6:34 A.M.	Sagittarius
13	Sagittarius		
14	Sagittarius	7:23 P.M.	Capricorn
15	Capricorn		
16	Capricorn		
17	Capricorn	8:19 A.M.	Aquarius
18	Aquarius		
19	Aquarius	8:02 P.M.	Pisces
20	Pisces		
21	Pisces		
22	Pisces	5:05 A.M.	Aries
23	Aries		
24	Aries	10:33 A.M.	Taurus
25	Taurus		
26	Taurus	12:33 P.M.	Gemini
27	Gemini		
28	Gemini	12:17 P.M.	Cancer
29	Cancer		
30	Cancer	11:36 A.M.	Leo
31	Leo		

MOON SIGN TABLES
1956

JANUARY			
1	Leo	12:31 P.M.	Virgo
2	Virgo		
3	Virgo	4:44 P.M.	Libra
4	Libra		
5	Libra		
6	Libra	1:00 A.M.	Scorpio
7	Scorpio		
8	Scorpio	12:32 P.M.	Sagittarius
9	Sagittarius		
10	Sagittarius		
11	Sagittarius	1:33 A.M.	Capricorn
12	Capricorn		
13	Capricorn	2:19 P.M.	Aquarius
14	Aquarius		
15	Aquarius		
16	Aquarius	1:47 A.M.	Pisces
17	Pisces		
18	Pisces	11:17 A.M.	Aries
19	Aries		
20	Aries	6:11 P.M.	Taurus
21	Taurus		
22	Taurus	10:06 P.M.	Gemini
23	Gemini		
24	Gemini	11:20 P.M.	Cancer
25	Cancer		
26	Cancer	11:06 P.M.	Leo
27	Leo		
28	Leo	11:17 P.M.	Virgo
29	Virgo		
30	Virgo		
31	Virgo	1:56 A.M.	Libra

FEBRUARY			
1	Libra		
2	Libra	8:33 A.M.	Scorpio
3	Scorpio		
4	Scorpio	7:13 P.M.	Sagittarius
5	Sagittarius		
6	Sagittarius		
7	Sagittarius	8:08 A.M.	Capricorn
8	Capricorn		
9	Capricorn	8:52 P.M.	Aquarius
10	Aquarius		
11	Aquarius		
12	Aquarius	7:52 A.M.	Pisces
13	Pisces		
14	Pisces	4:48 P.M.	Aries
15	Aries		
16	Aries	11:48 P.M.	Taurus
17	Taurus		
18	Taurus		
19	Taurus	4:50 A.M.	Gemini
20	Gemini		
21	Gemini	7:50 A.M.	Cancer
22	Cancer		
23	Cancer	9:10 A.M.	Leo
24	Leo		
25	Leo	10:05 A.M.	Virgo
26	Virgo		
27	Virgo	12:20 P.M.	Libra
28	Libra		
29	Libra	5:45 P.M.	Scorpio

MARCH			
1	Scorpio		
2	Scorpio		
3	Scorpio	3:09 A.M.	Sagittarius
4	Sagittarius		
5	Sagittarius	3:32 P.M.	Capricorn
6	Capricorn		
7	Capricorn		
8	Capricorn	4:19 A.M.	Aquarius
9	Aquarius		
10	Aquarius	3:11 P.M.	Pisces
11	Pisces		
12	Pisces	11:26 P.M.	Aries
13	Aries		
14	Aries		
15	Aries	5:32 A.M.	Taurus
16	Taurus		
17	Taurus	10:12 A.M.	Gemini
18	Gemini		
19	Gemini	1:47 P.M.	Cancer
20	Cancer		
21	Cancer	4:31 P.M.	Leo
22	Leo		
23	Leo	6:53 P.M.	Virgo
24	Virgo		
25	Virgo	10:00 P.M.	Libra
26	Libra		
27	Libra		
28	Libra	3:18 A.M.	Scorpio
29	Scorpio		
30	Scorpio	11:56 A.M.	Sagittarius
31	Sagittarius		

APRIL			
1	Sagittarius	11:37 P.M.	Capricorn
2	Capricorn		
3	Capricorn		
4	Capricorn	12:24 P.M.	Aquarius
5	Aquarius		
6	Aquarius	11:37 P.M.	Pisces
7	Pisces		
8	Pisces		
9	Pisces	7:46 A.M.	Aries
10	Aries		
11	Aries	1:03 P.M.	Taurus
12	Taurus		
13	Taurus	4:31 P.M.	Gemini
14	Gemini		
15	Gemini	7:15 P.M.	Cancer
16	Cancer		
17	Cancer	10:00 P.M.	Leo
18	Leo		
19	Leo		
20	Leo	1:17 A.M.	Virgo
21	Virgo		
22	Virgo	5:36 A.M.	Libra
23	Libra		
24	Libra	11:44 A.M.	Scorpio
25	Scorpio		
26	Scorpio	8:25 P.M.	Sagittarius
27	Sagittarius		
28	Sagittarius		
29	Sagittarius	7:44 A.M.	Capricorn
30	Capricorn		

MAY			
1	Capricorn	8:27 P.M.	Aquarius
2	Aquarius		
3	Aquarius		
4	Aquarius	8:15 A.M.	Pisces
5	Pisces		
6	Pisces	5:05 P.M.	Aries
7	Aries		
8	Aries	10:24 P.M.	Taurus
9	Taurus		
10	Taurus		
11	Taurus	1:00 A.M.	Gemini
12	Gemini		
13	Gemini	2:21 A.M.	Cancer
14	Cancer		
15	Cancer	3:52 A.M.	Leo
16	Leo		
17	Leo	6:40 A.M.	Virgo
18	Virgo		
19	Virgo	11:25 A.M.	Libra
20	Libra		
21	Libra	6:26 P.M.	Scorpio
22	Scorpio		
23	Scorpio		
24	Scorpio	3:46 A.M.	Sagittarius
25	Sagittarius		
26	Sagittarius	3:11 P.M.	Capricorn
27	Capricorn		
28	Capricorn		
29	Capricorn	3:52 A.M.	Aquarius
30	Aquarius		
31	Aquarius	4:09 P.M.	Pisces

JUNE			
1	Pisces		
2	Pisces		
3	Pisces	2:04 A.M.	Aries
4	Aries		
5	Aries	8:22 A.M.	Taurus
6	Taurus		
7	Taurus	11:09 A.M.	Gemini
8	Gemini		
9	Gemini	11:42 A.M.	Cancer
10	Cancer		
11	Cancer	11:45 A.M.	Leo
12	Leo		
13	Leo	1:03 P.M.	Virgo
14	Virgo		
15	Virgo	4:58 P.M.	Libra
16	Libra		
17	Libra		
18	Libra	12:03 A.M.	Scorpio
19	Scorpio		
20	Scorpio	9:55 A.M.	Sagittarius
21	Sagittarius		
22	Sagittarius	9:43 P.M.	Capricorn
23	Capricorn		
24	Capricorn		
25	Capricorn	10:26 A.M.	Aquarius
26	Aquarius		
27	Aquarius	10:54 P.M.	Pisces
28	Pisces		
29	Pisces		
30	Pisces	9:43 A.M.	Aries

JULY			
1	Aries		
2	Aries	5:26 P.M.	Taurus
3	Taurus		
4	Taurus	9:26 P.M.	Gemini
5	Gemini		
6	Gemini	10:20 P.M.	Cancer

7	Cancer	
8	Cancer	9:42 P.M. Leo
9	Leo	
10	Leo	9:34 P.M. Virgo
11	Virgo	
12	Virgo	11:54 P.M. Libra
13	Libra	
14	Libra	
15	Libra	5:56 A.M. Scorpio
16	Scorpio	
17	Scorpio	3:38 P.M. Sagittarius
18	Sagittarius	
19	Sagittarius	
20	Sagittarius	3:40 A.M. Capricorn
21	Capricorn	
22	Capricorn	4:28 P.M. Aquarius
23	Aquarius	
24	Aquarius	
25	Aquarius	4:50 A.M. Pisces
26	Pisces	
27	Pisces	3:54 P.M. Aries
28	Aries	
29	Aries	
30	Aries	12:40 A.M. Taurus
31	Taurus	

AUGUST

1	Taurus	6:16 A.M. Gemini
2	Gemini	
3	Gemini	8:32 A.M. Cancer
4	Cancer	
5	Cancer	8:27 A.M. Leo
6	Leo	
7	Leo	7:50 A.M. Virgo
8	Virgo	
9	Virgo	8:50 A.M. Libra
10	Libra	
11	Libra	1:20 P.M. Scorpio
12	Scorpio	
13	Scorpio	10:00 P.M. Sagittarius
14	Sagittarius	
15	Sagittarius	
16	Sagittarius	9:47 A.M. Capricorn
17	Capricorn	
18	Capricorn	10:38 P.M. Aquarius
19	Aquarius	
20	Aquarius	
21	Aquarius	10:47 A.M. Pisces
22	Pisces	
23	Pisces	9:30 P.M. Aries
24	Aries	
25	Aries	
26	Aries	6:23 A.M. Taurus
27	Taurus	
28	Taurus	12:59 P.M. Gemini
29	Gemini	
30	Gemini	4:51 P.M. Cancer
31	Cancer	

SEPTEMBER

1	Cancer	6:14 P.M. Leo
2	Leo	
3	Leo	6:20 P.M. Virgo
4	Virgo	
5	Virgo	7:04 P.M. Libra
6	Libra	
7	Libra	10:27 P.M. Scorpio
8	Scorpio	
9	Scorpio	
10	Scorpio	5:46 A.M. Sagittarius
11	Sagittarius	
12	Sagittarius	4:46 P.M. Capricorn
13	Capricorn	
14	Capricorn	
15	Capricorn	5:28 A.M. Aquarius
16	Aquarius	
17	Aquarius	5:34 P.M. Pisces
18	Pisces	
19	Pisces	
20	Pisces	3:47 A.M. Aries
21	Aries	
22	Aries	12:01 P.M. Taurus
23	Taurus	
24	Taurus	6:25 P.M. Gemini
25	Gemini	
26	Gemini	11:00 P.M. Cancer
27	Cancer	
28	Cancer	
29	Cancer	1:49 A.M. Leo
30	Leo	

OCTOBER

1	Leo	3:24 A.M. Virgo
2	Virgo	
3	Virgo	5:01 A.M. Libra
4	Libra	
5	Libra	8:19 A.M. Scorpio
6	Scorpio	
7	Scorpio	2:46 P.M. Sagittarius
8	Sagittarius	
9	Sagittarius	
10	Sagittarius	12:48 A.M. Capricorn
11	Capricorn	
12	Capricorn	1:09 P.M. Aquarius
13	Aquarius	
14	Aquarius	
15	Aquarius	1:25 A.M. Pisces
16	Pisces	
17	Pisces	11:35 A.M. Aries
18	Aries	
19	Aries	7:07 P.M. Taurus
20	Taurus	
21	Taurus	
22	Taurus	12:29 A.M. Gemini
23	Gemini	
24	Gemini	4:23 A.M. Cancer
25	Cancer	
26	Cancer	7:27 A.M. Leo
27	Leo	
28	Leo	10:09 A.M. Virgo
29	Virgo	
30	Virgo	1:10 P.M. Libra
31	Libra	

NOVEMBER

1	Libra	5:24 P.M. Scorpio
2	Scorpio	
3	Scorpio	11:56 P.M. Sagittarius
4	Sagittarius	
5	Sagittarius	
6	Sagittarius	9:24 A.M. Capricorn
7	Capricorn	
8	Capricorn	9:19 P.M. Aquarius
9	Aquarius	
10	Aquarius	
11	Aquarius	9:51 A.M. Pisces
12	Pisces	
13	Pisces	8:36 P.M. Aries
14	Aries	
15	Aries	
16	Aries	4:12 A.M. Taurus
17	Taurus	
18	Taurus	8:45 A.M. Gemini
19	Gemini	
20	Gemini	11:18 A.M. Cancer
21	Cancer	
22	Cancer	1:10 P.M. Leo
23	Leo	
24	Leo	3:32 P.M. Virgo
25	Virgo	
26	Virgo	7:11 P.M. Libra
27	Libra	
28	Libra	
29	Libra	12:34 A.M. Scorpio
30	Scorpio	

DECEMBER

1	Scorpio	7:59 A.M. Sagittarius
2	Sagittarius	
3	Sagittarius	5:36 P.M. Capricorn
4	Capricorn	
5	Capricorn	
6	Capricorn	5:16 A.M. Aquarius
7	Aquarius	
8	Aquarius	5:57 P.M. Pisces
9	Pisces	
10	Pisces	
11	Pisces	5:37 A.M. Aries
12	Aries	
13	Aries	2:15 P.M. Taurus
14	Taurus	
15	Taurus	7:06 P.M. Gemini
16	Gemini	
17	Gemini	8:52 P.M. Cancer
18	Cancer	
19	Cancer	9:11 P.M. Leo
20	Leo	
21	Leo	9:56 P.M. Virgo
22	Virgo	
23	Virgo	
24	Virgo	12:39 A.M. Libra
25	Libra	
26	Libra	6:09 A.M. Scorpio
27	Scorpio	
28	Scorpio	2:20 P.M. Sagittarius
29	Sagittarius	
30	Sagittarius	
31	Sagittarius	12:37 A.M. Capricorn

MOON SIGN TABLES
1957

JANUARY

1	Capricorn		
2	Capricorn	12:25 P.M.	Aquarius
3	Aquarius		
4	Aquarius		
5	Aquarius	1:04 A.M.	Pisces
6	Pisces		
7	Pisces	1:23 P.M.	Aries
8	Aries		
9	Aries	11:27 P.M.	Taurus
10	Taurus		
11	Taurus		
12	Taurus	5:44 A.M.	Gemini
13	Gemini		
14	Gemini	8:05 A.M.	Cancer
15	Cancer		
16	Cancer	7:50 A.M.	Leo
17	Leo		
18	Leo	7:03 A.M.	Virgo
19	Virgo		
20	Virgo	7:55 A.M.	Libra
21	Libra		
22	Libra	12:02 P.M.	Scorpio
23	Scorpio		
24	Scorpio	7:52 P.M.	Sagittarius
25	Sagittarius		
26	Sagittarius		
27	Sagittarius	6:32 A.M.	Capricorn
28	Capricorn		
29	Capricorn	6:42 P.M.	Aquarius
30	Aquarius		
31	Aquarius		

FEBRUARY

1	Aquarius	7:20 A.M.	Pisces
2	Pisces		
3	Pisces	7:42 P.M.	Aries
4	Aries		
5	Aries		
6	Aries	6:37 A.M.	Taurus
7	Taurus		
8	Taurus	2:34 P.M.	Gemini
9	Gemini		
10	Gemini	6:39 P.M.	Cancer
11	Cancer		
12	Cancer	7:18 P.M.	Leo
13	Leo		
14	Leo	6:17 P.M.	Virgo
15	Virgo		
16	Virgo	5:50 P.M.	Libra
17	Libra		
18	Libra	8:06 P.M.	Scorpio
19	Scorpio		
20	Scorpio		
21	Scorpio	2:23 A.M.	Sagittarius
22	Sagittarius		
23	Sagittarius	12:27 P.M.	Capricorn
24	Capricorn		
25	Capricorn		
26	Capricorn	12:42 A.M.	Aquarius
27	Aquarius		
28	Aquarius	1:25 P.M.	Pisces

MARCH

1	Pisces		
2	Pisces		
3	Pisces	1:31 A.M.	Aries
4	Aries		
5	Aries	12:20 P.M.	Taurus
6	Taurus		
7	Taurus	9:03 P.M.	Gemini
8	Gemini		
9	Gemini		
10	Gemini	2:45 A.M.	Cancer
11	Cancer		
12	Cancer	5:12 A.M.	Leo
13	Leo		
14	Leo	5:20 A.M.	Virgo
15	Virgo		
16	Virgo	4:59 A.M.	Libra
17	Libra		
18	Libra	6:15 A.M.	Scorpio
19	Scorpio		
20	Scorpio	10:54 A.M.	Sagittarius
21	Sagittarius		
22	Sagittarius	7:34 P.M.	Capricorn
23	Capricorn		
24	Capricorn		
25	Capricorn	7:17 A.M.	Aquarius
26	Aquarius		
27	Aquarius	8:00 P.M.	Pisces
28	Pisces		
29	Pisces		
30	Pisces	7:55 A.M.	Aries
31	Aries		

APRIL

1	Aries	6:11 P.M.	Taurus
2	Taurus		
3	Taurus		
4	Taurus	2:30 A.M.	Gemini
5	Gemini		
6	Gemini	8:37 A.M.	Cancer
7	Cancer		
8	Cancer	12:24 P.M.	Leo
9	Leo		
10	Leo	2:13 P.M.	Virgo
11	Virgo		
12	Virgo	3:08 P.M.	Libra
13	Libra		
14	Libra	4:45 P.M.	Scorpio
15	Scorpio		
16	Scorpio	8:43 P.M.	Sagittarius
17	Sagittarius		
18	Sagittarius		
19	Sagittarius	4:08 A.M.	Capricorn
20	Capricorn		
21	Capricorn	2:53 P.M.	Aquarius
22	Aquarius		
23	Aquarius		
24	Aquarius	3:23 A.M.	Pisces
25	Pisces		
26	Pisces	3:22 P.M.	Aries
27	Aries		
28	Aries		
29	Aries	1:18 A.M.	Taurus
30	Taurus		

MAY

1	Taurus	8:47 A.M.	Gemini
2	Gemini		
3	Gemini	2:08 P.M.	Cancer
4	Cancer		
5	Cancer	5:54 P.M.	Leo
6	Leo		
7	Leo	8:37 P.M.	Virgo
8	Virgo		
9	Virgo	10:57 P.M.	Libra
10	Libra		
11	Libra		
12	Libra	1:48 A.M.	Scorpio
13	Scorpio		
14	Scorpio	6:13 A.M.	Sagittarius
15	Sagittarius		
16	Sagittarius	1:13 P.M.	Capricorn
17	Capricorn		
18	Capricorn	11:12 P.M.	Aquarius
19	Aquarius		
20	Aquarius		
21	Aquarius	11:20 A.M.	Pisces
22	Pisces		
23	Pisces	11:34 P.M.	Aries
24	Aries		
25	Aries		
26	Aries	9:43 A.M.	Taurus
27	Taurus		
28	Taurus	4:47 P.M.	Gemini
29	Gemini		
30	Gemini	9:05 P.M.	Cancer
31	Cancer		

JUNE

1	Cancer	11:45 P.M.	Leo
2	Leo		
3	Leo		
4	Leo	1:59 A.M.	Virgo
5	Virgo		
6	Virgo	4:45 A.M.	Libra
7	Libra		
8	Libra	8:41 A.M.	Scorpio
9	Scorpio		
10	Scorpio	2:09 P.M.	Sagittarius
11	Sagittarius		
12	Sagittarius	9:36 P.M.	Capricorn
13	Capricorn		
14	Capricorn		
15	Capricorn	7:23 A.M.	Aquarius
16	Aquarius		
17	Aquarius	7:15 P.M.	Pisces
18	Pisces		
19	Pisces		
20	Pisces	7:46 A.M.	Aries
21	Aries		
22	Aries	6:38 P.M.	Taurus
23	Taurus		
24	Taurus		
25	Taurus	2:07 A.M.	Gemini
26	Gemini		
27	Gemini	6:01 A.M.	Cancer
28	Cancer		
29	Cancer	7:31 A.M.	Leo
30	Leo		

JULY

1	Leo	8:23 A.M.	Virgo
2	Virgo		
3	Virgo	10:16 A.M.	Libra
4	Libra		
5	Libra	2:10 P.M.	Scorpio
6	Scorpio		
7	Scorpio	8:20 P.M.	Sagittarius

8	Sagittarius		
9	Sagittarius		
10	Sagittarius	4:35 A.M.	Capricorn
11	Capricorn		
12	Capricorn	2:43 P.M.	Aquarius
13	Aquarius		
14	Aquarius		
15	Aquarius	2:32 A.M.	Pisces
16	Pisces		
17	Pisces	3:14 P.M.	Aries
18	Aries		
19	Aries		
20	Aries	2:58 A.M.	Taurus
21	Taurus		
22	Taurus	11:34 A.M.	Gemini
23	Gemini		
24	Gemini	4:05 P.M.	Cancer
25	Cancer		
26	Cancer	5:16 P.M.	Leo
27	Leo		
28	Leo	4:59 P.M.	Virgo
29	Virgo		
30	Virgo	5:20 P.M.	Libra
31	Libra		

AUGUST

1	Libra	8:01 P.M.	Scorpio
2	Scorpio		
3	Scorpio		
4	Scorpio	1:47 A.M.	Sagittarius
5	Sagittarius		
6	Sagittarius	10:23 A.M.	Capricorn
7	Capricorn		
8	Capricorn	9:01 P.M.	Aquarius
9	Aquarius		
10	Aquarius		
11	Aquarius	9:02 A.M.	Pisces
12	Pisces		
13	Pisces	9:46 P.M.	Aries
14	Aries		
15	Aries		
16	Aries	10:00 A.M.	Taurus
17	Taurus		
18	Taurus	7:51 P.M.	Gemini
19	Gemini		
20	Gemini		
21	Gemini	1:48 A.M.	Cancer
22	Cancer		
23	Cancer	3:51 A.M.	Leo
24	Leo		
25	Leo	3:26 A.M.	Virgo
26	Virgo		
27	Virgo	2:41 A.M.	Libra
28	Libra		
29	Libra	3:45 A.M.	Scorpio
30	Scorpio		
31	Scorpio	8:07 A.M.	Sagittarius

SEPTEMBER

1	Sagittarius		
2	Sagittarius	4:05 P.M.	Capricorn
3	Capricorn		
4	Capricorn		
5	Capricorn	2:50 A.M.	Aquarius
6	Aquarius		
7	Aquarius	3:04 P.M.	Pisces
8	Pisces		

9	Pisces		
10	Pisces	3:45 A.M.	Aries
11	Aries		
12	Aries	3:57 P.M.	Taurus
13	Taurus		
14	Taurus		
15	Taurus	2:26 A.M.	Gemini
16	Gemini		
17	Gemini	9:49 A.M.	Cancer
18	Cancer		
19	Cancer	1:31 P.M.	Leo
20	Leo		
21	Leo	2:11 P.M.	Virgo
22	Virgo		
23	Virgo	1:33 P.M.	Libra
24	Libra		
25	Libra	1:40 P.M.	Scorpio
26	Scorpio		
27	Scorpio	4:27 P.M.	Sagittarius
28	Sagittarius		
29	Sagittarius	10:59 P.M.	Capricorn
30	Capricorn		

OCTOBER

1	Capricorn		
2	Capricorn	9:04 A.M.	Aquarius
3	Aquarius		
4	Aquarius	9:17 P.M.	Pisces
5	Pisces		
6	Pisces		
7	Pisces	9:57 A.M.	Aries
8	Aries		
9	Aries	9:48 P.M.	Taurus
10	Taurus		
11	Taurus		
12	Taurus	8:01 A.M.	Gemini
13	Gemini		
14	Gemini	3:54 P.M.	Cancer
15	Cancer		
16	Cancer	8:59 P.M.	Leo
17	Leo		
18	Leo	11:23 P.M.	Virgo
19	Virgo		
20	Virgo		
21	Virgo	12:03 A.M.	Libra
22	Libra		
23	Libra	12:31 A.M.	Scorpio
24	Scorpio		
25	Scorpio	2:33 A.M.	Sagittarius
26	Sagittarius		
27	Sagittarius	7:41 A.M.	Capricorn
28	Capricorn		
29	Capricorn	4:32 P.M.	Aquarius
30	Aquarius		
31	Aquarius		

NOVEMBER

1	Aquarius	4:18 A.M.	Pisces
2	Pisces		
3	Pisces	5:00 P.M.	Aries
4	Aries		
5	Aries		
6	Aries	4:38 A.M.	Taurus
7	Taurus		
8	Taurus	2:09 P.M.	Gemini
9	Gemini		
10	Gemini	9:24 P.M.	Cancer

11	Cancer		
12	Cancer		
13	Cancer	2:36 A.M.	Leo
14	Leo		
15	Leo	6:07 A.M.	Virgo
16	Virgo		
17	Virgo	8:25 A.M.	Libra
18	Libra		
19	Libra	10:17 A.M.	Scorpio
20	Scorpio		
21	Scorpio	12:52 P.M.	Sagittarius
22	Sagittarius		
23	Sagittarius	5:29 P.M.	Capricorn
24	Capricorn		
25	Capricorn		
26	Capricorn	1:16 A.M.	Aquarius
27	Aquarius		
28	Aquarius	12:16 P.M.	Pisces
29	Pisces		
30	Pisces		

DECEMBER

1	Pisces	12:56 A.M.	Aries
2	Aries		
3	Aries	12:48 P.M.	Taurus
4	Taurus		
5	Taurus	10:00 P.M.	Gemini
6	Gemini		
7	Gemini		
8	Gemini	4:16 A.M.	Cancer
9	Cancer		
10	Cancer	8:23 A.M.	Leo
11	Leo		
12	Leo	11:28 A.M.	Virgo
13	Virgo		
14	Virgo	2:23 P.M.	Libra
15	Libra		
16	Libra	5:35 P.M.	Scorpio
17	Scorpio		
18	Scorpio	9:30 P.M.	Sagittarius
19	Sagittarius		
20	Sagittarius		
21	Sagittarius	2:47 A.M.	Capricorn
22	Capricorn		
23	Capricorn	10:19 A.M.	Aquarius
24	Aquarius		
25	Aquarius	8:41 P.M.	Pisces
26	Pisces		
27	Pisces		
28	Pisces	9:13 A.M.	Aries
29	Aries		
30	Aries	9:37 P.M.	Taurus
31	Taurus		

MOON SIGN TABLES
1958

JANUARY

1 Taurus		
2 Taurus	7:21 A.M.	Gemini
3 Gemini		
4 Gemini	1:22 P.M.	Cancer
5 Cancer		
6 Cancer	4:21 P.M.	Leo
7 Leo		
8 Leo	5:59 P.M.	Virgo
9 Virgo		
10 Virgo	7:52 P.M.	Libra
11 Libra		
12 Libra	11:02 P.M.	Scorpio
13 Scorpio		
14 Scorpio		
15 Scorpio	3:49 A.M.	Sagittarius
16 Sagittarius		
17 Sagittarius	10:13 A.M.	Capricorn
18 Capricorn		
19 Capricorn	6:22 P.M.	Aquarius
20 Aquarius		
21 Aquarius		
22 Aquarius	4:42 A.M.	Pisces
23 Pisces		
24 Pisces	5:03 P.M.	Aries
25 Aries		
26 Aries		
27 Aries	5:56 A.M.	Taurus
28 Taurus		
29 Taurus	4:47 P.M.	Gemini
30 Gemini		
31 Gemini	11:41 P.M.	Cancer

FEBRUARY

1 Cancer		
2 Cancer		
3 Cancer	2:37 A.M.	Leo
4 Leo		
5 Leo	3:11 A.M.	Virgo
6 Virgo		
7 Virgo	3:23 A.M.	Libra
8 Libra		
9 Libra	5:03 A.M.	Scorpio
10 Scorpio		
11 Scorpio	9:11 A.M.	Sagittarius
12 Sagittarius		
13 Sagittarius	3:55 P.M.	Capricorn
14 Capricorn		
15 Capricorn		
16 Capricorn	12:51 A.M.	Aquarius
17 Aquarius		
18 Aquarius	11:39 A.M.	Pisces
19 Pisces		
20 Pisces		
21 Pisces	12:02 A.M.	Aries
22 Aries		
23 Aries	1:05 P.M.	Taurus
24 Taurus		
25 Taurus		
26 Taurus	12:52 A.M.	Gemini
27 Gemini		
28 Gemini	9:17 A.M.	Cancer

MARCH

1 Cancer		
2 Cancer	1:27 P.M.	Leo
3 Leo		
4 Leo	2:15 P.M.	Virgo
5 Virgo		
6 Virgo	1:35 P.M.	Libra
7 Libra		
8 Libra	1:34 P.M.	Scorpio
9 Scorpio		
10 Scorpio	3:56 P.M.	Sagittarius
11 Sagittarius		
12 Sagittarius	9:36 P.M.	Capricorn
13 Capricorn		
14 Capricorn		
15 Capricorn	6:28 A.M.	Aquarius
16 Aquarius		
17 Aquarius	5:41 P.M.	Pisces
18 Pisces		
19 Pisces		
20 Pisces	6:17 A.M.	Aries
21 Aries		
22 Aries	7:16 P.M.	Taurus
23 Taurus		
24 Taurus		
25 Taurus	7:20 A.M.	Gemini
26 Gemini		
27 Gemini	4:53 P.M.	Cancer
28 Cancer		
29 Cancer	10:45 P.M.	Leo
30 Leo		
31 Leo		

APRIL

1 Leo	1:01 A.M.	Virgo
2 Virgo		
3 Virgo	12:54 A.M.	Libra
4 Libra		
5 Libra	12:16 A.M.	Scorpio
6 Scorpio		
7 Scorpio	1:07 A.M.	Sagittarius
8 Sagittarius		
9 Sagittarius	5:01 A.M.	Capricorn
10 Capricorn		
11 Capricorn	12:41 P.M.	Aquarius
12 Aquarius		
13 Aquarius	11:38 P.M.	Pisces
14 Pisces		
15 Pisces		
16 Pisces	12:23 P.M.	Aries
17 Aries		
18 Aries		
19 Aries	1:16 A.M.	Taurus
20 Taurus		
21 Taurus	1:03 P.M.	Gemini
22 Gemini		
23 Gemini	10:46 P.M.	Cancer
24 Cancer		
25 Cancer		
26 Cancer	5:44 A.M.	Leo
27 Leo		
28 Leo	9:40 A.M.	Virgo
29 Virgo		
30 Virgo	11:06 A.M.	Libra

MAY

1 Libra		
2 Libra	11:14 A.M.	Scorpio
3 Scorpio		
4 Scorpio	11:43 A.M.	Sagittarius
5 Sagittarius		

6 Sagittarius	2:21 P.M.	Capricorn
7 Capricorn		
8 Capricorn	8:29 P.M.	Aquarius
9 Aquarius		
10 Aquarius		
11 Aquarius	6:27 A.M.	Pisces
12 Pisces		
13 Pisces	6:58 P.M.	Aries
14 Aries		
15 Aries		
16 Aries	7:50 A.M.	Taurus
17 Taurus		
18 Taurus	7:14 P.M.	Gemini
19 Gemini		
20 Gemini		
21 Gemini	4:23 A.M.	Cancer
22 Cancer		
23 Cancer	11:14 A.M.	Leo
24 Leo		
25 Leo	4:00 P.M.	Virgo
26 Virgo		
27 Virgo	6:55 P.M.	Libra
28 Libra		
29 Libra	8:33 P.M.	Scorpio
30 Scorpio		
31 Scorpio	9:54 P.M.	Sagittarius

JUNE

1 Sagittarius		
2 Sagittarius		
3 Sagittarius	12:23 A.M.	Capricorn
4 Capricorn		
5 Capricorn	5:34 A.M.	Aquarius
6 Aquarius		
7 Aquarius	2:24 P.M.	Pisces
8 Pisces		
9 Pisces		
10 Pisces	2:20 A.M.	Aries
11 Aries		
12 Aries	3:12 P.M.	Taurus
13 Taurus		
14 Taurus		
15 Taurus	2:31 A.M.	Gemini
16 Gemini		
17 Gemini	11:04 A.M.	Cancer
18 Cancer		
19 Cancer	5:04 P.M.	Leo
20 Leo		
21 Leo	9:22 P.M.	Virgo
22 Virgo		
23 Virgo		
24 Virgo	12:42 A.M.	Libra
25 Libra		
26 Libra	3:30 A.M.	Scorpio
27 Scorpio		
28 Scorpio	6:11 A.M.	Sagittarius
29 Sagittarius		
30 Sagittarius	9:32 A.M.	Capricorn

JULY

1 Capricorn		
2 Capricorn	2:44 P.M.	Aquarius
3 Aquarius		
4 Aquarius	10:57 P.M.	Pisces
5 Pisces		
6 Pisces		
7 Pisces	10:18 A.M.	Aries

8	Aries		
9	Aries	11:09 P.M.	Taurus
10	Taurus		
11	Taurus		
12	Taurus	10:46 A.M.	Gemini
13	Gemini		
14	Gemini	7:15 P.M.	Cancer
15	Cancer		
16	Cancer		
17	Cancer	12:31 A.M.	Leo
18	Leo		
19	Leo	3:42 A.M.	Virgo
20	Virgo		
21	Virgo	6:11 A.M.	Libra
22	Libra		
23	Libra	8:57 A.M.	Scorpio
24	Scorpio		
25	Scorpio	12:25 P.M.	Sagittarius
26	Sagittarius		
27	Sagittarius	4:53 P.M.	Capricorn
28	Capricorn		
29	Capricorn	10:52 P.M.	Aquarius
30	Aquarius		
31	Aquarius		

AUGUST

1	Aquarius	7:11 A.M.	Pisces
2	Pisces		
3	Pisces	6:14 P.M.	Aries
4	Aries		
5	Aries		
6	Aries	7:04 A.M.	Taurus
7	Taurus		
8	Taurus	7:16 P.M.	Gemini
9	Gemini		
10	Gemini		
11	Gemini	4:25 A.M.	Cancer
12	Cancer		
13	Cancer	9:43 A.M.	Leo
14	Leo		
15	Leo	12:07 P.M.	Virgo
16	Virgo		
17	Virgo	1:17 P.M.	Libra
18	Libra		
19	Libra	2:50 P.M.	Scorpio
20	Scorpio		
21	Scorpio	5:48 P.M.	Sagittarius
22	Sagittarius		
23	Sagittarius	10:38 P.M.	Capricorn
24	Capricorn		
25	Capricorn		
26	Capricorn	5:28 A.M.	Aquarius
27	Aquarius		
28	Aquarius	2:25 P.M.	Pisces
29	Pisces		
30	Pisces		
31	Pisces	1:35 A.M.	Aries

SEPTEMBER

1	Aries		
2	Aries	2:24 P.M.	Taurus
3	Taurus		
4	Taurus		
5	Taurus	3:07 A.M.	Gemini
6	Gemini		
7	Gemini	1:22 P.M.	Cancer
8	Cancer		
9	Cancer	7:42 P.M.	Leo
10	Leo		
11	Leo	10:19 P.M.	Virgo
12	Virgo		
13	Virgo	10:44 P.M.	Libra
14	Libra		
15	Libra	10:49 P.M.	Scorpio
16	Scorpio		
17	Scorpio		
18	Scorpio	12:16 A.M.	Sagittarius
19	Sagittarius		
20	Sagittarius	4:13 A.M.	Capricorn
21	Capricorn		
22	Capricorn	11:03 A.M.	Aquarius
23	Aquarius		
24	Aquarius	8:33 A.M.	Pisces
25	Pisces		
26	Pisces		
27	Pisces	8:07 A.M.	Aries
28	Aries		
29	Aries	8:58 P.M.	Taurus
30	Taurus		

OCTOBER

1	Taurus		
2	Taurus	9:50 A.M.	Gemini
3	Gemini		
4	Gemini	9:00 P.M.	Cancer
5	Cancer		
6	Cancer		
7	Cancer	4:51 A.M.	Leo
8	Leo		
9	Leo	8:49 A.M.	Virgo
10	Virgo		
11	Virgo	9:44 A.M.	Libra
12	Libra		
13	Libra	9:11 A.M.	Scorpio
14	Scorpio		
15	Scorpio	9:09 A.M.	Sagittarius
16	Sagittarius		
17	Sagittarius	11:23 A.M.	Capricorn
18	Capricorn		
19	Capricorn	5:04 P.M.	Aquarius
20	Aquarius		
21	Aquarius		
22	Aquarius	2:19 A.M.	Pisces
23	Pisces		
24	Pisces	2:10 P.M.	Aries
25	Aries		
26	Aries		
27	Aries	3:07 A.M.	Taurus
28	Taurus		
29	Taurus	3:49 P.M.	Gemini
30	Gemini		
31	Gemini		

NOVEMBER

1	Gemini	3:09 A.M.	Cancer
2	Cancer		
3	Cancer	12:02 P.M.	Leo
4	Leo		
5	Leo	5:45 P.M.	Virgo
6	Virgo		
7	Virgo	8:16 P.M.	Libra
8	Libra		
9	Libra	8:30 P.M.	Scorpio
10	Scorpio		
11	Scorpio	8:03 P.M.	Sagittarius
12	Sagittarius		
13	Sagittarius	8:54 P.M.	Capricorn
14	Capricorn		
15	Capricorn		
16	Capricorn	12:53 A.M.	Aquarius
17	Aquarius		
18	Aquarius	8:56 A.M.	Pisces
19	Pisces		
20	Pisces	8:28 P.M.	Aries
21	Aries		
22	Aries		
23	Aries	9:30 A.M.	Taurus
24	Taurus		
25	Taurus	10:00 P.M.	Gemini
26	Gemini		
27	Gemini		
28	Gemini	8:51 A.M.	Cancer
29	Cancer		
30	Cancer	5:41 P.M.	Leo

DECEMBER

1	Leo		
2	Leo		
3	Leo	12:18 A.M.	Virgo
4	Virgo		
5	Virgo	4:31 A.M.	Libra
6	Libra		
7	Libra	6:28 A.M.	Scorpio
8	Scorpio		
9	Scorpio	7:02 A.M.	Sagittarius
10	Sagittarius		
11	Sagittarius	7:46 A.M.	Capricorn
12	Capricorn		
13	Capricorn	10:38 A.M.	Aquarius
14	Aquarius		
15	Aquarius	5:12 P.M.	Pisces
16	Pisces		
17	Pisces		
18	Pisces	3:45 A.M.	Aries
19	Aries		
20	Aries	4:38 P.M.	Taurus
21	Taurus		
22	Taurus		
23	Taurus	5:09 A.M.	Gemini
24	Gemini		
25	Gemini	3:33 P.M.	Cancer
26	Cancer		
27	Cancer	11:33 P.M.	Leo
28	Leo		
29	Leo		
30	Leo	5:41 A.M.	Virgo
31	Virgo		

MOON SIGN TABLES
1959

JANUARY

Day	Sign	Time	Sign
1	Virgo	10:21 A.M.	Libra
2	Libra		
3	Libra	1:42 P.M.	Scorpio
4	Scorpio		
5	Scorpio	3:55 P.M.	Sagittarius
6	Sagittarius		
7	Sagittarius	5:50 P.M.	Capricorn
8	Capricorn		
9	Capricorn	8:52 P.M.	Aquarius
10	Aquarius		
11	Aquarius		
12	Aquarius	2:39 A.M.	Pisces
13	Pisces		
14	Pisces	12:10 P.M.	Aries
15	Aries		
16	Aries		
17	Aries	12:33 A.M.	Taurus
18	Taurus		
19	Taurus	1:16 P.M.	Gemini
20	Gemini		
21	Gemini	11:47 P.M.	Cancer
22	Cancer		
23	Cancer		
24	Cancer	7:13 A.M.	Leo
25	Leo		
26	Leo	12:13 P.M.	Virgo
27	Virgo		
28	Virgo	3:54 P.M.	Libra
29	Libra		
30	Libra	7:05 P.M.	Scorpio
31	Scorpio		

FEBRUARY

Day	Sign	Time	Sign
1	Scorpio	10:11 P.M.	Sagittarius
2	Sagittarius		
3	Sagittarius		
4	Sagittarius	1:29 A.M.	Capricorn
5	Capricorn		
6	Capricorn	5:40 A.M.	Aquarius
7	Aquarius		
8	Aquarius	11:50 A.M.	Pisces
9	Pisces		
10	Pisces	8:55 P.M.	Aries
11	Aries		
12	Aries		
13	Aries	8:47 A.M.	Taurus
14	Taurus		
15	Taurus	9:39 P.M.	Gemini
16	Gemini		
17	Gemini		
18	Gemini	8:50 A.M.	Cancer
19	Cancer		
20	Cancer	4:38 P.M.	Leo
21	Leo		
22	Leo	9:06 P.M.	Virgo
23	Virgo		
24	Virgo	11:29 P.M.	Libra
25	Libra		
26	Libra		
27	Libra	1:14 A.M.	Scorpio
28	Scorpio		

MARCH

Day	Sign	Time	Sign
1	Scorpio	3:33 A.M.	Sagittarius
2	Sagittarius		
3	Sagittarius	7:05 A.M.	Capricorn
4	Capricorn		
5	Capricorn	12:16 P.M.	Aquarius
6	Aquarius		
7	Aquarius	7:25 P.M.	Pisces
8	Pisces		
9	Pisces		
10	Pisces	4:54 A.M.	Aries
11	Aries		
12	Aries	4:37 P.M.	Taurus
13	Taurus		
14	Taurus		
15	Taurus	5:31 A.M.	Gemini
16	Gemini		
17	Gemini	5:28 P.M.	Cancer
18	Cancer		
19	Cancer		
20	Cancer	2:22 A.M.	Leo
21	Leo		
22	Leo	7:28 A.M.	Virgo
23	Virgo		
24	Virgo	9:27 A.M.	Libra
25	Libra		
26	Libra	9:54 A.M.	Scorpio
27	Scorpio		
28	Scorpio	10:31 A.M.	Sagittarius
29	Sagittarius		
30	Sagittarius	12:49 P.M.	Capricorn
31	Capricorn		

APRIL

Day	Sign	Time	Sign
1	Capricorn	5:41 P.M.	Aquarius
2	Aquarius		
3	Aquarius		
4	Aquarius	1:23 A.M.	Pisces
5	Pisces		
6	Pisces	11:33 A.M.	Aries
7	Aries		
8	Aries	11:32 P.M.	Taurus
9	Taurus		
10	Taurus		
11	Taurus	12:25 P.M.	Gemini
12	Gemini		
13	Gemini		
14	Gemini	12:48 A.M.	Cancer
15	Cancer		
16	Cancer	10:55 A.M.	Leo
17	Leo		
18	Leo	5:27 P.M.	Virgo
19	Virgo		
20	Virgo	8:19 P.M.	Libra
21	Libra		
22	Libra	8:34 P.M.	Scorpio
23	Scorpio		
24	Scorpio	7:59 P.M.	Sagittarius
25	Sagittarius		
26	Sagittarius	8:32 P.M.	Capricorn
27	Capricorn		
28	Capricorn	11:55 P.M.	Aquarius
29	Aquarius		
30	Aquarius		

MAY

Day	Sign	Time	Sign
1	Aquarius	6:58 A.M.	Pisces
2	Pisces		
3	Pisces	5:19 P.M.	Aries
4	Aries		
5	Aries		
6	Aries	5:39 A.M.	Taurus
7	Taurus		
8	Taurus	6:34 P.M.	Gemini
9	Gemini		
10	Gemini		
11	Gemini	6:57 A.M.	Cancer
12	Cancer		
13	Cancer	5:40 P.M.	Leo
14	Leo		
15	Leo		
16	Leo	1:38 A.M.	Virgo
17	Virgo		
18	Virgo	6:06 A.M.	Libra
19	Libra		
20	Libra	7:24 A.M.	Scorpio
21	Scorpio		
22	Scorpio	6:51 A.M.	Sagittarius
23	Sagittarius		
24	Sagittarius	6:24 A.M.	Capricorn
25	Capricorn		
26	Capricorn	8:09 A.M.	Aquarius
27	Aquarius		
28	Aquarius	1:42 P.M.	Pisces
29	Pisces		
30	Pisces	11:18 P.M.	Aries
31	Aries		

JUNE

Day	Sign	Time	Sign
1	Aries		
2	Aries	11:37 A.M.	Taurus
3	Taurus		
4	Taurus		
5	Taurus	12:35 A.M.	Gemini
6	Gemini		
7	Gemini	12:44 P.M.	Cancer
8	Cancer		
9	Cancer	11:19 P.M.	Leo
10	Leo		
11	Leo		
12	Leo	7:50 A.M.	Virgo
13	Virgo		
14	Virgo	1:42 P.M.	Libra
15	Libra		
16	Libra	4:38 P.M.	Scorpio
17	Scorpio		
18	Scorpio	5:14 P.M.	Sagittarius
19	Sagittarius		
20	Sagittarius	5:01 P.M.	Capricorn
21	Capricorn		
22	Capricorn	6:00 P.M.	Aquarius
23	Aquarius		
24	Aquarius	10:09 P.M.	Pisces
25	Pisces		
26	Pisces		
27	Pisces	6:28 A.M.	Aries
28	Aries		
29	Aries	6:11 P.M.	Taurus
30	Taurus		

JULY

Day	Sign	Time	Sign
1	Taurus		
2	Taurus	7:05 A.M.	Gemini
3	Gemini		
4	Gemini	7:03 P.M.	Cancer
5	Cancer		
6	Cancer		
7	Cancer	5:08 A.M.	Leo

Day	Sign	Time	Change
8	Leo		
9	Leo	1:15 P.M.	Virgo
10	Virgo		
11	Virgo	7:26 P.M.	Libra
12	Libra		
13	Libra	11:33 P.M.	Scorpio
14	Scorpio		
15	Scorpio		
16	Scorpio	1:42 A.M.	Sagittarius
17	Sagittarius		
18	Sagittarius	2:42 A.M.	Capricorn
19	Capricorn		
20	Capricorn	4:05 A.M.	Aquarius
21	Aquarius		
22	Aquarius	7:41 A.M.	Pisces
23	Pisces		
24	Pisces	2:53 P.M.	Aries
25	Aries		
26	Aries		
27	Aries	1:43 A.M.	Taurus
28	Taurus		
29	Taurus	2:23 P.M.	Gemini
30	Gemini		
31	Gemini		

AUGUST

Day	Sign	Time	Change
1	Gemini	2:24 A.M.	Cancer
2	Cancer		
3	Cancer	12:09 P.M.	Leo
4	Leo		
5	Leo	7:29 P.M.	Virgo
6	Virgo		
7	Virgo		
8	Virgo	12:56 A.M.	Libra
9	Libra		
10	Libra	5:00 A.M.	Scorpio
11	Scorpio		
12	Scorpio	7:58 A.M.	Sagittarius
13	Sagittarius		
14	Sagittarius	10:18 A.M.	Capricorn
15	Capricorn		
16	Capricorn	12:53 P.M.	Aquarius
17	Aquarius		
18	Aquarius	4:59 P.M.	Pisces
19	Pisces		
20	Pisces	11:51 P.M.	Aries
21	Aries		
22	Aries		
23	Aries	9:58 A.M.	Taurus
24	Taurus		
25	Taurus	10:18 P.M.	Gemini
26	Gemini		
27	Gemini		
28	Gemini	10:33 A.M.	Cancer
29	Cancer		
30	Cancer	8:33 P.M.	Leo
31	Leo		

SEPTEMBER

Day	Sign	Time	Change
1	Leo		
2	Leo	3:31 A.M.	Virgo
3	Virgo		
4	Virgo	7:56 A.M.	Libra
5	Libra		
6	Libra	10:53 A.M.	Scorpio
7	Scorpio		
8	Scorpio	1:20 P.M.	Sagittarius
9	Sagittarius		
10	Sagittarius	4:04 P.M.	Capricorn
11	Capricorn		
12	Capricorn	7:43 P.M.	Aquarius
13	Aquarius		
14	Aquarius		
15	Aquarius	12:54 A.M.	Pisces
16	Pisces		
17	Pisces	8:16 A.M.	Aries
18	Aries		
19	Aries	6:12 P.M.	Taurus
20	Taurus		
21	Taurus		
22	Taurus	6:16 A.M.	Gemini
23	Gemini		
24	Gemini	6:49 P.M.	Cancer
25	Cancer		
26	Cancer		
27	Cancer	5:36 A.M.	Leo
28	Leo		
29	Leo	1:04 P.M.	Virgo
30	Virgo		

OCTOBER

Day	Sign	Time	Change
1	Virgo	5:08 P.M.	Libra
2	Libra		
3	Libra	6:54 P.M.	Scorpio
4	Scorpio		
5	Scorpio	7:54 P.M.	Sagittarius
6	Sagittarius		
7	Sagittarius	9:38 P.M.	Capricorn
8	Capricorn		
9	Capricorn		
10	Capricorn	1:12 A.M.	Aquarius
11	Aquarius		
12	Aquarius	7:06 A.M.	Pisces
13	Pisces		
14	Pisces	3:20 P.M.	Aries
15	Aries		
16	Aries		
17	Aries	1:40 A.M.	Taurus
18	Taurus		
19	Taurus	1:40 P.M.	Gemini
20	Gemini		
21	Gemini		
22	Gemini	2:22 A.M.	Cancer
23	Cancer		
24	Cancer	2:03 P.M.	Leo
25	Leo		
26	Leo	10:48 P.M.	Virgo
27	Virgo		
28	Virgo		
29	Virgo	3:41 A.M.	Libra
30	Libra		
31	Libra	5:14 A.M.	Scorpio

NOVEMBER

Day	Sign	Time	Change
1	Scorpio		
2	Scorpio	5:02 A.M.	Sagittarius
3	Sagittarius		
4	Sagittarius	5:05 A.M.	Capricorn
5	Capricorn		
6	Capricorn	7:14 A.M.	Aquarius
7	Aquarius		
8	Aquarius	12:35 P.M.	Pisces
9	Pisces		
10	Pisces	9:10 P.M.	Aries
11	Aries		
12	Aries		
13	Aries	8:04 A.M.	Taurus
14	Taurus		
15	Taurus	8:16 P.M.	Gemini
16	Gemini		
17	Gemini		
18	Gemini	8:56 A.M.	Cancer
19	Cancer		
20	Cancer	9:04 P.M.	Leo
21	Leo		
22	Leo		
23	Leo	7:08 A.M.	Virgo
24	Virgo		
25	Virgo	1:41 P.M.	Libra
26	Libra		
27	Libra	4:21 P.M.	Scorpio
28	Scorpio		
29	Scorpio	4:12 P.M.	Sagittarius
30	Sagittarius		

DECEMBER

Day	Sign	Time	Change
1	Sagittarius	3:11 P.M.	Capricorn
2	Capricorn		
3	Capricorn	3:35 P.M.	Aquarius
4	Aquarius		
5	Aquarius	7:16 P.M.	Pisces
6	Pisces		
7	Pisces		
8	Pisces	2:59 A.M.	Aries
9	Aries		
10	Aries	1:56 P.M.	Taurus
11	Taurus		
12	Taurus		
13	Taurus	2:24 A.M.	Gemini
14	Gemini		
15	Gemini	3:00 P.M.	Cancer
16	Cancer		
17	Cancer		
18	Cancer	2:58 A.M.	Leo
19	Leo		
20	Leo	1:29 P.M.	Virgo
21	Virgo		
22	Virgo	9:29 P.M.	Libra
23	Libra		
24	Libra		
25	Libra	2:01 A.M.	Scorpio
26	Scorpio		
27	Scorpio	3:16 A.M.	Sagittarius
28	Sagittarius		
29	Sagittarius	2:38 A.M.	Capricorn
30	Capricorn		
31	Capricorn	2:15 A.M.	Aquarius

MOON SIGN TABLES
1960

JANUARY

1	Aquarius		
2	Aquarius	4:19 A.M.	Pisces
3	Pisces		
4	Pisces	10:21 A.M.	Aries
5	Aries		
6	Aries	8:22 P.M.	Taurus
7	Taurus		
8	Taurus		
9	Taurus	8:45 A.M.	Gemini
10	Gemini		
11	Gemini	9:23 P.M.	Cancer
12	Cancer		
13	Cancer		
14	Cancer	8:59 A.M.	Leo
15	Leo		
16	Leo	7:03 P.M.	Virgo
17	Virgo		
18	Virgo		
19	Virgo	3:14 A.M.	Libra
20	Libra		
21	Libra	8:59 A.M.	Scorpio
22	Scorpio		
23	Scorpio	12:02 P.M.	Sagittarius
24	Sagittarius		
25	Sagittarius	12:59 P.M.	Capricorn
26	Capricorn		
27	Capricorn	1:19 P.M.	Aquarius
28	Aquarius		
29	Aquarius	2:56 P.M.	Pisces
30	Pisces		
31	Pisces	7:39 P.M.	Aries

FEBRUARY

1	Aries		
2	Aries		
3	Aries	4:16 A.M.	Taurus
4	Taurus		
5	Taurus	3:58 P.M.	Gemini
6	Gemini		
7	Gemini		
8	Gemini	4:37 A.M.	Cancer
9	Cancer		
10	Cancer	4:08 P.M.	Leo
11	Leo		
12	Leo		
13	Leo	1:35 A.M.	Virgo
14	Virgo		
15	Virgo	8:55 A.M.	Libra
16	Libra		
17	Libra	2:24 P.M.	Scorpio
18	Scorpio		
19	Scorpio	6:12 P.M.	Sagittarius
20	Sagittarius		
21	Sagittarius	8:39 P.M.	Capricorn
22	Capricorn		
23	Capricorn	10:32 P.M.	Aquarius
24	Aquarius		
25	Aquarius		
26	Aquarius	1:04 A.M.	Pisces
27	Pisces		
28	Pisces	5:38 A.M.	Aries
29	Aries		

MARCH

1	Aries	1:18 P.M.	Taurus
2	Taurus		

APRIL

3	Taurus		
4	Taurus	12:08 A.M.	Gemini
5	Gemini		
6	Gemini	12:37 P.M.	Cancer
7	Cancer		
8	Cancer		
9	Cancer	12:25 A.M.	Leo
10	Leo		
11	Leo	9:47 A.M.	Virgo
12	Virgo		
13	Virgo	4:19 P.M.	Libra
14	Libra		
15	Libra	8:37 P.M.	Scorpio
16	Scorpio		
17	Scorpio	11:37 P.M.	Sagittarius
18	Sagittarius		
19	Sagittarius		
20	Sagittarius	2:14 A.M.	Capricorn
21	Capricorn		
22	Capricorn	5:10 A.M.	Aquarius
23	Aquarius		
24	Aquarius	9:02 A.M.	Pisces
25	Pisces		
26	Pisces	2:29 P.M.	Aries
27	Aries		
28	Aries	10:13 P.M.	Taurus
29	Taurus		
30	Taurus		
31	Taurus	8:32 A.M.	Gemini

APRIL

1	Gemini		
2	Gemini	8:46 P.M.	Cancer
3	Cancer		
4	Cancer		
5	Cancer	9:01 A.M.	Leo
6	Leo		
7	Leo	7:02 P.M.	Virgo
8	Virgo		
9	Virgo		
10	Virgo	1:35 A.M.	Libra
11	Libra		
12	Libra	5:01 A.M.	Scorpio
13	Scorpio		
14	Scorpio	6:37 A.M.	Sagittarius
15	Sagittarius		
16	Sagittarius	8:01 A.M.	Capricorn
17	Capricorn		
18	Capricorn	10:32 A.M.	Aquarius
19	Aquarius		
20	Aquarius	2:55 P.M.	Pisces
21	Pisces		
22	Pisces	9:23 P.M.	Aries
23	Aries		
24	Aries		
25	Aries	5:50 A.M.	Taurus
26	Taurus		
27	Taurus	4:16 P.M.	Gemini
28	Gemini		
29	Gemini		
30	Gemini	4:22 A.M.	Cancer

MAY

1	Cancer		
2	Cancer	4:59 P.M.	Leo
3	Leo		
4	Leo		

5	Leo	3:59 A.M.	Virgo
6	Virgo		
7	Virgo	11:30 A.M.	Libra
8	Libra		
9	Libra	3:06 P.M.	Scorpio
10	Scorpio		
11	Scorpio	3:55 P.M.	Sagittarius
12	Sagittarius		
13	Sagittarius	3:50 P.M.	Capricorn
14	Capricorn		
15	Capricorn	4:51 P.M.	Aquarius
16	Aquarius		
17	Aquarius	8:23 P.M.	Pisces
18	Pisces		
19	Pisces		
20	Pisces	2:55 A.M.	Aries
21	Aries		
22	Aries	12:00 P.M.	Taurus
23	Taurus		
24	Taurus	10:55 P.M.	Gemini
25	Gemini		
26	Gemini		
27	Gemini	11:06 A.M.	Cancer
28	Cancer		
29	Cancer	11:50 P.M.	Leo
30	Leo		
31	Leo		

JUNE

1	Leo	11:38 A.M.	Virgo
2	Virgo		
3	Virgo	8:31 P.M.	Libra
4	Libra		
5	Libra		
6	Libra	1:20 A.M.	Scorpio
7	Scorpio		
8	Scorpio	2:31 A.M.	Sagittarius
9	Sagittarius		
10	Sagittarius	1:48 A.M.	Capricorn
11	Capricorn		
12	Capricorn	1:23 A.M.	Aquarius
13	Aquarius		
14	Aquarius	3:17 A.M.	Pisces
15	Pisces		
16	Pisces	8:42 A.M.	Aries
17	Aries		
18	Aries	5:33 P.M.	Taurus
19	Taurus		
20	Taurus		
21	Taurus	4:46 A.M.	Gemini
22	Gemini		
23	Gemini	5:10 P.M.	Cancer
24	Cancer		
25	Cancer		
26	Cancer	5:51 A.M.	Leo
27	Leo		
28	Leo	5:53 P.M.	Virgo
29	Virgo		
30	Virgo		

JULY

1	Virgo	3:46 A.M.	Libra
2	Libra		
3	Libra	10:08 A.M.	Scorpio
4	Scorpio		
5	Scorpio	12:42 P.M.	Sagittarius
6	Sagittarius		

7	Sagittarius	12:34 P.M.	Capricorn
8	Capricorn		
9	Capricorn	11:43 A.M.	Aquarius
10	Aquarius		
11	Aquarius	12:19 P.M.	Pisces
12	Pisces		
13	Pisces	4:07 P.M.	Aries
14	Aries		
15	Aries	11:48 P.M.	Taurus
16	Taurus		
17	Taurus		
18	Taurus	10:40 A.M.	Gemini
19	Gemini		
20	Gemini	11:09 P.M.	Cancer
21	Cancer		
22	Cancer		
23	Cancer	11:46 A.M.	Leo
24	Leo		
25	Leo	11:31 P.M.	Virgo
26	Virgo		
27	Virgo		
28	Virgo	9:33 A.M.	Libra
29	Libra		
30	Libra	4:55 P.M.	Scorpio
31	Scorpio		

AUGUST

1	Scorpio	9:04 P.M.	Sagittarius
2	Sagittarius		
3	Sagittarius	10:25 P.M.	Capricorn
4	Capricorn		
5	Capricorn	10:21 P.M.	Aquarius
6	Aquarius		
7	Aquarius	10:42 P.M.	Pisces
8	Pisces		
9	Pisces		
10	Pisces	1:21 A.M.	Aries
11	Aries		
12	Aries	7:36 A.M.	Taurus
13	Taurus		
14	Taurus	5:29 P.M.	Gemini
15	Gemini		
16	Gemini		
17	Gemini	5:43 A.M.	Cancer
18	Cancer		
19	Cancer	6:18 P.M.	Leo
20	Leo		
21	Leo		
22	Leo	5:41 A.M.	Virgo
23	Virgo		
24	Virgo	3:09 P.M.	Libra
25	Libra		
26	Libra	10:24 P.M.	Scorpio
27	Scorpio		
28	Scorpio		
29	Scorpio	3:19 A.M.	Sagittarius
30	Sagittarius		
31	Sagittarius	6:09 A.M.	Capricorn

SEPTEMBER

1	Capricorn		
2	Capricorn	7:35 A.M.	Aquarius
3	Aquarius		
4	Aquarius	8:51 A.M.	Pisces
5	Pisces		
6	Pisces	11:26 A.M.	Aries
7	Aries		

8	Aries	4:44 P.M.	Taurus
9	Taurus		
10	Taurus		
11	Taurus	1:31 A.M.	Gemini
12	Gemini		
13	Gemini	1:10 P.M.	Cancer
14	Cancer		
15	Cancer		
16	Cancer	1:46 A.M.	Leo
17	Leo		
18	Leo	1:07 P.M.	Virgo
19	Virgo		
20	Virgo	9:58 P.M.	Libra
21	Libra		
22	Libra		
23	Libra	4:18 A.M.	Scorpio
24	Scorpio		
25	Scorpio	8:42 A.M.	Sagittarius
26	Sagittarius		
27	Sagittarius	11:54 A.M.	Capricorn
28	Capricorn		
29	Capricorn	2:32 P.M.	Aquarius
30	Aquarius		

OCTOBER

1	Aquarius	5:14 P.M.	Pisces
2	Pisces		
3	Pisces	8:46 P.M.	Aries
4	Aries		
5	Aries		
6	Aries	2:09 A.M.	Taurus
7	Taurus		
8	Taurus	10:16 A.M.	Gemini
9	Gemini		
10	Gemini	9:18 P.M.	Cancer
11	Cancer		
12	Cancer		
13	Cancer	9:55 A.M.	Leo
14	Leo		
15	Leo	9:40 P.M.	Virgo
16	Virgo		
17	Virgo		
18	Virgo	6:32 A.M.	Libra
19	Libra		
20	Libra	12:06 P.M.	Scorpio
21	Scorpio		
22	Scorpio	3:16 P.M.	Sagittarius
23	Sagittarius		
24	Sagittarius	5:28 P.M.	Capricorn
25	Capricorn		
26	Capricorn	7:57 P.M.	Aquarius
27	Aquarius		
28	Aquarius	11:26 P.M.	Pisces
29	Pisces		
30	Pisces		
31	Pisces	4:11 A.M.	Aries

NOVEMBER

1	Aries		
2	Aries	10:27 A.M.	Taurus
3	Taurus		
4	Taurus	6:44 P.M.	Gemini
5	Gemini		
6	Gemini		
7	Gemini	5:26 A.M.	Cancer
8	Cancer		
9	Cancer	5:59 P.M.	Leo

10	Leo		
11	Leo		
12	Leo	6:24 A.M.	Virgo
13	Virgo		
14	Virgo	4:07 P.M.	Libra
15	Libra		
16	Libra	9:53 P.M.	Scorpio
17	Scorpio		
18	Scorpio		
19	Scorpio	12:17 A.M.	Sagittarius
20	Sagittarius		
21	Sagittarius	1:02 A.M.	Capricorn
22	Capricorn		
23	Capricorn	2:04 A.M.	Aquarius
24	Aquarius		
25	Aquarius	4:49 A.M.	Pisces
26	Pisces		
27	Pisces	9:51 A.M.	Aries
28	Aries		
29	Aries	5:00 P.M.	Taurus
30	Taurus		

DECEMBER

1	Taurus		
2	Taurus	2:01 A.M.	Gemini
3	Gemini		
4	Gemini	12:52 P.M.	Cancer
5	Cancer		
6	Cancer		
7	Cancer	1:21 A.M.	Leo
8	Leo		
9	Leo	2:13 P.M.	Virgo
10	Virgo		
11	Virgo		
12	Virgo	1:10 A.M.	Libra
13	Libra		
14	Libra	8:13 A.M.	Scorpio
15	Scorpio		
16	Scorpio	11:07 A.M.	Sagittarius
17	Sagittarius		
18	Sagittarius	11:16 A.M.	Capricorn
19	Capricorn		
20	Capricorn	10:49 A.M.	Aquarius
21	Aquarius		
22	Aquarius	11:47 A.M.	Pisces
23	Pisces		
24	Pisces	3:34 P.M.	Aries
25	Aries		
26	Aries	10:30 P.M.	Taurus
27	Taurus		
28	Taurus		
29	Taurus	8:01 A.M.	Gemini
30	Gemini		
31	Gemini	7:22 P.M.	Cancer

MOON SIGN TABLES
1961

JANUARY

1	Cancer		
2	Cancer		
3	Cancer	7:54 A.M.	Leo
4	Leo		
5	Leo	8:48 P.M.	Virgo
6	Virgo		
7	Virgo		
8	Virgo	8:31 A.M.	Libra
9	Libra		
10	Libra	5:09 P.M.	Scorpio
11	Scorpio		
12	Scorpio	9:40 P.M.	Sagittarius
13	Sagittarius		
14	Sagittarius	10:41 P.M.	Capricorn
15	Capricorn		
16	Capricorn	9:55 P.M.	Aquarius
17	Aquarius		
18	Aquarius	9:32 P.M.	Pisces
19	Pisces		
20	Pisces	11:26 P.M.	Aries
21	Aries		
22	Aries		
23	Aries	4:51 A.M.	Taurus
24	Taurus		
25	Taurus	1:50 P.M.	Gemini
26	Gemini		
27	Gemini		
28	Gemini	1:22 A.M.	Cancer
29	Cancer		
30	Cancer	2:05 P.M.	Leo
31	Leo		

FEBRUARY

1	Leo		
2	Leo	2:48 A.M.	Virgo
3	Virgo		
4	Virgo	2:27 P.M.	Libra
5	Libra		
6	Libra	11:51 P.M.	Scorpio
7	Scorpio		
8	Scorpio		
9	Scorpio	6:01 A.M.	Sagittarius
10	Sagittarius		
11	Sagittarius	8:50 A.M.	Capricorn
12	Capricorn		
13	Capricorn	9:14 A.M.	Aquarius
14	Aquarius		
15	Aquarius	8:53 A.M.	Pisces
16	Pisces		
17	Pisces	9:41 A.M.	Aries
18	Aries		
19	Aries	1:21 P.M.	Taurus
20	Taurus		
21	Taurus	8:51 P.M.	Gemini
22	Gemini		
23	Gemini		
24	Gemini	7:49 A.M.	Cancer
25	Cancer		
26	Cancer	8:34 P.M.	Leo
27	Leo		
28	Leo		

MARCH

1	Leo	9:12 A.M.	Virgo
2	Virgo		
3	Virgo	8:21 P.M.	Libra

4	Libra		
5	Libra		
6	Libra	5:24 A.M.	Scorpio
7	Scorpio		
8	Scorpio	12:04 P.M.	Sagittarius
9	Sagittarius		
10	Sagittarius	4:19 P.M.	Capricorn
11	Capricorn		
12	Capricorn	6:29 P.M.	Aquarius
13	Aquarius		
14	Aquarius	7:26 P.M.	Pisces
15	Pisces		
16	Pisces	8:32 P.M.	Aries
17	Aries		
18	Aries	11:25 P.M.	Taurus
19	Taurus		
20	Taurus		
21	Taurus	5:32 A.M.	Gemini
22	Gemini		
23	Gemini	3:22 P.M.	Cancer
24	Cancer		
25	Cancer		
26	Cancer	3:48 A.M.	Leo
27	Leo		
28	Leo	4:30 P.M.	Virgo
29	Virgo		
30	Virgo		
31	Virgo	3:21 A.M.	Libra

APRIL

1	Libra		
2	Libra	11:36 A.M.	Scorpio
3	Scorpio		
4	Scorpio	5:34 P.M.	Sagittarius
5	Sagittarius		
6	Sagittarius	9:52 P.M.	Capricorn
7	Capricorn		
8	Capricorn		
9	Capricorn	1:03 A.M.	Aquarius
10	Aquarius		
11	Aquarius	3:31 A.M.	Pisces
12	Pisces		
13	Pisces	5:55 A.M.	Aries
14	Aries		
15	Aries	9:16 A.M.	Taurus
16	Taurus		
17	Taurus	2:55 P.M.	Gemini
18	Gemini		
19	Gemini	11:50 P.M.	Cancer
20	Cancer		
21	Cancer		
22	Cancer	11:43 A.M.	Leo
23	Leo		
24	Leo		
25	Leo	12:31 A.M.	Virgo
26	Virgo		
27	Virgo	11:34 A.M.	Libra
28	Libra		
29	Libra	7:27 P.M.	Scorpio
30	Scorpio		

MAY

1	Scorpio		
2	Scorpio	12:25 A.M.	Sagittarius
3	Sagittarius		
4	Sagittarius	3:40 A.M.	Capricorn
5	Capricorn		

6	Capricorn	6:24 A.M.	Aquarius
7	Aquarius		
8	Aquarius	9:23 A.M.	Pisces
9	Pisces		
10	Pisces	12:56 P.M.	Aries
11	Aries		
12	Aries	5:25 P.M.	Taurus
13	Taurus		
14	Taurus	11:34 P.M.	Gemini
15	Gemini		
16	Gemini		
17	Gemini	8:17 A.M.	Cancer
18	Cancer		
19	Cancer	7:45 P.M.	Leo
20	Leo		
21	Leo		
22	Leo	8:38 A.M.	Virgo
23	Virgo		
24	Virgo	8:18 P.M.	Libra
25	Libra		
26	Libra		
27	Libra	4:34 A.M.	Scorpio
28	Scorpio		
29	Scorpio	9:11 A.M.	Sagittarius
30	Sagittarius		
31	Sagittarius	11:20 A.M.	Capricorn

JUNE

1	Capricorn		
2	Capricorn	12:45 P.M.	Aquarius
3	Aquarius		
4	Aquarius	2:50 P.M.	Pisces
5	Pisces		
6	Pisces	6:23 P.M.	Aries
7	Aries		
8	Aries	11:38 P.M.	Taurus
9	Taurus		
10	Taurus		
11	Taurus	6:40 A.M.	Gemini
12	Gemini		
13	Gemini	3:50 P.M.	Cancer
14	Cancer		
15	Cancer		
16	Cancer	3:16 A.M.	Leo
17	Leo		
18	Leo	4:12 P.M.	Virgo
19	Virgo		
20	Virgo		
21	Virgo	4:32 A.M.	Libra
22	Libra		
23	Libra	1:51 P.M.	Scorpio
24	Scorpio		
25	Scorpio	7:05 P.M.	Sagittarius
26	Sagittarius		
27	Sagittarius	9:00 P.M.	Capricorn
28	Capricorn		
29	Capricorn	9:18 P.M.	Aquarius
30	Aquarius		

JULY

1	Aquarius	9:52 P.M.	Pisces
2	Pisces		
3	Pisces		
4	Pisces	12:12 A.M.	Aries
5	Aries		
6	Aries	5:01 A.M.	Taurus
7	Taurus		

8	Taurus	12:27 P.M.	Gemini
9	Gemini		
10	Gemini	10:13 P.M.	Cancer
11	Cancer		
12	Cancer		
13	Cancer	9:56 A.M.	Leo
14	Leo		
15	Leo	10:55 P.M.	Virgo
16	Virgo		
17	Virgo		
18	Virgo	11:39 A.M.	Libra
19	Libra		
20	Libra	10:05 P.M.	Scorpio
21	Scorpio		
22	Scorpio		
23	Scorpio	4:42 A.M.	Sagittarius
24	Sagittarius		
25	Sagittarius	7:28 A.M.	Capricorn
26	Capricorn		
27	Capricorn	7:41 A.M.	Aquarius
28	Aquarius		
29	Aquarius	7:13 A.M.	Pisces
30	Pisces		
31	Pisces	7:56 A.M.	Aries

AUGUST

1	Aries		
2	Aries	11:19 A.M.	Taurus
3	Taurus		
4	Taurus	6:04 P.M.	Gemini
5	Gemini		
6	Gemini		
7	Gemini	3:56 A.M.	Cancer
8	Cancer		
9	Cancer	3:59 P.M.	Leo
10	Leo		
11	Leo		
12	Leo	5:00 A.M.	Virgo
13	Virgo		
14	Virgo	5:44 P.M.	Libra
15	Libra		
16	Libra		
17	Libra	4:44 A.M.	Scorpio
18	Scorpio		
19	Scorpio	12:44 P.M.	Sagittarius
20	Sagittarius		
21	Sagittarius	5:07 P.M.	Capricorn
22	Capricorn		
23	Capricorn	6:25 P.M.	Aquarius
24	Aquarius		
25	Aquarius	6:02 P.M.	Pisces
26	Pisces		
27	Pisces	5:49 P.M.	Aries
28	Aries		
29	Aries	7:37 P.M.	Taurus
30	Taurus		
31	Taurus		

SEPTEMBER

1	Taurus	12:52 A.M.	Gemini
2	Gemini		
3	Gemini	10:00 A.M.	Cancer
4	Cancer		
5	Cancer	10:01 P.M.	Leo
6	Leo		
7	Leo		
8	Leo	11:05 A.M.	Virgo
9	Virgo		
10	Virgo	11:33 P.M.	Libra
11	Libra		
12	Libra		
13	Libra	10:23 A.M.	Scorpio
14	Scorpio		
15	Scorpio	6:54 P.M.	Sagittarius
16	Sagittarius		
17	Sagittarius		
18	Sagittarius	12:42 A.M.	Capricorn
19	Capricorn		
20	Capricorn	3:43 A.M.	Aquarius
21	Aquarius		
22	Aquarius	4:36 A.M.	Pisces
23	Pisces		
24	Pisces	4:40 A.M.	Aries
25	Aries		
26	Aries	5:42 A.M.	Taurus
27	Taurus		
28	Taurus	9:31 A.M.	Gemini
29	Gemini		
30	Gemini	5:19 P.M.	Cancer

OCTOBER

1	Cancer		
2	Cancer		
3	Cancer	4:43 A.M.	Leo
4	Leo		
5	Leo	5:45 P.M.	Virgo
6	Virgo		
7	Virgo		
8	Virgo	6:04 A.M.	Libra
9	Libra		
10	Libra	4:19 P.M.	Scorpio
11	Scorpio		
12	Scorpio		
13	Scorpio	12:21 A.M.	Sagittarius
14	Sagittarius		
15	Sagittarius	6:24 A.M.	Capricorn
16	Capricorn		
17	Capricorn	10:37 A.M.	Aquarius
18	Aquarius		
19	Aquarius	1:10 P.M.	Pisces
20	Pisces		
21	Pisces	2:35 P.M.	Aries
22	Aries		
23	Aries	4:07 P.M.	Taurus
24	Taurus		
25	Taurus	7:24 P.M.	Gemini
26	Gemini		
27	Gemini		
28	Gemini	2:03 A.M.	Cancer
29	Cancer		
30	Cancer	12:30 P.M.	Leo
31	Leo		

NOVEMBER

1	Leo		
2	Leo	1:17 A.M.	Virgo
3	Virgo		
4	Virgo	1:42 P.M.	Libra
5	Libra		
6	Libra	11:40 P.M.	Scorpio
7	Scorpio		
8	Scorpio		
9	Scorpio	6:51 A.M.	Sagittarius
10	Sagittarius		
11	Sagittarius	11:59 A.M.	Capricorn
12	Capricorn		
13	Capricorn	3:59 P.M.	Aquarius
14	Aquarius		
15	Aquarius	7:18 P.M.	Pisces
16	Pisces		
17	Pisces	10:10 P.M.	Aries
18	Aries		
19	Aries		
20	Aries	1:03 A.M.	Taurus
21	Taurus		
22	Taurus	4:59 A.M.	Gemini
23	Gemini		
24	Gemini	11:20 A.M.	Cancer
25	Cancer		
26	Cancer	9:01 P.M.	Leo
27	Leo		
28	Leo		
29	Leo	9:25 A.M.	Virgo
30	Virgo		

DECEMBER

1	Virgo	10:08 P.M.	Libra
2	Libra		
3	Libra		
4	Libra	8:30 A.M.	Scorpio
5	Scorpio		
6	Scorpio	3:24 P.M.	Sagittarius
7	Sagittarius		
8	Sagittarius	7:31 P.M.	Capricorn
9	Capricorn		
10	Capricorn	10:11 P.M.	Aquarius
11	Aquarius		
12	Aquarius		
13	Aquarius	12:41 A.M.	Pisces
14	Pisces		
15	Pisces	3:44 A.M.	Aries
16	Aries		
17	Aries	7:39 A.M.	Taurus
18	Taurus		
19	Taurus	12:47 P.M.	Gemini
20	Gemini		
21	Gemini	7:50 P.M.	Cancer
22	Cancer		
23	Cancer		
24	Cancer	5:26 P.M.	Leo
25	Leo		
26	Leo	5:29 P.M.	Virgo
27	Virgo		
28	Virgo		
29	Virgo	6:26 A.M.	Libra
30	Libra		
31	Libra	5:42 P.M.	Scorpio

MOON SIGN TABLES
1962

January

1	Scorpio		
2	Scorpio		
3	Scorpio	1:23 A.M.	Sagittarius
4	Sagittarius		
5	Sagittarius	5:24 A.M.	Capricorn
6	Capricorn		
7	Capricorn	7:00 A.M.	Aquarius
8	Aquarius		
9	Aquarius	7:53 A.M.	Pisces
10	Pisces		
11	Pisces	9:34 A.M.	Aries
12	Aries		
13	Aries	1:01 P.M.	Taurus
14	Taurus		
15	Taurus	6:42 P.M.	Gemini
16	Gemini		
17	Gemini		
18	Gemini	2:39 A.M.	Cancer
19	Cancer		
20	Cancer	12:50 P.M.	Leo
21	Leo		
22	Leo		
23	Leo	12:53 A.M.	Virgo
24	Virgo		
25	Virgo	1:52 P.M.	Libra
26	Libra		
27	Libra		
28	Libra	1:54 A.M.	Scorpio
29	Scorpio		
30	Scorpio	10:59 A.M.	Sagittarius
31	Sagittarius		

February

1	Sagittarius	4:09 P.M.	Capricorn
2	Capricorn		
3	Capricorn	5:57 P.M.	Aquarius
4	Aquarius		
5	Aquarius	5:53 P.M.	Pisces
6	Pisces		
7	Pisces	5:50 P.M.	Aries
8	Aries		
9	Aries	7:35 P.M.	Taurus
10	Taurus		
11	Taurus		
12	Taurus	12:18 A.M.	Gemini
13	Gemini		
14	Gemini	8:20 A.M.	Cancer
15	Cancer		
16	Cancer	7:04 P.M.	Leo
17	Leo		
18	Leo		
19	Leo	7:27 A.M.	Virgo
20	Virgo		
21	Virgo	8:22 P.M.	Libra
22	Libra		
23	Libra		
24	Libra	8:36 A.M.	Scorpio
25	Scorpio		
26	Scorpio	6:46 P.M.	Sagittarius
27	Sagittarius		
28	Sagittarius		

March

1	Sagittarius	1:38 A.M.	Capricorn
2	Capricorn		
3	Capricorn	4:52 A.M.	Aquarius
4	Aquarius		
5	Aquarius	5:16 A.M.	Pisces
6	Pisces		
7	Pisces	4:32 A.M.	Aries
8	Aries		
9	Aries	4:40 A.M.	Taurus
10	Taurus		
11	Taurus	7:35 A.M.	Gemini
12	Gemini		
13	Gemini	2:25 P.M.	Cancer
14	Cancer		
15	Cancer		
16	Cancer	12:56 A.M.	Leo
17	Leo		
18	Leo	1:33 P.M.	Virgo
19	Virgo		
20	Virgo		
21	Virgo	2:28 A.M.	Libra
22	Libra		
23	Libra	2:29 P.M.	Scorpio
24	Scorpio		
25	Scorpio		
26	Scorpio	12:49 A.M.	Sagittarius
27	Sagittarius		
28	Sagittarius	8:46 A.M.	Capricorn
29	Capricorn		
30	Capricorn	1:43 P.M.	Aquarius
31	Aquarius		

April

1	Aquarius	3:42 P.M.	Pisces
2	Pisces		
3	Pisces	3:41 P.M.	Aries
4	Aries		
5	Aries	3:25 P.M.	Taurus
6	Taurus		
7	Taurus	5:00 P.M.	Gemini
8	Gemini		
9	Gemini	10:12 P.M.	Cancer
10	Cancer		
11	Cancer		
12	Cancer	7:36 A.M.	Leo
13	Leo		
14	Leo	7:57 P.M.	Virgo
15	Virgo		
16	Virgo		
17	Virgo	8:54 A.M.	Libra
18	Libra		
19	Libra	8:37 P.M.	Scorpio
20	Scorpio		
21	Scorpio		
22	Scorpio	6:27 A.M.	Sagittarius
23	Sagittarius		
24	Sagittarius	2:20 P.M.	Capricorn
25	Capricorn		
26	Capricorn	8:08 P.M.	Aquarius
27	Aquarius		
28	Aquarius	11:40 P.M.	Pisces
29	Pisces		
30	Pisces		

May

1	Pisces	1:12 A.M.	Aries
2	Aries		
3	Aries	1:49 A.M.	Taurus
4	Taurus		
5	Taurus	3:16 A.M.	Gemini
6	Gemini		
7	Gemini	7:28 A.M.	Cancer
8	Cancer		
9	Cancer	3:35 P.M.	Leo
10	Leo		
11	Leo		
12	Leo	3:11 A.M.	Virgo
13	Virgo		
14	Virgo	4:03 P.M.	Libra
15	Libra		
16	Libra		
17	Libra	3:43 A.M.	Scorpio
18	Scorpio		
19	Scorpio	1:02 P.M.	Sagittarius
20	Sagittarius		
21	Sagittarius	8:08 P.M.	Capricorn
22	Capricorn		
23	Capricorn		
24	Capricorn	1:31 A.M.	Aquarius
25	Aquarius		
26	Aquarius	5:29 A.M.	Pisces
27	Pisces		
28	Pisces	8:15 A.M.	Aries
29	Aries		
30	Aries	10:17 A.M.	Taurus
31	Taurus		

June

1	Taurus	12:40 P.M.	Gemini
2	Gemini		
3	Gemini	4:56 P.M.	Cancer
4	Cancer		
5	Cancer		
6	Cancer	12:23 A.M.	Leo
7	Leo		
8	Leo	11:12 A.M.	Virgo
9	Virgo		
10	Virgo	11:51 P.M.	Libra
11	Libra		
12	Libra		
13	Libra	11:45 A.M.	Scorpio
14	Scorpio		
15	Scorpio	9:03 P.M.	Sagittarius
16	Sagittarius		
17	Sagittarius		
18	Sagittarius	3:30 A.M.	Capricorn
19	Capricorn		
20	Capricorn	7:49 A.M.	Aquarius
21	Aquarius		
22	Aquarius	10:59 A.M.	Pisces
23	Pisces		
24	Pisces	1:43 P.M.	Aries
25	Aries		
26	Aries	4:34 P.M.	Taurus
27	Taurus		
28	Taurus	8:09 P.M.	Gemini
29	Gemini		
30	Gemini		

July

1	Gemini	1:19 A.M.	Cancer
2	Cancer		
3	Cancer	8:55 A.M.	Leo
4	Leo		
5	Leo	7:22 P.M.	Virgo
6	Virgo		
7	Virgo		

Day	Sign	Time	Enters
8	Virgo	7:48 A.M.	Libra
9	Libra		
10	Libra	8:05 P.M.	Scorpio
11	Scorpio		
12	Scorpio		
13	Scorpio	6:00 A.M.	Sagittarius
14	Sagittarius		
15	Sagittarius	12:32 P.M.	Capricorn
16	Capricorn		
17	Capricorn	4:07 P.M.	Aquarius
18	Aquarius		
19	Aquarius	6:00 P.M.	Pisces
20	Pisces		
21	Pisces	7:34 P.M.	Aries
22	Aries		
23	Aries	9:57 P.M.	Taurus
24	Taurus		
25	Taurus		
26	Taurus	1:57 A.M.	Gemini
27	Gemini		
28	Gemini	8:00 A.M.	Cancer
29	Cancer		
30	Cancer	4:21 P.M.	Leo
31	Leo		

AUGUST

Day	Sign	Time	Enters
1	Leo		
2	Leo	2:57 A.M.	Virgo
3	Virgo		
4	Virgo	3:17 P.M.	Libra
5	Libra		
6	Libra		
7	Libra	3:56 A.M.	Scorpio
8	Scorpio		
9	Scorpio	2:48 P.M.	Sagittarius
10	Sagittarius		
11	Sagittarius	10:18 P.M.	Capricorn
12	Capricorn		
13	Capricorn		
14	Capricorn	2:07 A.M.	Aquarius
15	Aquarius		
16	Aquarius	3:17 A.M.	Pisces
17	Pisces		
18	Pisces	3:25 A.M.	Aries
19	Aries		
20	Aries	4:20 A.M.	Taurus
21	Taurus		
22	Taurus	7:28 A.M.	Gemini
23	Gemini		
24	Gemini	1:34 P.M.	Cancer
25	Cancer		
26	Cancer	10:30 P.M.	Leo
27	Leo		
28	Leo		
29	Leo	9:36 A.M.	Virgo
30	Virgo		
31	Virgo	10:01 P.M.	Libra

SEPTEMBER

Day	Sign	Time	Enters
1	Libra		
2	Libra		
3	Libra	10:46 A.M.	Scorpio
4	Scorpio		
5	Scorpio	10:26 P.M.	Sagittarius
6	Sagittarius		
7	Sagittarius		
8	Sagittarius	7:20 A.M.	Capricorn
9	Capricorn		
10	Capricorn	12:26 P.M.	Aquarius
11	Aquarius		
12	Aquarius	2:02 P.M.	Pisces
13	Pisces		
14	Pisces	1:33 P.M.	Aries
15	Aries		
16	Aries	1:01 P.M.	Taurus
17	Taurus		
18	Taurus	2:29 P.M.	Gemini
19	Gemini		
20	Gemini	7:26 P.M.	Cancer
21	Cancer		
22	Cancer		
23	Cancer	4:07 A.M.	Leo
24	Leo		
25	Leo	3:31 P.M.	Virgo
26	Virgo		
27	Virgo		
28	Virgo	4:08 A.M.	Libra
29	Libra		
30	Libra	4:49 P.M.	Scorpio

OCTOBER

Day	Sign	Time	Enters
1	Scorpio		
2	Scorpio		
3	Scorpio	4:40 A.M.	Sagittarius
4	Sagittarius		
5	Sagittarius	2:35 P.M.	Capricorn
6	Capricorn		
7	Capricorn	9:22 P.M.	Aquarius
8	Aquarius		
9	Aquarius		
10	Aquarius	12:29 A.M.	Pisces
11	Pisces		
12	Pisces	12:41 A.M.	Aries
13	Aries	11:43 P.M.	Taurus
14	Taurus		
15	Taurus	11:50 P.M.	Gemini
16	Gemini		
17	Gemini		
18	Gemini	3:05 A.M.	Cancer
19	Cancer		
20	Cancer	10:30 A.M.	Leo
21	Leo		
22	Leo	9:31 P.M.	Virgo
23	Virgo		
24	Virgo		
25	Virgo	10:13 A.M.	Libra
26	Libra		
27	Libra	10:49 P.M.	Scorpio
28	Scorpio		
29	Scorpio		
30	Scorpio	10:19 A.M.	Sagittarius
31	Sagittarius		

NOVEMBER

Day	Sign	Time	Enters
1	Sagittarius	8:17 P.M.	Capricorn
2	Capricorn		
3	Capricorn		
4	Capricorn	4:02 A.M.	Aquarius
5	Aquarius		
6	Aquarius	8:52 A.M.	Pisces
7	Pisces		
8	Pisces	10:45 A.M.	Aries
9	Aries		
10	Aries	10:45 A.M.	Taurus
11	Taurus		
12	Taurus	10:43 A.M.	Gemini
13	Gemini		
14	Gemini	12:49 P.M.	Cancer
15	Cancer		
16	Cancer	6:40 P.M.	Leo
17	Leo		
18	Leo		
19	Leo	4:33 A.M.	Virgo
20	Virgo		
21	Virgo	4:58 P.M.	Libra
22	Libra		
23	Libra		
24	Libra	5:33 A.M.	Scorpio
25	Scorpio		
26	Scorpio	4:43 P.M.	Sagittarius
27	Sagittarius		
28	Sagittarius		
29	Sagittarius	2:00 A.M.	Capricorn
30	Capricorn		

DECEMBER

Day	Sign	Time	Enters
1	Capricorn	9:26 A.M.	Aquarius
2	Aquarius		
3	Aquarius	2:53 P.M.	Pisces
4	Pisces		
5	Pisces	6:17 P.M.	Aries
6	Aries		
7	Aries	7:59 P.M.	Taurus
8	Taurus		
9	Taurus	9:07 P.M.	Gemini
10	Gemini		
11	Gemini	11:21 P.M.	Cancer
12	Cancer		
13	Cancer		
14	Cancer	4:20 A.M.	Leo
15	Leo		
16	Leo	12:59 P.M.	Virgo
17	Virgo		
18	Virgo		
19	Virgo	12:41 A.M.	Libra
20	Libra		
21	Libra	1:18 P.M.	Scorpio
22	Scorpio		
23	Scorpio		
24	Scorpio	12:33 A.M.	Sagittarius
25	Sagittarius		
26	Sagittarius	9:19 A.M.	Capricorn
27	Capricorn		
28	Capricorn	3:42 P.M.	Aquarius
29	Aquarius		
30	Aquarius	8:20 P.M.	Pisces
31	Pisces		

MOON SIGN TABLES
1963

JANUARY

1	Pisces	11:48 P.M.	Aries
2	Aries		
3	Aries		
4	Aries	2:33 A.M.	Taurus
5	Taurus		
6	Taurus	5:14 A.M.	Gemini
7	Gemini		
8	Gemini	8:41 A.M.	Cancer
9	Cancer		
10	Cancer	2:01 P.M.	Leo
11	Leo		
12	Leo	10:07 P.M.	Virgo
13	Virgo		
14	Virgo		
15	Virgo	9:05 A.M.	Libra
16	Libra		
17	Libra	9:35 P.M.	Scorpio
18	Scorpio		
19	Scorpio		
20	Scorpio	9:20 A.M.	Sagittarius
21	Sagittarius		
22	Sagittarius	6:23 P.M.	Capricorn
23	Capricorn		
24	Capricorn		
25	Capricorn	12:14 A.M.	Aquarius
26	Aquarius		
27	Aquarius	3:35 A.M.	Pisces
28	Pisces		
29	Pisces	5:44 A.M.	Aries
30	Aries		
31	Aries	7:55 A.M.	Taurus

FEBRUARY

1	Taurus		
2	Taurus	11:03 A.M.	Gemini
3	Gemini		
4	Gemini	3:40 P.M.	Cancer
5	Cancer		
6	Cancer	10:06 P.M.	Leo
7	Leo		
8	Leo		
9	Leo	6:36 A.M.	Virgo
10	Virgo		
11	Virgo	5:18 P.M.	Libra
12	Libra		
13	Libra		
14	Libra	5:38 A.M.	Scorpio
15	Scorpio		
16	Scorpio	5:57 P.M.	Sagittarius
17	Sagittarius		
18	Sagittarius		
19	Sagittarius	4:00 A.M.	Capricorn
20	Capricorn		
21	Capricorn	10:23 A.M.	Aquarius
22	Aquarius		
23	Aquarius	1:17 P.M.	Pisces
24	Pisces		
25	Pisces	2:05 P.M.	Aries
26	Aries		
27	Aries	2:38 P.M.	Taurus
28	Taurus		

MARCH

1	Taurus	4:39 P.M.	Gemini
2	Gemini		
3	Gemini	9:08 P.M.	Cancer
4	Cancer		
5	Cancer		
6	Cancer	4:15 A.M.	Leo
7	Leo		
8	Leo	1:34 P.M.	Virgo
9	Virgo		
10	Virgo		
11	Virgo	12:35 A.M.	Libra
12	Libra		
13	Libra	12:51 P.M.	Scorpio
14	Scorpio		
15	Scorpio		
16	Scorpio	1:27 A.M.	Sagittarius
17	Sagittarius		
18	Sagittarius	12:35 P.M.	Capricorn
19	Capricorn		
20	Capricorn	8:21 P.M.	Aquarius
21	Aquarius		
22	Aquarius		
23	Aquarius	12:04 A.M.	Pisces
24	Pisces		
25	Pisces	12:38 A.M.	Aries
26	Aries	11:57 P.M.	Taurus
27	Taurus		
28	Taurus		
29	Taurus	12:13 A.M.	Gemini
30	Gemini		
31	Gemini	3:14 A.M.	Cancer

APRIL

1	Cancer		
2	Cancer	9:45 A.M.	Leo
3	Leo		
4	Leo	7:20 P.M.	Virgo
5	Virgo		
6	Virgo		
7	Virgo	6:49 A.M.	Libra
8	Libra		
9	Libra	7:14 P.M.	Scorpio
10	Scorpio		
11	Scorpio		
12	Scorpio	7:48 A.M.	Sagittarius
13	Sagittarius		
14	Sagittarius	7:27 P.M.	Capricorn
15	Capricorn		
16	Capricorn		
17	Capricorn	4:34 A.M.	Aquarius
18	Aquarius		
19	Aquarius	9:53 A.M.	Pisces
20	Pisces		
21	Pisces	11:30 A.M.	Aries
22	Aries		
23	Aries	10:51 A.M.	Taurus
24	Taurus		
25	Taurus	10:06 A.M.	Gemini
26	Gemini		
27	Gemini	11:27 A.M.	Cancer
28	Cancer		
29	Cancer	4:25 P.M.	Leo
30	Leo		

MAY

1	Leo		
2	Leo	1:13 A.M.	Virgo
3	Virgo		
4	Virgo	12:42 P.M.	Libra
5	Libra		

JUNE

(continued)

6	Libra		
7	Libra	1:16 A.M.	Scorpio
8	Scorpio		
9	Scorpio	1:42 P.M.	Sagittarius
10	Sagittarius		
11	Sagittarius		
12	Sagittarius	1:13 A.M.	Capricorn
13	Capricorn		
14	Capricorn	10:51 A.M.	Aquarius
15	Aquarius		
16	Aquarius	5:32 P.M.	Pisces
17	Pisces		
18	Pisces	8:48 P.M.	Aries
19	Aries		
20	Aries	9:21 P.M.	Taurus
21	Taurus		
22	Taurus	8:53 P.M.	Gemini
23	Gemini		
24	Gemini	9:29 P.M.	Cancer
25	Cancer		
26	Cancer		
27	Cancer	12:58 A.M.	Leo
28	Leo		
29	Leo	8:22 A.M.	Virgo
30	Virgo		
31	Virgo	7:09 P.M.	Libra

JUNE

1	Libra		
2	Libra		
3	Libra	7:38 A.M.	Scorpio
4	Scorpio		
5	Scorpio	8:01 P.M.	Sagittarius
6	Sagittarius		
7	Sagittarius		
8	Sagittarius	7:07 A.M.	Capricorn
9	Capricorn		
10	Capricorn	4:22 P.M.	Aquarius
11	Aquarius		
12	Aquarius	11:21 P.M.	Pisces
13	Pisces		
14	Pisces		
15	Pisces	3:46 A.M.	Aries
16	Aries		
17	Aries	5:54 A.M.	Taurus
18	Taurus		
19	Taurus	6:44 A.M.	Gemini
20	Gemini		
21	Gemini	7:46 A.M.	Cancer
22	Cancer		
23	Cancer	10:44 A.M.	Leo
24	Leo		
25	Leo	4:56 P.M.	Virgo
26	Virgo		
27	Virgo		
28	Virgo	2:41 A.M.	Libra
29	Libra		
30	Libra	2:48 P.M.	Scorpio

JULY

1	Scorpio		
2	Scorpio		
3	Scorpio	3:11 A.M.	Sagittarius
4	Sagittarius		
5	Sagittarius	2:03 P.M.	Capricorn
6	Capricorn		
7	Capricorn	10:36 P.M.	Aquarius

8	Aquarius		
9	Aquarius		
10	Aquarius	4:53 A.M.	Pisces
11	Pisces		
12	Pisces	9:16 A.M.	Aries
13	Aries		
14	Aries	12:15 P.M.	Taurus
15	Taurus		
16	Taurus	2:27 P.M.	Gemini
17	Gemini		
18	Gemini	4:45 P.M.	Cancer
19	Cancer		
20	Cancer	8:15 P.M.	Leo
21	Leo		
22	Leo		
23	Leo	2:06 A.M.	Virgo
24	Virgo		
25	Virgo	11:02 A.M.	Libra
26	Libra		
27	Libra	10:38 P.M.	Scorpio
28	Scorpio		
29	Scorpio		
30	Scorpio	11:08 A.M.	Sagittarius
31	Sagittarius		

AUGUST

1	Sagittarius	10:12 P.M.	Capricorn
2	Capricorn		
3	Capricorn		
4	Capricorn	6:25 A.M.	Aquarius
5	Aquarius		
6	Aquarius	11:46 A.M.	Pisces
7	Pisces		
8	Pisces	3:07 P.M.	Aries
9	Aries		
10	Aries	5:37 P.M.	Taurus
11	Taurus		
12	Taurus	8:16 P.M.	Gemini
13	Gemini		
14	Gemini	11:39 P.M.	Cancer
15	Cancer		
16	Cancer		
17	Cancer	4:17 A.M.	Leo
18	Leo		
19	Leo	10:40 A.M.	Virgo
20	Virgo		
21	Virgo	7:25 P.M.	Libra
22	Libra		
23	Libra		
24	Libra	6:39 A.M.	Scorpio
25	Scorpio		
26	Scorpio	7:15 P.M.	Sagittarius
27	Sagittarius		
28	Sagittarius		
29	Sagittarius	6:57 A.M.	Capricorn
30	Capricorn		
31	Capricorn	3:37 P.M.	Aquarius

SEPTEMBER

1	Aquarius		
2	Aquarius	8:37 P.M.	Pisces
3	Pisces		
4	Pisces	10:52 P.M.	Aries
5	Aries		
6	Aries		
7	Aries	12:02 A.M.	Taurus
8	Taurus		

9	Taurus	1:45 A.M.	Gemini
10	Gemini		
11	Gemini	5:08 A.M.	Cancer
12	Cancer		
13	Cancer	10:30 A.M.	Leo
14	Leo		
15	Leo	5:47 P.M.	Virgo
16	Virgo		
17	Virgo		
18	Virgo	3:00 A.M.	Libra
19	Libra		
20	Libra	2:10 P.M.	Scorpio
21	Scorpio		
22	Scorpio		
23	Scorpio	2:50 A.M.	Sagittarius
24	Sagittarius		
25	Sagittarius	3:15 P.M.	Capricorn
26	Capricorn		
27	Capricorn		
28	Capricorn	1:03 A.M.	Aquarius
29	Aquarius		
30	Aquarius	6:46 A.M.	Pisces

OCTOBER

1	Pisces		
2	Pisces	8:48 A.M.	Aries
3	Aries		
4	Aries	8:50 A.M.	Taurus
5	Taurus		
6	Taurus	8:58 A.M.	Gemini
7	Gemini		
8	Gemini	11:01 A.M.	Cancer
9	Cancer		
10	Cancer	3:54 P.M.	Leo
11	Leo		
12	Leo	11:34 P.M.	Virgo
13	Virgo		
14	Virgo		
15	Virgo	9:24 A.M.	Libra
16	Libra		
17	Libra	8:53 P.M.	Scorpio
18	Scorpio		
19	Scorpio		
20	Scorpio	9:32 A.M.	Sagittarius
21	Sagittarius		
22	Sagittarius	10:21 P.M.	Capricorn
23	Capricorn		
24	Capricorn		
25	Capricorn	9:20 A.M.	Aquarius
26	Aquarius		
27	Aquarius	4:36 P.M.	Pisces
28	Pisces		
29	Pisces	7:40 P.M.	Aries
30	Aries		
31	Aries	7:42 P.M.	Taurus

NOVEMBER

1	Taurus		
2	Taurus	6:48 P.M.	Gemini
3	Gemini		
4	Gemini	7:08 P.M.	Cancer
5	Cancer		
6	Cancer	10:24 P.M.	Leo
7	Leo		
8	Leo		
9	Leo	5:14 A.M.	Virgo
10	Virgo		

11	Virgo	3:07 P.M.	Libra
12	Libra		
13	Libra		
14	Libra	2:57 A.M.	Scorpio
15	Scorpio		
16	Scorpio	3:40 P.M.	Sagittarius
17	Sagittarius		
18	Sagittarius		
19	Sagittarius	4:23 A.M.	Capricorn
20	Capricorn		
21	Capricorn	3:51 P.M.	Aquarius
22	Aquarius		
23	Aquarius		
24	Aquarius	12:32 A.M.	Pisces
25	Pisces		
26	Pisces	5:25 A.M.	Aries
27	Aries		
28	Aries	6:49 A.M.	Taurus
29	Taurus		
30	Taurus	6:14 A.M.	Gemini

DECEMBER

1	Gemini		
2	Gemini	5:45 A.M.	Cancer
3	Cancer		
4	Cancer	7:20 A.M.	Leo
5	Leo		
6	Leo	12:26 P.M.	Virgo
7	Virgo		
8	Virgo	9:21 P.M.	Libra
9	Libra		
10	Libra		
11	Libra	9:04 A.M.	Scorpio
12	Scorpio		
13	Scorpio	9:53 P.M.	Sagittarius
14	Sagittarius		
15	Sagittarius		
16	Sagittarius	10:21 A.M.	Capricorn
17	Capricorn		
18	Capricorn	9:29 P.M.	Aquarius
19	Aquarius		
20	Aquarius		
21	Aquarius	6:28 A.M.	Pisces
22	Pisces		
23	Pisces	12:41 P.M.	Aries
24	Aries		
25	Aries	3:57 P.M.	Taurus
26	Taurus		
27	Taurus	4:58 P.M.	Gemini
28	Gemini		
29	Gemini	5:07 P.M.	Cancer
30	Cancer		
31	Cancer	6:09 P.M.	Leo

MOON SIGN TABLES
1964

JANUARY

1	Leo		
2	Leo	9:48 P.M.	Virgo
3	Virgo		
4	Virgo		
5	Virgo	5:10 A.M.	Libra
6	Libra		
7	Libra	4:04 P.M.	Scorpio
8	Scorpio		
9	Scorpio		
10	Scorpio	4:49 A.M.	Sagittarius
11	Sagittarius		
12	Sagittarius	5:14 P.M.	Capricorn
13	Capricorn		
14	Capricorn		
15	Capricorn	3:48 A.M.	Aquarius
16	Aquarius		
17	Aquarius	12:04 P.M.	Pisces
18	Pisces		
19	Pisces	6:10 P.M.	Aries
20	Aries		
21	Aries	10:23 P.M.	Taurus
22	Taurus		
23	Taurus		
24	Taurus	1:05 A.M.	Gemini
25	Gemini		
26	Gemini	2:51 A.M.	Cancer
27	Cancer		
28	Cancer	4:45 A.M.	Leo
29	Leo		
30	Leo	8:09 A.M.	Virgo
31	Virgo		

FEBRUARY

1	Virgo	2:25 P.M.	Libra
2	Libra		
3	Libra		
4	Libra	12:12 A.M.	Scorpio
5	Scorpio		
6	Scorpio	12:35 P.M.	Sagittarius
7	Sagittarius		
8	Sagittarius		
9	Sagittarius	1:11 A.M.	Capricorn
10	Capricorn		
11	Capricorn	11:39 A.M.	Aquarius
12	Aquarius		
13	Aquarius	7:09 P.M.	Pisces
14	Pisces		
15	Pisces		
16	Pisces	12:10 A.M.	Aries
17	Aries		
18	Aries	3:45 A.M.	Taurus
19	Taurus		
20	Taurus	6:48 A.M.	Gemini
21	Gemini		
22	Gemini	9:49 A.M.	Cancer
23	Cancer		
24	Cancer	1:11 P.M.	Leo
25	Leo		
26	Leo	5:30 P.M.	Virgo
27	Virgo		
28	Virgo	11:46 P.M.	Libra
29	Libra		

MARCH

1	Libra		
2	Libra	8:54 A.M.	Scorpio
3	Scorpio		
4	Scorpio	8:47 P.M.	Sagittarius
5	Sagittarius		
6	Sagittarius		
7	Sagittarius	9:35 A.M.	Capricorn
8	Capricorn		
9	Capricorn	8:35 P.M.	Aquarius
10	Aquarius		
11	Aquarius		
12	Aquarius	4:05 A.M.	Pisces
13	Pisces		
14	Pisces	8:15 A.M.	Aries
15	Aries		
16	Aries	10:30 A.M.	Taurus
17	Taurus		
18	Taurus	12:26 P.M.	Gemini
19	Gemini		
20	Gemini	3:11 P.M.	Cancer
21	Cancer		
22	Cancer	7:15 P.M.	Leo
23	Leo		
24	Leo		
25	Leo	12:42 A.M.	Virgo
26	Virgo		
27	Virgo	7:48 A.M.	Libra
28	Libra		
29	Libra	5:03 P.M.	Scorpio
30	Scorpio		
31	Scorpio		

APRIL

1	Scorpio	4:41 A.M.	Sagittarius
2	Sagittarius		
3	Sagittarius	5:36 P.M.	Capricorn
4	Capricorn		
5	Capricorn		
6	Capricorn	5:24 A.M.	Aquarius
7	Aquarius		
8	Aquarius	1:47 P.M.	Pisces
9	Pisces		
10	Pisces	6:08 P.M.	Aries
11	Aries		
12	Aries	7:37 P.M.	Taurus
13	Taurus		
14	Taurus	8:06 P.M.	Gemini
15	Gemini		
16	Gemini	9:23 P.M.	Cancer
17	Cancer		
18	Cancer		
19	Cancer	12:40 A.M.	Leo
20	Leo		
21	Leo	6:17 A.M.	Virgo
22	Virgo		
23	Virgo	2:08 P.M.	Libra
24	Libra		
25	Libra		
26	Libra	12:01 A.M.	Scorpio
27	Scorpio		
28	Scorpio	11:46 A.M.	Sagittarius
29	Sagittarius		
30	Sagittarius		

MAY

1	Sagittarius	12:42 A.M.	Capricorn
2	Capricorn		
3	Capricorn	1:06 P.M.	Aquarius
4	Aquarius		
5	Aquarius	10:43 P.M.	Pisces
6	Pisces		
7	Pisces		
8	Pisces	4:16 A.M.	Aries
9	Aries		
10	Aries	6:09 A.M.	Taurus
11	Taurus		
12	Taurus	6:01 A.M.	Gemini
13	Gemini		
14	Gemini	5:53 A.M.	Cancer
15	Cancer		
16	Cancer	7:31 A.M.	Leo
17	Leo		
18	Leo	12:02 P.M.	Virgo
19	Virgo		
20	Virgo	7:41 P.M.	Libra
21	Libra		
22	Libra		
23	Libra	5:58 A.M.	Scorpio
24	Scorpio		
25	Scorpio	6:03 P.M.	Sagittarius
26	Sagittarius		
27	Sagittarius		
28	Sagittarius	7:00 A.M.	Capricorn
29	Capricorn		
30	Capricorn	7:32 P.M.	Aquarius
31	Aquarius		

JUNE

1	Aquarius		
2	Aquarius	6:01 A.M.	Pisces
3	Pisces		
4	Pisces	1:03 P.M.	Aries
5	Aries		
6	Aries	4:20 P.M.	Taurus
7	Taurus		
8	Taurus	4:50 P.M.	Gemini
9	Gemini		
10	Gemini	4:16 P.M.	Cancer
11	Cancer		
12	Cancer	4:35 P.M.	Leo
13	Leo		
14	Leo	7:27 P.M.	Virgo
15	Virgo		
16	Virgo		
17	Virgo	1:54 A.M.	Libra
18	Libra		
19	Libra	11:49 A.M.	Scorpio
20	Scorpio		
21	Scorpio		
22	Scorpio	12:03 A.M.	Sagittarius
23	Sagittarius		
24	Sagittarius	1:02 P.M.	Capricorn
25	Capricorn		
26	Capricorn		
27	Capricorn	1:22 A.M.	Aquarius
28	Aquarius		
29	Aquarius	11:56 A.M.	Pisces
30	Pisces		

JULY

1	Pisces	7:52 P.M.	Aries
2	Aries		
3	Aries		
4	Aries	12:42 A.M.	Taurus
5	Taurus		
6	Taurus	2:43 A.M.	Gemini

Day	Sign	Time	Enters
7	Gemini		
8	Gemini	2:57 A.M.	Cancer
9	Cancer		
10	Cancer	3:01 A.M.	Leo
11	Leo		
12	Leo	4:44 A.M.	Virgo
13	Virgo		
14	Virgo	9:41 A.M.	Libra
15	Libra		
16	Libra	6:32 P.M.	Scorpio
17	Scorpio		
18	Scorpio		
19	Scorpio	6:28 A.M.	Sagittarius
20	Sagittarius		
21	Sagittarius	7:27 P.M.	Capricorn
22	Capricorn		
23	Capricorn		
24	Capricorn	7:30 A.M.	Aquarius
25	Aquarius		
26	Aquarius	5:36 P.M.	Pisces
27	Pisces		
28	Pisces		
29	Pisces	1:25 A.M.	Aries
30	Aries		
31	Aries	7:00 A.M.	Taurus

AUGUST

Day	Sign	Time	Enters
1	Taurus		
2	Taurus	10:28 A.M.	Gemini
3	Gemini		
4	Gemini	12:13 P.M.	Cancer
5	Cancer		
6	Cancer	1:11 P.M.	Leo
7	Leo		
8	Leo	2:50 P.M.	Virgo
9	Virgo		
10	Virgo	6:51 P.M.	Libra
11	Libra		
12	Libra		
13	Libra	2:31 A.M.	Scorpio
14	Scorpio		
15	Scorpio	1:44 P.M.	Sagittarius
16	Sagittarius		
17	Sagittarius		
18	Sagittarius	2:38 A.M.	Capricorn
19	Capricorn		
20	Capricorn	2:39 P.M.	Aquarius
21	Aquarius		
22	Aquarius		
23	Aquarius	12:13 A.M.	Pisces
24	Pisces		
25	Pisces	7:15 A.M.	Aries
26	Aries		
27	Aries	12:24 P.M.	Taurus
28	Taurus		
29	Taurus	4:16 P.M.	Gemini
30	Gemini		
31	Gemini	7:13 P.M.	Cancer

SEPTEMBER

Day	Sign	Time	Enters
1	Cancer		
2	Cancer	9:36 P.M.	Leo
3	Leo		
4	Leo		
5	Leo	12:12 A.M.	Virgo
6	Virgo		
7	Virgo	4:19 A.M.	Libra
8	Libra		
9	Libra	11:20 A.M.	Scorpio
10	Scorpio		
11	Scorpio	9:47 P.M.	Sagittarius
12	Sagittarius		
13	Sagittarius		
14	Sagittarius	10:30 A.M.	Capricorn
15	Capricorn		
16	Capricorn	10:47 P.M.	Aquarius
17	Aquarius		
18	Aquarius		
19	Aquarius	8:22 A.M.	Pisces
20	Pisces		
21	Pisces	2:44 P.M.	Aries
22	Aries		
23	Aries	6:46 P.M.	Taurus
24	Taurus		
25	Taurus	9:46 P.M.	Gemini
26	Gemini		
27	Gemini		
28	Gemini	12:39 A.M.	Cancer
29	Cancer		
30	Cancer	3:52 A.M.	Leo

OCTOBER

Day	Sign	Time	Enters
1	Leo		
2	Leo	7:42 A.M.	Virgo
3	Virgo		
4	Virgo	12:44 P.M.	Libra
5	Libra		
6	Libra	7:57 P.M.	Scorpio
7	Scorpio		
8	Scorpio		
9	Scorpio	6:02 A.M.	Sagittarius
10	Sagittarius		
11	Sagittarius	6:32 P.M.	Capricorn
12	Capricorn		
13	Capricorn		
14	Capricorn	7:15 A.M.	Aquarius
15	Aquarius		
16	Aquarius	5:33 P.M.	Pisces
17	Pisces		
18	Pisces		
19	Pisces	12:05 A.M.	Aries
20	Aries		
21	Aries	3:24 A.M.	Taurus
22	Taurus		
23	Taurus	5:03 A.M.	Gemini
24	Gemini		
25	Gemini	6:37 A.M.	Cancer
26	Cancer		
27	Cancer	9:14 A.M.	Leo
28	Leo		
29	Leo	1:25 P.M.	Virgo
30	Virgo		
31	Virgo	7:24 P.M.	Libra

NOVEMBER

Day	Sign	Time	Enters
1	Libra		
2	Libra		
3	Libra	3:25 A.M.	Scorpio
4	Scorpio		
5	Scorpio	1:43 P.M.	Sagittarius
6	Sagittarius		
7	Sagittarius		
8	Sagittarius	2:06 A.M.	Capricorn
9	Capricorn		
10	Capricorn	3:08 P.M.	Aquarius
11	Aquarius		
12	Aquarius		
13	Aquarius	2:28 A.M.	Pisces
14	Pisces		
15	Pisces	10:10 A.M.	Aries
16	Aries		
17	Aries	1:57 P.M.	Taurus
18	Taurus		
19	Taurus	2:58 P.M.	Gemini
20	Gemini		
21	Gemini	3:04 P.M.	Cancer
22	Cancer		
23	Cancer	3:59 P.M.	Leo
24	Leo		
25	Leo	7:03 P.M.	Virgo
26	Virgo		
27	Virgo		
28	Virgo	12:54 A.M.	Libra
29	Libra		
30	Libra	9:31 A.M.	Scorpio

DECEMBER

Day	Sign	Time	Enters
1	Scorpio		
2	Scorpio	8:24 P.M.	Sagittarius
3	Sagittarius		
4	Sagittarius		
5	Sagittarius	8:53 A.M.	Capricorn
6	Capricorn		
7	Capricorn	9:57 P.M.	Aquarius
8	Aquarius		
9	Aquarius		
10	Aquarius	10:00 A.M.	Pisces
11	Pisces		
12	Pisces	7:12 P.M.	Aries
13	Aries		
14	Aries		
15	Aries	12:33 A.M.	Taurus
16	Taurus		
17	Taurus	2:21 A.M.	Gemini
18	Gemini		
19	Gemini	2:02 A.M.	Cancer
20	Cancer		
21	Cancer	1:31 A.M.	Leo
22	Leo		
23	Leo	2:41 A.M.	Virgo
24	Virgo		
25	Virgo	7:04 A.M.	Libra
26	Libra		
27	Libra	3:11 P.M.	Scorpio
28	Scorpio		
29	Scorpio		
30	Scorpio	2:20 A.M.	Sagittarius
31	Sagittarius		

MOON SIGN TABLES
1965

JANUARY

1	Sagittarius	3:06 P.M.	Capricorn
2	Capricorn		
3	Capricorn		
4	Capricorn	4:04 A.M.	Aquarius
5	Aquarius		
6	Aquarius	4:06 P.M.	Pisces
7	Pisces		
8	Pisces		
9	Pisces	2:08 A.M.	Aries
10	Aries		
11	Aries	9:10 A.M.	Taurus
12	Taurus		
13	Taurus	12:48 P.M.	Gemini
14	Gemini		
15	Gemini	1:35 P.M.	Cancer
16	Cancer		
17	Cancer	12:57 P.M.	Leo
18	Leo		
19	Leo	12:55 P.M.	Virgo
20	Virgo		
21	Virgo	3:28 P.M.	Libra
22	Libra		
23	Libra	10:01 P.M.	Scorpio
24	Scorpio		
25	Scorpio		
26	Scorpio	8:32 A.M.	Sagittarius
27	Sagittarius		
28	Sagittarius	9:21 P.M.	Capricorn
29	Capricorn		
30	Capricorn		
31	Capricorn	10:17 A.M.	Aquarius

FEBRUARY

1	Aquarius		
2	Aquarius	9:56 P.M.	Pisces
3	Pisces		
4	Pisces		
5	Pisces	7:43 A.M.	Aries
6	Aries		
7	Aries	3:24 P.M.	Taurus
8	Taurus		
9	Taurus	8:36 P.M.	Gemini
10	Gemini		
11	Gemini	11:14 P.M.	Cancer
12	Cancer		
13	Cancer	11:54 P.M.	Leo
14	Leo		
15	Leo		
16	Leo	12:05 A.M.	Virgo
17	Virgo		
18	Virgo	1:45 A.M.	Libra
19	Libra		
20	Libra	6:45 A.M.	Scorpio
21	Scorpio		
22	Scorpio	3:57 P.M.	Sagittarius
23	Sagittarius		
24	Sagittarius		
25	Sagittarius	4:17 A.M.	Capricorn
26	Capricorn		
27	Capricorn	5:14 P.M.	Aquarius
28	Aquarius		

MARCH

1	Aquarius		
2	Aquarius	4:38 A.M.	Pisces
3	Pisces		

4	Pisces	1:45 P.M.	Aries
5	Aries		
6	Aries	8:49 P.M.	Taurus
7	Taurus		
8	Taurus		
9	Taurus	2:14 A.M.	Gemini
10	Gemini		
11	Gemini	6:03 A.M.	Cancer
12	Cancer		
13	Cancer	8:23 A.M.	Leo
14	Leo		
15	Leo	9:55 A.M.	Virgo
16	Virgo		
17	Virgo	12:04 P.M.	Libra
18	Libra		
19	Libra	4:32 P.M.	Scorpio
20	Scorpio		
21	Scorpio		
22	Scorpio	12:37 A.M.	Sagittarius
23	Sagittarius		
24	Sagittarius	12:07 P.M.	Capricorn
25	Capricorn		
26	Capricorn		
27	Capricorn	12:59 A.M.	Aquarius
28	Aquarius		
29	Aquarius	12:32 P.M.	Pisces
30	Pisces		
31	Pisces	9:19 P.M.	Aries

APRIL

1	Aries		
2	Aries		
3	Aries	3:29 A.M.	Taurus
4	Taurus		
5	Taurus	7:55 A.M.	Gemini
6	Gemini		
7	Gemini	11:24 A.M.	Cancer
8	Cancer		
9	Cancer	2:23 P.M.	Leo
10	Leo		
11	Leo	5:14 P.M.	Virgo
12	Virgo		
13	Virgo	8:38 P.M.	Libra
14	Libra		
15	Libra		
16	Libra	1:42 A.M.	Scorpio
17	Scorpio		
18	Scorpio	9:31 A.M.	Sagittarius
19	Sagittarius		
20	Sagittarius	8:24 P.M.	Capricorn
21	Capricorn		
22	Capricorn		
23	Capricorn	9:04 A.M.	Aquarius
24	Aquarius		
25	Aquarius	9:02 P.M.	Pisces
26	Pisces		
27	Pisces		
28	Pisces	6:12 A.M.	Aries
29	Aries		
30	Aries	12:03 P.M.	Taurus

MAY

1	Taurus		
2	Taurus	3:26 P.M.	Gemini
3	Gemini		
4	Gemini	5:39 P.M.	Cancer
5	Cancer		

6	Cancer	7:50 P.M.	Leo
7	Leo		
8	Leo	10:47 P.M.	Virgo
9	Virgo		
10	Virgo		
11	Virgo	3:04 A.M.	Libra
12	Libra		
13	Libra	9:10 A.M.	Scorpio
14	Scorpio		
15	Scorpio	5:32 P.M.	Sagittarius
16	Sagittarius		
17	Sagittarius		
18	Sagittarius	4:20 A.M.	Capricorn
19	Capricorn		
20	Capricorn	4:50 P.M.	Aquarius
21	Aquarius		
22	Aquarius		
23	Aquarius	5:14 A.M.	Pisces
24	Pisces		
25	Pisces	3:18 P.M.	Aries
26	Aries		
27	Aries	9:48 P.M.	Taurus
28	Taurus		
29	Taurus		
30	Taurus	12:58 A.M.	Gemini
31	Gemini		

JUNE

1	Gemini	2:05 A.M.	Cancer
2	Cancer		
3	Cancer	2:46 A.M.	Leo
4	Leo		
5	Leo	4:33 A.M.	Virgo
6	Virgo		
7	Virgo	8:29 A.M.	Libra
8	Libra		
9	Libra	3:04 P.M.	Scorpio
10	Scorpio		
11	Scorpio		
12	Scorpio	12:10 A.M.	Sagittarius
13	Sagittarius		
14	Sagittarius	11:20 A.M.	Capricorn
15	Capricorn		
16	Capricorn	11:51 P.M.	Aquarius
17	Aquarius		
18	Aquarius		
19	Aquarius	12:29 P.M.	Pisces
20	Pisces		
21	Pisces	11:29 P.M.	Aries
22	Aries		
23	Aries		
24	Aries	7:16 A.M.	Taurus
25	Taurus		
26	Taurus	11:18 A.M.	Gemini
27	Gemini		
28	Gemini	12:20 P.M.	Cancer
29	Cancer		
30	Cancer	11:59 P.M.	Leo

JULY

1	Leo		
2	Leo	12:11 P.M.	Virgo
3	Virgo		
4	Virgo	2:43 P.M.	Libra
5	Libra		
6	Libra	8:38 P.M.	Scorpio
7	Scorpio		

8	Scorpio		
9	Scorpio	5:53 A.M.	Sagittarius
10	Sagittarius		
11	Sagittarius	5:29 P.M.	Capricorn
12	Capricorn		
13	Capricorn		
14	Capricorn	6:08 A.M.	Aquarius
15	Aquarius		
16	Aquarius	6:45 P.M.	Pisces
17	Pisces		
18	Pisces		
19	Pisces	6:13 A.M.	Aries
20	Aries		
21	Aries	3:14 P.M.	Taurus
22	Taurus		
23	Taurus	8:48 P.M.	Gemini
24	Gemini		
25	Gemini	10:53 P.M.	Cancer
26	Cancer		
27	Cancer	10:37 P.M.	Leo
28	Leo		
29	Leo	9:55 P.M.	Virgo
30	Virgo		
31	Virgo	10:54 P.M.	Libra

AUGUST

1	Libra		
2	Libra		
3	Libra	3:20 A.M.	Scorpio
4	Scorpio		
5	Scorpio	11:49 A.M.	Sagittarius
6	Sagittarius		
7	Sagittarius	11:22 P.M.	Capricorn
8	Capricorn		
9	Capricorn		
10	Capricorn	12:09 P.M.	Aquarius
11	Aquarius		
12	Aquarius		
13	Aquarius	12:37 A.M.	Pisces
14	Pisces		
15	Pisces	11:57 A.M.	Aries
16	Aries		
17	Aries	9:27 P.M.	Taurus
18	Taurus		
19	Taurus		
20	Taurus	4:20 A.M.	Gemini
21	Gemini		
22	Gemini	8:04 A.M.	Cancer
23	Cancer		
24	Cancer	9:01 A.M.	Leo
25	Leo		
26	Leo	8:36 A.M.	Virgo
27	Virgo		
28	Virgo	8:52 A.M.	Libra
29	Libra		
30	Libra	11:54 A.M.	Scorpio
31	Scorpio		

SEPTEMBER

1	Scorpio	7:00 P.M.	Sagittarius
2	Sagittarius		
3	Sagittarius		
4	Sagittarius	5:51 A.M.	Capricorn
5	Capricorn		
6	Capricorn	6:34 P.M.	Aquarius
7	Aquarius		
8	Aquarius		
9	Aquarius	6:56 A.M.	Pisces
10	Pisces		
11	Pisces	5:50 P.M.	Aries
12	Aries		
13	Aries		
14	Aries	2:56 A.M.	Taurus
15	Taurus		
16	Taurus	10:06 A.M.	Gemini
17	Gemini		
18	Gemini	3:01 P.M.	Cancer
19	Cancer		
20	Cancer	5:35 P.M.	Leo
21	Leo		
22	Leo	6:30 P.M.	Virgo
23	Virgo		
24	Virgo	7:15 P.M.	Libra
25	Libra		
26	Libra	9:47 P.M.	Scorpio
27	Scorpio		
28	Scorpio		
29	Scorpio	3:42 A.M.	Sagittarius
30	Sagittarius		

OCTOBER

1	Sagittarius	1:29 P.M.	Capricorn
2	Capricorn		
3	Capricorn		
4	Capricorn	1:48 A.M.	Aquarius
5	Aquarius		
6	Aquarius	2:14 P.M.	Pisces
7	Pisces		
8	Pisces		
9	Pisces	12:54 A.M.	Aries
10	Aries		
11	Aries	9:16 A.M.	Taurus
12	Taurus		
13	Taurus	3:40 P.M.	Gemini
14	Gemini		
15	Gemini	8:27 P.M.	Cancer
16	Cancer		
17	Cancer	11:51 P.M.	Leo
18	Leo		
19	Leo		
20	Leo	2:13 A.M.	Virgo
21	Virgo		
22	Virgo	4:21 A.M.	Libra
23	Libra		
24	Libra	7:31 A.M.	Scorpio
25	Scorpio		
26	Scorpio	1:09 P.M.	Sagittarius
27	Sagittarius		
28	Sagittarius	10:05 P.M.	Capricorn
29	Capricorn		
30	Capricorn		
31	Capricorn	9:49 A.M.	Aquarius

NOVEMBER

1	Aquarius		
2	Aquarius	10:23 P.M.	Pisces
3	Pisces		
4	Pisces		
5	Pisces	9:21 A.M.	Aries
6	Aries		
7	Aries	5:29 P.M.	Taurus
8	Taurus		
9	Taurus	10:54 P.M.	Gemini
10	Gemini		
11	Gemini		
12	Gemini	2:29 A.M.	Cancer
13	Cancer		
14	Cancer	5:13 A.M.	Leo
15	Leo		
16	Leo	7:55 A.M.	Virgo
17	Virgo		
18	Virgo	11:10 A.M.	Libra
19	Libra		
20	Libra	3:37 P.M.	Scorpio
21	Scorpio		
22	Scorpio	9:57 P.M.	Sagittarius
23	Sagittarius		
24	Sagittarius		
25	Sagittarius	6:45 A.M.	Capricorn
26	Capricorn		
27	Capricorn	6:03 P.M.	Aquarius
28	Aquarius		
29	Aquarius		
30	Aquarius	6:40 A.M.	Pisces

DECEMBER

1	Pisces		
2	Pisces	6:22 P.M.	Aries
3	Aries		
4	Aries		
5	Aries	3:11 A.M.	Taurus
6	Taurus		
7	Taurus	8:27 A.M.	Gemini
8	Gemini		
9	Gemini	10:57 A.M.	Cancer
10	Cancer		
11	Cancer	12:08 P.M.	Leo
12	Leo		
13	Leo	1:35 P.M.	Virgo
14	Virgo		
15	Virgo	4:33 P.M.	Libra
16	Libra		
17	Libra	9:40 P.M.	Scorpio
18	Scorpio		
19	Scorpio		
20	Scorpio	5:01 A.M.	Sagittarius
21	Sagittarius		
22	Sagittarius	2:27 P.M.	Capricorn
23	Capricorn		
24	Capricorn		
25	Capricorn	1:44 A.M.	Aquarius
26	Aquarius		
27	Aquarius	2:17 P.M.	Pisces
28	Pisces		
29	Pisces		
30	Pisces	2:40 A.M.	Aries
31	Aries		

MOON SIGN TABLES
1966

JANUARY

1	Aries	12:46 P.M.	Taurus
2	Taurus		
3	Taurus	7:06 P.M.	Gemini
4	Gemini		
5	Gemini	9:40 P.M.	Cancer
6	Cancer		
7	Cancer	9:50 P.M.	Leo
8	Leo		
9	Leo	9:34 P.M.	Virgo
10	Virgo		
11	Virgo	10:53 P.M.	Libra
12	Libra		
13	Libra		
14	Libra	3:08 A.M.	Scorpio
15	Scorpio		
16	Scorpio	10:39 A.M.	Sagittarius
17	Sagittarius		
18	Sagittarius	8:45 P.M.	Capricorn
19	Capricorn		
20	Capricorn		
21	Capricorn	8:26 A.M.	Aquarius
22	Aquarius		
23	Aquarius	8:58 P.M.	Pisces
24	Pisces		
25	Pisces		
26	Pisces	9:33 A.M.	Aries
27	Aries		
28	Aries	8:43 P.M.	Taurus
29	Taurus		
30	Taurus		
31	Taurus	4:43 A.M.	Gemini

FEBRUARY

1	Gemini		
2	Gemini	8:41 A.M.	Cancer
3	Cancer		
4	Cancer	9:14 A.M.	Leo
5	Leo		
6	Leo	8:11 A.M.	Virgo
7	Virgo		
8	Virgo	7:50 A.M.	Libra
9	Libra		
10	Libra	10:15 A.M.	Scorpio
11	Scorpio		
12	Scorpio	4:33 P.M.	Sagittarius
13	Sagittarius		
14	Sagittarius		
15	Sagittarius	2:26 A.M.	Capricorn
16	Capricorn		
17	Capricorn	2:25 P.M.	Aquarius
18	Aquarius		
19	Aquarius		
20	Aquarius	3:05 A.M.	Pisces
21	Pisces		
22	Pisces	3:30 P.M.	Aries
23	Aries		
24	Aries		
25	Aries	2:53 A.M.	Taurus
26	Taurus		
27	Taurus	12:03 P.M.	Gemini
28	Gemini		

MARCH

1	Gemini	5:48 P.M.	Cancer
2	Cancer		
3	Cancer	7:56 P.M.	Leo

APRIL

4	Leo		
5	Leo	7:36 P.M.	Virgo
6	Virgo		
7	Virgo	6:49 P.M.	Libra
8	Libra		
9	Libra	7:47 P.M.	Scorpio
10	Scorpio		
11	Scorpio		
12	Scorpio	12:18 A.M.	Sagittarius
13	Sagittarius		
14	Sagittarius	8:55 A.M.	Capricorn
15	Capricorn		
16	Capricorn	8:35 P.M.	Aquarius
17	Aquarius		
18	Aquarius		
19	Aquarius	9:19 A.M.	Pisces
20	Pisces		
21	Pisces	9:33 A.M.	Aries
22	Aries		
23	Aries		
24	Aries	8:32 A.M.	Taurus
25	Taurus		
26	Taurus	5:41 P.M.	Gemini
27	Gemini		
28	Gemini		
29	Gemini	12:23 A.M.	Cancer
30	Cancer		
31	Cancer	4:12 A.M.	Leo

APRIL

1	Leo		
2	Leo	5:31 A.M.	Virgo
3	Virgo		
4	Virgo	5:40 A.M.	Libra
5	Libra		
6	Libra	6:30 A.M.	Scorpio
7	Scorpio		
8	Scorpio	9:54 A.M.	Sagittarius
9	Sagittarius		
10	Sagittarius	5:02 P.M.	Capricorn
11	Capricorn		
12	Capricorn		
13	Capricorn	3:42 A.M.	Aquarius
14	Aquarius		
15	Aquarius	4:13 P.M.	Pisces
16	Pisces		
17	Pisces		
18	Pisces	4:27 A.M.	Aries
19	Aries		
20	Aries	3:00 P.M.	Taurus
21	Taurus		
22	Taurus	11:27 P.M.	Gemini
23	Gemini		
24	Gemini		
25	Gemini	5:48 A.M.	Cancer
26	Cancer		
27	Cancer	10:09 A.M.	Leo
28	Leo		
29	Leo	12:50 P.M.	Virgo
30	Virgo		

MAY

1	Virgo	2:31 P.M.	Libra
2	Libra		
3	Libra	4:23 P.M.	Scorpio
4	Scorpio		
5	Scorpio	7:52 P.M.	Sagittarius

JUNE

6	Sagittarius		
7	Sagittarius		
8	Sagittarius	2:12 A.M.	Capricorn
9	Capricorn		
10	Capricorn	11:52 A.M.	Aquarius
11	Aquarius		
12	Aquarius	11:55 P.M.	Pisces
13	Pisces		
14	Pisces		
15	Pisces	12:15 P.M.	Aries
16	Aries		
17	Aries	10:49 P.M.	Taurus
18	Taurus		
19	Taurus		
20	Taurus	6:40 A.M.	Gemini
21	Gemini		
22	Gemini	12:00 P.M.	Cancer
23	Cancer		
24	Cancer	3:37 P.M.	Leo
25	Leo		
26	Leo	6:22 P.M.	Virgo
27	Virgo		
28	Virgo	9:00 P.M.	Libra
29	Libra		
30	Libra		
31	Libra	12:11 A.M.	Scorpio

JUNE

1	Scorpio		
2	Scorpio	4:38 A.M.	Sagittarius
3	Sagittarius		
4	Sagittarius	11:10 A.M.	Capricorn
5	Capricorn		
6	Capricorn	8:21 P.M.	Aquarius
7	Aquarius		
8	Aquarius		
9	Aquarius	7:57 A.M.	Pisces
10	Pisces		
11	Pisces	8:26 P.M.	Aries
12	Aries		
13	Aries		
14	Aries	7:30 A.M.	Taurus
15	Taurus		
16	Taurus	3:26 P.M.	Gemini
17	Gemini		
18	Gemini	8:05 P.M.	Cancer
19	Cancer		
20	Cancer	10:29 P.M.	Leo
21	Leo		
22	Leo		
23	Leo	12:08 A.M.	Virgo
24	Virgo		
25	Virgo	2:23 A.M.	Libra
26	Libra		
27	Libra	6:04 A.M.	Scorpio
28	Scorpio		
29	Scorpio	11:31 A.M.	Sagittarius
30	Sagittarius		

JULY

1	Sagittarius	6:51 P.M.	Capricorn
2	Capricorn		
3	Capricorn		
4	Capricorn	4:14 A.M.	Aquarius
5	Aquarius		
6	Aquarius	3:39 P.M.	Pisces
7	Pisces		

8	Pisces		
9	Pisces	4:16 A.M.	Aries
10	Aries		
11	Aries	4:03 P.M.	Taurus
12	Taurus		
13	Taurus		
14	Taurus	12:51 A.M.	Gemini
15	Gemini		
16	Gemini	5:44 A.M.	Cancer
17	Cancer		
18	Cancer	7:27 A.M.	Leo
19	Leo		
20	Leo	7:47 A.M.	Virgo
21	Virgo		
22	Virgo	8:38 A.M.	Libra
23	Libra		
24	Libra	11:32 A.M.	Scorpio
25	Scorpio		
26	Scorpio	5:04 P.M.	Sagittarius
27	Sagittarius		
28	Sagittarius		
29	Sagittarius	1:04 A.M.	Capricorn
30	Capricorn		
31	Capricorn	11:02 A.M.	Aquarius

AUGUST

1	Aquarius		
2	Aquarius	10:36 P.M.	Pisces
3	Pisces		
4	Pisces		
5	Pisces	11:15 A.M.	Aries
6	Aries		
7	Aries	11:38 P.M.	Taurus
8	Taurus		
9	Taurus		
10	Taurus	9:38 A.M.	Gemini
11	Gemini		
12	Gemini	3:41 P.M.	Cancer
13	Cancer		
14	Cancer	5:50 P.M.	Leo
15	Leo		
16	Leo	5:35 P.M.	Virgo
17	Virgo		
18	Virgo	5:05 P.M.	Libra
19	Libra		
20	Libra	6:24 P.M.	Scorpio
21	Scorpio		
22	Scorpio	10:51 P.M.	Sagittarius
23	Sagittarius		
24	Sagittarius		
25	Sagittarius	6:37 A.M.	Capricorn
26	Capricorn		
27	Capricorn	4:56 P.M.	Aquarius
28	Aquarius		
29	Aquarius		
30	Aquarius	4:48 A.M.	Pisces
31	Pisces		

SEPTEMBER

1	Pisces	5:27 P.M.	Aries
2	Aries		
3	Aries		
4	Aries	5:59 A.M.	Taurus
5	Taurus		
6	Taurus	4:52 P.M.	Gemini
7	Gemini		
8	Gemini		
9	Gemini	12:26 A.M.	Cancer
10	Cancer		
11	Cancer	4:01 A.M.	Leo
12	Leo		
13	Leo	4:26 A.M.	Virgo
14	Virgo		
15	Virgo	3:33 A.M.	Libra
16	Libra		
17	Libra	3:34 A.M.	Scorpio
18	Scorpio		
19	Scorpio	6:21 A.M.	Sagittarius
20	Sagittarius		
21	Sagittarius	12:52 P.M.	Capricorn
22	Capricorn		
23	Capricorn	10:48 P.M.	Aquarius
24	Aquarius		
25	Aquarius		
26	Aquarius	10:48 A.M.	Pisces
27	Pisces		
28	Pisces	11:29 P.M.	Aries
29	Aries		
30	Aries		

OCTOBER

1	Aries	11:47 A.M.	Taurus
2	Taurus		
3	Taurus	10:43 P.M.	Gemini
4	Gemini		
5	Gemini		
6	Gemini	7:12 A.M.	Cancer
7	Cancer		
8	Cancer	12:25 P.M.	Leo
9	Leo		
10	Leo	2:27 P.M.	Virgo
11	Virgo		
12	Virgo	2:29 P.M.	Libra
13	Libra		
14	Libra	2:21 P.M.	Scorpio
15	Scorpio		
16	Scorpio	3:59 P.M.	Sagittarius
17	Sagittarius		
18	Sagittarius	8:55 P.M.	Capricorn
19	Capricorn		
20	Capricorn		
21	Capricorn	5:41 A.M.	Aquarius
22	Aquarius		
23	Aquarius	5:20 P.M.	Pisces
24	Pisces		
25	Pisces		
26	Pisces	6:03 A.M.	Aries
27	Aries		
28	Aries	6:05 P.M.	Taurus
29	Taurus		
30	Taurus		
31	Taurus	4:28 A.M.	Gemini

NOVEMBER

1	Gemini		
2	Gemini	12:43 P.M.	Cancer
3	Cancer		
4	Cancer	6:36 P.M.	Leo
5	Leo		
6	Leo	10:10 P.M.	Virgo
7	Virgo		
8	Virgo	11:54 P.M.	Libra
9	Libra		
10	Libra		
11	Libra	12:53 A.M.	Scorpio
12	Scorpio		
13	Scorpio	2:36 A.M.	Sagittarius
14	Sagittarius		
15	Sagittarius	6:37 A.M.	Capricorn
16	Capricorn		
17	Capricorn	2:03 P.M.	Aquarius
18	Aquarius		
19	Aquarius		
20	Aquarius	12:53 A.M.	Pisces
21	Pisces		
22	Pisces	1:31 P.M.	Aries
23	Aries		
24	Aries		
25	Aries	1:37 A.M.	Taurus
26	Taurus		
27	Taurus	11:31 A.M.	Gemini
28	Gemini		
29	Gemini	6:50 P.M.	Cancer
30	Cancer		

DECEMBER

1	Cancer		
2	Cancer	12:02 A.M.	Leo
3	Leo		
4	Leo	3:48 A.M.	Virgo
5	Virgo		
6	Virgo	6:43 A.M.	Libra
7	Libra		
8	Libra	9:18 A.M.	Scorpio
9	Scorpio		
10	Scorpio	12:13 P.M.	Sagittarius
11	Sagittarius		
12	Sagittarius	4:30 P.M.	Capricorn
13	Capricorn		
14	Capricorn	11:19 P.M.	Aquarius
15	Aquarius		
16	Aquarius		
17	Aquarius	9:17 A.M.	Pisces
18	Pisces		
19	Pisces	9:39 P.M.	Aries
20	Aries		
21	Aries		
22	Aries	10:07 A.M.	Taurus
23	Taurus		
24	Taurus	8:14 P.M.	Gemini
25	Gemini		
26	Gemini		
27	Gemini	2:58 A.M.	Cancer
28	Cancer		
29	Cancer	6:57 A.M.	Leo
30	Leo		
31	Leo	9:33 A.M.	Virgo

MOON SIGN TABLES
1967

JANUARY

1	Virgo		
2	Virgo	12:04 P.M.	Libra
3	Libra		
4	Libra	3:16 P.M.	Scorpio
5	Scorpio		
6	Scorpio	7:28 P.M.	Sagittarius
7	Sagittarius		
8	Sagittarius		
9	Sagittarius	12:53 A.M.	Capricorn
10	Capricorn		
11	Capricorn	8:05 A.M.	Aquarius
12	Aquarius		
13	Aquarius	5:45 P.M.	Pisces
14	Pisces		
15	Pisces		
16	Pisces	5:48 A.M.	Aries
17	Aries		
18	Aries	6:39 P.M.	Taurus
19	Taurus		
20	Taurus		
21	Taurus	5:38 A.M.	Gemini
22	Gemini		
23	Gemini	12:51 P.M.	Cancer
24	Cancer		
25	Cancer	4:20 P.M.	Leo
26	Leo		
27	Leo	5:36 P.M.	Virgo
28	Virgo		
29	Virgo	6:33 P.M.	Libra
30	Libra		
31	Libra	8:44 P.M.	Scorpio

FEBRUARY

1	Scorpio		
2	Scorpio		
3	Scorpio	12:55 A.M.	Sagittarius
4	Sagittarius		
5	Sagittarius	7:10 A.M.	Capricorn
6	Capricorn		
7	Capricorn	3:17 P.M.	Aquarius
8	Aquarius		
9	Aquarius		
10	Aquarius	1:19 A.M.	Pisces
11	Pisces		
12	Pisces	1:17 P.M.	Aries
13	Aries		
14	Aries		
15	Aries	2:19 A.M.	Taurus
16	Taurus		
17	Taurus	2:15 P.M.	Gemini
18	Gemini		
19	Gemini	10:48 P.M.	Cancer
20	Cancer		
21	Cancer		
22	Cancer	3:04 A.M.	Leo
23	Leo		
24	Leo	4:04 A.M.	Virgo
25	Virgo		
26	Virgo	3:44 A.M.	Libra
27	Libra		
28	Libra	4:09 A.M.	Scorpio

MARCH

1	Scorpio		
2	Scorpio	6:53 A.M.	Sagittarius
3	Sagittarius		
4	Sagittarius	12:35 P.M.	Capricorn
5	Capricorn		
6	Capricorn	9:03 P.M.	Aquarius
7	Aquarius		
8	Aquarius		
9	Aquarius	7:41 A.M.	Pisces
10	Pisces		
11	Pisces	7:53 P.M.	Aries
12	Aries		
13	Aries		
14	Aries	8:54 A.M.	Taurus
15	Taurus		
16	Taurus	9:19 P.M.	Gemini
17	Gemini		
18	Gemini		
19	Gemini	7:10 A.M.	Cancer
20	Cancer		
21	Cancer	1:04 P.M.	Leo
22	Leo		
23	Leo	3:08 P.M.	Virgo
24	Virgo		
25	Virgo	2:50 P.M.	Libra
26	Libra		
27	Libra	2:10 P.M.	Scorpio
28	Scorpio		
29	Scorpio	3:08 P.M.	Sagittarius
30	Sagittarius		
31	Sagittarius	7:11 P.M.	Capricorn

APRIL

1	Capricorn		
2	Capricorn		
3	Capricorn	2:49 A.M.	Aquarius
4	Aquarius		
5	Aquarius	1:29 P.M.	Pisces
6	Pisces		
7	Pisces		
8	Pisces	1:57 A.M.	Aries
9	Aries		
10	Aries	2:56 P.M.	Taurus
11	Taurus		
12	Taurus		
13	Taurus	3:15 A.M.	Gemini
14	Gemini		
15	Gemini	1:37 P.M.	Cancer
16	Cancer		
17	Cancer	8:54 P.M.	Leo
18	Leo		
19	Leo		
20	Leo	12:43 A.M.	Virgo
21	Virgo		
22	Virgo	1:41 A.M.	Libra
23	Libra		
24	Libra	1:19 A.M.	Scorpio
25	Scorpio		
26	Scorpio	1:27 A.M.	Sagittarius
27	Sagittarius		
28	Sagittarius	3:54 A.M.	Capricorn
29	Capricorn		
30	Capricorn	9:57 A.M.	Aquarius

MAY

1	Aquarius		
2	Aquarius	7:47 P.M.	Pisces
3	Pisces		
4	Pisces		
5	Pisces	8:10 A.M.	Aries
6	Aries		
7	Aries	9:09 P.M.	Taurus
8	Taurus		
9	Taurus		
10	Taurus	9:08 A.M.	Gemini
11	Gemini		
12	Gemini	7:11 P.M.	Cancer
13	Cancer		
14	Cancer		
15	Cancer	2:49 A.M.	Leo
16	Leo		
17	Leo	7:52 A.M.	Virgo
18	Virgo		
19	Virgo	10:31 A.M.	Libra
20	Libra		
21	Libra	11:30 A.M.	Scorpio
22	Scorpio		
23	Scorpio	12:06 P.M.	Sagittarius
24	Sagittarius		
25	Sagittarius	1:58 P.M.	Capricorn
26	Capricorn		
27	Capricorn	6:44 P.M.	Aquarius
28	Aquarius		
29	Aquarius		
30	Aquarius	3:18 A.M.	Pisces
31	Pisces		

JUNE

1	Pisces	3:07 P.M.	Aries
2	Aries		
3	Aries		
4	Aries	4:04 A.M.	Taurus
5	Taurus		
6	Taurus	3:52 P.M.	Gemini
7	Gemini		
8	Gemini		
9	Gemini	1:18 A.M.	Cancer
10	Cancer		
11	Cancer	8:19 A.M.	Leo
12	Leo		
13	Leo	1:24 P.M.	Virgo
14	Virgo		
15	Virgo	4:58 P.M.	Libra
16	Libra		
17	Libra	7:25 P.M.	Scorpio
18	Scorpio		
19	Scorpio	9:20 P.M.	Sagittarius
20	Sagittarius		
21	Sagittarius	11:46 P.M.	Capricorn
22	Capricorn		
23	Capricorn		
24	Capricorn	4:11 A.M.	Aquarius
25	Aquarius		
26	Aquarius	11:49 A.M.	Pisces
27	Pisces		
28	Pisces	10:53 P.M.	Aries
29	Aries		
30	Aries		

JULY

1	Aries	11:43 A.M.	Taurus
2	Taurus		
3	Taurus	11:39 P.M.	Gemini
4	Gemini		
5	Gemini		
6	Gemini	8:47 A.M.	Cancer
7	Cancer		

8	Cancer	2:58 P.M.	Leo
9	Leo		
10	Leo	7:07 P.M.	Virgo
11	Virgo		
12	Virgo	10:20 P.M.	Libra
13	Libra		
14	Libra		
15	Libra	1:17 A.M.	Scorpio
16	Scorpio		
17	Scorpio	4:22 A.M.	Sagittarius
18	Sagittarius		
19	Sagittarius	7:59 A.M.	Capricorn
20	Capricorn		
21	Capricorn	12:59 P.M.	Aquarius
22	Aquarius		
23	Aquarius	8:28 P.M.	Pisces
24	Pisces		
25	Pisces		
26	Pisces	7:00 A.M.	Aries
27	Aries		
28	Aries	7:40 P.M.	Taurus
29	Taurus		
30	Taurus		
31	Taurus	8:00 A.M.	Gemini

AUGUST

1	Gemini		
2	Gemini	5:32 P.M.	Cancer
3	Cancer		
4	Cancer	11:26 P.M.	Leo
5	Leo		
6	Leo		
7	Leo	2:36 A.M.	Virgo
8	Virgo		
9	Virgo	4:34 A.M.	Libra
10	Libra		
11	Libra	6:44 A.M.	Scorpio
12	Scorpio		
13	Scorpio	9:52 A.M.	Sagittarius
14	Sagittarius		
15	Sagittarius	2:18 P.M.	Capricorn
16	Capricorn		
17	Capricorn	8:17 P.M.	Aquarius
18	Aquarius		
19	Aquarius		
20	Aquarius	4:18 A.M.	Pisces
21	Pisces		
22	Pisces	2:47 P.M.	Aries
23	Aries		
24	Aries		
25	Aries	3:21 A.M.	Taurus
26	Taurus		
27	Taurus	4:08 P.M.	Gemini
28	Gemini		
29	Gemini		
30	Gemini	2:34 A.M.	Cancer
31	Cancer		

SEPTEMBER

1	Cancer	9:08 A.M.	Leo
2	Leo		
3	Leo	12:07 P.M.	Virgo
4	Virgo		
5	Virgo	1:03 P.M.	Libra
6	Libra		
7	Libra	1:44 P.M.	Scorpio
8	Scorpio		
9	Scorpio	3:40 P.M.	Sagittarius
10	Sagittarius		
11	Sagittarius	7:43 P.M.	Capricorn
12	Capricorn		
13	Capricorn		
14	Capricorn	2:08 A.M.	Aquarius
15	Aquarius		
16	Aquarius	10:53 A.M.	Pisces
17	Pisces		
18	Pisces	9:46 P.M.	Aries
19	Aries		
20	Aries		
21	Aries	10:20 A.M.	Taurus
22	Taurus		
23	Taurus	11:21 P.M.	Gemini
24	Gemini		
25	Gemini		
26	Gemini	10:45 A.M.	Cancer
27	Cancer		
28	Cancer	6:41 P.M.	Leo
29	Leo		
30	Leo	10:38 P.M.	Virgo

OCTOBER

1	Virgo		
2	Virgo	11:34 P.M.	Libra
3	Libra		
4	Libra	11:14 P.M.	Scorpio
5	Scorpio		
6	Scorpio	11:32 P.M.	Sagittarius
7	Sagittarius		
8	Sagittarius		
9	Sagittarius	2:04 A.M.	Capricorn
10	Capricorn		
11	Capricorn	7:45 A.M.	Aquarius
12	Aquarius		
13	Aquarius	4:38 P.M.	Pisces
14	Pisces		
15	Pisces		
16	Pisces	3:58 A.M.	Aries
17	Aries		
18	Aries	4:41 P.M.	Taurus
19	Taurus		
20	Taurus		
21	Taurus	5:38 A.M.	Gemini
22	Gemini		
23	Gemini	5:27 P.M.	Cancer
24	Cancer		
25	Cancer		
26	Cancer	2:40 A.M.	Leo
27	Leo		
28	Leo	8:19 A.M.	Virgo
29	Virgo		
30	Virgo	10:31 A.M.	Libra
31	Libra		

NOVEMBER

1	Libra	10:26 A.M.	Scorpio
2	Scorpio		
3	Scorpio	9:51 A.M.	Sagittarius
4	Sagittarius		
5	Sagittarius	10:44 A.M.	Capricorn
6	Capricorn		
7	Capricorn	2:45 P.M.	Aquarius
8	Aquarius		
9	Aquarius	10:42 P.M.	Pisces
10	Pisces		
11	Pisces		
12	Pisces	9:58 A.M.	Aries
13	Aries		
14	Aries	10:52 P.M.	Taurus
15	Taurus		
16	Taurus		
17	Taurus	11:40 A.M.	Gemini
18	Gemini		
19	Gemini	11:13 P.M.	Cancer
20	Cancer		
21	Cancer		
22	Cancer	8:47 A.M.	Leo
23	Leo		
24	Leo	3:46 P.M.	Virgo
25	Virgo		
26	Virgo	7:48 P.M.	Libra
27	Libra		
28	Libra	9:13 P.M.	Scorpio
29	Scorpio		
30	Scorpio	9:10 P.M.	Sagittarius

DECEMBER

1	Sagittarius		
2	Sagittarius	9:25 P.M.	Capricorn
3	Capricorn		
4	Capricorn	11:57 P.M.	Aquarius
5	Aquarius		
6	Aquarius		
7	Aquarius	6:19 A.M.	Pisces
8	Pisces		
9	Pisces	4:43 P.M.	Aries
10	Aries		
11	Aries		
12	Aries	5:32 A.M.	Taurus
13	Taurus		
14	Taurus	6:18 P.M.	Gemini
15	Gemini		
16	Gemini		
17	Gemini	5:23 A.M.	Cancer
18	Cancer		
19	Cancer	2:21 P.M.	Leo
20	Leo		
21	Leo	9:21 P.M.	Virgo
22	Virgo		
23	Virgo		
24	Virgo	2:27 A.M.	Libra
25	Libra		
26	Libra	5:36 A.M.	Scorpio
27	Scorpio		
28	Scorpio	7:09 A.M.	Sagittarius
29	Sagittarius		
30	Sagittarius	8:11 A.M.	Capricorn
31	Capricorn		

MOON SIGN TABLES
1968

JANUARY

1	Capricorn	10:24 A.M.	Aquarius
2	Aquarius		
3	Aquarius	3:35 P.M.	Pisces
4	Pisces		
5	Pisces		
6	Pisces	12:45 A.M.	Aries
7	Aries		
8	Aries	1:02 P.M.	Taurus
9	Taurus		
10	Taurus		
11	Taurus	1:54 A.M.	Gemini
12	Gemini		
13	Gemini	12:54 P.M.	Cancer
14	Cancer		
15	Cancer	9:09 P.M.	Leo
16	Leo		
17	Leo		
18	Leo	3:11 A.M.	Virgo
19	Virgo		
20	Virgo	7:47 A.M.	Libra
21	Libra		
22	Libra	11:28 A.M.	Scorpio
23	Scorpio		
24	Scorpio	2:23 P.M.	Sagittarius
25	Sagittarius		
26	Sagittarius	4:57 P.M.	Capricorn
27	Capricorn		
28	Capricorn	8:06 P.M.	Aquarius
29	Aquarius		
30	Aquarius		
31	Aquarius	1:16 A.M.	Pisces

FEBRUARY

1	Pisces		
2	Pisces	9:39 A.M.	Aries
3	Aries		
4	Aries	9:15 P.M.	Taurus
5	Taurus		
6	Taurus		
7	Taurus	10:09 A.M.	Gemini
8	Gemini		
9	Gemini	9:34 P.M.	Cancer
10	Cancer		
11	Cancer		
12	Cancer	5:50 A.M.	Leo
13	Leo		
14	Leo	11:02 A.M.	Virgo
15	Virgo		
16	Virgo	2:21 P.M.	Libra
17	Libra		
18	Libra	5:00 P.M.	Scorpio
19	Scorpio		
20	Scorpio	7:48 P.M.	Sagittarius
21	Sagittarius		
22	Sagittarius	11:12 P.M.	Capricorn
23	Capricorn		
24	Capricorn		
25	Capricorn	3:37 A.M.	Aquarius
26	Aquarius		
27	Aquarius	9:42 A.M.	Pisces
28	Pisces		
29	Pisces	6:14 P.M.	Aries

MARCH

1	Aries		
2	Aries		
3	Aries	5:27 A.M.	Taurus
4	Taurus		
5	Taurus	6:17 P.M.	Gemini
6	Gemini		
7	Gemini		
8	Gemini	6:21 A.M.	Cancer
9	Cancer		
10	Cancer	3:27 P.M.	Leo
11	Leo		
12	Leo	8:51 P.M.	Virgo
13	Virgo		
14	Virgo	11:23 P.M.	Libra
15	Libra		
16	Libra		
17	Libra	12:33 A.M.	Scorpio
18	Scorpio		
19	Scorpio	1:54 A.M.	Sagittarius
20	Sagittarius		
21	Sagittarius	4:34 A.M.	Capricorn
22	Capricorn		
23	Capricorn	9:16 A.M.	Aquarius
24	Aquarius		
25	Aquarius	4:15 P.M.	Pisces
26	Pisces		
27	Pisces		
28	Pisces	1:32 A.M.	Aries
29	Aries		
30	Aries	12:55 P.M.	Taurus
31	Taurus		

APRIL

1	Taurus		
2	Taurus	1:40 A.M.	Gemini
3	Gemini		
4	Gemini	2:13 P.M.	Cancer
5	Cancer		
6	Cancer		
7	Cancer	12:28 A.M.	Leo
8	Leo		
9	Leo	7:04 A.M.	Virgo
10	Virgo		
11	Virgo	10:01 A.M.	Libra
12	Libra		
13	Libra	10:32 A.M.	Scorpio
14	Scorpio		
15	Scorpio	10:23 A.M.	Sagittarius
16	Sagittarius		
17	Sagittarius	11:23 A.M.	Capricorn
18	Capricorn		
19	Capricorn	2:57 P.M.	Aquarius
20	Aquarius		
21	Aquarius	9:46 P.M.	Pisces
22	Pisces		
23	Pisces		
24	Pisces	7:32 A.M.	Aries
25	Aries		
26	Aries	7:22 P.M.	Taurus
27	Taurus		
28	Taurus		
29	Taurus	8:11 A.M.	Gemini
30	Gemini		

MAY

1	Gemini	8:50 P.M.	Cancer
2	Cancer		
3	Cancer		
4	Cancer	7:54 A.M.	Leo
5	Leo		
6	Leo	3:58 P.M.	Virgo
7	Virgo		
8	Virgo	8:21 P.M.	Libra
9	Libra		
10	Libra	9:30 P.M.	Scorpio
11	Scorpio		
12	Scorpio	8:53 P.M.	Sagittarius
13	Sagittarius		
14	Sagittarius	8:31 P.M.	Capricorn
15	Capricorn		
16	Capricorn	10:22 P.M.	Aquarius
17	Aquarius		
18	Aquarius		
19	Aquarius	3:53 A.M.	Pisces
20	Pisces		
21	Pisces	1:14 P.M.	Aries
22	Aries		
23	Aries		
24	Aries	1:15 A.M.	Taurus
25	Taurus		
26	Taurus	2:12 P.M.	Gemini
27	Gemini		
28	Gemini		
29	Gemini	2:43 A.M.	Cancer
30	Cancer		
31	Cancer	1:53 P.M.	Leo

JUNE

1	Leo		
2	Leo	10:52 P.M.	Virgo
3	Virgo		
4	Virgo		
5	Virgo	4:49 A.M.	Libra
6	Libra		
7	Libra	7:30 A.M.	Scorpio
8	Scorpio		
9	Scorpio	7:42 A.M.	Sagittarius
10	Sagittarius		
11	Sagittarius	7:05 A.M.	Capricorn
12	Capricorn		
13	Capricorn	7:46 A.M.	Aquarius
14	Aquarius		
15	Aquarius	11:42 A.M.	Pisces
16	Pisces		
17	Pisces	7:50 P.M.	Aries
18	Aries		
19	Aries		
20	Aries	7:25 A.M.	Taurus
21	Taurus		
22	Taurus	8:22 P.M.	Gemini
23	Gemini		
24	Gemini		
25	Gemini	8:43 A.M.	Cancer
26	Cancer		
27	Cancer	7:30 P.M.	Leo
28	Leo		
29	Leo		
30	Leo	4:26 A.M.	Virgo

JULY

1	Virgo		
2	Virgo	11:10 A.M.	Libra
3	Libra		
4	Libra	3:20 P.M.	Scorpio
5	Scorpio		
6	Scorpio	5:04 P.M.	Sagittarius

7	Sagittarius		
8	Sagittarius	5:24 P.M.	Capricorn
9	Capricorn		
10	Capricorn	6:03 P.M.	Aquarius
11	Aquarius		
12	Aquarius	9:03 P.M.	Pisces
13	Pisces		
14	Pisces		
15	Pisces	3:51 A.M.	Aries
16	Aries		
17	Aries	2:30 P.M.	Taurus
18	Taurus		
19	Taurus		
20	Taurus	3:13 A.M.	Gemini
21	Gemini		
22	Gemini	3:31 P.M.	Cancer
23	Cancer		
24	Cancer		
25	Cancer	1:55 A.M.	Leo
26	Leo		
27	Leo	10:10 A.M.	Virgo
28	Virgo		
29	Virgo	4:32 P.M.	Libra
30	Libra		
31	Libra	9:11 P.M.	Scorpio

AUGUST

1	Scorpio		
2	Scorpio		
3	Scorpio	12:11 A.M.	Sagittarius
4	Sagittarius		
5	Sagittarius	1:57 A.M.	Capricorn
6	Capricorn		
7	Capricorn	3:37 A.M.	Aquarius
8	Aquarius		
9	Aquarius	6:45 A.M.	Pisces
10	Pisces		
11	Pisces	12:53 P.M.	Aries
12	Aries		
13	Aries	10:36 P.M.	Taurus
14	Taurus		
15	Taurus		
16	Taurus	10:51 A.M.	Gemini
17	Gemini		
18	Gemini	11:15 P.M.	Cancer
19	Cancer		
20	Cancer		
21	Cancer	9:40 A.M.	Leo
22	Leo		
23	Leo	5:21 P.M.	Virgo
24	Virgo		
25	Virgo	10:45 P.M.	Libra
26	Libra		
27	Libra		
28	Libra	2:38 A.M.	Scorpio
29	Scorpio		
30	Scorpio	5:40 A.M.	Sagittarius
31	Sagittarius		

SEPTEMBER

1	Sagittarius	8:22 A.M.	Capricorn
2	Capricorn		
3	Capricorn	11:19 A.M.	Aquarius
4	Aquarius		
5	Aquarius	3:27 P.M.	Pisces
6	Pisces		
7	Pisces	9:49 P.M.	Aries

8	Aries		
9	Aries		
10	Aries	7:06 A.M.	Taurus
11	Taurus		
12	Taurus	6:54 P.M.	Gemini
13	Gemini		
14	Gemini		
15	Gemini	7:28 A.M.	Cancer
16	Cancer		
17	Cancer	6:25 P.M.	Leo
18	Leo		
19	Leo		
20	Leo	2:15 A.M.	Virgo
21	Virgo		
22	Virgo	7:00 A.M.	Libra
23	Libra		
24	Libra	9:39 A.M.	Scorpio
25	Scorpio		
26	Scorpio	11:30 A.M.	Sagittarius
27	Sagittarius		
28	Sagittarius	1:44 P.M.	Capricorn
29	Capricorn		
30	Capricorn	5:11 P.M.	Aquarius

OCTOBER

1	Aquarius		
2	Aquarius	10:21 P.M.	Pisces
3	Pisces		
4	Pisces		
5	Pisces	5:35 A.M.	Aries
6	Aries		
7	Aries	3:07 P.M.	Taurus
8	Taurus		
9	Taurus		
10	Taurus	2:43 A.M.	Gemini
11	Gemini		
12	Gemini	3:23 P.M.	Cancer
13	Cancer		
14	Cancer		
15	Cancer	3:08 A.M.	Leo
16	Leo		
17	Leo	11:58 A.M.	Virgo
18	Virgo		
19	Virgo	5:05 P.M.	Libra
20	Libra		
21	Libra	7:05 P.M.	Scorpio
22	Scorpio		
23	Scorpio	7:32 P.M.	Sagittarius
24	Sagittarius		
25	Sagittarius	8:13 P.M.	Capricorn
26	Capricorn		
27	Capricorn	10:43 P.M.	Aquarius
28	Aquarius		
29	Aquarius		
30	Aquarius	3:54 A.M.	Pisces
31	Pisces		

NOVEMBER

1	Pisces	11:51 A.M.	Aries
2	Aries		
3	Aries	10:01 P.M.	Taurus
4	Taurus		
5	Taurus		
6	Taurus	9:48 A.M.	Gemini
7	Gemini		
8	Gemini	10:26 P.M.	Cancer
9	Cancer		

10	Cancer		
11	Cancer	10:45 A.M.	Leo
12	Leo		
13	Leo	8:55 P.M.	Virgo
14	Virgo		
15	Virgo		
16	Virgo	3:26 A.M.	Libra
17	Libra		
18	Libra	6:06 A.M.	Scorpio
19	Scorpio		
20	Scorpio	6:04 A.M.	Sagittarius
21	Sagittarius		
22	Sagittarius	5:20 A.M.	Capricorn
23	Capricorn		
24	Capricorn	6:02 A.M.	Aquarius
25	Aquarius		
26	Aquarius	9:52 A.M.	Pisces
27	Pisces		
28	Pisces	5:26 P.M.	Aries
29	Aries		
30	Aries		

DECEMBER

1	Aries	3:58 A.M.	Taurus
2	Taurus		
3	Taurus	4:06 P.M.	Gemini
4	Gemini		
5	Gemini		
6	Gemini	4:43 A.M.	Cancer
7	Cancer		
8	Cancer	5:02 P.M.	Leo
9	Leo		
10	Leo		
11	Leo	3:59 A.M.	Virgo
12	Virgo		
13	Virgo	12:08 P.M.	Libra
14	Libra		
15	Libra	4:31 P.M.	Scorpio
16	Scorpio		
17	Scorpio	5:27 P.M.	Sagittarius
18	Sagittarius		
19	Sagittarius	4:32 P.M.	Capricorn
20	Capricorn		
21	Capricorn	3:59 P.M.	Aquarius
22	Aquarius		
23	Aquarius	6:01 P.M.	Pisces
24	Pisces		
25	Pisces		
26	Pisces	12:02 A.M.	Aries
27	Aries		
28	Aries	9:57 A.M.	Taurus
29	Taurus		
30	Taurus	10:11 P.M.	Gemini
31	Gemini		

MOON SIGN TABLES
1969

JANUARY

Day	Sign	Time	Sign
1	Gemini		
2	Gemini	10:53 A.M.	Cancer
3	Cancer		
4	Cancer	10:55 P.M.	Leo
5	Leo		
6	Leo		
7	Leo	9:42 A.M.	Virgo
8	Virgo		
9	Virgo	6:32 P.M.	Libra
10	Libra		
11	Libra		
12	Libra	12:32 A.M.	Scorpio
13	Scorpio		
14	Scorpio	3:19 A.M.	Sagittarius
15	Sagittarius		
16	Sagittarius	3:39 A.M.	Capricorn
17	Capricorn		
18	Capricorn	3:17 A.M.	Aquarius
19	Aquarius		
20	Aquarius	4:20 A.M.	Pisces
21	Pisces		
22	Pisces	8:43 A.M.	Aries
23	Aries		
24	Aries	5:13 P.M.	Taurus
25	Taurus		
26	Taurus		
27	Taurus	4:53 A.M.	Gemini
28	Gemini		
29	Gemini	5:36 P.M.	Cancer
30	Cancer		
31	Cancer		

FEBRUARY

Day	Sign	Time	Sign
1	Cancer	5:29 A.M.	Leo
2	Leo		
3	Leo	3:40 P.M.	Virgo
4	Virgo		
5	Virgo		
6	Virgo	12:00 A.M.	Libra
7	Libra		
8	Libra	6:18 A.M.	Scorpio
9	Scorpio		
10	Scorpio	10:23 A.M.	Sagittarius
11	Sagittarius		
12	Sagittarius	12:28 P.M.	Capricorn
13	Capricorn		
14	Capricorn	1:30 P.M.	Aquarius
15	Aquarius		
16	Aquarius	3:03 P.M.	Pisces
17	Pisces		
18	Pisces	6:49 P.M.	Aries
19	Aries		
20	Aries		
21	Aries	2:02 A.M.	Taurus
22	Taurus		
23	Taurus	12:41 P.M.	Gemini
24	Gemini		
25	Gemini		
26	Gemini	1:11 A.M.	Cancer
27	Cancer		
28	Cancer	1:12 P.M.	Leo

MARCH

Day	Sign	Time	Sign
1	Leo		
2	Leo	11:07 P.M.	Virgo
3	Virgo		
4	Virgo		
5	Virgo	6:34 A.M.	Libra
6	Libra		
7	Libra	11:56 A.M.	Scorpio
8	Scorpio		
9	Scorpio	3:48 P.M.	Sagittarius
10	Sagittarius		
11	Sagittarius	6:40 P.M.	Capricorn
12	Capricorn		
13	Capricorn	9:09 P.M.	Aquarius
14	Aquarius		
15	Aquarius		
16	Aquarius	12:04 A.M.	Pisces
17	Pisces		
18	Pisces	4:27 A.M.	Aries
19	Aries		
20	Aries	11:20 A.M.	Taurus
21	Taurus		
22	Taurus	9:12 P.M.	Gemini
23	Gemini		
24	Gemini		
25	Gemini	9:18 A.M.	Cancer
26	Cancer		
27	Cancer	9:37 P.M.	Leo
28	Leo		
29	Leo		
30	Leo	7:54 A.M.	Virgo
31	Virgo		

APRIL

Day	Sign	Time	Sign
1	Virgo	3:03 P.M.	Libra
2	Libra		
3	Libra	7:22 P.M.	Scorpio
4	Scorpio		
5	Scorpio	9:57 P.M.	Sagittarius
6	Sagittarius		
7	Sagittarius		
8	Sagittarius	12:04 A.M.	Capricorn
9	Capricorn		
10	Capricorn	2:46 A.M.	Aquarius
11	Aquarius		
12	Aquarius	6:41 A.M.	Pisces
13	Pisces		
14	Pisces	12:13 P.M.	Aries
15	Aries		
16	Aries	7:43 P.M.	Taurus
17	Taurus		
18	Taurus		
19	Taurus	5:28 A.M.	Gemini
20	Gemini		
21	Gemini	5:17 P.M.	Cancer
22	Cancer		
23	Cancer		
24	Cancer	5:51 A.M.	Leo
25	Leo		
26	Leo	4:57 P.M.	Virgo
27	Virgo		
28	Virgo		
29	Virgo	12:44 A.M.	Libra
30	Libra		

MAY

Day	Sign	Time	Sign
1	Libra	4:49 A.M.	Scorpio
2	Scorpio		
3	Scorpio	6:19 A.M.	Sagittarius
4	Sagittarius		
5	Sagittarius	6:57 A.M.	Capricorn
6	Capricorn		
7	Capricorn	8:28 A.M.	Aquarius
8	Aquarius		
9	Aquarius	12:04 P.M.	Pisces
10	Pisces		
11	Pisces	6:09 P.M.	Aries
12	Aries		
13	Aries		
14	Aries	2:28 A.M.	Taurus
15	Taurus		
16	Taurus	12:41 P.M.	Gemini
17	Gemini		
18	Gemini		
19	Gemini	12:30 A.M.	Cancer
20	Cancer		
21	Cancer	1:12 P.M.	Leo
22	Leo		
23	Leo		
24	Leo	1:07 A.M.	Virgo
25	Virgo		
26	Virgo	10:07 A.M.	Libra
27	Libra		
28	Libra	3:05 P.M.	Scorpio
29	Scorpio		
30	Scorpio	4:30 P.M.	Sagittarius
31	Sagittarius		

JUNE

Day	Sign	Time	Sign
1	Sagittarius	4:07 P.M.	Capricorn
2	Capricorn		
3	Capricorn	4:04 P.M.	Aquarius
4	Aquarius		
5	Aquarius	6:13 P.M.	Pisces
6	Pisces		
7	Pisces	11:36 P.M.	Aries
8	Aries		
9	Aries		
10	Aries	8:06 A.M.	Taurus
11	Taurus		
12	Taurus	6:48 P.M.	Gemini
13	Gemini		
14	Gemini		
15	Gemini	6:52 A.M.	Cancer
16	Cancer		
17	Cancer	7:35 P.M.	Leo
18	Leo		
19	Leo		
20	Leo	7:53 P.M.	Virgo
21	Virgo		
22	Virgo	6:03 P.M.	Libra
23	Libra		
24	Libra		
25	Libra	12:31 A.M.	Scorpio
26	Scorpio		
27	Scorpio	3:00 A.M.	Sagittarius
28	Sagittarius		
29	Sagittarius	2:44 A.M.	Capricorn
30	Capricorn		

JULY

Day	Sign	Time	Sign
1	Capricorn	1:49 A.M.	Aquarius
2	Aquarius		
3	Aquarius	2:26 A.M.	Pisces
4	Pisces		
5	Pisces	6:16 A.M.	Aries
6	Aries		
7	Aries	1:53 P.M.	Taurus

8	Taurus			9	Leo			11	Sagittarius		
9	Taurus			10	Leo	2:20 A.M.	Virgo	12	Sagittarius	4:08 P.M.	Capricorn
10	Taurus	12:31 A.M.	Gemini	11	Virgo			13	Capricorn		
11	Gemini			12	Virgo	12:01 P.M.	Libra	14	Capricorn	5:53 P.M.	Aquarius
12	Gemini	12:47 P.M.	Cancer	13	Libra			15	Aquarius		
13	Cancer			14	Libra	7:25 P.M.	Scorpio	16	Aquarius	8:52 P.M.	Pisces
14	Cancer			15	Scorpio			17	Pisces		
15	Cancer	1:29 A.M.	Leo	16	Scorpio			18	Pisces		
16	Leo			17	Scorpio	12:42 A.M.	Sagittarius	19	Pisces	1:32 A.M.	Aries
17	Leo	1:42 P.M.	Virgo	18	Sagittarius			20	Aries		
18	Virgo			19	Sagittarius	4:14 A.M.	Capricorn	21	Aries	7:52 A.M.	Taurus
19	Virgo			20	Capricorn			22	Taurus		
20	Virgo	12:20 A.M.	Libra	21	Capricorn	6:31 A.M.	Aquarius	23	Taurus	3:59 P.M.	Gemini
21	Libra			22	Aquarius			24	Gemini		
22	Libra	8:04 A.M.	Scorpio	23	Aquarius	8:22 A.M.	Pisces	25	Gemini		
23	Scorpio			24	Pisces			26	Gemini	2:10 A.M.	Cancer
24	Scorpio	12:10 P.M.	Sagittarius	25	Pisces	10:55 A.M.	Aries	27	Cancer		
25	Sagittarius			26	Aries			28	Cancer	2:22 P.M.	Leo
26	Sagittarius	1:09 P.M.	Capricorn	27	Aries	3:29 P.M.	Taurus	29	Leo		
27	Capricorn			28	Taurus			30	Leo		
28	Capricorn	12:35 P.M.	Aquarius	29	Taurus	11:05 P.M.	Gemini				
29	Aquarius			30	Gemini			**DECEMBER**			
30	Aquarius	12:30 P.M.	Pisces					1	Leo	3:14 A.M.	Virgo
31	Pisces			**OCTOBER**				2	Virgo		
AUGUST				1	Gemini			3	Virgo	2:17 P.M.	Libra
1	Pisces	2:55 P.M.	Aries	2	Gemini	9:52 A.M.	Cancer	4	Libra		
2	Aries			3	Cancer			5	Libra	9:30 P.M.	Scorpio
3	Aries	9:02 P.M.	Taurus	4	Cancer	10:25 P.M.	Leo	6	Scorpio		
4	Taurus			5	Leo			7	Scorpio		
5	Taurus			6	Leo			8	Scorpio	12:43 A.M.	Sagittarius
6	Taurus	6:49 A.M.	Gemini	7	Leo	10:21 A.M.	Virgo	9	Sagittarius		
7	Gemini			8	Virgo			10	Sagittarius	1:20 A.M.	Capricorn
8	Gemini	6:57 P.M.	Cancer	9	Virgo	7:48 P.M.	Libra	11	Capricorn		
9	Cancer			10	Libra			12	Capricorn	1:27 A.M.	Aquarius
10	Cancer			11	Libra			13	Aquarius		
11	Cancer	7:38 A.M.	Leo	12	Libra	2:19 A.M.	Scorpio	14	Aquarius	2:56 A.M.	Pisces
12	Leo			13	Scorpio			15	Pisces		
13	Leo	7:32 P.M.	Virgo	14	Scorpio	6:33 A.M.	Sagittarius	16	Pisces	6:56 A.M.	Aries
14	Virgo			15	Sagittarius			17	Aries		
15	Virgo			16	Sagittarius	9:35 A.M.	Capricorn	18	Aries	1:35 P.M.	Taurus
16	Virgo	5:51 A.M.	Libra	17	Capricorn			19	Taurus		
17	Libra			18	Capricorn	12:21 P.M.	Aquarius	20	Taurus	10:28 P.M.	Gemini
18	Libra	1:54 P.M.	Scorpio	19	Aquarius			21	Gemini		
19	Scorpio			20	Aquarius	3:26 P.M.	Pisces	22	Gemini		
20	Scorpio	7:12 P.M.	Sagittarius	21	Pisces			23	Gemini	9:09 A.M.	Cancer
21	Sagittarius			22	Pisces	7:17 P.M.	Aries	24	Cancer		
22	Sagittarius	9:49 P.M.	Capricorn	23	Aries			25	Cancer	9:21 P.M.	Leo
23	Capricorn			24	Aries			26	Leo		
24	Capricorn	10:36 P.M.	Aquarius	25	Aries	12:32 A.M.	Taurus	27	Leo		
25	Aquarius			26	Taurus			28	Leo	10:20 A.M.	Virgo
26	Aquarius	11:03 P.M.	Pisces	27	Taurus	8:00 A.M.	Gemini	29	Virgo		
27	Pisces			28	Gemini			30	Virgo	10:18 P.M.	Libra
28	Pisces			29	Gemini	6:13 P.M.	Cancer	31	Libra		
29	Pisces	12:57 A.M.	Aries	30	Cancer						
30	Aries			31	Cancer						
31	Aries	5:50 A.M.	Taurus	**NOVEMBER**							
SEPTEMBER				1	Cancer	6:35 A.M.	Leo				
1	Taurus			2	Leo						
2	Taurus	2:23 P.M.	Gemini	3	Leo	7:00 P.M.	Virgo				
3	Gemini			4	Virgo						
4	Gemini			5	Virgo						
5	Gemini	1:57 A.M.	Cancer	6	Virgo	4:59 A.M.	Libra				
6	Cancer			7	Libra						
7	Cancer	2:36 P.M.	Leo	8	Libra	11:18 A.M.	Scorpio				
8	Leo			9	Scorpio						
				10	Scorpio	2:30 P.M.	Sagittarius				

MOON SIGN TABLES
1970

JANUARY

1	Libra		
2	Libra	7:03 A.M.	Scorpio
3	Scorpio		
4	Scorpio	11:33 A.M.	Sagittarius
5	Sagittarius		
6	Sagittarius	12:30 P.M.	Capricorn
7	Capricorn		
8	Capricorn	11:47 A.M.	Aquarius
9	Aquarius		
10	Aquarius	11:37 A.M.	Pisces
11	Pisces		
12	Pisces	1:48 P.M.	Aries
13	Aries		
14	Aries	7:20 P.M.	Taurus
15	Taurus		
16	Taurus		
17	Taurus	4:07 A.M.	Gemini
18	Gemini		
19	Gemini	3:13 P.M.	Cancer
20	Cancer		
21	Cancer		
22	Cancer	3:40 A.M.	Leo
23	Leo		
24	Leo	4:33 P.M.	Virgo
25	Virgo		
26	Virgo		
27	Virgo	4:42 A.M.	Libra
28	Libra		
29	Libra	2:34 P.M.	Scorpio
30	Scorpio		
31	Scorpio	8:50 P.M.	Sagittarius

FEBRUARY

1	Sagittarius		
2	Sagittarius	11:22 P.M.	Capricorn
3	Capricorn		
4	Capricorn	11:19 P.M.	Aquarius
5	Aquarius		
6	Aquarius	10:37 P.M.	Pisces
7	Pisces		
8	Pisces	11:17 P.M.	Aries
9	Aries		
10	Aries		
11	Aries	2:59 A.M.	Taurus
12	Taurus		
13	Taurus	10:29 A.M.	Gemini
14	Gemini		
15	Gemini	9:17 P.M.	Cancer
16	Cancer		
17	Cancer		
18	Cancer	9:53 A.M.	Leo
19	Leo		
20	Leo	10:42 P.M.	Virgo
21	Virgo		
22	Virgo		
23	Virgo	10:30 A.M.	Libra
24	Libra		
25	Libra	8:23 P.M.	Scorpio
26	Scorpio		
27	Scorpio		
28	Scorpio	3:38 A.M.	Sagittarius

MARCH

1	Sagittarius		
2	Sagittarius	7:54 A.M.	Capricorn
3	Capricorn		
4	Capricorn	9:34 A.M.	Aquarius
5	Aquarius		
6	Aquarius	9:49 A.M.	Pisces
7	Pisces		
8	Pisces	10:16 A.M.	Aries
9	Aries		
10	Aries	12:43 P.M.	Taurus
11	Taurus		
12	Taurus	6:37 P.M.	Gemini
13	Gemini		
14	Gemini		
15	Gemini	4:18 A.M.	Cancer
16	Cancer		
17	Cancer	4:39 P.M.	Leo
18	Leo		
19	Leo		
20	Leo	5:30 A.M.	Virgo
21	Virgo		
22	Virgo	4:56 P.M.	Libra
23	Libra		
24	Libra		
25	Libra	2:10 A.M.	Scorpio
26	Scorpio		
27	Scorpio	9:07 A.M.	Sagittarius
28	Sagittarius		
29	Sagittarius	2:00 P.M.	Capricorn
30	Capricorn		
31	Capricorn	5:08 P.M.	Aquarius

APRIL

1	Aquarius		
2	Aquarius	7:01 P.M.	Pisces
3	Pisces		
4	Pisces	8:32 P.M.	Aries
5	Aries		
6	Aries	11:02 P.M.	Taurus
7	Taurus		
8	Taurus		
9	Taurus	4:02 A.M.	Gemini
10	Gemini		
11	Gemini	12:33 P.M.	Cancer
12	Cancer		
13	Cancer		
14	Cancer	12:16 A.M.	Leo
15	Leo		
16	Leo	1:07 P.M.	Virgo
17	Virgo		
18	Virgo		
19	Virgo	12:35 A.M.	Libra
20	Libra		
21	Libra	9:15 A.M.	Scorpio
22	Scorpio		
23	Scorpio	3:15 P.M.	Sagittarius
24	Sagittarius		
25	Sagittarius	7:26 P.M.	Capricorn
26	Capricorn		
27	Capricorn	10:43 P.M.	Aquarius
28	Aquarius		
29	Aquarius		
30	Aquarius	1:37 A.M.	Pisces

MAY

1	Pisces		
2	Pisces	4:32 A.M.	Aries
3	Aries		
4	Aries	8:05 A.M.	Taurus
5	Taurus		
6	Taurus	1:17 P.M.	Gemini
7	Gemini		
8	Gemini	9:17 P.M.	Cancer
9	Cancer		
10	Cancer		
11	Cancer	8:22 A.M.	Leo
12	Leo		
13	Leo	9:10 P.M.	Virgo
14	Virgo		
15	Virgo		
16	Virgo	9:02 A.M.	Libra
17	Libra		
18	Libra	5:49 P.M.	Scorpio
19	Scorpio		
20	Scorpio	11:11 P.M.	Sagittarius
21	Sagittarius		
22	Sagittarius		
23	Sagittarius	2:13 A.M.	Capricorn
24	Capricorn		
25	Capricorn	4:25 A.M.	Aquarius
26	Aquarius		
27	Aquarius	6:59 A.M.	Pisces
28	Pisces		
29	Pisces	10:27 A.M.	Aries
30	Aries		
31	Aries	3:03 P.M.	Taurus

JUNE

1	Taurus		
2	Taurus	9:10 P.M.	Gemini
3	Gemini		
4	Gemini		
5	Gemini	5:25 A.M.	Cancer
6	Cancer		
7	Cancer	4:17 P.M.	Leo
8	Leo		
9	Leo		
10	Leo	5:02 A.M.	Virgo
11	Virgo		
12	Virgo	5:28 P.M.	Libra
13	Libra		
14	Libra		
15	Libra	3:01 A.M.	Scorpio
16	Scorpio		
17	Scorpio	8:39 A.M.	Sagittarius
18	Sagittarius		
19	Sagittarius	11:04 A.M.	Capricorn
20	Capricorn		
21	Capricorn	12:00 P.M.	Aquarius
22	Aquarius		
23	Aquarius	1:12 P.M.	Pisces
24	Pisces		
25	Pisces	3:52 P.M.	Aries
26	Aries		
27	Aries	8:35 P.M.	Taurus
28	Taurus		
29	Taurus		
30	Taurus	3:24 A.M.	Gemini

JULY

1	Gemini		
2	Gemini	12:21 P.M.	Cancer
3	Cancer		
4	Cancer	11:26 P.M.	Leo
5	Leo		
6	Leo		
7	Leo	12:11 P.M.	Virgo

Day	Sign	Time	Enters
8	Virgo		
9	Virgo		
10	Virgo	1:02 A.M.	Libra
11	Libra		
12	Libra	11:41 A.M.	Scorpio
13	Scorpio		
14	Scorpio	6:26 P.M.	Sagittarius
15	Sagittarius		
16	Sagittarius	9:19 P.M.	Capricorn
17	Capricorn		
18	Capricorn	9:44 P.M.	Aquarius
19	Aquarius		
20	Aquarius	9:36 P.M.	Pisces
21	Pisces		
22	Pisces	10:42 P.M.	Aries
23	Aries		
24	Aries		
25	Aries	2:18 A.M.	Taurus
26	Taurus		
27	Taurus	8:53 A.M.	Gemini
28	Gemini		
29	Gemini	6:14 P.M.	Cancer
30	Cancer		
31	Cancer		

AUGUST

Day	Sign	Time	Enters
1	Cancer	5:44 A.M.	Leo
2	Leo		
3	Leo	6:34 P.M.	Virgo
4	Virgo		
5	Virgo		
6	Virgo	7:33 A.M.	Libra
7	Libra		
8	Libra	6:57 P.M.	Scorpio
9	Scorpio		
10	Scorpio		
11	Scorpio	3:07 A.M.	Sagittarius
12	Sagittarius		
13	Sagittarius	7:25 A.M.	Capricorn
14	Capricorn		
15	Capricorn	8:31 A.M.	Aquarius
16	Aquarius		
17	Aquarius	8:01 A.M.	Pisces
18	Pisces		
19	Pisces	7:50 A.M.	Aries
20	Aries		
21	Aries	9:46 A.M.	Taurus
22	Taurus		
23	Taurus	3:03 P.M.	Gemini
24	Gemini		
25	Gemini	11:58 P.M.	Cancer
26	Cancer		
27	Cancer		
28	Cancer	11:38 A.M.	Leo
29	Leo		
30	Leo		
31	Leo	12:36 A.M.	Virgo

SEPTEMBER

Day	Sign	Time	Enters
1	Virgo		
2	Virgo	1:25 P.M.	Libra
3	Libra		
4	Libra		
5	Libra	12:54 A.M.	Scorpio
6	Scorpio		
7	Scorpio	9:58 A.M.	Sagittarius
8	Sagittarius		
9	Sagittarius	3:51 P.M.	Capricorn
10	Capricorn		
11	Capricorn	6:33 P.M.	Aquarius
12	Aquarius		
13	Aquarius	6:57 P.M.	Pisces
14	Pisces		
15	Pisces	6:35 P.M.	Aries
16	Aries		
17	Aries	7:21 P.M.	Taurus
18	Taurus		
19	Taurus	11:02 P.M.	Gemini
20	Gemini		
21	Gemini		
22	Gemini	6:41 A.M.	Cancer
23	Cancer		
24	Cancer	5:54 P.M.	Leo
25	Leo		
26	Leo		
27	Leo	6:53 A.M.	Virgo
28	Virgo		
29	Virgo	7:33 P.M.	Libra
30	Libra		

OCTOBER

Day	Sign	Time	Enters
1	Libra		
2	Libra	6:35 A.M.	Scorpio
3	Scorpio		
4	Scorpio	3:31 P.M.	Sagittarius
5	Sagittarius		
6	Sagittarius	10:10 P.M.	Capricorn
7	Capricorn		
8	Capricorn		
9	Capricorn	2:26 A.M.	Aquarius
10	Aquarius		
11	Aquarius	4:30 A.M.	Pisces
12	Pisces		
13	Pisces	5:12 A.M.	Aries
14	Aries		
15	Aries	6:00 A.M.	Taurus
16	Taurus		
17	Taurus	8:43 A.M.	Gemini
18	Gemini		
19	Gemini	2:59 P.M.	Cancer
20	Cancer		
21	Cancer		
22	Cancer	1:12 A.M.	Leo
23	Leo		
24	Leo	1:57 P.M.	Virgo
25	Virgo		
26	Virgo		
27	Virgo	2:37 A.M.	Libra
28	Libra		
29	Libra	1:15 P.M.	Scorpio
30	Scorpio		
31	Scorpio	9:24 P.M.	Sagittarius

NOVEMBER

Day	Sign	Time	Enters
1	Sagittarius		
2	Sagittarius		
3	Sagittarius	3:32 A.M.	Capricorn
4	Capricorn		
5	Capricorn	8:11 A.M.	Aquarius
6	Aquarius		
7	Aquarius	11:33 A.M.	Pisces
8	Pisces		
9	Pisces	1:52 P.M.	Aries
10	Aries		
11	Aries	3:50 P.M.	Taurus
12	Taurus		
13	Taurus	6:48 P.M.	Gemini
14	Gemini		
15	Gemini		
16	Gemini	12:23 A.M.	Cancer
17	Cancer		
18	Cancer	9:36 A.M.	Leo
19	Leo		
20	Leo	9:50 P.M.	Virgo
21	Virgo		
22	Virgo		
23	Virgo	10:39 A.M.	Libra
24	Libra		
25	Libra	9:25 P.M.	Scorpio
26	Scorpio		
27	Scorpio		
28	Scorpio	5:02 A.M.	Sagittarius
29	Sagittarius		
30	Sagittarius	10:06 A.M.	Capricorn

DECEMBER

Day	Sign	Time	Enters
1	Capricorn		
2	Capricorn	1:45 P.M.	Aquarius
3	Aquarius		
4	Aquarius	4:55 P.M.	Pisces
5	Pisces		
6	Pisces	8:03 P.M.	Aries
7	Aries		
8	Aries	11:24 P.M.	Taurus
9	Taurus		
10	Taurus		
11	Taurus	3:33 A.M.	Gemini
12	Gemini		
13	Gemini	9:32 A.M.	Cancer
14	Cancer		
15	Cancer	6:21 P.M.	Leo
16	Leo		
17	Leo		
18	Leo	6:04 A.M.	Virgo
19	Virgo		
20	Virgo	7:01 P.M.	Libra
21	Libra		
22	Libra		
23	Libra	6:27 A.M.	Scorpio
24	Scorpio		
25	Scorpio	2:27 P.M.	Sagittarius
26	Sagittarius		
27	Sagittarius	7:01 P.M.	Capricorn
28	Capricorn		
29	Capricorn	9:24 P.M.	Aquarius
30	Aquarius		
31	Aquarius	11:08 P.M.	Pisces

MOON SIGN TABLES
1971

JANUARY
1	Pisces		
2	Pisces		
3	Pisces	1:26 A.M.	Aries
4	Aries		
5	Aries	5:00 A.M.	Taurus
6	Taurus		
7	Taurus	10:08 A.M.	Gemini
8	Gemini		
9	Gemini	5:09 P.M.	Cancer
10	Cancer		
11	Cancer		
12	Cancer	2:24 A.M.	Leo
13	Leo		
14	Leo	1:57 P.M.	Virgo
15	Virgo		
16	Virgo		
17	Virgo	2:53 A.M.	Libra
18	Libra		
19	Libra	3:04 P.M.	Scorpio
20	Scorpio		
21	Scorpio		
22	Scorpio	12:16 A.M.	Sagittarius
23	Sagittarius		
24	Sagittarius	5:32 A.M.	Capricorn
25	Capricorn		
26	Capricorn	7:36 A.M.	Aquarius
27	Aquarius		
28	Aquarius	8:02 A.M.	Pisces
29	Pisces		
30	Pisces	8:36 A.M.	Aries
31	Aries		

FEBRUARY
1	Aries	10:49 A.M.	Taurus
2	Taurus		
3	Taurus	3:34 P.M.	Gemini
4	Gemini		
5	Gemini	11:07 P.M.	Cancer
6	Cancer		
7	Cancer		
8	Cancer	9:06 A.M.	Leo
9	Leo		
10	Leo	8:58 P.M.	Virgo
11	Virgo		
12	Virgo		
13	Virgo	9:50 A.M.	Libra
14	Libra		
15	Libra	10:22 P.M.	Scorpio
16	Scorpio		
17	Scorpio		
18	Scorpio	8:45 A.M.	Sagittarius
19	Sagittarius		
20	Sagittarius	3:37 P.M.	Capricorn
21	Capricorn		
22	Capricorn	6:43 P.M.	Aquarius
23	Aquarius		
24	Aquarius	7:05 P.M.	Pisces
25	Pisces		
26	Pisces	6:30 P.M.	Aries
27	Aries		
28	Aries	6:54 P.M.	Taurus

MARCH
1	Taurus		
2	Taurus	10:01 P.M.	Gemini
3	Gemini		

4	Gemini		
5	Gemini	4:47 A.M.	Cancer
6	Cancer		
7	Cancer	2:55 P.M.	Leo
8	Leo		
9	Leo		
10	Leo	3:10 A.M.	Virgo
11	Virgo		
12	Virgo	4:06 P.M.	Libra
13	Libra		
14	Libra		
15	Libra	4:31 A.M.	Scorpio
16	Scorpio		
17	Scorpio	3:23 P.M.	Sagittarius
18	Sagittarius		
19	Sagittarius	11:37 P.M.	Capricorn
20	Capricorn		
21	Capricorn		
22	Capricorn	4:29 A.M.	Aquarius
23	Aquarius		
24	Aquarius	6:07 A.M.	Pisces
25	Pisces		
26	Pisces	5:45 A.M.	Aries
27	Aries		
28	Aries	5:16 A.M.	Taurus
29	Taurus		
30	Taurus	6:43 A.M.	Gemini
31	Gemini		

APRIL
1	Gemini	11:51 A.M.	Cancer
2	Cancer		
3	Cancer	9:05 P.M.	Leo
4	Leo		
5	Leo		
6	Leo	9:16 A.M.	Virgo
7	Virgo		
8	Virgo	10:17 P.M.	Libra
9	Libra		
10	Libra		
11	Libra	10:28 A.M.	Scorpio
12	Scorpio		
13	Scorpio	9:03 P.M.	Sagittarius
14	Sagittarius		
15	Sagittarius		
16	Sagittarius	5:38 A.M.	Capricorn
17	Capricorn		
18	Capricorn	11:46 A.M.	Aquarius
19	Aquarius		
20	Aquarius	3:07 P.M.	Pisces
21	Pisces		
22	Pisces	4:08 P.M.	Aries
23	Aries		
24	Aries	4:06 P.M.	Taurus
25	Taurus		
26	Taurus	4:58 P.M.	Gemini
27	Gemini		
28	Gemini	8:43 P.M.	Cancer
29	Cancer		
30	Cancer		

MAY
1	Cancer	4:34 A.M.	Leo
2	Leo		
3	Leo	4:03 P.M.	Virgo
4	Virgo		
5	Virgo		

6	Virgo	4:59 A.M.	Libra
7	Libra		
8	Libra	5:03 P.M.	Scorpio
9	Scorpio		
10	Scorpio		
11	Scorpio	3:08 A.M.	Sagittarius
12	Sagittarius		
13	Sagittarius	11:09 A.M.	Capricorn
14	Capricorn		
15	Capricorn	5:19 P.M.	Aquarius
16	Aquarius		
17	Aquarius	9:39 P.M.	Pisces
18	Pisces		
19	Pisces		
20	Pisces	12:11 A.M.	Aries
21	Aries		
22	Aries	1:31 A.M.	Taurus
23	Taurus		
24	Taurus	3:01 A.M.	Gemini
25	Gemini		
26	Gemini	6:26 A.M.	Cancer
27	Cancer		
28	Cancer	1:16 P.M.	Leo
29	Leo		
30	Leo	11:48 P.M.	Virgo
31	Virgo		

JUNE
1	Virgo		
2	Virgo	12:26 P.M.	Libra
3	Libra		
4	Libra		
5	Libra	12:36 A.M.	Scorpio
6	Scorpio		
7	Scorpio	10:28 A.M.	Sagittarius
8	Sagittarius		
9	Sagittarius	5:45 P.M.	Capricorn
10	Capricorn		
11	Capricorn	11:03 P.M.	Aquarius
12	Aquarius		
13	Aquarius		
14	Aquarius	3:01 A.M.	Pisces
15	Pisces		
16	Pisces	6:06 A.M.	Aries
17	Aries		
18	Aries	8:39 A.M.	Taurus
19	Taurus		
20	Taurus	11:24 A.M.	Gemini
21	Gemini		
22	Gemini	3:30 P.M.	Cancer
23	Cancer		
24	Cancer	10:12 P.M.	Leo
25	Leo		
26	Leo		
27	Leo	8:06 A.M.	Virgo
28	Virgo		
29	Virgo	8:22 P.M.	Libra
30	Libra		

JULY
1	Libra		
2	Libra	8:46 A.M.	Scorpio
3	Scorpio		
4	Scorpio	6:59 P.M.	Sagittarius
5	Sagittarius		
6	Sagittarius		
7	Sagittarius	2:03 A.M.	Capricorn

Day	Sign	Time	Sign
8	Capricorn		
9	Capricorn	6:26 A.M.	Aquarius
10	Aquarius		
11	Aquarius	9:14 A.M.	Pisces
12	Pisces		
13	Pisces	11:32 A.M.	Aries
14	Aries		
15	Aries	2:10 P.M.	Taurus
16	Taurus		
17	Taurus	5:47 P.M.	Gemini
18	Gemini		
19	Gemini	10:56 P.M.	Cancer
20	Cancer		
21	Cancer		
22	Cancer	6:16 A.M.	Leo
23	Leo		
24	Leo	4:09 P.M.	Virgo
25	Virgo		
26	Virgo		
27	Virgo	4:12 A.M.	Libra
28	Libra		
29	Libra	4:50 P.M.	Scorpio
30	Scorpio		
31	Scorpio		

AUGUST

Day	Sign	Time	Sign
1	Scorpio	3:49 A.M.	Sagittarius
2	Sagittarius		
3	Sagittarius	11:32 A.M.	Capricorn
4	Capricorn		
5	Capricorn	3:46 P.M.	Aquarius
6	Aquarius		
7	Aquarius	5:34 P.M.	Pisces
8	Pisces		
9	Pisces	6:27 P.M.	Aries
10	Aries		
11	Aries	7:55 P.M.	Taurus
12	Taurus		
13	Taurus	11:10 P.M.	Gemini
14	Gemini		
15	Gemini		
16	Gemini	4:50 A.M.	Cancer
17	Cancer		
18	Cancer	12:57 P.M.	Leo
19	Leo		
20	Leo	11:19 P.M.	Virgo
21	Virgo		
22	Virgo		
23	Virgo	11:22 A.M.	Libra
24	Libra		
25	Libra		
26	Libra	12:09 A.M.	Scorpio
27	Scorpio		
28	Scorpio	11:56 A.M.	Sagittarius
29	Sagittarius		
30	Sagittarius	8:54 P.M.	Capricorn
31	Capricorn		

SEPTEMBER

Day	Sign	Time	Sign
1	Capricorn		
2	Capricorn	2:04 A.M.	Aquarius
3	Aquarius		
4	Aquarius	3:51 A.M.	Pisces
5	Pisces		
6	Pisces	3:43 A.M.	Aries
7	Aries		
8	Aries	3:37 A.M.	Taurus
9	Taurus		
10	Taurus	5:25 A.M.	Gemini
11	Gemini		
12	Gemini	10:21 A.M.	Cancer
13	Cancer		
14	Cancer	6:38 P.M.	Leo
15	Leo		
16	Leo		
17	Leo	5:29 A.M.	Virgo
18	Virgo		
19	Virgo	5:47 P.M.	Libra
20	Libra		
21	Libra		
22	Libra	6:33 A.M.	Scorpio
23	Scorpio		
24	Scorpio	6:43 P.M.	Sagittarius
25	Sagittarius		
26	Sagittarius		
27	Sagittarius	4:53 A.M.	Capricorn
28	Capricorn		
29	Capricorn	11:39 A.M.	Aquarius
30	Aquarius		

OCTOBER

Day	Sign	Time	Sign
1	Aquarius	2:36 P.M.	Pisces
2	Pisces		
3	Pisces	2:40 P.M.	Aries
4	Aries		
5	Aries	1:42 P.M.	Taurus
6	Taurus		
7	Taurus	1:53 P.M.	Gemini
8	Gemini		
9	Gemini	5:11 P.M.	Cancer
10	Cancer		
11	Cancer		
12	Cancer	12:30 A.M.	Leo
13	Leo		
14	Leo	11:16 A.M.	Virgo
15	Virgo		
16	Virgo	11:47 P.M.	Libra
17	Libra		
18	Libra		
19	Libra	12:31 P.M.	Scorpio
20	Scorpio		
21	Scorpio		
22	Scorpio	12:31 A.M.	Sagittarius
23	Sagittarius		
24	Sagittarius	11:05 A.M.	Capricorn
25	Capricorn		
26	Capricorn	7:11 P.M.	Aquarius
27	Aquarius		
28	Aquarius	11:57 P.M.	Pisces
29	Pisces		
30	Pisces		
31	Pisces	1:26 A.M.	Aries

NOVEMBER

Day	Sign	Time	Sign
1	Aries		
2	Aries	12:55 A.M.	Taurus
3	Taurus		
4	Taurus	12:27 A.M.	Gemini
5	Gemini		
6	Gemini	2:15 A.M.	Cancer
7	Cancer		
8	Cancer	7:56 A.M.	Leo
9	Leo		
10	Leo	5:44 P.M.	Virgo
11	Virgo		
12	Virgo		
13	Virgo	6:05 A.M.	Libra
14	Libra		
15	Libra	6:49 P.M.	Scorpio
16	Scorpio		
17	Scorpio		
18	Scorpio	6:30 A.M.	Sagittarius
19	Sagittarius		
20	Sagittarius	4:36 P.M.	Capricorn
21	Capricorn		
22	Capricorn		
23	Capricorn	12:52 A.M.	Aquarius
24	Aquarius		
25	Aquarius	6:48 A.M.	Pisces
26	Pisces		
27	Pisces	10:03 A.M.	Aries
28	Aries		
29	Aries	11:08 A.M.	Taurus
30	Taurus		

DECEMBER

Day	Sign	Time	Sign
1	Taurus	11:25 A.M.	Gemini
2	Gemini		
3	Gemini	12:51 P.M.	Cancer
4	Cancer		
5	Cancer	5:17 P.M.	Leo
6	Leo		
7	Leo		
8	Leo	1:40 A.M.	Virgo
9	Virgo		
10	Virgo	1:19 P.M.	Libra
11	Libra		
12	Libra		
13	Libra	2:01 A.M.	Scorpio
14	Scorpio		
15	Scorpio	1:37 P.M.	Sagittarius
16	Sagittarius		
17	Sagittarius	11:07 P.M.	Capricorn
18	Capricorn		
19	Capricorn		
20	Capricorn	6:32 A.M.	Aquarius
21	Aquarius		
22	Aquarius	12:10 P.M.	Pisces
23	Pisces		
24	Pisces	4:09 P.M.	Aries
25	Aries		
26	Aries	6:45 P.M.	Taurus
27	Taurus		
28	Taurus	8:38 P.M.	Gemini
29	Gemini		
30	Gemini	11:01 P.M.	Cancer
31	Cancer		

MOON SIGN TABLES
1972

JANUARY

1 Cancer		
2 Cancer	3:22 A.M.	Leo
3 Leo		
4 Leo	10:50 A.M.	Virgo
5 Virgo		
6 Virgo	9:33 P.M.	Libra
7 Libra		
8 Libra		
9 Libra	10:03 A.M.	Scorpio
10 Scorpio		
11 Scorpio	9:57 P.M.	Sagittarius
12 Sagittarius		
13 Sagittarius		
14 Sagittarius	7:26 A.M.	Capricorn
15 Capricorn		
16 Capricorn	2:04 P.M.	Aquarius
17 Aquarius		
18 Aquarius	6:28 P.M.	Pisces
19 Pisces		
20 Pisces	9:35 P.M.	Aries
21 Aries		
22 Aries		
23 Aries	12:17 A.M.	Taurus
24 Taurus		
25 Taurus	3:14 A.M.	Gemini
26 Gemini		
27 Gemini	7:01 A.M.	Cancer
28 Cancer		
29 Cancer	12:21 P.M.	Leo
30 Leo		
31 Leo	7:56 P.M.	Virgo

FEBRUARY

1 Virgo		
2 Virgo		
3 Virgo	6:06 A.M.	Libra
4 Libra		
5 Libra	6:18 P.M.	Scorpio
6 Scorpio		
7 Scorpio		
8 Scorpio	6:38 A.M.	Sagittarius
9 Sagittarius		
10 Sagittarius	4:50 P.M.	Capricorn
11 Capricorn		
12 Capricorn	11:36 P.M.	Aquarius
13 Aquarius		
14 Aquarius		
15 Aquarius	3:11 A.M.	Pisces
16 Pisces		
17 Pisces	4:51 A.M.	Aries
18 Aries		
19 Aries	6:11 A.M.	Taurus
20 Taurus		
21 Taurus	8:35 A.M.	Gemini
22 Gemini		
23 Gemini	12:52 P.M.	Cancer
24 Cancer		
25 Cancer	7:15 P.M.	Leo
26 Leo		
27 Leo		
28 Leo	3:39 A.M.	Virgo
29 Virgo		

MARCH

1 Virgo	2:00 P.M.	Libra
2 Libra		

3 Libra		
4 Libra	2:00 A.M.	Scorpio
5 Scorpio		
6 Scorpio	2:36 P.M.	Sagittarius
7 Sagittarius		
8 Sagittarius		
9 Sagittarius	1:49 A.M.	Capricorn
10 Capricorn		
11 Capricorn	9:42 A.M.	Aquarius
12 Aquarius		
13 Aquarius	1:39 P.M.	Pisces
14 Pisces		
15 Pisces	2:37 P.M.	Aries
16 Aries		
17 Aries	2:27 P.M.	Taurus
18 Taurus		
19 Taurus	3:12 P.M.	Gemini
20 Gemini		
21 Gemini	6:26 P.M.	Cancer
22 Cancer		
23 Cancer		
24 Cancer	12:46 A.M.	Leo
25 Leo		
26 Leo	9:48 A.M.	Virgo
27 Virgo		
28 Virgo	8:42 P.M.	Libra
29 Libra		
30 Libra		
31 Libra	8:48 A.M.	Scorpio

APRIL

1 Scorpio		
2 Scorpio	9:27 P.M.	Sagittarius
3 Sagittarius		
4 Sagittarius		
5 Sagittarius	9:20 A.M.	Capricorn
6 Capricorn		
7 Capricorn	6:37 P.M.	Aquarius
8 Aquarius		
9 Aquarius	11:58 P.M.	Pisces
10 Pisces		
11 Pisces		
12 Pisces	1:32 A.M.	Aries
13 Aries		
14 Aries	12:54 A.M.	Taurus
15 Taurus		
16 Taurus	12:16 A.M.	Gemini
17 Gemini		
18 Gemini	1:46 A.M.	Cancer
19 Cancer		
20 Cancer	6:47 A.M.	Leo
21 Leo		
22 Leo	3:24 P.M.	Virgo
23 Virgo		
24 Virgo		
25 Virgo	2:34 A.M.	Libra
26 Libra		
27 Libra	2:56 P.M.	Scorpio
28 Scorpio		
29 Scorpio		
30 Scorpio	3:31 A.M.	Sagittarius

MAY

1 Sagittarius		
2 Sagittarius	3:29 P.M.	Capricorn
3 Capricorn		
4 Capricorn		

5 Capricorn	1:35 A.M.	Aquarius
6 Aquarius		
7 Aquarius	8:28 A.M.	Pisces
8 Pisces		
9 Pisces	11:35 A.M.	Aries
10 Aries		
11 Aries	11:47 A.M.	Taurus
12 Taurus		
13 Taurus	10:57 A.M.	Gemini
14 Gemini		
15 Gemini	11:16 A.M.	Cancer
16 Cancer		
17 Cancer	2:38 P.M.	Leo
18 Leo		
19 Leo	9:56 P.M.	Virgo
20 Virgo		
21 Virgo		
22 Virgo	8:36 A.M.	Libra
23 Libra		
24 Libra	9:01 P.M.	Scorpio
25 Scorpio		
26 Scorpio		
27 Scorpio	9:33 A.M.	Sagittarius
28 Sagittarius		
29 Sagittarius	9:13 P.M.	Capricorn
30 Capricorn		
31 Capricorn		

JUNE

1 Capricorn	7:15 A.M.	Aquarius
2 Aquarius		
3 Aquarius	2:52 P.M.	Pisces
4 Pisces		
5 Pisces	7:27 P.M.	Aries
6 Aries		
7 Aries	9:14 P.M.	Taurus
8 Taurus		
9 Taurus	9:24 P.M.	Gemini
10 Gemini		
11 Gemini	9:45 P.M.	Cancer
12 Cancer		
13 Cancer		
14 Cancer	12:10 A.M.	Leo
15 Leo		
16 Leo	6:03 A.M.	Virgo
17 Virgo		
18 Virgo	3:39 P.M.	Libra
19 Libra		
20 Libra		
21 Libra	3:43 A.M.	Scorpio
22 Scorpio		
23 Scorpio	4:14 P.M.	Sagittarius
24 Sagittarius		
25 Sagittarius		
26 Sagittarius	3:36 A.M.	Capricorn
27 Capricorn		
28 Capricorn	1:02 P.M.	Aquarius
29 Aquarius		
30 Aquarius	8:18 P.M.	Pisces

JULY

1 Pisces		
2 Pisces		
3 Pisces	1:22 A.M.	Aries
4 Aries		
5 Aries	4:25 A.M.	Taurus
6 Taurus		

7	Taurus	6:05 A.M.	Gemini
8	Gemini		
9	Gemini	7:29 A.M.	Cancer
10	Cancer		
11	Cancer	10:05 A.M.	Leo
12	Leo		
13	Leo	3:16 P.M.	Virgo
14	Virgo		
15	Virgo	11:49 P.M.	Libra
16	Libra		
17	Libra		
18	Libra	11:15 A.M.	Scorpio
19	Scorpio		
20	Scorpio	11:46 P.M.	Sagittarius
21	Sagittarius		
22	Sagittarius		
23	Sagittarius	11:10 A.M.	Capricorn
24	Capricorn		
25	Capricorn	8:07 P.M.	Aquarius
26	Aquarius		
27	Aquarius		
28	Aquarius	2:29 A.M.	Pisces
29	Pisces		
30	Pisces	6:50 A.M.	Aries
31	Aries		

AUGUST

1	Aries	9:57 A.M.	Taurus
2	Taurus		
3	Taurus	12:33 P.M.	Gemini
4	Gemini		
5	Gemini	3:18 P.M.	Cancer
6	Cancer		
7	Cancer	6:56 P.M.	Leo
8	Leo		
9	Leo		
10	Leo	12:23 A.M.	Virgo
11	Virgo		
12	Virgo	8:27 A.M.	Libra
13	Libra		
14	Libra	7:19 P.M.	Scorpio
15	Scorpio		
16	Scorpio		
17	Scorpio	7:49 A.M.	Sagittarius
18	Sagittarius		
19	Sagittarius	7:38 P.M.	Capricorn
20	Capricorn		
21	Capricorn		
22	Capricorn	4:43 A.M.	Aquarius
23	Aquarius		
24	Aquarius	10:28 A.M.	Pisces
25	Pisces		
26	Pisces	1:40 P.M.	Aries
27	Aries		
28	Aries	3:43 P.M.	Taurus
29	Taurus		
30	Taurus	5:56 P.M.	Gemini
31	Gemini		

SEPTEMBER

1	Gemini	9:11 P.M.	Cancer
2	Cancer		
3	Cancer		
4	Cancer	1:54 A.M.	Leo
5	Leo		
6	Leo	8:15 A.M.	Virgo
7	Virgo		
8	Virgo	4:36 P.M.	Libra
9	Libra		
10	Libra		
11	Libra	3:15 A.M.	Scorpio
12	Scorpio		
13	Scorpio	3:42 P.M.	Sagittarius
14	Sagittarius		
15	Sagittarius		
16	Sagittarius	4:07 A.M.	Capricorn
17	Capricorn		
18	Capricorn	2:04 P.M.	Aquarius
19	Aquarius		
20	Aquarius	8:09 P.M.	Pisces
21	Pisces		
22	Pisces	10:44 P.M.	Aries
23	Aries		
24	Aries	11:27 P.M.	Taurus
25	Taurus		
26	Taurus		
27	Taurus	12:14 A.M.	Gemini
28	Gemini		
29	Gemini	2:39 A.M.	Cancer
30	Cancer		

OCTOBER

1	Cancer	7:25 A.M.	Leo
2	Leo		
3	Leo	2:31 P.M.	Virgo
4	Virgo		
5	Virgo	11:35 P.M.	Libra
6	Libra		
7	Libra		
8	Libra	10:27 A.M.	Scorpio
9	Scorpio		
10	Scorpio	10:52 P.M.	Sagittarius
11	Sagittarius		
12	Sagittarius		
13	Sagittarius	11:44 A.M.	Capricorn
14	Capricorn		
15	Capricorn	10:51 P.M.	Aquarius
16	Aquarius		
17	Aquarius		
18	Aquarius	6:12 A.M.	Pisces
19	Pisces		
20	Pisces	9:22 A.M.	Aries
21	Aries		
22	Aries	9:37 A.M.	Taurus
23	Taurus		
24	Taurus	9:02 A.M.	Gemini
25	Gemini		
26	Gemini	9:44 A.M.	Cancer
27	Cancer		
28	Cancer	1:14 P.M.	Leo
29	Leo		
30	Leo	7:59 P.M.	Virgo
31	Virgo		

NOVEMBER

1	Virgo		
2	Virgo	5:27 A.M.	Libra
3	Libra		
4	Libra	4:46 P.M.	Scorpio
5	Scorpio		
6	Scorpio		
7	Scorpio	5:16 A.M.	Sagittarius
8	Sagittarius		
9	Sagittarius	6:11 P.M.	Capricorn
10	Capricorn		
11	Capricorn		
12	Capricorn	6:02 A.M.	Aquarius
13	Aquarius		
14	Aquarius	2:56 P.M.	Pisces
15	Pisces		
16	Pisces	7:44 P.M.	Aries
17	Aries		
18	Aries	8:53 P.M.	Taurus
19	Taurus		
20	Taurus	8:05 P.M.	Gemini
21	Gemini		
22	Gemini	7:31 P.M.	Cancer
23	Cancer		
24	Cancer	9:12 P.M.	Leo
25	Leo		
26	Leo		
27	Leo	2:24 A.M.	Virgo
28	Virgo		
29	Virgo	11:15 A.M.	Libra
30	Libra		

DECEMBER

1	Libra	10:42 P.M.	Scorpio
2	Scorpio		
3	Scorpio		
4	Scorpio	11:22 A.M.	Sagittarius
5	Sagittarius		
6	Sagittarius		
7	Sagittarius	12:06 A.M.	Capricorn
8	Capricorn		
9	Capricorn	11:53 A.M.	Aquarius
10	Aquarius		
11	Aquarius	9:33 P.M.	Pisces
12	Pisces		
13	Pisces		
14	Pisces	3:59 A.M.	Aries
15	Aries		
16	Aries	6:59 A.M.	Taurus
17	Taurus		
18	Taurus	7:24 A.M.	Gemini
19	Gemini		
20	Gemini	6:57 A.M.	Cancer
21	Cancer		
22	Cancer	7:34 A.M.	Leo
23	Leo		
24	Leo	11:03 A.M.	Virgo
25	Virgo		
26	Virgo	6:21 P.M.	Libra
27	Libra		
28	Libra		
29	Libra	5:10 A.M.	Scorpio
30	Scorpio		
31	Scorpio	5:51 P.M.	Sagittarius

MOON SIGN TABLES
1973

JANUARY

1	Sagittarius		
2	Sagittarius		
3	Sagittarius	6:30 A.M.	Capricorn
4	Capricorn		
5	Capricorn	5:47 P.M.	Aquarius
6	Aquarius		
7	Aquarius		
8	Aquarius	3:03 A.M.	Pisces
9	Pisces		
10	Pisces	9:57 A.M.	Aries
11	Aries		
12	Aries	2:24 P.M.	Taurus
13	Taurus		
14	Taurus	4:41 P.M.	Gemini
15	Gemini		
16	Gemini	5:39 P.M.	Cancer
17	Cancer		
18	Cancer	6:40 P.M.	Leo
19	Leo		
20	Leo	9:24 P.M.	Virgo
21	Virgo		
22	Virgo		
23	Virgo	3:16 A.M.	Libra
24	Libra		
25	Libra	12:52 P.M.	Scorpio
26	Scorpio		
27	Scorpio		
28	Scorpio	1:10 A.M.	Sagittarius
29	Sagittarius		
30	Sagittarius	1:54 P.M.	Capricorn
31	Capricorn		

FEBRUARY

1	Capricorn		
2	Capricorn	12:55 A.M.	Aquarius
3	Aquarius		
4	Aquarius	9:22 A.M.	Pisces
5	Pisces		
6	Pisces	3:29 P.M.	Aries
7	Aries		
8	Aries	7:53 P.M.	Taurus
9	Taurus		
10	Taurus	11:10 P.M.	Gemini
11	Gemini		
12	Gemini		
13	Gemini	1:44 A.M.	Cancer
14	Cancer		
15	Cancer	4:12 A.M.	Leo
16	Leo		
17	Leo	7:31 A.M.	Virgo
18	Virgo		
19	Virgo	12:58 P.M.	Libra
20	Libra		
21	Libra	9:35 P.M.	Scorpio
22	Scorpio		
23	Scorpio		
24	Scorpio	9:14 A.M.	Sagittarius
25	Sagittarius		
26	Sagittarius	10:04 P.M.	Capricorn
27	Capricorn		
28	Capricorn		

MARCH

1	Capricorn	9:22 A.M.	Aquarius
2	Aquarius		
3	Aquarius	5:31 P.M.	Pisces
4	Pisces		
5	Pisces	10:37 P.M.	Aries
6	Aries		
7	Aries		
8	Aries	1:51 A.M.	Taurus
9	Taurus		
10	Taurus	4:31 A.M.	Gemini
11	Gemini		
12	Gemini	7:29 A.M.	Cancer
13	Cancer		
14	Cancer	11:07 A.M.	Leo
15	Leo		
16	Leo	3:42 P.M.	Virgo
17	Virgo		
18	Virgo	9:48 P.M.	Libra
19	Libra		
20	Libra		
21	Libra	6:15 A.M.	Scorpio
22	Scorpio		
23	Scorpio	5:26 P.M.	Sagittarius
24	Sagittarius		
25	Sagittarius		
26	Sagittarius	6:16 A.M.	Capricorn
27	Capricorn		
28	Capricorn	6:12 P.M.	Aquarius
29	Aquarius		
30	Aquarius		
31	Aquarius	2:55 A.M.	Pisces

APRIL

1	Pisces		
2	Pisces	7:48 A.M.	Aries
3	Aries		
4	Aries	9:58 A.M.	Taurus
5	Taurus		
6	Taurus	11:12 A.M.	Gemini
7	Gemini		
8	Gemini	1:04 P.M.	Cancer
9	Cancer		
10	Cancer	4:31 P.M.	Leo
11	Leo		
12	Leo	9:47 P.M.	Virgo
13	Virgo		
14	Virgo		
15	Virgo	4:50 A.M.	Libra
16	Libra		
17	Libra	1:51 P.M.	Scorpio
18	Scorpio		
19	Scorpio		
20	Scorpio	1:02 A.M.	Sagittarius
21	Sagittarius		
22	Sagittarius	1:49 P.M.	Capricorn
23	Capricorn		
24	Capricorn		
25	Capricorn	2:21 A.M.	Aquarius
26	Aquarius		
27	Aquarius	12:09 P.M.	Pisces
28	Pisces		
29	Pisces	5:53 P.M.	Aries
30	Aries		

MAY

1	Aries	8:01 P.M.	Taurus
2	Taurus		
3	Taurus	8:16 P.M.	Gemini
4	Gemini		
5	Gemini	8:35 P.M.	Cancer
6	Cancer		
7	Cancer	10:36 P.M.	Leo
8	Leo		
9	Leo		
10	Leo	3:13 A.M.	Virgo
11	Virgo		
12	Virgo	10:31 A.M.	Libra
13	Libra		
14	Libra	8:09 P.M.	Scorpio
15	Scorpio		
16	Scorpio		
17	Scorpio	7:41 A.M.	Sagittarius
18	Sagittarius		
19	Sagittarius	8:30 P.M.	Capricorn
20	Capricorn		
21	Capricorn		
22	Capricorn	9:17 A.M.	Aquarius
23	Aquarius		
24	Aquarius	8:05 P.M.	Pisces
25	Pisces		
26	Pisces		
27	Pisces	3:14 A.M.	Aries
28	Aries		
29	Aries	6:28 A.M.	Taurus
30	Taurus		
31	Taurus	6:53 A.M.	Gemini

JUNE

1	Gemini		
2	Gemini	6:21 A.M.	Cancer
3	Cancer		
4	Cancer	6:49 A.M.	Leo
5	Leo		
6	Leo	9:51 A.M.	Virgo
7	Virgo		
8	Virgo	4:16 P.M.	Libra
9	Libra		
10	Libra		
11	Libra	1:52 A.M.	Scorpio
12	Scorpio		
13	Scorpio	1:43 P.M.	Sagittarius
14	Sagittarius		
15	Sagittarius		
16	Sagittarius	2:37 A.M.	Capricorn
17	Capricorn		
18	Capricorn	3:19 P.M.	Aquarius
19	Aquarius		
20	Aquarius		
21	Aquarius	2:29 A.M.	Pisces
22	Pisces		
23	Pisces	10:48 A.M.	Aries
24	Aries		
25	Aries	3:37 P.M.	Taurus
26	Taurus		
27	Taurus	5:18 P.M.	Gemini
28	Gemini		
29	Gemini	5:08 P.M.	Cancer
30	Cancer		

JULY

1	Cancer	4:55 P.M.	Leo
2	Leo		
3	Leo	6:31 P.M.	Virgo
4	Virgo		
5	Virgo	11:23 P.M.	Libra
6	Libra		
7	Libra		

8	Libra	8:05 A.M.	Scorpio
9	Scorpio		
10	Scorpio	7:48 P.M.	Sagittarius
11	Sagittarius		
12	Sagittarius		
13	Sagittarius	8:45 A.M.	Capricorn
14	Capricorn		
15	Capricorn	9:15 P.M.	Aquarius
16	Aquarius		
17	Aquarius		
18	Aquarius	8:07 A.M.	Pisces
19	Pisces		
20	Pisces	4:43 P.M.	Aries
21	Aries		
22	Aries	10:41 P.M.	Taurus
23	Taurus		
24	Taurus		
25	Taurus	1:58 A.M.	Gemini
26	Gemini		
27	Gemini	3:10 A.M.	Cancer
28	Cancer		
29	Cancer	3:29 A.M.	Leo
30	Leo		
31	Leo	4:34 A.M.	Virgo

AUGUST

1	Virgo		
2	Virgo	8:12 A.M.	Libra
3	Libra		
4	Libra	3:35 P.M.	Scorpio
5	Scorpio		
6	Scorpio		
7	Scorpio	2:37 A.M.	Sagittarius
8	Sagittarius		
9	Sagittarius	3:30 P.M.	Capricorn
10	Capricorn		
11	Capricorn		
12	Capricorn	3:52 A.M.	Aquarius
13	Aquarius		
14	Aquarius	2:14 P.M.	Pisces
15	Pisces		
16	Pisces	10:16 P.M.	Aries
17	Aries		
18	Aries		
19	Aries	4:14 A.M.	Taurus
20	Taurus		
21	Taurus	8:26 A.M.	Gemini
22	Gemini		
23	Gemini	11:08 A.M.	Cancer
24	Cancer		
25	Cancer	12:49 P.M.	Leo
26	Leo		
27	Leo	2:33 P.M.	Virgo
28	Virgo		
29	Virgo	5:52 P.M.	Libra
30	Libra		
31	Libra		

SEPTEMBER

1	Libra	12:17 A.M.	Scorpio
2	Scorpio		
3	Scorpio	10:24 A.M.	Sagittarius
4	Sagittarius		
5	Sagittarius	11:01 P.M.	Capricorn
6	Capricorn		
7	Capricorn		
8	Capricorn	11:30 A.M.	Aquarius
9	Aquarius		
10	Aquarius	9:40 P.M.	Pisces
11	Pisces		
12	Pisces		
13	Pisces	4:56 A.M.	Aries
14	Aries		
15	Aries	9:59 A.M.	Taurus
16	Taurus		
17	Taurus	1:48 P.M.	Gemini
18	Gemini		
19	Gemini	5:01 P.M.	Cancer
20	Cancer		
21	Cancer	7:56 P.M.	Leo
22	Leo		
23	Leo	10:58 P.M.	Virgo
24	Virgo		
25	Virgo		
26	Virgo	3:00 A.M.	Libra
27	Libra		
28	Libra	9:18 A.M.	Scorpio
29	Scorpio		
30	Scorpio	6:47 P.M.	Sagittarius

OCTOBER

1	Sagittarius		
2	Sagittarius		
3	Sagittarius	7:02 A.M.	Capricorn
4	Capricorn		
5	Capricorn	7:49 P.M.	Aquarius
6	Aquarius		
7	Aquarius		
8	Aquarius	6:23 A.M.	Pisces
9	Pisces		
10	Pisces	1:29 P.M.	Aries
11	Aries		
12	Aries	5:36 P.M.	Taurus
13	Taurus		
14	Taurus	8:09 P.M.	Gemini
15	Gemini		
16	Gemini	10:28 P.M.	Cancer
17	Cancer		
18	Cancer		
19	Cancer	1:25 A.M.	Leo
20	Leo		
21	Leo	5:19 A.M.	Virgo
22	Virgo		
23	Virgo	10:28 A.M.	Libra
24	Libra		
25	Libra	5:28 P.M.	Scorpio
26	Scorpio		
27	Scorpio		
28	Scorpio	2:57 A.M.	Sagittarius
29	Sagittarius		
30	Sagittarius	2:57 P.M.	Capricorn
31	Capricorn		

NOVEMBER

1	Capricorn		
2	Capricorn	3:58 A.M.	Aquarius
3	Aquarius		
4	Aquarius	3:26 P.M.	Pisces
5	Pisces		
6	Pisces	11:19 P.M.	Aries
7	Aries		
8	Aries		
9	Aries	3:25 A.M.	Taurus
10	Taurus		
11	Taurus	4:59 A.M.	Gemini
12	Gemini		
13	Gemini	5:46 A.M.	Cancer
14	Cancer		
15	Cancer	7:20 A.M.	Leo
16	Leo		
17	Leo	10:41 A.M.	Virgo
18	Virgo		
19	Virgo	4:15 P.M.	Libra
20	Libra		
21	Libra		
22	Libra	12:06 A.M.	Scorpio
23	Scorpio		
24	Scorpio	10:11 A.M.	Sagittarius
25	Sagittarius		
26	Sagittarius	10:13 P.M.	Capricorn
27	Capricorn		
28	Capricorn		
29	Capricorn	11:17 A.M.	Aquarius
30	Aquarius		

DECEMBER

1	Aquarius	11:32 P.M.	Pisces
2	Pisces		
3	Pisces		
4	Pisces	8:50 A.M.	Aries
5	Aries		
6	Aries	2:08 P.M.	Taurus
7	Taurus		
8	Taurus	3:58 P.M.	Gemini
9	Gemini		
10	Gemini	3:52 P.M.	Cancer
11	Cancer		
12	Cancer	3:44 P.M.	Leo
13	Leo		
14	Leo	5:20 P.M.	Virgo
15	Virgo		
16	Virgo	9:53 P.M.	Libra
17	Libra		
18	Libra		
19	Libra	5:44 A.M.	Scorpio
20	Scorpio		
21	Scorpio	4:20 P.M.	Sagittarius
22	Sagittarius		
23	Sagittarius		
24	Sagittarius	4:41 A.M.	Capricorn
25	Capricorn		
26	Capricorn	5:43 P.M.	Aquarius
27	Aquarius		
28	Aquarius		
29	Aquarius	6:10 A.M.	Pisces
30	Pisces		
31	Pisces	4:34 P.M.	Aries

MOON SIGN TABLES
1974

JANUARY

1 Aries		
2 Aries	11:38 P.M.	Taurus
3 Taurus		
4 Taurus		
5 Taurus	3:00 A.M.	Gemini
6 Gemini		
7 Gemini	3:28 A.M.	Cancer
8 Cancer		
9 Cancer	2:42 A.M.	Leo
10 Leo		
11 Leo	2:41 A.M.	Virgo
12 Virgo		
13 Virgo	5:21 A.M.	Libra
14 Libra		
15 Libra	11:54 A.M.	Scorpio
16 Scorpio		
17 Scorpio	10:12 P.M.	Sagittarius
18 Sagittarius		
19 Sagittarius		
20 Sagittarius	10:47 A.M.	Capricorn
21 Capricorn		
22 Capricorn	11:50 P.M.	Aquarius
23 Aquarius		
24 Aquarius		
25 Aquarius	12:00 P.M.	Pisces
26 Pisces		
27 Pisces	10:32 P.M.	Aries
28 Aries		
29 Aries		
30 Aries	6:41 A.M.	Taurus
31 Taurus		

FEBRUARY

1 Taurus	11:53 A.M.	Gemini
2 Gemini		
3 Gemini	2:05 P.M.	Cancer
4 Cancer		
5 Cancer	2:11 P.M.	Leo
6 Leo		
7 Leo	1:52 P.M.	Virgo
8 Virgo		
9 Virgo	3:10 P.M.	Libra
10 Libra		
11 Libra	7:58 P.M.	Scorpio
12 Scorpio		
13 Scorpio		
14 Scorpio	5:01 A.M.	Sagittarius
15 Sagittarius		
16 Sagittarius	5:16 P.M.	Capricorn
17 Capricorn		
18 Capricorn		
19 Capricorn	6:21 A.M.	Aquarius
20 Aquarius		
21 Aquarius	6:15 P.M.	Pisces
22 Pisces		
23 Pisces		
24 Pisces	4:12 A.M.	Aries
25 Aries		
26 Aries	12:11 P.M.	Taurus
27 Taurus		
28 Taurus	6:10 P.M.	Gemini

MARCH

1 Gemini		
2 Gemini	9:59 P.M.	Cancer
3 Cancer		
4 Cancer	11:49 P.M.	Leo
5 Leo		
6 Leo		
7 Leo	12:33 A.M.	Virgo
8 Virgo		
9 Virgo	1:52 A.M.	Libra
10 Libra		
11 Libra	5:40 A.M.	Scorpio
12 Scorpio		
13 Scorpio	1:20 P.M.	Sagittarius
14 Sagittarius		
15 Sagittarius		
16 Sagittarius	12:41 A.M.	Capricorn
17 Capricorn		
18 Capricorn	1:38 P.M.	Aquarius
19 Aquarius		
20 Aquarius		
21 Aquarius	1:33 A.M.	Pisces
22 Pisces		
23 Pisces	11:02 A.M.	Aries
24 Aries		
25 Aries	6:09 P.M.	Taurus
26 Taurus		
27 Taurus	11:33 P.M.	Gemini
28 Gemini		
29 Gemini		
30 Gemini	3:40 A.M.	Cancer
31 Cancer		

APRIL

1 Cancer	6:40 A.M.	Leo
2 Leo		
3 Leo	8:56 A.M.	Virgo
4 Virgo		
5 Virgo	11:22 A.M.	Libra
6 Libra		
7 Libra	3:25 P.M.	Scorpio
8 Scorpio		
9 Scorpio	10:27 P.M.	Sagittarius
10 Sagittarius		
11 Sagittarius		
12 Sagittarius	8:56 A.M.	Capricorn
13 Capricorn		
14 Capricorn	9:34 P.M.	Aquarius
15 Aquarius		
16 Aquarius		
17 Aquarius	9:44 A.M.	Pisces
18 Pisces		
19 Pisces	7:20 P.M.	Aries
20 Aries		
21 Aries		
22 Aries	1:53 A.M.	Taurus
23 Taurus		
24 Taurus	6:11 A.M.	Gemini
25 Gemini		
26 Gemini	9:17 A.M.	Cancer
27 Cancer		
28 Cancer	12:03 P.M.	Leo
29 Leo		
30 Leo	3:00 P.M.	Virgo

MAY

1 Virgo		
2 Virgo	6:39 P.M.	Libra
3 Libra		
4 Libra	11:43 P.M.	Scorpio
5 Scorpio		
6 Scorpio		
7 Scorpio	7:05 A.M.	Sagittarius
8 Sagittarius		
9 Sagittarius	5:15 P.M.	Capricorn
10 Capricorn		
11 Capricorn		
12 Capricorn	5:34 A.M.	Aquarius
13 Aquarius		
14 Aquarius	6:03 P.M.	Pisces
15 Pisces		
16 Pisces		
17 Pisces	4:20 A.M.	Aries
18 Aries		
19 Aries	11:10 A.M.	Taurus
20 Taurus		
21 Taurus	2:54 P.M.	Gemini
22 Gemini		
23 Gemini	4:46 P.M.	Cancer
24 Cancer		
25 Cancer	6:12 P.M.	Leo
26 Leo		
27 Leo	8:25 P.M.	Virgo
28 Virgo		
29 Virgo		
30 Virgo	12:16 A.M.	Libra
31 Libra		

JUNE

1 Libra	6:10 A.M.	Scorpio
2 Scorpio		
3 Scorpio	2:21 P.M.	Sagittarius
4 Sagittarius		
5 Sagittarius		
6 Sagittarius	12:48 A.M.	Capricorn
7 Capricorn		
8 Capricorn	1:02 P.M.	Aquarius
9 Aquarius		
10 Aquarius		
11 Aquarius	1:43 A.M.	Pisces
12 Pisces		
13 Pisces	12:52 P.M.	Aries
14 Aries		
15 Aries	8:46 P.M.	Taurus
16 Taurus		
17 Taurus		
18 Taurus	12:59 A.M.	Gemini
19 Gemini		
20 Gemini	2:21 A.M.	Cancer
21 Cancer		
22 Cancer	2:30 A.M.	Leo
23 Leo		
24 Leo	3:11 A.M.	Virgo
25 Virgo		
26 Virgo	5:57 A.M.	Libra
27 Libra		
28 Libra	11:40 A.M.	Scorpio
29 Scorpio		
30 Scorpio	8:20 P.M.	Sagittarius

JULY

1 Sagittarius		
2 Sagittarius		
3 Sagittarius	7:19 A.M.	Capricorn
4 Capricorn		
5 Capricorn	7:41 P.M.	Aquarius
6 Aquarius		
7 Aquarius		

Day	Sign	Time	Change
8	Aquarius	8:25 A.M.	Pisces
9	Pisces		
10	Pisces	8:10 P.M.	Aries
11	Aries		
12	Aries		
13	Aries	5:21 A.M.	Taurus
14	Taurus		
15	Taurus	10:54 A.M.	Gemini
16	Gemini		
17	Gemini	12:56 P.M.	Cancer
18	Cancer		
19	Cancer	12:43 P.M.	Leo
20	Leo		
21	Leo	12:10 P.M.	Virgo
22	Virgo		
23	Virgo	1:19 P.M.	Libra
24	Libra		
25	Libra	5:45 P.M.	Scorpio
26	Scorpio		
27	Scorpio		
28	Scorpio	2:00 A.M.	Sagittarius
29	Sagittarius		
30	Sagittarius	1:11 P.M.	Capricorn
31	Capricorn		

AUGUST

Day	Sign	Time	Change
1	Capricorn		
2	Capricorn	1:46 A.M.	Aquarius
3	Aquarius		
4	Aquarius	2:26 P.M.	Pisces
5	Pisces		
6	Pisces		
7	Pisces	2:15 A.M.	Aries
8	Aries		
9	Aries	12:13 P.M.	Taurus
10	Taurus		
11	Taurus	7:15 P.M.	Gemini
12	Gemini		
13	Gemini	10:49 P.M.	Cancer
14	Cancer		
15	Cancer	11:26 P.M.	Leo
16	Leo		
17	Leo	10:42 P.M.	Virgo
18	Virgo		
19	Virgo	10:45 P.M.	Libra
20	Libra		
21	Libra		
22	Libra	1:37 A.M.	Scorpio
23	Scorpio		
24	Scorpio	8:34 A.M.	Sagittarius
25	Sagittarius		
26	Sagittarius	7:15 P.M.	Capricorn
27	Capricorn		
28	Capricorn		
29	Capricorn	7:52 A.M.	Aquarius
30	Aquarius		
31	Aquarius	8:29 P.M.	Pisces

SEPTEMBER

Day	Sign	Time	Change
1	Pisces		
2	Pisces		
3	Pisces	7:58 A.M.	Aries
4	Aries		
5	Aries	5:50 P.M.	Taurus
6	Taurus		
7	Taurus		
8	Taurus	1:36 A.M.	Gemini
9	Gemini		
10	Gemini	6:39 A.M.	Cancer
11	Cancer		
12	Cancer	8:54 A.M.	Leo
13	Leo		
14	Leo	9:12 A.M.	Virgo
15	Virgo		
16	Virgo	9:17 A.M.	Libra
17	Libra		
18	Libra	11:14 A.M.	Scorpio
19	Scorpio		
20	Scorpio	4:46 P.M.	Sagittarius
21	Sagittarius		
22	Sagittarius		
23	Sagittarius	2:22 A.M.	Capricorn
24	Capricorn		
25	Capricorn	2:38 P.M.	Aquarius
26	Aquarius		
27	Aquarius		
28	Aquarius	3:14 A.M.	Pisces
29	Pisces		
30	Pisces	2:25 P.M.	Aries

OCTOBER

Day	Sign	Time	Change
1	Aries		
2	Aries	11:39 P.M.	Taurus
3	Taurus		
4	Taurus		
5	Taurus	7:00 A.M.	Gemini
6	Gemini		
7	Gemini	12:30 P.M.	Cancer
8	Cancer		
9	Cancer	4:02 P.M.	Leo
10	Leo		
11	Leo	5:56 P.M.	Virgo
12	Virgo		
13	Virgo	7:11 P.M.	Libra
14	Libra		
15	Libra	9:23 P.M.	Scorpio
16	Scorpio		
17	Scorpio		
18	Scorpio	2:14 A.M.	Sagittarius
19	Sagittarius		
20	Sagittarius	10:44 A.M.	Capricorn
21	Capricorn		
22	Capricorn	10:20 P.M.	Aquarius
23	Aquarius		
24	Aquarius		
25	Aquarius	10:57 A.M.	Pisces
26	Pisces		
27	Pisces	10:13 P.M.	Aries
28	Aries		
29	Aries		
30	Aries	7:00 A.M.	Taurus
31	Taurus		

NOVEMBER

Day	Sign	Time	Change
1	Taurus	1:23 P.M.	Gemini
2	Gemini		
3	Gemini	6:01 P.M.	Cancer
4	Cancer		
5	Cancer	9:30 P.M.	Leo
6	Leo		
7	Leo		
8	Leo	12:18 A.M.	Virgo
9	Virgo		
10	Virgo	2:58 A.M.	Libra
11	Libra		
12	Libra	6:23 A.M.	Scorpio
13	Scorpio		
14	Scorpio	11:39 A.M.	Sagittarius
15	Sagittarius		
16	Sagittarius	7:42 P.M.	Capricorn
17	Capricorn		
18	Capricorn		
19	Capricorn	6:39 A.M.	Aquarius
20	Aquarius		
21	Aquarius	7:11 P.M.	Pisces
22	Pisces		
23	Pisces		
24	Pisces	6:59 A.M.	Aries
25	Aries		
26	Aries	4:05 P.M.	Taurus
27	Taurus		
28	Taurus	9:58 P.M.	Gemini
29	Gemini		
30	Gemini		

DECEMBER

Day	Sign	Time	Change
1	Gemini	1:22 A.M.	Cancer
2	Cancer		
3	Cancer	3:31 A.M.	Leo
4	Leo		
5	Leo	5:40 A.M.	Virgo
6	Virgo		
7	Virgo	8:42 A.M.	Libra
8	Libra		
9	Libra	1:13 P.M.	Scorpio
10	Scorpio		
11	Scorpio	7:34 P.M.	Sagittarius
12	Sagittarius		
13	Sagittarius		
14	Sagittarius	4:04 A.M.	Capricorn
15	Capricorn		
16	Capricorn	2:48 P.M.	Aquarius
17	Aquarius		
18	Aquarius		
19	Aquarius	3:12 A.M.	Pisces
20	Pisces		
21	Pisces	3:35 P.M.	Aries
22	Aries		
23	Aries		
24	Aries	1:45 A.M.	Taurus
25	Taurus		
26	Taurus	8:15 A.M.	Gemini
27	Gemini		
28	Gemini	11:15 A.M.	Cancer
29	Cancer		
30	Cancer	12:05 P.M.	Leo
31	Leo		

MOON SIGN TABLES
1975

JANUARY

Day	Sign	Time	Sign
1	Leo	12:33 P.M.	Virgo
2	Virgo		
3	Virgo	2:21 P.M.	Libra
4	Libra		
5	Libra	6:39 P.M.	Scorpio
6	Scorpio		
7	Scorpio		
8	Scorpio	1:39 A.M.	Sagittarius
9	Sagittarius		
10	Sagittarius	10:58 A.M.	Capricorn
11	Capricorn		
12	Capricorn	10:03 P.M.	Aquarius
13	Aquarius		
14	Aquarius		
15	Aquarius	10:23 A.M.	Pisces
16	Pisces		
17	Pisces	11:03 P.M.	Aries
18	Aries		
19	Aries		
20	Aries	10:21 A.M.	Taurus
21	Taurus		
22	Taurus	6:23 P.M.	Gemini
23	Gemini		
24	Gemini	10:20 P.M.	Cancer
25	Cancer		
26	Cancer	11:00 P.M.	Leo
27	Leo		
28	Leo	10:14 P.M.	Virgo
29	Virgo		
30	Virgo	10:13 P.M.	Libra
31	Libra		

FEBRUARY

Day	Sign	Time	Sign
1	Libra		
2	Libra	12:53 A.M.	Scorpio
3	Scorpio		
4	Scorpio	7:10 A.M.	Sagittarius
5	Sagittarius		
6	Sagittarius	4:42 P.M.	Capricorn
7	Capricorn		
8	Capricorn		
9	Capricorn	4:16 A.M.	Aquarius
10	Aquarius		
11	Aquarius	4:45 P.M.	Pisces
12	Pisces		
13	Pisces		
14	Pisces	5:22 A.M.	Aries
15	Aries		
16	Aries	5:09 P.M.	Taurus
17	Taurus		
18	Taurus		
19	Taurus	2:35 A.M.	Gemini
20	Gemini		
21	Gemini	8:18 A.M.	Cancer
22	Cancer		
23	Cancer	10:13 A.M.	Leo
24	Leo		
25	Leo	9:37 A.M.	Virgo
26	Virgo		
27	Virgo	8:38 A.M.	Libra
28	Libra		

MARCH

Day	Sign	Time	Sign
1	Libra	9:33 A.M.	Scorpio
2	Scorpio		
3	Scorpio	2:05 P.M.	Sagittarius
4	Sagittarius		
5	Sagittarius	10:39 P.M.	Capricorn
6	Capricorn		
7	Capricorn		
8	Capricorn	10:09 A.M.	Aquarius
9	Aquarius		
10	Aquarius	10:49 P.M.	Pisces
11	Pisces		
12	Pisces		
13	Pisces	11:18 A.M.	Aries
14	Aries		
15	Aries	10:52 P.M.	Taurus
16	Taurus		
17	Taurus		
18	Taurus	8:43 A.M.	Gemini
19	Gemini		
20	Gemini	3:48 P.M.	Cancer
21	Cancer		
22	Cancer	7:31 P.M.	Leo
23	Leo		
24	Leo	8:21 P.M.	Virgo
25	Virgo		
26	Virgo	7:51 P.M.	Libra
27	Libra		
28	Libra	8:08 P.M.	Scorpio
29	Scorpio		
30	Scorpio	11:10 P.M.	Sagittarius
31	Sagittarius		

APRIL

Day	Sign	Time	Sign
1	Sagittarius		
2	Sagittarius	6:08 A.M.	Capricorn
3	Capricorn		
4	Capricorn	4:45 P.M.	Aquarius
5	Aquarius		
6	Aquarius		
7	Aquarius	5:17 A.M.	Pisces
8	Pisces		
9	Pisces	5:44 P.M.	Aries
10	Aries		
11	Aries		
12	Aries	4:53 A.M.	Taurus
13	Taurus		
14	Taurus	2:14 P.M.	Gemini
15	Gemini		
16	Gemini	9:27 P.M.	Cancer
17	Cancer		
18	Cancer		
19	Cancer	2:14 A.M.	Leo
20	Leo		
21	Leo	4:42 A.M.	Virgo
22	Virgo		
23	Virgo	5:41 A.M.	Libra
24	Libra		
25	Libra	6:39 A.M.	Scorpio
26	Scorpio		
27	Scorpio	9:20 A.M.	Sagittarius
28	Sagittarius		
29	Sagittarius	3:08 P.M.	Capricorn
30	Capricorn		

MAY

Day	Sign	Time	Sign
1	Capricorn		
2	Capricorn	12:34 A.M.	Aquarius
3	Aquarius		
4	Aquarius	12:34 P.M.	Pisces
5	Pisces		
6	Pisces		
7	Pisces	1:03 A.M.	Aries
8	Aries		
9	Aries	12:03 P.M.	Taurus
10	Taurus		
11	Taurus	8:44 P.M.	Gemini
12	Gemini		
13	Gemini		
14	Gemini	3:08 A.M.	Cancer
15	Cancer		
16	Cancer	7:38 A.M.	Leo
17	Leo		
18	Leo	10:45 A.M.	Virgo
19	Virgo		
20	Virgo	1:05 P.M.	Libra
21	Libra		
22	Libra	3:25 P.M.	Scorpio
23	Scorpio		
24	Scorpio	6:51 P.M.	Sagittarius
25	Sagittarius		
26	Sagittarius		
27	Sagittarius	12:31 A.M.	Capricorn
28	Capricorn		
29	Capricorn	9:09 A.M.	Aquarius
30	Aquarius		
31	Aquarius	8:32 P.M.	Pisces

JUNE

Day	Sign	Time	Sign
1	Pisces		
2	Pisces		
3	Pisces	9:01 A.M.	Aries
4	Aries		
5	Aries	8:19 P.M.	Taurus
6	Taurus		
7	Taurus		
8	Taurus	4:49 A.M.	Gemini
9	Gemini		
10	Gemini	10:21 A.M.	Cancer
11	Cancer		
12	Cancer	1:45 P.M.	Leo
13	Leo		
14	Leo	4:11 P.M.	Virgo
15	Virgo		
16	Virgo	6:41 P.M.	Libra
17	Libra		
18	Libra	9:59 P.M.	Scorpio
19	Scorpio		
20	Scorpio		
21	Scorpio	2:34 A.M.	Sagittarius
22	Sagittarius		
23	Sagittarius	8:56 A.M.	Capricorn
24	Capricorn		
25	Capricorn	5:33 P.M.	Aquarius
26	Aquarius		
27	Aquarius		
28	Aquarius	4:33 A.M.	Pisces
29	Pisces		
30	Pisces	5:02 P.M.	Aries

JULY

Day	Sign	Time	Sign
1	Aries		
2	Aries		
3	Aries	4:54 A.M.	Taurus
4	Taurus		
5	Taurus	1:58 P.M.	Gemini
6	Gemini		
7	Gemini	7:23 P.M.	Cancer

8	Cancer		
9	Cancer	9:50 P.M.	Leo
10	Leo		
11	Leo	10:55 P.M.	Virgo
12	Virgo		
13	Virgo		
14	Virgo	12:21 A.M.	Libra
15	Libra		
16	Libra	3:23 A.M.	Scorpio
17	Scorpio		
18	Scorpio	8:32 A.M.	Sagittarius
19	Sagittarius		
20	Sagittarius	3:46 P.M.	Capricorn
21	Capricorn		
22	Capricorn		
23	Capricorn	12:56 A.M.	Aquarius
24	Aquarius		
25	Aquarius	11:58 A.M.	Pisces
26	Pisces		
27	Pisces		
28	Pisces	12:27 A.M.	Aries
29	Aries		
30	Aries	12:53 P.M.	Taurus
31	Taurus		

AUGUST

1	Taurus	11:02 P.M.	Gemini
2	Gemini		
3	Gemini		
4	Gemini	5:17 A.M.	Cancer
5	Cancer		
6	Cancer	7:44 A.M.	Leo
7	Leo		
8	Leo	7:53 A.M.	Virgo
9	Virgo		
10	Virgo	7:51 A.M.	Libra
11	Libra		
12	Libra	9:30 A.M.	Scorpio
13	Scorpio		
14	Scorpio	1:59 P.M.	Sagittarius
15	Sagittarius		
16	Sagittarius	9:25 P.M.	Capricorn
17	Capricorn		
18	Capricorn		
19	Capricorn	7:09 A.M.	Aquarius
20	Aquarius		
21	Aquarius	6:32 P.M.	Pisces
22	Pisces		
23	Pisces		
24	Pisces	7:02 A.M.	Aries
25	Aries		
26	Aries	7:45 P.M.	Taurus
27	Taurus		
28	Taurus		
29	Taurus	6:53 A.M.	Gemini
30	Gemini		
31	Gemini	2:35 P.M.	Cancer

SEPTEMBER

1	Cancer		
2	Cancer	6:08 P.M.	Leo
3	Leo		
4	Leo	6:29 P.M.	Virgo
5	Virgo		
6	Virgo	5:38 P.M.	Libra
7	Libra		
8	Libra	5:46 P.M.	Scorpio
9	Scorpio		
10	Scorpio	8:41 P.M.	Sagittarius
11	Sagittarius		
12	Sagittarius		
13	Sagittarius	3:11 A.M.	Capricorn
14	Capricorn		
15	Capricorn	12:51 P.M.	Aquarius
16	Aquarius		
17	Aquarius		
18	Aquarius	12:32 A.M.	Pisces
19	Pisces		
20	Pisces	1:07 P.M.	Aries
21	Aries		
22	Aries		
23	Aries	1:43 A.M.	Taurus
24	Taurus		
25	Taurus	1:13 P.M.	Gemini
26	Gemini		
27	Gemini	10:07 P.M.	Cancer
28	Cancer		
29	Cancer		
30	Cancer	3:20 A.M.	Leo

OCTOBER

1	Leo		
2	Leo	5:03 A.M.	Virgo
3	Virgo		
4	Virgo	4:39 A.M.	Libra
5	Libra		
6	Libra	4:09 A.M.	Scorpio
7	Scorpio		
8	Scorpio	5:35 A.M.	Sagittarius
9	Sagittarius		
10	Sagittarius	10:29 A.M.	Capricorn
11	Capricorn		
12	Capricorn	7:10 P.M.	Aquarius
13	Aquarius		
14	Aquarius		
15	Aquarius	6:40 A.M.	Pisces
16	Pisces		
17	Pisces	7:20 P.M.	Aries
18	Aries		
19	Aries		
20	Aries	7:43 A.M.	Taurus
21	Taurus		
22	Taurus	6:51 P.M.	Gemini
23	Gemini		
24	Gemini		
25	Gemini	3:57 A.M.	Cancer
26	Cancer		
27	Cancer	10:20 A.M.	Leo
28	Leo		
29	Leo	1:47 P.M.	Virgo
30	Virgo		
31	Virgo	2:55 P.M.	Libra

NOVEMBER

1	Libra		
2	Libra	3:07 P.M.	Scorpio
3	Scorpio		
4	Scorpio	4:10 P.M.	Sagittarius
5	Sagittarius		
6	Sagittarius	7:45 P.M.	Capricorn
7	Capricorn		
8	Capricorn		
9	Capricorn	2:59 A.M.	Aquarius
10	Aquarius		
11	Aquarius	1:42 P.M.	Pisces
12	Pisces		
13	Pisces		
14	Pisces	2:17 A.M.	Aries
15	Aries		
16	Aries	2:38 P.M.	Taurus
17	Taurus		
18	Taurus		
19	Taurus	1:14 A.M.	Gemini
20	Gemini		
21	Gemini	9:36 A.M.	Cancer
22	Cancer		
23	Cancer	3:48 P.M.	Leo
24	Leo		
25	Leo	8:04 P.M.	Virgo
26	Virgo		
27	Virgo	10:48 P.M.	Libra
28	Libra		
29	Libra		
30	Libra	12:37 A.M.	Scorpio

DECEMBER

1	Scorpio		
2	Scorpio	2:33 A.M.	Sagittarius
3	Sagittarius		
4	Sagittarius	5:58 A.M.	Capricorn
5	Capricorn		
6	Capricorn	12:12 P.M.	Aquarius
7	Aquarius		
8	Aquarius	9:52 P.M.	Pisces
9	Pisces		
10	Pisces		
11	Pisces	10:06 A.M.	Aries
12	Aries		
13	Aries	10:39 P.M.	Taurus
14	Taurus		
15	Taurus		
16	Taurus	9:12 A.M.	Gemini
17	Gemini		
18	Gemini	4:49 P.M.	Cancer
19	Cancer		
20	Cancer	9:54 P.M.	Leo
21	Leo		
22	Leo		
23	Leo	1:28 A.M.	Virgo
24	Virgo		
25	Virgo	4:27 A.M.	Libra
26	Libra		
27	Libra	7:28 A.M.	Scorpio
28	Scorpio		
29	Scorpio	10:53 A.M.	Sagittarius
30	Sagittarius		
31	Sagittarius	3:16 P.M.	Capricorn

MOON SIGN TABLES
1976

JANUARY

1	Capricorn		
2	Capricorn	9:33 P.M.	Aquarius
3	Aquarius		
4	Aquarius		
5	Aquarius	6:35 A.M.	Pisces
6	Pisces		
7	Pisces	6:21 P.M.	Aries
8	Aries		
9	Aries		
10	Aries	7:10 A.M.	Taurus
11	Taurus		
12	Taurus	6:19 P.M.	Gemini
13	Gemini		
14	Gemini		
15	Gemini	2:00 A.M.	Cancer
16	Cancer		
17	Cancer	6:15 A.M.	Leo
18	Leo		
19	Leo	8:25 A.M.	Virgo
20	Virgo		
21	Virgo	10:11 A.M.	Libra
22	Libra		
23	Libra	12:48 P.M.	Scorpio
24	Scorpio		
25	Scorpio	4:51 P.M.	Sagittarius
26	Sagittarius		
27	Sagittarius	10:24 P.M.	Capricorn
28	Capricorn		
29	Capricorn		
30	Capricorn	5:34 A.M.	Aquarius
31	Aquarius		

FEBRUARY

1	Aquarius	2:47 P.M.	Pisces
2	Pisces		
3	Pisces		
4	Pisces	2:17 A.M.	Aries
5	Aries		
6	Aries	3:13 P.M.	Taurus
7	Taurus		
8	Taurus		
9	Taurus	3:16 A.M.	Gemini
10	Gemini		
11	Gemini	11:59 A.M.	Cancer
12	Cancer		
13	Cancer	4:32 P.M.	Leo
14	Leo		
15	Leo	5:59 P.M.	Virgo
16	Virgo		
17	Virgo	6:14 P.M.	Libra
18	Libra		
19	Libra	7:14 P.M.	Scorpio
20	Scorpio		
21	Scorpio	10:18 P.M.	Sagittarius
22	Sagittarius		
23	Sagittarius		
24	Sagittarius	3:54 A.M.	Capricorn
25	Capricorn		
26	Capricorn	11:48 A.M.	Aquarius
27	Aquarius		
28	Aquarius	9:42 P.M.	Pisces
29	Pisces		

MARCH

1	Pisces		
2	Pisces	9:22 A.M.	Aries
3	Aries		
4	Aries	10:18 P.M.	Taurus
5	Taurus		
6	Taurus		
7	Taurus	10:56 A.M.	Gemini
8	Gemini		
9	Gemini	8:59 P.M.	Cancer
10	Cancer		
11	Cancer		
12	Cancer	2:55 A.M.	Leo
13	Leo		
14	Leo	4:59 A.M.	Virgo
15	Virgo		
16	Virgo	4:44 A.M.	Libra
17	Libra		
18	Libra	4:18 A.M.	Scorpio
19	Scorpio		
20	Scorpio	5:34 A.M.	Sagittarius
21	Sagittarius		
22	Sagittarius	9:48 A.M.	Capricorn
23	Capricorn		
24	Capricorn	5:19 P.M.	Aquarius
25	Aquarius		
26	Aquarius		
27	Aquarius	3:34 A.M.	Pisces
28	Pisces		
29	Pisces	3:37 P.M.	Aries
30	Aries		
31	Aries		

APRIL

1	Aries	4:34 A.M.	Taurus
2	Taurus		
3	Taurus	5:15 P.M.	Gemini
4	Gemini		
5	Gemini		
6	Gemini	4:06 A.M.	Cancer
7	Cancer		
8	Cancer	11:36 A.M.	Leo
9	Leo		
10	Leo	3:16 P.M.	Virgo
11	Virgo		
12	Virgo	3:54 P.M.	Libra
13	Libra		
14	Libra	3:14 P.M.	Scorpio
15	Scorpio		
16	Scorpio	3:15 P.M.	Sagittarius
17	Sagittarius		
18	Sagittarius	5:43 P.M.	Capricorn
19	Capricorn		
20	Capricorn	11:47 P.M.	Aquarius
21	Aquarius		
22	Aquarius		
23	Aquarius	9:28 A.M.	Pisces
24	Pisces		
25	Pisces	9:37 P.M.	Aries
26	Aries		
27	Aries		
28	Aries	10:37 A.M.	Taurus
29	Taurus		
30	Taurus	11:05 P.M.	Gemini

MAY

1	Gemini		
2	Gemini		
3	Gemini	9:53 A.M.	Cancer
4	Cancer		

MAY (continued)

5	Cancer	6:09 P.M.	Leo
6	Leo		
7	Leo	11:21 P.M.	Virgo
8	Virgo		
9	Virgo		
10	Virgo	1:39 A.M.	Libra
11	Libra		
12	Libra	2:03 A.M.	Scorpio
13	Scorpio		
14	Scorpio	2:04 A.M.	Sagittarius
15	Sagittarius		
16	Sagittarius	3:31 A.M.	Capricorn
17	Capricorn		
18	Capricorn	8:02 A.M.	Aquarius
19	Aquarius		
20	Aquarius	4:27 P.M.	Pisces
21	Pisces		
22	Pisces		
23	Pisces	4:07 A.M.	Aries
24	Aries		
25	Aries	5:07 P.M.	Taurus
26	Taurus		
27	Taurus		
28	Taurus	5:22 A.M.	Gemini
29	Gemini		
30	Gemini	3:39 P.M.	Cancer
31	Cancer		

JUNE

1	Cancer	11:37 P.M.	Leo
2	Leo		
3	Leo		
4	Leo	5:21 A.M.	Virgo
5	Virgo		
6	Virgo	9:00 A.M.	Libra
7	Libra		
8	Libra	10:58 A.M.	Scorpio
9	Scorpio		
10	Scorpio	12:07 P.M.	Sagittarius
11	Sagittarius		
12	Sagittarius	1:45 P.M.	Capricorn
13	Capricorn		
14	Capricorn	5:31 P.M.	Aquarius
15	Aquarius		
16	Aquarius		
17	Aquarius	12:43 A.M.	Pisces
18	Pisces		
19	Pisces	11:32 A.M.	Aries
20	Aries		
21	Aries		
22	Aries	12:21 A.M.	Taurus
23	Taurus		
24	Taurus	12:37 P.M.	Gemini
25	Gemini		
26	Gemini	10:29 P.M.	Cancer
27	Cancer		
28	Cancer		
29	Cancer	5:39 A.M.	Leo
30	Leo		

JULY

1	Leo	10:46 A.M.	Virgo
2	Virgo		
3	Virgo	2:34 P.M.	Libra
4	Libra		
5	Libra	5:33 P.M.	Scorpio
6	Scorpio		

7	Scorpio	8:05 P.M.	Sagittarius
8	Sagittarius		
9	Sagittarius	10:49 P.M.	Capricorn
10	Capricorn		
11	Capricorn		
12	Capricorn	2:53 A.M.	Aquarius
13	Aquarius		
14	Aquarius	9:36 A.M.	Pisces
15	Pisces		
16	Pisces	7:40 P.M.	Aries
17	Aries		
18	Aries		
19	Aries	8:11 A.M.	Taurus
20	Taurus		
21	Taurus	8:40 P.M.	Gemini
22	Gemini		
23	Gemini		
24	Gemini	6:39 A.M.	Cancer
25	Cancer		
26	Cancer	1:18 P.M.	Leo
27	Leo		
28	Leo	5:23 P.M.	Virgo
29	Virgo		
30	Virgo	8:13 P.M.	Libra
31	Libra		

AUGUST

1	Libra	10:55 P.M.	Scorpio
2	Scorpio		
3	Scorpio		
4	Scorpio	2:03 A.M.	Sagittarius
5	Sagittarius		
6	Sagittarius	5:54 A.M.	Capricorn
7	Capricorn		
8	Capricorn	10:57 A.M.	Aquarius
9	Aquarius		
10	Aquarius	6:00 P.M.	Pisces
11	Pisces		
12	Pisces		
13	Pisces	3:49 A.M.	Aries
14	Aries		
15	Aries	4:05 P.M.	Taurus
16	Taurus		
17	Taurus		
18	Taurus	4:54 A.M.	Gemini
19	Gemini		
20	Gemini	3:34 P.M.	Cancer
21	Cancer		
22	Cancer	10:31 P.M.	Leo
23	Leo		
24	Leo		
25	Leo	2:04 A.M.	Virgo
26	Virgo		
27	Virgo	3:42 A.M.	Libra
28	Libra		
29	Libra	5:05 A.M.	Scorpio
30	Scorpio		
31	Scorpio	7:28 A.M.	Sagittarius

SEPTEMBER

1	Sagittarius		
2	Sagittarius	11:29 A.M.	Capricorn
3	Capricorn		
4	Capricorn	5:20 P.M.	Aquarius
5	Aquarius		
6	Aquarius		
7	Aquarius	1:11 A.M.	Pisces
8	Pisces		
9	Pisces	11:18 A.M.	Aries
10	Aries		
11	Aries	11:30 P.M.	Taurus
12	Taurus		
13	Taurus		
14	Taurus	12:32 P.M.	Gemini
15	Gemini		
16	Gemini		
17	Gemini	12:07 A.M.	Cancer
18	Cancer		
19	Cancer	8:10 A.M.	Leo
20	Leo		
21	Leo	12:16 P.M.	Virgo
22	Virgo		
23	Virgo	1:28 P.M.	Libra
24	Libra		
25	Libra	1:34 P.M.	Scorpio
26	Scorpio		
27	Scorpio	2:22 P.M.	Sagittarius
28	Sagittarius		
29	Sagittarius	5:13 P.M.	Capricorn
30	Capricorn		

OCTOBER

1	Capricorn	10:49 P.M.	Aquarius
2	Aquarius		
3	Aquarius		
4	Aquarius	7:10 A.M.	Pisces
5	Pisces		
6	Pisces	5:50 P.M.	Aries
7	Aries		
8	Aries		
9	Aries	6:11 A.M.	Taurus
10	Taurus		
11	Taurus	7:14 P.M.	Gemini
12	Gemini		
13	Gemini		
14	Gemini	7:24 A.M.	Cancer
15	Cancer		
16	Cancer	4:49 P.M.	Leo
17	Leo		
18	Leo	10:25 P.M.	Virgo
19	Virgo		
20	Virgo		
21	Virgo	12:26 A.M.	Libra
22	Libra		
23	Libra	12:17 A.M.	Scorpio
24	Scorpio	11:49 P.M.	Sagittarius
25	Sagittarius		
26	Sagittarius		
27	Sagittarius	12:55 A.M.	Capricorn
28	Capricorn		
29	Capricorn	5:05 A.M.	Aquarius
30	Aquarius		
31	Aquarius	12:53 P.M.	Pisces

NOVEMBER

1	Pisces		
2	Pisces	11:46 P.M.	Aries
3	Aries		
4	Aries		
5	Aries	12:23 P.M.	Taurus
6	Taurus		
7	Taurus		
8	Taurus	1:21 A.M.	Gemini
9	Gemini		
10	Gemini	1:28 P.M.	Cancer
11	Cancer		
12	Cancer	11:36 P.M.	Leo
13	Leo		
14	Leo		
15	Leo	6:46 A.M.	Virgo
16	Virgo		
17	Virgo	10:34 A.M.	Libra
18	Libra		
19	Libra	11:31 A.M.	Scorpio
20	Scorpio		
21	Scorpio	11:03 A.M.	Sagittarius
22	Sagittarius		
23	Sagittarius	11:03 A.M.	Capricorn
24	Capricorn		
25	Capricorn	1:30 P.M.	Aquarius
26	Aquarius		
27	Aquarius	7:47 P.M.	Pisces
28	Pisces		
29	Pisces		
30	Pisces	6:01 A.M.	Aries

DECEMBER

1	Aries		
2	Aries	6:41 P.M.	Taurus
3	Taurus		
4	Taurus		
5	Taurus	7:38 A.M.	Gemini
6	Gemini		
7	Gemini	7:21 P.M.	Cancer
8	Cancer		
9	Cancer		
10	Cancer	5:12 A.M.	Leo
11	Leo		
12	Leo	12:55 P.M.	Virgo
13	Virgo		
14	Virgo	6:13 P.M.	Libra
15	Libra		
16	Libra	9:01 P.M.	Scorpio
17	Scorpio		
18	Scorpio	9:54 P.M.	Sagittarius
19	Sagittarius		
20	Sagittarius	10:12 P.M.	Capricorn
21	Capricorn		
22	Capricorn	11:48 P.M.	Aquarius
23	Aquarius		
24	Aquarius		
25	Aquarius	4:36 A.M.	Pisces
26	Pisces		
27	Pisces	1:32 P.M.	Aries
28	Aries		
29	Aries		
30	Aries	1:43 A.M.	Taurus
31	Taurus		

MOON SIGN TABLES
1977

JANUARY

1	Taurus	2:43 P.M.	Gemini
2	Gemini		
3	Gemini		
4	Gemini	2:12 A.M.	Cancer
5	Cancer		
6	Cancer	11:20 A.M.	Leo
7	Leo		
8	Leo	6:23 P.M.	Virgo
9	Virgo		
10	Virgo	11:48 P.M.	Libra
11	Libra		
12	Libra		
13	Libra	3:44 A.M.	Scorpio
14	Scorpio		
15	Scorpio	6:18 A.M.	Sagittarius
16	Sagittarius		
17	Sagittarius	8:02 A.M.	Capricorn
18	Capricorn		
19	Capricorn	10:12 A.M.	Aquarius
20	Aquarius		
21	Aquarius	2:30 P.M.	Pisces
22	Pisces		
23	Pisces	10:20 P.M.	Aries
24	Aries		
25	Aries		
26	Aries	9:41 A.M.	Taurus
27	Taurus		
28	Taurus	10:37 P.M.	Gemini
29	Gemini		
30	Gemini		
31	Gemini	10:20 A.M.	Cancer

FEBRUARY

1	Cancer		
2	Cancer	7:11 P.M.	Leo
3	Leo		
4	Leo		
5	Leo	1:17 A.M.	Virgo
6	Virgo		
7	Virgo	5:36 A.M.	Libra
8	Libra		
9	Libra	9:04 A.M.	Scorpio
10	Scorpio		
11	Scorpio	12:11 P.M.	Sagittarius
12	Sagittarius		
13	Sagittarius	3:14 P.M.	Capricorn
14	Capricorn		
15	Capricorn	6:45 P.M.	Aquarius
16	Aquarius		
17	Aquarius	11:45 P.M.	Pisces
18	Pisces		
19	Pisces		
20	Pisces	7:22 A.M.	Aries
21	Aries		
22	Aries	6:06 P.M.	Taurus
23	Taurus		
24	Taurus		
25	Taurus	6:50 A.M.	Gemini
26	Gemini		
27	Gemini	7:02 P.M.	Cancer
28	Cancer		

MARCH

1	Cancer		
2	Cancer	4:25 A.M.	Leo
3	Leo		
4	Leo	10:19 A.M.	Virgo
5	Virgo		
6	Virgo	1:34 P.M.	Libra
7	Libra		
8	Libra	3:37 P.M.	Scorpio
9	Scorpio		
10	Scorpio	5:42 P.M.	Sagittarius
11	Sagittarius		
12	Sagittarius	8:40 P.M.	Capricorn
13	Capricorn		
14	Capricorn		
15	Capricorn	1:00 A.M.	Aquarius
16	Aquarius		
17	Aquarius	7:06 A.M.	Pisces
18	Pisces		
19	Pisces	3:23 P.M.	Aries
20	Aries		
21	Aries		
22	Aries	2:05 A.M.	Taurus
23	Taurus		
24	Taurus	2:39 P.M.	Gemini
25	Gemini		
26	Gemini		
27	Gemini	3:16 A.M.	Cancer
28	Cancer		
29	Cancer	1:40 P.M.	Leo
30	Leo		
31	Leo	8:25 P.M.	Virgo

APRIL

1	Virgo		
2	Virgo	11:39 P.M.	Libra
3	Libra		
4	Libra		
5	Libra	12:40 A.M.	Scorpio
6	Scorpio		
7	Scorpio	1:09 A.M.	Sagittarius
8	Sagittarius		
9	Sagittarius	2:40 A.M.	Capricorn
10	Capricorn		
11	Capricorn	6:24 A.M.	Aquarius
12	Aquarius		
13	Aquarius	12:49 P.M.	Pisces
14	Pisces		
15	Pisces	9:52 P.M.	Aries
16	Aries		
17	Aries		
18	Aries	9:02 A.M.	Taurus
19	Taurus		
20	Taurus	9:37 P.M.	Gemini
21	Gemini		
22	Gemini		
23	Gemini	10:25 A.M.	Cancer
24	Cancer		
25	Cancer	9:43 P.M.	Leo
26	Leo		
27	Leo		
28	Leo	5:52 A.M.	Virgo
29	Virgo		
30	Virgo	10:12 A.M.	Libra

MAY

1	Libra		
2	Libra	11:23 A.M.	Scorpio
3	Scorpio		
4	Scorpio	10:59 A.M.	Sagittarius
5	Sagittarius		
6	Sagittarius	10:54 A.M.	Capricorn
7	Capricorn		
8	Capricorn	1:00 P.M.	Aquarius
9	Aquarius		
10	Aquarius	6:29 P.M.	Pisces
11	Pisces		
12	Pisces		
13	Pisces	3:29 A.M.	Aries
14	Aries		
15	Aries	3:04 P.M.	Taurus
16	Taurus		
17	Taurus		
18	Taurus	3:50 A.M.	Gemini
19	Gemini		
20	Gemini	4:35 P.M.	Cancer
21	Cancer		
22	Cancer		
23	Cancer	4:13 A.M.	Leo
24	Leo		
25	Leo	1:31 P.M.	Virgo
26	Virgo		
27	Virgo	7:28 P.M.	Libra
28	Libra		
29	Libra	9:57 P.M.	Scorpio
30	Scorpio		
31	Scorpio	9:54 P.M.	Sagittarius

JUNE

1	Sagittarius		
2	Sagittarius	9:07 P.M.	Capricorn
3	Capricorn		
4	Capricorn	9:44 P.M.	Aquarius
5	Aquarius		
6	Aquarius		
7	Aquarius	1:35 A.M.	Pisces
8	Pisces		
9	Pisces	9:34 A.M.	Aries
10	Aries		
11	Aries	8:56 P.M.	Taurus
12	Taurus		
13	Taurus		
14	Taurus	9:50 A.M.	Gemini
15	Gemini		
16	Gemini	10:28 P.M.	Cancer
17	Cancer		
18	Cancer		
19	Cancer	9:53 A.M.	Leo
20	Leo		
21	Leo	7:29 P.M.	Virgo
22	Virgo		
23	Virgo		
24	Virgo	2:35 A.M.	Libra
25	Libra		
26	Libra	6:42 A.M.	Scorpio
27	Scorpio		
28	Scorpio	8:02 A.M.	Sagittarius
29	Sagittarius		
30	Sagittarius	7:48 A.M.	Capricorn

JULY

1	Capricorn		
2	Capricorn	7:56 A.M.	Aquarius
3	Aquarius		
4	Aquarius	10:31 A.M.	Pisces
5	Pisces		
6	Pisces	5:03 P.M.	Aries
7	Aries		

8	Aries		
9	Aries	3:33 A.M.	Taurus
10	Taurus		
11	Taurus	4:15 P.M.	Gemini
12	Gemini		
13	Gemini		
14	Gemini	4:50 A.M.	Cancer
15	Cancer		
16	Cancer	3:51 P.M.	Leo
17	Leo		
18	Leo		
19	Leo	12:58 A.M.	Virgo
20	Virgo		
21	Virgo	8:09 A.M.	Libra
22	Libra		
23	Libra	1:13 P.M.	Scorpio
24	Scorpio		
25	Scorpio	4:04 P.M.	Sagittarius
26	Sagittarius		
27	Sagittarius	5:15 P.M.	Capricorn
28	Capricorn		
29	Capricorn	6:04 P.M.	Aquarius
30	Aquarius		
31	Aquarius	8:23 P.M.	Pisces

AUGUST

1	Pisces		
2	Pisces		
3	Pisces	1:54 A.M.	Aries
4	Aries		
5	Aries	11:18 A.M.	Taurus
6	Taurus		
7	Taurus	11:29 P.M.	Gemini
8	Gemini		
9	Gemini		
10	Gemini	12:04 P.M.	Cancer
11	Cancer		
12	Cancer	10:57 P.M.	Leo
13	Leo		
14	Leo		
15	Leo	7:26 A.M.	Virgo
16	Virgo		
17	Virgo	1:49 P.M.	Libra
18	Libra		
19	Libra	6:35 P.M.	Scorpio
20	Scorpio		
21	Scorpio	10:03 P.M.	Sagittarius
22	Sagittarius		
23	Sagittarius		
24	Sagittarius	12:30 A.M.	Capricorn
25	Capricorn		
26	Capricorn	2:41 A.M.	Aquarius
27	Aquarius		
28	Aquarius	5:46 A.M.	Pisces
29	Pisces		
30	Pisces	11:11 A.M.	Aries
31	Aries		

SEPTEMBER

1	Aries	7:52 P.M.	Taurus
2	Taurus		
3	Taurus		
4	Taurus	7:27 A.M.	Gemini
5	Gemini		
6	Gemini	8:03 P.M.	Cancer
7	Cancer		
8	Cancer		
9	Cancer	7:14 A.M.	Leo
10	Leo		
11	Leo	3:34 P.M.	Virgo
12	Virgo		
13	Virgo	9:07 P.M.	Libra
14	Libra		
15	Libra		
16	Libra	12:45 A.M.	Scorpio
17	Scorpio		
18	Scorpio	3:28 A.M.	Sagittarius
19	Sagittarius		
20	Sagittarius	6:04 A.M.	Capricorn
21	Capricorn		
22	Capricorn	9:12 A.M.	Aquarius
23	Aquarius		
24	Aquarius	1:30 P.M.	Pisces
25	Pisces		
26	Pisces	7:40 P.M.	Aries
27	Aries		
28	Aries		
29	Aries	4:21 A.M.	Taurus
30	Taurus		

OCTOBER

1	Taurus	3:33 P.M.	Gemini
2	Gemini		
3	Gemini		
4	Gemini	4:09 A.M.	Cancer
5	Cancer		
6	Cancer	3:58 P.M.	Leo
7	Leo		
8	Leo		
9	Leo	12:59 A.M.	Virgo
10	Virgo		
11	Virgo	6:29 A.M.	Libra
12	Libra		
13	Libra	9:11 A.M.	Scorpio
14	Scorpio		
15	Scorpio	10:27 A.M.	Sagittarius
16	Sagittarius		
17	Sagittarius	11:51 A.M.	Capricorn
18	Capricorn		
19	Capricorn	2:36 P.M.	Aquarius
20	Aquarius		
21	Aquarius	7:26 P.M.	Pisces
22	Pisces		
23	Pisces		
24	Pisces	2:34 A.M.	Aries
25	Aries		
26	Aries	11:53 A.M.	Taurus
27	Taurus		
28	Taurus	11:08 P.M.	Gemini
29	Gemini		
30	Gemini		
31	Gemini	11:40 A.M.	Cancer

NOVEMBER

1	Cancer		
2	Cancer		
3	Cancer	12:03 A.M.	Leo
4	Leo		
5	Leo	10:17 A.M.	Virgo
6	Virgo		
7	Virgo	4:51 P.M.	Libra
8	Libra		
9	Libra	7:42 P.M.	Scorpio
10	Scorpio		
11	Scorpio	8:03 P.M.	Sagittarius
12	Sagittarius		
13	Sagittarius	7:50 P.M.	Capricorn
14	Capricorn		
15	Capricorn	9:00 P.M.	Aquarius
16	Aquarius		
17	Aquarius		
18	Aquarius	12:58 A.M.	Pisces
19	Pisces		
20	Pisces	8:13 A.M.	Aries
21	Aries		
22	Aries	6:09 P.M.	Taurus
23	Taurus		
24	Taurus		
25	Taurus	5:48 A.M.	Gemini
26	Gemini		
27	Gemini	6:20 P.M.	Cancer
28	Cancer		
29	Cancer		
30	Cancer	6:53 A.M.	Leo

DECEMBER

1	Leo		
2	Leo	6:05 P.M.	Virgo
3	Virgo		
4	Virgo		
5	Virgo	2:18 A.M.	Libra
6	Libra		
7	Libra	6:33 A.M.	Scorpio
8	Scorpio		
9	Scorpio	7:22 A.M.	Sagittarius
10	Sagittarius		
11	Sagittarius	6:26 A.M.	Capricorn
12	Capricorn		
13	Capricorn	5:59 A.M.	Aquarius
14	Aquarius		
15	Aquarius	8:09 A.M.	Pisces
16	Pisces		
17	Pisces	2:11 P.M.	Aries
18	Aries		
19	Aries	11:54 P.M.	Taurus
20	Taurus		
21	Taurus		
22	Taurus	11:51 A.M.	Gemini
23	Gemini		
24	Gemini		
25	Gemini	12:30 A.M.	Cancer
26	Cancer		
27	Cancer	12:52 P.M.	Leo
28	Leo		
29	Leo		
30	Leo	12:13 A.M.	Virgo
31	Virgo		

MOON SIGN TABLES
1978

JANUARY

Day	Sign	Time	Ingress
1	Virgo	9:31 A.M.	Libra
2	Libra		
3	Libra	3:35 P.M.	Scorpio
4	Scorpio		
5	Scorpio	6:03 P.M.	Sagittarius
6	Sagittarius		
7	Sagittarius	5:55 P.M.	Capricorn
8	Capricorn		
9	Capricorn	5:05 P.M.	Aquarius
10	Aquarius		
11	Aquarius	5:50 P.M.	Pisces
12	Pisces		
13	Pisces	10:05 P.M.	Aries
14	Aries		
15	Aries		
16	Aries	6:30 A.M.	Taurus
17	Taurus		
18	Taurus	6:06 P.M.	Gemini
19	Gemini		
20	Gemini		
21	Gemini	6:50 A.M.	Cancer
22	Cancer		
23	Cancer	7:02 P.M.	Leo
24	Leo		
25	Leo		
26	Leo	5:56 A.M.	Virgo
27	Virgo		
28	Virgo	3:08 P.M.	Libra
29	Libra		
30	Libra	10:04 P.M.	Scorpio
31	Scorpio		

FEBRUARY

Day	Sign	Time	Ingress
1	Scorpio		
2	Scorpio	2:13 A.M.	Sagittarius
3	Sagittarius		
4	Sagittarius	3:50 A.M.	Capricorn
5	Capricorn		
6	Capricorn	4:04 A.M.	Aquarius
7	Aquarius		
8	Aquarius	4:47 A.M.	Pisces
9	Pisces		
10	Pisces	7:56 A.M.	Aries
11	Aries		
12	Aries	2:50 P.M.	Taurus
13	Taurus		
14	Taurus		
15	Taurus	1:24 A.M.	Gemini
16	Gemini		
17	Gemini	1:56 P.M.	Cancer
18	Cancer		
19	Cancer		
20	Cancer	2:09 A.M.	Leo
21	Leo		
22	Leo	12:39 P.M.	Virgo
23	Virgo		
24	Virgo	9:03 P.M.	Libra
25	Libra		
26	Libra		
27	Libra	3:28 A.M.	Scorpio
28	Scorpio		

MARCH

Day	Sign	Time	Ingress
1	Scorpio	8:02 A.M.	Sagittarius
2	Sagittarius		
3	Sagittarius	10:58 A.M.	Capricorn
4	Capricorn		
5	Capricorn	12:51 P.M.	Aquarius
6	Aquarius		
7	Aquarius	2:46 P.M.	Pisces
8	Pisces		
9	Pisces	6:08 P.M.	Aries
10	Aries		
11	Aries		
12	Aries	12:18 A.M.	Taurus
13	Taurus		
14	Taurus	9:48 A.M.	Gemini
15	Gemini		
16	Gemini	9:49 P.M.	Cancer
17	Cancer		
18	Cancer		
19	Cancer	10:12 A.M.	Leo
20	Leo		
21	Leo	8:49 P.M.	Virgo
22	Virgo		
23	Virgo		
24	Virgo	4:41 A.M.	Libra
25	Libra		
26	Libra	10:01 A.M.	Scorpio
27	Scorpio		
28	Scorpio	1:37 P.M.	Sagittarius
29	Sagittarius		
30	Sagittarius	4:23 P.M.	Capricorn
31	Capricorn		

APRIL

Day	Sign	Time	Ingress
1	Capricorn	7:05 P.M.	Aquarius
2	Aquarius		
3	Aquarius	10:20 P.M.	Pisces
4	Pisces		
5	Pisces		
6	Pisces	2:51 A.M.	Aries
7	Aries		
8	Aries	9:21 A.M.	Taurus
9	Taurus		
10	Taurus	6:27 P.M.	Gemini
11	Gemini		
12	Gemini		
13	Gemini	5:59 A.M.	Cancer
14	Cancer		
15	Cancer	6:30 P.M.	Leo
16	Leo		
17	Leo		
18	Leo	5:44 A.M.	Virgo
19	Virgo		
20	Virgo	1:53 P.M.	Libra
21	Libra		
22	Libra	6:39 P.M.	Scorpio
23	Scorpio		
24	Scorpio	9:00 P.M.	Sagittarius
25	Sagittarius		
26	Sagittarius	10:27 P.M.	Capricorn
27	Capricorn		
28	Capricorn		
29	Capricorn	12:28 A.M.	Aquarius
30	Aquarius		

MAY

Day	Sign	Time	Ingress
1	Aquarius	4:00 A.M.	Pisces
2	Pisces		
3	Pisces	9:27 A.M.	Aries
4	Aries		
5	Aries	4:52 P.M.	Taurus
6	Taurus		
7	Taurus		
8	Taurus	2:18 A.M.	Gemini
9	Gemini		
10	Gemini	1:41 P.M.	Cancer
11	Cancer		
12	Cancer		
13	Cancer	2:17 A.M.	Leo
14	Leo		
15	Leo	2:15 P.M.	Virgo
16	Virgo		
17	Virgo	11:24 P.M.	Libra
18	Libra		
19	Libra		
20	Libra	4:39 A.M.	Scorpio
21	Scorpio		
22	Scorpio	6:31 A.M.	Sagittarius
23	Sagittarius		
24	Sagittarius	6:41 A.M.	Capricorn
25	Capricorn		
26	Capricorn	7:10 A.M.	Aquarius
27	Aquarius		
28	Aquarius	9:36 A.M.	Pisces
29	Pisces		
30	Pisces	2:52 P.M.	Aries
31	Aries		

JUNE

Day	Sign	Time	Ingress
1	Aries	10:50 P.M.	Taurus
2	Taurus		
3	Taurus		
4	Taurus	8:53 A.M.	Gemini
5	Gemini		
6	Gemini	8:30 P.M.	Cancer
7	Cancer		
8	Cancer		
9	Cancer	9:07 A.M.	Leo
10	Leo		
11	Leo	9:35 P.M.	Virgo
12	Virgo		
13	Virgo		
14	Virgo	7:55 A.M.	Libra
15	Libra		
16	Libra	2:28 P.M.	Scorpio
17	Scorpio		
18	Scorpio	5:01 P.M.	Sagittarius
19	Sagittarius		
20	Sagittarius	4:52 P.M.	Capricorn
21	Capricorn		
22	Capricorn	4:07 P.M.	Aquarius
23	Aquarius		
24	Aquarius	4:57 P.M.	Pisces
25	Pisces		
26	Pisces	8:53 P.M.	Aries
27	Aries		
28	Aries		
29	Aries	4:21 A.M.	Taurus
30	Taurus		

JULY

Day	Sign	Time	Ingress
1	Taurus	2:37 P.M.	Gemini
2	Gemini		
3	Gemini		
4	Gemini	2:33 A.M.	Cancer
5	Cancer		
6	Cancer	3:13 P.M.	Leo
7	Leo		

8	Leo		
9	Leo	3:44 A.M.	Virgo
10	Virgo		
11	Virgo	2:48 P.M.	Libra
12	Libra		
13	Libra	10:47 P.M.	Scorpio
14	Scorpio		
15	Scorpio		
16	Scorpio	2:50 A.M.	Sagittarius
17	Sagittarius		
18	Sagittarius	3:33 A.M.	Capricorn
19	Capricorn		
20	Capricorn	2:41 A.M.	Aquarius
21	Aquarius		
22	Aquarius	2:26 A.M.	Pisces
23	Pisces		
24	Pisces	4:46 A.M.	Aries
25	Aries		
26	Aries	10:50 A.M.	Taurus
27	Taurus		
28	Taurus	8:31 P.M.	Gemini
29	Gemini		
30	Gemini		
31	Gemini	8:28 A.M.	Cancer

AUGUST

1	Cancer		
2	Cancer	9:10 P.M.	Leo
3	Leo		
4	Leo		
5	Leo	9:29 A.M.	Virgo
6	Virgo		
7	Virgo	8:30 P.M.	Libra
8	Libra		
9	Libra		
10	Libra	5:11 A.M.	Scorpio
11	Scorpio		
12	Scorpio	10:43 A.M.	Sagittarius
13	Sagittarius		
14	Sagittarius	1:03 P.M.	Capricorn
15	Capricorn		
16	Capricorn	1:15 P.M.	Aquarius
17	Aquarius		
18	Aquarius	1:04 P.M.	Pisces
19	Pisces		
20	Pisces	2:29 P.M.	Aries
21	Aries		
22	Aries	7:06 P.M.	Taurus
23	Taurus		
24	Taurus		
25	Taurus	3:31 A.M.	Gemini
26	Gemini		
27	Gemini	2:59 P.M.	Cancer
28	Cancer		
29	Cancer		
30	Cancer	3:40 A.M.	Leo
31	Leo		

SEPTEMBER

1	Leo	3:46 P.M.	Virgo
2	Virgo		
3	Virgo		
4	Virgo	2:15 A.M.	Libra
5	Libra		
6	Libra	10:38 A.M.	Scorpio
7	Scorpio		
8	Scorpio	4:39 P.M.	Sagittarius
9	Sagittarius		
10	Sagittarius	8:20 P.M.	Capricorn
11	Capricorn		
12	Capricorn	10:09 P.M.	Aquarius
13	Aquarius		
14	Aquarius	11:09 P.M.	Pisces
15	Pisces		
16	Pisces		
17	Pisces	12:50 A.M.	Aries
18	Aries		
19	Aries	4:43 A.M.	Taurus
20	Taurus		
21	Taurus	11:56 A.M.	Gemini
22	Gemini		
23	Gemini	10:31 P.M.	Cancer
24	Cancer		
25	Cancer		
26	Cancer	11:01 A.M.	Leo
27	Leo		
28	Leo	11:11 P.M.	Virgo
29	Virgo		
30	Virgo		

OCTOBER

1	Virgo	9:17 A.M.	Libra
2	Libra		
3	Libra	4:48 P.M.	Scorpio
4	Scorpio		
5	Scorpio	10:07 P.M.	Sagittarius
6	Sagittarius		
7	Sagittarius		
8	Sagittarius	1:52 A.M.	Capricorn
9	Capricorn		
10	Capricorn	4:42 A.M.	Aquarius
11	Aquarius		
12	Aquarius	7:12 A.M.	Pisces
13	Pisces		
14	Pisces	10:06 A.M.	Aries
15	Aries		
16	Aries	2:22 P.M.	Taurus
17	Taurus		
18	Taurus	9:05 P.M.	Gemini
19	Gemini		
20	Gemini		
21	Gemini	6:52 A.M.	Cancer
22	Cancer		
23	Cancer	7:04 P.M.	Leo
24	Leo		
25	Leo		
26	Leo	7:32 A.M.	Virgo
27	Virgo		
28	Virgo	5:51 P.M.	Libra
29	Libra		
30	Libra		
31	Libra	12:53 A.M.	Scorpio

NOVEMBER

1	Scorpio		
2	Scorpio	5:03 A.M.	Sagittarius
3	Sagittarius		
4	Sagittarius	7:40 A.M.	Capricorn
5	Capricorn		
6	Capricorn	10:04 A.M.	Aquarius
7	Aquarius		
8	Aquarius	1:06 P.M.	Pisces
9	Pisces		
10	Pisces	5:11 P.M.	Aries
11	Aries		
12	Aries	10:35 P.M.	Taurus
13	Taurus		
14	Taurus		
15	Taurus	5:45 A.M.	Gemini
16	Gemini		
17	Gemini	3:16 P.M.	Cancer
18	Cancer		
19	Cancer		
20	Cancer	3:09 A.M.	Leo
21	Leo		
22	Leo	3:57 P.M.	Virgo
23	Virgo		
24	Virgo		
25	Virgo	3:07 A.M.	Libra
26	Libra		
27	Libra	10:38 A.M.	Scorpio
28	Scorpio		
29	Scorpio	2:23 P.M.	Sagittarius
30	Sagittarius		

DECEMBER

1	Sagittarius	3:44 P.M.	Capricorn
2	Capricorn		
3	Capricorn	4:35 P.M.	Aquarius
4	Aquarius		
5	Aquarius	6:36 P.M.	Pisces
6	Pisces		
7	Pisces	10:40 P.M.	Aries
8	Aries		
9	Aries		
10	Aries	4:50 A.M.	Taurus
11	Taurus		
12	Taurus	12:54 P.M.	Gemini
13	Gemini		
14	Gemini	10:50 P.M.	Cancer
15	Cancer		
16	Cancer		
17	Cancer	10:37 A.M.	Leo
18	Leo		
19	Leo	11:34 P.M.	Virgo
20	Virgo		
21	Virgo		
22	Virgo	11:40 A.M.	Libra
23	Libra		
24	Libra	8:32 P.M.	Scorpio
25	Scorpio		
26	Scorpio		
27	Scorpio	1:07 A.M.	Sagittarius
28	Sagittarius		
29	Sagittarius	2:15 A.M.	Capricorn
30	Capricorn		
31	Capricorn	1:53 A.M.	Aquarius

MOON SIGN TABLES
1979

JANUARY

1	Aquarius		
2	Aquarius	2:08 A.M.	Pisces
3	Pisces		
4	Pisces	4:41 A.M.	Aries
5	Aries		
6	Aries	10:17 A.M.	Taurus
7	Taurus		
8	Taurus	6:42 P.M.	Gemini
9	Gemini		
10	Gemini		
11	Gemini	5:14 A.M.	Cancer
12	Cancer		
13	Cancer	5:16 P.M.	Leo
14	Leo		
15	Leo		
16	Leo	6:10 A.M.	Virgo
17	Virgo		
18	Virgo	6:40 P.M.	Libra
19	Libra		
20	Libra		
21	Libra	4:51 A.M.	Scorpio
22	Scorpio		
23	Scorpio	11:08 A.M.	Sagittarius
24	Sagittarius		
25	Sagittarius	1:27 P.M.	Capricorn
26	Capricorn		
27	Capricorn	1:12 P.M.	Aquarius
28	Aquarius		
29	Aquarius	12:25 P.M.	Pisces
30	Pisces		
31	Pisces	1:11 P.M.	Aries

FEBRUARY

1	Aries		
2	Aries	5:03 P.M.	Taurus
3	Taurus		
4	Taurus		
5	Taurus	12:33 A.M.	Gemini
6	Gemini		
7	Gemini	11:06 A.M.	Cancer
8	Cancer		
9	Cancer	11:25 P.M.	Leo
10	Leo		
11	Leo		
12	Leo	12:18 P.M.	Virgo
13	Virgo		
14	Virgo		
15	Virgo	12:37 A.M.	Libra
16	Libra		
17	Libra	11:12 A.M.	Scorpio
18	Scorpio		
19	Scorpio	6:51 P.M.	Sagittarius
20	Sagittarius		
21	Sagittarius	11:00 P.M.	Capricorn
22	Capricorn		
23	Capricorn		
24	Capricorn	12:12 A.M.	Aquarius
25	Aquarius	11:52 P.M.	Pisces
26	Pisces		
27	Pisces	11:54 P.M.	Aries
28	Aries		

MARCH

1	Aries		
2	Aries	2:09 A.M.	Taurus
3	Taurus		
4	Taurus	7:58 A.M.	Gemini
5	Gemini		
6	Gemini	5:34 P.M.	Cancer
7	Cancer		
8	Cancer		
9	Cancer	5:47 A.M.	Leo
10	Leo		
11	Leo	6:42 P.M.	Virgo
12	Virgo		
13	Virgo		
14	Virgo	6:42 A.M.	Libra
15	Libra		
16	Libra	4:49 P.M.	Scorpio
17	Scorpio		
18	Scorpio		
19	Scorpio	12:38 A.M.	Sagittarius
20	Sagittarius		
21	Sagittarius	5:56 A.M.	Capricorn
22	Capricorn		
23	Capricorn	8:52 A.M.	Aquarius
24	Aquarius		
25	Aquarius	10:04 A.M.	Pisces
26	Pisces		
27	Pisces	10:47 A.M.	Aries
28	Aries		
29	Aries	12:36 P.M.	Taurus
30	Taurus		
31	Taurus	5:08 P.M.	Gemini

APRIL

1	Gemini		
2	Gemini		
3	Gemini	1:24 A.M.	Cancer
4	Cancer		
5	Cancer	12:58 P.M.	Leo
6	Leo		
7	Leo		
8	Leo	1:52 A.M.	Virgo
9	Virgo		
10	Virgo	1:45 P.M.	Libra
11	Libra		
12	Libra	11:16 P.M.	Scorpio
13	Scorpio		
14	Scorpio		
15	Scorpio	6:18 A.M.	Sagittarius
16	Sagittarius		
17	Sagittarius	11:23 A.M.	Capricorn
18	Capricorn		
19	Capricorn	3:02 P.M.	Aquarius
20	Aquarius		
21	Aquarius	5:41 P.M.	Pisces
22	Pisces		
23	Pisces	7:51 P.M.	Aries
24	Aries		
25	Aries	10:27 P.M.	Taurus
26	Taurus		
27	Taurus		
28	Taurus	2:49 A.M.	Gemini
29	Gemini		
30	Gemini	10:11 A.M.	Cancer

MAY

1	Cancer		
2	Cancer	8:56 P.M.	Leo
3	Leo		
4	Leo		
5	Leo	9:41 A.M.	Virgo
6	Virgo		
7	Virgo	9:47 P.M.	Libra
8	Libra		
9	Libra		
10	Libra	7:10 A.M.	Scorpio
11	Scorpio		
12	Scorpio	1:25 P.M.	Sagittarius
13	Sagittarius		
14	Sagittarius	5:25 P.M.	Capricorn
15	Capricorn		
16	Capricorn	8:26 P.M.	Aquarius
17	Aquarius		
18	Aquarius	11:18 P.M.	Pisces
19	Pisces		
20	Pisces		
21	Pisces	2:30 A.M.	Aries
22	Aries		
23	Aries	6:20 A.M.	Taurus
24	Taurus		
25	Taurus	11:28 A.M.	Gemini
26	Gemini		
27	Gemini	6:51 P.M.	Cancer
28	Cancer		
29	Cancer		
30	Cancer	5:08 A.M.	Leo
31	Leo		

JUNE

1	Leo	5:41 A.M.	Virgo
2	Virgo		
3	Virgo		
4	Virgo	6:12 A.M.	Libra
5	Libra		
6	Libra	4:05 P.M.	Scorpio
7	Scorpio		
8	Scorpio	10:15 P.M.	Sagittarius
9	Sagittarius		
10	Sagittarius		
11	Sagittarius	1:23 A.M.	Capricorn
12	Capricorn		
13	Capricorn	3:06 A.M.	Aquarius
14	Aquarius		
15	Aquarius	4:56 A.M.	Pisces
16	Pisces		
17	Pisces	7:52 A.M.	Aries
18	Aries		
19	Aries	12:18 P.M.	Taurus
20	Taurus		
21	Taurus	6:23 P.M.	Gemini
22	Gemini		
23	Gemini		
24	Gemini	2:24 A.M.	Cancer
25	Cancer		
26	Cancer	12:47 P.M.	Leo
27	Leo		
28	Leo		
29	Leo	1:14 A.M.	Virgo
30	Virgo		

JULY

1	Virgo	2:08 P.M.	Libra
2	Libra		
3	Libra		
4	Libra	12:57 P.M.	Scorpio
5	Scorpio		
6	Scorpio	7:55 A.M.	Sagittarius
7	Sagittarius		

8	Sagittarius	11:07 A.M.	Capricorn
9	Capricorn		
10	Capricorn	11:59 A.M.	Aquarius
11	Aquarius		
12	Aquarius	12:23 P.M.	Pisces
13	Pisces		
14	Pisces	1:57 P.M.	Aries
15	Aries		
16	Aries	5:43 P.M.	Taurus
17	Taurus		
18	Taurus	12:00 P.M.	Gemini
19	Gemini		
20	Gemini		
21	Gemini	8:40 A.M.	Cancer
22	Cancer		
23	Cancer	7:30 P.M.	Leo
24	Leo		
25	Leo		
26	Leo	8:01 A.M.	Virgo
27	Virgo		
28	Virgo	9:06 P.M.	Libra
29	Libra		
30	Libra		
31	Libra	8:46 A.M.	Scorpio

AUGUST

1	Scorpio		
2	Scorpio	5:05 P.M.	Sagittarius
3	Sagittarius		
4	Sagittarius	9:23 P.M.	Capricorn
5	Capricorn		
6	Capricorn	10:28 P.M.	Aquarius
7	Aquarius		
8	Aquarius	10:05 P.M.	Pisces
9	Pisces		
10	Pisces	10:10 P.M.	Aries
11	Aries		
12	Aries		
13	Aries	12:21 A.M.	Taurus
14	Taurus		
15	Taurus	5:41 A.M.	Gemini
16	Gemini		
17	Gemini	2:17 P.M.	Cancer
18	Cancer		
19	Cancer		
20	Cancer	1:28 A.M.	Leo
21	Leo		
22	Leo	2:11 P.M.	Virgo
23	Virgo		
24	Virgo		
25	Virgo	3:13 A.M.	Libra
26	Libra		
27	Libra	3:12 P.M.	Scorpio
28	Scorpio		
29	Scorpio		
30	Scorpio	12:39 A.M.	Sagittarius
31	Sagittarius		

SEPTEMBER

1	Sagittarius	6:33 A.M.	Capricorn
2	Capricorn		
3	Capricorn	8:59 A.M.	Aquarius
4	Aquarius		
5	Aquarius	9:03 A.M.	Pisces
6	Pisces		
7	Pisces	8:29 A.M.	Aries
8	Aries		
9	Aries	9:12 A.M.	Taurus
10	Taurus		
11	Taurus	12:54 P.M.	Gemini
12	Gemini		
13	Gemini	8:27 P.M.	Cancer
14	Cancer		
15	Cancer		
16	Cancer	7:25 A.M.	Leo
17	Leo		
18	Leo	8:15 P.M.	Virgo
19	Virgo		
20	Virgo		
21	Virgo	9:11 A.M.	Libra
22	Libra		
23	Libra	8:54 P.M.	Scorpio
24	Scorpio		
25	Scorpio		
26	Scorpio	6:36 A.M.	Sagittarius
27	Sagittarius		
28	Sagittarius	1:40 P.M.	Capricorn
29	Capricorn		
30	Capricorn	5:49 P.M.	Aquarius

OCTOBER

1	Aquarius		
2	Aquarius	7:23 P.M.	Pisces
3	Pisces		
4	Pisces	7:28 P.M.	Aries
5	Aries		
6	Aries	7:45 P.M.	Taurus
7	Taurus		
8	Taurus	10:07 P.M.	Gemini
9	Gemini		
10	Gemini		
11	Gemini	4:09 A.M.	Cancer
12	Cancer		
13	Cancer	2:12 P.M.	Leo
14	Leo		
15	Leo		
16	Leo	2:51 A.M.	Virgo
17	Virgo		
18	Virgo	3:44 P.M.	Libra
19	Libra		
20	Libra		
21	Libra	3:02 A.M.	Scorpio
22	Scorpio		
23	Scorpio	12:09 P.M.	Sagittarius
24	Sagittarius		
25	Sagittarius	7:11 P.M.	Capricorn
26	Capricorn		
27	Capricorn		
28	Capricorn	12:16 A.M.	Aquarius
29	Aquarius		
30	Aquarius	3:29 A.M.	Pisces
31	Pisces		

NOVEMBER

1	Pisces	5:09 A.M.	Aries
2	Aries		
3	Aries	6:16 A.M.	Taurus
4	Taurus		
5	Taurus	8:26 A.M.	Gemini
6	Gemini		
7	Gemini	1:24 P.M.	Cancer
8	Cancer		
9	Cancer	10:14 P.M.	Leo
10	Leo		
11	Leo		
12	Leo	10:20 A.M.	Virgo
13	Virgo		
14	Virgo	11:16 P.M.	Libra
15	Libra		
16	Libra		
17	Libra	10:29 A.M.	Scorpio
18	Scorpio		
19	Scorpio	6:56 P.M.	Sagittarius
20	Sagittarius		
21	Sagittarius		
22	Sagittarius	1:01 A.M.	Capricorn
23	Capricorn		
24	Capricorn	5:37 A.M.	Aquarius
25	Aquarius		
26	Aquarius	9:17 A.M.	Pisces
27	Pisces		
28	Pisces	12:17 P.M.	Aries
29	Aries		
30	Aries	2:54 P.M.	Taurus

DECEMBER

1	Taurus		
2	Taurus	6:02 P.M.	Gemini
3	Gemini		
4	Gemini	11:01 P.M.	Cancer
5	Cancer		
6	Cancer		
7	Cancer	7:09 A.M.	Leo
8	Leo		
9	Leo	6:33 P.M.	Virgo
10	Virgo		
11	Virgo		
12	Virgo	7:29 A.M.	Libra
13	Libra		
14	Libra	7:08 P.M.	Scorpio
15	Scorpio		
16	Scorpio		
17	Scorpio	3:36 A.M.	Sagittarius
18	Sagittarius		
19	Sagittarius	8:55 A.M.	Capricorn
20	Capricorn		
21	Capricorn	12:13 P.M.	Aquarius
22	Aquarius		
23	Aquarius	2:50 P.M.	Pisces
24	Pisces		
25	Pisces	5:40 P.M.	Aries
26	Aries		
27	Aries	9:08 P.M.	Taurus
28	Taurus		
29	Taurus		
30	Taurus	1:32 A.M.	Gemini
31	Gemini		

MOON SIGN TABLES
1980

JANUARY

Day	Sign	Time	Sign
1	Gemini	7:29 A.M.	Cancer
2	Cancer		
3	Cancer	3:47 P.M.	Leo
4	Leo		
5	Leo		
6	Leo	2:48 A.M.	Virgo
7	Virgo		
8	Virgo	3:38 P.M.	Libra
9	Libra		
10	Libra		
11	Libra	3:55 A.M.	Scorpio
12	Scorpio		
13	Scorpio	1:17 P.M.	Sagittarius
14	Sagittarius		
15	Sagittarius	6:51 P.M.	Capricorn
16	Capricorn		
17	Capricorn	9:25 P.M.	Aquarius
18	Aquarius		
19	Aquarius	10:33 P.M.	Pisces
20	Pisces		
21	Pisces	11:52 P.M.	Aries
22	Aries		
23	Aries		
24	Aries	2:31 A.M.	Taurus
25	Taurus		
26	Taurus	7:11 A.M.	Gemini
27	Gemini		
28	Gemini	2:02 P.M.	Cancer
29	Cancer		
30	Cancer	11:08 P.M.	Leo
31	Leo		

FEBRUARY

Day	Sign	Time	Sign
1	Leo		
2	Leo	10:21 A.M.	Virgo
3	Virgo		
4	Virgo	11:04 P.M.	Libra
5	Libra		
6	Libra		
7	Libra	11:46 A.M.	Scorpio
8	Scorpio		
9	Scorpio	10:19 P.M.	Sagittarius
10	Sagittarius		
11	Sagittarius		
12	Sagittarius	5:12 A.M.	Capricorn
13	Capricorn		
14	Capricorn	8:19 A.M.	Aquarius
15	Aquarius		
16	Aquarius	8:54 A.M.	Pisces
17	Pisces		
18	Pisces	8:43 A.M.	Aries
19	Aries		
20	Aries	9:35 A.M.	Taurus
21	Taurus		
22	Taurus	12:58 P.M.	Gemini
23	Gemini		
24	Gemini	7:34 P.M.	Cancer
25	Cancer		
26	Cancer		
27	Cancer	5:10 A.M.	Leo
28	Leo		
29	Leo	4:53 P.M.	Virgo

MARCH

Day	Sign	Time	Sign
1	Virgo		
2	Virgo		
3	Virgo	5:40 A.M.	Libra
4	Libra		
5	Libra	6:23 P.M.	Scorpio
6	Scorpio		
7	Scorpio		
8	Scorpio	5:38 A.M.	Sagittarius
9	Sagittarius		
10	Sagittarius	2:02 P.M.	Capricorn
11	Capricorn		
12	Capricorn	6:45 P.M.	Aquarius
13	Aquarius		
14	Aquarius	8:10 P.M.	Pisces
15	Pisces		
16	Pisces	7:41 P.M.	Aries
17	Aries		
18	Aries	7:13 P.M.	Taurus
19	Taurus		
20	Taurus	8:47 P.M.	Gemini
21	Gemini		
22	Gemini		
23	Gemini	1:55 A.M.	Cancer
24	Cancer		
25	Cancer	10:58 A.M.	Leo
26	Leo		
27	Leo	10:52 P.M.	Virgo
28	Virgo		
29	Virgo		
30	Virgo	11:49 A.M.	Libra
31	Libra		

APRIL

Day	Sign	Time	Sign
1	Libra		
2	Libra	12:21 A.M.	Scorpio
3	Scorpio		
4	Scorpio	11:35 A.M.	Sagittarius
5	Sagittarius		
6	Sagittarius	8:43 P.M.	Capricorn
7	Capricorn		
8	Capricorn		
9	Capricorn	3:00 A.M.	Aquarius
10	Aquarius		
11	Aquarius	6:07 A.M.	Pisces
12	Pisces		
13	Pisces	6:40 A.M.	Aries
14	Aries		
15	Aries	6:11 A.M.	Taurus
16	Taurus		
17	Taurus	6:41 A.M.	Gemini
18	Gemini		
19	Gemini	10:11 A.M.	Cancer
20	Cancer		
21	Cancer	5:52 P.M.	Leo
22	Leo		
23	Leo		
24	Leo	5:12 A.M.	Virgo
25	Virgo		
26	Virgo	6:09 P.M.	Libra
27	Libra		
28	Libra		
29	Libra	6:35 A.M.	Scorpio
30	Scorpio		

MAY

Day	Sign	Time	Sign
1	Scorpio	5:22 P.M.	Sagittarius
2	Sagittarius		
3	Sagittarius		
4	Sagittarius	2:14 A.M.	Capricorn
5	Capricorn		
6	Capricorn	9:03 A.M.	Aquarius
7	Aquarius		
8	Aquarius	1:33 P.M.	Pisces
9	Pisces		
10	Pisces	3:44 P.M.	Aries
11	Aries		
12	Aries	4:24 P.M.	Taurus
13	Taurus		
14	Taurus	5:07 P.M.	Gemini
15	Gemini		
16	Gemini	7:52 P.M.	Cancer
17	Cancer		
18	Cancer		
19	Cancer	2:14 A.M.	Leo
20	Leo		
21	Leo	12:32 P.M.	Virgo
22	Virgo		
23	Virgo		
24	Virgo	1:11 A.M.	Libra
25	Libra		
26	Libra	1:37 P.M.	Scorpio
27	Scorpio		
28	Scorpio		
29	Scorpio	12:05 A.M.	Sagittarius
30	Sagittarius		
31	Sagittarius	8:14 A.M.	Capricorn

JUNE

Day	Sign	Time	Sign
1	Capricorn		
2	Capricorn	2:29 P.M.	Aquarius
3	Aquarius		
4	Aquarius	7:10 P.M.	Pisces
5	Pisces		
6	Pisces	10:23 P.M.	Aries
7	Aries		
8	Aries		
9	Aries	12:29 A.M.	Taurus
10	Taurus		
11	Taurus	2:22 A.M.	Gemini
12	Gemini		
13	Gemini	5:29 A.M.	Cancer
14	Cancer		
15	Cancer	11:22 A.M.	Leo
16	Leo		
17	Leo	8:47 P.M.	Virgo
18	Virgo		
19	Virgo		
20	Virgo	8:55 A.M.	Libra
21	Libra		
22	Libra	9:26 P.M.	Scorpio
23	Scorpio		
24	Scorpio		
25	Scorpio	8:02 A.M.	Sagittarius
26	Sagittarius		
27	Sagittarius	3:46 P.M.	Capricorn
28	Capricorn		
29	Capricorn	9:04 P.M.	Aquarius
30	Aquarius		

JULY

Day	Sign	Time	Sign
1	Aquarius		
2	Aquarius	12:48 A.M.	Pisces
3	Pisces		
4	Pisces	3:46 A.M.	Aries
5	Aries		
6	Aries	6:30 A.M.	Taurus

7	Taurus		
8	Taurus	9:33 A.M.	Gemini
9	Gemini		
10	Gemini	1:44 P.M.	Cancer
11	Cancer		
12	Cancer	8:03 P.M.	Leo
13	Leo		
14	Leo		
15	Leo	5:11 A.M.	Virgo
16	Virgo		
17	Virgo	4:55 P.M.	Libra
18	Libra		
19	Libra		
20	Libra	5:33 A.M.	Scorpio
21	Scorpio		
22	Scorpio	4:42 P.M.	Sagittarius
23	Sagittarius		
24	Sagittarius		
25	Sagittarius	12:45 A.M.	Capricorn
26	Capricorn		
27	Capricorn	5:34 A.M.	Aquarius
28	Aquarius		
29	Aquarius	8:11 A.M.	Pisces
30	Pisces		
31	Pisces	9:53 A.M.	Aries

AUGUST

1	Aries		
2	Aries	11:55 A.M.	Taurus
3	Taurus		
4	Taurus	3:10 P.M.	Gemini
5	Gemini		
6	Gemini	8:12 P.M.	Cancer
7	Cancer		
8	Cancer		
9	Cancer	3:23 A.M.	Leo
10	Leo		
11	Leo	12:54 P.M.	Virgo
12	Virgo		
13	Virgo		
14	Virgo	12:32 A.M.	Libra
15	Libra		
16	Libra	1:15 P.M.	Scorpio
17	Scorpio		
18	Scorpio		
19	Scorpio	1:08 A.M.	Sagittarius
20	Sagittarius		
21	Sagittarius	10:11 A.M.	Capricorn
22	Capricorn		
23	Capricorn	3:32 P.M.	Aquarius
24	Aquarius		
25	Aquarius	5:43 P.M.	Pisces
26	Pisces		
27	Pisces	6:11 P.M.	Aries
28	Aries		
29	Aries	6:41 P.M.	Taurus
30	Taurus		
31	Taurus	8:50 P.M.	Gemini

SEPTEMBER

1	Gemini		
2	Gemini		
3	Gemini	1:39 A.M.	Cancer
4	Cancer		
5	Cancer	9:22 A.M.	Leo
6	Leo		
7	Leo	7:31 P.M.	Virgo
8	Virgo		
9	Virgo		
10	Virgo	7:22 A.M.	Libra
11	Libra		
12	Libra	8:06 P.M.	Scorpio
13	Scorpio		
14	Scorpio		
15	Scorpio	8:28 A.M.	Sagittarius
16	Sagittarius		
17	Sagittarius	6:45 P.M.	Capricorn
18	Capricorn		
19	Capricorn		
20	Capricorn	1:31 A.M.	Aquarius
21	Aquarius		
22	Aquarius	4:27 A.M.	Pisces
23	Pisces		
24	Pisces	4:37 A.M.	Aries
25	Aries		
26	Aries	3:53 A.M.	Taurus
27	Taurus		
28	Taurus	4:21 A.M.	Gemini
29	Gemini		
30	Gemini	7:46 A.M.	Cancer

OCTOBER

1	Cancer		
2	Cancer	2:57 P.M.	Leo
3	Leo		
4	Leo		
5	Leo	1:19 A.M.	Virgo
6	Virgo		
7	Virgo	1:30 P.M.	Libra
8	Libra		
9	Libra		
10	Libra	2:15 A.M.	Scorpio
11	Scorpio		
12	Scorpio	2:37 P.M.	Sagittarius
13	Sagittarius		
14	Sagittarius		
15	Sagittarius	1:37 A.M.	Capricorn
16	Capricorn		
17	Capricorn	9:54 A.M.	Aquarius
18	Aquarius		
19	Aquarius	2:31 P.M.	Pisces
20	Pisces		
21	Pisces	3:43 P.M.	Aries
22	Aries		
23	Aries	2:55 P.M.	Taurus
24	Taurus		
25	Taurus	2:17 P.M.	Gemini
26	Gemini		
27	Gemini	4:00 P.M.	Cancer
28	Cancer		
29	Cancer	9:38 P.M.	Leo
30	Leo		
31	Leo		

NOVEMBER

1	Leo	7:18 A.M.	Virgo
2	Virgo		
3	Virgo	7:31 P.M.	Libra
4	Libra		
5	Libra		
6	Libra	8:19 A.M.	Scorpio
7	Scorpio		
8	Scorpio	8:25 P.M.	Sagittarius
9	Sagittarius		
10	Sagittarius		
11	Sagittarius	7:15 A.M.	Capricorn
12	Capricorn		
13	Capricorn	4:10 P.M.	Aquarius
14	Aquarius		
15	Aquarius	10:21 P.M.	Pisces
16	Pisces		
17	Pisces		
18	Pisces	1:22 A.M.	Aries
19	Aries		
20	Aries	1:51 A.M.	Taurus
21	Taurus		
22	Taurus	1:27 A.M.	Gemini
23	Gemini		
24	Gemini	2:18 A.M.	Cancer
25	Cancer		
26	Cancer	6:23 A.M.	Leo
27	Leo		
28	Leo	2:37 P.M.	Virgo
29	Virgo		
30	Virgo		

DECEMBER

1	Virgo	2:13 A.M.	Libra
2	Libra		
3	Libra	3:00 P.M.	Scorpio
4	Scorpio		
5	Scorpio		
6	Scorpio	2:57 A.M.	Sagittarius
7	Sagittarius		
8	Sagittarius	1:12 P.M.	Capricorn
9	Capricorn		
10	Capricorn	9:36 P.M.	Aquarius
11	Aquarius		
12	Aquarius		
13	Aquarius	4:03 A.M.	Pisces
14	Pisces		
15	Pisces	8:21 A.M.	Aries
16	Aries		
17	Aries	10:36 A.M.	Taurus
18	Taurus		
19	Taurus	11:39 A.M.	Gemini
20	Gemini		
21	Gemini	1:03 P.M.	Cancer
22	Cancer		
23	Cancer	4:34 P.M.	Leo
24	Leo		
25	Leo	11:32 P.M.	Virgo
26	Virgo		
27	Virgo		
28	Virgo	10:05 A.M.	Libra
29	Libra		
30	Libra	10:36 P.M.	Scorpio
31	Scorpio		

Your Inner Secretary—Mercury

"There can be no one best way of organizing a business."
SOCIOLOGIST JOAN WOODWARD

In case you're just starting out in business or the professional world, let me share my greatest secret to getting anything done in the free world: Make friends with the secretary. Though there are now many names for this role—administrative assistant, office manager, receptionist—this person is the eyes and ears (and sometimes the bullhorn) of any workplace, the point of entry to every organization. Want to talk to the big guy in the Oval Office? Unless you've got one of those special red phones minted in Moscow, get to know the secretary.

See, despite the brass nameplate, the executive behind closed doors doesn't have time to know beans about company paper policies or where they keep the extra supply of biodegradable coffee filters. And all those humorous memos that keep the crew on the floor on task and up to date? You think Mr. MBA wrote those? Not bloody likely, not with his schedule of 18 holes before power martinis at Bistro Mistral wooing potential investors. Enter the secretary. He helps the CEOs sound smart. He keeps them organized, scheduled, and saves them from embarrassment by remembering their kids' Little League championship play-offs.

Luckily we all have our very own inner secretary, symbolized by Mercury. Your Mercury sign represents your style of communication, how

you represent a product or company. In mythology Mercury was the messenger of the gods. He was a kind of an executive secretary, bike messenger, and sales rep all rolled into one. The ultimate Person Friday.

Pop astrologers who usually focus on romance think Mercury is insignificant. Hah! What do they know? In our current information economy our Mercury sign, that trusty inner secretary, matters more than ever. On the job, in the real world, when you want to get ahead, Mercury matters plenty. Without a strong Mercury, you seem incompetent, inarticulate, or just plain dumb.

THE MERCURY STRATEGY

By getting to know your Mercury sign, you can:

★ Express yourself more effectively

★ Get organized in ways that work for *you*

★ Hone your sales techniques, your talent for communicating features and benefits

★ Sound like an expert on Patagonia even when you know less about it than the average fifth-grade geography whiz

---

Mercury in Aries

Your inner secretary is a dynamo and stirs coworkers to action. A commanding presence, you often bark like a four-star general and wield authority whether you're the VP or the janitor. Yet your attention span is less suited to *60 Minutes* than to *Sesame Street*, where the subject changes every 22.5 seconds. You make quick decisions. You enjoy strategic thinking more than a warm bubble bath. But complications, like the fact your assistant is having a baby, can instantly send you into a tizzy. How dare she!

ORGANIZATION: Your desk is spartan and clean enough for surgery. Loose papers are trapped beneath a paperweight probably embossed with something like *Once I thought I was wrong, but I was mistaken.* You resent being restricted by others' organizational systems and would rather institute your own, even if your jam-packed schedule leaves little room for error or goofing off. Menial tasks don't just bore you; they offend you! In fact, you

may overlook the fact that humble chores, like taking careful inventory, will contribute to profitability.

COMMUNICATIONS: No doubt about it: You get your point across. A fast and eager talker, you're uninhibited about speaking out. In meetings, you're frank and forthright, willing to risk sounding stupid if there's a chance you might sound brilliant. Depending on your position in the chain of command, you may jump to decisions and conclusions without consulting everyone involved. When it comes to customer demands, you give them what they want—but not necessarily with a smile.

DR. MATT'S PRESCRIPTION FOR PEAK PERFORMANCE: Try many different tactics to capture people's attention. Screaming wears thin *fast*. Don't act too busy to see people. Make room for coworkers' opinions. Do tasks and fulfill responsibilities before they become critical or you'll always be sweating to meet the deadline. Though you may disagree, stress is not an aphrodisiac for most people! It tends to raise blood pressure, not profits.

Mercury in Taurus

Your inner secretary is a practical thinker. So you're slow, so what? A master of tact, you consider matters carefully and think before speaking. Anyone can bargain on a used car lot, hootin' and hollerin' over the figures, but *you've* got the cautious manners to haggle at Bloomingdale's! It takes your brain a while to warm up. Don't expect it to screech out of the driveway on a cold morning. You're a concrete thinker, interested in bottom lines—and lunch breaks.

ORGANIZATION: You spend a lot of time getting organized. Your desk is neat, but more for the sake of comfort than efficiency. Cautious, you plan in advance and know today if you can attend the company picnic six months away. If you need 10 copies, you'll make 20 so you won't have to stop and make 10 more later on. Expenses often weigh heavy on your mind. Before ordering a box of pencils, you check the three-year budget projection. Since you're a freak for quality control, leave the multitasking to Gemini—or at least be clear about the limits on your time.

COMMUNICATION: A little shy when it comes to public speaking, you might prefer talking on the phone to the honor of presenting at Carnegie Hall. You take orders dutifully, but respond defiantly to the crack of a whip. As

long as it doesn't break the budget, you treat clients with respect and courtesy. You sound as though you know more than you actually do, but you hate to waste time and money on idle gossip and arbitrary memos.

DR. MATT'S PRESCRIPTION FOR PEAK PERFORMANCE: Be careful that getting organized doesn't consume more time than getting the work done. Though the budget is your bible, don't be a zealot or you may overlook hidden costs, like a meticulous Pentagon accountant who routinely approves $400 toilet seat purchases! Open yourself up to new ideas, avoiding habitual ruts. You're gifted at presenting the facts; now work on sounding slick, delivering the hard cold figures in a pretty package. To get the boss's attention, toot your own horn more often.

Mercury in Gemini

Quick and precise, your inner secretary bounces around like Ping-Pong balls at a Chinese sports tournament. When you're in one of your stressed-out, obsessive-compulsive, note-taking moods, your supply of yellow legal pads runs dangerously low. Suddenly grouchy when there's nothing to do, you may hastily vow to clean out and refile old papers, but in 20 minutes you're caught reading the minutes from a 1924 board meeting. Gossip, trivia, and factoids turn you on. The nine-to-five day-in, day-out routine definitely doesn't.

ORGANIZATION: The immaculate work space is not for you. A heap of semi-organized clutter, your desktop needs to keep you stimulated, not just orderly. Determined to stay up to date, you make room for trade journals and professional publications. Whatever organizational system you choose, it *must* allow for flexibility and respond well to out-of-the-ordinary demands—otherwise you'll soon abandon it. And since you tend to over-schedule, consider techno options like video-conferencing, which let you be in two places at once.

COMMUNICATIONS: Silence inhibits you. Never at a loss for words and always pursuing diverse interests, you perform optimally wherever a free and easy exchange of ideas can take place. Since staying *in touch* is one of your professional hallmarks, you require three voice-mail boxes, two fax numbers, and seven e-mail accounts—but that means you spend most of your time checking them! Consider narrowing your focus so everyone gets

your full attention. Look for opportunities to use your wit and clever one-liners. In presentations, you can keep your audience enraptured but have to work extrahard to convey the *point* (learn to rely on boring structures like outlines). Consumers appreciate the way you serve up ideas in easy-to-digest portions.

DR. MATT'S PRESCRIPTION FOR PEAK PERFORMANCE: You can talk the talk—that's for sure. But it's less sure that you can *walk* your talk. So be careful not to promise more than you can deliver or make verbal agreements you'd rather not back up in writing. Also learn when *not* to talk. Take the hint when the person on the other end of the line wants to hang up. Though you have diverse interests and can speak intelligently on many subjects, choose one or two areas to master in depth. And—very important to peace of mind and peak performance—take time each day for not thinking. Note: Listening to your Walkman while glancing at the *Journal* and treading on the Stairmaster doesn't count as down time!

> **"The only competitive advantage today is the ability to 'morph' into new adaptive forms."**
> INTERNET CONSULTANT
> RICHARD THIEME

Mercury in Cancer

Your inner secretary tries very hard to sound cool and collected, like an astute and objective problem-solver. But nope! Secretly sappy and sentimental, you are seldom able to separate your heart from your head. Whatever your gender, you serve as workplace den mother, the confidant of coworkers and paragon of emotional intelligence. With a memory like a biblical scholar, you can recite chapter and verse of the *Standard & Poors Index* for your industry. And though you have a restless mind, it can obsess on one objective, especially when the price is right.

ORGANIZATION: You nest in your work space and cling to trustworthy operating methods, so when a new boss or project shows up you'll have to work extrahard to adjust. Although you crave easy access to files and stats, you may simply have too much *stuff* to be able to put your hands quickly on anything but towering paper piles. It's painful, but learn to trash irrelevant documents. When that's impossible, containers work well—not just filing cabinets but space-saving storage boxes. You might even want to try a scanner to zap all those research notes and magazine

clippings onto a computer disk. Above all, address workplace safety. You simply can't work well without a fire extinguisher nearby and a smoke detector that goes off on foggy mornings.

COMMUNICATION: Among your many interpersonal skills, you're able to express sincere concern for others' well-being. A good listener, sensitive to the nuances of body language and intonations, you can sway opinions by appealing to your listener's deepest drives and instincts. Don't overlook your talent for building coalitions and comforting irritable associates through graceful communications. To maintain your strong personal connections, consider starting a company newsletter or other nonadvertising communications that keep you in the public eye. Offering free information is a great way to serve and attract potential customers.

DR. MATT'S PRESCRIPTION FOR PEAK PERFORMANCE: According to human resources experts, coworkers are like family members: You can't choose them or get rid of them. But since workplace relations matter so much to your peak performance, do what you can: Pay special attention to selecting employees, training support staff, and processing grievances. Silent retreat is not an option! With practiced patience, you can use your common sense and pleasant communications style to become a sterling on-the-job mentor for new personnel.

Mercury in Leo

No offense, but your inner secretary probably types poorly and thinks "taking shorthand" is tennis lingo. On the other hand, Mercury in Leo means you possess a knock-out inner receptionist. You wear charisma like dime-store cologne and contribute personality to even the dreariest desk jobs. Quick on your feet, you're good at winging it. Don't know the answer? Can't think of what to say? You fake it splendidly, the artful improviser, a natural showperson. Learn to drive "shtick" and you'll go far.

ORGANIZATION: Despite your improvisational skills, when it comes to organization you hate to just "make do." You need state-of-the-art office supplies and software. Even if they're not furnished by your employer, consider investing in a few extravagances if it improves your efficiency. (One Mercury-in-Leo consultant I know refuses to write with anything but her Mont Blanc fountain pen!) Definitely don't forget a calendar—not one that sits on your desk and occasionally reminds you of birthdays but one that

goes where you go and keeps you on time. You have to manage your schedule vigilantly, including sufficient time for planning, brainstorming, and getting stuck in traffic.

COMMUNICATIONS: Grandiloquence and exaggeration are your native language. You adore superlatives like *best, cheapest,* and *most dazzling,* but this can backfire: When overused, these words sound hollow. So develop a communications style that conveys genuineness and sincerity, not get-rich-quick superficiality. You're at your best when you feel poised and professional in front of people. If that's difficult for you (which is hard to imagine with Mercury in Leo), take public speaking or acting lessons. Work with an image consultant to find the right wardrobe. Become a master of the lunch meeting, learning to casually pitch a product between mouthfuls. But remember: Good communicating depends on good listening. Work on it. Practice repeating back what others say so both of you know you get it.

DR. MATT'S PRESCRIPTION FOR PEAK PERFORMANCE: Learn to walk the fine line between being the helpful expert and the annoying know-it-all. Find your charisma button and figure out when to crank it up and when to cool it—you don't have to be on *all* the time. With Mercury in Leo, timing is everything. And since the instant gratification you desire is so hard to achieve, just put one foot in front of the other, taking the day task by task, not all in one giant leap. When trapped by writer's block or any creative impasse, try physical activity, music, a fascinating website—but make sure it's something truly inspirational, not mere work avoidance.

Mercury in Virgo

Your inner secretary is the quintessential switchboard operator. Remember the old-fashioned switchboards with 300 little holes and enough cords and plugs to electrocute all of Iowa? The technology has changed, but your inner secretary is still totally connected, totally wired. You know what everybody is doing (or should be doing), where to find them, and how to make them feel as worthless as a used postage stamp when they miss an important call. Organization is your middle name. But coworkers have all sorts of other pet names for you, too, like Little Miss Persnickety and Atilla the Meticulous. An insatiable problem-solver, prone to analyzing everything, you probably did profit-and-loss statements in the cradle.

ORGANIZATION: Look, it's OK if it makes everyone think you're anal-retentive: For your organizational well-being, you need to know your work is (1) accurate and (2) won't go to waste. So criticize mediocrity. Back up computer files constantly, or even get a "data safe" to do it automatically. Maximize your efforts and prevent the loss of hard-earned finished projects by any means necessary. And since you're better at data-crunching than the rest of us, make yourself popular, and indispensable, by distilling that daunting data into eye-catching, user-friendly charts and graphs so others can catch on as fast as you do.

COMMUNICATIONS: In a competitive environment, communicating *efficiently* (your forte) is nice but not sufficient. If you want people to remember you, add a little spice; stick to *more* than the facts. Personalize your exchanges.

> **"To avoid criticism, do nothing, say nothing, be nothing."**
> NOVELIST ELBERT HUBBARD

For example, add a thought-provoking quote to your e-mail's signature file—or go one step further and register your own distinctive Internet domain name. As for speaking in public, experts say the first and last 60 seconds of any presentation are the most memorable. So make 'em snazzy! No matter how many tasty morsels you sandwich in between that first and last minute, make sure you're doing it with something more memorable than white bread.

DR. MATT'S PRESCRIPTION FOR PEAK PERFORMANCE: For a competitive advantage in today's changing workforce, develop your natural adaptability. If you're concerned about losing your job as a librarian, secure your position by learning to design and maintain the library website.

Mercury in Libra

What charm! What finesse! What poise! You've got the only inner secretary that skipped the secretarial institute and won a scholarship to finishing school instead. When it comes to proper behavior in any setting, you out-manner Miss Manners and speak volumes with a simple but firm handshake. Always accommodating, you can quickly produce the safest, most mutually agreeable response to the problem client who insists on exchanging her chinchilla muff for mink slippers *without* a receipt. You're a gifted negotiator, who's good at keeping everyone happy, or at least notified of prices that may change without notice.

ORGANIZATION: Rational and level-headed, you thrive in an organizational system that's a lot like you: easygoing yet functional; able to deal with the facts—no matter how harsh or exciting—without falling to pieces. What won't work for you, however, is a setup where you or someone feels left out, so aim for *inclusivity* in your organizational design. When deadlines loom and the stress level heats up, value the team over the project. Next week the project will be done and gone but you'll *still* have to work with the team!

COMMUNICATIONS: You're a people person who benefits greatly from *making connections*. But how do you make them? Start with the art of good conversation and don't settle for idle gossip. Before entering the workplace each day, have at least two topics worth discussing—maybe the morning news or a book you just finished reading. In trying to reach new people, speak their language. Even if your foreign vocabulary is limited to *lasagna*, *Cabernet Sauvignon*, and *radical, dude,* you've got a sixth sense for communicating in unfamiliar territory. Always send a follow-up note—because *maintaining* the connection matters as much as making it.

DR. MATT'S PRESCRIPTION FOR PEAK PERFORMANCE: When some guy at a party asks what you do, be ready with more than the expeditious/generic *I'm a financial manager* response. Prepare (in advance!) a one-minute-or-less positioning statement that makes clear the value and benefits of your unique contributions to the professional world, such as, "I help educators find cost-effective ways to teach more subjects to more students in less time." While it doesn't have to get out of hand, don't be afraid to broadcast your work and make connections anywhere, anytime.

Mercury in Scorpio

Your inner secretary's got a mind like a steel trap. I'm not talking about one of those puny mousetraps. Think grizzly bear. Think brontosaurus. You absorb data quickly, relish complexity, and don't freak out when complications cross your desk. You get engrossed, and can easily spend hours in the library, the laboratory, or a virtual reality model of, well, reality. You do sarcasm well. But often you'd prefer to let other people do the talking while you're content to be a backup singer, clever enough to know when to avoid standing up front in the line of fire. Because you scrutinize so closely, you're excellent at checking facts, confirming

assertions, and witnessing white-collar crime like the impoverished temp who purloins TP from the janitorial closet.

ORGANIZATION: Since you're driven to cut costs and reduce taxes, you need an *easy* system for saving receipts and other relevant scraps of paper, no matter how irritating their presence. Stay on top of debt collection. To pacify your volatile stress level, account for every penny of your personal or company budget. This might sound anal, but when you lose financial and/or strategic control, you just plain lose your mind. To prevent losing all your computer files (or popsicle supplies) during a thunderstorm or other natural disaster, make a business emergency preparedness plan. You do your best thinking *after* taking certain precautions.

COMMUNICATIONS: Before walking into an interview or sales presentation, investigate your audience and their industry—you don't like to get caught off guard by hard-to-field questions. To sound yet more professional, be sensitive to your audience's sensitivities. While you're a master of expressing urgency, don't make every piece of business communication sound like a life-or-death situation. And since you get tired of answering the same questions repeatedly, consider creating a FAQ—a list of frequently asked questions for responding to forgetful colleagues and curious customers without wasting time.

DR. MATT'S PRESCRIPTION FOR PEAK PERFORMANCE: In working out the nitty-gritty of office life, remember that not every discussion has to be an argument.

Mercury in Sagittarius

OK, so you don't have the most organized inner secretary in the universe. It hasn't stopped you so far, even if you *are* still waiting for your 1989 tax return. A born communicator, capable of great eloquence, you often take this talent for granted. Use note cards! Practice your speech! You can't wing *everything!* Yet you try. You work a room well, if you care to bother. You could promise them condos on the Moon, and half of Houston would be on the next shuttle out of Texas. Never mind the fact there isn't enough oxygen to sustain a potted tumbleweed.

ORGANIZATION: Clutter is public enemy number one. Most days your work space looks like a pawnshop at an earthquake's epicenter. Then, suddenly

inspired and needing room to *think big*, you push the confusion aside. But watch out! Chaos can come back to overwhelm you. Try investing more time in getting organized so you'll waste less searching for lost paychecks. To prevent overdraft fees, for instance, consider computerizing your personal finances—but this only works if you commit to entering the data!

COMMUNICATION: You need the freedom to express yourself bluntly, without pussyfooting around. Even though you think about things way too much, sometimes you're capable of the darnedest indiscretions. While people may admire your dedication to principles, they resent your ascent to the pulpit. Don't use every meeting as an excuse to preach. Do, on the other hand, take advantage of being a born storyteller and an unconscious master of persuasion. You can win the favor of customers and coworkers with humor, lively debate, and colloquialisms that put people at ease.

DR. MATT'S PRESCRIPTION FOR PEAK PERFORMANCE: Rules and regulations drive you batty. That's why you need to address them up front, and *then* progress to doing what you love. If, for example, you're currently starting or expanding a business, you face the tough question of how to structure it legally. To incorporate or not to incorporate? Sole proprietorship or general partnership? Each has its pros and cons. Figure them out. Put it in writing with the state's seal of approval. Once the rules are in order, you can get back to eating bonbons!

Mercury in Capricorn

Put bluntly, your inner secretary is uptight, ideal for a stuffy, old-fashioned law firm. Hey, don't be offended. True, you're a bit retro. You may prefer an old Underwood manual typewriter to the laser printer, which isn't to your benefit in the computer age. But you *are* sober, dignified, and you do what you say you're going to do. You demand accuracy, even from your superiors. Often, you are mistaken for a VIP even if you aren't one, leading, more often than not, to promotions aplenty. But don't succumb to a tendency for small-mindedness and overspecialization. Read newspapers—and not just the business section. It's wise to keep your finger on the pulse of the rest of the world. Out

> "A . . . speech should be like a lady's dress—long enough to cover the subject and short enough to be interesting."
> BRITISH POLITICIAN RICHARD AUSTEN

there, in the larger universe, are people and opportunities you never dreamed of.

ORGANIZATION: Your desk *looks* dignified, topped by a brass letter opener and leather planner, but what's in the drawers may be another matter altogether. In a world of limited resources, you'll have to decide which is more important: time spent keeping up appearances or time spent accomplishing tasks. Whatever you do, you do it best if you know it is sound before you begin, but don't get hung up on your conception of proper procedure. You like to look organized, but you'll do really well if you can live up to your appearances.

COMMUNICATIONS: Let the public know what you're up to. If something noteworthy happens in your workplace, for instance, send a press release to the local papers. Dignified and standing on formality, you may wait too long for the public to come to you when it makes more sense to go to them. Though you're extremely articulate when talking of a subject you know, you fall to pieces in a situation where you are not the expert. Don't be afraid to ask a question. No one expects you to be as omniscient as Big Brother. And try shooting the breeze from time to time. Small talk is a key component in the art of networking.

DR. MATT'S PRESCRIPTION FOR PEAK PERFORMANCE: You've mastered the step-by-step approach; now, try the circuitous one. There's a deficit of spontaneity in your work habits; try going out on a limb, boarding new flights of fancy. Spout the facts and figures you need to spout in order to back your position up and use your expertise to finagle entree to the big shots in the executive penthouse suite. But don't talk through your nose or someone may punch it. And believe it or not, other people do have opinions, and it would be to your benefit to listen to them.

Mercury in Aquarius

Your inner secretary is like a visionary robot, R2D2 on a mission: feisty, productive, and communicating that message that can redeem the world or rejuvenate the corporate system. In Silicon Valley, your secretarial skills would be a dream come true: overqualified, quirky, and in natural possession of billions of mental gigabytes. You may invest wholeheartedly in gadgets or methods that promise to make you organized, but then get very disappointed when they don't work.

ORGANIZATION: You thrive in an office that's a lean, mean, techno machine. You're attuned to reaching goals and satisfying consumers, but may overlook government regulations and legal intricacies. You're happiest when figuring out new tricks to save time or increase productivity. Invent your own organizational system rather than stick to worn-out procedures. Room to experiment and a work space in tune with your individual eccentricities are prerequisites for your success. While you appreciate an orderly environment, you don't take kindly to arbitrary systems. So if you hire an organizational consultant, watch out! You might end up redoing everything you've just paid to have set up.

COMMUNICATIONS: You are a born motivational speaker. Convincing people you know a lot about a lot is no problem. Your CD-ROM of a brain, packed chock-full of tasty trivia, ought to impress the VIPs regularly. (Even if those factoids *were* learned from the back of cereal boxes.) Avoid assuming everyone understands insider jargon. Talk on their level, not over their heads—or over yours, for that matter. And while you don't want to offend anyone, don't get hung up on demanding political correctness in expression. You may be perceived as an ideologue rather than an independent thinker.

DR. MATT'S PRESCRIPTION FOR PEAK PERFORMANCE: Like an adoring mother, you won't depart from your brainchild easily. To be satisfied, stay involved with the development and implementation of your ideas. Plain vanilla intellectual property isn't your flavor. But even if the subject of discussion is plain and dull, don't tune people out. Try getting people out of their cubicles and into participatory dialogue. Without sacrificing your individual preferences, see if you can make your own goals resemble or at least line up with the goals of your company and comrades.

Mercury in Pisces

When your inner secretary isn't surfing the Web or sneaking off to meditate, you're cast in the dignified role of the workplace oracle of wisdom and arbiter of doing the right thing. A keen observer of human nature with the soul of a poet, Mercury in Pisces is the sign of the good listener. When people talk, you feel their pain. Or at least it looks like it. Chances are you're musing over the report due next Friday or the meaning of life, but coworkers appreciate your ears nonetheless. No, you don't always

make sense, but you're a fascinating talker, capable of great sensitivity and contemplation, with a flair for reading between the lines.

ORGANIZATION: Don't bother buying the *Moron's Guide to Getting Organized;* you learn best through observation and imitation, flourishing in a system that demands constant adaptability. You have a lot of *uncommon* sense—but whether you exercise it is another question. You can usually, for example, anticipate glitches before they glitch—but only if you're *present* and paying attention to what's under your nose, not in a galaxy far, far away. Your organization will run more smoothly if you insist on tying up loose ends, rather than harvesting a whole crop of *nearly done* projects.

> **"Things there are no solutions to: inflation, bureaucracy, dandruff."**
> PUBLISHING MOGUL
> MALCOLM FORBES

COMMUNICATION: As the Book of Ecclesiastes says, there's a time for everything under heaven. Likewise, there's a time for you to communicate clearly and directly (like when calling in a debt) and a time to leave room for doubt and equivocation (like when writing certain legal documents you want left open to interpretation). Distinguish the time and place for each style of communicating. Almost never, however, will it work well for you to fall into a mechanistic form of communicating that leaves no room for the personal touch. Nuance and subtlety are your specialty. Milk it!

DR. MATT'S PRESCRIPTION FOR PEAK PERFORMANCE: Your hungry imagination needs constant feeding, so fight the *blahs* and watch out for dull and mindless chores. Don't dismiss your instincts, articulate them. If you learn your instinctual language, it can guide you by revealing hitherto hidden drives and overlooked opportunities. Get over the feeling that anything you say can and will be used against you. Talk is cheap; don't be afraid to spend it. While your faith in humanity is commendable, a healthy dose of skepticism wouldn't hurt.

How to Find Your Mercury Sign—Easy as 1-2-3

1. In the following Mercury tables, look up the year of your birth.

2. The tables list every day on which Mercury *changed* signs, approximately every four weeks, so there's a good chance you won't find your exact date of birth and perhaps not even the month of your birth. That's OK!

Just find the dates that "sandwich" your birthday, the chunk of time during which you were born.

3. Way to go! Directly to the right of that chunk of time is your Mercury sign. When you find your Mercury sign, write it down in your Planetary Positions Chart on page 377.

But wait! Even though Mercury changes signs only about once a month, there's still a chance it changed signs right *on* your birthday. If so, you'll want to determine if you were born *before* or *after* the change. Simply refer to the section "Determining Your Sign Down to the Minute" on page 199.

EXAMPLE

Just for kicks, let's look up Oprah Winfrey's Mercury sign. Oprah was born on January 29, 1954.

1. We turn to 1954 in the Mercury tables.

2. At the start of the month we see Mercury was in Capricorn (having entered Capricorn on December 30 of 1953). But it shifted into Aquarius on January 18. Oprah was born on the 29th. Was Mercury still in Aquarius on January 29? Yep! (It stayed there until February 4, when it moved into Pisces.)

3. So on her Planetary Positions Chart at the line "My Mercury is in _____," Oprah would write "Aquarius."

MERCURY

1940
Jan.	6	2:56 A.M.		Capricorn
	25	5:15 A.M.		Aquarius
Feb.	11	9:01 A.M.		Pisces
March	4	5:07 A.M.		Aries
	7	8:23 A.M.	R	Pisces
April	16	11:57 P.M.		Aries
May	6	4:14 P.M.		Taurus
	21	8:59 A.M.		Gemini
June	4	5:29 P.M.		Cancer
	26	9:33 A.M.		Leo
July	20	8:39 P.M.	R	Cancer
Aug.	11	12:06 A.M.		Leo
	29	6:11 A.M.		Virgo
Sept.	14	6:34 A.M.		Libra
Oct.	3	7:14 A.M.		Scorpio
Dec.	9	7:45 A.M.		Sagittarius
	29	4:36 A.M.		Capricorn

1941
Jan.	16	5:37 P.M.		Aquarius
Feb.	3	8:09 A.M.		Pisces
March	6	9:21 P.M.	R	Aquarius
	16	7:27 A.M.		Pisces
April	12	2:19 A.M.		Aries
	28	6:10 P.M.		Taurus
May	12	7:51 P.M.		Gemini
	29	12:33 P.M.		Cancer
Aug.	6	12:58 A.M.		Leo
	21	12:18 A.M.		Virgo
Sept.	6	6:58 P.M.		Libra
	28	4:22 A.M.		Scorpio
Oct.	29	3:35 P.M.	R	Libra
Nov.	11	3:11 P.M.		Scorpio
Dec.	2	7:11 P.M.		Sagittarius
	21	10:54 P.M.		Capricorn

1942
Jan.	9	10:24 A.M.		Aquarius
March	16	7:11 P.M.		Pisces
April	5	2:07 A.M.		Aries
	20	8:43 A.M.		Taurus
May	4	11:38 P.M.		Gemini
July	12	3:25 P.M.		Cancer
	28	11:24 P.M.		Leo
Aug.	12	8:48 P.M.		Virgo
	31	3:28 A.M.		Libra
Nov.	6	8:45 P.M.		Scorpio
	25	3:26 P.M.		Sagittarius
Dec.	14	5:22 P.M.		Capricorn

1943
Jan.	3	3:27 A.M.		Aquarius
	27	6:43 P.M.	R	Capricorn
Feb.	15	2:00 P.M.		Aquarius
March	10	1:00 A.M.		Pisces
	28	6:20 A.M.		Aries
April	11	11:57 P.M.		Taurus
	30	10:56 A.M.		Gemini
May	26	5:05 A.M.	R	Taurus
June	13	7:46 P.M.		Gemini
July	6	4:05 A.M.		Cancer
	20	11:08 A.M.		Leo
Aug.	5	5:34 A.M.		Virgo
	26	7:37 P.M.		Libra
Sept.	25	4:56 A.M.	R	Virgo

Oct.	11	6:28 P.M.		Libra
	30	6:38 P.M.		Scorpio
Nov.	18	8:39 A.M.		Sagittarius
Dec.	7	8:48 P.M.		Capricorn

1944
Feb.	12	9:18 A.M.		Aquarius
March	2	9:45 P.M.		Pisces
	19	2:43 A.M.		Aries
April	3	12:29 P.M.		Taurus
June	11	6:47 A.M.		Gemini
	26	10:40 P.M.		Cancer
July	11	2:42 A.M.		Leo
	28	6:44 P.M.		Virgo
Oct.	4	10:18 P.M.		Libra
	22	6:33 A.M.		Scorpio
Nov.	10	6:10 A.M.		Sagittarius
Dec.	1	10:31 A.M.		Capricorn
	23	6:22 P.M.	R	Sagittarius

1945
Jan.	13	10:05 P.M.		Capricorn
Feb.	5	4:21 A.M.		Aquarius
	23	6:26 A.M.		Pisces
March	11	1:45 A.M.		Aries
May	16	10:22 A.M.		Taurus
June	4	5:30 A.M.		Gemini
	18	7:28 A.M.		Cancer
July	3	10:39 A.M.		Leo
	26	9:48 A.M.		Virgo
Aug.	17	3:50 A.M.	R	Leo
Sept.	10	2:21 A.M.		Virgo
	27	7:09 A.M.		Libra
Oct.	14	7:14 P.M.		Scorpio
Nov.	3	6:07 P.M.		Sagittarius

1946
Jan.	9	9:10 A.M.		Capricorn
	29	2:23 A.M.		Aquarius
Feb.	15	10:43 A.M.		Pisces
March	4	4:26 A.M.		Aries
April	1	1:17 P.M.	R	Pisces
	16	9:55 A.M.		Aries
May	11	9:29 A.M.		Taurus
	26	11:14 P.M.		Gemini
June	9	9:01 P.M.		Cancer
	27	2:08 P.M.		Leo
Sept.	3	11:30 A.M.		Virgo
	19	9:34 A.M.		Libra
Oct.	7	4:21 P.M.		Scorpio
	30	6:23 A.M.		Sagittarius
Nov.	20	3:16 P.M.	R	Scorpio
Dec.	12	7:03 P.M.		Sagittarius

1947
Jan.	2	8:47 P.M.		Capricorn
	21	4:06 P.M.		Aquarius
Feb.	7	8:32 P.M.		Pisces
April	15	11:31 P.M.		Aries
May	4	1:03 A.M.		Taurus
	18	8:34 A.M.		Gemini
June	2	8:41 A.M.		Cancer
Aug.	10	12:41 P.M.		Leo
	26	9:50 A.M.		Virgo
Sept.	11	3:55 P.M.		Libra
Oct.	1	10:26 A.M.		Scorpio

Dec.	7	7:32 A.M.		Sagittarius
	26	6:18 P.M.		Capricorn

1948
Jan.	14	5:07 A.M.		Aquarius
Feb.	1	7:46 P.M.		Pisces
	20	6:08 A.M.	R	Aquarius
March	18	3:14 A.M.		Pisces
April	8	9:26 P.M.		Aries
	24	8:39 P.M.		Taurus
May	8	11:39 P.M.		Gemini
	28	5:51 A.M.		Cancer
June	28	12:58 P.M.	R	Gemini
July	11	3:57 P.M.		Cancer
Aug.	2	8:55 A.M.		Leo
	17	3:44 A.M.		Virgo
Sept.	3	10:47 A.M.		Libra
	27	2:19 A.M.		Scorpio
Oct.	16	10:34 P.M.	R	Libra
Nov.	9	9:19 P.M.		Scorpio
	29	10:09 A.M.		Sagittarius
Dec.	18	11:47 A.M.		Capricorn

1949
Jan.	6	3:53 A.M.		Aquarius
March	14	4:52 A.M.		Pisces
April	1	11:02 A.M.		Aries
	16	9:56 A.M.		Taurus
May	1	9:19 P.M.		Gemini
July	9	10:20 P.M.		Cancer
	25	12:20 A.M.		Leo
Aug.	9	4:05 A.M.		Virgo
	28	10:48 A.M.		Libra
Nov.	3	1:58 P.M.		Scorpio
	22	4:07 P.M.		Sagittarius
Dec.	11	8:38 A.M.		Capricorn

1950
Jan.	1	7:40 A.M.		Aquarius
	15	2:36 A.M.	R	Capricorn
Feb.	14	2:13 P.M.		Aquarius
March	7	5:05 P.M.		Pisces
	24	10:52 A.M.		Aries
April	8	6:13 A.M.		Taurus
June	14	9:33 A.M.		Gemini
July	2	9:58 A.M.		Cancer
	16	12:09 P.M.		Leo
Aug.	1	9:44 P.M.		Virgo
	27	9:17 A.M.		Libra
Sept.	10	2:17 P.M.	R	Virgo
Oct.	9	9:41 A.M.		Libra
	27	5:37 A.M.		Scorpio
Nov.	14	10:11 P.M.		Sagittarius
Dec.	4	8:58 P.M.		Capricorn

1951
Feb.	9	12:51 P.M.		Aquarius
	28	8:05 A.M.		Pisces
March	16	6:54 A.M.		Aries
April	1	10:27 P.M.		Taurus
May	1	4:26 P.M.	R	Aries
	14	10:41 P.M.		Taurus
June	9	3:44 P.M.		Gemini
	23	10:14 P.M.		Cancer
July	8	8:39 A.M.		Leo
	27	10:24 P.M.		Virgo

MERCURY

Oct.	2	9:26 A.M.		Libra	Nov.	8	1:57 A.M.		Scorpio	Oct.	8	11:02 P.M.		Scorpio

Oct. 2 9:26 A.M. Libra
19 4:53 P.M. Scorpio
Nov. 7 11:59 P.M. Sagittarius
Dec. 1 3:41 P.M. Capricorn
12 7:40 A.M. R Sagittarius

1952
Jan. 13 1:45 A.M. Capricorn
Feb. 2 10:38 P.M. Aquarius
20 1:55 P.M. Pisces
March 7 12:10 P.M. Aries
May 14 9:44 A.M. Taurus
31 10:26 A.M. Gemini
June 14 7:22 A.M. Cancer
30 5:27 P.M. Leo
Sept. 7 7:03 A.M. Virgo
23 1:46 P.M. Libra
Oct. 11 8:06 A.M. Scorpio
Nov. 1 12:34 A.M. Sagittarius

1953
Jan. 6 8:24 A.M. Capricorn
25 2:11 P.M. Aquarius
Feb. 11 6:57 P.M. Pisces
March 2 2:22 P.M. Aries
15 4:17 P.M. R Pisces
April 17 11:48 A.M. Aries
May 8 1:24 A.M. Taurus
22 10:59 A.M. Gemini
June 6 3:24 A.M. Cancer
26 6:01 A.M. Leo
July 28 8:41 A.M. R Cancer
Aug. 11 9:05 A.M. Leo
30 5:59 P.M. Virgo
Sept. 15 4:45 P.M. Libra
Oct. 4 11:41 A.M. Scorpio
31 10:51 A.M. Sagittarius
Nov. 6 5:22 P.M. R Scorpio
Dec. 10 9:49 A.M. Sagittarius
30 12:14 P.M. Capricorn

1954
Jan. 18 2:44 A.M. Aquarius
Feb. 4 1:03 P.M. Pisces
April 13 6:35 A.M. Aries
30 6:26 A.M. Taurus
May 14 8:58 A.M. Gemini
30 11:13 A.M. Cancer
Aug. 7 9:44 A.M. Leo
22 12:42 P.M. Virgo
Sept. 8 3:06 A.M. Libra
28 11:07 P.M. Scorpio
Nov. 4 7:38 A.M. R Libra
11 5:25 A.M. Scorpio
Dec. 4 2:03 A.M. Sagittarius
23 7:10 A.M. Capricorn

1955
Jan. 10 6:05 P.M. Aquarius
March 17 3:50 P.M. Pisces
April 6 11:15 A.M. Aries
21 9:58 P.M. Taurus
May 6 8:05 A.M. Gemini
July 13 9:45 A.M. Cancer
30 12:23 P.M. Leo
Aug. 14 8:08 A.M. Virgo
Sept. 1 7:06 A.M. Libra

Nov. 8 1:57 A.M. Scorpio
26 11:35 P.M. Sagittarius
Dec. 16 1:07 A.M. Capricorn

1956
Jan. 4 4:17 A.M. Aquarius
Feb. 2 7:18 A.M. R Capricorn
15 1:34 A.M. Aquarius
March 11 5:28 A.M. Pisces
28 5:42 P.M. Aries
April 12 12:10 P.M. Taurus
29 5:42 P.M. Gemini
July 6 2:03 P.M. Cancer
21 12:35 A.M. Leo
Aug. 5 2:07 P.M. Virgo
26 8:30 A.M. Libra
Sept. 29 4:26 P.M. R Virgo
Oct. 11 2:30 A.M. Libra
31 3:20 A.M. Scorpio
Nov. 18 4:43 P.M. Sagittarius
Dec. 8 2:11 A.M. Capricorn

1957
Feb. 12 9:30 A.M. Aquarius
March 4 6:34 A.M. Pisces
20 2:48 P.M. Aries
April 4 6:38 P.M. Taurus
June 12 8:40 A.M. Gemini
28 12:09 P.M. Cancer
July 12 2:42 P.M. Leo
29 8:44 P.M. Virgo
Oct. 6 6:09 A.M. Libra
23 3:51 P.M. Scorpio
Nov. 11 1:01 P.M. Sagittarius
Dec. 2 6:19 A.M. Capricorn
28 12:31 P.M. R Sagittarius

1958
Jan. 14 5:03 A.M. Capricorn
Feb. 6 10:21 A.M. Aquarius
24 4:44 P.M. Pisces
March 12 12:32 P.M. Aries
April 2 2:20 P.M. Taurus
10 8:53 A.M. R Aries
May 16 8:53 P.M. Taurus
June 5 3:59 P.M. Gemini
19 9:21 P.M. Cancer
July 4 6:46 P.M. Leo
26 5:08 A.M. Virgo
Aug. 23 9:32 A.M. R Leo
Sept. 10 8:10 P.M. Virgo
28 5:46 P.M. Libra
Oct. 16 3:52 A.M. Scorpio
Nov. 4 9:36 P.M. Sagittarius

1959
Jan. 10 11:48 A.M. Capricorn
30 10:42 A.M. Aquarius
Feb. 16 9:15 P.M. Pisces
March 5 6:53 A.M. Aries
May 12 2:48 P.M. Taurus
28 12:36 P.M. Gemini
June 11 9:11 A.M. Cancer
28 11:32 A.M. Leo
Sept. 4 9:28 P.M. Virgo
20 8:20 P.M. Libra

Oct. 8 11:02 P.M. Scorpio
30 8:17 P.M. Sagittarius
Nov. 25 6:53 A.M. R Scorpio
Dec. 13 10:42 A.M. Sagittarius

1960
Jan. 4 3:25 A.M. Capricorn
23 1:17 A.M. Aquarius
Feb. 9 5:13 A.M. Pisces
April 15 9:22 P.M. Aries
May 4 11:46 A.M. Taurus
18 10:27 P.M. Gemini
June 2 3:31 P.M. Cancer
30 8:10 P.M. Leo
July 5 8:21 P.M. R Cancer
Aug. 10 12:50 P.M. Leo
26 10:12 P.M. Virgo
Sept. 12 1:30 A.M. Libra
Oct. 1 12:17 P.M. Scorpio
Dec. 7 12:30 P.M. Sagittarius
27 2:21 A.M. Capricorn

1961
Jan. 14 1:59 P.M. Aquarius
Feb. 1 4:40 P.M. Pisces
24 3:23 P.M. R Aquarius
March 18 5:16 A.M. Pisces
April 10 4:23 A.M. Aries
26 9:34 A.M. Taurus
May 10 11:34 A.M. Gemini
28 12:24 P.M. Cancer
Aug. 3 8:16 P.M. Leo
18 3:52 P.M. Virgo
Sept. 4 5:33 P.M. Libra
27 7:16 A.M. Scorpio
Oct. 21 9:30 P.M. R Libra
Nov. 10 6:54 P.M. Scorpio
30 5:55 P.M. Sagittarius
Dec. 19 8:05 P.M. Capricorn

1962
Jan. 7 10:08 A.M. Aquarius
March 15 6:43 A.M. Pisces
April 2 9:32 P.M. Aries
17 11:10 P.M. Taurus
May 3 1:05 A.M. Gemini
July 11 2:37 A.M. Cancer
26 1:50 P.M. Leo
Aug. 10 2:30 P.M. Virgo
29 10:48 A.M. Libra
Nov. 4 9:21 P.M. Scorpio
23 12:32 P.M. Sagittarius
Dec. 12 3:51 P.M. Capricorn

1963
Jan. 1 8:11 P.M. Aquarius
19 1:00 A.M. R Capricorn
Feb. 15 5:09 A.M. Aquarius
March 9 12:27 A.M. Pisces
25 10:53 P.M. Aries
April 9 5:04 P.M. Taurus
May 2 11:15 P.M. Gemini
10 3:41 P.M. R Taurus
June 14 6:21 P.M. Gemini
July 3 10:00 P.M. Cancer
18 1:20 A.M. Leo

MERCURY

Aug.	3	4:21 A.M.		Virgo
	26	3:34 P.M.		Libra
Sept.	16	3:30 P.M.	R	Virgo
Oct.	10	11:45 A.M.		Libra
	28	2:54 P.M.		Scorpio
Nov.	16	6:08 A.M.		Sagittarius
Dec.	6	12:18 A.M.		Capricorn

1964

Feb.	10	4:31 P.M.		Aquarius
	29	5:50 P.M.		Pisces
March	16	6:55 P.M.		Aries
April	1	7:58 P.M.		Taurus
June	9	10:46 A.M.		Gemini
	24	12:18 P.M.		Cancer
July	8	7:39 P.M.		Leo
	27	6:36 A.M.		Virgo
Oct.	2	7:13 P.M.		Libra
	20	2:12 A.M.		Scorpio
Nov.	8	6:02 A.M.		Sagittarius
	30	2:31 P.M.		Capricorn
Dec.	16	9:32 A.M.	R	Sagittarius

1965

Jan.	12	10:13 P.M.		Capricorn
Feb.	3	4:03 A.M.		Aquarius
	21	12:40 A.M.		Pisces
March	8	9:19 P.M.		Aries
May	15	8:20 A.M.		Taurus
June	1	10:48 P.M.		Gemini
	15	9:05 P.M.		Cancer
July	1	10:55 A.M.		Leo
	31	6:26 A.M.		Virgo
Aug.	3	2:57 A.M.	R	Virgo
Sept.	8	12:14 P.M.		Virgo
	25	12:50 A.M.		Libra
Oct.	12	4:16 P.M.		Scorpio
Nov.	2	1:05 A.M.		Sagittarius

1966

Jan.	7	1:26 P.M.		Capricorn
	26	11:10 P.M.		Aquarius
Feb.	13	5:18 A.M.		Pisces
March	11	9:58 P.M.		Aries
	21	9:34 P.M.	R	Pisces
April	17	4:32 P.M.		Aries
May	9	9:49 A.M.		Taurus
	24	12:60 P.M.		Gemini
June	7	2:12 P.M.		Cancer
	26	2:06 P.M.		Leo
Sept.	1	5:36 A.M.		Virgo
	17	3:20 A.M.		Libra
Oct.	5	5:03 P.M.		Scorpio
	30	2:39 A.M.		Sagittarius
Nov.	12	10:26 P.M.	R	Scorpio
Dec.	11	10:28 A.M.		Sagittarius
	31	7:52 P.M.		Capricorn

1967

Jan.	19	12:06 P.M.		Aquarius
Feb.	5	7:38 P.M.		Pisces
April	14	9:38 A.M.		Aries
May	1	6:27 P.M.		Taurus
	15	10:28 P.M.		Gemini
	31	1:03 P.M.		Cancer
Aug.	8	5:10 P.M.		Leo
	24	1:18 A.M.		Virgo

Sept.	9	11:54 A.M.		Libra
	29	8:47 P.M.		Scorpio
Dec.	5	8:42 A.M.		Sagittarius
	24	3:34 P.M.		Capricorn

1968

Jan.	12	2:20 A.M.		Aquarius
Feb.	1	7:58 A.M.		Pisces
	11	1:55 P.M.	R	Aquarius
March	17	9:46 A.M.		Pisces
April	6	8:02 P.M.		Aries
	22	11:19 A.M.		Taurus
May	6	5:56 P.M.		Gemini
	29	5:44 P.M.		Cancer
June	13	5:33 P.M.	R	Gemini
July	8	8:30 P.M.		Cancer
	31	1:11 A.M.		Leo
Aug.	14	7:54 P.M.		Virgo
Sept.	1	11:59 A.M.		Libra
	28	9:41 A.M.		Scorpio
Oct.	7	5:47 P.M.	R	Libra
Nov.	8	6:01 A.M.		Scorpio
	27	7:48 A.M.		Sagittarius
Dec.	16	9:11 A.M.		Capricorn

1969

Jan.	4	7:19 A.M.		Aquarius
March	12	10:20 A.M.		Pisces
	30	4:59 A.M.		Aries
April	14	12:55 A.M.		Taurus
	30	10:19 A.M.		Gemini
July	7	10:59 P.M.		Cancer
	22	2:12 P.M.		Leo
Aug.	6	11:21 P.M.		Virgo
	27	1:51 A.M.		Libra
Oct.	6	9:26 P.M.	R	Virgo
	9	12:16 P.M.		Libra
Nov.	1	11:54 A.M.		Scorpio
	20	1:01 A.M.		Sagittarius
Dec.	9	8:22 A.M.		Capricorn

1970

Feb.	13	8:09 A.M.		Aquarius
March	5	3:11 P.M.		Pisces
	22	4:59 A.M.		Aries
April	6	2:40 A.M.		Taurus
June	13	7:47 A.M.		Gemini
	30	1:23 A.M.		Cancer
July	14	3:07 A.M.		Leo
	31	12:22 A.M.		Virgo
Oct.	7	1:04 P.M.		Libra
	25	1:17 A.M.		Scorpio
Nov.	12	8:17 P.M.		Sagittarius
Dec.	3	5:15 A.M.		Capricorn

1971

Jan.	2	6:37 P.M.	R	Capricorn
	13	9:17 P.M.		Capricorn
Feb.	7	3:52 P.M.		Aquarius
	26	2:58 A.M.		Pisces
March	13	11:46 P.M.		Aries
April	1	9:12 A.M.		Taurus
	18	4:52 P.M.	R	Aries
May	16	10:33 P.M.		Taurus
June	7	1:45 A.M.		Gemini
	21	11:25 A.M.		Cancer
July	6	3:54 A.M.		Leo

	26	12:04 P.M.		Virgo
Aug.	29	3:42 P.M.	R	Leo
Sept.	11	1:45 A.M.		Virgo
	30	4:19 A.M.		Libra
Oct.	17	12:50 P.M.		Scorpio
Nov.	6	2:00 A.M.		Sagittarius

1972

Jan.	11	1:18 P.M.		Capricorn
	31	6:47 P.M.		Aquarius
Feb.	18	7:54 A.M.		Pisces
March	5	12:00 P.M.		Aries
May	12	6:46 P.M.		Taurus
	29	1:46 A.M.		Gemini
June	11	9:56 P.M.		Cancer
	28	11:53 A.M.		Leo
Sept.	5	6:37 A.M.		Virgo
	21	7:12 A.M.		Libra
Oct.	9	6:11 A.M.		Scorpio
	30	2:28 P.M.		Sagittarius
Nov.	29	2:08 A.M.	R	Scorpio
Dec.	12	6:21 P.M.		Sagittarius

1973

Jan.	4	9:42 A.M.		Capricorn
	23	10:24 A.M.		Aquarius
Feb.	9	2:30 P.M.		Pisces
April	16	4:18 P.M.		Aries
May	5	9:55 P.M.		Taurus
	20	12:24 P.M.		Gemini
June	3	11:43 P.M.		Cancer
	27	1:42 A.M.		Leo
July	16	3:04 A.M.	R	Cancer
Aug.	11	7:22 A.M.		Leo
	28	10:22 A.M.		Virgo
Sept.	13	11:17 A.M.		Libra
Oct.	2	3:13 P.M.		Scorpio
Dec.	8	4:30 P.M.		Sagittarius
	28	10:15 A.M.		Capricorn

1974

Jan.	15	10:57 P.M.		Aquarius
Feb.	2	5:42 P.M.		Pisces
March	2	12:50 P.M.	R	Aquarius
	17	3:12 P.M.		Pisces
April	11	10:21 A.M.		Aries
	27	10:11 P.M.		Taurus
May	11	11:55 P.M.		Gemini
	29	3:04 A.M.		Cancer
Aug.	5	6:42 A.M.		Leo
	20	4:04 P.M.		Virgo
Sept.	6	12:49 A.M.		Libra
	27	7:21 P.M.		Scorpio
Oct.	26	6:22 P.M.	R	Libra
Nov.	11	11:06 A.M.		Scorpio
Dec.	2	1:18 A.M.		Sagittarius
	21	4:17 A.M.		Capricorn

1975

Jan.	8	4:59 P.M.		Aquarius
March	16	6:51 A.M.		Pisces
April	4	7:28 A.M.		Aries
	19	12:21 P.M.		Taurus
May	4	6:55 P.M.		Gemini
July	12	3:57 A.M.		Cancer
	28	3:05 A.M.		Leo
Aug.	12	1:13 A.M.		Virgo

MERCURY

	30	12:21 P.M.		Libra
Nov.	6	3:58 A.M.		Scorpio
	24	8:45 P.M.		Sagittarius
Dec.	13	11:10 P.M.		Capricorn

1976

Jan.	2	3:23 P.M.		Aquarius
	24	8:31 P.M.	R	Aquarius
Feb.	15	2:03 P.M.		Aquarius
March	9	7:03 A.M.		Pisces
	26	10:37 A.M.		Aries
April	10	4:30 A.M.		Taurus
	29	6:12 P.M.		Gemini
May	19	2:22 P.M.	R	Taurus
June	13	2:21 P.M.		Gemini
July	4	9:19 A.M.		Cancer
	18	2:36 P.M.		Leo
Aug.	3	11:42 A.M.		Virgo
	25	3:53 P.M.		Libra
Sept.	21	2:15 A.M.	R	Virgo
Oct.	10	9:48 A.M.		Libra
	28	11:56 P.M.		Scorpio
Nov.	16	2:03 P.M.		Sagittarius
Dec.	6	4:25 A.M.		Capricorn

1977

Feb.	10	6:56 P.M.	Aquarius
March	2	3:09 A.M.	Pisces
	18	6:57 A.M.	Aries
April	2	9:46 P.M.	Taurus

June	10	4:07 P.M.		Gemini
	26	2:08 A.M.		Cancer
July	10	7:01 A.M.		Leo
	28	5:16 A.M.		Virgo
Oct.	4	4:17 A.M.		Libra
	21	11:24 A.M.		Scorpio
Nov.	9	12:21 P.M.		Sagittarius
Dec.	1	1:44 A.M.		Capricorn
	21	2:19 A.M.	R	Sagittarius

1978

Jan.	13	3:08 P.M.	Capricorn
Feb.	4	10:55 A.M.	Aquarius
	22	11:11 A.M.	Pisces
March	10	7:11 A.M.	Aries
May	16	3:21 A.M.	Taurus
June	3	10:27 A.M.	Gemini
	17	10:49 A.M.	Cancer
July	2	5:29 P.M.	Leo
	27	1:11 A.M.	Virgo
Aug.	13	2:06 A.M.	R Leo
Sept.	9	2:24 A.M.	Virgo
	26	11:41 A.M.	Libra
Oct.	14	12:30 A.M.	Scorpio
Nov.	3	2:49 A.M.	Sagittarius

1979

Jan.	8	5:34 P.M.	Capricorn
	28	7:50 A.M.	Aquarius
Feb.	14	3:39 P.M.	Pisces

March	3	4:33 P.M.		Aries
	28	5:40 A.M.	R	Pisces
April	17	7:49 A.M.		Aries
May	10	5:04 P.M.		Taurus
	26	2:45 A.M.		Gemini
June	9	1:33 A.M.		Cancer
	27	4:52 A.M.		Leo
Sept.	2	4:39 P.M.		Virgo
	18	2:00 P.M.		Libra
Oct.	6	10:55 P.M.		Scorpio
	30	2:06 A.M.		Sagittarius
Nov.	17	10:09 P.M.	R	Scorpio
Dec.	12	8:35 A.M.		Sagittarius

1980

Jan.	2	3:03 A.M.	Capricorn
	20	9:19 P.M.	Aquarius
Feb.	7	3:08 A.M.	Pisces
April	14	10:59 A.M.	Aries
May	2	5:56 A.M.	Taurus
	16	12:07 P.M.	Gemini
	31	5:06 P.M.	Cancer
Aug.	8	10:31 P.M.	Leo
	24	1:48 P.M.	Virgo
Sept.	9	9:01 P.M.	Libra
	29	8:17 P.M.	Scorpio
Dec.	5	2:46 P.M.	Sagittarius
	24	11:47 P.M.	Capricorn

Sizing Up Your Sales and Seduction Savvy—How Big Is Your Venus?

"A person without a smile should not open a shop."
CHINESE PROVERB

Actually it's not the size of your Venus but what you do with it that counts. Venus represents that integral part of you that *turns people on*. It symbolizes your powers of persuasion and promotion. It's about making connections and building relationships. For networking, marketing, and sales, you can't live without it. Having an impaired Venus is like being a brilliant software developer with no people skills or marketing flair. When you want to charm, negotiate, or seduce, turn on your Venus.

SIMPLY IRRESISTIBLE MARKETING

In classical mythology, Venus was the goddess of art, beauty, and love—and the mother of Cupid. This mischievous team made people fall in love, breaking even the hardest of hearts. No one could resist their charms. Traditional astrology sees Venus as the planet of relationships, and sales is all about getting into the *right* relationship with the consumer. Consumers relate to a brand's personality and a professional's reputation. To attract buyers, you often have to pump up your Venus to woo them as if they were potential mates.

Even if you hate sales, don't skip this chapter! Being a salesperson may not be for everyone. But to get a job—any job—in the first place, you have to "sell" yourself. Human resources studies have proven that most employees secure their positions through a personal connection, not a résumé in response to a help wanted ad. If you're participating in nearly any sector of our economy, you are selling. You sell your ideas, your credibility, your *self*. This doesn't mean you're selling out! So start networking with your built-in Venus talents!

OOH LA LA! NOW THAT'S ATTRACTION: NETWORKING

In the professional world, it takes more than a pretty face and pleasant demeanor to make connections. So you network: You meet people in all walks of life, talk to them, get to know them, and introduce what you can offer without an assaulting sales pitch. You stand out from the crowd in order to be *remembered*. For information on honing your networking and marketing energies, look up your individual Venus sign.

"LET'S MAKE A DEAL": YOUR SALES SAVVY

Once you've made the connection and established trust—either in person or through your marketing materials—it's time to make the sale. You can get to know what kind of salesperson you are and want to be by looking up your Venus sign, which can be found on pages 320–22 and then written into your Professional Planetary Profile.

WHAT'S LOVE GOT TO DO WITH IT?: WORKPLACE ROMANCE

While we're exploring the sales and marketing applications of your Venus energy, let's not overlook this planet's more traditional associations with love and romance. If you're doing work you're interested in, you're bound to meet someone on the job who shares your interests—and one thing may lead to another. Love seldom stops at the workplace door. But be forewarned: Workplace romances can be tricky! They fall under the jurisdiction of numerous laws and policies and create unforseeable complications. Before Cupid's arrow strikes, get the scoop on your—or your coworker's—romantic soft spots.

Venus in Aries

NETWORKING—MAKE THE CONNECTION: Given to random acts of impulsivity, you vow on Monday morning to follow up with your three best contacts this week. By Tuesday, however, you're distracted by three more fresh faces, leaving the previous prospects to wonder if you're full of hot air. By all means, take advantage of your Venus in Aries talents: Go up to people. Make cold calls. But don't let your love of schmoozing become more important than the relationships themselves. Convince everyone you're serious about doing business. Networking isn't a contest to see how many business cards you can distribute while sipping champagne. Instead, help prospective clients see how you can help them while they're helping you. In other words, no one-way streets!

SALES SAVVY—TURN THEM ON: By nature, you belong to the school of selling that tells the customer, "If you don't make up your mind in three minutes, I'll make it up for you!" As aggressive on the sales floor as in love, you can easily master the techniques of the "hard sell." But why limit yourself? Sure, when you come on strong *some* customers reach for their wallets, but others head for the nearest exit sign. So consider this bit of advice: Make it *easy* for the customer to do business with you. Don't rush them. Treat them like individuals, not replicas of "the perfect customer" described in the Marketing 101 textbook. Perhaps *you'd* never buy smooth peanut butter instead of chunky, but plenty of people do, and reaching both markets adds up to more jars sold.

> **"Meet me in the stockroom. I want to inspect your packaging."**
> A MISPLACED MEMO

WORKPLACE ROMANCE: Passions consume Venus in Aries. You love the thrill of the hunt, the smell of pheromones, the chance to clutch another conquest. And if a conquest happens to happen on company time, oh well! You'd never let it interfere with your work—at least you think you wouldn't. If you want to be safe not sorry, take workplace romances slowly. Even if you rush in and then rush right back out, you'll still have to see your ex-sweetheart every day of the work week. And people will talk. It's unavoidable. Keep your reputation intact by keeping hormones in check.

Venus in Taurus

NETWORKING—MAKE THE CONNECTION: With Venus in Taurus, you don't like to knock on doors. You prefer to stand behind a quality product and let it sell itself. It's a noble ideal. It doesn't make the most of your sales potential, however, especially since it neglects your inviting, welcoming warmth. At parties, don't just sit there—mingle. OK, maybe you shrink from saying something gauche and offensive like, "May I introduce myself?" So choose semifamiliar surroundings and branch out gradually. In new territory, take a friend. Invest in one or two *fabulous* networking outfits that make you feel as if you own the place—whether it's the Ritz or the wrecking yard.

SALES SAVVY—TURN THEM ON: Never overlook the power of a sale! You know the allure of red price tags that scream "half off!" Even if retail's not your gig, send announcements (bulk e-mail is a cheap way nowadays) to inform your entire mailing list you're offering a special this month. What's that? You don't have a mailing list? Get one, even if it's just a list of potential employers you've met and found intriguing. For in-person sales pitches, learn to use your voice. Business courses in every major city coach professionals to speak effectively. You've got gifted vocal cords—use them for more than singing in the shower. Don't let prospective clients slip through your fingers just because there are too many of them. Just as lovers have to kiss lots of frogs before finding their prince or princess, come to terms with approaching lots of prospective clients before you bag a deal.

WORKPLACE ROMANCE: Venus in Taurus is usually quite staid. *Love,* however, is one of the few forces that can knock Taurus out of a regular routine. It doesn't happen often—probably because you wait for the other person to make the first move—but when it does, *wow!*—you respond to the right person wholeheartedly. Despite your professionalism, you can't resist displaying affection. You go weak in the knees for simple romantic gestures like love notes or kitchen appliances, which you just happen to exhibit prominently on your desk for coworkers to see and envy. Nevertheless, you're better than most at handling the intrinsic tension between being in love and making a living.

Venus in Gemini

NETWORKING—MAKE THE CONNECTION: Venus in Gemini is the sign of a shameless flirt and congenial schmoozer, a better mixer than a cocktail straw. There's probably one of your business cards in every wallet on the block—when it comes to networking, you wrote the book. And by cultivating your innate ability to talk to anyone about anything, you can guarantee you'll always have an "in." If you're not living up to your goals for new leads, it probably means you need to do less mixing and more connecting; it suggests you're talking it up and picking people's brains, but offering little in return. To remedy this situation you might consider, for instance, sponsoring a luncheon or seminar and inviting prospective clients—a great opportunity to meet your community and discuss mutual issues. Don't spoil it by trying to sell then and there. Social occasions are foreplay.

SALES SAVVY—TURN THEM ON: What a telemarketer you would be! Upbeat and talkative, not too pushy, not too nonchalant, you've got the gift for selling in today's marketplace where consumers buy an idea, not just a product. And it doesn't matter *what you sell*—cars, consulting services, or sheep—because it's *how you sell* that counts. So if you enjoy sales of any kind, you stand to make big bucks in commission-based jobs. But if you don't enjoy it 50 weeks a year, don't do it. Sad and disillusioned is the Gemini salesperson who becomes a mechanized selling machine. Watch out! Sales pitches that sound like scripts seldom work, and playing games with people's emotions is a no-no. Remember, *even if you don't make the sale today with this particular customer, it doesn't mean they won't return tomorrow.* "I'll think about it" does not mean "No." Some people just think a lot.

WORKPLACE ROMANCE: You're at your most susceptible to on-the-job romantic overtures when you've already got 13 things to do and three clients on hold. Just for the fun of it, just to add a little more excitement to your already insane schedule, you make goo-goo eyes at the mail delivery person. It's harmless, right? Well maybe, maybe not. You see, since you often utter the perfect compliment at the right moment, unsuspecting colleagues can easily mistake your innocent intentions for something more than platonic good manners. Then, next time when that delivery person shows up not with a box of copy toner cartridges but a dozen red roses, you'll have some explaining to do. Fortunately, you're good at talking your way out of problems you've talked yourself into.

Venus in Cancer

NETWORKING—MAKING THE CONNECTION: You've got a knack for making people feel at ease, with some disarming mannerisms that render you a seductive listener. Your tender, sensitive nature makes you a good networker. You never forget a face or any of those important little details. The predatory approach doesn't work for you, but friendly personal interest does. If you're looking for new client prospects, turn to previously satisfied customers and old acquaintances—your most valuable sources for referrals. Stay in touch. Ask them for introductions to their friends and associates. Shyness mustn't stop you from drumming up business.

SALES SAVVY—TURN THEM ON: Advice isn't cheap anymore. Consumers pay for information. So don't unveil your repository of experience and expertise to just anyone. Guard your wisdom like a pricey silk suit under a dowdy raincoat—and titillate your prospects with just a glimpse of what they'll get once they commit. You need your clients' full attention, so sing your business's praises without immediately pitching a sale. Taking the time to assess your client's needs will put you in a better position to respond. (This needs-based marketing approach worked brilliantly for Nabisco 100 years ago when it launched its Uneeda Biscuits with the slogan, "You need these biscuits.") An ideal slogan for Venus in Cancer enterprises would sound something like "Exceptional care for exceptional customers."

> **"Publicity is stronger than sanity: Given the right PR, armpit hair on female singers could become a national fetish."**
> SOCIAL SATIRIST LENNY BRUCE

WORKPLACE ROMANCE: Though you're a sucker for sappy love songs, you're also a material girl or boy, so it's hard to say whether your favorite three words are "I love you" or "Wrap it up!" It follows, then, that when you're *single* you feel torn between looking for love in the workplace (anywhere you can, for that matter) and maintaining job security. If you're already *coupled*, you just covet the space and privacy to earn your paycheck and make the hours pass till you can return home to Sweetie. Either way, you appreciate a sweetheart who sticks around, calls when they say they will, and contributes a fair share to a lifestyle comfortable enough so you can both, at least once in a while, call in sick and hide under the covers.

Venus in Leo

NETWORKING—MAKE THE CONNECTION: If you feel on the verge of getting lost in a crowd, don't forget your talent for initiating a conversation or connections. Pay a compliment; ask relevant questions. You've got great entertainment value, but don't hog the conversation or hold up the buffet line with your latest joke, overexerting your "I'm the life of the party" efforts. Practice starting sentences with some word other than *I* and monitor that nasty habit of talking down to the common folk. You instinctively know how to work a room; now learn to enjoy the party. You think people are interested in what you say, but they're not. Not if you don't make them interested. So take a stand. Express a point of view. Better to be opinionated and memorable than wishy-washy and forgettable.

SALES SAVVY—TURN THEM ON: As a salesperson, you can make an old Formica desk seem like a precious antique. But don't exaggerate to the point of absurdity or dishonesty, like claiming to sell "calorie-free" chocolate cake. While your dynamic personality turns people on, it can also overwhelm them. The customer who has one sincere question before signing the sales contract may feel too intimidated to ever ask—and there goes the sale. Even if you're four feet tall, that Venus in Leo personality seems as big as Michael Jordan. Make sure your prospect has a chance to talk. Sit down with them, face to face; don't tower over them. Nervous Leos get particularly talkative, so if you're presenting, you can easily find yourself saying too much—like those Academy Award winners who get cut off by the music or a commercial.

WORKPLACE ROMANCE: Since the workplace often serves as your personal stage or screen, you're bound to attract numerous admirers there. But romances that begin where you both look and behave your best generally lead to unrealistic expectations. Don't broadcast your love over the company intranet until after you know if your new sweetie leaves dishes in the sink at home—or until they've seen you emerge disheveled to pick up the Sunday paper. Chances are that you're demanding in the boardroom *and* the bedroom. Chances are even greater that you get what you demand.

Venus in Virgo

NETWORKING—MAKE THE CONNECTION: In the networking department, you're probably as organized and methodical as in the rest of your relationships. You make lists of contacts; you keep track of people. But you may lack the initiative to call contacts out of the blue, to put yourself on the line, to ask someone for help. Yes, it's got to be done—so do it. Better sooner than later. Anyway, what you consider pushy, most people think of as normal, lively conversation. Since you're the kind of person who networks best when you have a specific job or role to perform, sign up for committees or volunteer to pass the hors d'ouevres—that way you have a *reason* to mingle and you'll meet people along the way.

SALES SAVVY—TURN THEM ON: On the showroom floor, you seldom resort to hard-sell tactics. Instead, you're terribly industrious and helpful, and can make customers feel you're doing them a favor. And if they don't buy from you, well, obviously they've made a grave, possibly irrevocable error! Occasionally, though, your sales approach verges on the excessively matter of fact. Try to invite qualitative responses from customers. Instead of asking, "May I help you?" (which invites a yes-or-no answer), ask "*How* can I help you?" (which invites a more detailed response so you really can know how to help). You'll find you can successfully sell many products and services with the "specs" alone, by outlining features and benefits and expecting the customer to see the usefulness of what you offer. But other times you'll have to stretch your sales savvy—experiment with psychology, special promotions, and even a price war with your competitors.

WORKPLACE ROMANCE: When romance intrudes on your career, you don't like it. It seems like an awful distraction. Even if you do fall for a coworker, you have a hard time showing affection, opting to keep it a *private* affair of the heart. You don't let your hair down for just anyone—you'll scratch lovers off the list who aren't squeaky clean, punctual, and hardworking. If you do succumb to Cupid's arrow, you'll require your on-the-job sweetie to diligently curry your favor—and stay out of your way during deadlines. Despite these drawbacks, the workplace isn't necessarily off-limits for romance. In fact it's a fine place to look for a date or a mate who shares your professional dedication. Just think of the fun you'll have commuting together!

Venus in Libra

NETWORKING—MAKE THE CONNECTION: With Venus in Libra, empathy ranks among your greatest assets. You can figure out what it's like to stand in someone else's wing tips or pumps for a day and use it to your advantage. Just remember: People love to talk about themselves and feel understood. Make eye contact. Show interest. Find common ground. Ask for *their* business cards before shoving yours in their faces. And since you tend to accumulate lots of friends and acquaintances, keep in mind that the best networkers don't just get introduced, they *make* introductions.

SALES SAVVY—TURN THEM ON: When it comes to sales you may lack aggression, but you can generate lots of contacts. You love to wheel and deal but find haggling and dickering much too crude. As a result your sales efforts may go far, but not far enough. To clinch more deals, consider cooperative marketing plans—joining forces with a company or professional who complements rather than competes with you—like a landscape architect with a gardener. Other than that, cultivate a loyal following so that word-of-mouth will make the sale for you. How to get a loyal following? When you've got a client at your desk or on the phone, give them your full attention. Don't take advantage of gullibility. Adopt a long-term vision for what kind of clientele you want to build up—most of them will pay the bills, but few will keep you interested enough to keep selling to them five years from now.

WORKPLACE ROMANCE: In astrological circles you've earned a dubious reputation for a willingness to do *anything* for love. As the ultimate romantic sucker, you seem to lap up affection and moonlight as a kitten laps up milk. You fall in love with love. Get over it, or find someone else who thinks life is a Broadway musical. Unless you've already snagged your long-term sweetheart, you're always on the prowl, whether there's a job to do or not. So, as much as you want to please the boss, romance comes first—unless of course the boss is the object of your affections! Alas, with Venus in Libra, true bliss only comes with a mate you can respect, so torrid desktop cybersex will quickly grow stale. If you've currently got your eye on a workplace comrade, make it a policy to be friends first. *Old friends* is even better.

> **"Kodak sells film, but they don't advertise film. They advertise memories."**
> EDUCATOR AND AUTHOR
> THEODORE LEVITT

Venus in Scorpio

NETWORKING—MAKE THE CONNECTION: A long time ago, you figured out it's not *what* you know or even *whom* you know that counts, but *what you know about whom you know.* You've got all the dirt. Oddly enough, this makes you very popular! Your dinner table conversation alone earns you plenty of invitations. What's not so easy, though, is for you to seem *familiar,* just one of the gang. Don't order three double vodkas, but loosen up. Just decide you're going to be easygoing at your next networking event. Tone down your "What's in it for me?" attitude. Ask questions that don't sound like interrogations or demands. Congratulate folks on their successes without having to "best" them. Remember, *networking* is no more than a fancy word for meeting people and making friends.

SALES SAVVY—TURN THEM ON: No matter what your actual field, you're a born life insurance salesperson. For you, it's a cinch to persuade folks they just can't live, or die, without $1 million in coverage. By accumulating relevant snippets of info about your prospective customer, you can create a proposition that's tailor-made to suit their desires, some of which they didn't even know they had. Your intensity, however, may scare off some hesitant consumers. Be up front about costs or you'll waste time seducing gullible but penniless clients. Though you may sometimes get clients to buy from you just to get you off their tail, this approach doesn't do much for repeat business. Make it your mission to incite desire—not to force it. Discerning what people want and how you can help them get it deserves to be an art, and you are the artiste. By helping others you may wind up helping yourself.

WORKPLACE ROMANCE: Remember "I can't get no satisfaction," from the Rolling Stones' song? That's Venus in Scorpio. Your passion is insatiable. You can't get enough. But you'd *never* stoop low enough to show it. A clandestine rendezvous in the supply closet? Perhaps. An open flirt fest with the field manager who flies in every other Thursday? No way, not in a million years. You'd rather maintain your separate lives, even if you two do hit it off. One word of warning: Jealousy boils your blood—rather inconvenient if you have to live with it Monday through Friday from nine to five—so choose your crushes wisely. On the other hand, don't be offended when half the office *doesn't* ask for your home phone number. Lots of people simply don't mix business with pleasure, whereas you rather like the business *of* pleasure.

Venus in Sagittarius

NETWORKING—MAKE THE CONNECTION: You're not so much a mingler as a *singler.* At parties and other networking events, you single out one or two interesting-looking professionals with whom to have deep and meaningful conversations and from whom you learn as much as you can. You get completely engrossed and before you know it the party ends and you realize you've made only one contact. If you want to expand your professional network, try making the rounds. Set a goal to pass out three business cards or résumés before you leave. You're not shy but you resent chitchat, so your ideal networking strategy is to act *terribly interested* in people and what they do. Call or approach a wide range of people with a big smile—one of the hallmarks of Venus in Saj—introduce yourself, and ask them to tell you about their work.

SALES SAVVY—TURN THEM ON: Whatever you sell, you sell excitement. You fire up your market like a coach whose players wouldn't dream of giving less than 100 percent. A zealot of whatever you believe in, you're a natural for the new "evangelism" marketing approach, which promotes with fervor and zeal, not just features and benefits. And practice what you preach—make sure you're as enthusiastic about, say, industrial-size pizza ovens as you want your pizza-baking customers to be. You're a born bluffer, but there are some things you simply can't fake. Make it your goal when you finish a sales meeting or interview to leave the impression that *Yeah, that Venus in Saj knows what they're talking about!* Finally, realize your sales and self-promotion efforts can't reach everyone. Often you'll find niche marketing (targeting specific groups with products or services especially suited to their needs and interests) is more effective than ballistic marketing (like advertising the same product in nine different magazines with nothing in common).

WORKPLACE ROMANCE: You bore quickly, so it makes sense your eyes would roam from the pie charts to the coworker who is *so* easy on the eyes. You chase and court more than you catch, desiring commitment but fearing it. You see everyone as fair game in your amorous intrigues—the boss, the customer, the wrong number whose husky voice you just couldn't get enough of. But it's hard to imagine you "settling" long term for a sweetheart so close to home as one of your coworkers. Nearly relentless in your quest for the perfect lover, you prefer to await lovey-dovey, long-distance faxes from your tall, dark and *strange* honey four time zones away. One insight from Dr. Matt: You treat friends and lovers an awful lot

alike, so sometimes they don't know if they're one or the other to you. Do you?

Venus in Capricorn

NETWORKING—MAKE THE CONNECTION: Actual networking is not the issue. You can work a room with the best of them. What matters more is how *seriously* you take this part of your career. There are two likely scenarios. Case one: not serious at all. It seems like a waste of time, frivolously waltzing around a hotel convention hall with a plastic cup of cheap wine and a dorky "Hello My Name Is" sticker on your lapel, yakking with out-of-towners who'll trash your card before they board their flight home. Case two: totally serious. Networking is your reason for living as you doggedly climb the social ladder by getting in good with seminar leaders, the rich and famous, and anyone else who'll let you fetch them a second cup of coffee. Unfortunately, neither extreme does you good. Networking is important—it's by far the best way to get job leads and meet important people—but it's not the end-all-be-all of the business world.

SALES SAVVY—TURN THEM ON: The well-seasoned Venus in Capricorn salesperson has it made. You're gutsy and confident, and having established yourself as an authority in your field, you're able to take no for an answer without falling into the *I'll-never-make-another-sale* pit of despair. But if you're a Venus in Capricorn who's new to sales, your powers of persuasion may need work. There's no question you satisfy your clients' needs with competence and even excellence. But what if you also want to impress them enough that they return for more, building up your "repeat business"? Make a relationship, not just a sale. Instead of a generic invoice, send a bill with a thank-you note. Casual is typical in today's business climate, so adapt to the given environment. Of course you want to look professional, but image consultants recommend that salespeople dress no more than one level more formally than their clients. In other words, don't wear a tux to a sporting goods convention and avoid those stuffy "To whom it may concern" letters.

WORKPLACE ROMANCE: Though you're serious about getting good at what you do, success turns you on. So even if you're married to the company, you'll have a hard time resisting the gallantry of Prince or Princess Charming, especially if he or she has a really big and impressive position. In less enlightened times, Venus in Capricorn was considered the sign of

someone who slept their way to the top. Nowadays, we know that's only vicious hearsay, but it's still true you value good deals in all things, including your relationships. Don't settle for less.

Venus in Aquarius

NETWORKING—MAKE THE CONNECTION: Do you ever wonder why you get all the weirdos; why the kooks come to you? It's because difficult people are your specialty. Some folks may even suspect *you* of being strange. No matter. You are who you are, and it's really pretty marvelous how you can hit it off with the visiting dignitary as well as with the waitperson who clears your plate. Yours is a charm that seems completely unrehearsed, never calculated. But watch out! Don't immediately stereotype or categorize the people you meet in social or professional settings. People want to be viewed as individuals, not "types" or representatives of a larger group. The best connections have a personal component. And while your tendency may be to stir up controversial conversation about giving employment opportunities to the homeless, let it be known you'll still want to play tennis with someone who doesn't share your views.

SALES SAVVY—TURN THEM ON: Sales jobs are not the natural habitat of Venus in Aquarius. The emotional roller-coaster ride of selling (for both seller and buyer) makes you dizzy, and while you love to argue a point, you seldom get jazzed about persuading people they need what you've got. But if you find yourself in a sales position, there is one approach that will work brilliantly for you: I call it "partnership selling." This tactic involves aligning yourself with the customer, assuring them "We're in this together." One Venus in Aquarius professional kept me as a long-term client by often saying "Stick with me, kid." Partnership selling succeeds especially well in a field like real estate, where home buyers want a partner in buying the best possible home for the money, not just a commission-hungry contract-writer. But partnership selling can serve you well in many areas. If, for instance, you're "selling" yourself at a job interview, try discarding the "I'm capable" approach and adopting an approach of "If you hire me, you and I (or this company and I) will improve productivity by 30 percent." Remember, it's much harder for a customer or employer to say no to a partner than to a salesperson.

WORKPLACE ROMANCE: With Venus in Aquarius, you're bound to practice a little harmless nepotism, paving the way for your collection of eccentric

friends and relatives (at least the ones you like) to join the team and advance right along with you. But while nepotism doesn't offend you, workplace incest does! A romance with your coworker? It seems positively unseemly, not to mention just way too generic and commonplace. Besides, you probably walk around thinking your soul mate is somewhere *out there*—certainly not under your nose at the office. But if you're determined to find a workplace sweetie, don't let me stand in your way. And don't stand in your own way, either, by seeming friendly but unapproachable—that catch-22 of having Venus in Aquarius. Remember, there's an elusive quality about you, as if no one could wrap their arms around you without you slipping away. Forget about dating—just let people get to know you!

Venus in Pisces

NETWORKING—MAKE THE CONNECTION: Venus in Pisces is not the sign of a born initiator. At monthly personnel meetings, you monopolize the two people you already know, ignore the 200 other "strangers," and wish you could return to your "real" work. But networking *is* real and yields very real results. Do you have to transform yourself into Supernetworker and "work" every room you enter? No; if it goes against your grain don't do it. But try getting people to come to you. Throw a party of your own. If you prefer the one-on-one setting, invite a potential contact to lunch. Send out "freebies"—not just monogrammed pens and key chains, but *helpful* goodies like free estimates or even juicy red tomatoes from your summer bumper crop. Write a column for your local newspaper—preferably with your phone number, e-mail address, and even a postage stamp–size photo. If you try these approaches, next time that meeting rolls around, lots of "strangers" will do the initiating for you—and hanging out near the cookie tray will no longer seem like your only option.

SALES SAVVY—TURN THEM ON: Two sales strategies come as naturally to you as tying your shoes: One: "Buy from me because you feel sorry for me and want to do a good deed." Two: "If you buy this it will save you and change your life." Both strategies have admirably secured millions of sales over the years. But if you'd like to further improve your sales skills, consider this: Astrological research indicates Venus in Pisces is the sign of the actor, a sympathetic person who can be many things to many people. Therefore, you need to size up your "audience" and determine what *they're* looking for—not only in a product or service, but also in a salesperson. Do they want an expert? A helpful friend? A problem-solver? Then, *play that role.*

It's not about being phony. It's about making people feel comfortable with a familiar *type* of interaction. One more tip: Establish sales goals. Objectively monitor your performance, and reward yourself if no one else is going to.

WORKPLACE ROMANCE: You go for strength of character. Though the workplace isn't your favorite mating territory, you'll look for love in all sorts of places, determined to find the prince in the pauper's hand-me-downs. When you fall in love, the world may as well stop and let you off, because gravity couldn't hold you down. In that case, work may suffer—especially if you and your sweetheart share an office or have access to each other in cyberspace. Whether it's romance, work, or your favorite soap opera, watch out for your reckless all-consuming tendencies. If not, coworkers may find you not capable but pathetic. Or worse, just plain easy and hard up for a date.

How to Find Your Venus Sign—Easy as 1-2-3

1. In the following Venus tables, look up the year of your birth.

2. The tables list every day on which Venus *changed* signs, approximately every four to six weeks, so there's a good chance you won't find your exact date of birth and perhaps not even the month of your birth. That's OK! You'll still have no trouble finding the dates that surround or "sandwich" your birthday, the chunk of time during which you were born.

3. There it is! Directly to the right of that chunk of time is your Venus sign. When you find your Venus sign, write it down in your Planetary Positions Chart on page 377.

But wait! Even though Venus changes signs only once a month or so, there's still a chance it changed signs right *on* your birthday. If so, you'll want to determine if you were born *before* or *after* the change. Simply refer to the section "Determining Your Sign Down to the Minute" on page 199, and then come back to the Venus tables.

EXAMPLE

Just for kicks, let's look up Oprah Winfrey's Venus sign. Oprah was born on January 29, 1954.

1. We turn to 1954 in the Venus tables.

2. At the start of the month we see Venus was in Scorpio, having entered Scorpio back on December 29, 1953. It shifted into Aquarius on January 22, 1954. Oprah was born on the 29th, and Venus was still in Aquarius. (See, the 29th is "sandwiched" between January 22, when Venus entered Aquarius, and February 15, when Venus departed into Pisces.)

3. So once again, Oprah writes "Aquarius" into her Planetary Positions Chart on page 377, this time in the slot where it says "My Venus is in _____."

VENUS

1940			
Jan.	18	9:00 A.M.	Pisces
Feb.	12	12:51 A.M.	Aries
March	8	11:26 A.M.	Taurus
April	4	1:10 P.M.	Gemini
May	6	1:47 P.M.	Cancer
July	5	11:17 P.M. R	Gemini
	31	9:20 A.M.	Cancer
Sept.	8	11:59 A.M.	Leo
Oct.	6	4:10 P.M.	Virgo
Nov.	1	12:24 P.M.	Libra
	26	7:32 A.M.	Scorpio
Dec.	20	2:37 P.M.	Sagittarius

1941			
Jan.	13	4:30 P.M.	Capricorn
Feb.	6	4:49 P.M.	Aquarius
March	2	5:33 P.M.	Pisces
	26	7:58 P.M.	Aries
April	20	12:54 A.M.	Taurus
May	14	8:37 A.M.	Gemini
June	7	6:53 P.M.	Cancer
July	2	7:33 A.M.	Leo
	26	11:13 P.M.	Virgo
Aug.	20	7:30 A.M.	Libra
Sept.	14	11:02 P.M.	Scorpio
Oct.	10	2:22 P.M.	Sagittarius
Nov.	6	5:17 A.M.	Capricorn
Dec.	5	6:05 P.M.	Aquarius

1942			
April	6	8:15 A.M.	Pisces
May	5	9:26 P.M.	Aries
June	1	7:26 A.M.	Taurus
	27	5:19 P.M.	Gemini
July	23	1:10 A.M.	Cancer
Aug.	16	10:05 P.M.	Leo
Sept.	10	9:38 A.M.	Virgo
Oct.	4	1:58 P.M.	Libra
	28	1:41 P.M.	Scorpio
Nov.	21	11:08 A.M.	Sagittarius
Dec.	15	7:53 A.M.	Capricorn

1943			
Jan.	8	5:03 A.M.	Aquarius
Feb.	1	4:02 A.M.	Pisces
	25	7:05 A.M.	Aries
March	21	5:25 P.M.	Taurus
April	15	3:12 P.M.	Gemini
May	11	6:57 A.M.	Cancer
June	7	7:09 A.M.	Leo
July	7	6:56 P.M.	Virgo
Nov.	9	1:26 A.M.	Libra
Dec.	8	2:45 A.M.	Scorpio

1944			
Jan.	2	11:44 P.M.	Sagittarius
	27	10:11 P.M.	Capricorn
Feb.	21	11:40 A.M.	Aquarius
March	16	9:47 P.M.	Pisces
April	10	7:10 A.M.	Aries
May	4	5:04 P.M.	Taurus
	29	3:40 A.M.	Gemini
June	22	2:12 P.M.	Cancer
July	17	11:47 P.M.	Leo
Aug.	10	8:13 A.M.	Virgo
Sept.	3	4:17 P.M.	Libra
	28	1:12 A.M.	Scorpio

Oct.	22	12:08 P.M.	Sagittarius
Nov.	16	2:26 A.M.	Capricorn
Dec.	10	11:48 P.M.	Aquarius

1945			
Jan.	5	2:19 P.M.	Pisces
Feb.	2	3:07 A.M.	Aries
March	11	6:18 A.M.	Taurus
April	7	2:16 P.M. R	Aries
June	4	5:58 A.M.	Taurus
July	7	11:21 A.M.	Gemini
Aug.	4	5:60 A.M.	Cancer
	30	8:05 A.M.	Leo
Sept.	24	11:07 A.M.	Virgo
Oct.	18	11:10 A.M.	Libra
Nov.	12	2:05 A.M.	Scorpio
Dec.	6	12:23 A.M.	Sagittarius
	29	8:57 P.M.	Capricorn

1946			
Jan.	22	5:28 P.M.	Aquarius
Feb.	15	3:12 P.M.	Pisces
March	11	3:32 P.M.	Aries
April	4	8:01 P.M.	Taurus
	29	5:60 A.M.	Gemini
May	23	10:40 P.M.	Cancer
June	18	12:01 A.M.	Leo
July	13	2:23 P.M.	Virgo
Aug.	9	3:35 A.M.	Libra
Sept.	6	7:16 P.M.	Scorpio
Oct.	16	5:45 A.M.	Sagittarius
Nov.	8	3:56 A.M. R	Scorpio

1947			
Jan.	5	11:46 A.M.	Sagittarius
Feb.	6	12:42 A.M.	Capricorn
March	5	12:09 A.M.	Aquarius
	30	5:15 P.M.	Pisces
April	24	10:03 P.M.	Aries
May	19	9:06 P.M.	Taurus
June	13	4:36 P.M.	Gemini
July	8	8:30 A.M.	Cancer
Aug.	1	8:07 P.M.	Leo
	26	3:18 A.M.	Virgo
Sept.	19	7:01 A.M.	Libra
Oct.	13	8:49 A.M.	Scorpio
Nov.	6	9:59 A.M.	Sagittarius
	30	11:23 A.M.	Capricorn
Dec.	24	2:13 P.M.	Aquarius

1948			
Jan.	17	9:14 A.M.	Pisces
Feb.	11	1:51 P.M.	Aries
March	8	1:60 A.M.	Taurus
April	4	7:40 A.M.	Gemini
May	7	3:28 A.M.	Cancer
June	29	2:58 A.M. R	Gemini
Aug.	2	9:16 P.M.	Cancer
Sept.	8	8:41 P.M.	Leo
Oct.	6	7:26 A.M.	Virgo
Nov.	1	1:42 A.M.	Libra
	25	7:55 P.M.	Scorpio
Dec.	20	2:29 A.M.	Sagittarius

1949			
Jan.	13	4:01 A.M.	Capricorn
Feb.	6	4:06 A.M.	Aquarius
March	2	4:39 A.M.	Pisces

	26	6:54 A.M.	Aries
April	19	11:44 A.M.	Taurus
May	13	7:26 P.M.	Gemini
June	7	5:48 A.M.	Cancer
July	1	6:41 P.M.	Leo
	26	10:44 A.M.	Virgo
Aug.	20	7:39 A.M.	Libra
Sept.	14	12:13 P.M.	Scorpio
Oct.	10	5:19 A.M.	Sagittarius
Nov.	5	11:54 P.M.	Capricorn
Dec.	6	1:06 A.M.	Aquarius

1950			
April	6	10:14 A.M.	Pisces
May	5	2:20 P.M.	Aries
June	1	9:19 A.M.	Taurus
	27	5:45 A.M.	Gemini
July	22	12:50 P.M.	Cancer
Aug.	16	9:18 A.M.	Leo
Sept.	9	8:38 P.M.	Virgo
Oct.	4	12:51 A.M.	Libra
	28	12:33 A.M.	Scorpio
Nov.	20	10:03 P.M.	Sagittarius
Dec.	14	6:54 P.M.	Capricorn

1951			
Jan.	7	4:11 P.M.	Aquarius
	31	3:15 P.M.	Pisces
Feb.	24	6:27 P.M.	Aries
March	21	5:06 A.M.	Taurus
April	15	3:34 A.M.	Gemini
May	10	8:42 P.M.	Cancer
June	7	12:10 A.M.	Leo
July	7	11:54 P.M.	Virgo
Nov.	9	1:48 P.M.	Libra
Dec.	7	7:19 P.M.	Scorpio

1952			
Jan.	2	1:45 P.M.	Sagittarius
	27	10:58 A.M.	Capricorn
Feb.	20	11:43 P.M.	Aquarius
March	16	9:18 A.M.	Pisces
April	9	6:18 P.M.	Aries
May	4	3:55 A.M.	Taurus
	28	2:19 P.M.	Gemini
June	22	12:47 A.M.	Cancer
July	16	10:23 A.M.	Leo
Aug.	9	6:58 P.M.	Virgo
Sept.	3	3:18 A.M.	Libra
	27	12:36 P.M.	Scorpio
Oct.	22	12:02 A.M.	Sagittarius
Nov.	15	3:03 P.M.	Capricorn
Dec.	10	1:31 P.M.	Aquarius

1953			
Jan.	5	6:11 A.M.	Pisces
Feb.	2	12:55 A.M.	Aries
March	14	1:59 P.M.	Taurus
	31	12:17 A.M. R	Aries
June	5	5:34 A.M.	Taurus
July	7	5:30 A.M.	Gemini
Aug.	3	8:09 P.M.	Cancer
	29	8:35 P.M.	Leo
Sept.	23	10:48 P.M.	Virgo
Oct.	18	10:27 A.M.	Libra
Nov.	11	1:13 P.M.	Scorpio
Dec.	5	11:24 A.M.	Sagittarius
	29	7:54 A.M.	Capricorn

VENUS

1954

Jan.	22	4:21 A.M.	Aquarius
Feb.	15	2:02 A.M.	Pisces
March	11	2:22 A.M.	Aries
April	4	6:56 A.M.	Taurus
	28	5:04 P.M.	Gemini
May	23	10:04 A.M.	Cancer
June	17	12:05 P.M.	Leo
July	13	3:43 A.M.	Virgo
Aug.	8	7:34 P.M.	Libra
Sept.	6	6:29 P.M.	Scorpio
Oct.	23	5:12 P.M.	Sagittarius
	27	5:38 A.M. R	Scorpio

1955

Jan.	6	1:49 A.M.	Sagittarius
Feb.	5	8:16 P.M.	Capricorn
March	4	3:22 A.M.	Aquarius
	30	6:31 A.M.	Pisces
April	24	10:14 A.M.	Aries
May	19	8:36 A.M.	Taurus
June	13	3:38 A.M.	Gemini
July	7	7:16 P.M.	Cancer
Aug.	1	6:43 A.M.	Leo
	25	1:53 P.M.	Virgo
Sept.	18	5:41 P.M.	Libra
Oct.	12	7:39 P.M.	Scorpio
Nov.	5	9:03 P.M.	Sagittarius
	29	10:43 P.M.	Capricorn
Dec.	24	1:53 A.M.	Aquarius

1956

Jan.	17	9:22 A.M.	Pisces
Feb.	11	2:47 A.M.	Aries
March	7	4:32 P.M.	Taurus
April	4	2:23 A.M.	Gemini
May	7	9:17 P.M.	Cancer
June	23	7:10 A.M. R	Gemini
Aug.	4	4:49 A.M.	Cancer
Sept.	8	4:24 A.M.	Leo
Oct.	5	10:13 P.M.	Virgo
	31	2:40 P.M.	Libra
Nov.	25	8:02 A.M.	Scorpio
Dec.	19	2:07 P.M.	Sagittarius

1957

Jan.	12	3:23 P.M.	Capricorn
Feb.	5	3:17 P.M.	Aquarius
March	1	3:40 P.M.	Pisces
	25	5:46 P.M.	Aries
April	18	10:29 P.M.	Taurus
May	13	6:08 A.M.	Gemini
June	6	4:35 P.M.	Cancer
July	1	5:43 A.M.	Leo
	25	10:10 P.M.	Virgo
Aug.	19	7:44 P.M.	Libra
Sept.	14	1:20 A.M.	Scorpio
Oct.	9	8:16 P.M.	Sagittarius
Nov.	5	6:46 P.M.	Capricorn
Dec.	6	10:26 A.M.	Aquarius

1958

April	6	11:00 A.M.	Pisces
May	5	6:60 A.M.	Aries
	31	11:08 P.M.	Taurus
June	26	6:09 P.M.	Gemini
July	22	12:26 A.M.	Cancer

Aug.	15	8:29 P.M.	Leo
Sept.	9	7:36 A.M.	Virgo
Oct.	3	11:44 A.M.	Libra
	27	11:27 A.M.	Scorpio
Nov.	20	8:60 A.M.	Sagittarius
Dec.	14	5:55 A.M.	Capricorn

1959

Jan.	7	3:17 A.M.	Aquarius
	31	2:29 A.M.	Pisces
Feb.	24	5:53 A.M.	Aries
March	20	4:56 P.M.	Taurus
April	14	4:08 P.M.	Gemini
May	10	10:45 A.M.	Cancer
June	6	5:43 P.M.	Leo
July	8	7:08 A.M.	Virgo
Sept.	19	9:56 P.M. R	Leo
	25	3:12 A.M.	Virgo
Nov.	9	1:11 P.M.	Libra
Dec.	7	11:42 A.M.	Scorpio

1960

Jan.	2	3:43 A.M.	Sagittarius
	26	11:46 P.M.	Capricorn
Feb.	20	11:48 A.M.	Aquarius
March	15	8:54 P.M.	Pisces
April	9	5:33 A.M.	Aries
May	3	2:56 P.M.	Taurus
	28	1:12 A.M.	Gemini
June	21	11:34 A.M.	Cancer
July	15	9:12 P.M.	Leo
Aug.	9	5:54 A.M.	Virgo
Sept.	2	2:30 P.M.	Libra
	27	12:13 A.M.	Scorpio
Oct.	21	12:13 P.M.	Sagittarius
Nov.	15	3:58 A.M.	Capricorn
Dec.	10	3:35 A.M.	Aquarius

1961

Jan.	4	10:31 P.M.	Pisces
Feb.	1	11:46 P.M.	Aries
June	5	2:25 P.M.	Taurus
July	6	11:33 P.M.	Gemini
Aug.	3	10:29 A.M.	Cancer
	29	9:19 A.M.	Leo
Sept.	23	10:43 A.M.	Virgo
Oct.	17	9:59 P.M.	Libra
Nov.	11	12:33 A.M.	Scorpio
Dec.	4	10:41 P.M.	Sagittarius
	28	7:07 P.M.	Capricorn

1962

Jan.	21	3:31 P.M.	Aquarius
Feb.	14	1:09 P.M.	Pisces
March	10	1:29 A.M.	Aries
April	3	6:05 P.M.	Taurus
	28	4:23 A.M.	Gemini
May	22	9:47 P.M.	Cancer
June	17	12:31 A.M.	Leo
July	12	5:32 P.M.	Virgo
Aug.	8	12:14 P.M.	Libra
Sept.	6	7:11 P.M.	Scorpio

1963

Jan.	6	12:36 P.M.	Sagittarius
Feb.	5	3:36 P.M.	Capricorn
March	4	6:42 A.M.	Aquarius

	29	8:00 P.M.	Pisces
April	23	10:40 P.M.	Aries
May	18	8:22 P.M.	Taurus
June	12	2:57 P.M.	Gemini
July	7	6:19 A.M.	Cancer
	31	5:39 P.M.	Leo
Aug.	25	12:49 A.M.	Virgo
Sept.	18	4:43 A.M.	Libra
Oct.	12	6:50 A.M.	Scorpio
Nov.	5	8:26 A.M.	Sagittarius
	29	10:22 A.M.	Capricorn
Dec.	23	1:54 P.M.	Aquarius

1964

Jan.	16	9:54 P.M.	Pisces
Feb.	10	4:10 P.M.	Aries
March	7	7:39 A.M.	Taurus
April	3	10:03 P.M.	Gemini
May	8	10:16 P.M.	Cancer
June	17	1:18 P.M. R	Gemini
Aug.	5	3:53 A.M.	Cancer
Sept.	7	11:54 P.M.	Leo
Oct.	5	1:11 P.M.	Virgo
	31	3:55 A.M.	Libra
Nov.	24	8:26 P.M.	Scorpio
Dec.	19	2:03 A.M.	Sagittarius

1965

Jan.	12	3:01 A.M.	Capricorn
Feb.	5	2:42 A.M.	Aquarius
March	1	2:56 A.M.	Pisces
	25	4:55 A.M.	Aries
April	18	9:31 A.M.	Taurus
May	12	5:08 P.M.	Gemini
June	6	3:39 A.M.	Cancer
	30	4:60 P.M.	Leo
July	25	9:52 A.M.	Virgo
Aug.	19	8:07 A.M.	Libra
Sept.	13	2:51 P.M.	Scorpio
Oct.	9	11:47 A.M.	Sagittarius
Nov.	5	2:36 P.M.	Capricorn
Dec.	6	11:37 P.M.	Aquarius

1966

Feb.	6	7:47 A.M. R	Capricorn
	25	5:55 P.M.	Aquarius
April	6	10:54 A.M.	Pisces
May	4	11:34 P.M.	Aries
	31	1:01 P.M.	Taurus
June	26	6:41 A.M.	Gemini
July	21	12:12 P.M.	Cancer
Aug.	15	7:48 A.M.	Leo
Sept.	8	6:41 P.M.	Virgo
Oct.	2	10:45 P.M.	Libra
	26	10:28 P.M.	Scorpio
Nov.	19	8:07 P.M.	Sagittarius
Dec.	13	5:09 P.M.	Capricorn

1967

Jan.	6	2:36 P.M.	Aquarius
	30	1:54 P.M.	Pisces
Feb.	23	5:30 P.M.	Aries
March	20	4:57 P.M.	Taurus
April	14	4:55 A.M.	Gemini
May	10	1:06 A.M.	Cancer
June	6	11:49 A.M.	Leo
July	8	5:12 P.M.	Virgo

VENUS

Sept.	9	6:58 A.M.	R	Leo
Oct.	1	1:08 P.M.		Virgo
Nov.	9	11:33 A.M.		Libra
Dec.	7	3:48 A.M.		Scorpio

1968

Jan.	1	5:38 P.M.	Sagittarius
	26	12:35 P.M.	Capricorn
Feb.	19	11:56 P.M.	Aquarius
March	15	8:32 A.M.	Pisces
April	8	4:49 P.M.	Aries
May	3	1:57 A.M.	Taurus
	27	12:03 P.M.	Gemini
June	20	10:21 P.M.	Cancer
July	15	7:60 A.M.	Leo
Aug.	8	4:49 P.M.	Virgo
Sept.	2	1:40 A.M.	Libra
	26	11:46 A.M.	Scorpio
Oct.	21	12:17 A.M.	Sagittarius
Nov.	14	4:48 P.M.	Capricorn
Dec.	9	5:40 P.M.	Aquarius

1969

Jan.	4	3:08 P.M.	Pisces
Feb.	1	11:45 P.M.	Aries
June	5	8:49 P.M.	Taurus
July	6	5:04 P.M.	Gemini
Aug.	3	12:31 A.M.	Cancer
	28	9:48 P.M.	Leo
Sept.	22	10:26 P.M.	Virgo
Oct.	17	9:18 A.M.	Libra
Nov.	10	11:40 A.M.	Scorpio
Dec.	4	9:41 A.M.	Sagittarius
	28	6:04 A.M.	Capricorn

1970

Jan.	21	2:27 A.M.	Aquarius
Feb.	14	12:05 A.M.	Pisces
March	10	12:25 A.M.	Aries
April	3	5:05 A.M.	Taurus
	27	3:34 P.M.	Gemini
May	22	9:20 A.M.	Cancer
June	16	12:50 P.M.	Leo
July	12	7:17 A.M.	Virgo
Aug.	8	5:00 A.M.	Libra
Sept.	6	8:54 P.M.	Scorpio

1971

Jan.	6	8:01 P.M.	Sagittarius
Feb.	5	9:57 A.M.	Capricorn
March	3	9:25 P.M.	Aquarius
	29	9:02 A.M.	Pisces
April	23	10:45 A.M.	Aries
May	18	7:49 A.M.	Taurus
June	12	1:58 A.M.	Gemini
July	6	5:03 P.M.	Cancer
	31	4:16 A.M.	Leo
Aug.	24	11:26 A.M.	Virgo
Sept.	17	3:26 P.M.	Libra
Oct.	11	5:43 P.M.	Scorpio
Nov.	4	7:31 P.M.	Sagittarius
	28	9:42 P.M.	Capricorn
Dec.	23	1:33 A.M.	Aquarius

1972

Jan.	16	10:02 A.M.	Pisces
Feb.	10	5:09 A.M.	Aries

March	6	10:26 P.M.		Taurus
April	3	5:49 P.M.		Gemini
May	10	8:52 A.M.		Cancer
June	11	3:09 P.M.	R	Gemini
Aug.	5	8:27 P.M.		Cancer
Sept.	7	6:28 P.M.		Leo
Oct.	5	3:34 A.M.		Virgo
	30	4:40 P.M.		Libra
Nov.	24	8:24 A.M.		Scorpio
Dec.	18	1:34 P.M.		Sagittarius

1973

Jan.	11	2:15 P.M.	Capricorn
Feb.	4	1:44 P.M.	Aquarius
	28	1:46 P.M.	Pisces
March	24	3:35 P.M.	Aries
April	17	8:06 P.M.	Taurus
May	12	3:43 A.M.	Gemini
June	5	2:21 P.M.	Cancer
	30	3:56 A.M.	Leo
July	24	9:14 P.M.	Virgo
Aug.	18	8:11 P.M.	Libra
Sept.	13	4:06 A.M.	Scorpio
Oct.	9	3:08 A.M.	Sagittarius
Nov.	5	10:40 A.M.	Capricorn
Dec.	7	4:38 P.M.	Aquarius

1974

Jan.	29	2:52 P.M.	R	Capricorn
Feb.	28	9:26 A.M.		Aquarius
April	6	9:18 A.M.		Pisces
May	4	3:22 P.M.		Aries
	31	2:19 A.M.		Taurus
June	25	6:44 P.M.		Gemini
July	20	11:35 P.M.		Cancer
Aug.	14	6:47 P.M.		Leo
Sept.	8	5:28 A.M.		Virgo
Oct.	2	9:28 A.M.		Libra
	26	9:13 A.M.		Scorpio
Nov.	19	6:57 A.M.		Sagittarius
Dec.	13	4:06 A.M.		Capricorn

1975

Jan.	6	1:40 A.M.		Aquarius
	30	1:05 A.M.		Pisces
Feb.	23	4:54 A.M.		Aries
March	19	4:43 P.M.		Taurus
April	13	5:26 P.M.		Gemini
May	9	3:12 P.M.		Cancer
June	6	5:55 A.M.		Leo
July	9	6:07 A.M.		Virgo
Sept.	2	10:35 A.M.	R	Leo
Oct.	4	12:20 A.M.		Virgo
Nov.	9	8:53 A.M.		Libra
Dec.	6	7:29 P.M.		Scorpio

1976

Jan.	1	7:15 A.M.	Sagittarius
	26	1:09 A.M.	Capricorn
Feb.	19	11:51 A.M.	Aquarius
March	14	7:60 A.M.	Pisces
April	8	3:57 A.M.	Aries
May	2	12:49 P.M.	Taurus
	26	10:44 P.M.	Gemini
June	20	8:57 A.M.	Cancer
July	14	6:37 P.M.	Leo
Aug.	8	3:36 A.M.	Virgo

Sept.	1	12:45 P.M.	Libra
	25	11:18 P.M.	Scorpio
Oct.	20	12:23 P.M.	Sagittarius
Nov.	14	5:43 A.M.	Capricorn
Dec.	9	7:54 A.M.	Aquarius

1977

Jan.	4	8:02 A.M.	Pisces
Feb.	2	12:55 A.M.	Aries
June	6	1:11 A.M.	Taurus
July	6	10:10 A.M.	Gemini
Aug.	2	2:19 P.M.	Cancer
	28	10:10 A.M.	Leo
Sept.	22	10:06 A.M.	Virgo
Oct.	16	8:38 P.M.	Libra
Nov.	9	10:52 P.M.	Scorpio
Dec.	3	8:50 P.M.	Sagittarius
	27	5:10 P.M.	Capricorn

1978

Jan.	20	1:30 P.M.	Aquarius
Feb.	13	11:07 A.M.	Pisces
March	9	11:30 A.M.	Aries
April	2	4:14 P.M.	Taurus
	27	2:54 A.M.	Gemini
May	21	9:04 P.M.	Cancer
June	16	1:20 A.M.	Leo
July	11	9:15 P.M.	Virgo
Aug.	7	10:09 P.M.	Libra
Sept.	7	12:08 A.M.	Scorpio

1979

Jan.	7	1:39 A.M.	Sagittarius
Feb.	5	4:16 A.M.	Capricorn
March	3	12:19 P.M.	Aquarius
	28	10:19 P.M.	Pisces
April	22	11:03 P.M.	Aries
May	17	7:30 P.M.	Taurus
June	11	1:14 P.M.	Gemini
July	6	4:03 A.M.	Cancer
	30	3:08 P.M.	Leo
Aug.	23	10:17 P.M.	Virgo
Sept.	17	2:22 A.M.	Libra
Oct.	11	4:49 A.M.	Scorpio
Nov.	4	6:51 A.M.	Sagittarius
	28	9:20 A.M.	Capricorn
Dec.	22	1:35 P.M.	Aquarius

1980

Jan.	15	10:37 P.M.		Pisces
Feb.	9	6:40 P.M.		Aries
March	6	1:55 P.M.		Taurus
April	3	2:47 P.M.		Gemini
May	12	3:54 P.M.		Cancer
June	5	12:45 A.M.	R	Gemini
Aug.	6	9:26 A.M.		Cancer
Sept.	7	12:58 P.M.		Leo
Oct.	4	6:08 P.M.		Virgo
	30	5:39 A.M.		Libra
Nov.	23	8:36 P.M.		Scorpio
Dec.	18	1:22 A.M.		Sagittarius

Where's Your Fearless Leader? Try Mars!

> **"It is time for a new generation of leadership, to cope with new problems and new opportunities. For there is a new world to be won."**
> U.S. PRESIDENT JOHN F. KENNEDY

The survival and success of every organization depends on its leaders. A teacher is a leader. So is a parent. So is a politician. If you want your career, small business, or even your family to thrive, you can't do it without stepping into a leadership role. And that demands courage! Finding a job, starting a business, standing up for your beliefs—it's all terrifying. It takes guts.

So if you're looking for your guts, don't rub your tummy! Find your Mars sign. In your Professional Planetary Profile, Mars symbolizes the part of you that takes charge, forges new enterprises, and resolves conflicts. It represents your nerve, ambition, and *chutzpah*. Your Mars energy makes you *hungry*. It rouses you out of bed in the morning and says, "Don't mess with me!" And it gets the job done.

In classical mythology, Mars was the god of war. In ancient history, Mars was the mascot of real-life military leaders such as Alexander the Great and Julius Caesar. In fact, civilizations throughout the world have equated this small but feisty red planet with fighting and conquest.

More recently, however, both Mars and the leadership qualities it represents have evolved. The business world no longer models itself on the military. If you want to command respect as a leader in today's economy,

you'll have to be more than a ruthless general or autocratic emperor. Since brains now matter more than brawn, you'll need to nurture and inspire. In our competitive market economy, you must champion progress and elicit people's best talents. Likewise, modern astrologers have realized that Mars personifies so much more than your aggression, dominance, and libido.

LEADERSHIP VERSUS MANAGEMENT

At one time *management* and *leadership* meant the same thing, but business experts now distinguish between the two. Management involves day-to-day operations like ensuring personnel arrive on time and seeing to it that customers receive fall catalogs before Christmas. Leadership, on the other hand, refers to creating the organization's vision and unifying the whole team behind a common purpose. If you're spending too much time managing employees—forever shrieking, "Don't be late," for example—it's time to hone your leadership skills. To start, read the leadership advice for your individual Mars sign.

WHEN IT HITS THE FAN: MANAGING CONFLICT

If you think you can avoid conflict, you're dead wrong. It's so pervasive, in fact, that courses about conflict management have become requirements in most MBA and other professional degree programs. That's because when dealt with effectively, conflict can produce results and yield progress. Try viewing competition, for example, as a form of collaboration. You can use a disagreement with a coworker to drive the cooperative project to new heights. But conflict can also hurt, particularly when taken personally. For customized conflict management tips, check out your Mars sign and integrate it into your Professional Planetary Profile.

> **"Two things are bad for the heart—running uphill and running down people."**
> RETAIL ENTREPRENEUR
> BERNARD GIMBEL

"BUT WHAT IF I WANT TO BE MY OWN BOSS?": ENTREPRENEURSHIP

Mars also represents your entrepreneurial spirit. Many of the greatest leaders work for themselves. With their vision and motivation, they're naturals for starting companies or succeeding as independent contractors and creators. Even if you run a business of one—just you!—good leadership counts more than ever. You have to motivate *yourself.* Remember, even a freelance painter who regards herself as an artist, not a business-

woman, is still an entrepreneur. By reading about your Mars sign, you'll discover your entrepreneurial spirit, plus get practical advice for starting or expanding your own business or private practice. Look up your individual Mars sign in the Mars tables, which begin on page 338.

SEIZE THE DAY: THE SELF-EMPOWERMENT BOOSTER

In the fourth and final section of your individual Mars sign, look up suggestions for becoming a stronger, more effective professional and a leader in any position, no matter what your job title. Standing up for yourself is tough. But with Dr. Matt's Booster Shot, get some ideas for making it easier.

Mars in Aries

LEADERSHIP: A management consultant once told me, "Leaders are made, not born." He must not have known you! As the original "I won't take *no* for an answer!" person, you possess an abundance of leadership potential. Develop that potential, no matter what your current position. Many of the best leaders don't have impressive titles or management degrees, but teammates turn to them for guidance. Why? Because they seem to have strength of character and everyone's best interests at heart. You've got what it takes to become a *great* leader. It requires, however, acquiring the right skills, controlling your temper, and *leading* rather than intimidating. Cultivate your credibility.

MANAGING CONFLICT: Never afraid to make a scene in public, or anywhere else for that matter, you quickly turn confrontational in conflicts. You're unstoppable—an admirable trait, but does it serve you well in every problematic situation? Make time to pause and reflect. Practice tact; take charm lessons. Even try a little scheming or cunning for a change of pace from your typical head-on-collision style of conflict-resolution.

ENTREPRENEURSHIP: Overflowing with enterprising gusto, you relish the challenge of starting your own business. But keep in mind you're more of a risk-taker than a problem-solver. In your urge to grow fast, it's important you keep overhead low. Because you're seldom content doing one thing for the rest of your life, design your business with a profitable "exit plan" so that you can sell it, move on, and start something bigger and better.

SELF-EMPOWERMENT BOOSTER: Given your built-in flair for leadership and entrepreneurship, do yourself a favor and acquire the basic skills that today's managers need. Winning means a lot to you, maybe so much that you're willing to sacrifice profits, personnel, or your kid's Little League game just to score the most points or pin your opponent. Choose your sacrifices wisely! Once you give something up, you can't get it back.

Mars in Taurus

LEADERSHIP: A productivity addict, you need to find ways of extracting high quality, plentiful results from staff members without turning them into uninspired workhorses. Don't give orders from on high. As many leaders are finding, it helps sometimes to work side by side with the rank and file, like the airline CEO who's famous for getting up and serving drinks with his flight attendants. Like nature, business thrives on diversity. By selecting a staff with widely varying strengths and backgrounds, you can create a team better able to meet the challenges of our times.

MANAGING CONFLICT: It takes a lot to make you mad. You do stubborn well. Eventually, however, you may have to do more than just dig in your heels to resolve conflicts, many of which are more complicated than you care to admit. End the struggle rather than perpetuate it and do it before it starts keeping you up nights. Keeping in mind the divide and conquer philosophy, be careful your firmness doesn't unite everyone against you.

ENTREPRENEURSHIP: Most entrepreneurs—and certainly almost all with Mars in Taurus—want to create a life, not just a business. So in starting your own business, pay special attention to lifestyle issues. What hours will you work? How much will you travel? Are you willing to sacrifice income for time or vice versa? By answering these issues *before* printing the letterhead for your new business, you're more likely to avoid the number-one reason most small businesses close: No, it's not financial failure, it's lack of motivation!

SELF-EMPOWERMENT BOOSTER: Confront your characteristic Mars in Taurus frugality. Though initially attractive, not all cost-cutting measures benefit the company's overall health. In the short run, for example, you might save on personnel expenses by replacing many permanent employees with long-term temps. But before you do, you'll need to assess the *long-term* effects of this plan on morale, training, and your ability to attract a

talented staff who won't flee at the first sign of a better offer elsewhere. If you want business longevity, practice business longsightedness.

Mars in Gemini

LEADERSHIP: You're a major *doer* and expect the same from your personnel. You can't tolerate, however, workers who don't think for themselves. For best results, you need a team of equals, not a staff of compliant yes-sayers. To accomplish these goals, invite dialogue between managers and managees. An open-door policy works splendidly for you. But don't hold countless meetings that keep staff jabbering, not working. And in your laudable effort to communicate, don't smother people with paperwork and clog their electronic mailboxes with interoffice memos. Since your greatest potential downfall as a leader is inconsistency, let employees know how they will be judged and stick to it. Even a small company or department should have a basic manual outlining benefits, holidays, sick leave, and so on. Discourage internal politics and favor concerted effort.

MANAGING CONFLICT: Before managing a conflict, you need to know what the conflict is. Discriminate between fact and fiction, truth and hearsay. Even if your opponent rages and threatens, take the high road: clarify misconceptions and take time to identify the real issues. You fare best when conflicts remain rational and you don't lose your chance to say, "Let's talk about it." For once the discussion is closed, you've lost one of your greatest tools: communicating through the difficulty. One more thing. Changing your mind is not necessarily an act of weakness, but a display of self-confidence—when backed up by solid reasoning, not a whim of fancy.

ENTREPRENEURSHIP: Many potential entrepreneurs, probably including you, start businesses because they want to make a living doing their hobby. Indeed, that is a fine way to keep yourself motivated. But bear in mind that if a baseball card shop emerges from your love of Babe Ruth, you'll not only be dealing cards but signing leases, paying self-employment tax, and marketing a retail establishment. Know what you're getting yourself into. Make sure you're ready to run a business, not a hobby.

SELF-EMPOWERMENT BOOSTER: If you need an assignment done, frame it as an authoritative directive, not merely a suggestion. Try to be consistent so that employees and associates don't expend a lot of energy figuring out what mind-set you're in today. Provide a clear sense of direction. With

Mars in Gemini, you rely heavily on knowing your material. So do your homework—with more facts you can make better decisions.

Mars in Cancer

LEADERSHIP: You can accomplish a lot with a little by selecting and retaining the right people. To do so, offer incentives for sticking around, such as generous retirement plans, stable and caring work environment, and possibilities for advancement. Sometimes, though, you care too much. Like an overprotective parent, you resist taking a vacation or leaving on business trips for fear that the office will collapse. But you can leave with a clear conscience and little or no anxiety if you've previously trained your staff to care for customers and meet responsibilities in your absence.

MANAGING CONFLICT: You may forgive, but it'd take a lobotomy to make you forget. Afraid of your own potential histrionics, you shy away from open conflict but head straight for the jugular with criticism and guilt trips. Tough situations make you sick to your stomach, even physically ill. But you needn't take every conflicting opinion as a threat. Our economy has room for many, many personalities and possibilities. Be careful that your directives don't sound naggy. Stay calm and professional. Express irritation diplomatically.

ENTREPRENEURSHIP: In starting your own business—depending more or less on your *complete* Professional Planetary Profile—you shy away from risk. That's OK! In an economy with frequent corporate downsizing, self-employment can be just as secure as a Fortune 500 occupation. But since uncertainty depletes your enterprising spirit, make sure you have plenty of cash stashed away for living expenses, especially in those fledgling early years when most new businesses operate in the red—a color you might like to wear but hate to see on a balance sheet!

SELF-EMPOWERMENT BOOSTER: Just get on with it! Adopt a forward-thinking attitude and focus less on the past while trying to learn from history. Even in our enlightened times, most professional settings make little room for matters of the heart. Don't however squelch your emotions; instead, harness them to drive up your energy levels. Fear and jealousy of the competition, for example, may give you and your team something to fight for.

Mars in Leo

LEADERSHIP: As a manager you run a tight ship, demanding total loyalty. If you're ever faced with a mutiny, you can dole out lots of rewards to keep everything shipshape. For example, each month identify a key staff member's contribution and share kudos with the staff when your division makes record fourth-quarter profits. As a famous lawyer once said, "Any leader worth following gives credit easily where credit is due." You understand that effective leadership doesn't mean bossiness; it means guiding ordinary people toward extraordinary achievements.

MANAGING CONFLICT: Demonstrative and sportsmanlike, you love a good fight. But it's an art to know the difference between combat for combat's sake and a clash of values or methods. Fight only when something of importance is at stake and respect your opponents. Though it's easy to pick on weaker opponents, consider the value of struggling with an antagonist who's smarter and more resourceful. If you win fairly and squarely, that's a trophy worth having: the trophy of self-improvement. Better by far than the limited satisfaction of nailing an easy target.

ENTREPRENEURSHIP: You want to leave your mark. Starting your own business might seem like the perfect way to do it, but you may not be prepared to deal with a small-time operation without a staff at your beck and call. At first, can you deal with staffing every position yourself from janitor to receptionist to chairman of the board? Eventually, however, look for ways to profit not only on your labor but also on your capital—such as a cartoonist who sells a daily comic strip and also licenses the cartoon's image on mugs and T-shirts.

SELF-EMPOWERMENT BOOSTER: Despite your alacrity, keep in mind leadership positions are seldom acquired overnight. But you can start inching your way toward one by taking charge of projects and displaying a cheerful willingness to assume ever-growing responsibilities. When colleagues and clients discover they can't get along without you, the ground will be fertile for you to lead.

Mars in Virgo

LEADERSHIP: You run a "meritocracy." You promote the people who serve you best. A bit of a fussbudget, you hold people highly accountable. You demand hard work. You're prone to be more of a *micro*manager than a leader. As a team or staff leader, you seek people's love but more often engender their fear. Give staff members their responsibilities and don't intrude until it's absolutely necessary. Train them as much with encouragement as with criticism.

MANAGING CONFLICT: You'd really prefer it if you could skip conflict management and get on with your work. But conflict is unavoidable and can even yield more creative solutions. Beware! Anger can eat at you physically. Even if you ignore it, it's likely to make you miss work with an excruciating migraine or tummy ache. If you're an employee in conflict with a coworker, first try to resolve the problem yourself, before tattling to a supervisor. And if you're a supervisor, don't bury your head in your paperwork. Conflict is OK, *really*.

ENTREPRENEURSHIP: With entrepreneurship, there are few guarantees. Health insurance, salary, and pensions—all of these are unknown factors, requiring a lot of day-to-day control for one person to handle. But if you decide to go for it, with Mars in Virgo you'll accomplish more if you establish a regular routine. When you run your own business, the boss and the employee are both in your head, and they have to get along. Develop self-discipline but don't flog yourself for underperformance. If you're unwilling to delegate authority, your business should be designed to stay small.

SELF-EMPOWERMENT BOOSTER: The higher you rise in your business or company, the greater your chances of becoming a slave to your career. Don't do it. Despite your gargantuan work ethic, a career can't and shouldn't take the place of getting a life. Given that you put a lot of effort into producing the best possible product, you don't take kindly to negative appraisals. Don't let that stop you. Just remember, they're criticizing your work, not you. Fight the stale factor! Find out how they're doing it! The best leaders and entrepreneurs regularly travel around observing success stories and integrating new ideas.

> **"Going into business for yourself, becoming an entrepreneur, is the modern-day equivalent of pioneering on the old frontier.**
>
> ECONOMIST PAULA NELSON

Mars in Libra

LEADERSHIP: Whether you're a teammate or head honcho, you encourage full participation. "Let's all get involved," you say. Maybe it's because you're full of goodwill, but more likely because you recognize that empowered employees perform better than drones. Whatever your reasons, keep it up. This does *not* mean you should give up your power. You have to want to be in charge. Establish a company or team culture based on respect for authority as well as team spirit. The two don't have to be mutually exclusive.

MANAGING CONFLICT: Conflict bothers you. It's unpleasant. As a result, you may be tempted to reach a resolution at any cost, perhaps one that's disadvantageous. Seeing every side of every issue tends to get you in the middle of things. Be careful of trying to stick up for everyone. Learn to trust your perceptions and don't be afraid to defend a viewpoint. Though you may look for it high and low, an objective reality cannot be found in all circumstances, so get used to resolving things with a degree of uncertainty. On a positive note, because you're good at anticipating strife, you can usually circumvent it: Your knack for seeing all sides lends nicely to the art of compromise.

ENTREPRENEURSHIP: Always looking to *buy low/sell high,* you're a prime candidate for investment-related enterprises. This, however, usually requires up-front capital or seed money. Before investing your life savings or going heavily into debt, investigate less conventional sources of investment capital, especially any plan that gets other interested parties involved in your idea, such as an investment club or a limited partnership. Most Mars-in-Libra entrepreneurs are attracted to partnerships; if that's you, make sure your goals are the same, from the start. With separate visions, you and your partners may start at the same point but forever tug in opposite directions.

SELF-EMPOWERMENT BOOSTER: They say it's lonely at the top. And it's true: Running your own business or managing a corporate division can be awfully isolating. Even if you interact with consumers and personnel all day long, chances are you'll miss having colleagues. You'll covet watercooler camaraderie. If so, try joining professional networking groups, a lunchtime exercise team, or even an on-line chat room for people like you worldwide. For Mars in Libra, a professional support system is vital.

Mars in Scorpio

LEADERSHIP: The mighty emperor Napoleon stated, "A throne is just a bench covered in velvet." You understand this implicitly. Not taken in by flashy fabrics, you evaluate employees, clients, and opportunities on authentic criteria. Avoid favoritism, nepotism, ruthless measures; in our interdependent economy, you can often help yourself by helping others. It's in your nature to move through the workplace checking up on people; make it seem like availability, not espionage. Because of your intensity, your staff may feel uncomfortable letting its guard down around you. Chill out. Show them you're human, too.

MANAGING CONFLICT: "Angry? Me, angry? No, I'm not angry that she stole my ideas and got the raise I deserved!" Hating public displays of antagonism, you don't like to admit your extreme feelings. But with Mars in Scorpio, you can prevent many conflicts by laying down the law. Set limits and make them known. Let people know where they stand with you. When boundaries break down, confusion ensues, pushing all your anger buttons. To deal with anger, expression and repression aren't the only two options. Stay with the anger; let it be. It doesn't have to erode your professionalism.

ENTREPRENEURSHIP: You sniff out weaknesses in the competition and possess the entrepreneur's gift for identifying underused or overlooked opportunities. On the other hand, you like to avoid personal financial and legal liability. So consider the pros and cons of, say, forming a *corporation* (which comes with legal safety nets) versus a *sole proprietorship* (easier to establish but lacks those protections). Whatever you decide, bear in mind that as your business grows you'll have to hire managers and other professionals—and you'll have to trust them. Are you ready to hand over some control?

SELF-EMPOWERMENT BOOSTER: Never content with just the bottom line, you can excite people (including yourself!) with *qualitative* goals, not *quantitative* ones. Nobody invests heart and soul in boosting second-quarter earnings. They *do* pledge allegiance to *delivering the finest service* or *creating the funniest sitcom*. Even if you have strong principles, you need to ensure your management practices don't look unfair and deceptive. One way to do this? Keep people informed of any change that affects their jobs or projects.

Mars in Sagittarius

LEADERSHIP: While you can command respect for your expertise, it's not always enough to establish authority. You tend to socialize with employees and foster their professional (and even personal) development, emphasizing continued training. Sometimes, you run the office more like a commune than a corporation, wanting every member to take responsibility and expecting employees to know more than they possibly could with limited experience. Though you do a good job articulating the overarching mission, don't let daily management slip through your fingers.

MANAGING CONFLICT: Perhaps a little too sue-happy, you always think you have the Law on your side. You'll spend three days and 20 phone calls just to get a parking ticket waived. You're endearingly confident about your own talents and abilities—until the deadline hits and you melt like chocolate on a hot dashboard. With Mars in Saj, though, the trick is to decide if you want to win or you want to be *right*. Unfortunately, you can't always have both. If, for instance, you have a problem with someone and quickly resort to legal action, the court may say you're right and rule in your favor, but meanwhile lawyers have cost you big bucks and lost time. Likewise, an articulate argument may prove your point but not without alienating your opponent. Always keep the goal in mind—you're probably not in business to educate the world.

ENTREPRENEURSHIP: You want to do a lot and you want to do it on your own. But most new enterprises start out small and thus lack the opportunities you crave. So your unique brand of entrepreneurship requires some fancy footwork and resourceful thinking. For example, let's say you want to start an archaeology business that digs up ancient relics. Such work normally requires funding from a big institution like a university. You, however, may find an independent route by securing government contracts, publishing books on your excavations, and consulting to museums. Unless your Sun and Mercury signs indicate otherwise, hire a business manager to relieve you of grunt work like writing checks.

SELF-EMPOWERMENT BOOSTER: With Mars in Sagittarius it helps to have a strong philosophy that guides you and gets you through the daily grind. Without that, you pursue endless sidelines. Increase your attention span! Dealings that compromise your ethics may leave you too confused to think straight. As people get more involved in their careers and higher up,

they often just stop learning. But your quest for knowledge is never-ending. Without lifelong learning, you risk fanaticism.

Mars in Capricorn

LEADERSHIP: A natural leader with sound administrative ability, you demand discipline from anyone on your payroll. Don't overlook the fact you're working with mere mortals, not those eminently capable computers you're so fond of. Consider the human factor. Lots of people out there look to you for guidance. You raise your hand to wipe something off your chin and they think you're pointing the way to Mecca. Don't abuse the respect you command, or you'll lose it.

MANAGING CONFLICT: Often you'd like to kick and scream, but since you worry what the neighbors would think, you tend to accomplish a lot with subtle scowls and thundering silences. Folks are probably too afraid to mess with you in the first place, but when conflict does arise, shoot for a win-win situation. No matter how much you need to exert your authority, never strip your staff of self-respect. To be effective, you need everyone you deal with to act like an adult—so steer clear of parent-child relationships in the workplace.

ENTREPRENEURSHIP: You can work the system. To start your own business, use this rare talent to obtain a Small Business Administration loan or government-sponsored grants. Whatever you do, don't overlook opportunities that lack prestige—huge computer companies have started in garages! As your own boss, you'll likely miss those affirming pats on the back from an authority figure. No matter how developed your self-esteem, find some strokes and positive reinforcement elsewhere.

SELF-EMPOWERMENT BOOSTER: Praise your opponents. They won't know what hit 'em. Be careful not to be the kind of boss who leads from a distance. It's best your employees know what you're talking about, or at least have five minutes to listen to the opposite point of view. People think you know what you're talking about. Why disappoint them by admitting you don't? But remember, no plan is ever executed exactly as conceived; no organizational guru can foresee all the problems that pop up. Make constant adjustments to bring performance in line with objectives. You're susceptible to nervous tension, so learn to relax—freeing the body can save the mind.

Mars in Aquarius

LEADERSHIP: A real visionary, you inspire men and women to reach goals. If you're a new leader, start by encouraging your employees. You can really sink your teeth into planning, but other than that you don't have much of a taste for the menial tasks of administration and organization. When problems arise, remind everybody why they're there. Make it clear that if you benefit, everybody benefits.

MANAGING CONFLICT: Guard against an "us against them" mentality, which pits labor against management or management against consumers. While you'll take sensible directives and go right to work, you loathe being told how to think. If that happens, reason will do more for you than a vicious fight. By prioritizing the issue over the person, you tend to burn bridges. But one argument need not eclipse an entire relationship. Above all, you must avoid falling into stereotypical antagonistic roles like victim and perpetrator.

ENTREPRENEURSHIP: Decidedly original, you want to make a contribution to society, so it's natural that entrepreneurship would make your mouth water. Here's your chance to be original, particularly if you can't find in a nine-to-five job the intellectual stimulation you're looking for. First, though, you face tough choices. For one: Will this enterprise revolve around you as a highly personal expression of your identity? Or will it have a strong enough personality of its own to endure when you move on?

SELF-EMPOWERMENT BOOSTER: Consider alternatives; then look for more alternatives. Whereas many professionals need to work within a conventional business model, you can survive, and even thrive, in a more creatively designed arrangement. If, for example, you're having trouble balancing work and family, think about telecommuting or running a home-based business. Technology opens up options. See what it can do for you. Chances are you'll try many before settling on one.

Mars in Pisces

LEADERSHIP: "Wait and see" characterizes your leadership style. You give few direct orders to your staff, expecting them to figure out what to do on their own. Your leadership strengths come out when you're in a position

to relate one on one with staff members. If you don't like giving spirited pep talks and issuing dictates, lead by example, instilling personnel with the confidence to take their own initiative. Give individual consultations concerning overall direction.

MANAGING CONFLICT: Because conflict management comes hard with Mars in Pisces, you often avoid it till it's too late and then, *bam!* you punish employees and affront customers. When you don't get what you want, you tend to cry or otherwise bemoan your misfortune. Scratch the silent treatment. Don't resort to manipulation. Be firm up front so you won't have to be a tyrant down the road.

ENTREPRENEURSHIP: You're not a natural entrepreneur, but that needn't stop you. Get comfortable with self-promotion. What you probably need is the right niche, catering to a market sector that wants a product or service not available just anywhere. That way you can distinguish yourself from those more macho entrepreneurs who fight for the same generic market share while you reach untapped markets with your unique, off-the-beaten-path approach. Caution! You can turn a real job off at the end of the day. Your own business, however, never goes away. Therefore you must schedule respites and find a place to get away from it all.

SELF-EMPOWERMENT BOOSTER: We all need feedback, especially employees and teammates who want to improve. Or those who require guidance to boost their performance. That's why it's important you review their work rather than just take what they deliver. This is a sound management practice and one that even small companies should consider, especially for new employees. Evaluating employees periodically gives them a chance to improve, a benefit for both of you.

How to Find Your Mars Sign—Easy as 1-2-3

1. In the following Mars tables, look up the year of your birth.

2. The tables only list the days on which Mars actually *changed* signs— approximately every few months—so there's a good chance you won't find your exact date of birth and perhaps not even the month of your birth. No problem! Simply look for the dates that surround or "sandwich" your birthday, the chunk of time during which you were born.

3. Congratulations! Directly to the right of that chunk of time is your Mars sign. When you find your Mars sign, write it down in your Planetary Positions Chart on page 377.

But wait! Even though Mars changes signs only a few times a year, there's still a slight chance it changed signs right *on* your birthday. If so, you'll want to determine if you were born *before* or *after* the change. Simply refer to the section "Determining Your Sign Down to the Minute" on page 199, then come back to these Mars tables.

EXAMPLE

If you're stuck, practice by looking up Oprah Winfrey's Mars sign. Oprah was born January 29, 1954.

1. Turn to 1954 in the Mars tables.

2. At the start of the 1954, you can see there's no January listed; it goes right to February. So go back a month to December 20, 1953, when Mars entered Scorpio. Oprah was born on January 29th, which is *between* those two dates (December 20, 1953, and February 9, 1954) during all of which Mars remained in Scorpio. (See how you just go back to the nearest date before your birthday?)

3. So this time Oprah writes "Scorpio" into her Planetary Positions Chart on page 377 in the slot on the line "My Mars is in _____."

MARS

1940			
Jan.	3	7:06 P.M.	Aries
Feb.	16	8:54 P.M.	Taurus
April	1	1:41 P.M.	Gemini
May	17	9:46 A.M.	Cancer
July	3	5:32 A.M.	Leo
Aug.	19	10:58 A.M.	Virgo
Oct.	5	9:22 A.M.	Libra
Nov.	20	12:16 P.M.	Scorpio

1941			
Jan.	4	2:43 P.M.	Sagittarius
Feb.	17	6:33 P.M.	Capricorn
April	2	6:46 A.M.	Aquarius
May	16	12:05 A.M.	Pisces
July	2	12:17 A.M.	Aries

1942			
Jan.	11	5:21 P.M.	Taurus
March	7	3:05 A.M.	Gemini
April	26	1:18 A.M.	Cancer
June	13	10:56 P.M.	Leo
Aug.	1	3:27 A.M.	Virgo
Sept.	17	5:11 A.M.	Libra
Nov.	1	5:37 P.M.	Scorpio
Dec.	15	11:51 A.M.	Sagittarius

1943			
Jan.	26	2:10 P.M.	Capricorn
March	8	7:42 A.M.	Aquarius
April	17	5:26 A.M.	Pisces
May	27	4:26 A.M.	Aries
July	7	6:05 P.M.	Taurus
Aug.	23	6:58 P.M.	Gemini

1944			
March	28	4:55 A.M.	Cancer
May	22	9:17 A.M.	Leo
July	11	9:55 P.M.	Virgo
Aug.	28	7:24 P.M.	Libra
Oct.	13	7:10 A.M.	Scorpio
Nov.	25	11:12 A.M.	Sagittarius

1945				
Jan.	5	2:31 P.M.		Capricorn
Feb.	14	4:58 A.M.		Aquarius
March	24	10:44 P.M.		Pisces
May	2	3:29 P.M.		Aries
June	11	6:53 A.M.		Taurus
July	23	3:59 A.M.		Gemini
Sept.	7	3:56 P.M.		Cancer
Nov.	11	4:05 P.M.		Leo
Dec.	26	10:05 A.M.	R	Cancer

1946			
April	22	2:32 P.M.	Leo
June	20	3:32 A.M.	Virgo
Aug.	9	8:17 A.M.	Libra
Sept.	24	11:35 A.M.	Scorpio
Nov.	6	1:23 P.M.	Sagittarius
Dec.	17	5:56 A.M.	Capricorn

1947			
Jan.	25	6:45 A.M.	Aquarius
March	4	11:47 A.M.	Pisces
April	11	6:03 P.M.	Aries
May	20	10:40 P.M.	Taurus
June	30	10:35 P.M.	Gemini
Aug.	13	4:26 P.M.	Cancer
Sept.	30	9:31 P.M.	Leo
Dec.	1	6:44 A.M.	Virgo

1948				
Feb.	12	5:28 A.M.	R	Leo
May	18	3:54 P.M.		Virgo
July	17	12:26 A.M.		Libra
Sept.	3	8:58 A.M.		Scorpio
Oct.	17	12:44 A.M.		Sagittarius
Nov.	26	4:59 P.M.		Capricorn

1949			
Jan.	4	12:50 P.M.	Aquarius
Feb.	11	1:06 P.M.	Pisces
March	21	5:03 P.M.	Aries
April	29	9:33 P.M.	Taurus
June	9	7:57 P.M.	Gemini
July	23	12:55 A.M.	Cancer
Sept.	6	11:52 P.M.	Leo
Oct.	26	7:59 P.M.	Virgo
Dec.	26	12:24 A.M.	Libra

1950				
March	28	6:05 A.M.	R	Virgo
June	11	3:27 P.M.		Libra
Aug.	10	11:48 A.M.		Scorpio
Sept.	25	2:49 P.M.		Sagittarius
Nov.	6	1:41 A.M.		Capricorn
Dec.	15	3:59 A.M.		Aquarius

1951			
Jan.	22	8:06 A.M.	Pisces
March	1	5:04 P.M.	Aries
April	10	4:37 P.M.	Taurus
May	21	10:32 A.M.	Gemini
July	3	6:42 P.M.	Cancer
Aug.	18	5:56 A.M.	Leo
Oct.	4	7:20 P.M.	Virgo
Nov.	24	1:12 A.M.	Libra

1952			
Jan.	19	8:33 P.M.	Scorpio
Aug.	27	1:54 P.M.	Sagittarius
Oct.	11	11:45 P.M.	Capricorn
Nov.	21	2:40 P.M.	Aquarius
Dec.	30	4:36 P.M.	Pisces

1953			
Feb.	7	8:07 P.M.	Aries
March	20	1:54 A.M.	Taurus
May	1	1:08 A.M.	Gemini
June	13	10:49 P.M.	Cancer
July	29	2:26 P.M.	Leo
Sept.	14	12:59 P.M.	Virgo
Nov.	1	9:19 A.M.	Libra
Dec.	20	6:23 A.M.	Scorpio

1954				
Feb.	9	2:18 P.M.		Sagittarius
April	12	11:28 A.M.		Capricorn
July	3	2:23 A.M.	R	Sagittarius
Aug.	24	8:23 A.M.		Capricorn
Oct.	21	7:03 A.M.		Aquarius
Dec.	4	2:42 A.M.		Pisces

1955			
Jan.	14	11:34 P.M.	Aries
Feb.	26	5:23 A.M.	Taurus
April	10	6:09 P.M.	Gemini
May	25	7:50 P.M.	Cancer
July	11	4:23 A.M.	Leo
Aug.	27	5:14 A.M.	Virgo
Oct.	13	6:20 A.M.	Libra
Nov.	28	8:34 P.M.	Scorpio

1956			
Jan.	13	9:28 P.M.	Sagittarius
Feb.	28	3:05 P.M.	Capricorn
April	14	6:40 P.M.	Aquarius
June	3	2:52 A.M.	Pisces
Dec.	6	6:24 A.M.	Aries

1957			
Jan.	28	9:19 A.M.	Taurus
March	17	4:34 P.M.	Gemini
May	4	10:22 A.M.	Cancer
June	21	7:18 A.M.	Leo
Aug.	8	12:28 A.M.	Virgo
Sept.	23	11:32 P.M.	Libra
Nov.	8	4:04 P.M.	Scorpio
Dec.	22	8:30 P.M.	Sagittarius

1958				
Feb.	3	1:57 P.M.		Capricorn
March	17	2:11 A.M.		Aquarius
April	26	9:31 P.M.		Pisces
June	7	1:21 A.M.		Aries
July	21	2:04 A.M.		Taurus
Sept.	21	12:26 A.M.		Gemini
Oct.	28	7:01 P.M.	R	Taurus

1959			
Feb.	10	8:58 A.M.	Gemini
April	10	4:47 A.M.	Cancer
May	31	9:26 P.M.	Leo
July	20	6:04 A.M.	Virgo
Sept.	5	5:47 P.M.	Libra
Oct.	21	4:41 A.M.	Scorpio
Dec.	3	1:09 P.M.	Sagittarius

1960			
Jan.	13	1:00 A.M.	Capricorn
Feb.	22	11:12 P.M.	Aquarius
April	2	1:25 A.M.	Pisces
May	11	2:20 A.M.	Aries
June	20	4:05 A.M.	Taurus
Aug.	1	11:32 P.M.	Gemini
Sept.	20	11:07 P.M.	Cancer

1961				
Feb.	4	7:09 P.M.	R	Gemini
	7	12:07 A.M.		Cancer
May	5	8:14 P.M.		Leo
June	28	6:48 P.M.		Virgo
Aug.	16	7:42 P.M.		Libra
Oct.	1	3:03 P.M.		Scorpio
Nov.	13	4:51 P.M.		Sagittarius
Dec.	24	12:51 P.M.		Capricorn

1962			
Feb.	1	6:07 P.M.	Aquarius
March	12	2:59 A.M.	Pisces

MARS

April	19	11:59 A.M.	Aries
May	28	6:48 P.M.	Taurus
July	8	10:51 P.M.	Gemini
Aug.	22	6:38 A.M.	Cancer
Oct.	11	6:55 P.M.	Leo

1963

June	3	1:30 A.M.	Virgo
July	26	11:15 P.M.	Libra
Sept.	12	4:12 A.M.	Scorpio
Oct.	25	12:32 P.M.	Sagittarius
Dec.	5	4:04 A.M.	Capricorn

1964

Jan.	13	1:14 A.M.	Aquarius
Feb.	20	2:33 A.M.	Pisces
March	29	6:25 A.M.	Aries
May	7	9:41 A.M.	Taurus
June	17	6:43 A.M.	Gemini
July	30	1:23 P.M.	Cancer
Sept.	15	12:23 A.M.	Leo
Nov.	5	10:20 P.M.	Virgo

1965

June	28	8:12 P.M.	Libra
Aug.	20	7:17 A.M.	Scorpio
Oct.	4	1:47 A.M.	Sagittarius
Nov.	14	2:20 A.M.	Capricorn
Dec.	23	12:37 A.M.	Aquarius

1966

Jan.	30	2:02 A.M.	Pisces
March	9	7:56 A.M.	Aries
April	17	3:35 P.M.	Taurus
May	28	5:08 P.M.	Gemini
July	10	10:15 P.M.	Cancer
Aug.	25	10:52 A.M.	Leo
Oct.	12	1:38 P.M.	Virgo
Dec.	3	7:55 P.M.	Libra

1967

Feb.	12	7:20 A.M.		Scorpio
March	31	1:10 A.M.	R	Libra
July	19	5:57 P.M.		Scorpio
Sept.	9	8:45 P.M.		Sagittarius
Oct.	22	9:15 P.M.		Capricorn
Dec.	1	3:12 P.M.		Aquarius

1968

Jan.	9	4:50 A.M.	Pisces
Feb.	16	10:18 P.M.	Aries
March	27	6:44 P.M.	Taurus
May	8	9:15 A.M.	Gemini
June	21	12:04 A.M.	Cancer
Aug.	5	12:08 P.M.	Leo
Sept.	21	1:39 P.M.	Virgo
Nov.	9	1:10 A.M.	Libra
Dec.	29	5:08 P.M.	Scorpio

1969

Feb.	25	1:21 A.M.	Sagittarius
Sept.	21	1:36 A.M.	Capricorn
Nov.	4	1:51 P.M.	Aquarius
Dec.	15	9:23 A.M.	Pisces

1970

Jan.	24	4:30 P.M.	Aries
March	6	8:29 P.M.	Taurus
April	18	1:59 P.M.	Gemini
June	2	1:51 A.M.	Cancer
July	18	1:44 A.M.	Leo
Sept.	2	11:58 P.M.	Virgo
Oct.	20	5:57 A.M.	Libra
Dec.	6	11:35 A.M.	Scorpio

1971

Jan.	22	8:35 P.M.	Sagittarius
March	12	5:12 A.M.	Capricorn
May	3	3:58 P.M.	Aquarius
Nov.	6	7:32 A.M.	Pisces
Dec.	26	1:05 P.M.	Aries

1972

Feb.	10	9:05 A.M.	Taurus
March	26	11:31 P.M.	Gemini
May	12	8:15 A.M.	Cancer
June	28	11:09 A.M.	Leo
Aug.	14	7:59 P.M.	Virgo
Sept.	30	6:24 P.M.	Libra
Nov.	15	5:18 P.M.	Scorpio
Dec.	30	11:13 A.M.	Sagittarius

1973

Feb.	12	12:51 A.M.		Capricorn
March	26	4:00 P.M.		Aquarius
May	7	11:10 P.M.		Pisces
June	20	3:54 P.M.		Aries
Aug.	12	9:57 A.M.		Taurus
Oct.	29	5:57 P.M.	R	Aries
Dec.	24	3:10 A.M.		Taurus

1974

Feb.	27	5:12 A.M.	Gemini
April	20	3:19 A.M.	Cancer
June	8	7:55 P.M.	Leo
July	27	9:05 A.M.	Virgo
Sept.	12	2:09 P.M.	Libra
Oct.	28	2:05 A.M.	Scorpio
Dec.	10	5:06 P.M.	Sagittarius

1975

Jan.	21	1:50 P.M.		Capricorn
March	3	12:32 A.M.		Aquarius
April	11	2:16 P.M.		Pisces
May	21	3:14 A.M.		Aries
June	30	10:54 P.M.		Taurus
Aug.	14	3:47 P.M.		Gemini
Oct.	17	3:44 A.M.		Cancer
Nov.	25	1:31 P.M.	R	Gemini

1976

March	18	8:15 A.M.	Cancer
May	16	6:11 A.M.	Leo
July	6	6:28 P.M.	Virgo
Aug.	24	12:55 A.M.	Libra
Oct.	8	3:24 P.M.	Scorpio
Nov.	20	6:54 P.M.	Sagittarius
Dec.	31	7:42 P.M.	Capricorn

1977

Feb.	9	6:58 A.M.	Aquarius
March	19	9:20 P.M.	Pisces
April	27	10:46 A.M.	Aries
June	5	10:00 P.M.	Taurus
July	17	10:13 A.M.	Gemini
Aug.	31	7:21 P.M.	Cancer
Oct.	26	1:57 P.M.	Leo

1978

Jan.	25	11:00 P.M.	R	Cancer
April	10	1:51 P.M.		Leo
June	13	9:39 P.M.		Virgo
Aug.	4	4:08 A.M.		Libra
Sept.	19	3:58 P.M.		Scorpio
Nov.	1	8:21 P.M.		Sagittarius
Dec.	12	12:40 P.M.		Capricorn

1979

Jan.	20	12:08 P.M.	Aquarius
Feb.	27	3:26 P.M.	Pisces
April	6	8:09 P.M.	Aries
May	15	11:26 P.M.	Taurus
June	25	8:56 P.M.	Gemini
Aug.	8	8:29 A.M.	Cancer
Sept.	24	4:22 P.M.	Leo
Nov.	19	4:37 P.M.	Virgo

1980

March	11	3:47 P.M.	R	Leo
May	3	9:27 P.M.		Virgo
July	10	1:00 P.M.		Libra
Aug.	29	12:51 A.M.		Scorpio
Oct.	12	1:27 A.M.		Sagittarius
Nov.	21	8:43 P.M.		Capricorn
Dec.	30	5:31 P.M.		Aquarius

Opportunity Knocks—Meet Jupiter

You've opened up the want ads. Perhaps you've opened up your own business. But have you opened yourself to the spirit of opportunity? An opportunity is an opening. In fact, the word *opportunity* comes from the same Latin root as "portal" and "harbor" and literally means "to stand in front of an open doorway."

Maybe you've got your act together. You've focused on your goals, polished your professional persona, honed your leadership skills, and harnessed your sales and seduction savvy. Hooray! You're ahead of the game. Does that mean you can kick back and let the good times roll?

No. Sorry. It doesn't work that way. You won't land every promotion for which you're qualified, just as every talented actor in Hollywood won't become a star. In fact, it sometimes seems that qualifications and talent matter *less* than being willing to take chances, being in the right place at the right time, and finding opportunities. It's the combination of these three that astrologers call Jupiter.

Jupiter represents the part of you that lays out the welcome mat for opportunity. It symbolizes how you can put yourself in the right place at the right time. Jupiter reflects your attitude toward expanding your horizons and the inner voice that says, "Yes, I believe it's possible!" Getting to

know your Jupiter can help you unlock the creativity you need to open up opportunities.

DUMB LUCK OR HARD WORK?

Traditional astrology viewed Jupiter as a cosmic fairy godmother. If she liked you, good fortune fell on you like chocolate-covered manna from heaven. If not, you'd better invest in sensible shoes for standing in soup lines. Today, we postmodern astrologers recognize Jupiter is more complicated. Good fortune and prosperity emerge from an unpredictable mixture of hard work, vision, and what you've had for lunch that day. Take, for example, the case of my former client, a British-educated chemist. Though it was a long shot, he applied for a job at a top-notch think tank. Lo and behold, it turned out that a member of the search committee was a friend of my client's former professor, now on his list of references. My client landed the job.

Sure, he was lucky that an unlikely personal connection made his résumé stand out, but didn't he help enable that luck? He revealed that his former professor was so impressed by his research that he actually *offered* to recommend my client for any job. So Jupiter, his inner opportunist, played a large role in my client's success. Luck doesn't just show up; it has to be invited.

OPEN THE DOOR—BUT WHICH DOOR? FIND THE KEY

You'll find lots of books and seminars that tell you how to create abundance in your life, why you aren't more prosperous, and even where to find lucky numbers for playing the lottery. Most of this advice, however, overlooks the personal factor. It assumes that universal principles work the same for everybody in every case. By looking up your Jupiter sign, you can pinpoint the key for unlocking your doors of opportunity.

OVERDOSE! TOO MUCH OF A GOOD THING

Jupiter has a tendency to overdo it. And why not? We always want more of good thing. We eat till we're sick. We work till we drop. We spend till the credit cards melt from the friction of overswiping. Just another reason to know Jupiter intimately—otherwise you may suffer from too much of a good thing.

Find your Jupiter in the Jupiter table on page 352. It'll suggest how and where you're likely to bump into your lucky breaks and a sense of *anything's possible.*

Jupiter in Aries

THE KEY: *CONFIDENCE.* "I can do it!" says Jupiter in Aries. You benefit from the gift of confidence. And with confidence comes energy and vitality, hallmarks of any great leader. Having confidence means you can defy limits and take risks, emboldened by the youthful delusion that you'll live forever. So you're a little cocky. Who wouldn't be? Confidence opens many doors. You make your own breaks in life. You don't rely on institutions, bosses, or your business astrologer to cultivate luck. When you're confident, you can afford to be generous, and like attracts like. To get the most out of your Jupiter sign, put yourself out there and try new experiences. Invest in more than your IRA; invest in your own abilities.

TOO MUCH OF A GOOD THING? Where your good fortune can run out, however, is where your confidence turns into mere bravado—performing a Clint Eastwood impersonation when you really feel like Elmer Fudd. You take foolish risks and bully your way to the front. With a confidence overdose, minor disappointments feel like unbearable setbacks. Unless you're very clear on your reasons, Dr. Matt doesn't recommend accepting challenges just for the heck of it, just so you can prove you've got *cajones.* Those aren't opportunities; they're stunts—unless you can see how they'll lead you in the direction where you want to go.

Jupiter in Taurus

THE KEY: *PERSEVERANCE.* "No matter what, I'll stick with it," says Jupiter in Taurus. Good fortune comes your way through diligence and tenacity. You don't have the fastest Jupiter sign, so forget get-rich-quick schemes, but nobody can say you lack endurance. As a result, your ability to arrive at your destination is seldom in doubt. Look for opportunities where perseverance pays off. You might, for example, want to invest in real estate in an up-and-coming neighborhood where, through gentrification and patience, you'll accrue a handsome rise in equity.

TOO MUCH OF A GOOD THING? Since we live in a culture that looks down on quitters, perseverance is bound to open many doors for you. But sometimes quitting makes sense. In that case, when letting go and walking away is the most appropriate, even advantageous, response, can you do it without feeling like a loser? Avoid the self-destructive perseverance of my

Jupiter-in-Taurus client who had to fail out of law school before she'd admit she wanted to leave and do something else. So don't cling to just one opportunity to the exclusion of all others. Expand your horizons. Venture out of your comfort zone. Apply your perseverance not only to one goal but also to opening up more opportunities.

Jupiter in Gemini

THE KEY: *KNOW-HOW.* "I know how to do it, and I can make it work," says Jupiter in Gemini. You'll go far with your brains. Whether you've got a Ph.D. from MIT or a GED and plenty of street smarts, your fortune is not so much what you know already, but a talent for learning new things. Learn all you can. If you're a dancer, read about physics; if you're a banker, visit art museums. Information seldom goes to waste. I cast a chart, for example, for a Jupiter-in-Gemini waitress who gobbled up TV trivia, and was forever singing *Partridge Family* songs or telling *Seinfeld* jokes. Though it may sound frivolous, this knowledge helped her

> **"When considering choices in your life, the 'most alive choice' feels like a bit of a risk, makes you giggle, or makes the hairs at the back of your neck stand up."**
> AUTHOR SARK

land a screenwriting job in L.A.—she impressed the studio execs with her ability to schmooze about all their shows. If you're starved for opportunities, try sharing what you know. Give, and thou shalt receive. Start a website or write a column about your area of expertise. Teach a course. At social events, make a point of discovering more about fellow guests than their names and occupations. Embrace discussion and dissension. Get out of the office more.

TOO MUCH OF A GOOD THING? Your Jupiter-in-Gemini know-how can pry open a wealth of opportunities. But look out! That treasure chest may explode into a Pandora's box. If indulged too far, your Jupiter can go from smart to just plain cunning, crafty, and tricky. You complicate matters. You spend more time scheming than working. You invent fabulous lies that belong in a bestselling novel, not in a memo or quarterly report. But perhaps more importantly, you need to distinguish between opportunities and *distractions.* Just because you know *how* to accomplish a goal, does that mean you *want* to? If you really cultivate your know-how, you'll likely suffer from a dearth of time, not chances. So take some advice from the author Ernest Hemingway: "Read only the best books first, for you cannot read them all."

Jupiter in Cancer

THE KEY: *FORTITUDE*. "I'll always land on my feet," says Jupiter in Cancer. To others it may simply look like you have your stuff together, but actually you've been gifted with fortitude and strength of character. No matter where you go, what you do, or whom you encounter, you know you can depend on yourself. Traditionally, Jupiter in Cancer signified you would have victory over incredible odds. Maybe that's still true, because you can enter risky, uncharted territory. It means that you can go wherever your destiny calls, knowing that you can always fall back on yourself. You feel at home wherever you go, which is probably all over the place. Since Jupiter in Cancer suggests you've got big strong shoulders, you can support many of the people around you, creating an atmosphere of inclusion. At your table there's room for everyone, and the opportunities they may bring with them. Furthermore, your fortitude allows you to be receptive to opportunities without feeling threatened by them.

TOO MUCH OF A GOOD THING? Opportunities tend to dry up when your fortitude turns into a fortress. Determined never to lose control over your options, you may react defensively when unexpected help comes your way. Let's say you're at a convention and someone says, "I saw your presentation. It was great, but you ought to use different colors." Thank him for the advice though you may not appreciate this unsolicited criticism. Allow him to give you valuable yet free feedback—and if he thought your presentation was so great, sell him your services!

Jupiter in Leo

THE KEY: *PANACHE*. "I've got something nobody else has—*me*!" says Jupiter in Leo. Call it what you will—a flair, a style, pizzazz—but, baby, you got it. It's your key to opportunity. Traditionally Jupiter in Leo meant you were lucky in romance. But you can imbue your work with sex appeal, even outside the boudoir. This kind of panache creates excitement. You just got fired? Throw a party. Creating opportunities isn't a job, it's a lifestyle. Don't overlook the opportunities associated with having a good time. Many deals are made on tennis courts. Extend your panache to all of your opportunity-enhancing endeavors. Print your résumé on tastefully colored paper. Choose a distinctive wardrobe style—and always wear at least one item that'll invite a comment or compliment. Identify the person who

has your dream job and invite them to lunch: "I think what you do is so cool! Tell me about it." And remember: If at first you don't succeed, you can always reinvent yourself. In the personality department, Jupiter in Leo knows no limits.

TOO MUCH OF A GOOD THING? Panache can, of course, go too far. Your ambition to reach people might swell into an arrogant attempt to impress them. And if you overlook opportunities that lack panache, you may limit your options. Beware of opportunities with a patina of gold but an inside of stainless steel. This doesn't mean, however, that you should squelch your panache. Instead, channel it into activities that directly promote opportunities as opposed to outrageousness. You can, for example, emphasize other people's achievements as much as your own. Encourage an atmosphere with room for everyone to shine. Congratulate coworkers. Help them celebrate their successes. Fame comes easily to Jupiter-in-Leo professionals. But not all fame is an opportunity. Keep in mind your goals: Which opportunities will help you reach them? Those deserve more attention than the so-called opportunities that promise to put your name in lights.

Jupiter in Virgo

THE KEY: *COMMITMENT.* "I'm committed to making the most of this opportunity," says Jupiter in Virgo. Remember, an opportunity is a door, a portal to someplace where you want to go. Fully seizing an opportunity means you walk through the door—all the way through, not one foot in, one foot out. That's the key of Jupiter in Virgo. Forget the just-get-it-done approach; commit yourself to doing it right. Practice discipline. Reduce distractions. Keep it simple. If nothing is calling out your name right now, dedicate yourself to something, *anything*. Take up a devotional practice—meditate, train for a marathon, learn Japanese calligraphy.

TOO MUCH OF A GOOD THING? Commitment can become counterproductive when it turns fanatical. You run so hard and fast that you injure your knee and miss the marathon altogether! Commitment relies on awareness, not blindness. Don't commit prematurely. Allow yourself time to explore and make choices. Be careful you don't dedicate yourself to unworthy projects or organizations. And be aware that the various parts of your life must work together to work well.

Jupiter in Libra

THE KEY: *SYNERGY*. "I can bring all the pieces together," says Jupiter in Libra. World-class chefs don't adhere to recipes. They develop an instinct for combining distinct flavors into a unique blend that makes the most of each individual taste. That's *synergy* ("energy working together"), and it can open up many opportunities for you. If you're looking for good fortune, try combining forces: Form a job-seekers' support group or join a networking club. If something comes your way but you can't act on it right now, call a friend and offer it to them. Perhaps opportunities won't come to you prepackaged and ready to serve. But with a little finesse, you might make them quite palatable. By providing opportunities for others you may ensure that opportunities will be provided for you. Synergy means you value the working relationships as much as the work itself. And— very important!—it means you can ask for help. One more hint: Don't neglect other parts of your life during your job search. With Jupiter in Libra, opportunities come from the momentum of energy working together, not in isolation.

> **"Jupiter enlarges awareness through seeking a broader vision of reality."**
> ASTROLOGY AUTHORS
> DOUGLAS BLOCH AND
> DEMETRA GEORGE

TOO MUCH OF A GOOD THING? This working-together approach can burgeon out of control. In your efforts to keep harmony, you may get tangled in a web of compromises. By relying on other people, you might become dependent on favors and overlook real opportunities—or wind up granting favors and receive nothing in return. Or in your eagerness to incorporate all aspects of yourself and your life in your work, you may create a jumbled organization rather than a unified entity. Remember, not all combinations work; to develop your opportunities, you may have to sacrifice some parts for the good of the whole.

Jupiter in Scorpio

THE KEY: *RESOURCEFULNESS*. "Where there's a will there's a way—and I'll find it!" says Jupiter in Scorpio. You can find the opportunities that other folks can't. Being resourceful means being able to get in the back door if the front is locked. If, for instance, you want desperately to break into the fashion design industry but keep getting turned down, try your hand at a re-

lated profession—like modeling, fashion journalism, or photography—that'll get you into the inner circle. Traditionally the sign of wealth through inheritance or marriage, Jupiter in Scorpio suggests that you can go quickly from being down on your luck to holding the winning ticket. Develop your resources. Don't settle for the opportunities that providence drops at your doorstep. Instead, make lists of people, talents, and assets that you'd like to benefit from. And remember, opportunities don't always look like opportunities, so it's up to you to recognize potential—and to believe you can turn negative or neutral situations to your advantage.

TOO MUCH OF A GOOD THING? Put some holds on your "resourceful" instincts or they'll take you places you don't want to go, like into the murky realm of unethical behavior. Making your own luck is fine, but an overactive Jupiter in Scorpio bent on "milking" everyone and everything tends to manipulate people—even to the point of blackmail. Remember, resourcefulness doesn't mean underhandedness! You don't have to abuse rules or take advantage of people. By all means, push the envelope. Find legal loopholes. Coax and cajole people to go along with your plan. But stop short of sleaze. And keep in mind that you can occasionally seize an opportunity simply by walking straight through the front door.

Jupiter in Sagittarius

THE KEY: *EXPERIENCE.* "I've done it before and I can do it again," says Jupiter in Sagittarius. Traditionally, this Jupiter sign signified great wisdom. Even today, your good fortune hinges on a simple formula: The more experiences you have, the more opportunities open up before you. Intrinsically growth-oriented, you can enhance your opportunities by making your world as big as possible. If you follow developments in the U.S. advertising industry, for example, why not read about ad agencies and trends overseas, too? General Motors Corporation bumbled a golden opportunity in the 1970s: It marketed its Chevy Nova—a big North American seller—to the Latin American market, and it busted. Not only that, but consumers there laughed at the car! Why? Because *no va* in Spanish means "It doesn't go." So get comfortable in a wide variety of situations. The next time you go to a convention, don't sit next to the same people you sat with last time. If you typically listen to the classical radio station, tune into country/western for a change—not just for kicks, but to understand a different market together with a different marketing approach.

TOO MUCH OF A GOOD THING? You have a huge appetite for experience, so you're often tempted to overfill your plate. Moderate your enthusiasm. You don't need to leap at every opportunity. If you do, you may not be able to take on the perfect opportunity when it comes your way. Choose your experiences carefully. Try to identify the "gaps" in your résumé—those areas where you have relatively few experiences—and make it a point to fill them. Finally, don't overlook the experience of just *being*. Opportunities don't arise only in the midst of "great experiences," but also during the quiet moments. So while you should seek out the experiences that'll likely bring you opportunities, don't ignore the ones that fall in your lap!

Jupiter in Capricorn

THE KEY: *APLOMB.* "I'm comfortable enough with myself to follow opportunity wherever it might lead me," says Jupiter in Capricorn. *Aplomb* combines the qualities of "poise," "dignity," and "imperturbable self-possession."

> **"When one door closes another door opens; but we so often look so long and so regretfully upon the closed door, that we do not see the ones which open for us."**
> INVENTOR ALEXANDER GRAHAM BELL

A professional with aplomb quickly sizes up the rules of the game—and how to win. You can always work the system—whether it's big business, bureaucracies, or social cliques—because it doesn't overshadow who you are. Jupiter in Capricorn traditionally promised its owner a prestigious destiny, a first-class ticket and muckety-muck status. Finding Jupiter in Capricorn in your birth chart, fortune-tellers would proclaim, "You should go far in life." But today's astrologers know that inviting opportunity into your life requires believing you're worthy of good fortune. With aplomb you can feel and look successful in spite of your circumstances; your identity needn't depend on your job title or bank balance. Inwardly, aplomb means you don't stress out over one golden opportunity; outwardly it means you present a poised and comfortable image without bragging or threatening. If you strive toward this sort of self-assurance, you'll gain a reputation for personality plus professionalism and golden opportunities will unfold just as the fortune-teller predicted.

TOO MUCH OF A GOOD THING? Aplomb is tough to maintain in every situation. No one can remain completely self-composed when starting a new venture or walking into unfamiliar territory. In situations like those, if you in-

sist on remaining as dignified as ever, you may stumble in the dark—or, worse yet, you may avoid the situations in the first place and miss out on their potential. Some opportunities are bound to throw you into temporary turmoil.

Jupiter in Aquarius

THE KEY: *OPEN-MINDEDNESS*. "I'll try anything!" says Jupiter in Aquarius. Traditionally, Jupiter in Aquarius meant you'd have weird luck and find fortune in strange, unexpected places. You do. By keeping an open mind, you come in contact with movers and shakers. Eager to associate with people of diverse backgrounds, you may see opportunities that everyone else overlooked. Think of a Scrabble board congested with a bunch of one-syllable words, when someone lays down *xenophobic* and opens up the entire game. That's Jupiter in Aquarius. Your ability to think outside the box makes you lucky, and it also helps out the rest of us, too. To enhance your opportunities, resist the urge to categorize people. Pigeonholes simply aren't big enough for human beings. The same goes for situations—you needn't immediately evaluate them as "good" or "bad." If you walk into a meeting without a lot of preconceived negative ideas, you're bound to find more chances for success and cooperation.

TOO MUCH OF A GOOD THING? Don't feel that to be open-minded you must remain totally impartial. If you're rigidly open-minded, you may never form opinions of your own. Or you may mistakenly believe that all approaches have equal merit. Being open-minded doesn't mean you need to accept every idea that comes your way. Be wary, for example, of embracing inventions and innovations that are cool but unprofitable.

Jupiter in Pisces

THE KEY: *FAITH*. "It'll all work out," says Jupiter in Pisces. Back in astrology's early days, Jupiter in Pisces was the sign of martyrs, gurus, and saints. But since martyrdom is out of fashion, guru jobs are hard to come by, and you have to die to be canonized, let's consider the practical applications of your Jupiter placement. If you believe good things will happen, they usually do. So keep the faith. When you encounter a new person or situation, hold off judgment. Could it be an opportunity in disguise? Perhaps. Put

yourself in the best of all possible circumstances—and then see what happens. Your strong sense of faith wins friends and influences people. You have this quality about you that tells people you can make dreams come true. Only you know whether that's the case, but let them believe it and they'll keep coming back for more. When it comes to opportunity, there are no guarantees. That's what makes faith so valuable. Walk through the door. See what's there.

> **"Fortune is the chance we take on the roulette wheel of life. . . . For Fortune, to play the game is more important than winning or losing."**
> MERRILL-WEST PUBLISHING COMPANY FOUNDER JIM WANLESS, PH.D.

TOO MUCH OF A GOOD THING? Faith used indiscriminately becomes gullibility. You can be taken advantage of easily. Don't invest in opportunities that sound too good to be true. It's your tendency to forgive and forget but be wary of those who may walk all over you again. Plan for the future—don't get lost in fantasy. Keep your expectations realistic—rather than waiting around for good things to happen, follow a true belief wherever it may lead you.

How to Find Your Jupiter Sign—Easy as 1-2-3

1. In the following Jupiter tables, look up the year of your birth.

2. The tables only list the days on which Jupiter actually *changed* signs—approximately once a year. So look for the nearest date listed that comes before your birthday.

3. Land ho! That's your Jupiter sign, right there in the far-right column across from the date you found in Step 2. When you find your Jupiter sign, write it down in your Planetary Positions Chart on page 377.

But wait! Even though Jupiter changes signs only once a year, there's still a slim chance it changed signs right *on* your birthday. If so, you'll want to determine if you were born *before* or *after* the change. Simply refer to the section "Determining Your Sign Down to the Minute" on page 199, then come back to these Jupiter tables.

EXAMPLE

If you need help, let's practice by looking up Oprah Winfrey's Jupiter sign. Oprah was born January 29, 1954.

1. Turn to 1954 in the Jupiter tables.

2. At the start of 1954, you can see there's no January listed. So go *back* to the next nearest date, which happens to be May 9, 1953, when Jupiter entered Gemini. Oprah's got Jupiter in Gemini (which makes sense, considering her stellar success in the media business!).

3. In her Planetary Positions Chart on page 377, Oprah would write this down and read the entry in this chapter for Jupiter in Gemini.

JUPITER

1940			
May	16	2:55 A.M.	Taurus

1941			
May	26	7:48 A.M.	Gemini

1942			
June	10	5:36 A.M.	Cancer

1943			
June	30	4:46 P.M.	Leo

1944			
July	25	8:04 P.M.	Virgo

1945			
Aug.	25	1:06 A.M.	Libra

1946			
Sept.	25	5:19 A.M.	Scorpio

1947			
Oct.	23	10:00 P.M.	Sagittarius

1948			
Nov.	15	5:38 A.M.	Capricorn

1949				
April	12	2:18 P.M.		Aquarius
June	27	1:30 P.M.	R	Capricorn
Nov.	30	3:08 P.M.		Aquarius

1950				
April	15	3:59 A.M.		Pisces
Sept.	14	9:23 P.M.	R	Aquarius
Dec.	1	2:57 P.M.		Pisces

1951			
April	21	9:57 A.M.	Aries

1952			
April	28	3:51 P.M.	Taurus

1953			
May	9	10:34 A.M.	Gemini

1954			
May	23	11:44 P.M.	Cancer

1955			
June	12	7:07 P.M.	Leo
Nov.	16	10:59 P.M.	Virgo

1956				
Jan.	17	9:05 P.M.	R	Leo
July	7	2:02 P.M.		Virgo
Dec.	12	9:17 P.M.		Libra

1957				
Feb.	19	10:38 A.M.	R	Virgo
Aug.	6	9:11 P.M.		Libra

1958				
Jan.	13	7:52 A.M.		Scorpio
March	20	2:14 P.M.	R	Libra
Sept.	7	3:52 A.M.		Scorpio

1959				
Feb.	10	8:46 A.M.		Sagittarius
April	24	9:11 A.M.	R	Scorpio
Oct.	5	9:40 A.M.		Sagittarius

1960				
March	1	8:10 A.M.		Capricorn
June	9	8:53 P.M.	R	Sagittarius
Oct.	25	10:01 P.M.		Capricorn

1961				
March	15	3:02 A.M.		Aquarius
Aug.	12	3:55 A.M.	R	Capricorn
Nov.	3	9:49 P.M.		Aquarius

1962			
March	25	5:08 P.M.	Pisces

1963			
April	3	10:20 P.M.	Aries

1964			
April	12	1:53 A.M.	Taurus

1965				
April	22	9:33 A.M.		Gemini
Sept.	20	11:40 P.M.		Cancer
Nov.	16	10:09 P.M.	R	Gemini

1966			
May	5	9:52 A.M.	Cancer
Sept.	27	8:20 A.M.	Leo

1967				
Jan.	15	10:50 P.M.	R	Cancer
May	23	3:21 A.M.		Leo
Oct.	19	5:52 A.M.		Virgo

1968				
Feb.	26	10:34 P.M.	R	Leo
June	15	9:44 A.M.		Virgo
Nov.	15	5:44 P.M.		Libra

1969				
March	30	4:37 P.M.	R	Virgo
July	15	8:30 A.M.		Libra
Dec.	16	10:56 A.M.		Scorpio

1970				
April	30	1:45 A.M.	R	Libra
Aug.	15	12:58 P.M.		Scorpio

1971				
Jan.	14	3:50 A.M.		Sagittarius
June	4	9:13 P.M.	R	Scorpio
Sept.	11	10:33 A.M.		Sagittarius

1972				
Feb.	6	2:37 P.M.		Capricorn
July	24	11:43 A.M.	R	Sagittarius
Sept.	25	1:20 P.M.		Capricorn

1973			
Feb.	23	4:28 A.M.	Aquarius

1974			
March	8	6:12 A.M.	Pisces

1975			
March	18	11:48 A.M.	Aries

1976				
March	26	5:25 A.M.		Taurus
Aug.	23	5:25 A.M.		Gemini
Oct.	16	3:25 P.M.	R	Taurus

1977				
April	3	10:43 A.M.		Gemini
Aug.	20	7:43 A.M.		Cancer
Dec.	30	6:51 P.M.	R	Gemini

1978			
April	11	7:12 P.M.	Cancer
Sept.	5	3:31 A.M.	Leo

1979				
Feb.	28	6:36 P.M.	R	Cancer
April	20	3:30 A.M.		Leo
Sept.	29	5:24 A.M.		Virgo

1980			
Oct.	27	5:11 A.M.	Libra

Get Over It—Your Saturn Sign

"Once you have felt the rush of conquering your own fear, it will become an addiction. That's where you'll get the strength to go forward and keep trying new things. Things you've always wanted to do."

AUTHOR LUCINDA BASSETT

I once had a client come to me for his birth chart, looking to answer some pretty serious questions. He explained that he had paid his dues and played by all the rules. He was the youngest graduate in his Ivy League law school class, and had spent three years on the partnership track at a prestigious law firm. His life was neat, tidy, and studded with luxuries. But not satisfying.

Though his résumé and credentials were the envy of many young professionals, he felt stuck, always doing what he thought he *should* do instead of what he *wanted* to do. I knew it right away—he had met his Saturn. By analyzing his Saturn self, though, he came to feel good about articulating what he really wanted, changing jobs, and adopting a new outlook about himself and his career. You can, too.

Saturn represents your *rut*. It symbolizes the traps you tend to get stuck in, the ways you hold yourself back from reaching your potential, or how you overcompensate for what you perceive as a personal deficiency. Saturn stands for your petty fears and worst nightmares. Avoid Saturn and you'll never dare to climb the mountain. Face it, and you're already halfway up.

"HELP! I'VE FALLEN AND I CAN'T GET UP!"—THE TRAPS

Studying your Saturn sign can help you identify the ruts and self-defeating myths or behavior patterns that you fall back on when you don't know what else to do—or simply because of bad habits. These are the traps that might keep you stuck on the treadmill. Awareness is the first step toward freedom.

BREAK FREE!

If you get caught in a Saturn "trap," are you doomed to stay there? Not at all. But in order to unlock the trap, you can't ignore its existence; you have to learn the mechanism by which it functions. Don't get discouraged! Mastering your Saturn can take years, because once you overcome one obstacle you'll naturally gravitate toward bigger ones. For a while, you may react to your trap by ignoring it or covering it up. But nearly every professional I interviewed and cast a chart for—from psychologist to financier—explained that by standing and confronting them, their fears and failures eventually became some of their greatest strengths.

Saturn in Aries

THE TRAP: *WEAKNESS*. "I'm vulnerable and might break if not handled with care," says the voice of Saturn in Aries. If you fall into the weakness trap, you'll have a hard time asserting yourself. Everyone seems to pose a threat. You'll run from conflict and avoid activities that draw attention to you. On the flip side, you might overcompensate for your perceived weakness by covering it up. You won't ask for help. You'll bully people. You'll be as strict and demanding with them as you are with yourself, always fearing that your weakness will be discovered.

BREAK FREE! Weakness has a bum rap in our bigger-is-better society. That's unfortunate, because weakness is surprisingly powerful. A small fledgling company will often out-compete a mighty corporation by identifying a crack in the market, innovating a new product, and keeping overhead low. To break free of the weakness trap, take stock of your abilities objectively. Evaluate your strengths and weaknesses. Show this "inventory" to people you trust and ask for feedback. Compare your self-evaluation with their eval-

> **"The trouble with the rat race is that even if you win, you're still a rat."**
> COMEDIENNE LILY TOMLIN

uation of you. How do they compare? Do you accentuate or cover up your weaknesses? Don't view disappointments as signs of your intrinsic "weakness." If you survived the letdown, you're obviously stronger than you thought!

Saturn in Taurus

THE TRAP: *SCARCITY*. "There's never enough to go around," says the voice of Saturn in Taurus, exhibiting an astrological symptom of what some psychologists call the "Bag Lady Syndrome." No matter how impressive your résumé or bank account, you dread going broke. You fear you can't afford to think fresh thoughts. You take obsessive precautions. On the other hand, you might overcompensate by pinching pennies till it hurts or swing to the opposite extreme and spend every last dime on worthless trinkets or foolhardy investments.

BREAK FREE! To release yourself from the scarcity trap, take a few reasonable precautions. For instance, work with a personal financial advisor to ensure you'll have enough assets when you retire—and enough spending money *now*. Then catch yourself when you start dwelling on want. There are only two positions available and 18 candidates? Who cares? You have everything to lose and nothing to gain by applying for the position. Heck, it's better odds than roulette in Vegas.

Saturn in Gemini

THE TRAP: *BOREDOM*. "There's nothing new under the Sun; it's all been done before; I've never had an original idea in my entire life," says the voice of Saturn in Gemini. If you fall into the boredom trap, you might be able to identify with 19th-century fictional characters who suffer ennui, an overwhelming feeling of *blah*. You seesaw from drudgery to chaos, from doing nothing to making to-do lists longer than ticker tape—all in an effort to stimulate your mind and make yourself feel like more than a bump on a log. The boredom trap produces either an abject couch potato or a raving busybody—unless, of course, you break free.

BREAK FREE! Ours is a culture of doing, not being. Perhaps if you don't do enough, you feel worthless; if you do too much, you burn out. But it's

possible to extricate yourself from this boredom trap. First, keep yourself *engaged*. Even if you're between jobs, stay active and open-minded; even if you've landed your dream job, maintain outside interests. Fight staleness and entropy! Decline to go to lunch with colleagues if all they'll discuss is work. You need more stimulation than that over your tuna fish sandwich. Next, get comfortable with down time. Be careful not to overschedule—you need room to breathe. If you have to make agendas, list the things you accomplish, not the things that need to be accomplished. Focus your energy on the tasks you're doing, not on what you're not doing.

Saturn in Cancer

THE TRAP: *INSECURITY.* "There's no safety net to catch me if I fall!" says the voice of Saturn in Cancer. If you get caught in the insecurity trap, the professional world must seem like a mighty threatening place. Every step you take in any different direction jeopardizes the status quo. You won't do anything at which you don't excel. You take every little comment as a personal injury. You exude emotional neediness, demanding constant reassurance about your own worth—or you defend yourself ruthlessly. You go to ridiculous lengths to maintain stability, or perhaps you go to the other extreme and throw all caution to the wind, changing jobs every six months. Neither tactic, unfortunately, makes the fear of change any easier to bear.

BREAK FREE! Sometimes you have to swim with the sharks even if you feel more like a dolphin. That doesn't mean, however, you must *become* a shark—you simply need to be a more self-assured dolphin! Gradually coax yourself to enter more insecure situations. Don't make coworkers treat you with kid gloves. Attempt endeavors at which you have no experience, particularly if you're allowed to have room for "failure." That way, even if you don't "succeed" at the endeavor, you will have succeeded at letting down your defenses without having the world fall apart.

Saturn in Leo

THE TRAP: *INHIBITION.* "Nobody likes me; nobody likes what I do," says the voice of Saturn in Leo. Though you probably long to express yourself, if

you fall into the inhibition trap, it's likely to stifle your creativity. You never want to risk the "humiliation" of holding yourself up for judgment. If you think your first portrait can't rival the *Mona Lisa*, you'll find it nearly impossible to approach your easel each morning, constantly "blocked" or "uninspired" but not sure why. Stage fright and performance anxiety hold you back. Then again, the inhibition trap might make you react just the opposite, by insisting your work is brilliant, or altering your work to fit the "judges'" idea of brilliant. Either way, inhibition prevents you from realizing your true vision.

BREAK FREE! Start by separating yourself from your profession. Your work may partly shape your identity—but only partly. Next, determine *why* you want to do what you do. To help people? Get rich? Show off? Create beauty? Knowing this will make it easier, when the job is done, for you to assess your success—and stop thinking your career is over because the "critics" didn't like you. Maybe you never intended to please the critics!

Saturn in Virgo

THE TRAP: *FUTILITY.* "It's just useless. *I'm* just useless," says the voice of Saturn in Virgo. When life doesn't go according to plan—and it rarely does—you're terrified. "Why didn't my career come with an instruction manual?" you wonder, afraid that every choice you make is the wrong one, that you'll never help make the world a better place or contribute anything of value. As a result, you're bound to become a committed, faithless cynic, afraid to make a difference—or take everything you do so seriously that it's almost laughable, and ultimately disappointing.

BREAK FREE! Start by choosing or shaping a career that feels intrinsically *worthwhile*. If in your eyes that means earning a good living, identify the steps needed to get a raise—and then take them, congratulating yourself for each milestone you pass en route to your objective. Don't berate yourself for previous choices—undoubtedly, almost all of them opened up options you now take for granted; if necessary, make lists of those options so you see how each choice produced both pluses and minuses. Finally, keep perspective. In the course of things, who's to say that helping three customers matters less than enacting congressional legislation?

Saturn in Libra

THE TRAP: *LONELINESS.* "I can't do it on my own," says the voice of Saturn in Libra. If you fall into the loneliness trap, you may get stuck in dependency. Too afraid to face your true abilities, you scream, "Don't leave me!" Rather than risk finding out the results of your decision, you rely on someone else to choose for you. You're always seeking to define yourself through others, petrified by rejection or accountability. As a result, you might rush into partnerships and alliances, frantic for cooperation. But if you try to break out of the loneliness trap by pretending it doesn't exist, you might go too far in the other direction: absolute independence, avoiding partnerships for fear they will overshadow your individuality, passing up opportunities at relationships with a mate, a date, or anyone else who gets too close.

BREAK FREE! Many experts now agree that workplace relationships needn't fall into one of two opposing categories: *dependence* or *independence*. A third category, *interdependence*, is a theory of mutual reliance that consultants earn big bucks for teaching to corporations worldwide. With practice you can master interdependence, simply by smashing Saturn in Libra's loneliness trap. Start by taking responsibility for your actions—don't pass the buck or say, as Adam did in Eden, "She made me do it!" Next, value each person's contribution. Think of ballroom dancing. Though one person "leads," it takes two to tango; one dancer isn't doing it *for* or *to* the other. Finally, beware of unreasonable commitments. If someone is clearly asking too much of you, and you consent, you're returning to the loneliness trap. Don't do it!

Saturn in Scorpio

THE TRAP: *DANGER.* "The world's a dangerous place; I must never let down my guard. In order to win, I must vanquish," says the voice of Saturn in Scorpio. If you get caught in the danger trap, you perceive every disappointment (whether real or not) as a major catastrophe. So you demand total control, possessive of your projects. "This is my baby," you insist like an overprotective parent. Seeing danger all around, you do things like abstain from starting your dream business for fear of lawsuits and liability. On the other hand, you may go to the other extreme, taking no precau-

tions for the future. You relish risky business. Expecting crisis, you may create it—the self-fulfilling prophecy of an underdeveloped Saturn in Scorpio.

BREAK FREE! Find and rely on trustworthy confidants; you need someone objective on your side. Confront the sources of danger. If it's a person, ask them about their motives. If it's a situation, get all the facts. Finally, realize that life is inherently dangerous. You'll never avoid danger altogether—nor should you. The key is to respond to each "danger" individually, not as though the gods had conspired to test your reflexes!

Saturn in Sagittarius

THE TRAP: *IGNORANCE.* "The world's too big and complicated; I can't possibly understand how to succeed," says the voice of Saturn in Sagittarius. If you fall into the ignorance trap, you'll feel dumb. Even when your smarts open doors, you fear you're faking it—and a more clever individual will expose your "sham" the minute you slip up. Furthermore, you may never feel *ready*—how could you when you haven't read *every* book a lawyer or landscape architect, for example, *ought* to read? Possibly afraid to show your "ignorance," you may put on airs of intelligence. You assert that you've got the answers, all the *right* answers. And then, believing this yourself, you stop learning for fear you'll discover that you, like everyone else, still have a lot to learn.

BREAK FREE! With a Sagittarian Saturn, you understand that you can't make it without using your noggin, but the ignorance trap can strap you onto a treadmill of always seeking more information or insisting that you know best. The truly intelligent professional runs free. Start by conquering the fear of appearing stupid. If, for instance, you're looking for a job, don't pretend to be an expert on finding one. Instead, set up informational interviews with friends of friends who already have a foot in the door. Ask what it's like to do what they do and how they got their start.

> **"And only if [our] visions can stand alone, unassisted, in the face of absolute impossibility, can we say that we truly have faith. Until then we are still riding with training wheels."**
> AUTHOR STEVEN FORREST

Next, get over the myth that there's one right solution to a problem. Since life is not a multiple-choice test, most questions have, in fact, many an-

swers. Finally, allow yourself to change your mind or say you were wrong. Newspapers print retractions all the time. Remember, nothing's written in stone anymore; it's all digital and highly likely to change by next month.

Saturn in Capricorn

> **"Notice the difference between what happens when a man says to himself, 'I have failed three times,' and what happens when he says, 'I am a failure.'"**
>
> FORMER U.S. SENATOR
> S. I. HAYAKAWA

THE TRAP: *INADEQUACY*. "I'm not good enough," says the voice of Saturn in Capricorn. Though highly responsible, you worry you can't bear the burdens the world heaps atop your shoulders. Or is it actually a case of *you* asking for more and more burdens in a desperate quest to prove your adequacy? No matter what you do it never lives up to your expectations. You overlook accomplishments and focus on short-comings. Eventually resigning yourself to inadequacy, you might stop trying, and decline the challenges where you could really shine. On the other hand, some Saturn-in-Capricorn professionals respond to the inadequacy trap by fishing for compliments or coveting prizes or hot-shot titles—all of which provide only a temporary respite from an ongoing, destructive treadmill ride.

BREAK FREE! You first need to define, according to *your* values, what it means to be good enough. You won't be good at everything, but you can be great where you choose to concentrate your efforts. Second, realistically calculate how much time and effort it takes. Don't berate yourself for failing to build a house in two months when it takes the average human three months. Finally, remember that life is not a race. Another person's accomplishments needn't diminish your own.

Saturn in Aquarius

THE TRAP: *CHANGE*. "The world moves too fast! I've got to rush to keep up," says the voice of Saturn in Aquarius. If you fall into the change trap, you'll always look for trouble—or maybe it will just find you. Everything needs fixing. Committed to progress, fearing you'll be left behind, you contend

that tomorrow will be a better day, and forget to live *today*. Perhaps you'll defer gratification, procrastinate vacations till you have more time (which never seems to arrive), or even disregard friends and colleagues who may move next week. Goals and objectives lead you around like a dog on a leash. Then again, the reverse may happen: Overwhelmed by the idea of change, you hold tight, intolerant of new ideas.

BREAK FREE! Recently I overheard a woman tell a salesman she'd buy a professional wardrobe *later*, after she'd lost 15 pounds. The smart suits that might enhance her image and boost her confidence had to wait till she eradicated her "flaws." Start freeing yourself from the change trap by setting goals but not living for them. It might help to write them down on a calendar so you can see they exist in the future, not today. Next, agree to work with imperfection; if you do, eventually you can become a master of your circumstances, rather than feeling you must change your circumstances before being able to work with them. Furthermore, don't feel that once you make a change you can't go back. (Consider the case of a Chicago company that, when its employees want to quit, encourages them to leave for a month while their jobs remain available.) Finally, realize that change is usually a process, not an event. Giraffes didn't evolve long necks overnight, you know!

Saturn in Pisces

THE TRAP: *SUFFERING.* "It's not my fault. It's *theirs*," says the voice of Saturn in Pisces. If you fall into the suffering trap, you'll suffer rather than change your situation. You fear you have no control over your own life. Every little detail—right down to the raise you deserved but didn't get last week— seems determined by an "external locus of control." The government, the gods, your parents who dropped you, your boss who fired you—all of them seem to have a hand in making you or breaking you. Alternatively, succumbing to the other extreme, you may overcompensate for this anxiety by trying to control factors outside your reach, from the global economy to the weather.

BREAK FREE! Identify your part in the circumstances. How can you effect change in your own life? Don't waste your energy on factors over which you can never gain control. Take steps to gain control over the factors within in your grasp. Next, commit yourself to the idea that you're the

master of your own destiny. No, you can't alter your DNA and grow six inches taller, but you *can* play the hand that life deals you. If, for example, you're suddenly fired, go ahead and suffer awhile; it's human and healthy. Get mad, get sad, *respond* with your true emotions. Then try to look at the situation objectively: *What part of it lies in your hands?* Did you deserve to be fired? If not, do you have any recourse? Are you prepared at this juncture to pursue a different goal and make a career change? Remember that no matter what the circumstances, you retain the power to *choose* your own reaction.

How to Find Your Saturn Sign—Easy as 1-2-3

1. In the following Saturn tables, look up the year of your birth—or, if that's not listed, the year right *before* your birth year.

2. Saturn moves very slowly (the most slowly of all the planets covered in your Professional Planetary Profile). These tables tell you the days—approximately two years apart—on which Saturn actually *changed* signs. So look for the two-year chunk of time during which you were born.

3. Holy ringed planets! That's your Saturn sign, right there in the far-right column across from the date that *starts* the two-year chunk of time you found in Step 2. When you find your Saturn sign, write it down in your Planetary Positions Chart on page 377.

But wait! Even though Saturn changes signs rather rarely, there's still a *minute* chance it changed signs right *on* your birthday. If so, you'll want to determine if you were born *before* or *after* the change. Simply refer to the section "Determining Your Sign Down to the Minute" on page 199, then come back to these Saturn tables.

EXAMPLE

If you want a trial run, let's experiment by looking up Oprah Winfrey's Saturn sign. Oprah was born January 29, 1954.

1. Turn to 1954 in the Saturn tables.

2. It's not listed. But you do see 1953 and 1956, and Oprah's 1954 birthday comes right between those two. So go *back* to 1953 and discover that

Saturn entered Scorpio on October 22, 1953. (Note, then, how Saturn was in Scorpio for that entire period between October 1953 and January 1956, a little over two years.) Well, Oprah clearly has Saturn in Scorpio.

3. At this point, Oprah would complete filling in her Planetary Positions Chart on page 377 and read the entry for Saturn in Scorpio in this chapter.

SATURN

1940			
March	20	4:41 A.M.	Taurus

1942			
May	8	2:40 P.M.	Gemini

1944			
June	20	2:48 A.M.	Cancer

1946			
Aug.	2	9:42 A.M.	Leo

1948			
Sept.	18	11:36 P.M.	Virgo

1949				
April	2	10:40 P.M.	R	Leo
May	29	7:58 A.M.		Virgo

1950			
Nov.	20	10:50 A.M.	Libra

1951				
March	7	7:14 A.M.	R	Virgo
Aug.	13	11:44 A.M.		Libra

1953			
Oct.	22	10:36 A.M.	Scorpio

1956				
Jan.	12	1:45 P.M.		Sagittarius
May	13	10:47 P.M.	R	Scorpio
Oct.	10	10:11 A.M.		Sagittarius

1959			
Jan.	5	8:33 A.M.	Capricorn

1962			
Jan.	3	2:02 P.M.	Aquarius

1964				
March	23	11:18 P.M.		Pisces
Sept.	15	4:05 P.M.	R	Aquarius
Dec.	16	12:39 A.M.		Pisces

1967			
March	3	4:32 P.M.	Aries

1969			
April	29	5:24 P.M.	Taurus

1971			
June	18	11:10 A.M.	Gemini

1972				
Jan.	9	10:43 P.M.	R	Taurus
Feb.	21	9:53 A.M.		Gemini

1973			
Aug.	1	5:21 P.M.	Cancer

1974				
Jan.	7	3:28 P.M.	R	Gemini
April	18	5:34 P.M.		Cancer

1975			
Sept.	16	11:57 P.M.	Leo

1976				
Jan.	14	8:17 A.M.	R	Cancer
June	5	12:09 A.M.		Leo

1977			
Nov.	16	9:42 P.M.	Virgo

1978				
Jan.	4	7:48 P.M.	R	Leo
July	26	7:02 A.M.		Virgo

1980			
Sept.	21	5:48 A.M.	Libra

What's Up with Uranus?— Megatrends, Macroplanets . . . and Other Insider Secrets

Congratulations! By coming this far in *Work Your Stars!* you've crisscrossed the solar system, assembling all of the most important factors in your birth chart. Just like a professional business and career astrologer, you're using the tools of the trade to interpret and maximize any individual's *personal* potential, drives, and workplace relationships. Focus on these factors—the Sun, Moon, rising sign, and Inner Planets—and you'll create an insightful, inspiring Professional Planetary Profile.

BUT WAIT, THERE'S MORE!

Astrology doesn't end with the study of the individual. Just as psychology branches into social psychology, and microeconomics into *macro*economics, business astrology extends to organizations, institutions, national economies, and the global marketplace. It emphasizes astrological phenomena that matter less in a birth chart's individual career profile. If you're starting a business venture or working with marketing or demographics, you might want to have a chart cast for your organization. In a future book, I'll explain how astrologers assess mass-market influences and forecast future trends. But if you can't wait till then, here's what you need to know for further study or discussion with your professional astrologer:

THE BIG GUYS OUT THERE

Discovered late in the history of astrology, the outer planets—Uranus, Neptune, and Pluto—occupy a special category in business forecasting. These "transpersonal" planets symbolize *generational*, rather than personal, forces at work. If, for example, you were born with Pluto in Virgo in 1967, so was your coworker who popped into the world four years later. As children of the '70s, you share a lot in common, having grown up with the same sitcoms and social forces, despite huge differences in your personalities.

So, as markers of a zeitgeist or spirit of an age, the outer planets are the favorites of marketing and advertising professionals who want to reach masses of consumers, not just individual purchasers. You wouldn't, for example, appeal to baby boomer tastes with the same ad campaign that successfully reached generation x'ers. Likewise, astrology can help you anticipate your target market's behavior and desires.

Perhaps you don't give two hoots about marketing, but you do care about the job outlook for, say, computer programmers or Latin professors 20 years from now. That's outer planet territory, too, because various trends and collective movements are represented by these slow-moving giants with lengthy cycles.

GOT AN ITCH? THAT'S URANUS!

With an 84-year cycle, Uranus spends approximately seven years in each zodiac sign. Ever heard of the "seven-year itch" in relationships? Uranus shakes things up. It represents *the force of change*. Just as the freewheeling 1960s reacted against the straitlaced values of the '50s, Uranus symbolizes a group's urge to react to or against the status quo.

If you play the stock market, keep your eye on Uranus. It can indicate sudden shifts in consumer behavior and revolutionary advancements in technology.

NAME THAT TUNE . . . IT'S *NEPTUNE*

Neptune's complete cycle lasts even longer—165 years—with approximately 14 years in each sign. Much as the Moon symbolizes an individual's deepest needs and desires, Neptune reflects a community's or an era's *yearnings and longings*. Collectively, some generations seem to yearn for personal growth while others long for material accumulation. That's Neptune, representing ideals, closely held beliefs, and the pursuit of pleasure or satisfaction.

Why do products and brands that our grandparents cherished no longer excite us? Which types of movies will draw huge audiences next summer while others stumble at the box office? How will upcoming generations satisfy their desire to lead meaningful, productive lives? Social historians and market researchers propose many theories. Meanwhile, if you want to sing along with the times—or anticipate the next big music craze—listen to Neptune.

THAT'S NO MICKEY MOUSE PLANET—THAT'S PLUTO!

Small and cold with an erratic orbit, Pluto has the longest cycle of all: 245 years or so, with very roughly 20 years in each sign, making its passage through a zodiac sign the delineator of an entire generation. The best astrological signifier of sweeping social movements, Pluto symbolizes *values worth fighting for* and how *power is concentrated*. We currently live in a time and place that values the individual and the free market. Maybe democracy and consumerism haven't reached every corner of the globe, but they represent the dominant paradigm, along with almost universal faith in science and progress. But will it always be like this, or will history invent a new way of life, as it has in the past? Such is the stuff of Pluto, emblem of transformation, control, and the search for ultimate truths.

If you want to understand economics and market fluctuations within the context of larger political and societal forces, it's worth taking a look at Pluto. It reminds us that a record-breaking harvest in the Szechuan province of China can influence the price of eggplants in Tucson.

THE HOROSCOPE OF A BUSINESS?

How about my cat? Yep, both have horoscopes. In fact, if your business already exists, find its "birth time" by looking up the date when it incorporated, or when its doors first opened, or any other moment that you consider its inception. You can then cast its chart just as you've done for yourself. If, on the other hand, you want to start a business in the future, consider using the specialized field of "electional astrology." This branch of astrology—long favored by Hong Kong captains of industry—can help you determine in advance the most auspicious time to start your business, accounting for who you are, what your mission is, and external circumstances.

As for your feline friends, try a Libran cat for affection or a four-legged Sagittarian for fun and frolic!

Part Three

PUTTING IT TOGETHER: YOUR PROFESSIONAL PLANETARY PROFILE

A diploma, a résumé, and a little investment capital are all you need to start a business or career, right? No way! You have to know yourself, your talents, and what'll get you out of bed in the morning. And you have to know people and how to get along with them in the workplace and the marketplace.

How can you bring all of these things together? Make a plan, as any business or company does—one comprehensive document that outlines your past, present, and future, your goals and aspirations, and what you have to work with.

You've examined not only your Sun sign, but also the other planets and aspects of your astrological chart. Your horoscope is like a snapshot of the entire sky as seen from earth at the time and place of your birth. By examining the multiple energies represented in your birth chart, you can get the big picture as well as the nitty-gritty details of your professional potentials and pitfalls.

The Professional Planetary Profile (PPP) comprises:

★ Your Sun sign: Your sense of purpose, your motivation and personal portfolio of assets and liabilities.

★ Your rising sign: Your public persona and ability to get your foot in the door.

★ Your Mercury sign: Your strategies for communicating and organizing.

★ Your Venus sign: Your approach to networking, marketing, and flirting!

★ Your Mars sign: Your energies for leading, managing, competing, and resolving conflicts.

★ Your Jupiter sign: Your drive to create good luck and prosperity, abundance and community.

★ Your Saturn sign: Your capacity for overcoming obstacles and breaking free of limits.

How to Create Your Profile

★ Look up all of your planets, plus your rising sign, in the tables at the end of the corresponding chapters in *Work Your Stars!* and fill them into your Professional Planetary Profile (PPP) work sheet.

★ Read Dr. Matt's descriptions and suggestions for each of your planetary placements (e.g., Moon in Libra, Venus in Scorpio, etc.).

★ Using the text to stimulate your thoughts and jump-start your imagination, complete the profile to create a document that describes who you are and what you want to do, and a sensible strategy for going for it.

How to Use Your Profile

★ Make it gel. If your profile, like most people's, contains contradictions and competing factors, think about how various parts of yourself and your ambitions can get along better. Include those compromises and resolutions in an updated version of your PPP.

★ Milk your profile for answers. If you're currently searching for a career path or choosing your life's objectives, analyze your PPP. Writing a document like this can help clarify what you really want.

★ Turn to your profile for inspiration. When you're writing your résumé or business plan, refer to your PPP. It can help you summarize your strengths and promote yourself based on more than the merits or good name of your last job.

★ Assess your goals. When you're setting goals or making big decisions, consult your PPP. How do your new goals help you achieve the mission contained in your PPP? How will the choice to move cross-country affect your opportunities?

★ Update your profile. Like you, your planetary energies and inclinations don't remain stagnant over a lifetime. At certain junctures—like changing careers, expanding a business, or embarking on a big creative

project—return to your PPP. Reread the corresponding sections of the book, ask yourself these questions once again, and create a PPP that reflects the new you.

Before you take the plunge, here's a sample version of a completed PPP. The blank PPP work sheet follows the sample.

Sample Professional Planetary Profile

Profile for _Stella Smithfield_

Birth date _Sept. 3_ Birth time _9:30 p.m. (Daylight Savings Time)_ Birthplace _Savannah, Georgia_

Profile creation date _March 29_

MISSION

Sun in _Virgo_

The greatest inspiration for my career is _my belief system._

My hero(es) is/are _my grandmother, who started her own organic foods business, and the founder of Healthy Prospects Company, which provides low-cost, complementary health care._

My guiding motivation is a desire to _help people and improve their health-care options._

The personal strengths and assets I most want to capitalize on are _an attention to detail, compassion, and my unique experience in both Western and alternative medicine._

The personal weaknesses and liabilities I want to overcome are _self-criticism, too narrow a focus on just a few aspects of my work, and intolerance for health-care options I disagree with._

PUBLIC AND PROFESSIONAL IMAGE

Rising Sign: _Taurus_

The image I most want to present in the workplace is of someone who is _capable and dependable but not so set in her ways that she can't adapt to changes and advances._

I want to enhance my public and professional image by _letting my enthusiasm and passion come through and by responding quickly to calls, questions, and requests so that people know I'm on top of things._

ENVIRONMENT

Moon in _Sagittarius_

I thrive in an environment where _I am constantly learning new things and meeting people from all walks of life._

I can handle stress by _exercising, practicing hobbies that have nothing to do with work, and maintaining my killer sense of humor in every situation._

Eventually I want to work in a setting where I can _come and go as I like and travel frequently._

ORGANIZATION AND COMMUNICATION

Mercury in _Leo_

I communicate effectively by _having a flair for colorful language, coming across as deeply sincere, and practicing active listening._

I excel at organizing by _having the right tools for the job and making enough time to do all I have to do._

I can achieve my peak performance by _tackling tasks piece by piece. I want to choose one or two priorities and do them so well that they make me proud._

PROMOTION AND MARKETING

Venus in _Cancer_

I am a great networker when I _take an interest in other people and put them at ease—and also when I remember to call old friends and coworkers to ask for leads._

My sales savvy shines when I _figure out how my services can help each of my individual clients and sell not only my time but also my brand—which is ME._

I want to improve my networking and sales by _confidently promoting myself as a valuable contribution to my customers, not as an intrusion on their time._

LEADERSHIP

Mars in _Aquarius_

I want to develop my leadership qualities by _sharing my vision with the people I work with._

When conflicts arise, I can resolve them by _not personalizing criticism and realizing that one disagreement doesn't destroy my "ideal" collaborative team._

I want to express my entrepreneurial spirit by/with _becoming a well-known expert in my field who has a totally unique set of skills so that I can offer the discriminating consumer something totally original._

I can become more self-empowered by _fighting against conventional wisdom that says a young woman from the South can't succeed in the Big Leagues, and by not feeling that I have to play or live up to a stereotype in order to succeed._

OPPORTUNITY

Jupiter in _Scorpio_

My key to opening up greater opportunities is _resourcefulness._

I want to develop this quality by *getting to know the key players in my field and, even while I'm working at my current job, start making the contacts I'll need if I start my own consulting business. But I'm not interested in opportunities that compromise my values or take advantage of anyone.*

REACHING OPTIMUM POTENTIAL

Saturn in *Aries*

I sometimes hold myself back by *feeling I can't compete against tougher, better-educated professionals in my field.*

Recognizing this, I can break free by *taking stock every year on my birthday of how much I've achieved. I'll also stop comparing myself to others and start trying to live up to goals that suit me and my individual sense of destiny.*

Planetary Positions Chart

Consult the charts found throughout part two to complete the rising sign, Moon sign, and planet information.

My Sun is in _____

My rising sign is _____

My Moon is in _____

My Mercury is in _____

My Venus is in _____

My Mars is in _____

My Jupiter is in _____

My Saturn is in _____

The Professional Planetary Profile

Profile for _____

Birth date _____ Birth time _____ Birthplace _____

Profile creation date _____

MISSION

Sun in _____

The greatest inspiration for my career is _____.

My hero(es) is/are _____.

My guiding motivation is a desire to _____.

The personal strengths and assets I most want to capitalize on are _____

_____.

The personal weaknesses and liabilities I want to overcome are _____

_____.

PUBLIC AND PROFESSIONAL IMAGE

Rising sign: _____

The image I most want to present in the workplace is of someone who is _____

_____.

I want to enhance my public and professional image by _____

_____.

ENVIRONMENT

Moon in _____

I thrive in an environment where _____.

I can handle stress by _____.

Eventually I want to work in a setting where I can _____

_____.

ORGANIZATION AND COMMUNICATION

Mercury in _____

I communicate effectively by _____.

I excel at organizing by _____.

I can achieve my peak performance by _____

_____.

PROMOTION AND MARKETING

Venus in _____

I am a great networker when I _____.

My sales savvy shines when I _____.

I want to improve my networking and sales by _____

_____.

LEADERSHIP

Mars in _____

I want tc develop my leadership qualities by _____

_____.

When conflicts arise, I can resolve them by _____

_____.

I want to express my entrepreneurial spirit by/with _____

_____.

I can become more self-empowered by _____.

OPPORTUNITY

Jupiter in _____

My key to opening up greater opportunities is _____

_____.

I want to develop this quality by _____.

REACHING OPTIMUM POTENTIAL

Saturn in _____

I sometimes hold myself back by _____.

Recognizing this, I can break free by _____.